Happy Birthday

Love, Mom "88"

Karen Brechin and Catherine Garrison, Editorial Assistants

Charles Walton IV, Senior Foods Photographer; Beverly Morrow and Cindy Manning, Photo Stylists

Above: *Judy Feagin and Diane Hogan, Test Kitchens Staff*

Left: *Jane Cairns and Peggy Smith, Test Kitchens Staff*

Southern Living

1987 ANNUAL RECIPES

Oxmoor
House

Copyright 1987 by Oxmoor House, Inc.
Book Division of Southern Progress Corporation
P.O. Box 2463, Birmingham, Alabama 35201

Southern Living®, *Cooking Light*®, *Breakfasts & Brunches*®,
Summer Suppers®, and *Holiday Dinners*®, are federally
registered trademarks of Southern Living, Inc.

Library of Congress Catalog Number: 79-88364
ISBN: 0-8487-0717-6
ISSN: 0272-2003

Manufactured in the United States of America
First Printing 1987

Southern Living®
   Foods Editor: Jean Wickstrom Liles
   Associate Foods Editors: Deborah G. Lowery,
      Susan Payne
   Assistant Foods Editors: Phyllis Young Cordell,
      Susan Dosier, B. Ellen Templeton
   Editorial Assistants: Karen Brechin, Catherine Garrison
   Test Kitchens Director: Kaye Adams
   Assistant Test Kitchens Director: Patty Vann
   Test Kitchens Staff: Jane Cairns, Judy Feagin, Diane
      Hogan, Peggy Smith
   Photo Stylists: Cindy Manning, Beverly Morrow
   Senior Foods Photographer: Charles E. Walton IV
      Additional photography by *Southern Living*
      photographers: Jim Bathie, pages 73, 148, 169; Gary
      Clark, ii bottom left; Colleen Duffley, ii top left, ii top
      right, ii bottom right, iii top left, iii bottom left, iii
      bottom right, 86; Sylvia Martin, vii center, 7, 39, 44,
      47, 56, 65, 66, 97, 100, 101, 104, 112, 117, 119, 132,
      133, 135, 136, 214, 223, 234, 236, 304; John O'Hagan,
      iii top right, vii right, 148, 298; Mary-Gray Hunter, 148
   Production Manager: Clay Nordan
   Assistant Production Manager: Wanda Butler

Oxmoor House, Inc.
   Executive Editor: Ann H. Harvey
   Production Manager: Jerry Higdon
   Associate Production Manager: Rick Litton
   Art Director: Bob Nance
   Production Assistant: Theresa Beste

Southern Living® *1987 Annual Recipes*

   Editor: Olivia Kindig Wells
   Copy Editor: Mary Ann Laurens
   Editorial Assistant: Pam Beasley Bullock
   Designer: Carol Middleton
   Illustrator: Barbara Ball

Cover: *Bake these desserts, and your whole house will smell like
Christmas. From front, Spiced Christmas Cookies, Spiced Carrot
Cake, Festive Braids, and Pumpkin Pie in Spiced Nut Crust.
(Recipes begin on page 294.)*

Page i: *Stuffed Chicken Breasts Sardou (page 269) is topped with a
Mock Mustard-Hollandaise Sauce that contains mushrooms and
low-fat yogurt.*

Page iv: *Let Heart Tarts (page 14) be a special ending to your
Valentine's Day meal.*

Back cover: *Nutty-tasting Light Wheat Rolls (page 254) or a loaf
of Cheese-Wine Bread (page 254) adds flavor to any holiday meal.*

To find out how you can receive *Southern Living* magazine, write
to *Southern Living*®, P.O. Box C-119, Birmingham, AL 35283.

Table of Contents

Good Luck Jambalaya (page 11)

Cornbread Sticks (page 15)

Pumpkin-Ice Cream Pie (page 243)

**Our Year
at *Southern Living***   x

January   1

It's A Snap To Make These
  Crackers   2
Burgoo And Brunswick Stew   3
Cooking Light: Fish Is Fine On
  Your Low-Sodium Diet   4
Microwave Cookery: Soup And
  Sandwich—A Natural Combo   6
Snacks To Keep You Cheering   7
New Variations On An Old
  Favorite   8
Salads From Your Pantry   9
No-Fuss Supper Ideas   10
Bring On Black-Eyed Peas   11
Try Feta Cheese   12
From Our Kitchen To Yours   12

February   13

Dessert For The Sentimental   14
Southerners Love These Oldtime
  Breads   15
From Our Kitchen To Yours   16
Bake A Dainty Party Cookie   16

Cooking Light® Special
  Section   17
  Lighten Up For A Livelier
    You   17
  Make Your Own Frozen
    Entrées   17

Chocolate—The Ultimate In
  Desserts   21
Special Equipment   21
Start Your Day With A
  Piping-Hot Muffin   23
Add A Chilled Vegetable
  Salad To The Menu   24

Tasty Substitutions Keep Dips
  Lower In Calories   25
Sauces Slim On Calories   26
A Menu For The Two Of You   31
Iron Is Important In Your
  Low-Calorie Diet   32
Enjoy Fresh Basil   33
The Keys To Weight Loss   34
Simple But Savory Entrées   35
Spice Up Dishes With Italian
  Seasonings   36
Microwave Cookery: Favorite
  Recipes—Only Faster   36
Enjoy The Taste Of Sour Cream   37
Caramel Makes It Rich   38
Oysters Are Versatile   39
Serve Carrots Anytime   40
Avocado Salad Ideas   41
Cabbage Patch Favorites   42

March   43

Puzzled About White Chocolate?   44
Rice—A Versatile Southern
  Tradition   45
From Our Kitchen To Yours   46
Cheese Invites A Party   46
English Muffins For Breakfast   49
Cooking Light: Stir-Fry To Keep
  Calories Low   50
Microwave Cookery: Helpful Hints
  And A Few Good Tips   52
Potato Yeast Rolls   53
Have Fun With Phyllo Appetizers   53
Have You Cooked Corned Beef
  Lately?   54
Accent Meals With Kiwifruit   55
Spring Vegetables Are Here   55
Offer A Fruit Salad   56
Tea Is The Basis Of These
  Beverages   57

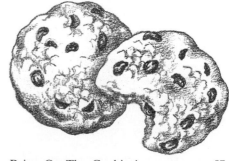

Bring On The Cookies!   57
Processor-Quick Frostings And
  Toppings   58

April   59

Look What's Sizzling On The
  Grill   60
The Freshest, Prettiest Salads   61

Breakfasts & Brunches® Special
   Section 67
  Can't Wait For Breakfast! 67
  Make The Entrée A Quiche
   Or Tart 70
  Cooking Light: Cholesterol Is
   Low In These Dishes 71
  Toast The Morning 72
  Plan A Great Brunch 72
  Fruit Instead Of Flowers 73
Let's Have Lunch! 74
Cooking Light: Low-Calorie
  Desserts With High Appeal 75
Use Up That Leftover Ham 78
Microwave Cookery: Fish In A
  Flash 78
From Our Kitchen To Yours 79
Appetizers And Salads For Two 80
Salad Dressings To Boast About 81
Pork Pleasers For Two 81
Use Your Canned Beans 82
Oranges Add Tangy Flavor 83
No-Frost Cakes 84
Fast-Rising Rolls 85

Luscious Whole-Grain Bread 85
Peanut Butter Eggs For Your
  Easter Basket 86

May 87

Cheese Served With Flair 88
Get Ready For Fresh Vegetables 89
Try A Seafood Entrée For Two 91
Scrumptious Picnic Fare 91
Celebrate With A Party 92
Appetizers From The Sea 94
Entrées Men Like To Cook 95
Microwave Cookery: Quick And
  Easy Cakes 96
Basil-Cheese Tart 98
Surprise Her With Breakfast 98
Put A Salad On The Menu 103
A New Twist For Chicken 103
Cooking Light: Take A New Look
  At Sandwiches 104
Get A Crush On Mint 107

Look What's Happening
  With Pasta 108
Desserts From The Freezer 109
Grind, Chop, Or Slice Meat In
  The Processor 110
Hot Stuffing For Shrimp 112
From Our Kitchen To Yours 112

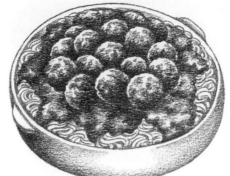

June 113

Pretty To Look At, Good To Eat 114
Come For Dinner! 115
Expect The Unexpected In New
  Southwestern Cuisine 119
Make Extra Soup, And Freeze It 123
Microwave Cookery: Quick
  Cooking For Summer 124
Cooking Light: It's Yogurt—Not
  Ice Cream 125
End The Meal With Crêpes 126
Perk Up Vegetables With A
  Cream Sauce 126
Add A Chilled Sauce To Meat 127
This Menu Is For Two 128
It's Time To Pick Blackberries 129
From Our Kitchen To Yours 130

July 131

Present Dessert In A Shell
  Of Chocolate 132
Delicious Summer Gifts 134
Summer Suppers® Special
  Section 137
  Summertime Food And Fun 137
  Hot Days Call For Cool
   Desserts 139
  Blueberries At Their Best 140
  Grilled Meats For Lazy
   Evenings 140
  Cooking Light: Spirited Main
   Dishes 142
  Easy Ways With Dinner
   Breads 143
  When The Entrée Is A Salad 144
  Appetizers For Summer 146
  Beverages On Ice 146
  Yummy Ice Cream Sandwiches 147
  Put Together A Summer
   Bouquet 147
  Set The Mood With Candles 148

Pickles: The Quick Way 149
From Our Kitchen To Yours 150
Microwave Cookery:
  Quick-Cooking Garden Fare 150
Cooking Light: Cool, Crisp Salads
  To Beat The Heat 152
Casseroles For Potluck Dinners 154
Mighty Flavor From Tarragon 155
A Southern Breakfast In Just
  Minutes 156
Try Warm-Weather Soups 156
Party Spreads And Sandwich
  Fillings 157
Kids Will Love These Snacks 158
Chicken With A Cajun Flair 159
Ice Cream Parlor Beverages 159
Baked Ham Stretches Summer
  Menus 160

August 161

Not Your Everyday Melon 162
Cooking Light: Traditional
  Southern Foods Go Light 162
Microwave Cookery: Dessert Is
  Easy With Fruit Sauces 164
Add Eggplant To The Menu 166
Dinner's Ready In Less Than
  An Hour 167
Treats From The Freezer 168
It's Better With Fresh Basil 171
Cornbread Mix Offers Possibilities 171

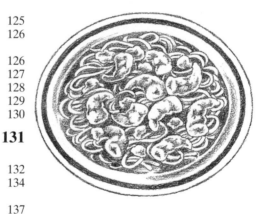

Shrimp, Wonderful Shrimp! 172
These Appetizers Are Really Hot 173
Cooking Smart Means Cooking
  Healthy 174
Chicken—Fried Crisp And
  Delicious 175
Try Hot Salads For A Change 176
From Our Kitchen To Yours 177
Favorite Family Desserts 178

September 179

Picante Sauce Burns With Flavor 180
Not The Same Old Pizza 181
Pecans And Peanuts, Plain And
  Fancy 183
Perk Up Your Burgers 185

Cooking Light: Color Is The Key To Vitamins 186
Microwave Cookery: Try Your Hand At Adapting Recipes 188
Vegetables You Can Rely On 189
Stir In Flavor With Cottage Cheese 190
For The Love Of Potatoes 191
Add Pasta To These Entrées 192
Entrées To Bake Or Broil 193
Flavor The Entrée With Fruit 194
Eggs Benedict With A Twist 195
Kick Off With Snacks 195
Fry This Appetizer 196
Tex-Mex Dip Starts The Party 196
Celebrate Victory With A Buffet 197
Invite Friends For Dainties 198
You Can't Resist Brownies 198
Energizing Blender Beverages 199
Carrot Dishes That Satisfy 200
A Relish You'll Rave About 200
Tuna Salads To Rave About 200
Stuff A Pita With Flavor 202

Fresh-Baked Sugar Cake 228
Dried Fruit Is Always In Season 228
Fruit And Spices Flavor Pork 229
It's Ravioli, And It's Homemade! 230
Cauliflower Is Best Now 231
Spoon On Sauces For Flavor 232
Celebrate Fall With A Salad 233
What A Salad! 233
Make A Soufflé To Brag About 234

November 235
Tangy, Crunchy Holiday Salads 236
Sausage—A Texas Tradition 237
From Our Kitchen To Yours 238
Holiday Dinners® Special Section 239
  Bring On The Holidays! 239
  Sippers For The Holidays 241
  Entertaining: Casual And Easy 242
  The Berries Of The Holidays 243
  Relishes And Chutneys Add Color, Flavor 245
  Appetizers That Say Cheese 246
  Delicious Entrées To Carve 248
  Dinner Entrées For Two 249
  Cooking Light: It's Open House, And The Menu Is Light 250
  New Ideas For Side Dishes 252
  More Flavor In These Breads 254
  Make Breads With Fruit And Nuts 255
  Food Gifts To Mail 256
  Splurge With Cream-Filled Chocolates 258
  Baked Or Chilled, Pies Make Grand Finales 259
  Marvelous Marbled Desserts 261
  Make A Cake From Popcorn 262
  Cakes And Pies For The Season 263
  A Different Fruitcake 264
  A Prize-Winning Cheesecake 265
  When Dinner Is At Your House 266
  A Fresh Greeting For Guests 266
Entrées For Everyday 267
Cooking Light: Sensational Stuffed Entrées 268

Beautiful Pastries—Without The Trouble 275
Microwave Cookery: Holiday Baking In Minutes 278
Hot Sandwiches To Satisfy 278
Try These Sweet Potato Favorites 280
Serve Mushrooms Anytime 280
Warm Up With Dried-Bean Soup 282
Serve Chicken Nuggets 283
Ground Beef Tastes Better Than Ever 283
Casseroles For Busy Days 284
Toss Turkey Into A Salad 285
A Salad To Rave About 285
Chicken As An Elegant Entrée 286
Take A Look At These Sunday Suppers 286
Wow! Pasta Salad 288
This Salad Is A Group Project 288
Processor Crêpes And Fillings 289

December 291
Recipes For A Tree-Hunt Tradition 292
A Fruit Wreath To Eat 294
Holiday Baking Spices The Air 294
From Our Kitchen To Yours 297
Coffee Cake For Christmas 298
Start With A Can Of Pie Filling 298
A Cheese-And-Date Delight 299

Making The Best Cream Pie 207
From Our Kitchen To Yours 208

October 209
Cooked Up In The Bayous 210
From Our Kitchen To Yours 211
Traditional Fall Pies 212
Treat Your Friends To A Halloween Buffet 213
Savory Pot Roasts 215
Meat Loaf, An Old Favorite 216
Keep Chicken On The Menu 217
Microwave Cookery: Timesaving Entrées 218
Savor Veal 219
Cooking Light: Low In Cholesterol, Not In Flavor 220
Sheet Cakes To Enjoy 222
Sample A Chip Off The Old Chocolate Block 223
Pancakes And Waffles For Breakfast And More 224
A Bread Made With Beer 226
French Bread Baked Like The Pros 226

Breads For Now And Later 300
Leftover Turkey For Company 301
Microwave Cookery: Promote Even Cooking With Foil 302
He's A Serious Chili Cook 303
It's Time For Venison 304
Cooking Light: Enjoy A Candlelight Dinner For Two 304
Entrées With Flair 306
Salads That Fit The Season 311

Glossary 312

Recipe Title Index 314

Month-by-Month Index 320

General Recipe Index 328

Our Year At Southern Living®

I t's hard to believe we're putting the finishing touches on the ninth volume of *Annual Recipes*. It seems like yesterday that *you*, our readers, were begging us to compile a cookbook containing all the recipes published during a year in *Southern Living*.

The avalanche of letters since our first *Annual Recipes* in 1979 confirms that you have enjoyed the convenience of not having to clip each month's recipes, allowing you to keep each issue of *Southern Living* magazine intact.

In your letters you've told us of your many successes with our recipes, often describing occasions you've served particular recipes or even sending snapshots of your finished dish. Our recipes have encouraged you to try new cooking techniques or to experiment with new or unusual ingredients on the market.

Many of you have inquired how we select recipes for our stories or how we test them in our kitchens. After our story topics are planned for the year, our food editors select appropriate recipes from the thousands submitted each month by our readers. Before any recipe is published, it is tested once or twice by one of the home economists in our test kitchens. As the testing takes place, brand names and package sizes of ingredients plus any changes made in the list of ingredients and the recipe procedure are recorded on each recipe test sheet.

The highlight of each day for the foods staff is the taste-testing of 20 to 25 dishes. This is a critical process as each recipe undergoes the most rigorous scrutiny in terms of taste, appearance, practicality, and ease of preparation. Often technical adjustments in testing must be made, resulting in a retest using a different cooking time, temperature, pan size, or alternate ingredients. And those recipes selected for photography are prepared

again for the photo and savored one more time! Only the best recipes are selected for publication in the magazine. It is our goal to select recipes and create stories that appeal to you.

Our foods staff works diligently to make *Southern Living* very special for our audience. The results of this effort are apparent on every page of all nine volumes of *Annual Recipes*.

And to aid you in finding the ideal recipe for each occasion, we've responded to your recent request for a cumulative index of all recipes from our

Annual Recipes collection. We now have available the *Annual Recipes Master Index*, listing all the *Southern Living* recipes appearing in the last nine years. It's a ready source for convenient, easy access to a treasury of Southern recipes. This cumulative index can be ordered from Oxmoor House®.

As you use this *1987 Annual Recipes*, think of the many carefully selected and tested recipes as ingredients in themselves. These recipes range from quick-and-easy to gourmet fare, but all have a special flair that will delight your family and friends. Choose your favorites, and create your own blend of hospitality from our *Southern Living* kitchens.

Jean Wickstrom Liles

January

It's A Snap To Make These Crackers

Cracker bread is the thin, crisp flatbread that's popping up on restaurant menus across the country. And at home it's easy to make crackers these days.

Team Fennel-Rye Crackers with soup or with your favorite cheese or appetizer spread. They're equally good for just plain munching, too. Large flatbreads, such as Sesame Cracker Bread, are commonly seen tucked into baskets on appetizer tables. They're intended for breaking into bite-size pieces and serving with dips and spreads. Sprinkled with cinnamon sugar instead of sesame seeds, the flatbread becomes a teatime treat, while grated Parmesan cheese or seasoned salt dress it for snack time.

Traditionally, flatbreads were not leavened, but our version is updated with yeast to make a more tender product. Prepare the dough as for any basic yeast dough, but roll it into wafer-thin rounds, and don't allow it to rise. Brush it with water to help it crisp, and then sprinkle with the desired topping. Prick it with a fork so it doesn't form too many air bubbles, and bake until crisp and golden.

Serve these treats hot or at room temperature. They'll stay fresh and crisp several days stored in airtight containers. And don't worry if they don't bake up perfectly shaped, perfectly flat, or evenly browned. Irregularity in their looks gives them individuality.

On a lightly floured surface, roll equal portions of dough for Sesame Cracker Bread into 10-inch rounds.

Transfer rounds to baking sheets; brush with water, sprinkle with sesame seeds, and prick with a fork. Bake as directed.

Roll dough for Fennel-Rye Crackers to ⅛-inch thickness, and cut into diamond shapes, using a fluted pastry cutter.

Transfer diamonds to ungreased baking sheets; brush with egg white, and sprinkle with fennel seeds before baking.

SESAME CRACKER BREAD
(pictured on page 64)

5½ to 6 cups all-purpose flour, divided
1 package dry yeast
1 teaspoon salt
2 cups warm water (105° to 115°)
⅓ cup butter or margarine, melted
2 tablespoons sesame seeds, toasted

Combine 4 cups flour, yeast, and salt; stir well. Gradually add water to mixture, stirring well. Add butter; beat at medium speed of an electric mixer until blended. Gradually stir in enough remaining flour to make a stiff dough.

Turn dough out onto a floured surface, and knead until smooth and elastic (about 4 minutes). Place in a well-greased bowl, turning to grease top. Cover and let rise in a warm place (85°), free from drafts, 1 hour or until doubled in bulk.

Punch dough down, and divide into 10 equal portions. Shape each portion into a smooth ball on a lightly floured surface, and let rest for 10 minutes.

Roll each ball into a 10-inch circle on a lightly floured surface, rolling only enough to bake at one time. Chill extra balls of dough to slow down the rising process as you await oven space. Place rolled rounds on lightly greased baking sheets. Brush lightly with cold water, and sprinkle with sesame seeds. Prick entire surface liberally with a fork. (Do not allow to rise.)

Bake rounds at 350° for 25 minutes or until they are lightly browned and crisp. Let cool on wire racks. Repeat procedure with remaining balls of dough. Yield: 10 crackers.

Note: Cinnamon sugar, seasoned salt, or grated Parmesan cheese may be substituted for sesame seeds.

FENNEL-RYE CRACKERS
(pictured on page 64)

1¼ cups all-purpose flour
1¼ cups rye flour
1 tablespoon sugar
¾ teaspoon salt
½ teaspoon dry mustard
⅔ cup butter or margarine, softened
6 to 8 tablespoons cold water
1 egg white, lightly beaten
Fennel seeds

Combine flour, sugar, salt, and mustard in a large bowl; cut in butter with pastry blender until mixture resembles coarse meal. Sprinkle water (1 tablespoon at a time) evenly over surface; stir with a fork until dry ingredients are moistened. Shape into a ball.

Roll dough to ⅛-inch thickness on a lightly floured surface. Cut dough into 1½-inch diamonds, using a fluted pastry cutter; place on ungreased baking sheets. Brush with egg white; sprinkle lightly with fennel seeds. Bake at 375° for 12 to 14 minutes or until golden brown. Yield: 6 dozen.

DESSERT CRACKERS
(pictured on page 64)

⅓ cup butter or margarine, softened
⅓ cup sugar
2 eggs
½ teaspoon anise oil
2 cups all-purpose flour

Cream butter; gradually add sugar, and beat until light and fluffy. Add eggs; beat well. Stir in anise oil and flour. Turn dough out onto a lightly floured surface, and shape into a ball. Divide dough into 16 equal portions; shape each portion into a smooth ball.

Place each ball between 2 sheets of lightly floured wax paper, and roll to a 5-inch circle. Place rounds on lightly greased baking sheets. Prick entire surface liberally with a fork. Bake at 375° for 8 to 10 minutes or until lightly browned. Cool on wire racks. Serve with fruited cream cheese spread and fresh fruit. Yield: 16 crackers.

Burgoo And Brunswick Stew

Since pioneer times, inventive cooks have added harvest vegetables and flavorful seasonings to their hunter's stews. As a result, today we have Kentucky's burgoo and Brunswick stew, two classic Southern stews.

Traditionally, these stews are cooked slowly in huge iron pots over a smoldering fire, which imparts a rich smoky flavor. We reduced the recipes for kitchen cooking. We also used frozen and canned vegetables for convenience in winter months, but seasonal vegetables may be substituted. Because cooking time has been decreased, you may want to cook the stew in advance and refrigerate it to mellow the flavors.

FIVE-MEAT BURGOO

1 pound lean pork, cut into 1-inch cubes
1 pound lean beef, cut into 1-inch cubes
1 pound lean lamb, cut into 1-inch cubes
1 pound veal, cut into 1-inch cubes
1 (2-pound) broiler-fryer
1 gallon water
1 cup chopped cabbage
1 green pepper, finely chopped
1 cup frozen whole kernel corn
¾ cup chopped fresh parsley
2 carrots, scraped and diced
2 onions, chopped
2 medium potatoes, peeled and cubed
1 (16-ounce) can whole tomatoes, undrained and chopped
½ cup frozen lima beans
1 hot red pepper
2 teaspoons Worcestershire sauce
¼ teaspoon ground red pepper (optional)
1 tablespoon salt

Combine pork, beef, lamb, veal, chicken, and water in a large Dutch oven; bring to a boil. Cover, reduce heat, and simmer 2 hours. Drain meat, reserving broth. Skin, bone, and shred chicken. Shred other meats. Return all meat to broth. Add remaining ingredients; return to a boil. Reduce heat, and simmer, uncovered, 4 hours, stirring often. Add water for a thinner consistency, if desired. Yield: 1¼ gallons.
Mrs. Walter Kimbell,
Frankfort, Kentucky.

HARRY YOUNG'S BURGOO

1 (2- to 2½-pound) pork loin roast
1 (2- to 2½-pound) broiler-fryer
12 to 14 cups water
4 pounds ground beef
6 cups frozen whole kernel corn
5 cups frozen purple hull peas
5 cups frozen lima beans
3 cups chopped cabbage
2 medium potatoes, peeled and cubed
2 medium onions, chopped
1 (46-ounce) can tomato juice
1 (16-ounce) can whole tomatoes, undrained and chopped
2 cups frozen cut okra
1 (1-pound) bag carrots, scraped and diced
1 green pepper, chopped
¾ cup chopped celery
¼ cup chopped fresh parsley
1 to 2 tablespoons crushed red pepper
1 tablespoon salt
1 tablespoon celery salt
1½ teaspoons pepper

Combine pork, chicken, and 12 cups water in a large Dutch oven; bring to a boil. Cover, reduce heat, and simmer 2

hours. Drain meat, reserving broth. Remove bone, and shred pork. Skin, bone, and shred chicken. Return meat to broth.

Brown ground beef in a large skillet, stirring to crumble; drain. Add ground beef and remaining ingredients to broth. Return to a boil. Reduce heat, and simmer, uncovered, 2 hours; stir often. Add water for a thinner consistency, if desired. Yield: 2½ gallons.
Harry M. Young, Jr.
Herndon, Kentucky.

OLD-FASHIONED BURGOO

1 cup dried Great Northern beans
¾ cup dried baby lima beans
¼ cup dried split peas
8 slices bacon
1 pound beef or ham bones with meat or 1 pound beef short ribs
1 (3-pound) broiler-fryer
1½ quarts water
2 large potatoes, peeled and chopped
1 large onion, chopped
1 large cooking apple, peeled and chopped
5 stalks celery, including leaves, sliced
3 large carrots, scraped and sliced
2 large turnips, peeled and chopped
1 large green pepper, chopped
1 medium-size hot pepper, seeded
½ cup sliced okra
1 cup shredded cabbage
½ cup chopped fresh parsley
1 (8½-ounce) can English peas, undrained
1 (17-ounce) can whole kernel corn, undrained
3 (16-ounce) cans whole tomatoes, undrained and chopped
2 teaspoons salt
1 teaspoon pepper
¼ teaspoon ground red pepper
¼ teaspoon chili powder

Sort and wash beans and peas; place in a medium bowl. Cover with water 2 inches above beans, and let soak at least 8 hours.

Fry bacon in a large Dutch oven. Add soup bone, chicken, and water. Bring to a boil. Cover, reduce heat, and simmer 2 hours. Remove chicken and soup bone from broth, reserving broth; let meat cool completely. Bone and coarsely chop meat; set aside.

Drain beans, and add to broth. Cover and cook over medium heat 30 minutes or until beans are almost tender. Add chicken and remaining ingredients. Cover, reduce heat, and simmer 2 to 3 hours, stirring often. Add water for a thinner consistency, if desired. Yield: about 1½ gallons.

BAMA BRUNSWICK STEW

1 (2½- to 3-pound) broiler-fryer
1 (2- to 2½-pound) boneless pork loin
   roast
1 (2-pound) chuck roast
2½ quarts water
3 large potatoes, peeled and finely
   chopped
3 large onions, finely chopped
1 (28-ounce) can tomatoes, undrained and
   chopped
1 (17-ounce) can cream-style corn
1 (14-ounce) bottle catsup
1 small hot pepper
¼ cup red wine
2 to 3 tablespoons lemon juice
2 tablespoons dry sherry
1½ teaspoons paprika
1 teaspoon brown sugar
1 teaspoon pepper
½ teaspoon ground red pepper
½ teaspoon dried red pepper flakes

Combine chicken, roasts, and water in a large Dutch oven; cover and bring to a boil. Reduce heat, and simmer 1 hour or until meat is tender. Remove meat from broth, reserving broth. Cool meat completely. Remove meat from bones. Grind meat in food processor or food grinder.

Add potatoes and onions to broth; cook over medium heat 20 to 25 minutes or until tender. Add meat and remaining ingredients; bring to a boil. Reduce heat; simmer, uncovered, 2½ hours, stirring often. Add water for a thinner consistency, if desired. Yield: 1½ gallons.
James A. Christian,
River View, Alabama.

SONNY FRYE'S BRUNSWICK STEW

1 (5-pound) pork loin roast
2 (3-pound) broiler-fryers
3 quarts water
3 pounds onions, ground or chopped
4½ pounds potatoes, peeled and ground
   or coarsely shredded
1 (28-ounce) can whole tomatoes,
   undrained and mashed
2 (14-ounce) bottles catsup
1 (10-ounce) bottle mustard/mayonnaise
   sauce
1 (5-ounce) bottle Worcestershire sauce
Juice of 2 lemons
1 cup margarine
1 tablespoon salt
1 teaspoon pepper
2 (17-ounce) cans cream-style corn
1 (16-ounce) can whole-kernel corn,
   drained (optional)
1 (16-ounce) package frozen lima beans,
   thawed and drained (optional)

Combine pork, chicken, and water in a large Dutch oven; bring to a boil. Cover, reduce heat, and simmer 2 hours. Remove meat from broth, reserving broth. Skin, bone, and shred meat; cover and chill. Cover and chill broth 8 hours or overnight; remove solidified fat.

Heat broth; add onions, potatoes, tomatoes, catsup, mustard/mayonnaise sauce, Worcestershire sauce, lemon juice, margarine, salt, and pepper. Bring to a boil; reduce heat, and simmer, uncovered, 2 hours, stirring often.

Add reserved meat, cream-style corn and, if desired, whole-kernel corn, and lima beans to vegetable mixture. Bring to a boil. Reduce heat and simmer, uncovered, 2 hours or until desired consistency, stirring often. Add additional water for a thinner consistency, if desired. Yield: about 2¼ gallons.
James Frank Ragland,
Montgomery, Alabama.

BLAKELY BRUNSWICK STEW

1 (6- to 8-pound) fully cooked ham
4 medium onions, chopped
3 tablespoons vegetable oil
4 (16-ounce) cans tomatoes, undrained and
   chopped
2 (16-ounce) cans English peas, undrained
2 (16-ounce) cans cream-style corn
2 cups catsup
1 (15-ounce) can tomato sauce
⅓ to ½ cup Worcestershire sauce
2 tablespoons hot sauce
¼ lemon, chopped

Remove skin from ham; place ham, fat side up, in a shallow baking pan. Insert meat thermometer, making sure it does not touch fat or bone. Bake, uncovered, at 325° for 2 to 3 hours or until meat thermometer registers 140°. Cool completely in refrigerator.

Cut ham into large cubes, removing as much fat as possible. Grind ham in food processor or food grinder. Set ground ham aside.

Sauté onion in vegetable oil in a large Dutch oven. Add ground ham and remaining ingredients; bring to a boil. Reduce heat, and simmer, uncovered, 3 hours; stir often. Yield: 6 quarts.
Wayne Foster,
Blakely, Georgia.

BRUNSWICK CHICKEN STEW

1 (2½- to 3-pound) broiler-fryer
1 tablespoon salt
2 quarts water
¼ pound cooked pork or ham, cut into
   cubes
2 large onions, chopped
1 green pepper, chopped
2 tablespoons chopped fresh parsley
1 (16-ounce) can tomatoes, undrained and
   chopped
1 (16-ounce) can whole kernel corn,
   drained
1 (10-ounce) package frozen lima beans
1 (10-ounce) package frozen sliced okra
1 teaspoon salt
½ teaspoon black pepper
½ teaspoon dried whole thyme
1 bay leaf
1¼ teaspoons hot sauce

Combine first 3 ingredients in a large Dutch oven; bring to a boil. Cover, reduce heat, and simmer 1 hour. Remove chicken from broth, reserving broth. Cool chicken completely. Skin, bone, and coarsely chop meat.

Combine 2 quarts of reserved chicken broth, chicken, pork, and remaining ingredients in a large Dutch oven. Cover and simmer 2 hours or until mixture is desired consistency, stirring often. Add chicken broth or water for a thinner consistency, if desired. Discard bay leaf. Yield: 1 gallon.
Carol S. Noble,
Burgaw, North Carolina.

Fish Is Fine On Your Low-Sodium Diet

If you're trying to lower the sodium content of your diet and keep down calories, these fish recipes are for you. Most varieties of fish from the sea contain less than 60 milligrams of sodium per 3-ounce serving. Flounder, sole, and other flatfish are slightly higher.

If snapper fillets are not available for making Caribbean Snapper, other lean white fish fillets (of the same thickness) can be substituted. However, baking time may change—just watch carefully.

Fish is done when it flakes easily with a fork. Swordfish, however, is an exception. Use tenderness as your guide to doneness.

In our recipe for Curried Baked Fish we use low-sodium reduced-calorie mayonnaise to keep the sodium content at a low 53.5 milligrams per serving. If you don't need to cut the sodium in your diet quite so low, regular reduced-calorie mayonnaise can be used. The sodium content will be just 129 milligrams per serving. Tangy Broiled Scamp uses low-sodium breadcrumbs for 86 milligrams sodium per serving. If you use regular breadcrumbs, it will be increased to only 236 milligrams.

CARIBBEAN SNAPPER

Vegetable cooking spray
1 large onion, sliced
2 large tomatoes, peeled and chopped
1 teaspoon sugar
½ teaspoon dried whole oregano
¼ teaspoon dried whole thyme
1½ teaspoons chopped fresh parsley
½ bay leaf, crumbled
¼ cup water
Dash of hot sauce
3 pounds red snapper fillets or other lean white fish fillets
1½ tablespoons lemon juice
1 small clove garlic, minced
1 large onion, chopped
½ cup chopped green pepper
1 tablespoon olive oil
¼ cup sliced almonds, toasted

Coat a 13- x 9- x 2-inch baking dish with vegetable cooking spray. Arrange sliced onion in dish; add tomatoes, sugar, oregano, thyme, parsley, and ½ bay leaf.

Combine water and hot sauce; gently pour over tomato mixture. Rub fillets with lemon juice; arrange in dish.

Sauté garlic, onion, and green pepper in olive oil about 3 minutes; spoon over fillets. Cover and bake at 400° for 40 to 45 minutes or until fish flakes easily when tested with a fork. Garnish with almonds. Yield: 12 servings.

☐ 147 calories, 23.5 grams protein, 3.4 grams fat, 4.8 grams carbohydrate, 62 milligrams cholesterol, 80 milligrams sodium, and 36 milligrams calcium per 3-ounce serving. Linda R. Giar, Garland, Texas.

Tip: A fresh fish has practically no "fish" odor. The fish odor becomes more pronounced with the passage of time, but should not be strong when fish are bought.

CURRIED BAKED FISH

Vegetable cooking spray
8 (4-ounce) orange roughy fillets or other lean white fish fillets
½ cup low-sodium reduced-calorie mayonnaise
1 tablespoon Chablis or other dry white wine
1 tablespoon lemon juice
½ teaspoon dried whole dillweed
½ teaspoon curry powder

Coat a broiling rack with cooking spray. Place rack in a shallow baking pan; arrange fillets on rack.

Combine remaining ingredients; spread over fillets. Bake at 350° for 25 minutes or until fish flakes easily when tested with a fork. Yield: 8 servings.

☐ 147 calories, 22.6 grams protein, 5.1 grams fat, 1.3 grams carbohydrate, 67 milligrams cholesterol, 111 milligrams sodium, and 20 milligrams calcium per 3-ounce serving. Alice McNamara, Eucha, Oklahoma.

TANGY BROILED SCAMP

3 tablespoons lemon juice
½ teaspoon dry mustard
½ teaspoon dried whole tarragon
½ teaspoon garlic powder
½ teaspoon paprika
1 teaspoon dried whole oregano
1 pound scamp fillets or other lean white fish fillets
1 cup soft low-sodium breadcrumbs
Vegetable cooking spray
1 tablespoon reduced-calorie margarine, melted

Combine lemon juice, mustard, tarragon, garlic powder, paprika, and oregano in a shallow dish. Dip fish fillets into lemon juice mixture; lightly coat with breadcrumbs. Place on a broiler pan coated with cooking spray. Drizzle margarine over fish.

Broil 7 inches from heat about 7 minutes or until fish flakes easily when tested with a fork. Yield: 4 servings.

☐ 224 calories, 25.9 grams protein, 3.8 grams fat, 20.1 grams carbohydrate, 64 milligrams cholesterol, 144 milligrams sodium, and 60 milligrams calcium per 3-ounce serving. Margaret E. Carr, Hixson, Tennessee.

FOIL-BAKED SWORDFISH

1 medium onion, sliced
1 cup sliced fresh mushrooms
2 tablespoons chopped fresh parsley
2 tablespoons tarragon-flavored wine vinegar
2 tablespoons olive oil
½ teaspoon dill seeds
1½ pounds (1-inch-thick) swordfish steaks
⅛ teaspoon white pepper
6 small bay leaves

Combine onion, mushrooms, parsley, vinegar, olive oil, and dill seeds in a bowl; place half of mushroom mixture in a foil-lined 13- x 9- x 2-inch baking pan. Top with swordfish steaks. Sprinkle with white pepper, and place a bay leaf on each piece of fish.

Top with remaining mushroom mixture. Cover and bake at 425° for 45 minutes or until tender. Remove bay leaves. Yield: 6 servings.

☐ 186 calories, 22.4 grams protein, 9.2 grams fat, 2.8 grams carbohydrate, 62.3 milligrams cholesterol, 62.8 milligrams sodium, and 32.8 milligrams calcium per 3-ounce serving. Wilmina R. Smith, St. Petersburg, Florida.

Our Nutrition Analysis

—Each "Cooking Light" recipe has been analyzed for calories, protein, fat, carbohydrate, cholesterol, sodium, and calcium per serving.

—Nutrition analysis of each recipe is provided for people on normal diets to plan healthier, more balanced meals. People following physician-prescribed diets should consult a registered dietitian to see how "Cooking Light" recipes can fit into specific meal plans.

—Ingredients that appear as optional items (2 lemon slices, optional) in a recipe are not calculated.

—When ingredient options are given within a recipe (1 teaspoon fresh basil or ¼ teaspoon dried basil), only the first item has been calculated.

—Nutrition analysis is based on a stated serving size of the prepared recipe. If a recipe does not give a specific serving size (cake yields 12 servings), assume that all serving sizes are equal.

MARINATED SALMON STEAKS

2 (8-ounce) salmon steaks, 1¼ to 1½
   inches thick
½ cup sliced green onions with tops
½ cup Chablis or other dry white wine
1½ teaspoons fresh dillweed or ½
   teaspoon dried whole dillweed
¼ teaspoon ground mace
¼ teaspoon pepper
Lemon slices (optional)
Fresh dillweed sprigs (optional)

Place salmon steaks in an 8-inch square baking dish; add green onions, wine, dillweed, mace, and pepper. Cover and chill 45 minutes, turning once. Remove salmon from refrigerator, and let stand 20 minutes.

Bake, uncovered, at 350° for 35 minutes or until fish flakes easily when tested with a fork, basting with any remaining marinade. Garnish with lemon slices and dillweed, if desired. Yield: 4 servings.

☐ *146 calories, 23 grams protein, 4.3 grams fat, 2.5 grams carbohydrate, 39.5 milligrams cholesterol, 75 milligrams sodium, and 156.75 milligrams calcium per 3-ounce serving.*

Pauline J. Thompson,
Lenoir, North Carolina.

VEGETABLE-STUFFED FLOUNDER ROLLS

Vegetable cooking spray
1 (10-ounce) package frozen chopped
   broccoli, thawed and well drained
½ cup shredded carrots
¼ cup chopped green onions
¼ cup chopped green pepper
¼ cup chopped celery
1 clove garlic, minced
1½ teaspoons low-sodium herb-and-spice
   steak sauce
¼ teaspoon ground ginger
⅛ teaspoon pepper
½ teaspoon low-sodium chicken-flavored
   bouillon granules
2 tablespoons lemon juice, divided
8 (4-ounce) flounder fillets
Paprika
Parsley sprigs (optional)
Lemon slices (optional)

Place a skillet over medium heat until hot; coat with cooking spray. Sauté broccoli, carrots, green onions, green pepper, celery, and garlic until vegetables are crisp-tender; stir in steak sauce, ginger, pepper, bouillon granules, and 1 tablespoon lemon juice.

Spoon one-eighth of vegetable mixture onto each fillet; carefully roll up,

and place seam side down in a 12- x 8- x 2-inch baking dish coated with cooking spray. Brush with remaining 1 tablespoon lemon juice, and sprinkle with paprika. Bake, uncovered, at 350° for 20 to 25 minutes or until fish flakes easily when tested with a fork. Garnish with parsley and lemon slices, if desired. Yield: 8 servings.

☐ *86 calories, 15.5 grams protein, .8 grams fat, 3.9 grams carbohydrate, 42.5 milligrams cholesterol, 82.3 milligrams sodium, and 36.5 milligrams calcium per 3-ounce serving.*

MICROWAVE COOKERY

Soup And Sandwich–A Natural Combo

A cup of soup and a sandwich team up for a quick meal on cold days, and with the microwave, preparation of this simple combo can be even easier. Our recipes here feature Hot Pita Sandwiches and Brown Bread-Cream Cheese Sandwiches. For homemade soup, try our version of Cream of Cauliflower Soup or Bacon-Beer Cheese Soup. Just be sure to cook the soup in the specified dish size; milk-based soups bubble up high when they are cooked in the microwave oven.

Even if you use the microwave only for heating canned soup and deli-style sandwiches, here are some tips.

—To prepare canned soup, combine soup and water in a 1½-quart casserole. Microwave at HIGH for 5 to 7 minutes. If you use a temperature probe, set it for 150° to 170°.

—If you add milk instead of water to the canned soup, heat it at MEDIUM HIGH (70% power).

—One serving of soup will heat in the microwave in 2½ to 3½ minutes.

—For a hot deli-style sandwich, place slices of cheese between layers of meat. Cheese attracts microwaves, so placing it in the center will keep it from overcooking and will help the rest of the sandwich to heat quickly. When microwaving, wrap the sandwich in a paper towel to absorb moisture from the bread.

HOT PITA SANDWICHES

2 medium tomatoes, chopped
1 small green pepper, chopped
½ cup chopped green onions
1 small cucumber, peeled and chopped
3 tablespoons commercial Italian salad
   dressing
1 pound ground beef
¾ cup chopped onion
3 tablespoons catsup
1 tablespoon water
½ teaspoon ground allspice
Dash of ground cinnamon
¼ teaspoon salt
Dash of pepper
5 (6-inch) pita bread rounds
10 lettuce leaves
Crumbled feta cheese

Combine tomatoes, green pepper, green onions, cucumber, and salad dressing in a bowl; toss to mix. Cover and chill.

Crumble ground beef into a 1½-quart microwave-safe casserole. Add onion, and cover with heavy-duty plastic wrap. Microwave at HIGH for 5 to 6 minutes or until ground beef is done, stirring at 2-minute intervals. Drain well. Add catsup, water, allspice, cinnamon, salt, and pepper; mix well. Cover and microwave at HIGH for 1 minute.

Cut pita bread rounds in half; place on a microwave-safe glass plate. Microwave, uncovered, at HIGH for 1 minute or until warm. Line bread halves with lettuce; spoon ground beef mixture evenly into bread. Fill each sandwich with vegetable mixture. Top with feta cheese. Serve sandwiches immediately. Yield: 5 servings.

BROWN BREAD-CREAM CHEESE SANDWICHES

½ cup all-purpose flour
½ cup whole wheat flour
½ cup cornmeal
1 cup buttermilk
⅓ cup molasses
1 teaspoon baking soda
½ teaspoon salt
1 cup raisins
2 (3-ounce) packages cream cheese,
   softened

Combine flours, cornmeal, buttermilk, molasses, soda, and salt; beat at low speed of an electric mixer 30 seconds. Beat at medium speed until blended. Stir in raisins. Pour half of batter into a greased 2-cup glass measure. Cover with wax paper, and microwave at MEDIUM (50% power) for 3 minutes; rotate. Continue to microwave

Serve Brown Bread-Cream Cheese Sandwiches and Cream of Cauliflower Soup for a quick homemade meal from the microwave.

BACON-BEER CHEESE SOUP

6 slices bacon
1 cup chicken broth
1 (12-ounce) can beer, divided
½ teaspoon Worcestershire sauce
3 dashes of hot sauce
1 (16-ounce) jar process cheese spread
2 cups milk
3 tablespoons cornstarch

Place bacon on a rack in a 12- x 8- x 2-inch baking dish; cover with paper towels. Microwave at HIGH for 5 to 7 minutes or until bacon is crisp. Drain bacon; crumble and set aside.

Combine broth, ¾ cup beer, Worcestershire sauce, and hot sauce in a 3-quart casserole. Microwave at HIGH for 3½ to 4 minutes or until hot. Stir in cheese and milk; cover and microwave at MEDIUM HIGH (70% power) for 6 to 7 minutes, stirring after 1 minute.

Combine cornstarch and remaining beer; add to cheese mixture. Cover and microwave at MEDIUM HIGH for 7 to 8 minutes. Ladle into serving bowls; top each with bacon. Yield: about 7 cups.

Snacks To Keep You Cheering

During the "fourth quarter" of the football season, many of us will watch the championship bowl games on television. If the cook at your house is also an avid football fan, we have some snack recipes that can be made quickly before the game.

at MEDIUM for 2 to 4 minutes or until edge is no longer doughy. Let stand 5 minutes; unmold. Cool. Repeat procedure with remaining batter.

Cut loaves into ¼-inch slices. Spread half of bread slices with cream cheese. Top with remaining bread slices, matching sizes. (Sandwiches will vary in size.) Yield: 10 sandwiches.

CREAM OF CAULIFLOWER SOUP

1 (1-pound) head cauliflower, broken into
   flowerets
1 small onion, chopped
¼ cup water
3 tablespoons butter or margarine
1 tablespoon chicken-flavored bouillon
   granules
2 cups milk
½ teaspoon salt
¼ teaspoon ground nutmeg
¼ to ½ teaspoon white pepper
Chopped parsley or shredded Cheddar
   cheese

Combine cauliflower, onion, and water in a 2-quart microwave-safe casserole. Cover and microwave at HIGH for 4 to 7 minutes, stirring once. Let stand, covered, 2 to 3 minutes.

Spoon cauliflower mixture into container of electric blender or food processor. Add butter, bouillon, milk, salt, nutmeg, and pepper. Cover and process at low speed 3 to 4 seconds; process at high speed until mixture is smooth, about 1 minute.

Return mixture to casserole, and microwave at HIGH for 4 minutes, stirring once. Sprinkle each serving with parsley or shredded cheese; serve immediately. Yield: 4 cups.

Tip: If you use a lot of instant nonfat dry milk, measure the easy way: Mark the level of powder and water on the side of a plastic container with an indelible marker. There will be no need to measure the next time.

MEAT-AND-CHEESE APPETIZERS

1 (8-ounce) package cream cheese,
   softened
¼ cup chopped marinated artichokes,
   drained and chopped
¼ cup chopped water chestnuts, drained
36 (6- x 4-inch) thin slices cooked
   pastrami or ham

Combine cream cheese, artichokes, and water chestnuts in a small bowl; mix until blended. Place 1 teaspoon cream cheese mixture in center of pastrami slice; fold sides over filling. Fold edges of pastrami slice over filling; secure with a wooden pick. Repeat with remaining ingredients. Yield: 3 dozen appetizer servings.   *Lyn Renwick, Charlotte, North Carolina.*

COUNTRY HAM SPREAD

1 cup chopped cooked country ham
¾ cup mayonnaise
1 tablespoon brandy
1 tablespoon sweet pickle relish

Position knife blade in food processor bowl; add ham. Top with cover, and process until ham is coarsely ground. Combine remaining ingredients; stir in ham. Serve with crackers or toast points. Yield: 2 cups.

James E. Boggess,
North Miami, Florida.

MEXICAN CHEESE PUFFS

¾ cup water
¼ cup plus 2 tablespoons butter or
    margarine
¾ cup all-purpose flour
3 eggs
¼ cup grated Parmesan cheese
1 (8-ounce) package cream cheese,
    softened
1 (3-ounce) package cream cheese,
    softened
¾ cup ripe olives, chopped
1 (4-ounce) can chopped green chiles,
    undrained
2 tablespoons finely chopped onion
¾ teaspoon chicken-flavored bouillon
    granules

Combine water and butter in a medium saucepan; bring to a boil. Add flour, all at once, stirring vigorously over medium-high heat until mixture leaves sides of pan and forms a smooth ball. Remove from heat.

Add eggs, one at a time, beating thoroughly with a wooden spoon after each addition; beat until dough is smooth. Drop dough by rounded teaspoonfuls onto ungreased baking sheets. Sprinkle with Parmesan cheese. Bake at 400° for 25 to 30 minutes or until puffed and golden. Cool on wire racks.

Combine cream cheese and remaining ingredients; blend well.

Just before serving, cut top one-third off cream puffs. Spoon cream cheese filling into cream puffs; replace tops. Yield: about 3 dozen.

Marian C. Brown,
Simpsonville, South Carolina.

SPICED POPCORN SNACK

6 cups freshly popped corn, unsalted
3 cups small pretzel twists
2 cups unsalted peanuts
¼ cup butter or margarine, melted
1 teaspoon curry powder
¼ teaspoon hot sauce
¼ teaspoon salt
1½ cups raisins

Combine popcorn, pretzels, and peanuts in a roasting pan. Combine butter, curry powder, and hot sauce; drizzle over popcorn mixture, and gently toss to mix. Bake at 300° for 30 minutes; stir occasionally. Sprinkle with salt; let cool. Stir in raisins just before serving. Yield: 12½ cups.

Donna Hebson,
Sylacauga, Alabama.

ORIENTAL HOT MUNCH

¼ cup butter or margarine, melted
2 tablespoons soy sauce
2 teaspoons Worcestershire sauce
½ teaspoon hot sauce
1 teaspoon seasoning salt
¼ teaspoon garlic powder
1 cup chow mein noodles
1 cup crispy rice cereal squares
1 cup crispy wheat cereal squares
1 cup broken pretzel sticks
½ cup pecan halves
½ cup cashews

Combine butter, soy sauce, Worcestershire sauce, hot sauce, seasoning salt, and garlic powder. Combine remaining ingredients in a 15- x 10- x 1-inch jellyroll pan. Drizzle butter mixture over cereal mixture; toss gently. Bake at 250° for 1 hour, stirring occasionally. Cool and store in an airtight container. Yield: 5 cups.

Sharon Cotton,
Rogersville, Missouri.

New Variations
On An Old Favorite

When you think of upside-down cake, pineapple probably comes to mind. But here are three delicious variations of the classic upside-down cake, using other kinds of fruit.

You don't have to wait for fresh fruit to enjoy two of these desserts. Peach Upside-Down Cake and Upside-Down Sunburst Cake call for canned fruit.

PEACH UPSIDE-DOWN CAKE

¼ cup butter or margarine, softened
½ cup firmly packed brown sugar
1 (16-ounce) can peach slices, drained
18 maraschino cherries
½ cup shortening
1 cup sugar
2 eggs
1 teaspoon vanilla extract
2 cups sifted cake flour
1 tablespoon baking powder
1 teaspoon salt
⅔ cup milk

Combine butter and brown sugar; stir and spread in a 13- x 9- x 2-inch pan. Arrange peach slices in a single layer over brown sugar mixture. Place cherries between peach slices; set aside.

Cream shortening; gradually add sugar, beating until smooth. Add eggs and vanilla; beat until combined. Combine flour, baking powder, and salt; add to creamed mixture alternately with milk. Spoon batter evenly over peach slices. Bake at 350° for 40 minutes or until cake tests done. Cool 5 minutes; invert cake onto serving platter. Yield: 15 servings.

Marie A. Davis,
Drexel, North Carolina.

CRANBERRY UPSIDE-DOWN CAKE

1⅓ cups sugar, divided
4 cups fresh cranberries, divided
5 egg yolks
1½ cups sugar
¾ cup water
½ cup vegetable oil
2 teaspoons vanilla extract
2 teaspoons grated lemon rind
2 cups all-purpose flour
1 tablespoon baking powder
1 teaspoon salt
7 egg whites
½ teaspoon cream of tartar
Crème Chantilly

Grease two 8-inch square baking pans; sprinkle ⅓ cup sugar in each pan. Place 2 cups cranberries evenly in each pan. Sprinkle ⅓ cup sugar over cranberries in each pan; cover with foil. Bake mixture at 325° for 30 minutes. Uncover and cool.

Combine egg yolks, 1½ cups sugar, water, oil, vanilla, and lemon rind in a large bowl; beat well. Combine flour, baking powder, and salt; add to egg yolk mixture, beating until smooth. Combine egg whites (at room temperature) and cream of tartar; beat until soft peaks form, and fold into batter. Spoon batter evenly into pans. Bake at 350° for 35 to 40 minutes or until cake tests done. Cool for 5 minutes; invert cake onto a cooling rack.

Stack layers onto a plate, and frost sides with Crème Chantilly. Yield: one 8-inch cake.

Crème Chantilly:

2 cups whipping cream
2 tablespoons powdered sugar
2 teaspoons cream sherry

Combine all ingredients in a large mixing bowl; beat until soft peaks form. Spread or pipe around sides of cake. Yield: enough for one 8-inch cake.
Mrs. Raymond E. Pierce,
Hartselle, Alabama.

UPSIDE-DOWN SUNBURST CAKE

2 tablespoons butter
2 tablespoons light corn syrup
½ cup firmly packed brown sugar
4 canned pear halves, drained
10 maraschino cherries, quartered
¼ cup chopped pecans
½ cup butter
1¼ cups sugar
2 eggs
1½ cups all-purpose flour
¼ cup cocoa
½ teaspoon baking soda
½ teaspoon salt
½ cup buttermilk
1 teaspoon vanilla extract
Whipped cream (optional)

Melt 2 tablespoons butter and syrup in a 9-inch square pan. Sprinkle brown sugar evenly over butter mixture. Cut each pear half into 4 wedges. Arrange pears and cherries in sunburst design over brown sugar. Sprinkle chopped pecans over fruit.

Combine ½ cup butter and 1¼ cups sugar, beating at medium speed of an electric mixer until light and fluffy. Add eggs, one at a time, beating well after each addition.

Combine flour, cocoa, baking soda, and salt. Add to creamed mixture alternately with milk, beginning and ending with flour mixture. Stir in vanilla.

Spoon batter evenly over pear slices. Bake at 350° for 40 to 45 minutes or until cake tests done. Cool 5 minutes, and invert cake onto serving plate. Serve warm with whipped cream, if desired. Yield: one 9-inch cake.
Mrs. Stanley Pichon, Jr.
Slidell, Louisiana.

Salads From Your Pantry

Although winter is upon us and some fresh vegetables are scarce, you can still enjoy the variety and texture offered by winter salads. A combination of canned vegetables or fruit makes a colorful and nutritious addition to any meal.

SALMON-PASTA SALAD

1 (7¾-ounce) can salmon, undrained
2 tablespoons olive oil
2 tablespoons white wine vinegar
1 teaspoon Dijon mustard
½ teaspoon sugar
¼ teaspoon salt
Dash of pepper
2 cups cooked shell macaroni
1 Red Delicious apple, unpeeled and diced
½ cup chopped walnuts
2 tablespoons chopped green onions
2 tablespoons chopped fresh parsley
Lettuce

Drain salmon, reserving 2 tablespoons salmon liquid; flake with a fork. Set salmon aside.

Combine reserved salmon liquid, olive oil, vinegar, mustard, sugar, salt, and pepper in a small bowl; blend well. Pour over pasta. Cover and refrigerate at least 1 hour. Add reserved salmon, apple, walnuts, green onions, and parsley. Stir well. Serve in lettuce-lined bowl. Yield: 4 servings. *Cathy Darling, Grafton, West Virginia.*

CRUNCHY SAUERKRAUT SALAD

1 (16-ounce) can sauerkraut, drained
1 (15-ounce) can garbanzo beans, drained
1 (2-ounce) jar diced pimiento, drained
1 cup chopped onion
1 cup chopped celery
½ cup sugar
½ cup vinegar
½ cup vegetable oil
Lettuce leaves (optional)

Combine sauerkraut, beans, pimiento, onion, and celery in a large bowl, and set aside.

Combine sugar and vinegar in a small saucepan; bring to a boil. Stir in oil. Remove from heat. Pour over sauerkraut mixture; cover and chill overnight. Serve on bed of lettuce, if desired. Yield: about 6 servings.
Alice Slaton Grant,
Concord, North Carolina.

MARINATED CORN-BEAN SALAD

¾ cup sugar
¾ cup vinegar
½ cup vegetable oil
1 tablespoon water
1 teaspoon pepper
½ teaspoon salt
1 (17-ounce) can whole kernel corn, drained
1 (16-ounce) can French-style green beans, drained
1 (16-ounce) can English peas, drained
1 cup chopped onion
1 cup chopped green pepper

Combine sugar, vinegar, oil, water, pepper, and salt in a small saucepan; bring to a boil. Remove from heat; cool. Place remaining ingredients in a large bowl. Pour vinegar mixture over vegetables; cover and chill at least 4 hours. To serve, use a slotted spoon. Yield: 6 to 8 servings.
Diane L. Watson,
Thomson, Georgia.

ICY PINEAPPLE-FRUIT SALAD

1 (17-ounce) can apricots, undrained and sliced
1 (15¼-ounce) can crushed pineapple, undrained
½ cup sugar
3 (10-ounce) packages frozen strawberries, thawed and drained
3 bananas, sliced
1 (6-ounce) can frozen orange juice concentrate, thawed and undiluted
2 tablespoons lemon juice

Drain apricots and pineapple, reserving 1 cup juice. Combine sugar and reserved juice in a small saucepan; boil 2 minutes. Cool. Set aside.

Combine apricots, pineapple, strawberries, bananas, orange juice concentrate, lemon juice, and cooled syrup; stir gently. Pour mixture into a lightly oiled 6½-cup mold; cover and freeze until firm. Yield: 12 servings.
Jackie Helen Bergenheier,
Wichita Falls, Texas.

No-Fuss Supper Ideas

Today's busy families want good meals prepared with ease. For a delicious and colorful supper with a special dessert, try our menu featuring Baked Mustard Chicken. After the chicken is in the oven, assemble the Green Beans Italian so that the two recipes can bake together during the last 30 minutes. You'll then have time to make the salad. Make the Banana Split Alaska in advance and refreeze before baking.

Our second menu features cooking with soup—a convenient way to trim time in the kitchen. You may want to start the bread first to allow for rising time. While it's baking, prepare Chili Chops and Easy-Crust Apple Pie, which can be baked at the same time. As they bake, prepare the slaw.

Baked Mustard Chicken
Green Beans Italian
Carrot-Raisin Salad
Commercial Rolls
Banana Split Alaskas
Iced Tea   Coffee

BAKED MUSTARD CHICKEN

4 chicken breast halves, skinned
¼ cup spicy brown mustard
½ cup Italian-flavored breadcrumbs
¼ cup butter or margarine, melted
2 tablespoons lemon juice
2 tablespoons water or white wine
Paprika

Brush chicken with mustard, and dredge in breadcrumbs. Place in a 13- x 9- x 2-inch baking dish.

Combine butter, lemon juice, and water; drizzle 1 tablespoon over each piece of chicken, and pour remainder in dish. Cover and bake at 350° for 45 minutes. Remove cover, sprinkle with paprika, and bake an additional 15 minutes. Yield: 4 servings.
Marie Liggan Magennis,
Holiday, Florida.

Tip: When buying fresh sprouts, remember that they spoil after a day or two, losing their white color and crispness. Sprouts that are brownish colored or coated with film have already begun to spoil.

GREEN BEANS ITALIAN

1 (16-ounce) can cut green beans, drained
1 small onion, diced
1 (14½-ounce) can Italian-style stewed tomatoes, undrained
⅔ cup (2½ ounces) shredded mozzarella cheese

Place beans in a lightly greased 1½-quart casserole. Sprinkle onion over beans. Arrange stewed tomatoes evenly over onion.

Bake, uncovered, at 350° for 30 minutes. Add cheese, and bake an additional 5 minutes or until cheese melts. Serve immediately. Yield: 4 servings.
Donna Taylor,
Eads, Tennessee.

CARROT-RAISIN SALAD

¾ pound carrots, scraped and shredded
¼ cup plus 2 tablespoons raisins
¼ cup plus 2 tablespoons chopped walnuts
½ cup mayonnaise
1½ tablespoons cider vinegar
1 tablespoon sugar
⅛ teaspoon lemon juice

Combine carrots, raisins, and chopped walnuts in a bowl. Combine remaining ingredients, stirring well; add to carrot mixture. Toss gently. Yield: 4 servings.
Kaye Hagler,
Dothan, Alabama.

BANANA SPLIT ALASKAS

2 cake doughnuts, cut in half horizontally
1 banana, sliced
2 cups strawberry ice cream, divided
2 tablespoons plus 2 teaspoons chocolate syrup
¼ cup finely chopped pecans
4 egg whites
½ teaspoon cream of tartar
½ cup sugar
1 teaspoon vanilla extract
¼ cup coconut, toasted

Place doughnut halves, cut side up, on an ovenproof wooden board. Cover each half with banana slices. Spoon ½ cup ice cream over bananas, making an indentation in center of the ice cream. Fill each indentation with 2 teaspoons chocolate syrup and 1 tablespoon pecans. Then place in freezer.

Beat egg whites (at room temperature) and cream of tartar at high speed of an electric mixer 1 minute. Gradually add sugar, 1 tablespoon at a time, beating until stiff peaks form and sugar dissolves (2 to 4 minutes); add vanilla.

Remove doughnut halves from freezer, and quickly spread meringue over entire surface, making sure edges are sealed. Swirl meringue to make peaks. Sprinkle sides with coconut; cover and freeze until firm.

Remove from freezer and bake, uncovered, at 450° for 2 to 3 minutes or until meringue is lightly browned. Serve immediately. Yield: 4 servings.
Mrs. C. D. Marshall,
Boston, Virginia.

Chili Chops
Sour Cream Slaw
Cheese Bread
Easy-Crust Apple Pie
Milk

CHILI CHOPS

2 tablespoons vegetable oil
6 (¼-inch-thick) pork chops
1 teaspoon salt
⅛ teaspoon pepper
1 (10¾-ounce) can tomato soup, undiluted
1 (15-ounce) can kidney beans, undrained
½ cup sliced onion
1 tablespoon chili powder
½ teaspoon garlic powder
6 green pepper rings
Vegetable oil
Hot cooked rice

Heat 2 tablespoons oil in a large ovenproof skillet; brown pork chops on both sides. Remove chops and sprinkle with salt and pepper. Combine soup, beans, onion, chili powder, and garlic powder in skillet. Place chops over soup mixture. Cover and bake at 325° for 45 minutes or until chops are tender. Top each chop with a green pepper ring brushed with vegetable oil during last 10 minutes. Serve over hot cooked rice. Yield: 6 servings.
Thelma Peedin,
Newport News, Virginia.

SOUR CREAM SLAW

¾ cup commercial sour cream
1 tablespoon vinegar
½ teaspoon dill seeds
¼ teaspoon celery seeds
½ teaspoon salt
½ teaspoon pepper
5 cups shredded cabbage
½ cup thinly cut green pepper strips

Combine sour cream, vinegar, dill seeds, celery seeds, salt, and pepper in a small bowl; cover and chill 1 hour. Combine cabbage and green pepper; pour dressing over cabbage mixture. Toss to mix. Yield: 6 servings.

Judy Guilliams,
Clarksville, Texas.

CHEESE BREAD

1 (10¾-ounce) can Cheddar cheese soup, undiluted
¼ cup butter or margarine
½ cup cornmeal
1 tablespoon sugar
1 package dry yeast
2 eggs, slightly beaten
3½ cups all-purpose flour, divided
Melted butter or margarine

Combine soup and butter in a small saucepan; cook over low heat until butter melts and soup is smooth, stirring constantly. Remove from heat, and cool to 105° to 115°.

Combine cornmeal, sugar, yeast, and soup mixture in a large bowl. Stir in eggs, mixing until blended. Add 3 cups flour, 1 cup at a time, beating well after each addition. (Dough will be sticky.)

Place dough in a well-greased bowl, turning to grease top. Cover and let rise in a warm place (85°), free from drafts, 1 hour or until doubled in bulk.

Punch dough down; turn out onto a floured surface. Knead, adding remaining ½ cup flour as needed, until dough is smooth and elastic.

Divide dough in half. Shape each half into a loaf, and place in a well-greased 7- x 3- x 2-inch loafpan. Cover and let rise in a warm place, free from drafts, 25 minutes or until doubled in bulk.

Bake at 400° for 20 to 25 minutes or until bread sounds hollow when tapped. Remove from pans, and let cool on wire racks; brush tops of bread with melted butter. Yield: 2 loaves.

Martha Edington,
Knoxville, Tennessee.

EASY-CRUST APPLE PIE

6 cups sliced apples
1¼ teaspoons ground cinnamon
¼ teaspoon ground nutmeg
1 cup sugar
1½ cups biscuit mix, divided
¾ cup milk
2 eggs
2 tablespoons butter or margarine
½ cup chopped pecans
⅓ cup firmly packed brown sugar
3 tablespoons butter or margarine

Combine apples and spices in a large bowl; place in a greased 9-inch pieplate. Combine sugar, ½ cup biscuit mix, milk, eggs, and 2 tablespoons butter; beat until smooth, and pour mixture over apples.

Combine remaining 1 cup biscuit mix, pecans, brown sugar, and 3 tablespoons butter; sprinkle over apples. Bake at 325° for 50 to 55 minutes or until apples are tender. Yield: one 9-inch pie.

Mrs. Clifford B. Smith, Sr.,
White Hall, Maryland.

Bring On Black-Eyed Peas

Call them cowpeas, "Texas caviar," or black-eyed beans and you'll still be talking about the same tasty Southern specialty—black-eyed peas. Actually, they aren't peas or even beans at all. The correct name is "black-pigmented lentils," but Southerners will always know them as black-eyed peas.

To prepare dried peas, you'll need to soak them overnight before cooking, or you can use the quick-soak method. For the faster method of soaking, boil the peas in water for 2 minutes. Then remove them from heat; cover and let soak 1 hour. Be sure to cook the peas in the same water they soak in to preserve the most nutrients.

Also keep in mind when you cook dried peas that they will be less likely to split and break if they are simmered slowly. Acidic ingredients, such as wine, lemon juice, vinegar, or tomatoes, keep the peas from softening to the correct texture. So if your recipe calls for them, add these ingredients close to the end of cooking time.

GOOD LUCK JAMBALAYA

½ cup salt pork strips
2 cloves garlic, minced
1 large onion, chopped
1 medium-size green pepper, chopped
2 (16-ounce) cans black-eyed peas with jalapeño peppers, undrained
⅔ cup Bloody Mary mix
⅓ cup uncooked long-grain rice
1 pound raw shrimp, peeled and deveined or 1 (8-ounce) package dried shrimp
Additional cooked shrimp
Celery leaves

Cook salt pork in a large skillet until golden brown. Add garlic, onion, and green pepper; sauté until tender. Add peas, Bloody Mary mix, and rice. Bring mixture to a boil over medium heat; cover, reduce heat to low, and simmer 20 minutes. Add shrimp; cover and cook 5 minutes. Transfer to serving platter; garnish with shrimp and celery leaves. Yield: 6 to 8 servings.

W. C. Johnston,
Huntsville, Texas.

REUNION PEA CASSEROLE

1 pound bulk pork sausage
2 (16-ounce) cans black-eyed peas, drained
1 (4-ounce) can chopped green chiles, drained
1 teaspoon garlic powder
¼ teaspoon ground cumin
¼ teaspoon dried whole oregano
½ teaspoon pepper
¼ teaspoon salt
2 cups sliced yellow squash
2 cups sliced zucchini
1 cup chopped onion
2 tablespoons butter or margarine, melted
4 eggs, well beaten
2 cups (8 ounces) shredded mozzarella cheese
2 cups (8 ounces) shredded Cheddar cheese
2 (8-ounce) packages refrigerated crescent dinner rolls

Cook sausage in a skillet over medium heat until browned, stirring to crumble. Drain well. Combine with peas, chiles, garlic powder, cumin, oregano, pepper, and salt; set aside.

Sauté squash, zucchini, and onion in butter until tender, and drain well. Cool 5 minutes. Combine eggs and cheeses; fold into squash mixture; set aside.

Separate crescent roll dough into 2 long rectangles; pinch dough together. Roll out to a 17- x 13-inch rectangle. Place dough in a lightly greased 13- x 9- x 2-inch baking dish; press on bottom and up sides to form crust. Layer sausage and pea mixture on dough, and top with squash mixture.

Bake at 350° for 30 to 35 minutes. Let stand 15 minutes before serving. Yield: 8 servings.

Joyce Carroll,
Athens, Texas.

BLACK-EYED PEA GRAVY

½ cup vermouth
1 cup finely chopped green onions
⅔ cup finely chopped carrots
1 bay leaf
1 teaspoon freshly ground pepper
½ teaspoon dry mustard
Dash of red pepper
1 (10¼-ounce) can beef gravy
1 (16-ounce) can black-eyed peas, undrained
¼ cup butter or margarine
⅛ teaspoon lemon juice

Combine vermouth, green onions, carrots, bay leaf, ground pepper, mustard, and red pepper in a saucepan; stir well. Bring to a boil. Cover, reduce heat, and simmer 15 minutes. Add gravy, peas, butter, and lemon juice; cook, stirring occasionally, until mixture is thoroughly heated. Remove bay leaf, and serve mixture over beef, venison, or hot cooked rice. Yield: 3⅔ cups.

Dan Burger,
Euless, Texas.

PLENTIFUL P'S SALAD

4 cups cooked, drained black-eyed peas
2 cups cooked rotelle macaroni
1 medium-size red pepper, chopped
1 medium-size green pepper, chopped
1 medium-size purple onion, chopped
1 (6-ounce) package sliced provolone cheese, cut into strips
1 (3-ounce) package sliced pepperoni, cut into strips
1 (2-ounce) jar diced pimiento, drained
1 (4.5-ounce) jar sliced mushrooms, drained
2 tablespoons minced fresh parsley
1 (0.7-ounce) package Italian salad dressing mix
¼ teaspoon pepper
¼ cup sugar
½ cup vinegar
¼ cup vegetable oil

Combine peas, macaroni, red and green peppers, onion, cheese, pepperoni, pimiento, mushrooms, and parsley in a large bowl, and set aside.

Combine Italian salad dressing mix, pepper, sugar, vinegar, and oil in a jar; cover tightly, and shake. Pour salad dressing mixture over pea mixture; cover and chill salad at least 2 hours before serving. Yield: 8 servings.

Anna Ardinger,
Dallas, Texas.

Try Feta Cheese

Turn a macaroni-and-beef casserole into a family favorite or company fare by adding feta cheese. Pastitsio, a popular Greek casserole, is our selection for this idea.

Made with goat's milk, this white, crumbly cheese is cured in a salty brine and packed in jars. Consider feta a savory, slightly salty cream cheese, and its uses will be countless. Due to its slightly sharp flavor, feta makes a tasty bread spread when mixed with butter and cream cheese.

PASTITSIO

1½ pounds ground beef
1 cup chopped onion
1 (16-ounce) can tomatoes, undrained and chopped
1 (6-ounce) can tomato paste
¼ teaspoon dried whole thyme
1¾ teaspoons salt, divided
1 (8-ounce) package elbow macaroni
½ cup crumbled feta cheese
4 egg whites, slightly beaten
½ cup butter or margarine
½ cup all-purpose flour
¼ teaspoon ground cinnamon
1 quart milk
4 egg yolks, slightly beaten
Paprika (optional)

Combine ground beef and onion in a large skillet. Cook over medium heat until beef browns, stirring to crumble beef; drain. Stir in tomatoes, tomato paste, thyme, and ¾ teaspoon salt; bring to a boil. Cover, reduce heat, and simmer 30 minutes, stirring often.

Cook macaroni according to package directions, adding ¼ teaspoon salt; drain. Stir in feta cheese and egg whites. Add to beef mixture; stir well. Spoon mixture into a lightly greased 13- x 9- x 2-inch baking dish.

Melt butter in a heavy saucepan over low heat; add flour and cinnamon, stirring until smooth. Cook 1 minute, stirring constantly. Gradually add milk; cook over medium heat, stirring constantly, until mixture is thickened and bubbly. Stir in remaining ¾ teaspoon salt. Gradually stir about one-fourth of hot mixture into yolks; add to remaining hot mixture, stirring constantly. Cook 1 minute, stirring constantly. Pour sauce over beef mixture; bake at 350° for 35 to 40 minutes. Remove from oven; let stand 10 minutes before serving. Sprinkle with paprika, if desired. Yield: 8 servings. *Mrs. P. J. Davis,*
Drexel, North Carolina.

From Our Kitchen To Yours

When home economists join our staff, we acquaint them with our standard cooking procedures and terms. Understanding these procedures should help you, too, in using our recipes.

For instance, many of our recipes call for **chopped cooked chicken.** In our test kitchens, here's how we cook it. Place a whole chicken in a large Dutch oven, cover with water, and add ½ teaspoon salt. Bring water to a boil; cover, reduce heat, and simmer 45 minutes to 1 hour. Remove chicken and let cool; reserve broth, if desired. Remove meat from bone, discarding skin and fat; then chop the meat. (Removing skin and visible fat before cooking reduces the amount of fat even more.)

When a recipe calls for **cooked shrimp,** we use 6 cups water per 2 pounds unpeeled, fresh shrimp. Bring water to a boil in a Dutch oven; add shrimp, and cook 3 to 5 minutes only. (Keep in mind that overcooking will make the shrimp tough.) Drain shrimp, and rinse with cold water; peel and devein shrimp.

Some recipes require that ingredients be drained. We use two different procedures, depending on whether the recipe states to **drain** or to **drain well.** A colander or sieve is used to simply drain ingredients. To drain well, the ingredients are pressed between paper towels until all moisture is absorbed.

Recipes for yeast bread usually say to cover dough and let rise in a warm place (85°), free from drafts. We have found that the following **rising procedure** provides the best results. Place dough in a lightly greased bowl, and cover with plastic wrap or a towel. Place a pan of hot water on lower rack of unheated oven, and place dough on center rack; close door and turn on light. Let dough rise for the specified time or until doubled in bulk.

Cake flour and powdered sugar are always sifted for accurate measurement. **Sifting** lightens and removes lumps from cake flour. Powdered sugar must be sifted. All-purpose flour is no longer lumpy and compact; we now just stir it with a spoon before measuring.

Cheese placed on top of a casserole becomes tough and stringy when overcooked. To prevent this problem, we bake the casserole, without cheese, for 5 minutes less than the recipe indicates. Then we sprinkle the casserole with cheese, and bake 5 minutes longer.

February

Dessert For The Sentimental

If you're searching for a special treat to bake, try these Heart Tarts. To make them, we used one 11- x 8-inch aluminum pan that has six heart-shaped molds. Each mold measures 3½- x 3½- x 1¼-inches. The pan is available from stores that carry cake-decorating equipment. Substitute other ovenproof pans of a similar size if you can't find this particular set.

HEART TARTS
(pictured on page iv)

1 recipe Heart Tart Pastry
1 recipe choice of fillings
About 3 cups fruit
1 recipe choice of glazes

Prepare Heart Tart Pastry; remove from pans, and let cool.

Spoon desired filling evenly into pastry shells. Top with desired fruit: fresh strawberries, kiwifruit, or grapes; thawed frozen raspberries, blueberries, or blackberries; or canned sliced peaches, apricot halves, or mandarin oranges. Brush glaze lightly over fruit. Yield: 6 servings.

Heart Tart Pastry

1½ cups all-purpose flour
½ teaspoon baking powder
½ teaspoon salt
¼ cup butter
¼ cup shortening
4 to 5 tablespoons milk

Combine flour, baking powder, and salt; cut in butter and shortening with pastry blender until mixture resembles coarse meal. Sprinkle milk evenly over surface; stir with a fork until dry ingredients are moistened. Shape dough into a ball; chill.

Divide dough into 6 equal portions. Roll one portion at a time on a lightly floured surface just larger than 3½-inch heart-shaped pans. Fit pastry gently into pans; trim edges as needed. Fold edges under, and flute. Repeat procedure with remaining pastry.

Prick bottom of pastries with a fork. Bake at 450° for 10 minutes or until pastries are lightly browned. Remove pastries to wire rack to cool. Yield: six 3½-inch tarts.

EGG CUSTARD FILLING

⅓ cup sugar
1 tablespoon all-purpose flour
1 egg
1 egg yolk
¾ cup milk
3 tablespoons butter or margarine
1 teaspoon vanilla extract

Combine sugar and flour in top of a double boiler; stir well. Add egg, egg yolk, and milk; beat well with a wire whisk. Cook over boiling water, stirring constantly, until smooth and thickened. Remove from heat; add butter and vanilla, stirring until butter melts. Place plastic wrap directly on top of pudding; chill thoroughly. Yield: 1 cup.

LEMON CREAM FILLING

4 egg yolks
⅔ cup sugar
3 to 4 tablespoons lemon juice
½ cup butter or margarine, cut into pieces

Combine all ingredients in a saucepan; cook over medium heat, stirring constantly, until mixture thickens (about 10 minutes). Let cool. Yield: 1 cup.

GROUND ALMOND FILLING

¾ cup slivered almonds
⅓ cup sifted powdered sugar
1 egg
1 tablespoon butter or margarine, softened
⅛ teaspoon almond extract

Position knife blade in food processor bowl. Add slivered almonds; process 30 seconds or until finely ground. Add remaining ingredients; process until blended. Yield: ¾ cup.

APRICOT-KIRSCH GLAZE

¼ cup apricot preserves
2 tablespoons water
1 tablespoon sugar
1½ teaspoons kirsch

Combine preserves, water, and sugar in a saucepan; cook over low heat until sugar dissolves. Press mixture through a sieve, reserving syrup; discard pulp. Stir kirsch into syrup. Yield: ⅓ cup.

Roll Heart Tart Pastry just a little larger than the pans. Fit the pastry into the pans; then trim and flute edges.

Spoon a filling of your choice evenly into baked pastry shells, and spread the filling with the back of the spoon.

Arrange fruit over the filling, and brush with your choice of glazes. You can make the fruit arrangements alike or different.

HONEY-NUT GLAZE

½ cup sugar
3 tablespoons water
1 teaspoon lemon juice
1½ tablespoons honey
2 tablespoons finely chopped pecans or
   almonds

Combine sugar, water, and lemon juice in a saucepan; bring to a boil. Reduce heat, and simmer 3 minutes. Stir in honey and pecans. Serve warm. Yield: ⅓ cup.

Southerners Love These Oldtime Breads

"Just add flour till it *looks* right; then stir in some milk till it *feels* right." You've probably heard these words a thousand times as friends and relatives have shared their secrets for fluffy biscuits or rolls. It's the same story for cornbread, hush puppies, and other breads so common to this region that many folks whip them up without ever using a measuring cup or a recipe.

Fortunately, some people did write down their recipes, and the breads we love the most today are amazingly similar to the Southern favorites of centuries ago. Some of these recipes may differ from your standbys, but we hope you'll find a new favorite.

SPOON ROLLS

1 package dry yeast
2 cups warm water (105° to 115°)
½ cup butter or margarine, melted
4 cups self-rising flour
1 egg, slightly beaten
¼ cup sugar

Dissolve yeast in warm water; let stand 5 minutes. Combine yeast mixture, butter, and flour in a large bowl, mixing well. Stir in egg and sugar. (Mixture will be a very soft batter.) Cover and refrigerate batter overnight.

Spoon batter into greased muffin pans, filling two-thirds full. Bake at 350° for 25 minutes. Yield: 16 rolls.

Note: Batter may be stored, covered, in refrigerator up to 4 days.

Betty B. Lawrence,
Cadiz, Kentucky.

CLOUD BISCUITS

2¼ cups self-rising flour
1 tablespoon sugar
½ cup butter-flavored shortening
1 egg, beaten
⅔ cup milk
1 tablespoon butter or margarine,
   melted

Combine flour and sugar in a medium bowl; mix well. Cut in shortening with a pastry blender until mixture resembles coarse meal.

Combine egg and milk; add to flour mixture, stirring just until dry ingredients are moistened. Turn dough out onto a floured surface, and knead dough 3 or 4 times.

Roll dough to ½-inch thickness; cut with a 2½-inch biscuit cutter. Place biscuits on an ungreased baking sheet. Bake at 450° for 10 to 12 minutes or until biscuits are golden. Remove baking sheet from oven; brush biscuits with melted butter. Yield: 12 biscuits.

Mrs. Ken Altizer,
Charlotte, North Carolina.

REFRIGERATOR POTATO ROLLS

2 medium potatoes, peeled and
   chopped
1 package dry yeast
1 cup warm water (105° to 115°)
¾ cup sugar
½ cup butter
½ cup shortening
1½ teaspoons salt
About 7 cups all-purpose flour

Cook potatoes in boiling water to cover 10 minutes or until tender. Drain potatoes, reserving 1 cup liquid (add water to equal 1 cup liquid, if necessary). Set potato water aside. Mash potatoes. Measure 1 cup mashed potatoes; set aside.

Dissolve yeast in warm water; let stand 5 minutes. Set aside. Combine 1 cup mashed potatoes, sugar, butter, and shortening in a large mixing bowl. Cool to 105° to 115°; stir in yeast mixture, mixing well. Let stand at room temperature 2 hours.

Add salt and potato water; gradually stir in enough flour to make a soft dough. Place the dough in a well-greased bowl, turning to grease top. Cover bowl, and refrigerate the dough overnight.

Punch dough down; divide into thirds. Shape each portion into 12 (1½-inch) balls. Place in 3 greased 9-inch round cakepans; cover and let rise in a warm place (85°), free from drafts, 40 minutes or until doubled in bulk. Bake at 400° for 18 to 20 minutes or until golden. Yield: 3 dozen.

Emma Lee Hester,
Creedmoor, North Carolina.

CORNBREAD STICKS

1 cup cornmeal
3 tablespoons all-purpose flour
1 teaspoon baking powder
¼ teaspoon baking soda
¼ teaspoon salt
1 cup buttermilk
1 egg, slightly beaten
2 tablespoons shortening, melted

Combine cornmeal, flour, baking powder, soda, and salt, mixing well. Combine buttermilk and egg, mixing well; add to dry ingredients, stirring until dry ingredients are moistened. Stir shortening into batter.

Place a well-greased cast-iron corn stick pan in a 475° oven for 3 minutes or until hot. Remove pan from oven; spoon batter into pan, filling two-thirds full. Bake at 475° for 12 to 15 minutes. Yield: 11 corn sticks.

Mrs. J. W. Riley, Jr.,
Kingsport, Tennessee.

HUSH PUPPIES

2 cups yellow cornmeal
1 cup all-purpose flour
1 tablespoon sugar
1 tablespoon baking powder
½ teaspoon baking soda
1 teaspoon salt
1 teaspoon coarsely ground
   pepper
1 egg
½ to 1 teaspoon hot sauce
1½ cups buttermilk
1 cup minced onion
1 cup whole kernel corn
Vegetable oil

Combine cornmeal, flour, sugar, baking powder, soda, salt, and pepper in a medium bowl; set aside. Combine egg and hot sauce; stir in buttermilk. Pour into dry ingredients, stirring just to mix. Stir in onion and corn. (Do not overmix batter.)

Drop batter by tablespoonfuls into deep, hot oil (350°); cook only a few at a time, turning once. Fry 3 minutes or until golden brown. Drain on paper towels. Yield: 3 dozen.

Mrs. John Montgomery,
Pensacola, Florida.

CORNMEAL BATTER CAKES

1 cup cornmeal
½ teaspoon baking soda
½ teaspoon salt
2 eggs, beaten
1¼ cups buttermilk
2 tablespoons melted shortening or bacon
   drippings
Syrup (optional)

Combine cornmeal, soda, and salt in a small bowl; set aside. Combine eggs and buttermilk; stir into dry ingredients. Stir in melted shortening.

For each cake, pour about 2 tablespoons batter onto a hot, lightly greased griddle. Turn when tops are covered with bubbles and edges are browned. Serve cakes with syrup, if desired. Yield: 20 (3-inch) cakes.

T. C. Dedman,
Harrodsburg, Kentucky.

QUICK SALLY LUNN

¼ cup shortening
¼ cup sugar
3 eggs, beaten
2 cups all-purpose flour
2½ teaspoons baking powder
1 teaspoon salt
1 cup milk

Cream shortening; gradually add sugar, beating at medium speed of an electric mixer until light and fluffy. Stir in eggs, mixing well.

Combine flour, baking powder, and salt. Stir flour mixture into creamed mixture alternately with milk, beginning and ending with flour mixture. (Do not overmix; batter should be lumpy.)

Spoon batter into a greased 6-cup Bundt pan or ring mold. Bake at 350° for 45 to 50 minutes or until a wooden pick inserted in center comes out clean. Remove from pan, and transfer to a wire rack to cool. Yield: 1 loaf.

Charlotte Watkins,
Lakeland, Florida.

From Our Kitchen To Yours

Hush puppies piled high in a bread basket, a skillet of piping-hot cornbread rich with melting butter, and a bowl of crispy fried okra bring the warmth of tradition to our supper tables. These simple foods make cornmeal a staple on Southerners' pantry shelves. (See "Southerners Love These Oldtime Breads" beginning on page 15.)

Understanding the Label

Cornmeal is coarsely ground corn. When ground between two large rocks, it is labeled **water ground** or **rock ground** and has a soft texture. **Roller ground,** which usually feels like fine crystals, is ground between steel cylinders or rollers.

The word **enriched** on cornmeal's label signifies that iron, calcium, and B vitamins have been added.

Cornmeal is made from either white or yellow corn. The yellow type is more familiar in the North, while white cornmeal, which is milder in flavor, is usually preferred by Southern cooks.

Consumers also have the choice of **plain** or **self-rising cornmeal.** Self-rising cornmeal has leavening agents and salt blended in the correct proportions to ensure leavening accuracy and save the cook steps.

With the rapid shift to convenience products, supermarkets stock many **cornmeal mixes.** You add only water to some, while other mixes call for milk or buttermilk. Adding an egg is usually optional. Some mixes contain sugar, resulting in a sweet cornbread.

Making Good Cornbread

—Some recipes team flour with the cornmeal. The proportion of cornmeal to flour determines the texture of the baked product. More flour results in a softer, lighter texture.

—Fat added to cornmeal helps make breads tender. Just stir melted shortening or vegetable oil into the batter. Bacon drippings, butter, and margarine add extra flavor with the fat.

—Eggs help bind the batter and add lightness and volume. They also increase the food value of cornbread.

—Milk or buttermilk provides additional food value as well as good flavor.

—Sugar, used in small amounts in some cornbreads, helps bring out the sweet, nutlike flavor of cornmeal.

—Spices, onion, and other condiments add extra flavor to many breads made from cornmeal.

Bake A Dainty Party Cookie

If the only pirouette cookies you've had are the commercial kind, you'll enjoy seeing how easy they are to make at home. Jean Voan of Shepherd, Texas, sends us her version of French Curled Cookies.

The crisp, thin cookies are rolled around a wooden spoon handle as soon as they come from the oven. It's important to work quickly because the cookies get brittle as they cool.

FRENCH CURLED COOKIES

¼ cup plus 2 tablespoons butter or
   margarine, softened
1 cup sifted powdered sugar
⅔ cup all-purpose flour
4 egg whites
1 teaspoon vanilla extract

Cream butter; gradually add sugar, beating well at medium speed of an electric mixer. Add flour, egg whites, and vanilla; mix well.

Bake only 4 cookies at a time on a greased cookie sheet. Spoon 1½ teaspoons of batter in the center of each of 4 sections on cookie sheet. Spread each portion of batter evenly with a spatula to make a 3- x 4-inch oval. Bake at 425° for 3 minutes or until edges are golden.

Loosen cookies with a metal spatula, but leave on cookie sheet. Place one cookie upside down on counter, and quickly roll it around the handle of a wooden spoon. Remove cookie, and let cool on wire racks. Repeat procedure with remaining cookies as quickly as possible. (If cookies become too stiff before rolling, return cookie sheet to oven briefly to soften them.) Continue procedure with remaining cookie batter. Yield: 3 dozen.

Tip: Keep butter, margarine, and fat drippings tightly covered in the refrigerator. Vegetable shortening can be kept covered at room temperature. Homemade salad dressing should be kept in the refrigerator; mayonnaise and commercial salad dressings should be refrigerated after opening. Foods mixed with mayonnaise, such as potato salad or egg salad, should be refrigerated and used within a couple of days.

COOKING Light

Lighten Up For A Livelier You

Today's society places a high value on being thin, and it's not all a matter of vanity. The more you weigh above your ideal body weight, the more your health risks are increased. Overweight people are more likely to have hypertension, diabetes, elevated blood cholesterol levels, and cardiovascular disease, as well as certain types of cancer. And, of course, being overweight has an adverse effect on longevity.

At least 28% of the population age 25 to 74 is overweight. And for many, dieting has become a way of life. At any point, it is estimated that one out of every five adults is dieting. One in three goes on some type of crash diet and ends up dieting repeatedly. This "rhythm method of girth control," however, is not the healthiest way to shed extra pounds.

Some research suggests that the reason so many people are overweight is the lack of physical activity, rather than eating too many calories. Reports also indicate that only about 50% of the people exercise in conjunction with a reasonable weight-loss diet. This combination, however, is the safest way to permanently lose unwanted pounds.

To find out more about the role of exercise with diet in weight loss, be sure to read our article "The Keys to Weight Loss" on page 34 in this section. And once you're convinced that you don't have to starve to lose weight, you can sit back and enjoy our article on chocolate desserts found on page 21.

In this section you'll also find ideas for making your own single-portion frozen entrées and for making sauces that fit into your diet plan. And for adventurous cooks, we'll show ways to use some special equipment that will make this kind of cooking easier. Some of this equipment includes a loaf pan with drainage holes, a wok, and a vegetable steamer. So regardless of your health and nutrition interests, we think we've got them covered in this tempting special section.

Make Your Own Frozen Entrées

Juggling work schedules, household responsibilities, recreational activities, and errands often leaves little time for preparing meals. But instead of giving in to the lure of fast-food restaurants and their high-fat, high-calorie offerings, be prepared with your own homemade fast food in the form of single-portion frozen entrées.

You can make light frozen entrées from scratch at about half the cost of commercial ones. And you'll have control over ingredients, so that you can minimize fat and sodium, and eliminate additives and preservatives.

In making Spinach-Stuffed Shells (page 20), you'll probably notice that the tomato sauce which covers them calls for no-salt-added tomato products, yet we added salt to the recipe. This may seem a bit strange, but by doing this, we kept the sodium at a lower level than if all regular tomato products had been used and no salt added to the recipe. If you taste the sauce before freezing, you may want to add more seasonings, but wait. The taste of certain herbs and spices is more intense after freezing.

Other foods will need to be added to your homemade frozen main dishes to round out the meal, but these can also be prepared quickly if you keep the dishes simple.

CHILI

Vegetable cooking spray
9 ounces ground round
¼ cup chopped onion
¼ cup chopped green pepper
3 cloves garlic, minced
2 (14½-ounce) cans no-salt-added whole tomatoes, undrained and chopped
1 (8-ounce) can no-salt-added tomato sauce
¾ cup water
1 tablespoon chili powder
1 teaspoon ground cumin
½ teaspoon salt
¼ teaspoon dried whole oregano
1 (16-ounce) can kidney beans, drained

Place a large skillet over medium heat until hot; coat with cooking spray. Add ground round, onion, green pepper, and garlic; cook until beef is browned, stirring to crumble meat. Drain. Add tomatoes, tomato sauce, water, chili powder, cumin, salt, and oregano to meat mixture; stir well. Bring mixture to a boil; reduce heat, and simmer, uncovered, 15 minutes, stirring occasionally. Stir in kidney beans.

Ladle 1 cup chili into 6 sealable boiling bags or microwave-safe containers. Remove as much air as possible; seal boiling bags or cover microwave-safe containers with heavy-duty plastic wrap and then with heavy-duty aluminum foil. Freeze.

To heat frozen chili in sealable boiling bag, submerge in boiling water 20 minutes. To heat frozen chili in microwave-safe container, remove foil, and vent plastic wrap. Microwave at HIGH for 5 to 6 minutes or until heated, rotating dish a half-turn after 2½ to 3 minutes. Yield: 6 servings.

□ *134 calories, 12.6 grams protein, 3.9 grams fat, 15.1 grams carbohydrate, 21 milligrams cholesterol, 387 milligrams sodium, and 62 milligrams calcium per 1-cup serving.* Fran Williamson, *Baton Rouge, Louisiana.*

BEEF-AND-ONION STEW

1 tablespoon vegetable oil
2 pounds lean boneless sirloin, cut into
 1-inch cubes
3 whole cloves
1 (4-inch) stick cinnamon
1 cup Burgundy or other dry red wine
¾ cup water
3 tablespoons no-salt-added tomato sauce
2 tablespoons red wine vinegar
1 bay leaf
4 cloves garlic, minced
2 teaspoons dark brown sugar
½ teaspoon salt
½ teaspoon ground cumin
¼ teaspoon pepper
1½ pounds pearl onions

Heat vegetable oil in a Dutch oven. Add beef cubes, browning on all sides; drain off drippings.

Tie cloves and cinnamon stick in a spice bag. Add spice bag, wine, water, tomato sauce, vinegar, bay leaf, garlic, brown sugar, salt, cumin, and pepper to beef; stir well. Bring to a boil; cover, reduce heat, and simmer 40 minutes. Add onions; cover and simmer 20 minutes. Discard bay leaf and spice bag.

Spoon ¾ cup stew into each of 6 sealable boiling bags or microwave-safe containers. Remove as much air as possible, and seal bags or cover microwave-safe containers with heavy-duty aluminum foil; freeze.

To heat frozen stew in boiling bag, submerge in boiling water for 15 minutes or until thoroughly heated.

To heat frozen stew in microwave oven, remove foil; cover with heavy-duty plastic wrap, venting it on one side. Microwave at HIGH for 5 to 7 minutes or until thoroughly heated, rotating dish after 2½ to 3½ minutes. Yield: 6 servings.

☐ *233 calories, 25.4 grams protein, 8.3 grams fat, 13.8 grams carbohydrate, 68.8 milligrams cholesterol, 276.3 milligrams sodium, and 58.6 milligrams calcium per ¾-cup serving.* Ruth A. Colosimo, *Copperas Cove, Texas.*

Tip: When browning food in a skillet, dry the food first on paper towels.

SHRIMP CREOLE

2 quarts water
2 pounds unpeeled fresh medium shrimp
1 cup chopped onion
1 cup chopped green pepper
1 tablespoon vegetable oil
2 (14½-ounce) cans no-salt-added whole
 tomatoes, drained and chopped
1 (6-ounce) can no-salt-added tomato paste
1 bay leaf
1 teaspoon Worcestershire sauce
½ teaspoon dried whole oregano
¼ teaspoon salt
¼ teaspoon lemon-pepper seasoning
¼ teaspoon freshly ground pepper
Dash of red pepper
2 cups hot cooked rice (cooked without
 salt or fat)

Bring water to a boil in a large Dutch oven; add shrimp, and cook 3 to 5 minutes. Drain well; rinse with cold water. Chill. Peel and devein shrimp. Set aside 1 pound of shrimp; reserve the rest for other uses.

Sauté onion and green pepper in oil in a large skillet until tender. Add tomatoes, tomato paste, bay leaf, Worcestershire sauce, oregano, salt, lemon-pepper seasoning, pepper, and red pepper; stir well. Bring to a boil; reduce heat, and simmer, uncovered, 15 minutes, stirring occasionally (sauce will be thick). Remove from heat; discard bay leaf. Stir in shrimp.

Spoon 1 cup Shrimp Creole into 4 sealable boiling bags or microwave-safe containers. Seal boiling bags, or cover microwave-safe containers with heavy-duty plastic wrap and then heavy-duty aluminum foil. Freeze.

Spoon ½ cup rice into each of 4 sealable boiling bags or microwave-safe containers. Remove as much air as possible; seal boiling bags, or cover microwave-safe containers with heavy-duty plastic wrap and then with heavy-duty aluminum foil. Freeze.

To heat frozen Shrimp Creole and rice in sealable boiling bags, submerge both bags in boiling water; return to a boil, and cook 10 minutes.

To heat frozen Shrimp Creole and rice in microwave-safe containers, remove foil, and vent plastic wrap on one side. Microwave at HIGH for 5 to 7 minutes or until heated, rotating dish a half-turn after 2½ to 3 minutes. Yield: 4 servings.

☐ *228 calories, 26.2 grams protein, 4.8 grams fat, 20.9 grams carbohydrate, 189 milligrams cholesterol, 501.1 milligrams sodium, and 154 milligrams calcium per 1-cup serving Shrimp Creole plus 118 calories, 2.2 grams protein, 0.1 gram fat, 25.9 grams carbohydrate, 0 milligrams cholesterol, 1 milligram sodium, and 8 milligrams calcium per ½-cup serving rice.* Joyce Spears, *Arlington, Texas.*

TURKEY PATTIES IN VEGETABLE-TOMATO SAUCE

1 pound raw frozen ground turkey,
 thawed
¼ teaspoon salt
⅛ teaspoon garlic powder
⅛ teaspoon pepper
⅛ teaspoon celery seeds
1 teaspoon browning and seasoning sauce
Vegetable cooking spray
2 (8-ounce) cans no-salt-added tomato
 sauce
2 medium-size yellow squash, thinly sliced
1 medium zucchini, thinly sliced
1 small onion, thinly sliced
2 teaspoons chopped fresh parsley
¼ teaspoon ground savory
⅛ teaspoon dried whole thyme
½ teaspoon salt

Combine turkey, salt, garlic powder, pepper, celery seeds, and browning sauce in a medium bowl; stir well. Shape into 4 patties. Place on a broiling rack coated with cooking spray. Bake at 350° for 15 to 20 minutes; let cool.

Combine tomato sauce and remaining ingredients in a medium saucepan. Bring to a boil; reduce heat, and simmer 3 minutes. Let cool.

Place each turkey patty with ⅔ cup sauce and vegetables into ovenproof or microwave-safe container. Cover with heavy-duty plastic wrap and then with heavy-duty aluminum foil. Freeze.

To heat patties in conventional oven, remove foil and plastic wrap; re-cover with foil. Bake at 375° for 30 minutes.

To heat patties in microwave oven, remove foil, and vent plastic wrap. Microwave at HIGH for 7 to 9 minutes or until heated, rotating every 2 minutes. Yield: 4 servings.

☐ *237 calories, 16 grams protein, 14.4 grams fat, 13.2 grams carbohydrate, 59 milligrams cholesterol, 509.5 milligrams sodium, and 56 milligrams calcium per patty with ⅔ cup sauce and vegetables.*

CURRIED CHICKEN-STUFFED PEPPERS

6 medium-size green peppers (about 2 pounds)
Vegetable cooking spray
1 cup peeled and chopped cooking apple
1 cup chopped celery
½ cup chopped onion
2 tablespoons cornstarch
1 (12-ounce) can evaporated skim milk
2 cups chopped cooked chicken (cooked without salt)
1½ cups cooked brown rice (cooked without salt or fat)
¼ cup raisins
¼ teaspoon plus ⅛ teaspoon salt
¼ teaspoon white pepper
⅛ teaspoon coconut extract
2 teaspoons curry powder
¼ cup chopped unsalted almonds

Cut off tops of peppers, and remove seeds. Wash peppers, and set aside.

Coat a skillet with cooking spray; place over medium-high heat until hot. Add apple, celery, and onion; sauté until crisp-tender. Dissolve cornstarch in milk; add to vegetable mixture. Cook over medium heat, stirring constantly, until thickened. Stir in chicken, rice, raisins, salt, white pepper, coconut extract, and curry. Spoon ¾ cup mixture into each pepper; top with almonds.

Place each pepper into ovenproof or microwave-safe container; cover with heavy-duty aluminum foil. Freeze.

To heat frozen stuffed peppers in ovenproof container, vent foil and bake at 400° for 60 to 70 minutes.

To heat frozen stuffed peppers in microwave-safe container, remove foil; cover with heavy-duty plastic wrap, venting it on one side. Microwave at HIGH 5 to 7½ minutes or until heated, rotating dish a half-turn after 3 minutes. Yield: 6 servings.

☐ *313 calories, 25.6 grams protein, 7.4 grams fat, 36.1 grams carbohydrate, 48 milligrams cholesterol, 213.5 milligrams sodium, and 53.7 milligrams calcium per pepper.*

COLORFUL VEGETABLE LASAGNA

6 lasagna noodles, uncooked
2 (10-ounce) packages frozen chopped spinach, thawed and drained
1 egg, beaten
3 cloves garlic, minced
2 cups 1% low-fat cottage cheese
1 teaspoon dried whole basil
½ teaspoon Italian seasoning
3 cups coarsely shredded carrots, steamed
¼ cup chopped onion
1½ cups chicken broth
¾ cup instant nonfat dry milk powder
1 tablespoon cornstarch
¼ teaspoon salt
⅛ teaspoon white pepper
⅛ teaspoon ground nutmeg
Vegetable cooking spray
½ cup (2 ounces) shredded 40% less-fat mozzarella cheese

Cook lasagna noodles according to package directions, omitting salt. Drain and set aside.

Press spinach between paper towels. Combine chopped spinach, egg, garlic, cottage cheese, basil, and Italian seasoning; set aside.

Press steamed carrots between paper towels. Combine carrots and chopped onion; set aside.

Combine broth, milk powder, and cornstarch in a heavy saucepan. Stir until smooth; cook over medium heat, stirring constantly, until sauce is thickened and bubbly. Stir in salt, white pepper, and nutmeg; set aside.

Coat a 12- x 8- x 2-inch baking dish with cooking spray. Spread ½ cup sauce in dish, and top with 3 lasagna noodles. Top noodles with spinach and cottage cheese mixture; top with remaining 3 noodles. Add carrot mixture and remaining sauce.

Cover and bake at 350° for 15 minutes; uncover and let cool completely. Sprinkle with mozzarella cheese, and cut into 8 (3- x 4-inch) servings. Place each serving in an ovenproof or a microwave-safe container. Cover with heavy-duty aluminum foil, removing as much air as possible. Freeze.

To heat frozen lasagna in ovenproof container, leave foil intact. Bake at 375° for 40 minutes.

To heat frozen lasagna in microwave-safe container, remove foil; cover with heavy-duty plastic wrap, venting the wrap on one side. Microwave at HIGH 6 to 8 minutes or until thoroughly heated, rotating every 2 minutes. Yield: 8 servings.

☐ *217 calories, 18.7 grams protein, 3.3 grams fat, 28.3 grams carbohydrate, 43 milligrams cholesterol, 604.5 milligrams sodium, and 311.4 milligrams calcium per 4- x 3-inch serving.*

Tip: When food boils over in the oven, sprinkle the burned surface with a little salt. This will stop smoke and odor from forming and make the spot easier to clean. Also, rubbing damp salt on dishes in which food has been baked will remove brown spots.

Tips for Making Frozen Entrées at Home

- Use cornstarch rather than flour for thickening sauces to prevent separation during thawing and heating.
- Reduce amount of seasonings that become stronger during freezing (oregano, thyme, parsley, black pepper, cloves, onion, garlic, and vanilla flavoring).
- Undercook dishes slightly before freezing. Vegetables need only to be blanched, and meats browned.
- Cool food completely before packaging and freezing. Quickly cool foods, uncovered, in the refrigerator, stirring occasionally. Cooling at room temperature encourages food spoilage.
- Freeze food in moisture/vapor-proof packaging. Use disposable aluminum pans for heating in a conventional oven; use glass dishes for the microwave oven. For items to be heated in boiling water, use sealable boiling bags, not bags with zip-type closures.
- Cover dishes containing fruit juice or tomatoes first with heavy-duty plastic wrap, then with heavy-duty aluminum foil. Acid from these two ingredients will sometimes discolor or form a hole in foil placed directly on the food.
- Arrange food in shallow layers in containers for even heating.
- Choose containers that are similar in size to the product being frozen. Remove as much air as possible before sealing and freezing. Extra airspace encourages freezer burn.
- Allow space for expansion when packaging foods with a lot of liquid, such as soups or dishes in a sauce.
- Place entrées in a single layer in the freezer for fast freezing, a necessity to maintain food quality.
- Use homemade frozen entrées within 3 months, sooner if your freezer temperature is above 0° F.

Spinach-Stuffed Shells don't look like a diet entrée, but they are. A serving of three is only 237 calories. And they're full of calcium and other nutrients.

SPINACH-STUFFED SHELLS

Vegetable cooking spray
1 small onion, diced
2 (14½-ounce) cans no-salt-added whole tomatoes, undrained and chopped
1 (6-ounce) can no-salt-added tomato paste
1 (8-ounce) can no-salt-added tomato sauce
2 teaspoons brown sugar
½ teaspoon salt
¼ teaspoon pepper
1 teaspoon dried whole oregano
24 jumbo macaroni shells, uncooked
2 (10-ounce) packages frozen chopped spinach, thawed and drained
1 (16-ounce) container 1% low-fat cottage cheese
1 cup (4 ounces) shredded 40% less-fat mozzarella cheese
¼ teaspoon pepper

Place a large saucepan over medium heat until hot; coat with vegetable cooking spray. Sauté onion until tender.

Add tomatoes, tomato paste, tomato sauce, brown sugar, salt, ¼ teaspoon pepper, and oregano; stir well. Bring to a boil. Cover, reduce heat, and simmer 20 minutes, stirring occasionally.

Cook shells according to package directions, omitting salt. Drain.

Drain spinach; press between layers of paper towels. Combine spinach, cheeses, and ¼ teaspoon pepper; stir well. Fill each shell with 2 tablespoons spinach mixture.

Spoon ¼ cup sauce into each of 8 ovenproof containers or microwave-safe containers. Place 3 filled shells in each, and top with ¼ cup sauce. Cover with heavy-duty plastic wrap, removing as much air as possible. Then cover with heavy-duty aluminum foil. Freeze.

To heat frozen Spinach-Stuffed Shells in ovenproof container, remove foil and plastic wrap, and re-cover dish with foil. Bake at 350° for 1 hour and 10 to 15 minutes or until heated.

To heat frozen Spinach-Stuffed Shells in microwave-safe container, remove foil, and vent plastic wrap on one side. Microwave at HIGH 5 to 7 minutes or until heated, rotating container a half-turn after 2½ to 3½ minutes. Yield: 8 servings.

□ *237 calories, 17.3 grams protein, 3.6 grams fat, 21.3 grams carbohydrate, 10 milligrams cholesterol, 514.8 milligrams sodium, and 244.4 milligrams calcium per 3 filled shells with sauce.*
Linda McIntosh,
Tyler, Texas.

Chocolate—The Ultimate In Desserts

Some people will exercise and sacrifice most favorite foods to shed pounds. But they draw the line at giving up chocolate. That's why these dessert recipes at only 132 calories a serving will delight dieting chocolate lovers.

CHOCOLATE-ORANGE ROLL

Vegetable cooking spray
3 eggs
½ cup sugar
2 tablespoons strong brewed coffee
1 teaspoon vanilla extract
½ cup all-purpose flour
¼ cup cocoa
¼ teaspoon salt
2 tablespoons cocoa
1 cup reduced-calorie orange marmalade
or red raspberry spread
1 teaspoon powdered sugar or cocoa
Orange rind strips (optional)

Coat a 15- x 10- x 1-inch jellyroll pan with cooking spray, and line with foil. Coat foil with cooking spray, and dust with flour; set aside.

Beat eggs at medium speed of an electric mixer until light and fluffy. Gradually add sugar, beating until thick and lemon colored. Add brewed coffee and vanilla; beat well. Combine flour,

¼ cup cocoa, and salt; fold into egg mixture. Spread batter evenly in prepared pan. Bake at 350° for 15 minutes.

Sift 2 tablespoons cocoa in a 15- x 10- x 1-inch rectangle on a towel. When cake is done, immediately loosen from sides of pan, and turn out onto cocoa. Peel off foil. Starting at narrow end, roll up cake and towel together; cool on a wire rack, seam side down, about 10 minutes.

Unroll cake; remove towel. Spread with marmalade, and reroll. Place on serving plate, seam side down; let cool completely. Dust with powdered sugar, and garnish with orange-rind strips, if desired. Yield: 10 servings.

□ *132 calories, 2.8 grams protein, 2.2 grams fat, 25.4 grams carbohydrate, 82 milligrams cholesterol, 80 milligrams sodium, and 17.6 milligrams calcium per 1-inch slice.*
Ethel Murray,
Huntsville, Arkansas.

CHOCOLATE ANGEL FOOD CAKE

12 egg whites
¼ teaspoon salt
1½ teaspoons cream of tartar
1¼ cups sugar, divided
1 cup sifted cake flour
¼ cup cocoa
½ teaspoon almond extract
1 teaspoon vanilla extract

Beat egg whites (at room temperature) and salt until foamy. Add cream of tartar; beat until soft peaks form. Add 1 cup sugar, 2 tablespoons at a time, and beat until stiff peaks form.

Sift remaining ¼ cup sugar, flour, and cocoa together; gently fold into egg whites. Add flavorings.

Spoon batter into an ungreased 10-inch tube pan. Bake at 375° for 30 to 35 minutes. Invert cake; let cool completely. Remove cake from pan. Yield: 12 servings.

□ *132 calories, 4.1 grams protein, 0.3 gram fat, 28.2 grams carbohydrate, 0 milligrams cholesterol, 125 milligrams sodium, and 11 milligrams calcium per slice.*

Special Equipment

"Cooking Light" involves not only the selection of lower fat, lower calorie foods, but also preparation techniques that retain nutrients and help minimize unwanted calories. Poultry shears, a wok, nonstick skillets, a blender, a broiling pan, a vegetable steamer, and a gravy skimmer are pieces of equipment you may want in your kitchen.

SOLE DIVAN

¾ pound fresh broccoli
Vegetable cooking spray
4 (4-ounce) sole fillets
1 cup sliced fresh mushrooms
Vegetable cooking spray
1 cup skim milk, divided
1 teaspoon chicken-flavored bouillon
granules
1 tablespoon cornstarch
4 (⅔-ounce) slices reduced-calorie process
American cheese
¼ teaspoon paprika

Trim off any large leaves of broccoli; remove tough ends of lower stalks. Wash broccoli thoroughly, and separate into spears.

Arrange broccoli in a steaming rack with stalks to center of rack. Place over boiling water; cover and steam 8 minutes. Coat a 10- x 6- x 2-inch baking dish with cooking spray. Arrange broccoli in baking dish; top with fish.

Sauté mushrooms in a nonstick skillet coated with cooking spray until tender; spoon over fish. Combine ¾ cup milk and bouillon granules in skillet. Combine remaining ¼ cup milk and cornstarch; add to skillet, stirring well. Cook 1 minute or until thickened and bubbly. Add cheese, and stir until cheese melts. Pour sauce over fish. Bake, uncovered, at 350° for 25 minutes or until fish flakes easily when tested with a fork. Sprinkle with paprika. Yield: 4 servings.

□ *179 calories, 27.8 grams protein, 2.65 grams fat, 9.6 grams carbohydrate, 58 milligrams cholesterol, 595 milligrams sodium, and 250 milligrams calcium per serving.*
Abby Moore,
Ballwin, Missouri.

FISH FLORENTINE IN PARCHMENT

Vegetable cooking spray
½ pound fresh mushrooms, sliced
1 clove garlic, minced
¼ teaspoon salt
1 (10-ounce) package frozen chopped spinach, thawed and well drained
4 (4-ounce) orange roughy fillets, or other lean white fish fillets
1 teaspoon dried whole thyme
¼ teaspoon white pepper
2 tablespoons malt vinegar
Mustard sauce (recipe follows)

Cut four 15- x 12-inch pieces parchment paper; fold in half lengthwise, creasing firmly. Trim each into a large heart shape. Place parchment hearts on baking sheets. Coat one side of each heart with cooking spray, leaving edges ungreased; set aside.

Place a skillet over medium-high heat until hot; coat with cooking spray. Sauté mushrooms until tender; add garlic, salt, and spinach, stirring well. Spoon one-fourth of spinach mixture on the side of each parchment heart coated with cooking spray. Top each with a fish fillet, and sprinkle with thyme, pepper, and malt vinegar.

Fold over remaining halves of hearts. Starting with rounded edge of each heart, pleat and crimp edges together to make a seal. Twist end tightly to seal.

Bake at 450° for 10 to 12 minutes or until parchment is puffed and lightly browned and fish flakes easily when tested with a fork. Serve with mustard sauce. Yield: 4 servings.

Note: Aluminum foil may be substituted for parchment paper.

☐ *139 calories, 25.3 grams protein, 1.6 grams fat, 5.8 grams carbohydrate, 62 milligrams cholesterol, 209 milligrams sodium, and 318 milligrams calcium per 3-ounce serving fish plus 26 calories, 0.5 gram protein, 2.2 grams fat, 1.1 grams carbohydrate, 3 milligrams cholesterol, 267 milligrams sodium, and 93 milligrams calcium per tablespoon sauce.*

Mustard Sauce:
¼ cup reduced-calorie mayonnaise
¼ cup plain low-fat yogurt
1 tablespoon spicy brown mustard

Combine all ingredients; stir well. Chill. Yield: ½ cup.

PARSLEY MEAT LOAF

2 pounds ground chuck
1¼ cups soft breadcrumbs
1 cup chopped fresh parsley
¾ cup chopped onion
1 egg, beaten
2 tablespoons chopped green pepper
1 large clove garlic, minced
½ teaspoon salt
½ teaspoon dried whole thyme
½ teaspoon freshly ground pepper
¼ teaspoon ground allspice
⅛ teaspoon ground nutmeg
⅛ teaspoon red pepper
3 bay leaves
1 tablespoon catsup

Combine all ingredients except bay leaves and catsup; stir well. Shape into a loaf, and place in a 9- x 5- x 3-inch two-piece loafpan with drain holes in the bottom. Arrange bay leaves on top; bake at 350° for 1 hour and 20 to 25 minutes or until done. Remove from pan, and discard bay leaves; spread catsup over meat loaf. Yield: 10 servings.

☐ *217 calories, 13.6 grams protein, 15.3 grams fat, 5.4 grams carbohydrate, 115 milligrams cholesterol, 220.9 milligrams sodium, and 30 milligrams calcium per slice.* Jeanette Thompson, Lexington, Kentucky.

DEVILED-BEEF PATTIES

1 pound ground chuck
¼ cup chili sauce
1 tablespoon minced onion
1 teaspoon prepared mustard
1 teaspoon prepared horseradish
1 teaspoon Worcestershire sauce
⅛ teaspoon pepper
Vegetable cooking spray

Combine ground chuck, chili sauce, onion, mustard, horseradish, Worcestershire sauce, and pepper; stir well. Shape into 4 patties. Place patties on broiler pan coated with cooking spray. Broil 5 inches from heat 4 minutes on each side. Yield: 4 servings.

☐ *251 calories, 15.7 grams protein, 18.4 grams fat, 4.9 grams carbohydrate, 80 milligrams cholesterol, 313 milligrams sodium, and 16 milligrams calcium per 3-ounce patty.* Sandra Pierson, Tyner, Kentucky.

BEEF-AND-VEGETABLE STIR-FRY

½ pound lean boneless top round steak
1 tablespoon reduced-sodium soy sauce
1 tablespoon dry sherry
⅛ teaspoon garlic powder
1 tablespoon cornstarch
¾ cup water
2 low-sodium beef bouillon cubes
1½ teaspoons minced fresh gingerroot
1 tablespoon hoisin sauce
1½ tablespoons reduced-sodium soy sauce
1½ tablespoons dry sherry
1½ tablespoons cornstarch
¼ teaspoon crushed red pepper flakes
1 teaspoon vegetable oil
1 cup sliced onion
1 clove garlic, minced
1 cup cubed sweet red pepper
½ pound snow peas, trimmed
½ cup diagonally sliced celery
¼ pound fresh bean sprouts
2½ cups hot cooked rice (cooked without salt or fat)

Partially freeze steak; slice diagonally across grain into thin strips. Combine meat, 1 tablespoon soy sauce, 1 tablespoon sherry, garlic powder, and 1 tablespoon cornstarch; set aside.

Combine water, bouillon cubes, and gingerroot in a small saucepan; bring to a boil. Reduce heat, and simmer 10 minutes. Let cool. Add hoisin sauce, 1½ tablespoons soy sauce, 1½ tablespoons sherry, 1½ tablespoons cornstarch, and red pepper flakes; set aside.

Preheat wok or heavy skillet to 325°; add oil. Stir-fry meat mixture until browned. Add onion and garlic; cook 2 minutes. Add sweet red pepper and snow peas; stir-fry 2 minutes. Add celery; cook 1 minute. Add bean sprouts;

stir-fry 1 minute. Pour sauce over mixture; stir-fry until mixture is thickened. Serve over rice. Yield: 5 servings.

☐ *145 calories, 13.9 grams protein, 3 grams fat, 15.1 grams carbohydrate, 22 milligrams cholesterol, 335.8 milligrams sodium, 41.4 milligrams calcium per 1-cup beef and vegetables plus 118 calories, 2.2 grams protein, 0.1 gram fat, 25.9 grams carbohydrate, 0 milligrams cholesterol, 1.4 milligrams sodium, and 7.8 milligrams calcium per ½-cup rice.*
Sally Murphy,
Allen, Texas.

CHICKEN IN A BAG

1 (4¼-pound) broiler-fryer
½ cup beef broth
1 tablespoon reduced-sodium soy sauce
½ teaspoon ground ginger
½ teaspoon garlic powder
½ cup coarsely chopped onion
½ cup shredded cabbage
¾ pound pearl onions, peeled
½ pound baby carrots, scraped
¾ pound medium-size fresh mushrooms
1 tablespoon plus 1 teaspoon cornstarch

Remove skin from chicken, using poultry shears. Combine broth, soy sauce, ginger, and garlic powder. Place chicken in a bowl; pour marinade over chicken; cover and chill 8 hours or overnight, turning occasionally.

Remove chicken from marinade, reserving marinade. Stuff cavity of chicken with chopped onion and cabbage. Place chicken in a large cooking bag; add pearl onions, carrots, and mushrooms. Pour reserved marinade into cavity of chicken. Seal bag; cut a slit in top of bag to allow steam to escape. Place in a 13- x 9- x 2-inch baking dish. Bake at 350° for 1½ hours.

Arrange chicken and vegetables on a serving platter. Pour chicken broth

through a gravy skimmer; reserve 1¼ cups broth, and discard fat. Combine cornstarch with broth in a small saucepan; bring to a boil. Reduce heat, and stir constantly until thickened and bubbly. Serve with chicken and vegetables. Yield: 6 servings.

☐ *208 calories, 24.2 grams protein, 5.6 grams fat, 15.1 grams carbohydrate, 67.3 milligrams cholesterol, 246.5 milligrams sodium, and 50.5 milligrams calcium per serving with sauce.*
Doris Phillips,
Springdale, Arkansas.

FROSTY FRUIT SHAKE

1 (6-ounce) can frozen orange juice
  concentrate, thawed and undiluted
1 cup skim milk
1 cup frozen unsweetened strawberries
1 medium banana, peeled and frozen
1 teaspoon vanilla extract
12 ice cubes
1 (8-ounce) carton plain low-fat yogurt

Combine all ingredients except yogurt in container of an electric blender; process until smooth. Add yogurt, and process just until blended. Yield: 5 servings.

☐ *135 calories, 5.2 grams protein, 1 gram fat, 27 grams carbohydrate, 4 milligrams cholesterol, 59 milligrams sodium, and 161 milligrams calcium per 1-cup serving.*
Carol Schulz,
Crossville, Tennessee.

Start Your Day With A Piping-Hot Muffin

For breakfast on the run, nothing beats a homemade muffin with fresh fruit or juice and a tall glass of skim milk. It's a nutritious way to get the morning off to a good start. Our recipes contain fruit and/or vegetables, and are lower in fat and sugar and higher in fiber than most muffins.

High-fiber whole wheat flour in combination with all-purpose flour provides the basis for Apple Muffins. It's important to combine whole wheat flour with all-purpose flour in baked goods to get a successful product. Whole wheat flour contains less gluten-yielding properties, which give baked products a good structure, than all-purpose flour and will produce a coarser, denser product when used alone. Cinnamon and nutmeg make these muffins seem sweeter than you might expect for the small amount of sugar.

In Blueberry-Oatmeal Muffins (recipe on following page), oats provide the dietary fiber, and buttermilk lends special flavor and texture.

APPLE MUFFINS
(pictured on page 27)

1 cup all-purpose flour
1 cup whole wheat flour
⅓ cup wheat germ
¼ cup firmly packed brown sugar
1 teaspoon baking powder
1 teaspoon baking soda
¼ teaspoon salt
1 teaspoon ground cinnamon
¼ teaspoon ground nutmeg
2 eggs, beaten
¼ cup skim milk
¼ cup vegetable oil
2 cups peeled, shredded apple
1 tablespoon grated lemon rind
Vegetable cooking spray

Combine flours, wheat germ, brown sugar, baking powder, soda, salt, cinnamon, and nutmeg in a large bowl; make a well in center of mixture. Combine eggs, milk, and oil; add to dry ingredients, stirring just until moistened. Stir in apple and lemon rind.

Spoon into muffin pans coated with cooking spray, filling two-thirds full. Bake at 400° for 10 to 12 minutes. Yield: 1½ dozen.

☐ *108 calories, 3 grams protein, 4.3 grams fat, 15.4 grams carbohydrate, 31 milligrams cholesterol, 80 milligrams sodium, and 38 milligrams calcium per muffin.*
Mrs. James A. Tuthill,
Virginia Beach, Virginia.

BLUEBERRY-OATMEAL MUFFINS

1 cup quick-cooking oats
1 cup nonfat buttermilk
1 cup all-purpose flour
¼ cup sugar
1 tablespoon baking powder
¼ teaspoon salt
⅛ teaspoon ground cinnamon
1 egg, beaten
¼ cup vegetable oil
¾ cup frozen unsweetened blueberries, thawed and drained
Vegetable cooking spray

Combine oats and buttermilk; let stand 5 minutes. Combine flour, sugar, baking powder, salt, and cinnamon in a large bowl; make a well in center of mixture.

Combine oat mixture, egg, and oil; stir well. Add to dry ingredients, stirring just until moistened. Stir in blueberries. Spoon into muffin pans coated with cooking spray, filling two-thirds full. Bake at 425° for 20 minutes or until browned. Yield: 16 muffins.

☐ *104 calories, 2.4 grams protein, 4.4 grams fat, 13.9 grams carbohydrate, 17 milligrams cholesterol, 118 milligrams sodium, and 61 milligrams calcium per muffin.*

CARROT-AND-RAISIN MUFFINS

1 cup all-purpose flour
1 cup whole wheat flour
2 teaspoons baking powder
¼ teaspoon salt
¼ teaspoon pumpkin pie spice
¾ cup finely shredded carrots
⅓ cup raisins
1 egg, beaten
1 cup skim milk
2 tablespoons vegetable oil
2 tablespoons molasses
Vegetable cooking spray

Combine flour, baking powder, salt, and pumpkin pie spice in a large bowl; stir in shredded carrots and raisins. Make a well in the center of mixture.

Combine egg, milk, oil, and molasses; stir well. Add to dry ingredients, stirring just until moistened. Spoon into muffin pans coated with cooking spray, filling three-fourths full. Bake at 425° for 15 minutes or until lightly browned. Yield: 1 dozen.

☐ *127 calories, 3.7 grams protein, 3.2 grams fat, 21.6 grams carbohydrate, 23 milligrams cholesterol, 120 milligrams sodium, and 75 milligrams calcium per muffin.*

Add A Chilled Vegetable Salad To The Menu

Even on a cold winter day, a chilled vegetable salad brings life to a meal of hot foods. It's the contrast of temperature, texture, color, and shape that makes the difference.

Confetti-Stuffed Lettuce is an interesting way to serve a lettuce wedge. It comes with its own dressing made from Neufchâtel cheese and reduced-calorie mayonnaise, lower-calorie counterparts to cream cheese and regular mayonnaise. Serve with a steaming bowl of chili or homemade soup.

Beef stew or broiled fish makes a good main-dish choice for Broccoli-Corn Salad. Most vegetable salad marinades call for equal amounts of vinegar and oil and a lot of sugar to balance the two. But this recipe substitutes the mild flavor of rice vinegar, allowing less oil and no sugar to be used.

ENGLISH PEA-AND-APPLE SALAD

2 cups frozen English peas, thawed and drained
½ cup thinly sliced celery
½ cup unpeeled and chopped red apple
2 teaspoons diced onion
1 teaspoon chopped fresh mint (optional)
3 tablespoons reduced-calorie mayonnaise
3 tablespoons plain low-fat yogurt
2 teaspoons grated Parmesan cheese

Combine peas, celery, apple, onion, and mint in a medium bowl; set aside. Combine mayonnaise, yogurt, and Parmesan cheese; pour over pea mixture, tossing gently. Cover and chill. Yield: 5 servings.

☐ *85 calories, 3.8 grams protein, 3 grams fat, 11.1 grams carbohydrate, 4 milligrams cholesterol, 144 milligrams sodium, and 43 milligrams calcium per ½-cup serving.*

BROCCOLI-CORN SALAD

4 cups broccoli flowerets
2 cups frozen whole kernel corn, thawed and drained
½ cup chopped sweet red pepper
¼ cup plus 2 tablespoons rice vinegar
3 tablespoons vegetable oil
¼ teaspoon salt
⅛ teaspoon freshly ground pepper
⅛ teaspoon ground cumin
⅛ teaspoon chili powder
⅛ teaspoon dried whole oregano

Place broccoli in a vegetable steamer. Place over a small amount of boiling water; cover and steam 2 to 3 minutes or until crisp-tender. Let cool. Combine broccoli, corn, and red pepper in a shallow container; set aside.

Combine vinegar and remaining ingredients in a jar. Cover tightly; shake well. Pour over vegetables; toss gently. Cover and chill. Yield: 8 servings.

☐ *96 calories, 2.6 grams protein, 5.6 grams fat, 1.5 grams carbohydrate, 0 milligrams cholesterol, 87 milligrams sodium, and 24 milligrams calcium per ½-cup serving.*

CONFETTI-STUFFED LETTUCE

1 small firm head iceberg lettuce (about 1 pound)
3 ounces Neufchâtel cheese, softened
2 tablespoons reduced-calorie mayonnaise
¼ cup thinly sliced green onions
¾ cup shredded carrots
½ cup chopped radishes
3 drops hot sauce
Radicchio leaves (optional)

Wash and core lettuce; discard outer leaves. Let drain. Gently remove heart of lettuce to enlarge the center cavity; reserve heart for other uses.

Combine Neufchâtel cheese, mayonnaise, onions, carrots, radishes, and hot sauce in a medium bowl; stir well. Stuff mixture firmly into cavity of lettuce. Cover and chill.

Cut lettuce into wedges. Serve wedges on radicchio leaves, if desired. Yield: 4 servings.

☐ *102 calories, 3.5 grams protein, 7.3 grams fat, 6.4 grams carbohydrate, 19 milligrams cholesterol, 148 milligrams sodium, and 47 milligrams calcium per wedge.* Susan Buckmaster, *Charlotte, North Carolina.*

Tasty Substitutions Keep Dips Lower In Calories

Dips are a trusty appetizer or party snack, but they can also be a high-calorie pitfall for people concerned about their weight. The problem is the base used for most dips. Sour cream, cream cheese, mayonnaise, and creamed cottage cheese are all favorites, but they're high in fat and calories. Our recipes trim calories and increase nutrients in different ways.

Delicious Spinach Dip is made from 1% low-fat cottage cheese (which has 25% fewer calories than creamed cottage cheese) and reduced-calorie mayonnaise (which has about half the calories of regular mayonnaise). Chopped fresh spinach and various seasonings are added, and the mixture is processed in an electric blender for a thick, smooth, creamy consistency.

Deviled Dip relies on plain low-fat yogurt, which has 71% fewer calories, 93% less fat, and about 1½ times more calcium than the sour cream it replaces. The ingredients for this dip are stirred together by hand. When processed in a

blender, yogurt breaks down and becomes runny.

Low-Cal Tuna Dip substitutes light cream cheese for half the calories of regular cream cheese. We used tuna packed in water rather than oil to save another 196 calories.

LOW-CAL TUNA DIP

1 (8-ounce) container light process cream cheese, softened
2 tablespoons reduced-calorie mayonnaise
2 teaspoons prepared horseradish
⅛ teaspoon hot sauce
Dash of Worcestershire sauce
¼ cup diced green onions
¼ cup diced celery
¼ cup diced green pepper
1 (6½-ounce) can 60% less-salt tuna packed in water, drained and flaked
Paprika

Combine cream cheese, mayonnaise, horseradish, hot sauce, and Worcestershire sauce in a medium bowl; stir well. Add onions, celery, and green pepper; stir well. Stir in tuna. Cover and chill. Sprinkle with paprika. Serve with raw vegetables. Yield: 1¼ cups.

☐ *24 calories, 2.2 grams protein, 1.8 grams fat, 0.86 gram carbohydrate, 4.6 milligrams cholesterol, 64.8 milligrams sodium, and 7.7 milligrams calcium per tablespoon.* Teresa Duncan, *Dyersburg, Tennessee.*

SPINACH DIP

(pictured on page 30)

1 cup chopped fresh spinach
1 cup 1% low-fat cottage cheese
½ cup chopped green onions
½ cup reduced-calorie mayonnaise
1 tablespoon reduced-sodium soy sauce
1 clove garlic, minced
Sweet red pepper strips (optional)

Combine spinach, and next 5 ingredients in container of an electric blender; process until smooth. Cover and chill. Garnish with red pepper strips, if desired. Serve with raw vegetables. Yield: 1⅔ cups.

☐ *18 calories, 1.1 grams protein, 1.2 grams fat, 0.8 gram carbohydrate, 2 milligrams cholesterol, 77 milligrams sodium, and 8 milligrams calcium per tablespoon.* Ginny Whitt, *Mount Washington, Kentucky.*

CURRY DIP

1 (12-ounce) carton 1% low-fat cottage cheese
2 tablespoons skim milk
1 teaspoon vinegar
⅓ cup peeled, seeded, chopped cucumber
¼ to ½ teaspoon curry powder
⅛ teaspoon garlic powder
⅓ cup minced green onions

Combine cottage cheese, milk, and vinegar in container of an electric blender; process until smooth. Add cucumber, curry powder, and garlic powder; process 30 seconds. Add onions, and process 10 seconds. Yield: 2 cups.

☐ *9 calories, 1.4 grams protein, 0.1 gram fat, 0.5 gram carbohydrate, 0 milligrams cholesterol, 44 milligrams sodium, and 9 milligrams calcium per tablespoon.* Mrs. W. R. Brennan, *Macon, Georgia.*

DEVILED DIP

1 (8-ounce) carton plain low-fat yogurt
2 teaspoons prepared mustard
2 teaspoons Pickapeppa sauce
2 teaspoons green pepper flakes
1½ teaspoons dry onion flakes
⅛ teaspoon white pepper
⅛ teaspoon garlic powder
⅛ teaspoon hot sauce

Combine all ingredients in a small bowl; stir well. Cover and chill. Serve with raw vegetables. Yield: 1 cup.

☐ *11 calories, 0.8 gram protein, 0.3 gram fat, 1.4 grams carbohydrate, 1 milligram cholesterol, 30 milligrams sodium, and 27 milligrams calcium per tablespoon.*

Mrs. Kenneth B. Waldron, *Mountain Rest, South Carolina.*

Sauces Slim On Calories

Let's face it—most sauces are high in fat and calories. And one way to make dishes lighter is to eliminate these culprits. But sometimes, plain steamed vegetables or basic broiled meats need something extra to perk up flavor.

Low-Calorie Medium White Sauce is the answer. It's unlike the sauces you often get in restaurants made by cooking down cream, which makes the sauce even higher in calories. It's also different from a basic white sauce made at home using butter, flour, and milk. Our version has several advantages. It has 36% fewer calories than a regular basic white sauce, one-sixth the cholesterol, and no added fat; yet it also contains over twice as much protein and over 2½ times as much calcium. The basic recipe can be adapted for a number of tasty variations.

Curry Sauce makes a great accompaniment for steamed vegetables. Serve Hot Horseradish Sauce alongside plain roast beef. Try Wine and Cheese Sauce with everything—it goes well with almost any food.

LOW-CALORIE MEDIUM WHITE SAUCE

1 cup water
½ cup instant nonfat dry milk powder
1½ tablespoons all-purpose flour
¼ teaspoon salt
Pinch of white pepper
3 drops of butter flavoring

Combine water, milk powder, and flour in a heavy saucepan, stirring until smooth. Cook over medium heat, stirring constantly, until mixture is thickened and bubbly. Stir in remaining ingredients. Yield: 1 cup.

☐ *16 calories, 1.4 grams protein, 0 grams fat, 2.5 grams carbohydrate, 1 milligram cholesterol, 57 milligrams sodium, and 48 milligrams calcium per tablespoon.*

For thin white sauce, decrease flour to 1 tablespoon. Yield: 1 cup.

☐ *15 calories, 1.4 grams protein, 0 grams fat, 2.3 grams carbohydrate, 1 milligram cholesterol, 57 milligrams sodium, and 48 milligrams calcium per tablespoon.*

For thick white sauce, increase flour to 2 tablespoons. Yield: 1 cup.

☐ *17 calories, 1.5 grams protein, 0 grams fat, 2.6 grams carbohydrate, 1 milligram cholesterol, 57 milligrams sodium, and 48 milligrams calcium per tablespoon.*

Variations

CHEESE SAUCE: Add ¼ cup (2 ounces) shredded sharp Cheddar cheese and ⅛ teaspoon dry mustard to Low-Calorie Medium White Sauce. Cook and stir until cheese melts. Yield: 1 cup plus 2 tablespoons.

☐ *27 calories, 2.1 grams protein, 1.1 grams fat, 2.2 grams carbohydrate, 4 milligrams cholesterol, 70 milligrams sodium, and 65 milligrams calcium per tablespoon.*

CURRY SAUCE: Add ¼ to ½ teaspoon curry powder to Low-Calorie Medium White Sauce. Stir sauce well. Yield: 1 cup.

☐ *16 calories, 1.4 grams protein, 0 grams fat, 2.5 grams carbohydrate, 1 milligram cholesterol, 57 milligrams sodium, and 48 milligrams calcium per tablespoon.*

HERB SAUCE: Add 2 teaspoons chopped chives, 2 teaspoons minced fresh parsley, and ⅛ teaspoon dried whole thyme to Low-Calorie Medium White Sauce. Stir sauce to blend. Yield: 1 cup.

☐ *16 calories, 1.4 grams protein, 0 grams fat, 2.5 grams carbohydrate, 1 milligram cholesterol, 57 milligrams sodium, and 48 milligrams calcium per tablespoon.*

HOT HORSERADISH SAUCE: Add 2 to 2½ tablespoons drained prepared horseradish to Low-Calorie Medium White Sauce. Stir to blend. Yield: 1 cup plus 2 tablespoons.

☐ *15 calories, 1.3 grams protein, 0 grams fat, 2.4 grams carbohydrate, 1 milligram cholesterol, 52 milligrams sodium, and 43.2 milligrams calcium per tablespoon.*

EGG SAUCE: Add one grated hard-cooked egg and ¼ teaspoon Worcestershire sauce to Low-Calorie Medium White Sauce. Stir to blend. Yield: 1 cup plus 2 tablespoons.

☐ *19 calories, 1.6 grams protein, 0.3 gram fat, 2.2 grams carbohydrate, 16 milligrams cholesterol, 55 milligrams sodium, and 44 milligrams calcium per tablespoon.*

WINE AND CHEESE SAUCE: Add ¼ cup (2 ounces) shredded sharp Cheddar cheese, 2 tablespoons sherry, ¼ teaspoon dry mustard, dash of ground nutmeg, and dash of red pepper to Low-Calorie Medium White Sauce. Cook; stir until cheese melts. Yield: 1 cup plus 2 tablespoons.

☐ *27 calories, 2.1 grams protein, 1.1 grams fat, 2.3 grams carbohydrate, 4 milligrams cholesterol, 70 milligrams sodium, and 65 milligrams calcium per tablespoon.*   Mrs. W. Keaton, Muskogee, Oklahoma.

Right: *Shredded apple and a small amount of oil help make Apple Muffins (page 23) deliciously moist.*

Pages 28 and 29: *Make wholesome, nutritious foods the basis of your healthy, low-calorie eating plan. ("Cooking Light" section begins on page 17.)*

Page 30: *Surprise guests by serving Spinach Dip (page 25) with an array of colorful vegetables. Sliced turnips, Belgian endive, red and yellow pepper strips, radishes, mushrooms, snow peas, and cherry tomatoes make interesting dippers.*

A Menu For The Two Of You

Preparing a meal for two may be an everyday occurrence at your house, or it might be the sign of an anniversary, birthday, or other special event. Whatever the occasion, it's often difficult to find a good selection of tasty recipes for two that won't leave you with a lot of leftovers. This menu that we've planned offers a variety of taste-pleasing dishes especially for two.

Veal Picante
Zucchini With Pecans
Herbed Carrots And Onions
Red Cabbage-And-Apple Slaw
Orange Tapioca Fluff
or
Fruited Meringue Shells

VEAL PICANTE

2 tablespoons all-purpose flour
⅛ teaspoon salt
Pinch of pepper
⅛ teaspoon paprika
2 (4-ounce) slices veal
Vegetable cooking spray
¼ cup water
2 tablespoons vinegar
1 teaspoon brown sugar
1 bay leaf
2 thin lemon slices
Additional lemon slices (optional)

Combine flour, salt, pepper, and paprika; stir well. Dredge veal slices in flour mixture; pound with a meat mallet until thin.

Heat a heavy skillet over medium heat; spray with cooking spray. Add veal; brown on both sides.

Combine water, vinegar, and brown sugar; stir well. Pour over veal; add bay leaf. Place a lemon slice on each veal piece. Bring to a boil; reduce heat, and simmer 5 minutes or until done. Discard bay leaf and lemon slices. Garnish with fresh lemon slices, if desired. Yield: 2 servings.

☐ *178 calories, 17.4 grams protein, 8.2 grams fat, 7.8 grams carbohydrate, 86.5 milligrams cholesterol, 223.5 milligrams sodium, and 14 milligrams calcium per 3-ounce serving.* Patty McCoy Horton, *Demopolis, Alabama.*

ZUCCHINI WITH PECANS

Vegetable cooking spray
1½ cups julienne strips of zucchini
½ teaspoon olive oil
⅛ teaspoon garlic salt
⅛ teaspoon white pepper
2 tablespoons chopped pecans, toasted

Coat skillet with cooking spray; sauté zucchini in oil until crisp-tender. Add remaining ingredients, tossing gently. Yield: 2 servings.

☐ *78 calories, 1.7 grams protein, 6.7 grams fat, 4.3 grams carbohydrate, 0 milligrams cholesterol, 134 milligrams sodium, and 19 milligrams calcium per ½-cup serving.*

HERBED CARROTS AND ONIONS

1 cup diagonally sliced carrots
1 small onion, sliced
Pinch of dry rosemary leaves, crushed
Pinch of dried whole thyme
Pinch of dry marjoram leaves
Pinch of salt
Pinch of pepper
1 teaspoon reduced-calorie margarine
1 tablespoon chopped fresh parsley

Place carrots and onion in a vegetable steamer. Place rack over boiling water in a Dutch oven; sprinkle with herbs, salt, and pepper. Cover and steam 10 to 15 minutes or until carrots are crisp-tender. Spoon into serving dish; stir in margarine, and sprinkle with parsley. Yield: 2 servings.

☐ *63 calories, 1.6 grams protein, 1.2 grams fat, 12.8 grams carbohydrate, 0 milligrams cholesterol, 124.5 milligrams sodium, and 42.5 milligrams calcium per ½-cup serving.* Kate Yoffy, *Richmond, Virginia.*

RED CABBAGE-AND-APPLE SLAW

½ small green apple, unpeeled and thinly sliced
2 tablespoons lemon juice
1 tablespoon reduced-calorie mayonnaise
2 tablespoons vanilla low-fat yogurt
Dash of celery seeds
Dash of onion salt
Dash of white pepper
1¼ cups coarsely shredded red cabbage

Coat apple slices with lemon juice; set aside.

Combine reduced-calorie mayonnaise, yogurt, celery seeds, onion salt, and pepper in a small bowl. Pour over cabbage, tossing gently. To serve, spoon cabbage mixture onto salad plates; arrange apple slices on top of cabbage. Yield: 2 servings.

☐ *63 calories, 1.4 grams protein, 2.5 grams fat, 10.4 grams carbohydrate, 3 milligrams cholesterol, 126 milligrams sodium, and 49 milligrams calcium per ¾-cup serving.*

ORANGE TAPIOCA FLUFF

2 tablespoons quick-cooking tapioca
1 cup unsweetened orange juice
1 egg, separated
1 tablespoon sugar
Orange rind (optional)

Combine tapioca, orange juice, and egg yolk in a saucepan; let stand 5 minutes. Bring to a boil over medium heat, stirring constantly. Remove from heat.

Beat egg white (at room temperature) until soft peaks form. Gradually add sugar; beat until stiff peaks form. Fold into the orange mixture. Spoon into 2 dessert glasses. Chill. To serve, garnish tapioca with orange rind, if desired. Yield: 2 servings.

☐ *151 calories, 4 grams protein, 2.9 grams fat, 27.6 grams carbohydrate, 137 milligrams cholesterol, 36 milligrams sodium, and 26 milligrams calcium per ¾-cup serving.* Mrs. Charles DeHaven, *Owensboro, Kentucky.*

FRUITED MERINGUE SHELLS

1 egg white
⅛ teaspoon cream of tartar
¼ cup sugar
1 kiwifruit, peeled and sliced
2 tablespoons reduced-calorie red
    raspberry spread
1 teaspoon lemon juice

Line a baking sheet with aluminum foil; draw 2 (3-inch) circles on foil.

Beat egg white (at room temperature) in a bowl at high speed of an electric mixer until foamy. Sprinkle cream of tartar over egg white; continue beating until soft peaks form. Gradually add sugar, 1 tablespoon at a time, beating until stiff peaks form.

Spoon half of meringue mixture onto each circle. Using the back of a spoon, shape mixture into circles, mounding sides ½ inch higher than centers.

Bake at 225° for 45 minutes. Turn oven off, and let meringue shells cool at least 1 hour before opening oven door. Carefully peel aluminum foil from shells; cool meringue shells completely on wire racks.

Arrange half of kiwifruit slices in each shell.

Combine raspberry spread and lemon juice in a small saucepan; stir well. Cook over low heat, stirring constantly, until drizzling consistency. Drizzle mixture over kiwifruit. Yield: 2 servings.

☐ *143 calories, 2 grams protein, 0 grams fat, 34.1 grams carbohydrate, 0 milligrams cholesterol, 38 milligrams sodium, and 2 milligrams calcium per meringue with fruit.*

Iron Is Important In Your Low-Calorie Diet

If you're following a low-calorie diet, chances are you may not be getting enough iron. Iron intake is closely tied to calorie intake—about 6 milligrams of iron is taken into the body per 1,000 calories. Women need more iron than men, and pre-menopausal women have increased needs for it in their diets. Menus that provide enough iron must be carefully planned because relatively few foods offer the mineral in significant amounts.

Iron is needed by the body to help produce hemoglobin, the oxygen-carrying red blood pigment. If you don't get enough iron, you may feel tired, lethargic, or irritable.

Dietary iron comes in two forms: heme and nonheme. Heme iron comes from animal sources and is well absorbed and utilized by the body. But nonheme, which comes from plant sources, accounts for most of the iron we eat. Its absorption and use by the body is not as good as heme iron, but this can be enhanced by eating meat or foods high in ascorbic acid (vitamin C) along with the iron-rich foods. Oranges, grapefruit, strawberries, cantaloupe, watermelon, tomato juice, broccoli, and dark-green leafy vegetables contain appreciable amounts of ascorbic acid.

For example, have Apricot-Raisin Bars and a glass of orange juice as a snack. The ascorbic acid in the juice will help your body to better use the iron from the enriched flour, molasses, raisins, and apricots in the bars.

You'll also want to give Marinated London Broil a try. Marinated in a pungent mixture of mustard, red wine, lemon juice, soy sauce, and Worcestershire sauce, this lean flank steak is a good source of iron.

APRICOT-RAISIN BARS

¼ cup vegetable oil
¼ cup molasses
1 egg, slightly beaten
1 teaspoon vanilla extract
1½ cups all-purpose flour
2 teaspoons baking powder
1 teaspoon apple pie spice
¼ teaspoon salt
¾ cup raisins
¾ cup chopped dried apricots
1¼ cups peeled, grated apple
Vegetable cooking spray

Combine oil, molasses, egg, and vanilla in a medium bowl; set aside. Combine flour, baking powder, apple pie spice, and salt; add to molasses mixture, stirring well. Stir in raisins, apricots, and apple.

Spread mixture in a 9-inch square baking pan coated with cooking spray. Bake at 350° for 20 minutes or until done. Let cool; cut into 1½-inch squares. Yield: 3 dozen.

☐ *62 calories, 0.9 gram protein, 1.8 grams fat, 11.1 grams carbohydrate, 8 milligrams cholesterol, 37 milligrams sodium, 21 milligrams calcium per 1½-inch square.*

MARINATED LONDON BROIL

1 (1¼-pound) flank steak
1 tablespoon prepared mustard
2 tablespoons Burgundy or other dry red
    wine
2 tablespoons lemon juice
2 tablespoons reduced-sodium soy sauce
2 tablespoons Worcestershire sauce

Score steak on both sides in a diamond pattern. Brush mustard on both sides; place in a large shallow dish. Combine Burgundy, lemon juice, soy sauce, and Worcestershire sauce; pour over steak. Cover and marinate 8 hours in refrigerator.

Remove steak from marinade; place on a broiling pan. Broil steak 5 inches from heat 4 to 5 minutes on each side or to desired degree of doneness, basting with remaining marinade.

To serve, thinly slice steak diagonally across grain. Yield: 5 servings.

☐ *170 calories, 25 grams protein, 6.5 grams fat, 1.3 grams carbohydrate, 107 milligrams cholesterol, 329 milligrams sodium, 20 milligrams calcium per 3-ounce serving.*   Susan M. Baker, *Louisville, Kentucky.*

LIVER IN CREOLE SAUCE

¼ cup reduced-calorie Italian dressing
1 pound (½-inch-thick slice) calf's liver,
   cut into ½-inch strips
1 cup chopped onion
1 cup chopped green pepper
¾ cup chopped celery
1 clove garlic, crushed
2 medium tomatoes, peeled and quartered
1 (8-ounce) can tomato sauce
1 teaspoon chili powder
1 teaspoon dried whole oregano
¼ teaspoon salt
2 cups hot cooked rice (cooked without
   salt or fat)

Combine reduced-calorie Italian dressing, liver, onion, green pepper, celery, and garlic in a large skillet, and cook over medium heat until vegetables are tender (2 to 3 minutes).

Add tomatoes, tomato sauce, chili powder, oregano, and salt. Bring to a boil. Cover, reduce heat, and simmer 10 minutes or until liver is tender. Serve over rice. Yield: 4 servings.

☐ *223 calories, 24.4 grams protein, 6.1 grams fat, 20.4 grams carbohydrate, 340 milligrams cholesterol, 620.3 milligrams sodium, and 55 milligrams calcium per 3-ounce serving plus 112 calories, 2.1 grams protein, 0.1 gram fat, 24.8 grams carbohydrate, 0 milligrams cholesterol, 2 milligrams sodium, and 10.3 milligrams calcium per ½-cup serving rice.*
            Frank H. Fogg,
            Tulsa, Oklahoma.

Enjoy Fresh Basil

It won't be long until many health-conscious cooks plant their herb gardens. Besides having wonderful aromas, fresh herbs can be substituted for fat and salt to flavor foods.

One of the most popular herbs is basil. To get you started with a conventional use of basil, try Pasta-Basil Toss. Considered an Italian seasoning, basil is a natural in this dish, which also calls for pasta and Parmesan cheese.

Growing Basil at Home

Basil is a tender annual that is simple to grow but needs to be replanted each spring. It thrives in hot, humid weather and grows well throughout the South until fall frost.

Plant basil in full sun and a loose, well-drained soil. Because it will not grow in cold soil, it is best to wait until the ground warms up and all danger of frost is past. Plant basil seeds in a shallow furrow, and cover them with ¼ inch soil. When the plants are 2 to 3 inches tall, thin to 18 to 24 inches apart.

One of the beauties of basil is that the plants require little maintenance. For bushier growth, fertilize after a heavy clipping with liquid 18-18-18 or 20-20-20 diluted according to label directions. And it's important to keep the soil moist.

To extend the life of the basil plant, just pinch off the flower stalks. Remember that the flavor of the leaves is strongest just before the flowers open.

PASTA-BASIL TOSS

1 cup broccoli flowerets
1 cup cauliflower flowerets
½ pound fresh snow peas
2 cloves garlic, minced
3 tablespoons chopped fresh basil
1 tablespoon reduced-calorie margarine,
   melted
3 cups cooked, drained rotelle macaroni
   (cooked without salt or fat)
⅓ cup grated Parmesan cheese
1 (2-ounce) jar diced pimiento, drained
⅛ teaspoon salt
⅛ teaspoon pepper

Blanch broccoli and cauliflower in boiling water 4 minutes; add snow peas, and blanch an additional minute. Drain and set aside.

Sauté garlic and basil in margarine until tender. Combine macaroni, vegetables, basil mixture, Parmesan cheese, and remaining ingredients in a medium bowl; toss gently. Serve warm or chilled. Yield: 7 servings.

☐ *133 calories, 6.1 grams protein, 2.4 grams fat, 22 grams carbohydrate, 3 milligrams cholesterol, 142 milligrams sodium, and 101 milligrams calcium per 1-cup serving.*
       Mrs. John A. Kinniburgh,
         McLean, Virginia.

CUCUMBER-YOGURT SALAD

5 cups thinly sliced cucumbers (about 2
   large)
¾ cup thinly sliced red onion (about 1
   small)
1 (8-ounce) carton plain low-fat yogurt
3 tablespoons wine vinegar
1 tablespoon lemon juice
1 tablespoon minced fresh basil
1 clove garlic, crushed
1 teaspoon Dijon mustard
⅛ teaspoon salt
⅛ teaspoon pepper

Combine cucumbers and onion in a large bowl; cover and chill.

Combine yogurt and remaining ingredients in a small bowl; stir to blend. Cover and chill. Pour mixture over vegetables, and toss. Serve salad immediately. Yield: 6 servings.

☐ *45 calories, 2.8 grams protein, 0.8 gram fat, 7.5 grams carbohydrate, 2 milligrams cholesterol, 102 milligrams sodium, and 99 milligrams calcium per 1-cup serving. Mary Beth McCormack,*
         Austin, Texas.

ZUCCHINI-BASIL SCRAMBLE

4¾ cups thinly sliced zucchini (about 3 medium)
1 cup thinly sliced onion
1 clove garlic, minced
2 tablespoons minced fresh basil
1 teaspoon vegetable-flavored bouillon granules
¼ teaspoon freshly ground pepper
2 medium tomatoes, peeled and cut into wedges
¼ cup grated Parmesan cheese

Combine zucchini, onion, garlic, basil, bouillon granules, and pepper in a skillet; cook over medium heat 5 minutes, stirring occasionally. Add tomatoes; cook 3 to 5 minutes or until done. Sprinkle with cheese, and serve immediately. Yield: 4 servings.

☐ *73 calories, 5.1 grams protein, 2 grams fat, 11 grams carbohydrate, 4 milligrams cholesterol, 225 milligrams sodium, and 140 milligrams calcium per 1-cup serving.*

The Keys To Weight Loss

Calories and weight loss are popular topics these days. Yet in spite of a multitude of information in newspapers, magazines, and books, the subject of permanent weight loss is still a mystery to many.

Weight loss involves a very simple formula: Expend more calories than you take in. For example, you will lose weight if you eat 1,500 calories and expend 2,000 calories that day. Eating more calories than you burn up will cause you to put on pounds.

Over the years you may have noticed a slow weight gain. The weight was probably added at the rate of a pound or two a year. Known as "creeping obesity," these pounds are generally hard to lose. Inactivity is often the culprit in creeping obesity.

Basal metabolic rate (BMR) and body metabolism are two important terms associated with weight loss. Basal metabolic rate is the minimum amount of calories required by the body to sustain life. This includes calories needed for breathing, body temperature, blood circulation, and other basic functions during sleep. Additional calories are needed for any activity, such as sitting up, moving, or exercising. Most people require 35 to 55 calories per hour while sleeping. An individual's body metabolism is unique. Depending on the types of activities you participate in daily, anywhere from 1,000 to 5,000 calories per day may be used (refer to the chart). The great difference between these two numbers can be attributed to exercise in addition to individual metabolic requirements.

Basal metabolic rates vary considerably among individuals. Men, pregnant and nursing women, people with fevers, those who have more muscle than fat, and people who exercise regularly all tend to have higher BMR's. Undernourished or starved people have a lower BMR. An adult's BMR also decreases with age. It's a common misconception that many people are overweight due to a malfunctioning thyroid gland that causes a lower BMR. In fact, fewer than 1% of all overweight people really have abnormal thyroid function.

Researchers have found that many people who lose weight while dieting often return to their original weight, as if their bodies want to weigh that certain amount. This "set-point theory" states that the body alters its BMR to expend more or fewer calories depending on the amount of food eaten. When following a strict, low-calorie diet without increasing activity, the body reacts as if it's being starved and will slow down its metabolism to compensate. However, if you follow a diet with moderate calorie restriction and exercise regularly, the body's set point can be changed. That's why the best way to lose weight involves a combination of diet and exercise.

Dieting alone causes you to lose both fat and muscle tissue; for that reason, a very-low-calorie diet will cheat the body of necessary nutrients. A very-low-calorie level also causes your metabolism to slow down to compensate for the loss of calories. Even after you reach a desired weight, you may find that the body needs fewer calories.

Exercise combined with diet for a gradual weight loss has psychological and physical benefits. You'll probably feel better and have more energy. Exercise reduces stress. It also helps to increase muscle tone and keep skin from sagging. And it raises your body's metabolism, causing it to burn more calories at rest and during exercise.

To gain the most benefit, choose exercises that are rhythmic and continuous, such as walking, swimming, cycling, and jogging. Work up to a goal of participating in these activities at least three times a week at a pace that is not too strenuous. Exercise does not have to be exhausting to benefit your body. Your physician can help you with an individualized program.

Calories Used Per Hour During Various Activities

Activity	Calories Used
Aerobic dancing, medium	400-445
Bicycling, 6 minutes/mile	415
Calisthenics, vigorous	300-400
Dancing	250
Dishwashing (by hand)	100-135
Driving a car	80-100
Eating, reading, writing	80-90
Gardening and heavy yard work	300-390
Jogging, 11 minutes/mile	600
Squash, racquetball	600-775
Stationary bicycling, brisk	300-400
Swimming, moderate	300-400
Tennis, singles	425
Walking, 15 minutes/mile	345-400
Walking, 25 minutes/mile	200-250
Washing, showering, shaving	150-205
Washing windows	250
Watching TV	70-80

The bigger and more active you are, the more calories you burn for any given activity. The calories listed above are approximate for a 158-pound adult.

Simple But Savory Entrées

Today's busy life-styles require simplified cooking. A list of ingredients that fills half a page is bound to mean an evening's worth of cooking and a sink full of dirty utensils. But taking shortcuts doesn't necessarily mean curtailing flavor. A few well-chosen ingredients that are already packed with seasonings decrease the number of ingredients needed to obtain good flavor. You can, for instance, use condiments to create savory entrées and homemade sauces or use commercial sauces for marinades.

BEER-MARINATED FLANK STEAK

1 large onion, chopped
½ to 1 teaspoon ground cumin
3 cloves garlic, crushed
⅛ teaspoon salt
⅛ teaspoon pepper
1 (12-ounce) can beer
1 (1½-pound) flank steak

Combine all ingredients except steak in a large shallow dish, mixing well. Place steak in dish; cover and refrigerate 12 hours.

Remove steak from marinade. Broil 5 inches from heat 4 to 5 minutes on each side or until desired degree of doneness. To serve, thinly slice steak diagonally across grain. Yield: 4 to 6 servings.
Mrs. E. W. Hanley,
Palm Harbor, Florida.

BRAISED ROUND STEAK

2 to 2½ pounds boneless top round steak, ½ inch thick
¾ teaspoon seasoning salt
½ teaspoon pepper
2 tablespoons butter or margarine, divided
1 cup beef broth
¼ cup half-and-half
2 tablespoons steak sauce

Trim excess fat from steak. Cut steak into serving-size pieces; pound to ¼-inch thickness. Sprinkle with seasoning salt and pepper.

Melt 1 tablespoon butter in a large skillet; add half of steak, and brown on both sides. Remove steak pieces; set aside. Repeat procedure with remaining 1 tablespoon butter and remaining steak

pieces. Return steak to skillet. Add beef broth; bring to a boil. Cover, reduce heat, and simmer 1 hour or until steak is tender.

Remove steak from skillet; keep warm. Stir half-and-half and steak sauce into drippings in skillet; simmer 3 minutes. Return steak to skillet; simmer 2 minutes or until steak is heated. Yield: 6 to 8 servings. *Minnie Young,*
Montgomery, Alabama.

BAKED SHRIMP

¼ cup butter
1 (8-ounce) bottle commercial Italian dressing
Juice of 2 lemons
¼ teaspoon freshly ground pepper
3 pounds large shrimp, peeled with tails intact

Melt butter in a 13- x 9- x 2-inch baking dish. Add dressing, lemon juice, and pepper. Add shrimp to sauce, mixing well. Bake at 325° for 25 to 30 minutes, stirring several times. Yield: 6 to 8 servings. *Teresa Davenport,*
Fort Walton Beach, Florida.

APPLE-GLAZED PORK CHOPS

½ cup teriyaki sauce
1 tablespoon lemon juice
6 (½-inch-thick) center-cut pork chops
1 cup unsweetened applesauce
¼ cup orange marmalade
Apple slices (optional)
Parsley sprigs (optional)

Combine teriyaki sauce and lemon juice in a 13- x 9- x 2-inch baking dish. Arrange pork chops in dish, turning to coat. Cover and marinate 8 hours in refrigerator, turning meat once.

Remove from refrigerator; let stand 30 minutes. Cover and bake at 350° for 45 minutes; drain drippings from dish. Combine applesauce and marmalade; stir well. Spoon a thin layer over each pork chop; bake, uncovered, an additional 15 minutes or until done. Serve with remaining applesauce mixture. Garnish with apple slices and parsley, if desired. Yield: 6 servings.
Cindy Murphy,
McDonald, Tennessee.

PORK MEDALLIONS WITH CHUTNEY SAUCE

2 (¾-pound) pork tenderloins, divided
2 tablespoons olive oil, divided
1 clove garlic, minced, divided
⅛ teaspoon salt
⅛ teaspoon pepper
½ cup chutney
Rind and juice of 1 orange
Parsley sprigs (optional)
Orange slices (optional)

Partially freeze tenderloins; cut into ¼-inch slices, and set aside.

Heat 1 tablespoon oil in a large skillet; sauté half of garlic and half of pork slices about 3 minutes on each side or until pork is done. Remove to serving platter, and keep warm. Repeat procedure with remaining oil, garlic, and pork; add to serving platter. Sprinkle with salt and pepper; keep warm.

Add chutney and rind and juice of 1 orange to skillet; cook over medium heat, stirring constantly, until thoroughly heated. Serve pork medallions with sauce. Garnish with parsley and orange slices, if desired. Yield: 6 servings.
Lynn Joy,
Gadsden, Alabama.

TANGY CHICKEN

½ cup commercial mustard/mayonnaise sauce, divided
Grated rind of 1 lemon
1 tablespoon minced parsley
6 chicken breast halves with skin
Juice of 1 lemon
⅓ cup dry white wine

Combine 3 tablespoons sauce, lemon rind, and parsley. Using fingers, carefully lift chicken skin (do not detach). Insert 2 teaspoons sauce mixture under skin of each breast. Press outside of skin to spread sauce mixture evenly over chicken. Place chicken, skin side down, in a 13- x 9- x 2-inch baking dish.

Combine remaining sauce, lemon juice, and wine; pour mixture over chicken. Cover and refrigerate 8 hours, turning once.

Bake, skin side down, uncovered, at 350° for 30 minutes, basting occasionally. Turn skin side up, and bake an additional 30 minutes or until chicken is done. Yield: 6 servings.

Tip: Never use a dish towel to handle hot utensils. Loose ends of the towel may touch a burner and catch on fire.

SAUTÉED CHICKEN BREASTS

1 clove garlic, minced
3 tablespoons olive oil
4 chicken breast halves, skinned
¼ cup red wine vinegar
1 teaspoon dried whole basil
¼ teaspoon salt
⅛ teaspoon pepper

Sauté garlic in oil in a large skillet. Add chicken, and cook 15 minutes or until chicken is lightly browned. Add remaining ingredients; cover, reduce heat, and simmer 30 minutes or until chicken is done. Yield: 4 servings.

Chris Singley,
Selma, Alabama.

HONEY-CURRY CHICKEN

¼ cup butter or margarine, melted
¼ cup honey
¼ cup prepared mustard
¼ teaspoon salt
½ to 1 teaspoon curry powder
3 pounds chicken pieces, skinned
Parsley sprigs (optional)

Combine butter, honey, mustard, salt, and curry; stir well. Dip chicken into honey sauce, coating all sides. Place chicken in a greased 13- x 9- x 2-inch baking dish. Reserve remaining sauce. Bake, uncovered, at 375° for 1 hour, basting occasionally with remaining sauce. Garnish with parsley, if desired. Yield: 4 servings.

Midge Finnerty,
Washington, Virginia.

Spice Up Dishes With Italian Seasonings

Reach for the spice rack, and enjoy the flavors of Italy. For centuries, Italians have created zesty, aromatic dishes. Basil, oregano, and herb blends, such as Italian seasoning, are the key.

Basil, known as the "king of the herbs," enhances tomato, meat, and vegetable dishes. Oregano complements tomatoes and pasta. Italian seasoning—usually a combination of oregano, rosemary, savory, fennel, basil, and thyme—is well suited to chicken entrées, tomato dishes, stews, meat loaves, and casseroles.

PASTA SALAD

4 ounces uncooked spaghetti
1 (6-ounce) jar marinated artichokes
¾ cup sliced fresh zucchini
⅔ cup shredded carrots
2 ounces sliced salami, cut into strips
1 cup (4 ounces) shredded mozzarella cheese
2 tablespoons grated Parmesan cheese
2 tablespoons vegetable oil
2 tablespoons vinegar
¾ teaspoon dry mustard
½ teaspoon dried whole oregano
½ teaspoon dried whole basil
1 clove garlic, crushed

Break spaghetti in half, and cook according to package directions, omitting salt. Drain and cool.

Drain artichokes, reserving the liquid, and chop.

Combine spaghetti, artichokes, zucchini, carrots, salami, and cheeses, and set mixture aside.

Combine reserved artichoke liquid and remaining ingredients in a jar. Cover tightly, and shake vigorously. Pour over spaghetti mixture; toss gently to coat. Cover and chill 2 to 3 hours. Yield: 6 to 8 servings.

Connie Burgess,
Knoxville, Tennessee.

STUFFED CHICKEN BREASTS

8 chicken breast halves, boned and skinned
4 (1-ounce) slices cooked ham, cut in half
4 (1-ounce) slices Swiss cheese, cut in half
1 egg, beaten
2 teaspoons water
1 cup seasoned, dry breadcrumbs
½ cup butter or margarine
1 teaspoon Italian seasoning
Mushroom Sauce

Place each chicken breast half on a sheet of wax paper; flatten to ¼-inch thickness, using a meat mallet or rolling pin. Place 1 piece of ham and 1 piece of cheese in center of each chicken piece. Roll up lengthwise, and secure meat and cheese with wooden picks.

Combine egg and water; dip each chicken breast in egg, and coat well with breadcrumbs.

Melt butter in a large skillet; stir in Italian seasoning. Add chicken, and cook over low heat 30 to 40 minutes, browning all sides. Serve with Mushroom Sauce. Yield: 8 servings.

Mushroom Sauce:

½ pound fresh mushrooms, sliced
¼ cup chopped onion
3 tablespoons butter or margarine, melted
3 tablespoons white wine
½ cup milk
1 (10¾-ounce) can cream of mushroom soup, undiluted

Sauté mushrooms and onion in butter in a medium saucepan until vegetables are tender. Stir in remaining ingredients. Yield: 2 cups. *Sally Murphy,*
Allen, Texas.

ITALIAN WAFERS

½ cup butter or margarine, softened
½ cup (2 ounces) shredded mozzarella cheese
¼ cup (1 ounce) grated Parmesan cheese
1 cup all-purpose flour
½ teaspoon dried whole oregano
Pinch of salt
Dash of red pepper
1 tablespoon diced pimiento

Combine butter and cheeses in a large bowl, stirring to mix. Stir in flour, oregano, salt, and red pepper. Add diced pimiento, and mix well. Divide dough in half; shape dough into two 6-inch rolls. Cover and chill rolls several hours or overnight.

Slice dough into ¼-inch slices; place on a lightly greased baking sheet. Bake at 375° for 10 to 12 minutes. Transfer wafers to wire racks; cool completely. Yield: 4 dozen. *Kristy LeFevre,*
Arlington, Virginia.

MICROWAVE COOKERY

Favorite Recipes— Only Faster

Microwave ovens are quickly becoming a necessity in busy households. The recipes here are some favorites that our readers use to save time.

Besides saving time, fruit and vegetables from the microwave are often tastier than those cooked conventionally. Moisture does not escape during microwave cooking as quickly as in conventional methods, so that fruit and vegetables stay moist and retain more nutrients.

CHICKEN AND VEGETABLES VERMOUTH

4 chicken breast halves, skinned and
  boned
3 tablespoons grated Parmesan cheese
⅛ teaspoon pepper
¼ cup butter or margarine
2 tablespoons vermouth
2 tablespoons water
1 chicken-flavored bouillon cube
4 carrots, scraped and sliced diagonally
1 large onion, cut into eighths
1 cup sliced fresh mushrooms

Cut chicken into bite-size pieces; set aside. Combine cheese and pepper in a plastic bag; close bag securely, and shake to mix. Add chicken to cheese mixture; close bag securely, and shake well to coat chicken.

Place butter in an 8-inch square baking dish; microwave at HIGH for 55 seconds or until melted. Remove chicken from plastic bag, and place in baking dish. Cover with wax paper, and microwave at MEDIUM HIGH (70% power) for 6 to 7½ minutes, stirring after 3 minutes. Set aside.

Combine vermouth and water in a 1½-quart casserole; microwave 1 minute and 15 seconds at HIGH or until boiling. Add bouillon cube; stir until dissolved. Add carrots and onion; cover with heavy-duty plastic wrap, and microwave at HIGH for 4 minutes. Add mushrooms and chicken mixture; stir gently, cover, and microwave at HIGH for 1 minute or until thoroughly heated. Yield: 4 servings. *Aimee Goodman, Knoxville, Tennessee.*

ROSY CINNAMON APPLES

½ cup red cinnamon candies
¼ cup water
6 medium-size cooking apples, peeled and
  cut into wedges

Combine candies and water in a 2-cup glass measure. Microwave at HIGH for 3 to 4 minutes, stirring at 1-minute intervals until candies dissolve. Place apples in a 1½-quart casserole. Pour melted candy mixture over apples; cover and microwave at HIGH for 7 to 9 minutes or until apples are tender, stirring after 4 minutes. Yield: 6 servings. *Mrs. Billie Taylor, Fork Union, Virginia.*

Tip: Reheat single servings in a microwave or toaster oven; these use less energy than a standard range.

CHOCOLATE-TOPPED AMARETTO CUSTARD

3 eggs, beaten
¼ cup sugar
1 teaspoon vanilla extract
⅛ teaspoon salt
¼ cup amaretto
1¼ cups milk
⅓ cup commercial chocolate syrup
Sliced almonds

Combine eggs, sugar, vanilla, and salt in a bowl; blend well. Stir in amaretto; set aside.

Place milk in a 2-cup glass measure; microwave at HIGH for 2 to 3 minutes or until milk is scalded (do not boil). Gradually stir about one-fourth of hot milk into egg mixture; add to remaining hot milk, stirring constantly. Pour mixture into 4 (6-ounce) custard cups. Place cups in a circle in microwave oven, and microwave at MEDIUM (50% power) for 6 to 10 minutes or until almost set in the center, rearranging cups every 2 minutes. Chill thoroughly.

Heat chocolate syrup in microwave according to container directions. Invert custard onto serving plates; spoon one-fourth of chocolate syrup over each serving. Top with sliced almonds. Yield: 4 servings. *Vivian Levine, Oak Ridge, Tennessee.*

Enjoy The Taste Of Sour Cream

Sour cream gives tangy flavor to many new dishes as well as traditional ones. And there is another bonus; with only 26 calories per tablespoon, sour cream has fewer calories than whipped cream or mayonnaise.

Sour cream is especially popular in sauces, dressings, and dips. When adding it to a heated sauce, remember to remove the mixture from the cooking surface before adding the sour cream. It curdles when combined with liquids that are too hot.

Be sure to check the freshness date when buying sour cream, and keep it refrigerated and covered. If it separates, simply stir it.

CHILLED AVOCADO SOUP

1 large avocado, coarsely chopped
¼ cup coarsely chopped onion
2 (10½-ounce) cans consommé, divided
1 (8-ounce) carton commercial sour cream
⅛ teaspoon chili powder
⅛ teaspoon ground red pepper

Combine avocado, onion, and 1 can consommé in container of electric blender. Cover and blend at high speed 1 to 2 minutes or until pureed. Pour into a mixing bowl; stir in remaining consommé, sour cream, chili powder, and pepper. Cover and chill 1 to 2 hours. Yield: 5¼ cups. *Hazel Sellers, Albany, Georgia.*

SOUR CREAM ENCHILADAS

1 pound ground beef
½ cup chopped onion
1 teaspoon garlic powder
1 teaspoon ground cumin
½ teaspoon salt
1 tablespoon chili powder
1 (10¾-ounce) can cream of mushroom
  soup, undiluted
½ cup milk
1 (8-ounce) carton commercial sour cream
8 corn tortillas
2 tablespoons vegetable oil
2 cups (8 ounces) shredded sharp Cheddar
  cheese, divided
1 (2.2-ounce) can sliced ripe olives,
  drained

Cook ground beef and onion in a heavy skillet until brown; drain off drippings. Stir in garlic powder, cumin, salt, and chili powder. Set aside.

Combine soup and milk in a small saucepan. Cook over medium heat, stirring constantly, until bubbly. Remove from heat, and add sour cream; stir until well blended. Set aside.

Fry tortillas, one at a time, in 2 tablespoons hot oil (375°) for 3 to 5 seconds on each side or just until tortillas are softened. Drain on paper towels.

Place 2 heaping tablespoonfuls beef mixture in center of each tortilla. Sprinkle each with 1 tablespoon cheese, and roll up. Place tortillas, seam side down, in a 12- x 8- x 2-inch baking dish.

Pour sour cream mixture over tortillas. Cover and bake at 350° for 25 minutes. Sprinkle with remaining cheese, and garnish with ripe olives. Bake, uncovered, an additional 5 minutes. Yield: 4 servings. *Jeri Phillips, Allen, Texas.*

SALMON QUICHE

1 cup whole wheat flour
⅔ cup shredded sharp Cheddar cheese
¼ cup chopped almonds
¼ teaspoon salt
¼ teaspoon paprika
¼ cup plus 2 tablespoons vegetable oil
3 eggs, beaten
1 (8-ounce) carton commercial sour cream
¼ cup mayonnaise
½ cup (2 ounces) shredded Cheddar cheese
1 tablespoon grated onion
¼ teaspoon dried whole dillweed
3 drops hot sauce
1 (15½-ounce) can salmon, undrained
Celery leaves (optional)
Cherry tomato (optional)

Combine flour, ⅔ cup cheese, almonds, salt, paprika, and vegetable oil; mix well. Reserve ½ cup crust mixture, and set aside.

Press crust mixture into bottom and up sides of a 9-inch quiche dish. Bake crust at 400° for 10 minutes. Reduce oven heat to 325°. Remove crust from oven, and set aside.

Combine eggs, sour cream, mayonnaise, ½ cup cheese, onion, dillweed, and hot sauce in a large bowl; stir well. Drain salmon, reserving liquid; flake. Remove and discard bones and skin from salmon, if desired; add salmon to egg mixture. Add water to reserved liquid to measure ½ cup; add to salmon mixture, stirring well. Spoon salmon mixture into crust; sprinkle reserved crust mixture over top. Bake at 325° for 45 minutes. Garnish with celery leaves and a cherry tomato, if desired. Yield: one 9-inch quiche.

Janice E. Stephens,
Richardson, Texas.

MACARONI SHELL SALAD

8 ounces small shell macaroni
½ cup mayonnaise
½ cup commercial sour cream
¼ cup half-and-half
½ teaspoon salt
¼ teaspoon pepper
1 cup chopped celery
¼ cup chopped green pepper
¼ cup chopped red pepper
¼ cup chopped purple onion

Cook macaroni according to package directions; drain. Rinse with cold water; drain again.

Combine mayonnaise, sour cream, half-and-half, salt, and pepper in a large bowl; stir until smooth. Add macaroni and remaining ingredients; toss lightly until well coated. Chill 2 hours before serving. Yield: 6 servings.

Marilee Chapman,
Greer, South Carolina.

LEMON-SOUR CREAM POUND CAKE

1 cup butter or margarine, softened
½ cup shortening
3 cups sugar
5 eggs
1 (8-ounce) carton commercial sour cream
¼ cup milk
3 cups all-purpose flour
½ teaspoon baking powder
2 teaspoons lemon extract
1 teaspoon vanilla extract

Cream butter and shortening; gradually add sugar, beating well at medium speed of an electric mixer. Add eggs, one at a time, beating mixture after each addition.

Combine sour cream and milk; stir until smooth. Combine flour and baking powder; add to creamed mixture alternately with sour cream mixture, beginning and ending with flour mixture. Mix just until blended after each addition. Stir in lemon and vanilla flavorings.

Pour batter into a greased and floured 10-inch tube pan. Bake at 325° for 1 hour and 40 to 45 minutes or until a wooden pick inserted in center comes out clean. Cool cake in pan 10 to 15 minutes; remove from pan, and cool completely. Yield: one 10-inch cake.

Myrtle C. Merritt,
Rural Hall, North Carolina.

Caramel Makes It Rich

You'll be right on either count if you think of caramel as a delicious "burnt-sugar" flavoring or as a smooth, sticky candy. Actually, the process of caramelizing sugar gives the chewy candy its name. But the same caramelized sugar flavor is stirred into sauces, frostings, and other foods as well.

Caramel candy (called *Quemada*) is a traditional Mexican treat found many times as the prize inside a piñata. The candy is made with only three ingredients: caramelized sugar, milk, and butter. The version here is a little different from the traditional recipe—it has pecans.

Caramelizing sugar can be tricky, so it's best to use a heavy skillet, such as cast iron, over very low heat to keep from burning the sugar. Just cook the sugar slowly, stirring constantly, until it melts to a golden syrup.

QUEMADA (BURNT-SUGAR CANDY)

3 cups sugar, divided
1 cup milk
½ cup butter
½ cup chopped pecans

Combine 2 cups sugar, milk, and butter in a heavy 3-quart saucepan; stir well. Cook over medium heat, stirring often, until butter melts.

Place remaining 1 cup sugar in a heavy skillet; cook over medium heat, stirring constantly, until sugar melts and syrup is light golden brown. Gradually stir into butter mixture. Cook over medium heat, stirring often, until mixture reaches soft ball stage (240°). Remove from heat. Let mixture cool to 110°. Beat at high speed of an electric mixer until mixture is cool and holds its shape. Shape candy into two 7- x 1½-inch logs; roll in pecans. Wrap in plastic wrap, and chill 1 to 2 hours. Cut into ½-inch slices. Yield: about 2 pounds.

Jennie Kinnard,
Mabank, Texas.

EASY CARAMEL SAUCE

1 (14-ounce) can sweetened condensed milk
¾ cup light corn syrup
½ cup sugar
⅓ cup firmly packed brown sugar
¼ cup butter or margarine
¼ cup whipping cream
1½ teaspoons vanilla extract

Combine first 4 ingredients in a heavy saucepan; mix well. Cook over medium heat until mixture reaches 220°, stirring constantly. Remove from heat; stir in butter, whipping cream, and vanilla. Serve sauce warm over ice cream or pound cake. Yield: 3 cups.

Sharon McClatchey,
Muskogee, Oklahoma.

For the easy way to enjoy rich caramel flavor, use brown sugar in the frosting of Pound Cake With Caramel Frosting.

OYSTER-AND-MUSHROOM SOUP

2 (12-ounce) containers Standard oysters
½ pound fresh mushrooms, sliced
3 tablespoons chopped green onions
1 tablespoon butter or margarine, melted
¼ cup butter or margarine
¼ cup all-purpose flour
½ cup half-and-half
3 tablespoons chopped fresh parsley
2 tablespoons Sauterne
¼ teaspoon salt
¼ teaspoon pepper

Drain oysters, reserving the liquid. Set aside. Sauté mushrooms and green onions in 1 tablespoon butter; do not drain. Set mixture aside.

Melt ¼ cup butter in a heavy 3-quart saucepan over low heat; add flour, stirring until smooth. Cook, stirring constantly, until golden brown. Gradually add reserved oyster liquid and half-and-half; cook over medium heat, stirring constantly, until mixture is thickened and bubbly. Stir in reserved mushroom mixture, oysters, and remaining ingredients. Reduce heat, and simmer 5 to 8 minutes or until edges of oysters curl. If desired, add more half-and-half for a thinner soup. Yield: 4 cups.

Rose Alleman,
Prairieville, Louisiana.

POUND CAKE
WITH CARAMEL FROSTING

2 cups butter, softened
2⅔ cups sugar, divided
8 eggs, separated
3½ cups all-purpose flour
½ cup half-and-half
1 teaspoon vanilla extract
Easy Caramel Frosting
Pecan halves (optional)

Cream butter; gradually add 2 cups sugar, beating at medium speed of an electric mixer until light and fluffy. Add the egg yolks, one at a time, beating after each addition.

Add flour to creamed mixture alternately with half-and-half, beginning and ending with flour. Stir in vanilla.

Beat egg whites (at room temperature) at high speed of an electric mixer until foamy. Gradually add remaining ⅔ cup sugar, 1 tablespoon at a time, beating until stiff peaks form; fold into batter. Pour batter into a greased and floured 10-inch tube pan; bake at 325° for 1 hour and 25 minutes or until a wooden pick inserted in center comes out clean. Cool in pan 10 minutes; remove from pan, and cool completely on a rack. Frost cake with Easy Caramel Frosting; garnish with pecan halves, if desired. Yield: one 10-inch cake.

Easy Caramel Frosting:

½ cup butter or margarine
1 cup firmly packed brown
   sugar
¼ cup whipping cream
2½ cups sifted powdered sugar
1 teaspoon vanilla extract

Melt butter in a heavy saucepan. Add brown sugar; cook over low heat, stirring constantly, until sugar dissolves. (Do not boil.) Remove from heat. Stir in whipping cream. Add powdered sugar and vanilla; beat at high speed of an electric mixer until smooth. Yield: enough frosting for one 10-inch cake.

Mrs. J. W. Riley, Jr.,
Kingsport, Tennessee.

Oysters Are Versatile

If you prefer oysters cooked, you'll undoubtedly be enticed to try these recipes. In three of them, oysters are seasoned and sauced and returned to their shells to bake, while a fourth one is for a sandwich of fried oysters. For starters, try our recipe for soup.

TEXAS OYSTER NACHOS

2 dozen unshucked oysters
1 (4-pound) package rock salt
¾ cup cocktail sauce
1 cup crushed tortilla chips
½ cup (2 ounces) shredded Monterey Jack
   cheese
4 jalapeño peppers, sliced
Whole tortilla chips

Wash and rinse oysters in cold water. Shuck oysters, reserving deep half of shells; place oysters in colander to drain.

Sprinkle rock salt in a 15- x 10- x 1-inch jellyroll pan; arrange half of the reserved shells on rock salt. Place 1 oyster in each half shell. Dollop 1 heaping teaspoon cocktail sauce on each oyster. Broil 4 inches from heat 3 to 4 minutes or until edges of oysters begin to curl. Top each oyster with 2 teaspoons crushed tortilla chips and 1 teaspoon cheese. Broil 30 seconds or until cheese melts. Top each with a pepper slice. Repeat with remaining oysters, cocktail sauce, crushed chips, cheese, and peppers. Serve oysters with tortilla chips. Yield: 4 to 6 servings.

Ginny Munsterman,
Garland, Texas.

OYSTERS IN SHRIMP SAUCE

2 tablespoons butter or margarine
2 tablespoons all-purpose flour
⅛ teaspoon ground nutmeg
¾ cup milk
1 egg yolk, beaten
⅓ cup dry white wine
1 (4¼-ounce) can shrimp, rinsed, drained, and chopped
2 tablespoons chopped fresh parsley
2 dozen unshucked oysters
1 (4-pound) package rock salt
¾ cup grated Parmesan cheese

Melt butter in a heavy saucepan over low heat; add flour and nutmeg, stirring until smooth. Cook 1 minute, stirring constantly. Gradually add milk; cook over medium heat, stirring constantly, until mixture is thickened and bubbly. Combine egg yolk and wine, mixing well. Gradually stir about one-fourth of hot mixture into yolk mixture; add to remaining hot mixture, stirring constantly. Cook over low heat, stirring constantly, 1 to 2 minutes or until mixture is thickened and bubbly. Stir in shrimp and parsley. Set aside.

Wash and rinse oysters thoroughly in cold water. Shuck oysters, reserving deep half of shells; place oysters in colander to drain. Set aside.

Sprinkle rock salt in a 15- x 10- x 1-inch jellyroll pan; arrange half the reserved shells on rock salt. Place 1 oyster in each half shell. Top each with 1 tablespoon shrimp sauce, and sprinkle with 1 teaspoon cheese. Bake at 400° for 10 to 12 minutes or until oysters begin to curl. Repeat with remaining oysters, sauce, and cheese. Yield: 4 to 6 servings.

Marie A. Davis,
Drexel, North Carolina.

OYSTERS BUCCANEER

½ pound fresh lump crabmeat
1½ cups herb-seasoned stuffing mix
½ cup butter or margarine, melted
1 (2-ounce) jar diced pimiento, undrained
¼ cup lemon juice
¼ teaspoon salt
⅛ teaspoon pepper
32 unshucked oysters
1 (4-pound) package rock salt
⅔ cup shredded Cheddar cheese
Cocktail sauce

Combine crabmeat, stuffing mix, butter, pimiento, lemon juice, salt, and pepper, mixing well; set aside.

Wash and rinse oysters thoroughly in cold water. Shuck oysters, reserving deep half of shells; place oysters in colander to drain.

Sprinkle rock salt in a 15- x 10- x 1-inch jellyroll pan; arrange half of the reserved shells on rock salt. Place 1 oyster in each half shell. Top each with 1 tablespoon crabmeat dressing.

Bake at 350° for 10 minutes or until oysters begin to curl and dressing is hot. Top with half the cheese, and cook 2 minutes or until cheese melts. Repeat with remaining oysters, dressing, and cheese. Serve with cocktail sauce. Yield: 6 to 8 servings.

Rita W. Cook,
Corpus Christi, Texas.

OYSTER-AND-BACON POOR BOYS

4 slices bacon
⅓ cup chopped onion
¼ cup chopped green pepper
¼ cup chopped celery
1 teaspoon garlic powder
½ teaspoon seasoned salt
1 tomato, chopped and drained
2 tablespoons chopped fresh parsley
⅓ cup mayonnaise
¼ teaspoon hot sauce
1 cup cracker meal
½ cup cornmeal
¼ teaspoon seasoned salt
⅛ teaspoon pepper
1 (12-ounce) container fresh Select oysters, drained
2 eggs, beaten
Vegetable oil
4 (6- to 7-inch) French bread loaves, sliced lengthwise and lightly toasted
Lettuce

Cook bacon in a large skillet until crisp; remove bacon, reserving 1 tablespoon drippings in skillet. Set bacon aside. Sauté onion, green pepper, celery, and garlic powder in drippings 2 to 3 minutes. Add ½ teaspoon seasoned salt, tomato, and parsley; drain and place in bowl. Add mayonnaise and hot sauce, mixing well. Set mixture aside.

Combine cracker meal, cornmeal, ¼ teaspoon seasoned salt, and pepper in a medium bowl. Dip oysters in eggs; dredge in cornmeal mixture. Fry oysters in deep, hot oil (375°) for 1½ minutes or until golden, turning once. Drain on paper towels.

Spread mayonnaise mixture on each bread half. Place bacon, lettuce, and oysters on bottom halves; cover with top half. Serve with remaining mayonnaise mixture. Yield: 4 servings.

Margaret Brantley,
Montgomery, Alabama.

Serve Carrots Anytime

Carrots are available all year long, so you have more than just one season to find creative ways to put them on the table. These recipes will help you make fresh carrots something special every time you serve them.

Unlike many other vegetables, carrots will keep well in a refrigerator for as long as a month. If you purchase them with tops, be sure to remove the tops before storing or the carrots will quickly become limp.

TIPSY CARROTS

1 pound carrots, scraped and diagonally sliced
½ cup rum
½ cup water
2 tablespoons butter or margarine
Dash of ground nutmeg
Dash of ground cinnamon

Combine carrots, rum, and water in a saucepan. Bring to a boil; reduce heat, and simmer 10 to 12 minutes or until carrots are crisp-tender. Add remaining ingredients; toss gently until butter melts. Yield: 4 servings.

Patsy Layer,
Galveston, Texas.

STUFFED CARROTS

6 medium carrots, scraped
10 saltine crackers, finely crushed
2 hard-cooked eggs, mashed
¼ cup minced celery
¼ cup minced onion
¼ cup butter or margarine, softened
¼ teaspoon pepper
⅛ teaspoon salt

Cut carrots 5 inches from top, reserving smaller end for another use. Cook carrots, covered, in a small amount of water 10 minutes or until crisp-tender. Let cool. Cut carrots in half lengthwise, and scoop out center of each.

Combine cracker crumbs and remaining ingredients; toss to mix. Stuff carrots with mixture; place in a lightly greased 13- x 9- x 2-inch baking dish. Bake, uncovered, at 350° for 30 minutes or until carrots are hot. Yield: 6 servings.

Clara June Waldrop,
Prairie Hill, Texas.

SAUCY CARROTS

8 medium carrots, scraped and thinly
  sliced (about 1 pound)
1 tablespoon butter or margarine
1 tablespoon all-purpose flour
1 cup milk
1 teaspoon Dijon mustard
½ teaspoon salt
⅛ teaspoon pepper
1 tablespoon chopped chives

Cook carrots, covered, in a small amount of water for 10 to 12 minutes or just until tender. Remove from heat, and drain.

Melt butter in a heavy saucepan over low heat; add flour, stirring until smooth. Cook 1 minute, stirring constantly. Gradually add milk; cook over medium heat, stirring constantly, until mixture is thickened and bubbly. Stir in mustard, salt, and pepper. Add carrots to sauce, and heat. Spoon into serving dish. Sprinkle with chives. Yield: 4 servings. *Michele Oswald, Dallas, Texas.*

CARROT POUND CAKE

1 cup butter or margarine, softened
1 (16-ounce) package powdered sugar,
  sifted
6 eggs
3 cups all-purpose flour
1½ teaspoons baking soda
1 teaspoon salt
2 teaspoons ground cinnamon
3 cups grated carrots (about 1 pound)
¼ cup wheat germ
1½ cups chopped pecans
1 tablespoon lemon juice
1 tablespoon vanilla extract
Lemon glaze (recipe follows)

Cream butter; gradually add sugar, beating well at medium speed of an electric mixer. Add eggs, one at a time, beating after each addition.

Combine flour, soda, salt, and cinnamon; add to creamed mixture; blend well. Stir in carrots, wheat germ, pecans, lemon juice, and vanilla. Spoon batter into a greased and floured 10-inch tube pan. Bake at 325° for 1 hour and 10 minutes or until a wooden pick

inserted in center comes out clean. Cool cake in pan 10 to 15 minutes; remove from pan. Drizzle top of cake with lemon glaze; cool completely. Yield: one 10-inch cake.

Lemon Glaze:

2 tablespoons butter or margarine, melted
2 tablespoons lemon juice
½ teaspoon vanilla extract
1¼ cups sifted powdered sugar

Combine butter, lemon juice, and vanilla in a small bowl; stir in powdered sugar. Drizzle over warm cake. Yield: about ½ cup. *Karen Eaker, Uvalde, Texas.*

Avocado Salad Ideas

Avocados are available year-round in pear, egg, or round shapes, and in a range of colors from green to almost black. In the winter, look for avocados that have a glossy green rind; the darker skinned variety with a rough, pebbly texture is available in the summer. The avocado has a creamy, butter-like texture, and a subtle nutlike flavor that complements assorted fruits and vegetables.

It's best to purchase avocados before they fully ripen because once ripened, they have a relatively short shelf life. They will ripen in three to five days at room temperature. To hasten the process, store the fruit in a brown paper bag. A ripe avocado should yield to gentle pressure.

FRUITED CHICKEN SALAD
IN AVOCADOS

2 cups chopped cooked chicken
½ cup orange sections, halved
½ cup seedless green grapes, halved
¼ cup chopped onion
¼ cup coarsely chopped walnuts
¼ cup plus 1 tablespoon olive oil
2 tablespoons fresh lemon juice
2 tablespoons chopped fresh parsley
1 tablespoon chopped fresh basil or 1
  teaspoon dried whole basil
½ teaspoon salt
¼ teaspoon pepper
2 large ripe avocados, peeled and halved
Lemon juice
Lettuce leaves

Combine chicken, oranges, grapes, onion, and walnuts in a mixing bowl;

mix well. Chill 1 hour. Combine olive oil, lemon juice, parsley, basil, salt, and pepper in a jar; cover tightly, and shake vigorously. Chill 1 hour.

Brush avocado halves with lemon juice. Shake dressing vigorously; pour over chicken mixture, and toss gently. Spoon chicken salad evenly into the avocado cavities. Serve on lettuce-lined plates. Yield: 4 servings. *Jeannette Safford, Mobile, Alabama.*

AVOCADO FRUIT SALAD

⅓ cup vegetable oil
3 tablespoons vinegar
½ teaspoon garlic powder
¼ teaspoon salt
⅛ teaspoon pepper
2 oranges
1 pink grapefruit
1 avocado
1 apple
Lettuce leaves

Combine oil, vinegar, garlic powder, salt, and pepper in a jar. Cover tightly, and shake vigorously. Set aside.

Peel oranges, grapefruit, and avocado; core apple, and cut all fruit into bite-size pieces. Combine fruit in a bowl. Pour dressing over fruit; toss. Cover and chill.

To serve, use a slotted spoon to arrange the fruit on a lettuce-lined platter. Yield: 6 servings. *Barbara Carson, Hollywood, Florida.*

SPANISH AVOCADO SALAD

1 pint cherry tomatoes, halved
1 (6-ounce) can pitted ripe olives, drained
1 small onion, sliced
1 (4-ounce) can chopped green chiles,
  drained
¼ cup plus 2 tablespoons vegetable oil
3 tablespoons vinegar
1 teaspoon garlic salt
3 dashes of hot sauce
Lettuce leaves
2 avocados, peeled and sliced

Combine tomatoes, olives, onion, and chiles in a medium bowl; set aside. Combine oil, vinegar, garlic salt, and hot sauce in a jar; cover tightly, and shake vigorously. Reserve 3 tablespoons dressing; pour remaining dressing over tomato mixture, and toss. Line a serving platter with lettuce. Arrange avocado on lettuce; brush avocado slices with reserved dressing. Mound tomato mixture in center. Serve immediately. Yield: 6 servings. *Karen Herrin, Arlington, Texas.*

CONGEALED AVOCADO SALADS

2 envelopes unflavored gelatin
½ cup cold water
¾ cup boiling water
2 tablespoons lemon juice
1¼ teaspoons salt
1 teaspoon grated onion
2 dashes of hot sauce
2½ cups mashed avocado
1 (8-ounce) carton commercial sour cream
1 cup mayonnaise
Lettuce leaves
1 (8-ounce) can mandarin orange sections, drained

Soften gelatin in ½ cup cold water. Add ¾ cup boiling water; stir until gelatin dissolves. Add lemon juice, salt, onion, and hot sauce; stir well, and cool to room temperature. Stir in avocado, sour cream, and mayonnaise. Pour mixture into 10 lightly oiled individual molds; cover and chill until firm. Unmold onto lettuce leaves. Garnish with oranges. Yield: 10 servings.
Mrs. Irving M. Day, Jr.,
Swanton, Maryland.

Cabbage Patch Favorites

No matter how you enjoy cabbage, you'll want to try Hot Cabbage Creole and Cabbage With Apples and Franks. If cabbage and sausage is more to your liking, make Cabbage Kielbasa. With beer or iced tea and lots of rye bread with butter, it's a wholesome, sustaining dish. For those who like casseroles, we suggest Italian Cabbage Casserole. It's like lasagna with cabbage used instead of noodles.

ITALIAN CABBAGE CASSEROLE

1 medium cabbage, shredded
2 pounds lean ground beef
1 medium onion, chopped
1 green pepper, chopped
1 (6-ounce) can tomato paste
1 (8-ounce) can tomato sauce
1 teaspoon dried whole oregano
1 teaspoon salt
⅛ teaspoon pepper
¼ teaspoon garlic powder
1 cup (4 ounces) shredded mozzarella cheese

Steam cabbage 8 to 10 minutes; drain and set aside. Combine ground beef, onion, and green pepper in a skillet; cook over medium heat until beef is browned and vegetables are tender, stirring to crumble meat. Drain well. Add tomato paste, tomato sauce, oregano, salt, pepper, and garlic powder to beef mixture, and mix well.

Spoon half of cabbage into a lightly greased 13- x 9- x 2-inch baking dish. Cover with half of meat mixture. Repeat layers of cabbage and meat mixture. Cover and bake at 350° for 25 minutes. Sprinkle with cheese; bake, uncovered, an additional 5 minutes. Yield: 6 to 8 servings.
Mary Kay Menees,
White Pine, Tennessee.

CABBAGE WITH APPLES AND FRANKS

3 cups shredded cabbage
3 cooking apples, cored and sliced
5 frankfurters, cut into 1-inch lengths
2 tablespoons butter or margarine
¼ cup firmly packed brown sugar
½ cup water, divided
¼ cup vinegar
½ teaspoon salt
1 tablespoon cornstarch
2 tablespoons cracker crumbs

Steam cabbage in a covered saucepan with a small amount of water for 2 minutes. Drain.

Layer apples, steamed cabbage, and frankfurters in a lightly greased 2-quart baking dish.

Melt butter in a small saucepan; stir in sugar, ¼ cup water, vinegar, and salt. Dissolve cornstarch in remaining ¼ cup water; add to hot mixture, stirring until thick and clear. Pour over casserole. Cover and bake at 350° for 25 minutes. Sprinkle cracker crumbs over top of casserole; bake, uncovered, an additional 5 minutes. Yield: 4 to 6 servings.
Mrs. John A. Shoemaker,
Louisville, Kentucky.

CABBAGE KIELBASA

1 medium cabbage, coarsely chopped
1 to 1½ pounds kielbasa, cut into 1-inch pieces
1 large onion, cut into wedges
1 teaspoon paprika
¼ cup water

Combine all ingredients in a large Dutch oven. Cover and cook over medium heat 10 to 15 minutes, stirring occasionally. Yield: 6 servings.
Louis Joyner,
Birmingham, Alabama.

HOT CABBAGE CREOLE

2 slices bacon, cut into 1-inch pieces
1 large onion, chopped
1 large green pepper, chopped
1 (28-ounce) can whole tomatoes, chopped
1 medium cabbage, chopped
⅓ cup vinegar
1 teaspoon salt
¼ teaspoon pepper
Dash of red pepper

Fry bacon in a Dutch oven. Add onion and green pepper; sauté until vegetables are tender. Add remaining ingredients; cover and bring to a boil. Reduce heat; simmer 15 minutes, stirring occasionally. Yield: 8 to 10 servings.
Virginia Laux,
Toney, Alabama.

NUTTY CABBAGE SALAD

2 cups finely chopped cabbage
½ cup shredded carrot
⅓ cup unsalted sunflower kernels
¼ cup salted peanuts
¼ cup seedless raisins
¼ cup diced apple
¼ cup ricotta cheese
3 tablespoons buttermilk
3 tablespoons apple juice

Combine cabbage, carrot, sunflower kernels, peanuts, raisins, and apple; toss gently. Combine remaining ingredients; stir until smooth. Pour over cabbage mixture; toss gently to coat. Chill until serving time. Yield: 3½ cups.
Cathy Darling,
Grafton, West Virginia.

Tip: When selecting fresh cabbage, choose heads that are solid and heavy in relation to their size. The cabbage leaves should be fresh, crisp, and free from bruises.

March

Puzzled About White Chocolate?

Despite its name, texture, and flavor that remind us of traditional dark chocolate, white chocolate is actually not chocolate. Instead, it's a mixture of cocoa butter, milk solids, sugar, and vanilla; it lacks the cocoa solids that give dark chocolate its characteristic color and some of its flavor.

The taste of white chocolate comes mainly from sugar and vanilla, but the cocoa butter gives a hint of dark chocolate flavor and fragrance. You can use it in ways you traditionally use the dark form. Our cheesecake, cookies, and truffles are spectacular examples.

The easiest place to find white chocolate may be at the candy counter of large department stores, which usually has large chunks of it for sale by the pound. The department stores also sometimes carry white chocolate candy bars, as do some large supermarkets and food specialty shops.

Don't confuse white chocolate with something similar called "summer coating." The texture and look of white summer coating and white chocolate are much the same. The ingredients are similar, too, except that in summer coating the cocoa butter is replaced with vegetable fat. It doesn't have the flavor of chocolate.

Coarsely chop white chocolate before melting. Be sure to melt it slowly—we suggest a double boiler. Remove it from the heat as soon as it is melted; overheating can cause it to separate or become grainy. In general, white chocolate will handle much like dark chocolate, but the flavor and the look are uniquely its own.

White chocolate makes an unusual base for common desserts: (from front) Chocolate Teasers, White Chocolate Cheesecake, and White Chocolate Truffles.

CHOCOLATE TEASERS

1 cup butter or margarine, softened
1 cup sugar
1 egg
1 teaspoon vanilla extract
2 ounces white chocolate, coarsely chopped
¼ cup semisweet chocolate morsels
2½ to 3 cups all-purpose flour
1½ teaspoons baking powder
¼ teaspoon salt

Cream butter; gradually add sugar, beating at medium speed of an electric mixer until light and fluffy. Add egg and vanilla; beat well. Divide mixture in half, putting halves in separate bowls. Set aside.

Place white chocolate in top of a double boiler; bring water to a boil. Reduce heat to low; cook until chocolate melts. Remove from heat, and let cool slightly.

Place chocolate morsels in top of double boiler; bring water to a boil. Reduce heat to low; cook until chocolate melts. Remove from heat, and let cool slightly.

Stir white chocolate into one portion of creamed mixture; stir semisweet chocolate into remaining portion of creamed mixture. Combine flour, baking powder, and salt. Stir 1¼ to 1½ cups flour mixture into each portion of chocolate mixture, stirring well. Cover and refrigerate both portions.

On floured wax paper, roll each half of dough into a 15- x 8-inch rectangle. Invert white dough carefully onto dark dough; peel wax paper from white dough. Tightly roll dough jellyroll fashion, starting at long end, and peeling wax paper from dough as you roll. Cover and chill 1 hour. Slice dough about ¼ inch thick, and place on ungreased cookie sheets. Bake at 350° for 10 to 12 minutes. Remove to wire rack to cool. Yield: about 5 dozen.

WHITE CHOCOLATE CHEESECAKE

1½ cups graham cracker crumbs
¼ cup ground pecans
¼ cup plus 1 tablespoon butter or margarine, melted
1 pound white chocolate, coarsely chopped
2 (8-ounce) packages cream cheese, softened
½ cup commercial sour cream
3 eggs
1 teaspoon vanilla extract
1 (11-ounce) can mandarin oranges, undrained
¼ cup Cointreau or other orange-flavored liqueur
½ cup orange juice
1 tablespoon plus 1 teaspoon cornstarch

Combine graham cracker crumbs, pecans, and butter, stirring until blended. Press mixture into bottom and 1 inch up sides of a 9-inch springform pan. Bake at 375° for 8 minutes; cool.

Place white chocolate in top of a double boiler; bring water to a boil. Reduce heat to low; cook until chocolate melts. Let cool slightly.

Combine cream cheese and sour cream in a large mixing bowl; beat at medium speed of an electric mixer until fluffy. Add eggs, one at a time, beating after each addition. Add vanilla and chocolate, stirring just until blended.

Pour filling into prepared pan; bake at 300° for 50 minutes or until cheesecake is almost set. Turn oven off, and partially open oven door. Leave cake in oven 30 minutes. Cool cake on wire rack; chill.

Drain mandarin oranges, reserving ½ cup liquid. Combine mandarin oranges and Cointreau; stir gently. Set aside for 30 minutes, stirring occasionally.

Drain oranges, reserving Cointreau; set oranges aside. Combine reserved ½ cup orange liquid, reserved Cointreau, orange juice, and cornstarch in a saucepan; stir well. Cover and cook over medium heat 5 minutes or until thickened, stirring constantly; cool slightly.

Remove outer rim of springform pan, and place cheesecake on serving plate. Arrange orange sections in center and around outer edge of cheesecake. Spoon glaze over top of cheesecake; chill. Yield: one 9-inch cheesecake.

WHITE CHOCOLATE TRUFFLES

½ pound white chocolate, coarsely
  chopped
⅓ cup butter
1 egg yolk
¾ cup minced blanched almonds, toasted

Combine chocolate and butter in top of a double boiler; bring water to a boil. Reduce heat to low; cook until chocolate melts. Remove from heat. Add egg yolk, and beat at medium speed of an electric mixer until fluffy and cooled. Cover and let sit 12 to 24 hours in a cool, dry place. (Do not refrigerate mixture.)

Shape mixture into 1-inch balls; roll in almonds. Cover and chill. Let stand at room temperature before serving. Serve truffles in miniature foil cups. Yield: 2 dozen.

Note: If mixture is too soft to shape into balls after standing, stir in 1 to 3 tablespoons powdered sugar, a tablespoon at a time, to make desired consistency. Do not chill before shaping.

Rice—A Versatile Southern Tradition

Enjoy the rich heritage of rice in our featured Southern recipes. The delicate, versatile grain complements the flavor and variety of regional cooking. (You'll find tips on selecting and cooking rice on page 46.)

NORTHSHORE JAMBALAYA

½ pound smoked sausage, cut into ½-inch
  slices
½ pound sirloin steak or pork tenderloin,
  finely chopped
¼ cup vegetable oil
¼ cup all-purpose flour
1 cup chopped onion
1 cup chopped celery
1 bunch green onions, chopped and
  divided
4 cloves garlic, minced
1 tablespoon chopped fresh parsley
1 (8-ounce) can tomato sauce
1 teaspoon garlic salt
½ teaspoon pepper
½ teaspoon hot Hungarian paprika
½ teaspoon dried whole thyme
¼ teaspoon red pepper
2 cups uncooked long-grain rice

Cook sausage and sirloin in a skillet until browned; drain well. Set aside.

Heat oil in a large Dutch oven. Add flour, and cook over medium-high heat, stirring constantly, until mixture turns the color of a copper penny (about 8 minutes). Stir in onion, celery, half of green onions, garlic, and parsley. Cook over medium heat 10 minutes, stirring frequently. Add tomato sauce and seasonings. Reduce heat, and simmer 5 minutes, stirring occasionally. Stir in meat and remaining green onions; cook until thoroughly heated. Cook rice according to package directions. Add rice, and mix well. Yield: 4 to 6 servings.
Joanne Champagne,
Covington, Louisiana.

RICE CASSEROLE

1 (10½-ounce) can beef consommé,
  undiluted
1 (10½-ounce) can French onion soup,
  undiluted
2 tablespoons butter or margarine, melted
1 cup uncooked long-grain rice
½ cup chopped onion
½ cup golden raisins
½ cup chopped cashews
1 tablespoon butter or margarine, melted

Combine first 4 ingredients in a lightly greased 10- x 6- x 2-inch baking dish. Cover and bake at 350° for 1 hour or until all liquid is absorbed.

Sauté onion, raisins, and cashews in 1 tablespoon butter until onion is tender. Sprinkle mixture over cooked rice. Yield: 6 servings.
Betty Baird,
Utica, Kentucky.

RED BEANS AND RICE

1 (16-ounce) package dried red kidney
  beans
6 cups water
1 large smoked ham hock
1 large onion, chopped
2 cloves garlic, minced
½ pound ground beef
2 tablespoons chopped fresh parsley
½ teaspoon crushed red pepper
1 teaspoon salt
3 bay leaves
1½ cups uncooked long-grain rice
Parsley sprigs (optional)

Sort and wash beans; place in a large Dutch oven. Cover with water; let soak overnight. Drain. Add 6 cups water, ham hock, onion, and garlic; boil 10 minutes. Cook ground beef, and drain well. Add ground beef, parsley, red pepper, salt, and bay leaves to beans; cover and simmer 2 hours. Remove ham bone and bay leaves; discard fat, bone, and bay leaves. Shred ham, and return to bean mixture.

Cook rice according to package directions. Serve bean mixture over rice. Garnish with fresh parsley, if desired. Yield: 6 to 8 servings. *Lucille James,*
New Orleans, Louisiana.

RICE WITH GREEN PEAS

2 cups uncooked long-grain rice
1 medium onion, chopped
1 to 2 tablespoons caraway seeds
3 tablespoons butter or margarine, melted
1 (10¾-ounce) can chicken broth,
  undiluted
4 cups water
¼ teaspoon salt
¼ teaspoon pepper
1 (10-ounce) package frozen English peas,
  thawed

Sauté first 3 ingredients in butter in a Dutch oven 5 minutes, stirring constantly. Stir in broth, water, salt, and pepper. Bring to a boil; cover, reduce heat, and simmer 20 minutes. Add peas, and cook 5 additional minutes. Yield: 8 servings. *Jeanne S. Hotaling,*
Augusta, Georgia.

RAISIN-RICE PUDDING

4 eggs
¾ cup sugar
2 cups milk
1⅓ cups cooked long-grain rice
1½ teaspoons lemon juice
1½ teaspoons vanilla extract
1 tablespoon butter or margarine, melted
1 teaspoon ground nutmeg
⅔ cup raisins

Combine eggs, sugar, and milk; beat at medium speed of an electric mixer 1 to 2 minutes or until sugar dissolves. Add remaining ingredients; stir well. Pour into a greased 1½-quart casserole; place casserole in a baking pan. Pour boiling water into baking pan to depth of 1 inch. Bake, uncovered, at 350° for 40 to 45 minutes or until mixture is slightly thickened. Stir and bake an additional 10 to 15 minutes or until set. Serve warm or at room temperature. Yield: 6 servings.   *Jennie Callahan,*
Louisville, Kentucky.

From Our Kitchen To Yours

Rice, a staple in our test kitchens' pantry, is nutritious and easy to prepare. Our story "Rice—A Versatile Southern Tradition" on page 45 includes recipes that demonstrate rice's versatility. Offering endless opportunities for complementing many foods, rice goes with meat, poultry, and seafood, or it can be used in casseroles, soups, salads, or desserts.

If you take a close look at the rice on supermarket shelves, you may be surprised at the wide variety available.

Types of Rice

The primary differences are in their cooking characteristics.

Short-grain rice, usually found in specialized markets, cooks up softer than the longer grain. As a rule, the shorter the grain, the more tender and clingy the cooked rice. This characteristic makes short-grain rice ideal for dishes such as sushi, but it's almost too clingy for molded-rice dishes.

Medium-grain rice is also shorter and plumper than the long grain. These moist, tender cooked grains also have a tendency to cling, producing a product that adheres well for molding. For those recipes that have creamier textures, such as risotto, molds, or rice desserts, the medium-grain type is a good choice.

Long-grain rice, the type commonly preferred in the South, is four to five times as long as the grain is wide. When cooked, the distinct grains become separate and fluffy, making this type desirable for recipes such as Rice With Green Peas on page 45.

Forms of Rice

Rice undergoes varying degrees of processing that give consumers a number of choices between forms.

Regular-milled white rice is the least expensive and most common form of rice. The outer husk is removed, and the bran layers are milled away until the grain is white.

Parboiled rice (also called converted) becomes hard, translucent, and shiny when treated with a steam-pressure process before milling. More cooking liquid and a longer cooking time are required to cook this form. Parboiled rice cooks fluffier and drier than regular rice.

Precooked rice is milled, cooked, and dried. The porous, open appearance enables boiling water to penetrate and rehydrate the grains in a short time period. Precooked rice is ideal for hurry-up meals.

The least processed form is **brown rice.** The outer hull is removed, but the bran layers are retained to produce the characteristic tan color and nutlike flavor. When cooked, the inner part of the grain becomes tender, while the outer bran layers are slightly crunchy. Brown rice requires a longer cooking time and a slight increase in liquid.

Storage

Regular-milled white, parboiled, and precooked rice can be stored indefinitely on your pantry shelf. To keep out dust and moisture, be sure to store in airtight containers.

Brown rice has a limited shelf life (about six months) because of the oil in the bran. Refrigeration slows spoilage.

Cooked rice, stored in the refrigerator, keeps its quality and flavor six to seven days. Cover tightly to prevent the grains from drying out or absorbing flavors of other foods.

Cooked rice freezes well by itself or combined with other foods that are suitable for freezing. It may be frozen for up to four months.

Preparation

You can cook rice on a cooking surface, in the oven, in the microwave, or in automatic or nonautomatic rice cookers. The amount of liquid and cooking time will vary, depending on the cooking method and the form of rice used.

Tips

—Cook rice in a flavorful liquid, such as chicken broth, beef broth, or fruit juice, instead of water.

—Herbs and spices, such as thyme, curry, basil, and parsley, add extra flavor to rice. Be sure to choose a seasoning that will complement your entrée as well as the rice.

—Cooked rice can be reheated without loss of texture or flavor. Place rice in a colander or strainer; place colander over simmering water in a Dutch oven. Cover and steam until rice is hot. To reheat rice in the microwave, add 2 tablespoons water for each cup of cooked rice. Cover and cook at HIGH about 1 minute per cup.

Cheese Invites A Party

With our love for entertaining and attractive tables of food, it's only natural that Southerners enjoy cheese, a feast for the eyes and a pleasure for the palate. Whatever the occasion, cheese brings elegance to a gathering. (For ideas, see the photograph on page 65.)

To help you choose and serve cheese with confidence, we've included a brief explanation of the varieties. There are also tips on buying, storing, and serving cheese and some information on "what goes with what." It's impossible to cover everything in this article, and of course, the very best way to learn about eating and serving cheese is to do it.

There are seven categories of cheeses for eating and one for cooking. The eating types include soft ripened, semisoft, semihard, chèvre, blue vein, fresh creamy, and processed. Grating cheeses are used for cooking. (See cheese chart on page 48.)

The popularity of Brie and Camembert has introduced **soft-ripened** cheeses to the South. They're round and coated with a white or golden crust, and will run or ooze at room temperature. Brie and Camembert come in many sizes. Soft-ripened cheeses are the hardest to buy because you can't tell if a cheese is ripe until you cut it. To test a wrapped wheel, press the top. It should spring back to your touch.

Double and triple crèmes are also included in this group. These are richer, creamier versions of the soft-ripened favorites, but have 60% to 70% butterfat and are softer after sitting at room temperature. Other soft-ripened cheeses have only 50% butterfat.

In the group called **semisoft,** you'll find a wide variety of shapes and flavors, ranging from mild to sharp. Most are soft and light in color.

The semisoft group includes the monastery cheeses, created by meticulous French Trappist monks during the Middle Ages as a food to eat during fasts from meat. All have wax coatings or rinds washed with curing solutions, such as beer, wine, and herbs or spices.

Semihard cheeses include familiar ones such as Cheddar and Swiss. These are made mostly from cow's or sheep's milk and are then pressed for a firm texture. In the processing of Swiss cheese, tiny bubbles of carbon dioxide form during cooking. These bubbles give Swiss its characteristic holes.

In French, **chèvre** means goat. And this group naturally includes the tangy, full-flavored cheeses made from goat's milk. Usually, people either love or hate their strong flavor. At a wine-and-cheese tasting, guests should start with mild-flavored cheeses and work their way up to the strong goat cheeses, which are often shaped in cones, logs, and pyramids and sometimes rolled in cinders or herbs.

You'll probably enjoy **blue-vein** cheeses better if you don't know exactly how they're made. But it's the processing that gives blue cheese its distinctive flavor and soft texture. A mold is injected into the cheese during curing to create the delicate, recognizable blue-green veins. Most of these cheeses are then aged in caves. Roquefort, the most well-known blue cheese, gets its name from the famous Roquefort caves of France. Stilton is the English answer to blue cheese. And Gorgonzola is a blue-vein cheese from Italy.

Fresh creamy cheeses, produced by separating the curds and whey in cow's milk, were probably some of the first ones made in America. Cottage cheese and cream cheese are the best known of this group. Cream cheese, blended with herbs and fruit or stirred into dips and spreads, is a favorite. Neufchâtel is an alternative for weight-conscious eaters. The cream cheese of France, it has fewer calories than its American counterpart and has a mildly acidic flavor.

American cheese is the best seller of the **processed** cheese group. Because it is heated to high temperatures during

These are just a few of the over 1,000 varieties of cheese produced worldwide.

processing, it keeps longer than other cheeses. Moisture is added to make these processed cheeses spreadable and easy to melt. Keep in mind that canned cheese foods and cheese spreads, also in this category, are handy for snacks and quick entertaining.

Grating cheeses bear mentioning here, although they're used only for cooking and are much firmer than their semihard cousins. Parmesan and Romano are the best known of this group. You can grate these in your food processor or by hand. They have a long shelf life, and you'll find the fresh grated flavor to be much livelier and more pungent than the flavor of the cheeses that have been grated beforehand and then processed.

When You Buy Cheese

First, find a reputable dealer who will let you sample, sample, sample. The more business a dealer does, the more likely you are to find fresh cheeses that have not been abused in shipping.

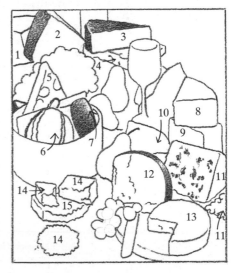

1. *Fontina* 2. *American Cheddar*
3. *Wisconsin Cheddar* 4. *Emmentaler*
5. *Jarlsberg* 6. *Provolone* 7. *Gouda*
8. *Bel Paese* 9. *Muenster* 10. *Port Salut*
11. *Roquefort* 12. *Doux de Montagne*
13. *Camembert* 14. *Parmesan* 15. *Romano*

CHEESE	DESCRIPTION
Soft-Ripened	
Brie, Camembert, double and triple crèmes	White or golden powdery crust that's safe to eat; may run at room temperature; creamy, delicate flavors
Boursin	A white triple crème, flavored with garlic, herbs, or pepper
Semisoft	
Liederkranz	Similar to Brie; strong flavor and aroma
Doux de Montagne	Brown wax covering; creamy-ivory color with small eyes; sweet, tangy flavor
Muenster	Orange rind; small holes, sweet, mild to strong flavor; similar to fontina
Port Salut	Pale yellow with orange and brown wrapping; buttery texture, distinctive flavor
Bel Paese	Ivory-colored with map on package; buttery smooth; mild to strong flavor
Fontina	Red wrapper; buttery smooth; nutty flavor; ivory color
Semihard	
Cheddar	Red or black wrapper, depending on origin; naturally white or orange colored; mild to sharp flavor
Edam, Gouda	Pale color with red or pale-gold wax rind; semisoft to firm; nutlike flavor; Gouda has a higher fat content than Edam.
Emmentaler (Swiss)	Granddaddy of Swiss cheese; large holes, smooth texture, mild to sharp nutty taste
Jarlsberg	Norwegian Swiss; creamy white with holes; nutty though somewhat bland flavor
Provolone	Many shapes; smooth, hard, creamy white body; mild to sharp smoky flavor
Double Gloucester	Cheddar relative; rich, orange color and pungent flavor; often packaged with Stilton
Mozzarella	Creamy white; mild flavor; elastic and springy when hot; cooking cheese

CHEESE	DESCRIPTION
Grating	
Parmesan	Pale yellow; hard; sharp flavor
Romano	Pale yellow; grainy; very sharp flavor
Chèvre	
Ste. Maure	Very strong; creamy outside, chalky inside
Montrachet	Medium-strong; log shaped and occasionally rolled in charcoal; salty
Blue Vein	
Roquefort	Soft texture; sharp flavor; used in dressings, cooking, eating; cave ripened
Stilton	English, crumbly, marbled cheese; sharp, rich flavor
Gorgonzola	Italian blue; soft texture; very strong, pungent flavor and smell
Fresh Creamy	
Cottage cheese	Large or small soft curds, creamed or uncreamed; mild flavor; whitish color
Feta	White, crumbly; usually packaged in salty brine; Greek cooking cheese
Cream cheese	White, soft, mild in flavor. Often whipped or combined with fruits and herbs
Processed	
American pasteurized process	Pale yellow to orange; smooth, semisoft to soft; mild Cheddarlike flavor
Pasteurized process cheese food	American cheese is base; moisture added; cheese food very creamy, spreadable
Pasteurized process cheese spread	Uses American cheese as base; extra moisture added, with pickles, pimientos, or spices

Look at the product before buying; dried out or oily cheeses will taste the way they look. Avoid those with an ammonia smell (Liederkranz and Limburger are exceptions). Blue-veined cheeses should look moist rather than grainy. The body should be ivory or white with the veins running through it. Avoid brown, gray, or yellow streaks. Canned cheeses usually don't have the flavor of fresh. (Feta and processed cheese spreads are exceptions.)

What Kind To Serve

Offering too many cheeses all at once is overwhelming. Strike a balance between strong and mild flavors and hard and soft textures. An evening buffet or cheese board might include Brie or Camembert; a double or triple crème; a semisoft, such as Port Salut or fontina; a Swiss; American or New York Cheddar; and a blue. You might add an herbed goat cheese if serving red wine. Highlight the creamy, milder cheeses on a dessert tray. Include Brie, a triple crème, Bel Paese, a cream cheese whipped by itself or with fruit, gingersnaps, strawberries, apples, and small chocolates. You may also like a sharper cheese for contrast, such as a sharp Cheddar, Colby, or Monterey Jack.

Plan on serving what you buy, and expect little to be left over. Purchase 2 ounces of cheese per person if other food is being served. If only cheese, bread, and crackers are planned, buy 3 to 4 ounces per person. Whole forms weighing about a pound are better for smaller groups. For large groups, consider buying whole or half wheels.

The Many Ways To Slice It

Shape and texture determine how cheese should be cut. Forked cheese knives are best for pre-cut cheeses or cutting individual portions. Use a cheese wire for soft, creamy varieties and for blues. A cheese plane works best on semihard varieties. For Brie and Camembert, cut a whole round into quarters, and then split each quarter to get eight wedges. Place the slices together after cutting so that the wedges are still arranged in the shape of a wheel. Large Bries may need to be cut into more pieces.

Tips for Serving Cheese

Cheeses taste best at room temperature. Set out hard varieties about an hour before guests arrive. Bring out Brie and other soft varieties 30 minutes before serving.

Present cheese naturally. It is beautiful on its own, served as chunks or in wheels with as few frills as possible. Avoid cutting it into cubes; the air dries it out, and the flavor is lost. Wooden slabs, marble, or wicker trays make simple yet elegant serving pieces. You might want to group cheeses on a table or sideboard. Arrange cheeses from the mildest to the strongest flavors.

What Goes With Cheese

Wine and cheese have been eaten together for centuries. For tasty combinations, match the flavor of the cheese to the flavor of the wine. Rich, tangy, or sharp cheeses work best with full-bodied red wines. Light, delicate cheeses are best with dry white wines. You'll also find that wine and cheese from the same country may complement each other well. For example, English Stilton and port are natural partners.

Appetizer wines include sherry and dry vermouth. Boursin, mild Cheddar, Brie, and Colby are appetizer cheeses.

Pair well-chilled **white table wines,** such as Sauterne, Zinfandel, Chablis, and Chardonnay, with Edam, Monterey Jack, Muenster, Gouda, Colby, mild Swiss, and Gruyère, as well as other mild, medium-flavored cheeses.

Burgundy, claret, Cabernet Sauvignon, Bordeaux, and Chianti are among the **red table wines** that are best at room temperature. Cheeses that go well with them are medium to sharp in flavor. Swiss, Port Salut, fontina, and provolone are among the suitable choices.

Dessert wines include port, muscatel, Tokay, cream sherry, and Madeira. Champagne is also a popular one.

Beer or **robust red wines** enhance the flavor of hearty blues and goat cheeses.

Some refreshing **nonalcoholic beverages** are chilled apple cider, ice water with fresh lemon slices, and iced tea.

As for accompaniments, whole grain crackers are excellent choices for any cheese. Save garlic, onion, and herb-flavored crackers for medium and sharp cheeses. You might also offer fresh fruit. Grapes, apples, pears, and strawberries are fine choices. If you slice fruit, dip the pieces in lemon juice to keep them from turning dark. Arrange fruit around the cheese, and let guests help themselves.

After the Party

Seal any leftover cheese tightly in plastic wrap to keep moisture in and air out. If it molds, don't throw it out. Cut ¼ inch into the cheese, and remove the mold. You may also lightly wipe the cheese with a solution of vinegar and water to stop mold growth.

English Muffins For Breakfast

If the only English muffins you've ever eaten have come out of a package, then you'll want to try this homemade version from Mrs. Harland J. Stone of Ocala, Florida.

The dough is prepared just as in most yeast bread recipes, and then cut into rounds for the second rising.

After muffins rise, an electric skillet is used to cook them. The skillet keeps the heat constant for more even cooking. The muffins should be turned often, about every three minutes.

These muffins freeze well; just store them in an airtight container in the freezer.

ENGLISH MUFFINS

1 package dry yeast
½ cup warm water (105° to 115°)
2 tablespoons sugar
1½ cups milk, scalded
¼ cup shortening, melted
1 teaspoon salt
6 cups all-purpose flour, divided

Dissolve yeast in warm water; add sugar, and stir until dissolved. Set aside.

Combine milk, shortening, and salt in a large bowl; mix well. Cool to 105° to 115°. Stir in yeast mixture. Add 3 cups flour; beat mixture until smooth and elastic. Add remaining flour; knead until smooth (8 to 10 minutes). Place in a well-greased bowl, turning to grease top. Cover and let rise in a warm place (85°), free from drafts, 1 hour or until doubled in bulk.

Punch dough down. Turn dough out onto a lightly floured surface. Roll dough to ¾-inch thickness, and cut with a 3-inch cutter; put each round on a 4-inch square of wax paper placed on a baking sheet. Cover and let rise in a warm place, 1 hour or until dough is doubled in bulk.

Transfer muffins carefully to a well-greased electric skillet preheated to 350°. Cook 12 to 15 minutes, turning frequently. Yield: 1½ dozen.

Stir-Fry To Keep Calories Low

"Cooking Light" means more than just the substitution of certain ingredients to make foods lower in calories and higher in nutrients. It sometimes involves a change in cooking method. Stir-frying is a technique that uses little oil to cook foods quickly, so that they keep their natural flavor and nutrient value. Any food can be stir-fried, and the seasonings to use are limited only by your imagination.

Many people use a wok to stir-fry and for a good reason. The shape and design of the utensil make it ideal for this type of cookery. Its shallow bottom and sloping sides allow even heating and a large surface area to gently toss and constantly stir the food for quick cooking. But in the absence of a wok, a large, heavy, flat-bottom skillet with sloping sides can be used successfully.

Casseroles are a Southern favorite, and they traditionally call for creamy soup, sour cream, lots of cheese, or a heavy gravy. These ingredients add lots of fat and calories and actually mask the flavor of the meats and vegetables they're supposed to enhance. But you can stir-fry the same meat-and-vegetable combinations with only a change of seasonings and still preserve the basis of the dish in a low-calorie way.

Our Chinese-Style Beef is similar to pepper steak. It calls for reduced-sodium soy sauce, which has 40% less sodium than regular soy sauce.

CHINESE-STYLE BEEF

2 (1-pound) flank steaks, trimmed
1 tablespoon peanut oil
2 cloves garlic, crushed
¼ teaspoon ground ginger
⅛ teaspoon pepper
3 tablespoons reduced-sodium soy sauce
1 teaspoon sugar
2 cups coarsely chopped green pepper
2 cups fresh bean sprouts
2 medium tomatoes, peeled and quartered
1 tablespoon cornstarch
¼ cup water
4 cups hot cooked rice (cooked without salt or fat)

Partially freeze steaks; slice diagonally across grain into ½-inch strips.

Add oil to wok or heavy skillet, and heat to medium high (325°) for 1 minute. Add steak, garlic, ginger, and pepper; stir-fry 5 minutes or until browned. Add soy sauce and sugar; cook 1 minute. Add green pepper and bean sprouts; stir well. Cover and cook 3 minutes; stir in tomatoes.

Combine cornstarch and water; stir until cornstarch dissolves. Stir into beef mixture; stir-fry 2 minutes. Serve immediately over rice. Yield: 8 servings.

☐ *206 calories, 28.9 grams protein, 7.6 grams fat, 7.1 grams carbohydrate, 55 milligrams cholesterol, 273 milligrams sodium, and 22 milligrams calcium per ⅞ cup beef and vegetables plus 118 calories, 2.2 grams protein, 0.1 gram fat, 25.9 grams carbohydrate, 0 milligrams cholesterol, 1 milligram sodium, and 8 milligrams calcium per ½ cup rice.*
Mrs. Hugh F. Mosher,
Huntsville, Alabama.

FAST-AND-EASY STIR-FRIED STEAK

1 pound lean boneless top round steak, trimmed
2 cloves garlic, minced
2 tablespoons Worcestershire sauce
3 tablespoons water
½ teaspoon seasoned salt
¼ teaspoon pepper
Vegetable cooking spray
12 small pearl onions, peeled
2 cups sliced fresh mushrooms
½ cup sweet red pepper strips
3 cups chopped fresh broccoli
1 (10-ounce) package frozen French-style green beans, thawed
1 tablespoon cornstarch
2 cups hot cooked thin egg noodles (cooked without salt or fat)

Partially freeze steak; slice diagonally across grain into ¼-inch strips; set aside. Combine garlic, Worcestershire sauce, water, seasoned salt, and pepper, stirring well; add steak. Cover and refrigerate 4 hours.

Coat a wok or heavy skillet with vegetable cooking spray; heat to medium high (325°) for 2 minutes. Drain beef, reserving marinade; add beef, and stir-fry 3 minutes. Add onions, mushrooms, pepper strips, broccoli, and green beans, and stir-fry 5 minutes or until vegetables are crisp-tender.

Combine cornstarch and reserved marinade; stir well. Pour over meat mixture, and stir-fry until thickened and bubbly. Serve immediately over noodles. Yield: 4 servings.

☐ *232 calories, 31.4 grams protein, 5.3 grams fat, 16.2 grams carbohydrate, 55.5 milligrams cholesterol, 416 milligrams sodium, and 90.8 milligrams calcium per 2 cups steak and vegetables plus 100 calories, 3.2 grams protein, 1.2 grams fat, 18.6 grams carbohydrate, 25 milligrams cholesterol, 2 milligrams sodium, and 8 milligrams calcium per ½ cup noodles.*
Nell Balmaseda,
Miami, Florida.

QUICK SHRIMP SKILLET

1 tablespoon reduced-calorie margarine
½ cup sliced green onions
2 cups diagonally sliced celery
½ cup sliced carrot
1 cup sliced fresh mushrooms
2 cloves garlic, minced
½ teaspoon ground ginger
⅛ teaspoon pepper
2 teaspoons reduced-sodium soy sauce
¾ pound shelled and deveined medium shrimp
2 tablespoons water
1½ cups hot cooked rice (cooked without salt or fat)

Add margarine to a wok or heavy skillet; heat to medium high (325°) for 1 minute. Add onions, celery, carrot, mushrooms, and garlic, and stir-fry until vegetables are crisp-tender. Add ginger, pepper, soy sauce, shrimp, and water; stir-fry until shrimp are pink. Serve over rice. Yield: 3 servings.

☐ *156 calories, 21.7 grams protein, 3 grams fat, 10.1 grams carbohydrate, 164 milligrams cholesterol, 408 milligrams sodium, and 120 milligrams calcium per 1⅓ cups shrimp and vegetables plus 118 calories, 2.2 grams protein, 0.1 gram fat, 25.9 grams carbohydrate, 0 milligrams cholesterol, 1 milligram sodium, and 8 milligrams calcium per ½ cup rice.*
Ruby Kirkes,
Tuskahoma, Oklahoma.

STIR-FRIED PORK

1 pound lean pork tenderloin, trimmed
½ cup unsweetened orange juice
1½ tablespoons cornstarch
3 tablespoons reduced-sodium soy sauce
1 tablespoon dry sherry
⅛ teaspoon pepper
Vegetable cooking spray
1 tablespoon vegetable oil
1 cup thinly sliced onion
2 medium zucchini, cut into ⅛-inch slices
1 medium-size sweet red pepper, cut into
  ¼-inch slices
2 cups unsweetened pineapple chunks,
  drained

Partially freeze pork tenderloin; slice diagonally across grain into ¼-inch strips. Set aside.

Combine orange juice, cornstarch, soy sauce, sherry, and pepper; stir well, and set aside.

Coat a wok or heavy skillet with cooking spray; heat to medium high (325°) for 1 to 2 minutes. Add pork, and stir-fry 3 to 5 minutes. Remove pork from skillet. Add oil to skillet; allow to heat 1 minute. Add onion, zucchini, and red pepper; stir-fry 4 minutes or until vegetables are crisp-tender. Return pork to skillet.

Pour orange juice mixture over pork, stirring well. Cover, reduce heat to low (225°), and cook 2 to 3 minutes or until slightly thickened. Add pineapple; stir well. Yield: 4 servings.

☐ 252 calories, 20.6 grams protein, 6.5 grams fat, 28.5 grams carbohydrate, 55 milligrams cholesterol, 483 milligrams sodium, and 37 milligrams calcium per 1½-cup serving.   Kathy Henry,
Jefferson City, Tennessee.

STIR-FRIED CHICKEN CURRY

1 pound boneless chicken breasts,
  skinned
1 (20-ounce) can unsweetened pineapple
  chunks, undrained
1 teaspoon curry powder
1 tablespoon cornstarch
1 teaspoon chicken-flavored bouillon
  granules
Vegetable cooking spray
¼ teaspoon red pepper flakes
4 cups coarsely shredded cabbage
½ cup sliced green onions
¼ cup raisins
¼ cup dry roasted peanuts
2 cups hot cooked rice (cooked without
  salt or fat)
2 tablespoons flaked coconut

Cut chicken into thin strips. Drain pineapple, reserving juice; set pineapple aside. Combine pineapple juice and curry powder in a shallow dish; add chicken. Cover and chill 4 hours.

Drain chicken, reserving marinade. Combine marinade, cornstarch, and bouillon granules; stir until cornstarch dissolves. Set aside.

Coat a wok or heavy skillet with cooking spray; heat to medium high (325°) for 2 minutes. Add chicken and red pepper flakes; stir-fry 2 to 3 minutes. Add cabbage and green onions; stir-fry 2 minutes. Add cornstarch mixture; stir-fry until thickened and bubbly. Add pineapple, raisins, and peanuts. Serve over rice, and garnish with coconut. Yield: 4 servings.

☐ 299 calories, 24.3 grams protein, 7.9 grams fat, 35.4 grams carbohydrate, 50 milligrams cholesterol, 242 milligrams sodium, and 76 milligrams calcium per 1½ cups chicken and vegetables plus 118 calories, 2.2 grams protein, 0.1 gram fat, 25.9 grams carbohydrate, 0 milligrams cholesterol, 1 milligram sodium, and 8 milligrams calcium per ½ cup rice.

STIR-FRIED VEGETABLES
WITH CURRY

1½ teaspoons vegetable oil
2 cloves garlic, minced
7 cups coarsely shredded cabbage
1 cup sliced celery
⅓ cup chopped green onions
2 cups fresh bean sprouts
1 tablespoon reduced-sodium soy sauce
1 teaspoon curry powder
¼ teaspoon sugar
¼ teaspoon vinegar

Add oil to wok or heavy skillet, and heat to medium high (325°) for 1 minute. Add garlic; stir-fry 1 minute. Add cabbage, celery, and green onions; stir-fry 3 minutes or until crisp-tender. Add remaining ingredients; stir-fry 1 to 2 minutes or until thoroughly heated. Yield: 5 servings.

☐ 61 calories, 3.1 grams protein, 1.7 grams fat, 10.3 grams carbohydrate, 0 milligrams cholesterol, 158 milligrams sodium, and 68 milligrams calcium per 1-cup serving.   Anne Rob,
Murfreesboro, Tennessee.

Stir-Frying Pointers

■ Prior to cooking, assemble everything you need. Once you start the cooking process, there's no time to stop and hunt anything or to prepare ingredients, without overcooking the ingredients already in the wok.

■ Partially freeze meat, and slice it diagonally across the grain into thin strips so that more surface area is exposed to heat, cooking the meat faster. Slice or chop vegetables in uniform pieces that will cook in the same amount of time.

■ First add ingredients that need to cook longest. Then add other ingredients based on how long they need to cook.

■ Use a lift-and-stir motion to move the food constantly during cooking.

■ Cook vegetables only until they are crisp-tender.

STIR-FRIED PEAS AND PEPPERS

Vegetable cooking spray
1 teaspoon vegetable oil
½ pound snow peas, trimmed
1½ cups sweet red pepper strips
1 (8-ounce) can sliced water chestnuts,
  drained
1 teaspoon sugar
½ teaspoon cornstarch
¼ teaspoon chicken-flavored bouillon
  granules
Dash of pepper
2 teaspoons reduced-sodium soy sauce
¼ cup water
1 teaspoon sesame seeds, toasted

Coat a wok or heavy skillet with cooking spray; add oil, and heat to medium high (325°) for 2 minutes. Add peas, pepper strips, and water chestnuts; stir-fry 3 to 5 minutes or until vegetables are crisp-tender.

Combine sugar, cornstarch, bouillon granules, and pepper in a small bowl. Add soy sauce and water; stir well. Pour over vegetables; cook, stirring constantly, 1 minute or until sauce is thickened. Sprinkle with sesame seeds. Yield: 6 servings.

☐ 49 calories, 1.6 grams protein, 1.3 grams fat, 8 grams carbohydrate, 0 milligrams cholesterol, 106 milligrams sodium, and 23.5 milligrams calcium per ½-cup serving.

STIR-FRIED ASPARAGUS

1 (13½-ounce) bunch fresh asparagus
Vegetable cooking spray
1 tablespoon reduced-calorie margarine
2¼ teaspoons grated fresh gingerroot
½ clove garlic, minced
Dash of crushed red pepper
¼ cup sweet red pepper strips
1½ tablespoons reduced-sodium soy sauce
2 tablespoons dry sherry

Snap off tough ends of asparagus, and remove scales from stalks with a knife or vegetable peeler, if desired. Slice diagonally into 1½- to 2-inch pieces.

Coat a wok or heavy skillet with cooking spray; add margarine, and heat to medium high (325°) for 1 minute. Add remaining ingredients; stir-fry 8 to 10 minutes or until asparagus is crisp-tender. Yield: 3 servings.

☐ *50 calories, 3.4 grams protein, 2.4 grams fat, 5.2 grams carbohydrate, 0 milligrams cholesterol, 340 milligrams sodium, and 22 milligrams calcium per ½-cup serving.*

MICROWAVE COOKERY

Helpful Hints And A Few Good Tips

Getting the best results from your microwave oven requires an understanding of how the appliance cooks food and the use of a few easy techniques.

Microwaving differs from conventional cooking. To put it simply, microwaves strike the food and start molecules moving, creating heat that is then conducted throughout the food. Thus, food is cooked by the heat generated when microwaves strike the surface of food and by the conduction of heat inside the food. By conventional methods, food is cooked by contact with hot air or a hot pan.

The difference in these cooking methods makes a difference in the way food appears after it is cooked. Baked goods and some meats have a paler color when cooked in the microwave. We've included information on how to enhance the appearance of microwaved food in the tips below.

Yet another challenge for the microwave cook is to cook food evenly. Microwave ovens can have uneven cooking patterns; some areas of a dish will receive more microwaves and cook quickly while others will receive fewer microwaves and cook slowly.

Here are some tips on solving these problems as well as other helpful hints.

Browning

—Use toppings and sauces to give food a darker color. Worcestershire, soy, and browning and seasoning sauces are a few of the available items that improve the color of meat and add flavor. Pour or brush on before cooking.

—Use a browning utensil, which works like a grill. A special coating absorbs microwave energy and gets hot enough to sear meat and other food. You can even stir-fry on it. When using a browning utensil, use caution with nonstick vegetable cooking sprays. The spray turns brown upon contact with the heated browning utensil. This is to be expected. You may prefer using vegetable or peanut oil and following the manufacturer's instructions.

Cooking Evenly

—Stir foods such as vegetables or soups a few times during cooking.

—Rotate dishes of food that can't be stirred, such as a casserole or soufflé; or use a turntable to mechanically rotate food during cooking.

—Some foods, such as potatoes and corn on the cob, should be turned over halfway through cooking time.

—When cooking several similar items at the same time, arrange them in a circle; rearrange the items halfway through cooking time.

—Use round dishes whenever you can. Food in square dishes gets higher concentration of microwaves at the corners. If you use a square dish, rotate it during cooking and shield corners with aluminum foil, if necessary; see oven manual on using aluminum foil.

—The edge of a dish receives more energy than the center. For that reason, you should place foods so that more dense portions are near the outside and delicate pieces are in the center.

—Small quantities of food cook faster than large quantities. Cooking 2 to 3 potatoes at a time will be faster than cooking 4 to 6 all at once.

—Cover dishes to save moisture and speed up cooking. Use microwave-safe casserole lids, heavy-duty plastic wrap, paper towels, or wax paper.

—Vent dishes covered with plastic wrap. The vent allows steam to escape and prevents the wrap from splitting. Be careful not to get burned by steam when removing plastic wrap.

More Microwave Hints

—Use nonmetal cookware in your oven. Some shallow heat-and-serve foil pans are safe; they will have microwave instructions printed on the label. If the label is *not* marked safe for microwave use, don't use the pan in your microwave oven. White, non-recycled paper products are also safe to use.

—Glass cookware should be microwave-tested for safety unless the manufacturer says it is microwave safe. Testing is easy: Fill a glass measure with one cup of water. Place it beside the dish to be tested, and put both in the microwave oven. Heat the dish at HIGH for 1 minute. If the dish is hot to touch after heating, it is *not* safe for use in a microwave oven. On the other hand, if the water is hot and the dish is cool, the dish is microwave safe.

—Know the wattage of your oven. It is listed in your owner's manual or on the metal plate attached to the back of the oven. The less expensive 500-watt ovens are designed for lighter cooking tasks, such as defrosting and reheating. If you plan to cook full meals in these ovens, be sure to expect longer microwave cooking times.

—Beware of popping corn in a 500-watt oven—unless it is microwave popping corn designed specifically for 500-watt ovens.

—If you have a 700-watt oven rather than a 600- to 650-watt oven, you may notice shorter cooking times. Power flow into your house during peak usage will also affect cooking times.

—Melt chocolate in the microwave at MEDIUM HIGH (70% power). You can melt chocolate in its paper wrapper, or place it in a custard cup. If you're melting a lot of chocolate, use a glass bowl, and stir at 1-minute intervals.

—Microwave a lemon at HIGH for 20 to 30 seconds before juicing; you'll get more juice.

—Soften one-half gallon of ice cream at HIGH for 30 seconds.

—Remove wrapper, and soften 3 ounces cream cheese at HIGH for 10 to 15 seconds.

—Defrost meat fast. Dense meat, such as steak, will take 5 to 6 minutes per pound to defrost. Leave the ends of the freezer wrapping open so air can circulate during the first half of the defrost time. Remove wrappings for the second half, and use a plate to catch meat drippings.

—Use the microwave in combination with conventional cooking methods. Partially cook chicken in the microwave, and finish cooking it on the grill or in a skillet to get moist chicken and grilled or fried flavor.

—Experiment with oven-cooking bags for stews, vegetables, and meats. Use nylon ties; paper-covered metal ones may cause an electrical arc (a giant spark) in your oven and damage it.

—If you like microwave equipment, shop for utensils that go from the freezer to the microwave to the conventional oven. You'll save time and enjoy the convenience.

—Dry herbs in the microwave. Place a few sprigs or ½ cup of leaves between paper towels; microwave at HIGH for ½ to 1 minute.

—Microwaved food is still cooking when it's removed from the oven, so allow time to let food stand and finish cooking, about 5 to 10 minutes. Meanwhile, microwave quick-cooking vegetables while meats or casseroles stand.

Potato Yeast Rolls

Even before commercial yeast was readily available, homemade bread was standard fare at mealtime. Housewives usually made their own liquid yeast mixture from potatoes or potato water, sugar, and a small amount of commercial yeast. Remember the unique flavor and the delicate texture of the rolls Grandma used to make? Chances are she used a liquid potato yeast mixture.

POTATO YEAST ROLLS

½ cup milk, scalded
3 tablespoons shortening
2 tablespoons sugar
1 teaspoon salt
1 cup Potato Yeast
1 egg, beaten
3 to 3½ cups all-purpose flour, divided

Combine milk, shortening, sugar, and salt; stir until sugar dissolves. Cool to lukewarm (105° to 115°). Add Potato Yeast, egg, and 1½ cups flour; beat at medium speed of an electric mixer until smooth. Stir in enough of remaining flour to make a soft dough.

Turn dough out onto a floured surface, and knead until smooth and elastic (about 5 minutes). Place in a well-greased bowl, turning to grease top. Cover and let rise in a warm place (85°), free from drafts, 1½ to 2 hours or until doubled in bulk.

Punch dough down; shape into 2-inch balls. Place in a greased 13- x 9- x 2-inch pan. Cover and let rise in a warm place (85°), free from drafts, 1 hour or until doubled in bulk. Bake at 400° for 15 to 17 minutes or until golden. Yield: 2 dozen.

Potato Yeast:

4 cups peeled and cubed potatoes (about 4 medium)
1 package dry yeast
2 cups warm water (105° to 115°), divided
¼ cup sugar
1½ teaspoons salt

Cook potatoes in boiling water to cover 10 minutes or until tender; drain. Mash potatoes, and let cool.

Dissolve yeast in ½ cup warm water; let stand 5 minutes. Combine yeast mixture, sugar, salt, and mashed potatoes in a medium-size nonmetal bowl; stir well. Add remaining 1½ cups water; stir well. Cover loosely with plastic wrap or cheesecloth, and let stand in a warm place (80° to 85°) for 72 hours, stirring 2 or 3 times daily. Place fermented mixture in refrigerator 24 hours before making Potato Yeast Rolls.

To use, remove Potato Yeast from refrigerator, and let stand at room temperature at least 1 hour. Yield: 4 cups.

Note: Yeast mixture will keep in refrigerator up to 14 days; stir daily.

Pansy G. Edwards,
Wilkesboro, North Carolina.

Have Fun With Phyllo Appetizers

If you've seen phyllo, also spelled fillo (and pronounced fēlō), in the frozen food case but don't know what to do with it, here are two suggestions. Use the parchment-thin pastry to make Phyllo-Spinach Triangles. Feta cheese and nutmeg carry the distinctive flavor in these Greek pastries. And best of all, they can be made ahead of time, frozen, and then baked without thawing.

Another appetizer idea to try is Artichoke-Parmesan Phyllo Bites. Individual servings are shaped to resemble small bags, with corners gathered and gently twisted.

You'll find phyllo in 1-pound packages at the grocery store. For best results, follow directions for storing and thawing. Phyllo is a simple dough of flour and water mixed into a stiff paste and rolled thin. To prevent the pastry from drying out and cracking during use, keep covered with a slightly damp towel until you're ready to work with it. Brushing the phyllo sheets with melted butter during handling will keep the pastry pliable. This will also aid in making the pastry flaky and brown.

PHYLLO-SPINACH TRIANGLES

1 small onion, grated
2 tablespoons butter or margarine, melted
2 (10-ounce) packages frozen chopped spinach, thawed and drained well
2 eggs, slightly beaten
4 egg yolks, slightly beaten
1⅔ cups (½ pound) feta cheese
1 teaspoon chopped fresh parsley
½ teaspoon ground nutmeg
1 tablespoon dry breadcrumbs
½ pound frozen phyllo pastry, thawed
½ cup butter or margarine, melted

Sauté onion in 2 tablespoons butter; add spinach, and cook until dry. Let cool slightly. Add eggs, egg yolks, cheese, parsley, nutmeg, and breadcrumbs; stir well.

Keep phyllo covered with a slightly damp towel until ready for use. Cut phyllo sheets lengthwise into 3-inch strips. Brush 1 strip with melted butter. Place a rounded teaspoonful of spinach mixture at base of phyllo strip; fold the right bottom corner over to form a triangle. Continue folding back and forth into a triangle, gently pressing corners together, to end of strip. Repeat procedure with remaining phyllo sheets and spinach filling. Brush tops of triangles with ½ cup melted butter.

Place triangles seam side down on greased baking sheets. Bake at 325° for 35 minutes or until golden. Serve hot. Yield: 3½ dozen.

Note: Phyllo triangles may be frozen, if desired. Place unbaked triangles on baking sheets in freezer until hard. Remove from baking sheet, and store in airtight container in freezer. To serve, place on greased baking sheets, and bake at 325° for 35 minutes.

Kate Morris,
South Charleston, West Virginia.

ARTICHOKE-PARMESAN PHYLLO BITES

3 (6-ounce) jars marinated artichoke hearts, undrained
¾ cup freshly grated Parmesan cheese, divided
1 clove garlic, minced
10 sheets frozen phyllo pastry, thawed

Drain artichoke hearts, reserving marinade; set marinade aside.

Position knife blade in food processor bowl; add artichoke hearts, ½ cup cheese, and garlic. Top with cover; pulse 2 or 3 times until artichokes are finely chopped.

Keep phyllo covered with a slightly damp towel until ready for use. Place 1 phyllo sheet horizontally on a flat surface; brush lightly with reserved marinade, and sprinkle with about 2 teaspoons of remaining cheese. Top with another phyllo sheet; brush lightly with reserved marinade. With a sharp knife, halve phyllo sheets lengthwise; then cut crosswise into thirds, making 6 sections, each approximately 6 x 5 inches. Place a rounded teaspoon of artichoke filling in center of each phyllo section; working with 1 section at a time, gather corners of phyllo over the filling, and gently twist to close pastry. Place on a lightly greased baking sheet. Repeat procedure with remaining phyllo sheets and artichoke filling. Bake at 350° for 15 to 17 minutes or until golden. Serve hot. Yield: 2½ dozen.
Joanne Warner Gross,
Lufkin, Texas.

Have You Cooked Corned Beef Lately?

Do you often order a Reuben sandwich at the deli but never cook corned beef at home? It's a traditional Saint Patrick's Day favorite that's too good to save for just that day. After you try these recipes, you'll agree there's got to be a little Irish in our readers who sent us these ideas.

CORNED BEEF WITH DIJON GLAZE

1 (3-pound) corned beef brisket, trimmed
4 cups water
¼ cup vinegar
¼ cup Worcestershire sauce
2 bay leaves
8 whole cloves
3 cloves garlic, split
Dijon Glaze

Place brisket in a large Dutch oven. Add water, vinegar, Worcestershire sauce, bay leaves, cloves, and garlic; bring to a boil. Cover, reduce heat, and simmer 2½ to 3 hours or until tender. Drain. Return to Dutch oven. Spread with ½ cup Dijon Glaze. Bake at 350° for 20 minutes. Serve with remaining glaze. Yield: 6 to 8 servings.

Dijon Glaze:

½ cup Dijon mustard
½ cup orange marmalade
2 tablespoons prepared horseradish
2 tablespoons Worcestershire sauce

Combine all ingredients in a small saucepan. Cook over medium heat, stirring mixture constantly, until bubbly. Yield: 1¼ cups. *Beppy Hassey,*
Montgomery, Alabama.

FRENCH ONION-BEEF SOUP

1 (3½-pound) corned beef brisket, trimmed
7 cups water, divided
½ cup reduced-sodium soy sauce
l clove garlic
½ teaspoon Beau Monde seasoning
1½ teaspoons browning-and-seasoning sauce
1 (1.25-ounce) package dry onion soup mix
2 large onions, sliced and separated into rings
¼ cup butter or margarine, melted
4 (6-inch) French rolls
1½ cups (6 ounces) shredded Swiss cheese

Place brisket in a large Dutch oven. Set aside.

Combine 2 cups water, soy sauce, garlic clove, Beau Monde seasoning, browning-and-seasoning sauce, and soup mix in container of an electric blender; cover and process until mixture is smooth. Pour mixture over brisket; add 3 cups water; mix well. Bake, covered, at 350° for 2 hours.

Sauté onion in butter until tender; add to brisket. Bake, covered, an additional hour or until brisket is tender.

Remove brisket from liquid, and let cool 20 minutes; cut meat across grain into thin, bite-size pieces. Return to broth mixture, and add remaining 2 cups water. Cook over medium heat until thoroughly heated.

Slice rolls in half lengthwise; toast until golden brown. Spoon onion soup and beef slices into ovenproof individual bowls. Top each with a bread slice; sprinkle with Swiss cheese.

Bake at 350° for 5 minutes or until cheese melts. Yield: 8 servings.
Mary Kay Menees,
White Pine, Tennessee.

CORNED BEEF DINNER

1 (3-pound) corned beef brisket, trimmed
4 cups water
2 cloves garlic, minced
2 bay leaves
½ teaspoon salt
8 small new potatoes, unpeeled
4 medium carrots, scraped and quartered
4 small boiling onions, halved
1 medium head cabbage, cut into thin wedges

Place brisket in a Dutch oven. Add water, garlic, bay leaves, and salt; bring to a boil. Cover, reduce heat, and simmer 2½ hours. Add potatoes, carrots, and onions; cook, covered, 10 minutes. Add cabbage; cook, covered, 15 to 20 minutes. Remove the bay leaves. Yield: 6 to 8 servings. *Christine McQueen,*
Annville, Kentucky.

GRILLED CORNED BEEF SANDWICHES

¼ cup spicy brown mustard
8 slices rye bread
1 pound thinly sliced corned beef
4 slices Swiss cheese
1 (8-ounce) can shredded sauerkraut, drained
½ cup commercial sour cream
¼ cup butter or margarine, melted

Spread mustard on one side of 4 slices of bread. Arrange corned beef, cheese, and sauerkraut evenly over each slice. Spread sour cream over remaining bread slices; place over sauerkraut. Brush butter on one side of each sandwich. Grill, buttered side down, in hot skillet until golden brown. Brush butter on top slice of sandwich; turn and grill until golden brown. Serve sandwiches hot. Yield: 4 servings.

Accent Meals With Kiwifruit

Next time you're shopping the produce section of the grocery store, think twice before you pass up the funny-looking egg-shaped fruit with the fuzzy brown skin. The outside of a kiwifruit may not be very appealing, but inside there's a stunning emerald-green flesh surrounding tiny black edible seeds.

Juicy and tangy-sweet, the flavor of kiwifruit has been compared to a blend of strawberry, pineapple, and lime. The texture is similar to a strawberry or a fresh fig. Besides being delicious, one medium-size kiwifruit contains only about 36 calories, and it is an excellent source of vitamin C (ascorbic acid) and potassium, as well.

The enchanting, nutritious kiwifruit is practically a year-round item. Although harvested when fully mature, the fruit may still need to ripen further once purchased. Choose a kiwifruit that is plump and not shriveled. If fruit is hard, let it ripen at room temperature. Once it has ripened, store in the refrigerator up to two weeks.

KIWI PARFAIT

1 (3-ounce) package lemon-flavored gelatin
1½ cups boiling water
1 tablespoon grated lemon rind
1 (8-ounce) carton frozen whipped
    topping, thawed
3 kiwifruit, peeled

Dissolve gelatin in boiling water. Stir in lemon rind; chill until consistency of unbeaten egg white. Fold in whipped topping; set aside. Cut 1 kiwifruit into 8 slices; chop remaining 2.

Alternate layers of gelatin mixture and chopped kiwifruit into 8 parfait glasses; chill 1 hour. Garnish with sliced kiwifruit. Yield: 8 servings.

Louise Denmon,
Silsbee, Texas.

KIWI-BERRY PIZZA

1 (9-ounce) package golden yellow cake
    mix
⅔ cup strawberry preserves
1 tablespoon water
1 (1.4-ounce) envelope whipped topping
    mix
3 to 4 kiwifruit, peeled and thinly sliced
1 pint small strawberries, sliced

Prepare cake mix according to package directions. Pour into a greased and floured 12-inch pizza pan. Bake at 350° for 20 minutes. Let cool in pan 10 minutes; remove to wire rack, and cool completely.

Combine preserves and water in a small saucepan; heat until preserves melt; cool. Set aside.

Prepare whipped topping mix according to package directions. Spread over cake. Top with preserves. Arrange fruit over preserves. Yield: one 12-inch pie.

Kaye Rousseau,
Taylor, Louisiana.

Spring Vegetables Are Here

They're here! Artichokes, asparagus, and English peas—all fresh, available, and ready for spring menus.

The recipe for Chilled Artichokes With Lemon-Pepper Dressing explains how to cook artichokes. If you've never eaten an artichoke, now's your opportunity. Simply pull off a leaf, and dip the fleshy end into the dressing. Draw the leaf between your teeth, scraping off the tender part. Discard the tough end.

CHILLED ARTICHOKES WITH LEMON-PEPPER DRESSING

5 whole artichokes
Lemon wedge
2 lemons, sliced
2 cloves garlic, minced
1 teaspoon salt
Lemon-Pepper Dressing
Lemon slices (optional)
Parsley sprigs (optional)

Wash artichokes by plunging them up and down in cold water. Cut off the stem end; trim about ½ inch from top of each artichoke. Remove any loose bottom leaves. Trim away about a fourth of each outer leaf with scissors. Rub top and edges of leaves with lemon wedge. Place artichokes in a large Dutch oven; cover with water.

Add 2 sliced lemons, garlic, and salt. Cover and bring to a boil; reduce heat and simmer, 40 to 45 minutes or until leaves pull out easily. Arrange artichokes on serving plates, if desired, and serve with Lemon-Pepper Dressing. Garnish with lemon slices and parsley, if desired. Yield: 5 servings.

Lemon-Pepper Dressing:

1 cup vegetable oil
¼ cup lemon juice
¼ cup red wine vinegar
2 tablespoons brown mustard
4 cloves garlic, minced
1 teaspoon salt
1 teaspoon pepper
2 tablespoons sliced green onions
½ cup chopped green pepper

Combine oil, lemon juice, vinegar, brown mustard, garlic, salt, and pepper; let dressing mixture stand 30 minutes. Stir in sliced green onions and chopped green pepper. Yield: 2 cups.

Mary Hamblen,
New Orleans, Louisiana.

SHRIMP-STUFFED ARTICHOKES

6 medium artichokes
Lemon wedge
1½ pounds unpeeled medium-size fresh
    shrimp
2 cloves garlic, minced
⅓ cup minced onion
¼ cup butter or margarine, melted
¼ cup white wine
¼ cup grated Parmesan cheese
1 cup soft breadcrumbs
2 tablespoons lemon juice
1 to 2 tablespoons minced parsley
6 lemon wedges (optional)
Parsley sprigs (optional)
Paprika (optional)

Wash artichokes by plunging them up and down in cold water. Cut off stem end, and trim about ½ inch from the top of each artichoke. Remove any loose bottom leaves. Trim away about a fourth of each outer leaf with scissors. Rub top of each artichoke and edge of leaves with lemon wedge.

Place artichokes in a large Dutch oven and cover with water. Cover and bring to a boil; reduce heat, and simmer 35 to 45 minutes or until leaves pull out easily. Remove artichokes from water; scrape out each fuzzy thistle center (choke) with a spoon.

Peel and devein shrimp. Chop shrimp; set aside.

Sauté garlic and onion in butter in a large skillet. Add shrimp and wine; cook about 3 minutes, stirring often. Add cheese, breadcrumbs, and lemon juice; stir well.

Spoon shrimp stuffing into center of artichokes. Sprinkle minced parsley over artichokes. Garnish with lemon wedges, parsley sprigs, and paprika, if desired. Yield: 6 servings.

ASPARAGUS WITH CASHEW BUTTER

1½ pounds fresh asparagus
1 cup chicken broth
½ cup butter or margarine, softened
¼ cup chopped cashews

Snap off tough ends of asparagus. Remove scales with a knife or vegetable peeler, if desired. Place asparagus in a large skillet. Pour chicken broth over asparagus; bring to a boil over medium heat. Cover, reduce heat, and simmer about 8 minutes. Drain.

Combine butter and cashews; beat at high speed of an electric mixer until fluffy. Serve cashew butter with cooked asparagus. Yield: 4 to 6 servings.

Tony Jones,
Atlanta, Georgia.

MINTED PEAS

2½ pounds fresh English peas
2 tablespoons jellied mint sauce
1 tablespoon butter or margarine
½ teaspoon salt
¼ teaspoon pepper

Shell and rinse peas.

Cook peas in boiling water to cover 10 to 12 minutes or until tender. Drain, reserving ¼ cup liquid. Return peas and reserved liquid to pan; add remaining ingredients. Cook over medium heat, stirring constantly, 2 to 3 minutes or until mint sauce melts. Yield: 4 servings.

Cathy Powell,
Claxton, Georgia.

Offer A Fruit Salad

Crunchy apples, mellow pears, succulent pineapples, and sweet strawberries are some of the fruit available during the early days of spring. If you are tired of your tossed salad standby, try these fruit salads to add some natural sweetness to your menu.

For salads, as well as appetizers and snacks, cheese and fruit are favored accompaniments. When combined in a salad with tart dressing and crisp lettuce, they're sure to be winners.

Pears, fresh or canned, are a dependable salad choice year-round. For a spruced up salad variety that's not camouflaged with dressing, try Pear-and-Celery Salad.

Fan out the pear slices, scoop up the celery-and-raisin mixture, and sprinkle on the blue cheese to make an appealing presentation for Pear-and-Celery Salad.

PEAR-AND-CELERY SALAD

1½ cups chopped celery
½ cup golden raisins
⅓ cup mayonnaise
1 tablespoon honey
1 tablespoon lemon juice
Lettuce leaves
2 large pears, unpeeled and cored
Lemon juice
¼ cup crumbled blue cheese

Combine celery, raisins, mayonnaise, honey, and lemon juice; mix well. Cover and chill.

Arrange lettuce on individual salad plates. Slice each pear into 10 slices; brush with lemon juice. Arrange 5 pear slices on each plate. Spoon about ½ cup celery mixture on each salad; sprinkle with cheese. Yield: 4 servings.

Louise Osborne,
Lexington, Kentucky.

CHEESY FRUIT-'N'-NUT SALAD

3 medium apples, unpeeled and chopped
2 cups thinly sliced celery
1 (20-ounce) can unsweetened pineapple tidbits, drained
8 ounces sharp Cheddar cheese, diced
¾ cup slivered almonds, toasted
½ cup commercial sour cream
½ cup mayonnaise
Lettuce leaves (optional)

Combine apples, celery, pineapple, cheese, and almonds in a large bowl; toss gently. Combine sour cream and mayonnaise; add to apple mixture, tossing gently to coat. Serve on lettuce leaves, if desired. Yield: 6 servings.

Phyllis Dupont,
Concord, Virginia.

COTTAGE CHEESE-BANANA SPLITS

Lettuce leaves
4 bananas
Lemon juice
2 cups cream-style cottage cheese
½ cup flaked coconut, toasted
1 (15¼-ounce) can crushed pineapple, drained
1 cup strawberry halves
French salad dressing (optional)

Line banana split dishes or salad plates with lettuce.

Cut bananas in half lengthwise; sprinkle with lemon juice. Place 2 banana halves in each dish. Combine cottage cheese and coconut; place a scoop in each dish.

Combine pineapple and strawberries; spoon around cottage cheese. Serve with French salad dressing, if desired. Yield: 4 servings.

Edith Askins,
Greenville, Texas.

FRUIT SALAD WITH DATE DRESSING

1 pineapple
2 oranges
2 bananas, sliced
Lettuce leaves
Date Dressing

Peel and core pineapple; cut into wedges. Peel and section oranges. Combine pineapple and oranges in a bowl; cover and chill. Add bananas, and toss fruit gently.

Line a serving platter with lettuce. Spoon fruit over lettuce. Serve with Date Dressing. Yield: 4 to 6 servings.

Date Dressing:

1 tablespoon butter or margarine
1 tablespoon all-purpose flour
½ cup milk
1 egg yolk, slightly beaten
¼ teaspoon prepared mustard
¼ cup orange juice
1½ tablespoons lemon juice
2 tablespoons sugar
¼ teaspoon salt
¼ cup chopped dates

Melt butter in a small saucepan over low heat. Add flour, stirring until smooth. Cook 1 minute, stirring constantly. Gradually add milk; cook over medium heat, stirring constantly, until mixture is thickened and bubbly. Gradually stir about one-fourth of hot mixture into yolk; add to remaining hot mixture, stirring constantly. Cook 1 minute over low heat. Remove from heat; stir in remaining ingredients. Chill thoroughly. Yield: about 1 cup.
Sarah Watson,
Knoxville, Tennessee.

Tea Is the Basis Of These Beverages

Tea may have been discovered in China, but its popularity here in the South might lead you to believe otherwise. Served hot, iced, or in combination with other ingredients, tea is a refreshing way to quench your thirst.

Our readers have shared some delicious recipes for beverages that start with tea. Fruit juice, spices, different sweeteners, and even liquor make interesting variations to the popular drink.

WHITE GRAPE JUICE TEA

1 gallon water
3 family-size tea bags
2 to 2½ cups sugar
¾ cup white grape juice
1 (.32-ounce) envelope unsweetened lemonade-flavored drink mix

Bring water to a boil, and pour over tea bags. Cover and let stand 5 minutes. Discard tea bags; add remaining ingredients. Stir well. Serve chilled. Yield: 1 gallon.
Melinda Pipes,
Hartford, Kentucky.

HAWAIIAN TEA

2 quarts water
6 regular tea bags
1 (8-ounce) jar maraschino cherries, undrained
½ cup water
1 cup sugar
1½ cups lemon juice
2½ cups pineapple juice
Lemon slices (optional)
Mint sprigs (optional)

Bring 2 quarts water to a boil, and pour over tea bags. Cover and let stand 5 minutes. Discard tea bags.

Drain cherries, reserving juice (reserve cherries for other uses). Combine ½ cup water and sugar; boil 5 minutes. Add sugar mixture, lemon juice, pineapple juice, and cherry juice to tea. Serve hot or chilled. Garnish with lemon slices and mint sprigs, if desired. Yield: 3 quarts.
Emma Prillhart,
Kingsport, Tennessee.

BOURBON-TEA PUNCH

2 cups water
3 regular tea bags
3 to 4 cups bourbon
2 cups orange juice
1 cup sugar
1 cup lemon juice
1 cup Curaçao or other orange-flavored liqueur
3 (33.8-ounce) bottles club soda, chilled

Bring water to a boil, and pour over tea bags. Cover and let stand 15 minutes. Discard tea bags. Add remaining ingredients except club soda, stirring until sugar dissolves.

To serve, pour over decorated ice ring in punch bowl, and add club soda. Yield: 5½ quarts.
Lana J. Tabb,
Lakeland, Florida.

HOT APPLE-CINNAMON TEA

½ gallon apple cider
¼ cup unsweetened instant tea mix
2 tablespoons honey
1 teaspoon ground cinnamon

Combine all ingredients in a Dutch oven; stir well. Cook over medium heat until hot. Serve hot. Yield: 2 quarts.
Dorothy Burgess,
Huntsville, Texas.

Bring On The Cookies!

It's a fact: Kids love cookies. But we bet you'll catch adults, as well, sneaking a few of these treats. Whatever your taste, you'll find favorites here.

If you need a quick sweet, try Chocolate Macaroons. Made with pudding mix and sweetened condensed milk, they're rich in flavor.

CHOCOLATE MACAROONS

½ cup all-purpose flour
1 (4-ounce) package chocolate instant pudding mix
1 (7-ounce) can flaked coconut
1 cup sweetened condensed milk
½ teaspoon almond extract

Combine all ingredients, mixing well. Drop by rounded teaspoonfuls onto greased cookie sheets. Bake at 325° for 10 to 12 minutes. Remove to wire rack; let cool. Yield: 3½ dozen.
Mrs. Charles DeHaven,
Owensboro, Kentucky.

ORANGE FINGERS

3½ cups vanilla wafer crumbs
1 (16-ounce) package powdered sugar, sifted
1½ cups chopped pecans
1 (6-ounce) can frozen orange juice concentrate, thawed and undiluted
½ cup butter or margarine, melted
1 (7-ounce) package flaked coconut

Combine vanilla wafer crumbs, powdered sugar, and pecans; mix well. Stir in orange juice concentrate and butter. Shape into 2-inch fingers; roll in coconut. Refrigerate. Yield: 4½ dozen.
Carol C. Gibson,
Martin, Tennessee.

PEANUT BUTTER COOKIES

1 cup butter or margarine, softened
1 cup sugar
1 cup firmly packed brown sugar
2 eggs
2½ cups all-purpose flour
2 teaspoons baking soda
¼ teaspoon salt
1 cup peanut butter
1 teaspoon vanilla extract

Cream butter; gradually add sugars, beating well. Add eggs, one at a time, beating well after each addition.

Combine flour, soda, and salt; add to creamed mixture alternately with peanut butter, beginning and ending with flour mixture. Stir in vanilla. Cover and chill 1 to 2 hours. Shape dough into 1-inch balls, and place on ungreased cookie sheets. Press with a fork to flatten cookies; bake at 375° for 10 minutes. Yield: about 10 dozen.   *James A. Christian, Riverview, Alabama.*

SHORTBREAD COOKIES

½ cup shortening
½ cup butter or margarine, softened
1 cup sugar
2 tablespoons corn syrup
2 cups all-purpose flour
1 teaspoon baking soda
⅔ cup chopped almonds
½ teaspoon almond extract

Cream shortening and butter; gradually add sugar and syrup, beating at medium speed of an electric mixer until mixture is light and fluffy.

Combine flour and soda; add to creamed mixture, stirring well. Stir in almonds and almond extract. Shape mixture into one 12- x 1½-inch log; wrap in wax paper, and chill at least 2 hours.

Cut dough with an electric knife into ¼-inch slices; place on ungreased cookie sheets. Bake at 350° for 8 to 10 minutes. Let stand 1 minute; remove to wire racks, and cool completely. Yield: about 3½ dozen.   *Jean Voan, Shepherd, Texas.*

BUTTERSCOTCH COOKIES

1 cup butter or margarine, softened
¾ cup sugar
¾ cup firmly packed dark brown sugar
2 eggs
1 teaspoon vanilla extract
2¼ cups all-purpose flour
1 teaspoon baking soda
½ teaspoon salt
1 (12-ounce) package butterscotch morsels

Cream butter; gradually add sugars, beating at medium speed of an electric mixer until light and fluffy. Add eggs, one at a time, beating after each addition. Add vanilla; mix well.

Combine flour, baking soda, and salt; add to creamed mixture. Stir in butterscotch morsels.

Drop dough by heaping teaspoonfuls onto ungreased cookie sheets. Bake at 375° for 10 minutes or until golden brown. Remove to wire racks to cool completely. Yield: 7 dozen.

Bettye Cortner, Cerulean, Kentucky.

Processor-Quick Frostings And Toppings

If a fine cloud of powdered sugar coats your kitchen when you mix up a frosting, then you'll welcome these food processor versions. They make an easy task of preparing frosting.

And because sweet sauces are increasingly popular with unfrosted cakes, we've included some dessert toppings that are just suited for serving with slices of pound cake, angel food cake, or even fresh fruit.

As with most food processor recipes, there's no need to soften cream cheese for frosting and dessert-topping recipes; cut it into small chunks right from the refrigerator. For the smoothest consistency, it will help to soften butter before mixing.

FLUFFY CHOCOLATE FROSTING

½ cup butter, softened
4 cups sifted powdered sugar
¾ cup cocoa
½ cup evaporated milk
1 teaspoon Grand Marnier or other orange-flavored liqueur

Position knife blade in food processor bowl; add all ingredients in order listed. Top with cover; pulse 2 or 3 times. Process about 1 minute, scraping sides of processor bowl occasionally. Yield: 2 cups or enough for one 2-layer cake.

Joanie Meyer, Okarche, Oklahoma.

CREAM CHEESE FROSTING

1 (8-ounce) package cream cheese, cubed
1 tablespoon butter or margarine
1 (16-ounce) package powdered sugar, sifted
½ teaspoon vanilla extract

Position knife blade in food processor bowl; add all ingredients. Top with cover, and process 15 seconds or until mixture is well creamed, scraping sides of processor bowl occasionally. Yield: 1¾ cups or enough for one 13- x 9- x 2-inch cake.   *Katy Holt, Arkadelphia, Arkansas.*

PROCESSOR DEVONSHIRE SAUCE

2 lemons
1 (3⅜-ounce) package vanilla instant pudding mix, divided
2 (3-ounce) packages cream cheese, cubed
2 cups milk

Cut four 4-inch strips from lemons. Extract juice from lemons; set aside.

Position knife blade in food processor bowl; add lemon strips. Top with cover, and process 1 minute. Add 1 teaspoon instant pudding mix to processor bowl; process 1 minute or until lemon rind is finely chopped. Add cream cheese and process until smooth. Gradually pour milk and reserved lemon juice through food chute with processor running. Add remaining pudding mix, and process 1 minute. Refrigerate the sauce. Serve over fresh fruit. Yield: 3 cups.

Margaret L. Hunter, Princeton, Kentucky.

ORANGE DESSERT SAUCE

1 (3-ounce) package cream cheese, cubed
2 tablespoons sugar
¼ cup commercial sour cream
1 (11-ounce) can mandarin oranges, drained and divided
Mint leaves (optional)

Position knife blade in food processor bowl. Combine cream cheese, sugar, and sour cream in processor bowl; process 1 minute, scraping sides of processor bowl occasionally. Add ¼ cup mandarin oranges to mixture, and pulse 3 times; chill.

Arrange remaining mandarin oranges over slices of cake; spoon orange sauce over oranges. Garnish with mint leaves, if desired. Yield: ¾ cup.

Mrs. Bruce Fowler, Woodruff, South Carolina.

April

Look What's Sizzling On The Grill

If the first sign of spring finds you dusting off the grill and longing for the aroma of meat searing over hot coals, then these recipes are for you. They offer variations of poultry, seafood, and cuts of meat that you might ordinarily reserve for company. But you'll find them right for any occasion.

Instead of typical beef steaks, try our version of Teriyaki Lamb Chops. As in cooking any chops or steaks, trim away excess fat to avoid flare-ups. Scoring the fat on the outside edges will keep the meat from curling as it cooks.

Meat is often seared in a skillet over high heat to seal in juices, but you can do this on the grill. Place the meat 2 to 3 inches above the coals for the first three minutes of cooking; then raise the rack to 4 to 5 inches above the coals. The thinner the chops or steaks, the closer the rack should be to the coals. The thicker cuts should be cooked farther away from the heat so that they will cook more thoroughly. Turn meat only once while cooking, and use tongs instead of a fork to keep from piercing it and losing flavorful juices.

Beef tenderloin is expensive, so when you plan to serve it, you might want to use Curt Treloar's recipe for Tournedos Diables. Sherry, cognac, and seasonings, along with the smoked flavor, give each bite a rich taste.

You'll find that tenderloin, other roasts, and lean meat (such as chicken) take longer to grill than well-marbled steaks or any meat with more fat. Because of this, use more charcoal briquets to keep the heat constant for a longer cooking time. Be sure that the briquets extend at least 1 inch beyond each outer edge of the meat on the grill rack. For gas grills, double-check to see that the volcanic rock or briquets are in an even layer.

You might not think of grilling oysters on the half shell, but our recipe for Smoky Oysters Supreme offers an easy and flavorful example. If you want to save time, you can purchase oyster half shells and a carton of shucked oysters. Arrange the oysters in the half shells, matching sizes.

Use these additional tips for successful outdoor grilling.

■ If the grill is too hot, raise the rack, and move coals to each side of the meat. To increase the temperature, lower the rack, and move the coals closer together.

■ You can test the temperature of the coals with your hand. Place open palm at cooking height over the heat. If you can hold it there 2 seconds, the temperature is hot; 3 seconds, medium hot; 4 seconds, medium; and 5 seconds, low.

■ If the air is cold or windy or if the meat is still refrigerator cold, count on extra grilling time.

■ Chicken has a tendency to burn on the grill, so cook over medium-hot coals for best results. If it begins to burn, place a disposable aluminum pan directly under the chicken to catch drippings, and push coals to both sides of the pan.

■ When grilling fish, be sure to brush the rack with vegetable oil to prevent the tender skin from sticking.

■ To add an aromatic wood-smoke flavor to grilled food, toss a few chips of green wood onto the briquets. If the chips are dry, soak in water for at least 30 minutes.

SMOKY OYSTERS SUPREME
(pictured on page 63)

24 oysters in shells
3 tablespoons chopped onion
⅓ cup butter or margarine, melted
2 tablespoons chopped pimiento
1 tablespoon chopped parsley
¼ teaspoon salt
¼ teaspoon dry mustard
¼ teaspoon hot pepper sauce
¼ teaspoon Worcestershire sauce

Shuck and drain oysters. Place oysters in deep halves of shells. Set aside.

Sauté onion in butter until tender; add remaining ingredients, mixing well. Spoon mixture evenly over oysters.

Arrange oyster shells evenly on grill rack; grill over medium coals 20 minutes or until edges of oysters begin to curl. Serve oysters immediately. Yield: 4 servings.

Note: Shucked oysters may be used if you have your own shells.

TERIYAKI LAMB CHOPS
(pictured on page 63)

6 (1-inch-thick) lamb sirloin chops
½ cup finely chopped onion
¼ cup soy sauce
¼ cup cider vinegar
2 cloves garlic, sliced
2 tablespoons honey
2 teaspoons ground ginger
¼ teaspoon dry mustard
¼ teaspoon pepper

Trim excess fat from lamb; place lamb in a shallow dish. Combine remaining ingredients, mixing well; pour over lamb. Cover; refrigerate 8 hours.

Grill chops over medium coals 8 to 10 minutes on each side or to desired degree of doneness, basting frequently with marinade. Yield: 6 servings.

George Darling,
Grafton, West Virginia.

TOURNEDOS DIABLES
(pictured on page 63)

1 (5- to 7-pound) beef tenderloin, trimmed
Coarsely ground pepper
Garlic salt
1 (6-ounce) package long grain and wild rice
2 cups beef bouillon
⅓ cup sherry
¼ cup cognac
2 teaspoons butter or margarine
1 tablespoon plus 1 teaspoon Dijon mustard
1 tablespoon tomato paste
1 teaspoon Worcestershire sauce
½ teaspoon vinegar
½ teaspoon garlic powder
1 cup sliced fresh mushrooms
1 cup chopped green onions

Sprinkle tenderloin with pepper and garlic salt. Grill over medium coals 15 minutes on each side or until desired degree of doneness.

Prepare rice according to package directions. Set aside, and keep warm.

Bring bouillon to a boil in a heavy saucepan; reduce heat, and simmer.

Heat sherry and cognac in a small saucepan just until hot (do not boil); remove from heat, ignite, and pour over bouillon. When flames die down, add remaining ingredients except mushrooms and green onions. Cook over low heat 15 minutes. Stir in mushrooms and green onions; simmer 5 minutes. Cut meat into ½-inch slices. Place rice on platter; top with meat and sauce. Yield: 8 to 10 servings. *Curt Treloar,*
Largo, Florida.

FLANK STEAK AND MUSHROOMS

1½ cups red wine
½ cup soy sauce
¼ cup plus 2 tablespoons Worcestershire
  sauce
1 clove garlic, crushed
1½ tablespoons ground ginger
¼ teaspoon pepper
1 (1- to 1½-pound) flank steak
1 (8-ounce) package fresh mushrooms,
  sliced
1 tablespoon butter or margarine,
  melted

Combine wine, soy sauce, Worcestershire sauce, garlic, ginger, and pepper in a shallow dish, mixing well. Place steak in dish. Cover and refrigerate 8 to 12 hours, turning steak occasionally.

Remove steak from marinade, reserving marinade. Grill steak 4 inches from hot coals 5 to 7 minutes on each side or until desired degree of doneness, basting occasionally with reserved marinade.

Sauté mushrooms in butter in a skillet 5 minutes; add 1 cup reserved marinade. Bring to a boil; reduce heat, and simmer 5 minutes. Drain.

To serve, thinly slice steak diagonally across the grain. Spoon mushrooms over steak. Yield: 3 to 4 servings.
Bob Grossman,
Boca Raton, Florida.

TEXAS-STYLE GAME HENS

4 (1¼-pound) Cornish hens
½ teaspoon salt
½ teaspoon garlic powder
½ teaspoon chili powder
½ cup apple jelly
½ cup catsup
1 tablespoon vinegar
½ teaspoon chili powder

Rinse hens with cold water, and pat dry. Split Cornish hens in half. Combine salt, garlic powder, and ½ teaspoon chili powder; sprinkle both sides of halves with seasonings.

Grill hens over medium coals 45 minutes, turning occasionally.

Combine apple jelly, catsup, vinegar, and ½ teaspoon chili powder in a small saucepan. Cook apple jelly mixture over medium heat, stirring constantly, until jelly melts.

Brush Cornish hens with apple jelly sauce, and grill an additional 15 minutes, turning and basting frequently with the sauce. Yield: 4 to 6 servings.
Marcy Hart,
Killeen, Texas.

MARINATED CHICKEN

¼ cup vegetable oil
¼ cup white wine
2 tablespoons lemon juice
1 teaspoon salt
½ teaspoon dry mustard
½ teaspoon dried whole rosemary
½ teaspoon parsley flakes
Dash of garlic powder
1 (2½- to 3-pound) broiler-fryer, cut up

Combine all ingredients except chicken; mix well. Place chicken in a 13- x 9- x 2-inch dish; pour marinade over chicken. Cover and refrigerate 2 to 4 hours.

Remove chicken from marinade, reserving marinade. Place chicken on grill over medium coals; baste with reserved marinade. Grill chicken 55 to 60 minutes or until done, turning chicken and basting every 10 minutes. Yield: 4 servings.
Nancy Handley,
Elizabethtown, Kentucky.

The Freshest, Prettiest Salads

Iceberg lettuce makes a great salad, but don't stop there. As popular and as good as iceberg is, it's only one of many choices of greens for salads.

Bibb lettuce is a small cup-shaped head of deep green leaves that is whitish green toward the core. Belgian endive looks more like a small stalk with flat leaves. The colors vary from white to light greenish yellow. At the opposite end, curly endive is usually a large bunchy head of tightly curled, lacy, green leaves. The outside leaves tend to be slightly bitter.

Escarole has broad, flat leaves with ruffled edges that range in color from rich green at the outer end to yellowish in the center. And, of course, iceberg lettuce is firm and crisp textured, with green leaves on the outside and a pale-green core.

Leaf lettuce has long, delicate leaves that grow loosely from a small slender stalk. Leaf lettuce can be all green or have red-tipped leaves. Radicchio has tightly crimped, heavily veined, red leaves and is fairly new to some produce markets.

Romaine lettuce has coarse, crisp leaves with heavy ribs and forms an elongated head. The outer leaves are dark green and are a lighter shade at the root end. And almost everyone is familiar with the dark green, slightly curly leaves of spinach.

Watercress has crisp, dark green leaves. The small leaves have a spicy, peppery flavor that perks up a salad.

Once you've decided on the salad greens you will use, be sure to purchase only those that are fresh and crisp. Then take the time to prepare them properly. Make sure the greens are cleaned and any wilted or bruised spots removed. Wash the leaves in a colander under slightly warm, running water; then rinse with cold water. Put the greens in a wire basket, and shake to remove water; any excess can be removed by blotting with a paper towel. The cleaned greens should be wrapped in a paper towel and stored in a plastic container in the refrigerator's crisper.

To prepare your salad, tear the greens into bite-size pieces. Cutting or chopping will bruise the greens and cause them to brown. Also, be sure the greens are dry before starting.

FLIPPO CAESAR SALAD

1 small clove garlic
1 egg
1 tablespoon olive oil
1 teaspoon Worcestershire sauce
1 teaspoon Dijon mustard
½ teaspoon lemon juice
20 romaine lettuce leaves, torn (about 2
  heads)
½ cup freshly grated Parmesan cheese
1 (2-ounce) can anchovy fillets
Salt and pepper to taste
1 cup seasoned croutons

Crush garlic in large salad bowl (or use garlic press). Add egg, olive oil, Worcestershire sauce, mustard, and lemon juice; beat well, using a wire whisk. Add lettuce; toss to coat. Add remaining ingredients; toss again. Serve immediately. Yield: 6 servings.
Patricia Boschen,
Ashland, Virginia.

SPRING SALAD

4 hard-cooked eggs
3 tablespoons vegetable oil
1½ teaspoons sugar
¾ teaspoon salt
¼ teaspoon dry mustard
⅛ teaspoon pepper
3 tablespoons cider vinegar
⅓ cup milk
2½ cups torn iceberg lettuce (about 1
    small head)
2½ cups torn escarole (about 1 small
    head)
1 cup shredded carrots
2 tablespoons finely chopped onion

Separate egg whites and yolks. Slice egg whites; set aside. Mash egg yolks; add vegetable oil, sugar, salt, mustard, and pepper. Slowly stir in cider vinegar; mix well. Gradually add milk, and mix well. Refrigerate.

Combine remaining ingredients and sliced egg whites; refrigerate.

Just before serving, pour dressing mixture over salad; toss gently. Yield: 6 servings.   *Mrs. Randall L. Wilson,*
Louisville, Kentucky.

SPRING SALAD WEDGES

1 cup mayonnaise
1 cup chili sauce
1 hard-cooked egg, shredded
½ cup chopped green onions
½ cup chopped celery
¼ cup chopped sweet pickle
1 large head iceberg lettuce, cut into 8
    wedges

Combine mayonnaise, chili sauce, egg, green onions, celery, and pickle; mix well. Cover and chill. Serve over lettuce wedges. Yield: 8 servings.
Doris Tibbs,
New Port Richey, Florida.

DELICATE GARDEN LETTUCE

1 clove garlic, cut in half
3 tablespoons vegetable oil
1 tablespoon lemon juice
¼ teaspoon salt
4 cups torn leaf lettuce (about 1 head)

Rub a large wooden bowl with cut sides of garlic. Add oil, lemon juice, and salt to bowl; stir well. Add lettuce; gently toss. Chill 30 minutes before serving. Yield: 4 servings.
Mrs. Ernest Harmon,
Elk Park, North Carolina.

MIXED GREENS SALAD

2 cups (½-inch) French bread cubes
¾ cup vegetable oil, divided
1 clove garlic, minced
4 cups torn endive (about 1 small head)
4 cups torn romaine (about 1 small head)
4 cups torn iceberg lettuce (about ½
    medium head)
1 large cucumber, sliced
6 to 8 green onions, cut into 1-inch pieces
¼ cup (1 ounce) Roquefort cheese,
    crumbled
1 tablespoon lemon juice
⅛ teaspoon salt
⅛ teaspoon coarsely ground pepper

Place bread cubes in a shallow baking pan; bake at 400° for 8 to 10 minutes or until brown, stirring occasionally. Set bread cubes aside.

Combine ¼ cup oil and garlic; stir well. Let stand at least 30 minutes. Combine endive, romaine, iceberg lettuce, cucumber, onions, and cheese in a bowl. Combine remaining ½ cup oil, lemon juice, salt, and pepper; stir well. Pour over salad, and toss gently.

Pour garlic mixture over croutons; stir. Sprinkle over salad. Serve immediately. Yield: 8 servings.
Mrs. Bob Nester,
Charleston, West Virginia.

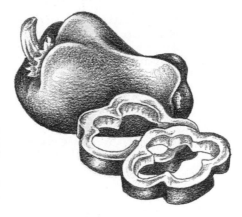

GARDEN SALAD

⅔ cup vegetable oil
⅓ cup lemon juice
2 cloves garlic, minced
1 teaspoon salt
1 medium-size green pepper, cut into
    rings
2 medium tomatoes, cut into wedges
1 medium cucumber, peeled and diced
½ cup sliced green onions
12 Bibb lettuce leaves (about 1 head)
12 radicchio leaves (about 1 head)

Combine oil, lemon juice, garlic, and salt in a jar. Cover tightly, and shake vigorously; set aside.

Layer half each of green pepper, tomatoes, cucumber, and green onions in a 1-quart casserole; repeat layers. Pour dressing mixture over vegetables. Cover and marinate vegetables for 4 hours in the refrigerator.

Arrange 2 Bibb lettuce leaves and 2 radicchio leaves on a salad plate; spoon drained vegetables in center. Repeat procedure for other servings. Yield: 6 servings.   *Doris Garton,*
Shenandoah, Virginia.

SPINACH SALAD

1 pound spinach, torn
3 hard-cooked eggs, cut into wedges
3 small green onions, chopped
2 medium tomatoes, cut into wedges
1 medium avocado, peeled and sliced
4 slices bacon, cooked and crumbled
½ cup (2 ounces) shredded mozzarella
    cheese
Dressing (recipe follows)

Place spinach on a large serving platter or individual plates; arrange eggs, onions, tomatoes, and avocado on top. Sprinkle with bacon and cheese. Serve with dressing. Yield: 6 to 8 servings.

Dressing:
½ cup catsup
¼ cup vegetable oil
¼ cup wine vinegar
1 teaspoon Worcestershire sauce
½ teaspoon lemon juice
⅛ teaspoon garlic powder
Dash of hot sauce

Combine all ingredients in a jar; cover tightly, and shake vigorously. Yield: 1 cup.   *Sonya Smith,*
Daphne, Alabama.

Right: *You might not expect to cook (front to back) Teriyaki Lamb Chops, Tournedos Diables, or Smoky Oysters Supreme outdoors, but the grilled flavor makes them extra special. (Recipes begin on page 60.)*

Page 66: *Omelet Primavera (page 71) makes a tasty low-cholesterol alternative for brunch.*

Page 66 inset: *Yeast Biscuits (page 71) as smooth as rolls and Banana Bread (page 72) with a hint of wheat germ offer flavor variety and virtually no cholesterol.*

Above: *Pop the cork on the champagne, and serve cheese for dessert: (top to bottom) Whipped cream cheese, St. André (triple crème), and Brie. (See page 46 for information on cheese and tips for a successful cheese party.)*

Left: *These crackers and flatbreads rival those from the box: (from front) Fennel-Rye Crackers, Sesame Cracker Bread, and Dessert Crackers (Recipes begin on page 2.)*

BREAKFASTS&BRUNCHES®

Can't Wait For Breakfast!

In this ninth annual "Breakfasts and Brunches" special section, we'll show you how to make planning a brunch a breeze. And we'll share how Sherrel and Stephen Jones of Enid, Oklahoma, celebrate the arrival of spring with a morning party in their garden.

There are ideas for quiches and tarts using plenty of eggs. And there's a "Cooking Light" article that uses no eggs at all so that cholesterol is kept to a minimum. To help you make your table as attractive as it can be, we'll give you suggestions for colorful and decorative fruit arrangements.

A Garden Brunch

Sherrel Jones's menu offers a choice of breads for everyone. The large braided loaf of County Fair Egg Bread is served with orange-honey butter and sand plum jelly, a local specialty. Cinnamon-Pecan Coffee Cake poses no problem for a morning party because the yeast dough is shaped and then rises in the refrigerator overnight. Lemon-Raisin Scones are best made the day they are to be eaten.

Sherrel's culinary creativity doesn't stop with breads. The menu includes a grilled chicken recipe, as well as several delectable vegetables. A special dessert tops off the brunch.

Oklahoma Sunrise
Spinach Quichelets
Chicken Bundles With Bacon Ribbons
Asparagus in Squash Rings
Ginger-Glazed Carrots
County Fair Egg Bread
Cinnamon-Pecan Coffee Cake
Lemon-Raisin Scones
Poached Pears With Raspberry Sauce
Praline-Flavored Coffee

OKLAHOMA SUNRISE

1 (12-ounce) can frozen orange juice concentrate, thawed and undiluted
1 (12-ounce) can apricot nectar, chilled
1½ pints commercial strawberry sorbet, softened
3 cups water
1 (25.4-ounce) bottle champagne, chilled
3 cups crushed ice
Whole strawberries (optional)

Combine orange juice concentrate, apricot nectar, sorbet, and water in a large container; stir until blended. Chill. To serve, pour mixture into a punch bowl; add champagne and ice, and stir gently to blend. Serve in stemmed glasses, and garnish with strawberries, if desired. Yield: 1 gallon.

SPINACH QUICHELETS

1 (10-ounce) package fresh spinach
3 tablespoons butter or margarine, melted
2 eggs
1 egg yolk
1 tablespoon all-purpose flour
2 (0.6-ounce) envelopes cream of chicken-flavored soup mix
1 (5-ounce) can evaporated milk
½ cup (2 ounces) shredded Swiss cheese
Processor Pastry
Pimiento strips

Wash spinach, and remove stems; pat dry with paper towels. Set aside 2½ cups firmly packed spinach. (Reserve any remaining spinach for other uses.) Sauté spinach in butter in a large skillet until spinach begins to wilt; cover and cook spinach 1 minute (do not overcook); set aside.

Combine eggs, egg yolk, flour, soup mix, and milk in container of an electric blender; process until smooth. Add cheese and spinach; process just until spinach is chopped (do not puree). Pour mixture into unbaked Processor Pastry shells, filling three-fourths full. Bake at 375° for 18 to 20 minutes. Garnish with pimiento strips. Yield: 3 dozen.

Processor Pastry:

1¾ cups all-purpose flour
¾ teaspoon salt
½ cup plus 2 tablespoons butter or margarine, chilled
2 tablespoons butter-flavored shortening, chilled
¼ cup plus 2 tablespoons ice water

Position knife blade in food processor bowl; add flour and salt. Cover and process, pulsing 3 or 4 times, until combined. Cut butter into 1-inch pieces; add butter and shortening to flour mixture. Process, pulsing 5 or 6 times, or until mixture resembles coarse meal. With processor running, slowly add water, one teaspoon at a time, until dough forms a ball leaving sides of processor bowl. Cover and chill 30 minutes. Divide dough into 36 balls; shape in ungreased miniature muffin pans. Yield: 3 dozen.

Tip: Every time the door is opened to the oven, the temperature drops 25 to 30 degrees. Use the oven window so as not to waste energy.

CHICKEN BUNDLES WITH BACON RIBBONS

12 whole chicken breasts, skinned and boned
1 cup molasses
½ teaspoon ground ginger
¼ teaspoon garlic powder
2 tablespoons Worcestershire sauce
¼ cup soy sauce
¼ cup olive oil
¼ cup lemon juice
2 pounds mushrooms, sliced and divided
20 green onions, sliced and divided
½ cup butter, melted and divided
½ to 1 teaspoon spike seasoning, divided
24 slices bacon

Place chicken between two sheets of heavy-duty plastic wrap; pound to ¼-inch thickness, using a meat mallet or rolling pin. Place chicken in a large shallow container, and set aside.

Combine molasses, ginger, garlic powder, Worcestershire sauce, soy sauce, oil, and lemon juice; stir well. Pour mixture over chicken breasts, and marinate 8 hours in refrigerator.

Sauté half each of mushrooms and green onions in ¼ cup butter, stirring constantly until liquid has evaporated; add half of spike seasoning; stir well. Repeat process with remaining mushrooms, green onions, butter, and spike seasoning.

For each chicken bundle, lay 2 slices bacon in a crosswise pattern on a flat surface. Place a chicken breast in center of bacon. Top each with 3 tablespoons mushroom mixture. Fold over sides and ends of chicken to make a square-shaped pouch. Pull bacon around, and tie ends under securely.

Grill chicken over low coals 45 to 55 minutes or until done, turning and basting with remaining marinade every 15 minutes. Yield: 12 servings.

Note: Spike seasoning may be purchased from health food stores.

Tip: Remember that the darker the orange color of carrots, the greater the content of vitamin A.

ASPARAGUS IN SQUASH RINGS

3 pounds fresh asparagus spears
4 to 5 small yellow squash, cut into ½-inch-thick slices
½ cup butter or margarine
¼ cup lemon juice
1 teaspoon fines herbes

Snap off tough ends of asparagus. Remove scales from stalks with a knife or vegetable peeler, if desired. Cook asparagus, covered, in boiling water 6 to 8 minutes or until crisp-tender; drain.

Place squash in a vegetable steamer over boiling water. Cover and steam 3 minutes or until tender. Remove centers of squash slices, leaving ¼-inch flesh with skin.

Insert 3 to 4 asparagus spears in center of each squash ring; place on a serving platter, and set aside.

Combine remaining ingredients in a saucepan; heat until butter melts. Pour over asparagus. Yield: 12 servings.

GINGER-GLAZED CARROTS

3 pounds carrots, scraped and sliced
¾ cup minced onion
1 teaspoon ground ginger
¼ cup butter or margarine, melted
¼ cup firmly packed brown sugar
¼ cup honey
¼ cup frozen orange juice concentrate, thawed and undiluted
¼ cup orange-flavored liqueur
1 to 2 teaspoons minced fresh thyme or ¼ to ½ teaspoon dried whole thyme
Fresh thyme sprig (optional)

Place carrots in a vegetable steamer over boiling water. Cover and steam 8 to 10 minutes or until crisp-tender. Spoon into serving dish; set aside.

Sauté onion and ginger in butter in a heavy saucepan until onion is tender. Add remaining ingredients except fresh thyme sprig, and cook until mixture is bubbly and thickened. Pour ginger mixture over carrots, tossing gently to coat. Garnish with fresh thyme sprig, if desired. Yield: 12 servings.

COUNTY FAIR EGG BREAD

1 package dry yeast
¼ cup warm water (105° to 115°)
¼ cup sugar
¼ cup shortening
2 teaspoons salt
1 cup milk, scalded
¼ cup water
2 eggs, beaten
4 to 5 cups all-purpose flour, divided
Butter or margarine, melted

Dissolve yeast in warm water. Combine sugar, shortening, salt, and milk in a large bowl; stir until shortening melts. Add water; let mixture cool.

Add yeast mixture, eggs, and 2 cups flour; beat at low speed of an electric mixer until mixture is smooth. Stir in enough of the remaining flour to make a soft dough.

Place dough in a greased bowl, turning to grease top. Cover and let rise in a warm place (85°), free from drafts, 1½ hours or until doubled in bulk. Punch dough down; cover and let rise in a warm place (85°), free from drafts, 30 minutes.

Divide dough into thirds. Shape each third into a 12- to 14-inch rope. Place ropes on a greased baking sheet (do not stretch); pinch ropes together at one end to seal. Braid ropes; pinch ends to seal. Tuck ends under, and spread braids apart in center to form an oval shape. Cover and let rise 45 minutes or until doubled in bulk.

Bake at 375° for 20 to 25 minutes or until golden; brush bread with butter. Yield: 1 loaf.

CINNAMON-PECAN COFFEE CAKE

2 packages dry yeast
2½ cups water (105° to 115°)
¾ cup sugar
¾ cup vegetable oil
2 eggs
2½ teaspoons salt
7½ cups all-purpose flour, divided
2 cups sugar
2 tablespoons ground cinnamon
1 cup butter, melted
2 cups chopped pecans
Topping Glaze

Dissolve yeast in warm water; set mixture aside.

Combine sugar, oil, eggs, salt, and yeast mixture in a large mixing bowl. Beat at medium speed of an electric mixer 1 minute. Add 4 cups flour, beating at low speed, scraping bowl occasionally, until mixture is smooth and elastic. Stir in remaining 3½ cups flour to make a soft dough.

Place dough in a greased bowl, turning to grease top. Cover and let rise in a warm place (85°), free from drafts, 1 hour or until doubled in bulk.

Combine sugar and cinnamon in a small bowl; set aside.

Punch dough down; shape into 1-inch balls. Dip balls in melted butter, then in cinnamon mixture. Layer half of balls in a well-greased 10-inch Bundt pan, sprinkling with pecans after each layer. Repeat procedure with balls, butter, cinnamon mixture, and pecans in another well-greased 10-inch Bundt pan. Cover both Bundt pans, and chill dough 8 hours.

Pour Topping Glaze over dough. Bake at 325° for 40 minutes. Invert both cakes onto a large serving platter; drizzle with glaze formed in pan. Yield: 2 (10-inch) coffee cakes.

Topping Glaze:

1 cup whipping cream
1 cup firmly packed brown sugar
2 teaspoons ground cinnamon

Beat whipping cream until consistency of a thick milk shake; stir in brown sugar and cinnamon. Yield: glaze for 2 (10-inch) coffee cakes.

LEMON-RAISIN SCONES

4½ cups biscuit mix
¼ cup firmly packed brown sugar
1 cup golden raisins
1 tablespoon grated lemon rind
1 egg, beaten
1 cup milk
1 egg white
1 teaspoon water
Raw sugar

Combine biscuit mix and brown sugar, stirring well. Stir in raisins and lemon rind.

Combine egg and milk; add to flour mixture, stirring until dry ingredients are moistened. Turn dough out onto a lightly floured surface. Pat dough to ½-inch thickness; cut with a 2½-inch biscuit cutter. Place scones on a greased baking sheet.

Combine egg white and water; brush tops of scones. Sprinkle with raw sugar.

Bake at 400° for 10 to 12 minutes or until golden. Yield: About 2 dozen.

POACHED PEARS WITH RASPBERRY SAUCE

2 cups water
⅓ cup lemon juice
12 medium-size firm, ripe pears
2 cups Chablis or other dry white wine
4 cups apple cider
Chocolate Truffle Filling
Raspberry Sauce

Combine 2 cups water and ⅓ cup lemon juice; set the mixture aside.

Peel pears, removing core from bottom end and leaving stems intact. Scoop a slightly larger area from bottom end of pear cavity using a small melon baller. Cut a thin slice from bottoms so pears stand upright. Dip pears in lemon water, coating well.

Combine wine and apple cider in a large Dutch oven; bring to a boil. Add pears, standing upright; cover, reduce heat, and simmer 15 to 20 minutes or until pears are tender but still hold their shape. Let pears cool in cooking liquid. Fill cavity with Chocolate Truffle Filling. Chill. Serve with Raspberry Sauce. Yield: 12 servings.

Chocolate Truffle Filling:

1 (6-ounce) package semisweet chocolate morsels, melted
½ (8-ounce) package cream cheese, softened
1 teaspoon vanilla extract

Combine all ingredients in a small bowl; stir until smooth. Pipe filling into cavity of pears using a pastry bag fitted with a No. 4 tip. Yield: 1 cup.

Raspberry Sauce:

2 (10-ounce) packages frozen raspberries in heavy syrup, thawed
⅔ cup rosé wine
⅓ cup raspberry Schnapps or other raspberry-flavored liqueur

Place raspberries in container of an electric blender; process until smooth. Strain mixture; discard seeds. Add wine and liqueur; stir well. Chill. Yield: about 3 cups.

PRALINE-FLAVORED COFFEE

2 cups coffee beans, divided (or 1¾ cups plus 2 tablespoons ground coffee)
⅔ cup chopped pecans
15 cups cold water
1 cup praline-flavored liqueur
Half-and-half (optional)
Sugar (optional)

Combine ½ cup coffee beans and pecans in a shallow pan. Bake at 350° for 12 minutes. Cool. Combine baked mixture and remaining 1½ cups coffee beans; place in coffee grinder or food processor, and grind to desired coarseness. (If the grinder is small, procedure may need to be repeated.)

Pour water and liqueur into percolator or coffee pot. Place pecan mixture in basket. Cover and follow manufacturer's directions. Serve coffee with half-and-half and sugar, if desired. Yield: 16 cups.

Make The Entrée A Quiche Or Tart

Quiche and main-dish tarts have become popular brunch items. We've included three interesting recipes for you to choose from.

If you like seafood, Shrimp Tart is sure to be a favorite. It also contains Cheddar cheese, green onions, and the surprising crunch of chopped pecans.

Tart Milan is time consuming to make, but we thought it was outstanding in terms of both taste and eye appeal. After taking the dish from the oven, be sure to wait at least 10 minutes before cutting it so that the wedges will hold their shape.

Crustless Sausage-Apple Quiche contains some of the same ingredients as apple pie. It's an unusual combination that also includes cheese, cinnamon, and nutmeg. Biscuit mix makes it quick to prepare.

SHRIMP TART

Pastry for 11-inch pie
4 cups water
1¼ pounds fresh unpeeled shrimp
1½ cups (6 ounces) shredded Cheddar cheese
⅓ cup sliced green onions
4 eggs, beaten
1½ cups half-and-half
½ teaspoon salt
¼ teaspoon paprika
⅛ teaspoon red pepper
½ cup coarsely chopped pecans
Onion fan

Line an 11-inch tart pan or quiche dish with pastry; trim off excess pastry around edges. Prick bottom and sides of pastry with a fork. Bake at 400° for 3 minutes; remove from oven, and gently prick with a fork. Bake an additional 5 minutes. Cool.

Bring water to a boil; add shrimp, and cook 3 to 5 minutes. Drain well; rinse with cold water. Chill. Peel and devein shrimp; set aside 8 shrimp for garnish. Chop remaining shrimp. Layer chopped shrimp, cheese, and green onions in tart pan.

Combine eggs, half-and-half, salt, paprika, red pepper, and pecans in a small bowl; pour over shrimp mixture. Bake at 325° for 50 minutes or until set. Garnish with reserved shrimp and onion fan. Yield: one 11-inch tart.

Janet M. Filer,
Arlington, Virginia.

TART MILAN

1 pound fresh spinach
1 large sweet red pepper, chopped
2 cloves garlic, minced
1 tablespoon butter or margarine, melted
1 tablespoon vegetable oil
¼ to ½ teaspoon ground nutmeg
⅛ teaspoon salt
Pinch of pepper
1 (1-pound) package commercial puff pastry, divided
9 eggs
1 tablespoon chopped fresh chives
1 tablespoon chopped fresh parsley
¾ teaspoon dried whole tarragon
¼ teaspoon salt
2 tablespoons plus 2 teaspoons butter or margarine, divided
3 cups (12 ounces) shredded Swiss cheese, divided
12 ounces thinly sliced ham, divided
1 egg, beaten
Fresh parsley sprigs

Remove stems from spinach; wash leaves thoroughly in lukewarm water. Drain and set aside.

Sauté red pepper and garlic in butter and oil in a Dutch oven; remove red pepper and garlic, reserving drippings in pan. Add spinach, nutmeg, ⅛ teaspoon salt, and pepper, stirring gently. Cover and cook over high heat 3 to 5 minutes. Drain and press between paper towels.

Line a greased 8-inch springform pan with 1 sheet of puff pastry, leaving a ½-inch overhang; set aside. Cut remaining sheet of puff pastry into a 9-inch circle; cover with a damp cloth, and set pastry aside.

Combine 9 eggs, chives, parsley, tarragon, and ¼ teaspoon salt; beat well. Heat an 8-inch omelet pan or heavy skillet until it is hot enough to sizzle a drop of water. Add 2 teaspoons butter; tilt pan to coat bottom. Pour about one-fourth of egg mixture into pan. As mixture starts to cook, gently lift edges of omelet with a spatula, and tilt pan so uncooked portion flows underneath. Cook until eggs are set and top is still moist and creamy. Loosen omelet with spatula; transfer to pastry-lined pan. Repeat procedure for second, third, and fourth omelet, transferring omelets to wax paper. Set aside.

Layer one-third of spinach, ½ cup cheese, one-third of ham, ½ cup cheese, and one-third red pepper over omelet in pan. Top with second omelet and the same amount of layered ingredients. Repeat with third omelet and remaining layered ingredients; end with fourth omelet.

Top with pastry circle; seal well, crimping edges, if desired. Make indentations in pastry with a knife, dividing pie into 6 or 8 portions; brush with beaten egg. Place springform pan in a shallow baking pan. Position oven rack in lower third of oven; bake at 350° for 60 to 65 minutes. Remove from oven; let stand at least 10 minutes before serving. Remove from pan, and place on platter. Garnish with parsley. Yield: 6 to 8 servings.

Jane King Moore,
Norfolk, Virginia.

CRUSTLESS SAUSAGE-APPLE QUICHE

½ pound bulk pork sausage
1½ cups finely chopped apple
½ teaspoon ground cinnamon
½ teaspoon ground nutmeg
1 cup (4 ounces) shredded sharp Cheddar cheese
4 eggs, beaten
1 cup half-and-half
½ cup biscuit mix

Cook sausage until browned, stirring to crumble; drain well. Set aside.

Combine apple, spices, cheese, and sausage. Spoon into a 9-inch quiche dish or deep-dish pieplate.

Combine eggs, half-and-half, and biscuit mix in a mixing bowl; mix well. Pour over apple mixture. Bake at 375° for 40 minutes or until set. Yield: one 9-inch quiche. *Ruth Sherrer, Fort Worth, Texas.*

COOKING LIGHT®

Cholesterol Is Low In These Dishes

If reducing dietary cholesterol is a concern, use our low-cholesterol recipes to add variety to the morning menu.

Dietary cholesterol comes from animal foods only; no plant foods contain the compound. Let this be your guide to determine whether or not a food has cholesterol in it. Egg yolks and organ meats (such as liver and kidney) are particularly rich in this substance. And while scientists have designated an elevated blood-cholesterol level as a risk factor for heart disease, the compound is not totally bad. In fact, our bodies manufacture cholesterol because it's an essential part of cell membranes. It's also required to form bile acids, which help in the digestion and absorption of fats in the diet. However, it's prudent to become more aware of the amount and sources of the dietary cholesterol you consume. A reduction to 300 milligrams a day has been recommended by some groups.

To help in lessening dietary cholesterol in your diet, try Omelet Primavera using an egg substitute. Nestled inside the omelet are carrots, zucchini, and herbs. When selecting an egg substitute, read the label. Some brands have almost twice as much sodium as a large egg; others have less than two-thirds the calories of a large egg.

Fill the breakfast bread basket with Yeast Biscuits and Banana Bread. Each uses nonfat buttermilk and vegetable oil to keep the cholesterol content low. The biscuit recipe yields 4½ dozen, so you can make some now and save the extra dough for later. It keeps well in the refrigerator up to 7 days.

OMELET PRIMAVERA
(pictured on page 66)

¼ cup julienne-cut carrots
¼ cup julienne-cut zucchini
1½ teaspoons chopped fresh chives
1½ teaspoons fresh dillweed
3 tablespoons part-skim ricotta cheese
½ cup egg substitute
2 teaspoons water
⅛ teaspoon salt
Vegetable cooking spray
Steamed julienne-cut carrots (optional)
Steamed julienne-cut zucchini (optional)

Place carrots and zucchini in a vegetable steamer over boiling water; steam 2 to 3 minutes. Drain well. Combine carrot mixture, chives, dillweed, and ricotta cheese; stir well, and set aside. Combine egg substitute, water, and salt in a small bowl, and stir well.

Coat a 6-inch skillet with cooking spray; place over medium heat until hot enough to sizzle a drop of water.

Pour egg mixture into pan. As mixture starts to cook, gently lift edges of omelet with a spatula, and tilt pan so uncooked portion flows underneath.

When egg mixture is almost set, spoon vegetable mixture over half of omelet; continue cooking until eggs are set.

Loosen omelet with a spatula, and fold in half. Slide omelet onto a plate. Garnish with steamed carrots and zucchini, if desired. Yield: 1 serving.

☐ *150 calories, 18.1 grams protein, 4.6 grams fat, 8.4 grams carbohydrate, 14 milligrams cholesterol, 555 milligrams sodium, and 190 milligrams calcium per omelet.* *Marian J. Brown, Lynchburg, Virginia.*

YEAST BISCUITS
(pictured on page 66)

1 package dry yeast
1 cup warm water (105°-115°)
7 cups all-purpose flour
2 teaspoons baking powder
¼ teaspoon baking soda
½ teaspoon salt
2 cups nonfat buttermilk
¾ cup vegetable oil
¼ cup sugar
Vegetable cooking spray

Dissolve yeast in warm water; let stand 5 minutes. Combine flour and next 3 ingredients; set aside. Combine buttermilk, oil, and sugar in a large bowl; add yeast mixture and 2 cups flour mixture. Beat at low speed of an electric mixer until smooth. Add remaining 5 cups flour mixture; stir until well blended. Cover and chill 8 hours.

Turn dough out onto a lightly floured surface; roll to ½-inch thickness, and cut with a 2-inch cutter. Place on ungreased baking sheets. Bake at 400° for 15 to 18 minutes or until lightly browned. Remove from baking sheets; spray biscuits lightly with cooking spray. Yield: 4½ dozen.

☐ *89 calories, 1.9 grams protein, 3.3 grams fat, 12.8 grams carbohydrate, 0 milligrams cholesterol, 47 milligrams sodium, and 21 milligrams calcium per biscuit.*
Note: Dough may be kept in refrigerator for 7 days. *Judi Grigoraci, Charleston, West Virginia.*

BANANA BREAD

(pictured on page 66)

1½ cups all-purpose flour
2 teaspoons baking powder
½ teaspoon baking soda
⅛ teaspoon salt
½ cup wheat germ
⅓ cup firmly packed brown sugar
¼ teaspoon ground cinnamon
¼ teaspoon ground cardamom
½ cup egg substitute
¼ cup nonfat buttermilk
¼ cup vegetable oil
1 cup mashed, very ripe banana
Vegetable cooking spray

Combine flour, baking powder, soda, salt, wheat germ, brown sugar, cinnamon, and cardamom in a medium mixing bowl; set aside.

Combine egg substitute, buttermilk, and oil in a large bowl; stir well. Stir in mashed banana. Add flour mixture, stirring just until moistened.

Pour batter into an 8½- x 4½- x 3-inch loafpan coated with cooking spray. Bake at 350° for 45 minutes or until a wooden pick inserted in center comes out clean. Cool in pan 10 minutes; remove from pan, and cool completely on a wire rack. Yield: 16 servings.

☐ *116 calories, 3.2 grams protein, 4.1 grams fat, 17.7 grams carbohydrate, 0 milligrams cholesterol, 99.4 milligrams sodium, and 45.3 milligrams calcium per ½-inch slice.* Lana Coan, *Plantation, Florida.*

PEAR BREAKFAST TREAT

1 medium pear, peeled, cored, and thinly sliced
¼ teaspoon lime or lemon juice
1 tablespoon plus 1 teaspoon brown sugar
¼ teaspoon pumpkin pie spice
¼ cup egg substitute
1 tablespoon plus 1 teaspoon skim milk
1 tablespoon reduced-calorie margarine, melted
1 teaspoon vanilla extract
¾ cup 40% bran flakes cereal
Vegetable cooking spray

Combine sliced pear and lime juice in a bowl; toss gently to coat. Set aside.

Combine brown sugar, pumpkin pie spice, egg substitute, milk, margarine, and vanilla; stir well. Add pear and bran flakes; stir well.

Spoon mixture into an 8-inch piepan coated with cooking spray. Bake at 350° for 30 to 35 minutes. Cool slightly before serving. Yield: 2 servings.

☐ *175 calories, 5.6 grams protein, 3.9 grams fat, 31.7 grams carbohydrate, 0 milligrams cholesterol, 258 milligrams sodium, and 47 milligrams calcium per serving.* Rhunella Johnson, *Bay Springs, Mississippi.*

Toast the Morning

Whether your favorite beverage is cranapple juice, lemonade, or orange juice, you'll find something here to celebrate the morning. Magnolia Blossoms combines orange juice, Chablis, and Triple Sec for a simple, tasty drink. Cranapple-Vodka Punch brings a deep burgundy hue to your table. The cranapple juice is mixed with cinnamon, cloves, ginger ale, and vodka.

CRANAPPLE-VODKA PUNCH

4 (3-inch) cinnamon sticks
1 teaspoon whole cloves
1 gallon cranapple juice
1 (33.8-ounce) bottle ginger ale, chilled
2 cups vodka

Combine cinnamon sticks and cloves in a piece of cheesecloth; tie tightly. Combine cranapple juice and spices in a Dutch oven. Heat to boiling; cover, reduce heat, and simmer 10 minutes. Let cool. Remove spice bag.

Pour cranapple juice into a punch bowl. Add ginger ale and vodka, stirring well. Serve over ice. Yield: 5½ quarts. Kristie Gareis, *Charles Town, West Virginia.*

MAGNOLIA BLOSSOMS

1 (6-ounce) can frozen orange juice concentrate, thawed and undiluted
3 cups Chablis
1½ cups water
½ cup Triple Sec
Orange slices (optional)

Combine all ingredients except orange slices; mix well. Serve over ice. Garnish with orange slices, if desired. Yield: 6 cups. Betty Joyce Mills, *Birmingham, Alabama.*

BRANDY SLUSH PUNCH

1 (6-ounce) can frozen orange juice concentrate, thawed and undiluted
1 (6-ounce) can frozen lemonade concentrate, thawed and undiluted
1 quart plus ½ cup water
1 cup apricot brandy
¾ cup sugar
1 quart lemon-lime carbonated beverage, divided

Combine all ingredients except lemon-lime beverage; stir until sugar dissolves. Freeze 24 hours. Spoon 3 cups frozen mixture into container of an electric blender; add 2 cups lemon-lime beverage. Blend 20 seconds on high speed; pour into serving glasses. Repeat procedure with remaining frozen mixture and lemon-lime beverage. Serve immediately. Yield: 2½ quarts.
Peggy Fowler Revels, *Woodruff, South Carolina.*

Plan A Great Brunch

Brunches are popular ways to dine. It seems everyone has a fondness for relaxing and letting breakfast run over into lunch. It's a good time for friends to gather, and brunch can extend naturally into other activities, such as going to a matinee, a sporting event, or even on a shopping spree.

Most hostesses enjoy giving brunches. They agree that brunch is more relaxed than a formal dinner, and guests find morning a good time to attend a party. Brunch usually takes place between 10 a.m. and 1 p.m., so there's time to tend to last-minute details before guests arrive. And the afternoon can be spent cleaning up.

Brunch menus allow for lots of flexibility. This is the ideal time to be creative and add a surprise or two to the menu. You might consider serving anything from eggs to seafood.

The secret to a successful brunch is planning ahead. By doing as much in advance as possible, you will have more time to have fun with your guests. Here are some tips to make it all run smoothly.

■ Decide what type of brunch you are going to have. Consider the occasion and your resources, such as space, time, budget, and talents.
■ Select a theme, if desired. Sometimes this helps when you're planning the menu and decorations.
■ Plan the menu well in advance, and carefully select the wine, champagne, or other beverages.
■ Use recipes you have prepared before that can be assembled ahead of time.
■ Make a list of all jobs and errands that need to be done—clean house, polish silver, set table, shop, and cook—and delegate what you can.
■ Record plans in a notebook or file for future use. This way, when you entertain the same people again, you won't repeat the menu or theme.

Fruit Instead Of Flowers

When we gather with our friends and families, there's usually an abundance of warmth, laughter, and tempting food. And in making our homes a welcoming place, quite often the preparations include an arrangement, especially one made from fresh materials. Flowers and foliage are the most commonly used materials, and often they come right from our garden or the neighbor's. You can take the idea a step further by using fresh fruit. It can be made into a distinctive creation—whether it's to be used in a country kitchen or an elegant dining room.

The shape, color, and aroma of fruit are guaranteed to do more than attract the senses. Admirers are likely to inspect your arrangement, trying to identify each element and probing to figure out how it is constructed. How did you stack the apples? Why don't they roll? What is that frozen fuzzy fruit?

Naomi Thomason, a floral designer in Birmingham, suggests fruit as a very cost-effective decoration. She explains, "If you don't want to spend a lot of money on flowers, you can buy a sack of small apples and a few other items to arrange—and then you could eat them the next day!" She adds, "You'll find all kinds of interesting things to put fruit in that you'd never use for flowers. It can be just a bowl or a sieve from the kitchen."

As you put arrangements together, it is important that you anchor the fruit in place. To keep it from shifting, use rounded wooden toothpicks. First, determine the angle at which you want to place the fruit, and then place a wooden pick into the back side so that half the pick protrudes. Use it to anchor the fruit into other pieces of the arrangement. When working with a bowl, you can use a large, heavy item as an anchor in the bottom; grapefruit is a perfect example. Use long florist picks or a hyacinth stick to elevate pieces of fruit.

Here, we present two examples—each made with an assortment of fruit. Use these suggestions as a springboard for ideas. Then use your ingenuity to make your own arrangements with available containers and fruit from the garden or local market.

An Irish potato ring forms a base for pineapple, pears, limes, figs, and unusual fruit such as pomegranates and prickly pears. Two bunches of grapes balance the design, and begonia foliage fills spaces.

Fruit may also be used with flowers and foliage. A shallow basket of apples, pears, grapes, lemons, and limes accents a tall arrangement of fresh branches combined with silk flowers.

Let's Have Lunch!

Invite the ladies to lunch, and greet them with Sherry Sour, a sweet and tangy, slushy lemonade with a kick. Then head to the dining room, garden room, or patio. Use your finest china for a fancy luncheon, or keep it simple on the patio by setting out your casual tableware.

Sherry Sour
Chutney-Chicken Salad
Marinated Asparagus
Easy Whole Wheat Rolls
Chocolate Charlotte Russe

SHERRY SOUR

1 (25.4-ounce) bottle cream sherry
Juice of 1 lemon
1 (6-ounce) can frozen lemonade
    concentrate, undiluted
Ice cubes

Combine half each of sherry, lemon juice, and lemonade concentrate in container of an electric blender; add ice cubes to bring up to 3-cup mark. Process until smooth. Repeat with remaining ingredients. Yield: 5 cups.

Sara Cairns,
Montevallo, Alabama.

CHUTNEY-CHICKEN SALAD

4½ cups chopped cooked chicken
¾ cup mayonnaise
½ cup commercial chutney
1½ teaspoons curry powder
¼ teaspoon salt
1 tablespoon lime juice
1½ cups sliced almonds, toasted
Lettuce leaves
Apple slices (optional)

Combine chicken, mayonnaise, chutney, curry, salt, and lime juice in a large bowl; toss to mix. Cover and let chill thoroughly.

Stir in toasted almonds before serving. Serve salad on lettuce leaves. Garnish salad with apple slices, if desired. Yield: 4½ cups.

Jeanne S. Hotaling,
Augusta, Georgia.

MARINATED ASPARAGUS

2 pounds fresh asparagus spears
½ cup vegetable oil
¼ cup white wine vinegar
¼ cup lemon juice
¼ cup chopped green onion
2 tablespoons chopped parsley
½ teaspoon sugar
½ teaspoon dry mustard
¼ teaspoon salt
⅛ teaspoon freshly ground pepper

Snap off tough ends of asparagus. Remove scales from stalks with a knife or vegetable peeler, if desired. Cover asparagus, and cook in a small amount of water 6 to 8 minutes or until asparagus is crisp-tender; drain.

Combine remaining ingredients in a jar; cover tightly, and shake vigorously. Place asparagus in a shallow container; pour marinade over asparagus. Cover and chill 8 hours. To serve, drain off marinade. Yield: 8 servings.

Norval Springfield,
Birmingham, Alabama.

EASY WHOLE WHEAT ROLLS

½ cup shortening
¼ cup butter or margarine
½ cup water
1 package dry yeast
¼ cup warm water (105° to 115°)
1 egg, beaten
½ cup cold water
½ cup sugar
2½ cups self-rising flour
1½ cups whole wheat flour
½ teaspoon salt
2 tablespoons butter or margarine,
    melted

Combine shortening, butter, and ½ cup water in a saucepan; cook over low heat until shortening and butter melt. Cool to lukewarm.

Dissolve yeast in ¼ cup warm water in a large bowl; let stand 5 minutes. Add egg, ½ cup cold water, sugar, and butter mixture; mix well.

Combine flours and salt. Gradually stir into yeast mixture; mix well. Place dough in a well-greased bowl, turning to grease top. Cover and refrigerate mixture at least 8 hours.

Remove dough from refrigerator; turn out onto a lightly floured surface. Knead until smooth and elastic (about 2 minutes). Roll dough to ¼-inch thickness on a lightly floured surface; cut into 3-inch circles.

Make a crease across each circle, and fold one half over; gently press edges to seal. Place 2 inches apart on greased baking sheets. Brush with melted butter; cover. Let rise in a warm place (85°), free from drafts, 1 hour or until doubled in bulk. Bake at 450° for 8 to 10 minutes. Yield: 2½ dozen.

Barbara Ruth,
Kingsport, Tennessee.

CHOCOLATE CHARLOTTE RUSSE

1 envelope unflavored gelatin
2 tablespoons cold water
3 (1-ounce) squares unsweetened
    chocolate
½ cup water
4 eggs, separated
¾ cup sugar, divided
1 teaspoon vanilla extract
Dash of salt
½ teaspoon cream of tartar
1 cup whipping cream, whipped
1 cup chopped pecans, divided
24 ladyfingers, split
Additional whipped cream for garnish
Chocolate leaves (optional)

Soften gelatin in 2 tablespoons cold water, and let stand 5 minutes.

Combine chocolate and ½ cup water in top of a double boiler; bring to a boil. Reduce heat to low; cook until the chocolate melts. Remove from heat; add the softened gelatin, and mix thoroughly. Set aside.

Beat egg yolks at medium speed of an electric mixer until thick and lemon colored; gradually add ½ cup sugar. Add vanilla and salt. Gradually add chocolate mixture, and mix well.

Beat egg whites (at room temperature) and ½ teaspoon cream of tartar at high speed of an electric mixer 1 minute. Gradually add remaining ¼ cup sugar, 1 tablespoon at a time, beating until stiff peaks form. Fold egg white mixture, 2 cups whipped cream, and ¾ cup plus 2 tablespoons chopped pecans into chocolate mixture.

Line bottom and sides of a 9-inch springform pan with ladyfingers, reserving 10 ladyfinger halves for center layer. Spoon half of chocolate mixture into pan. Layer reserved ladyfingers; spoon remaining chocolate mixture over ladyfingers. Cover and chill 8 hours or until dessert is firm.

Place dessert on a serving platter, and remove rim from pan. Garnish with additional whipped cream, remaining 2 tablespoons pecans, and if desired, chocolate leaves. Yield: 10 to 12 servings.

Donna Taylor,
Eads, Tennessee.

COOKING LIGHT®

Low-Calorie Desserts With High Appeal

Rich, luscious, and creamy aren't words that usually come to mind when someone talks about low-calorie desserts. But we think these recipes may just change your thoughts. Each is less than 200 calories per serving—quite a contrast to regular desserts that can contain several hundred calories.

This is the season for plump, fresh strawberries, and what better way to use them than in White Cake With Strawberries and Chocolate Glaze or in Strawberry-Lemon Cream Puffs. The cake recipe, which you'll find on the next page, uses cake flour, giving it a tender texture and allowing less fat and sugar to be used. The cholesterol conscious will be glad to know there's no cholesterol in this recipe. Egg whites are used instead of whole eggs, and vegetable oil, a polyunsaturated fat, has been substituted for shortening, a saturated fat. Melted semisweet chocolate morsels serve as a quick glaze for the decorative strawberry topping.

Our recipe for Dainty Strawberry-Lemon Cream Puffs makes a great dessert idea for a light luncheon or bridal shower. Lemon low-fat yogurt and sliced strawberries are the basis for the tasty filling, and a serving of two filled cream puffs is only 169 calories.

Canned peaches and frozen raspberries are used for Peach Melba Meringues, so you can make this dessert any time of the year. (The recipe is on the next page.) Home-baked meringues give the dessert an elegant look. But if you don't have time to make the meringues, try spooning ⅓-cup portions of vanilla ice milk over the cut side of the peach half, and top with the Melba Sauce and almonds. Regardless of which you choose, either option is about the same number of calories, 140 per serving.

Blueberry Chiffon Cheesecake is as light as a cloud in texture but very rich tasting. Skim milk, light cream cheese, part-skim ricotta cheese, and plain low-fat yogurt help keep the calorie count much lower than in a regular cheesecake. We thickened the blueberry glaze with cornstarch instead of flour to keep the mixture translucent. And it saves calories since you need to use only half as much cornstarch as flour for the same thickening effect. (The recipe for this dessert is on the following page.)

You'll find fresh, frozen, and canned fruits are used in these enticing low-calorie desserts: (front to back) Strawberry-Lemon Cream Puffs, Blueberry Chiffon Cheesecake, Peach Melba Meringues, and White Cake With Strawberries and Chocolate Glaze.

STRAWBERRY-LEMON CREAM PUFFS

1 cup water
¼ cup margarine
1 cup all-purpose flour
4 eggs
1½ tablespoons cornstarch
½ cup evaporated skim milk
¼ teaspoon butter flavoring
½ teaspoon vanilla extract
¼ cup sugar
1 (8-ounce) container lemon low-fat yogurt
1 cup sliced fresh strawberries
¼ teaspoon powdered sugar

Combine water and margarine in a saucepan; bring to a boil. Add flour all at once, stirring vigorously over low heat about 1 minute or until mixture leaves sides of pan and forms a smooth ball. Remove from heat, and cool slightly.

Add eggs to flour mixture, one at a time, beating with a wooden spoon after each addition; beat until batter is smooth. Drop batter by slightly rounded tablespoonfuls 2 inches apart on an ungreased baking sheet.

Bake at 400° for 30 minutes or until golden and puffed. Cool away from drafts. Cut tops off cream puffs; pull out and discard soft dough inside.

Combine cornstarch, milk, flavorings, and sugar in a heavy saucepan. Cook until mixture comes to a boil, stirring constantly; boil 1 minute. Let cool.

Add yogurt to cooled cornstarch mixture; stir to blend. Fold in sliced strawberries. Fill cream puffs evenly with strawberry mixture; replace tops. Sift powdered sugar over cream puff tops. Yield: 9 servings.

☐ *169 calories, 5.3 grams protein, 7.1 grams fat, 21.1 grams carbohydrate, 106.3 milligrams cholesterol, 112.4 milligrams sodium, and 73.1 milligrams calcium per 2 filled cream puffs.*

WHITE CAKE WITH STRAWBERRIES AND CHOCOLATE GLAZE

Vegetable cooking spray
¾ cup plus 2 tablespoons sifted cake flour
½ cup superfine sugar
1 teaspoon baking powder
¼ cup vegetable oil
¼ cup water
1 teaspoon vanilla extract
3 egg whites
½ teaspoon cream of tartar
1 cup sliced small fresh strawberries
¼ cup semisweet chocolate morsels
1 whole strawberry

Coat a 10-inch flan pan with cooking spray; set aside.

Combine flour, sugar, and baking powder in a medium bowl; make a well in center of mixture. Combine oil, water, and vanilla; add to dry ingredients, stirring well. Set aside.

Beat egg whites (at room temperature) at high speed of an electric mixer until frothy; add cream of tartar and beat until stiff peaks form. Fold egg white mixture into flour mixture.

Pour batter into prepared pan. Bake at 350° for 18 to 20 minutes or until a wooden pick inserted in center comes out clean. Cool in pan 10 minutes; remove from pan, and cool completely on a wire rack.

Arrange strawberries over the cake, and set aside.

Place chocolate morsels in a heavy-duty zip-top plastic bag; seal bag. Submerge bag in boiling water until chocolate melts. Snip a tiny whole in the end of bag, using scissors; drizzle chocolate over strawberries. Garnish with a whole strawberry. Yield: 8 servings.

□ *190 calories, 2.3 grams protein, 9 grams fat, 25.8 grams carbohydrate, 0 milligrams cholesterol, 69.3 milligrams sodium, and 32.4 milligrams calcium per slice.*

APPLE-NUT CAKE

1 egg
⅓ cup sugar
1 teaspoon vanilla extract
½ cup all-purpose flour
1 teaspoon baking powder
Dash of salt
1 cup peeled diced apple
½ cup finely chopped walnuts
Vegetable cooking spray
6 thinly sliced apple wedges
Lemon juice
Ground cinnamon (optional)

Combine egg, sugar, and vanilla in a medium bowl; stir well. Add flour, baking powder, and salt; stir until smooth. Stir in 1 cup diced apple and walnuts, blending well.

Coat a 9-inch pieplate with cooking spray. Spread batter evenly in pieplate. Bake at 325° for 25 to 30 minutes or until a wooden pick inserted in center comes out clean. Let cake cool completely in pieplate.

Coat 6 apple wedges with lemon juice, and arrange in a pinwheel design over cake. Sprinkle with cinnamon, if desired. Yield: 6 servings.

□ *171 calories, 3.5 grams protein, 7.4 grams fat, 23.5 grams carbohydrate, 45.7 milligrams cholesterol, 63 milligrams sodium, and 48.5 milligrams calcium per slice.* Bruce D. Craft, Jr., Exmore, Virginia.

BLUEBERRY CHIFFON CHEESECAKE

⅔ cup graham cracker crumbs
3 tablespoons reduced-calorie margarine
Vegetable cooking spray
3 eggs, separated
1 cup skim milk
2 envelopes unflavored gelatin
¼ cup sugar
⅛ teaspoon salt
1 (8-ounce) container light processed cream cheese product
1 (16-ounce) container part-skim ricotta cheese
1 (8-ounce) carton plain low-fat yogurt
2 tablespoons grated lemon rind
2 tablespoons lemon juice
1 teaspoon vanilla extract
¼ teaspoon cream of tartar
1 tablespoon cornstarch
1 tablespoon lemon juice
¼ cup sugar
½ cup water
1½ cups frozen blueberries, thawed and divided
Lemon rind (optional)

Combine graham cracker crumbs and margarine; stir well. Set aside. Coat a 9-inch springform pan with cooking spray. Firmly press crumb mixture into bottom of pan. Bake at 350° for 5 minutes. Let cool, and chill.

Combine egg yolks, milk, gelatin, ¼ cup sugar, and salt in a small saucepan. Cook over medium heat, stirring constantly, until gelatin is dissolved and mixture is slightly thickened. Let cool.

Combine cream cheese, ricotta cheese, yogurt, lemon rind, lemon juice, and vanilla in a large mixing bowl; beat at medium speed of an electric mixer until mixture is smooth. Stir in gelatin mixture; set aside.

Beat egg whites (at room temperature) at high speed of an electric mixer until foamy. Add cream of tartar, and continue to beat until stiff peaks form. Fold egg whites into cheese mixture. Pour over prepared crust. Cover and refrigerate for 8 hours.

Combine cornstarch, lemon juice, ¼ cup sugar, water, and ½ cup blueberries in a small saucepan. Cook over medium heat, stirring constantly, until mixture comes to a boil; cook 1 minute. Cool slightly; stir in the remaining blueberries. Cool completely.

Remove sides of springform pan. Spread blueberry mixture over cheesecake. Garnish with lemon rind, if desired. Yield: 14 servings.

□ *183 calories, 9.5 grams protein, 8.6 grams fat, 18.2 grams carbohydrate, 78.6 milligrams cholesterol, 254 milligrams sodium, and 177.9 milligrams calcium per slice.* Pearl Lakey, Seymour, Missouri.

PEACH MELBA MERINGUES

2 egg whites
¼ teaspoon cream of tartar
½ cup sugar
Melba Sauce
1 (16-ounce) can peach halves in light syrup, drained
1 tablespoon sliced almonds, toasted

Beat egg whites (at room temperature) in a small bowl at high speed of an electric mixer until foamy. Add cream of tartar, and beat until soft peaks form. Gradually add sugar, 1 tablespoon at a time, beating until stiff peaks form.

Spoon meringue mixture into 6 mounds on a baking sheet lined with brown paper. Shape meringue mixture into circles using the back of a spoon, mounding the sides at least ½ inch higher than centers.

Bake at 225° for 45 minutes. Turn oven off, and let meringues cool at least 1 hour before opening oven door. Carefully remove meringue shells from brown paper; cool meringue shells completely on wire racks.

Spoon Melba Sauce evenly into meringue shells. Top each with a peach half, cut side down. Garnish with almonds. Yield: 6 servings.

Melba Sauce:

2 cups frozen raspberries, thawed
1 tablespoon Chambord or other raspberry-flavored liqueur
2 tablespoons powdered sugar
2 teaspoons cornstarch

Mash and strain raspberries. Combine raspberries and remaining ingredients in a small saucepan. Cook over medium heat, stirring constantly, until mixture comes to a boil; cook 1 minute. Cool mixture completely. Yield: ¾ cup plus 1 tablespoon.

RANGE-TOP AMARETTO CUSTARD

2 eggs, beaten
2 tablespoons sugar
¼ teaspoon vanilla extract
¼ teaspoon almond extract
1½ cups skim milk, scalded
Vegetable cooking spray
1 tablespoon plus 1 teaspoon amaretto
1 tablespoon sliced almonds, toasted
Ground allspice

Combine eggs, sugar, and flavorings in a medium bowl; stir well. Pour milk slowly over egg mixture, stirring constantly. Coat four ½-cup metal molds with cooking spray. Pour custard into molds; place in a large skillet. Add boiling water to skillet until it comes two-thirds of the way up sides of mold. Cover and cook (do not let water boil) 12 minutes or until a knife inserted in center comes out clean. Remove molds from water; let stand 5 minutes.

To serve, invert molds onto dessert plates; spoon 1 teaspoon amaretto over each custard. Garnish each with almonds and allspice. Yield: 4 servings.

TROPICAL FRUIT CRÊPES

1 (8-ounce) can unsweetened pineapple tidbits, undrained
1 (11-ounce) can mandarin oranges in light syrup, drained
⅔ cup thinly sliced banana
1 teaspoon rum flavoring
1 (8-ounce) container Piña Colada low-fat yogurt, divided
Low-Calorie Crêpes
2 tablespoons coconut, toasted

Drain pineapple tidbits, reserving juice; set juice aside.

Combine pineapple tidbits and mandarin oranges in a medium bowl. Pour reserved pineapple juice over banana; drain and add banana to fruit mixture. Toss gently to mix; set aside.

Mix rum flavoring with yogurt. Reserve ¼ cup yogurt; set aside. Spread remaining ¾ cup yogurt evenly down center of 10 crêpes. (Reserve remaining crêpes for other uses.) Spoon about 3 tablespoons fruit mixture on each crêpe; roll up. Place on serving dish. Top crêpes evenly with reserved yogurt, and sprinkle each evenly with coconut. Yield: 10 servings.

Low-Calorie Crêpes:

3 eggs
1½ cups skim milk
1⅓ cups all-purpose flour
½ teaspoon salt
2 teaspoons vegetable oil
Vegetable cooking spray

Combine eggs, milk, flour, salt, and vegetable oil in container of an electric blender; process 30 seconds. Scrape down sides of blender container with rubber spatula; process an additional 30 seconds or until batter is smooth. Refrigerate batter 1 hour. (This allows flour particles to swell and soften so that crêpes are light in texture.)

Coat the bottom of a 6-inch crêpe pan or nonstick skillet with cooking spray; place the pan over medium heat until hot, but not smoking.

Pour 2 tablespoons batter into pan. Quickly tilt pan in all directions so batter covers pan in a thin film; cook about 1 minute.

Lift edge of crêpe to test for doneness. Crêpe is ready for flipping when it can be shaken loose from pan. Flip crêpe, and cook about 30 seconds on other side. (This side is usually spotty brown and is the side on which the filling is placed.)

When crêpe is done, place on a towel to cool. Stack between layers of wax paper to prevent sticking. Repeat until all batter is used, stirring batter occasionally. Yield: 20 (6-inch) crêpes.

Note: To freeze unfilled crêpes, stack between wax paper, and wrap securely in heavy-duty aluminum foil, or place in an airtight container. Crêpes may be frozen up to 4 months. Thaw crêpes before using.

GREEN GRAPE TART

½ cup ground almonds
3 tablespoons sugar
2 tablespoons egg substitute
3 tablespoons reduced-calorie margarine, melted
¼ teaspoon grated lemon rind
Tart shell (recipe follows)
1⅔ cups green grape halves (about ¾ pound)
1 tablespoon reduced-calorie imitation apple jelly
½ teaspoon lemon juice

Combine almonds, sugar, egg substitute, margarine, and lemon rind in a small bowl, stirring well. Spread mixture into prepared tart shell. Bake at 350° for 10 to 12 minutes. Let cool slightly. Arrange grapes over filling.

Combine apple jelly and lemon juice in a small saucepan. Cook over low heat until jelly melts. Brush grapes with jelly mixture. Yield: 8 servings.

Tart Shell:

1 cup all-purpose flour
Pinch of salt
¼ cup plus 1 tablespoon reduced-calorie margarine, chilled
4 to 5 tablespoons cold water

Combine flour and salt; cut in margarine with pastry blender until mixture resembles coarse meal. Sprinkle cold water, 1 tablespoon at a time, evenly over surface; stir with a fork until dry ingredients are moistened. Shape into a ball; chill.

Roll dough to ⅛-inch thickness; transfer to 9-inch tart pan. Prick bottom and sides of shell with a fork. Bake at 350° for 20 to 22 minutes. Yield: one 9-inch tart shell. Judi Grigoraci, Charleston, West Virginia.

Use Up That Leftover Ham

If there's leftover ham at your house after Easter dinner, plan on using it in these recipes. Golden Ham Pie contains chopped onion, green pepper, and chicken soup. And Cheese Biscuits are baked atop the pie during the last 20 minutes of cooking.

If a skillet dish is more to your fancy, try Ham-Noodle Skillet. Served with a green salad or your favorite vegetables, it makes a tasty Sunday night supper.

HAM-NOODLE SKILLET

1 (4-ounce) can whole mushrooms
2 cups cubed cooked ham
¼ cup chopped green pepper
¼ cup chopped onion
2 tablespoons butter or margarine, melted
⅛ teaspoon pepper
Dash of paprika
1 teaspoon Worcestershire sauce
1 cup water
4 ounces uncooked medium egg noodles
1 cup commercial sour cream

Drain mushrooms, reserving ¼ cup liquid. Set aside.

Sauté ham, green pepper, and onion in butter in a large skillet. Stir in pepper, paprika, and Worcestershire sauce. Add water, reserved mushroom liquid, and noodles; bring to a boil. Cover, reduce heat, and simmer 20 minutes, adding mushrooms the last 5 minutes. Stir in sour cream; cook just until thoroughly heated. (Do not boil.) Yield: 4 servings. *Helen Dill, Oklahoma City, Oklahoma.*

GOLDEN HAM PIE

3 tablespoons finely chopped onion
¼ cup finely chopped green pepper
¼ cup butter or margarine, melted
¼ cup plus 2 tablespoons all-purpose flour
¼ teaspoon pepper
2 cups milk
1 (10¾-ounce) can cream of chicken soup, undiluted
3 cups chopped ham
1 tablespoon lemon juice
Cheese Biscuits

Sauté onion and green pepper in butter until tender in a large saucepan. Add flour and pepper; cook 1 minute, stirring mixture constantly.

Gradually add milk and soup; cook over medium heat, stirring constantly, until thickened and bubbly. Stir in ham and lemon juice.

Pour ham mixture into a lightly greased 12- x 8- x 2-inch baking dish. Bake at 350° for 30 minutes. Top casserole with Cheese Biscuits. Bake an additional 20 minutes or until biscuits are golden brown. Yield: 6 servings.

Cheese Biscuits:

1 cup all-purpose flour
1½ teaspoons baking powder
½ teaspoon salt
2½ tablespoons shortening
¾ cup (3 ounces) shredded Cheddar cheese
⅓ cup milk

Combine first 3 ingredients; cut in shortening until mixture is crumbly. Stir in Cheddar cheese and milk, and mix until blended.

Turn dough out on a lightly floured surface; knead lightly 4 or 5 times.

Roll dough to ¼-inch thickness; cut 12 biscuits with a 2½-inch biscuit cutter. Yield: 12 biscuits. *Mrs. Kirby Smith, Millbrook, Alabama.*

HAM-AND-CHEESE CASSEROLE

8 ounces seashell macaroni
½ pound fresh mushrooms, sliced
¼ cup chopped onion
¼ cup butter or margarine, melted
¼ cup all-purpose flour
2 cups chicken broth
1¼ cups half-and-half
1 cup (4 ounces) shredded Cheddar cheese
1 teaspoon lemon juice
⅛ teaspoon pepper
3 cups diced cooked ham
¼ cup grated Parmesan cheese

Cook seashell macaroni according to package directions, omitting salt; drain and set aside.

Sauté mushrooms and onion in butter in a large skillet. Add flour, stirring until smooth. Cook 1 minute, stirring constantly. Gradually add chicken broth and half-and-half; cook over medium heat, stirring constantly, until mixture is thickened and bubbly. Add cheese, lemon juice, and pepper; stir until cheese melts. Reduce heat, and simmer, uncovered, 10 minutes. Add macaroni and ham. Spoon into a greased 2½-quart casserole. Sprinkle with Parmesan cheese. Bake, uncovered, at 350° for 30 minutes or until bubbly. Yield: 6 to 8 servings. *Mrs. Peter Rosato III, Memphis, Tennessee.*

HAM-RICE-TOMATO BAKE

2 cups cooked diced ham
1 cup cooked rice
½ cup chopped onion
¼ cup chopped green pepper
1 (4-ounce) can mushrooms, stems and pieces, drained
1 (16-ounce) can stewed tomatoes, chopped and undrained
¼ teaspoon salt
¼ teaspoon pepper
1 cup soft breadcrumbs
¼ cup butter or margarine, melted

Combine ham, rice, onion, green pepper, mushrooms, tomatoes, salt, and pepper; mix well. Spoon into a greased 2-quart casserole. Combine breadcrumbs and butter; toss to mix well. Sprinkle on top of casserole. Bake, uncovered, at 350° for 30 minutes. Yield: 4 servings. *Sara McNeil, Mooresburg, Tennessee.*

MICROWAVE COOKERY

Fish In A Flash

Fish and shellfish are naturally tender and require minimal cooking. A microwave oven helps preserve their natural juices and delicate textures.

Fish fillets and steaks cook best in shallow round or square baking dishes that can be rotated in the oven. For even cooking, arrange fillets with thickest portions at the edge of the dish. Thinner portions of fillets should overlap in the center.

Juice from extremely moist fish, especially flounder, collects on the surface as it cooks and detracts from the appearance. To prevent this, line the dish with paper towels to absorb the liquid. Or arrange the fish on a trivet placed inside the dish.

It's easy to overcook fish. Always test for doneness after the minimum time suggested in the recipe and after it stands covered 3 to 5 minutes. For standing time, place the dish flat on the counter to hold in heat that continues to cook the fish.

For microwave cooking, when fish turns opaque, it's done. If you follow the rule for conventional cooking (cook until fish flakes with a fork), you will have gone too far. The center should be slightly translucent at the end of the cooking time and will become opaque during the standing time. If after standing the fish doesn't appear done, microwave an additional 30 seconds. Keep fish covered so that edges stay moist and center cooks completely.

Fish and seafood do not retain heat as well as some other foods. Make sure the rest of the meal—vegetables, salad, bread—is near completion before microwaving fish.

The microwave can even make shucking oysters easier. While the shells will not open completely, the muscles will relax, making the job easier. Use WARM (30% power) to open the shells but not cook the oysters. For fully cooked oysters and ease of opening in one step, use HIGH power. See specific instructions for shucking in Dressed Oysters on the Half Shell. Arrange the oysters on a platter with the hinges toward the center of the plate so that you can watch for the shells to open.

For tips on buying and storing fish, see "From Our Kitchen" on this page.

CREOLE FISH

1 clove garlic, minced
1 medium onion, sliced
½ cup chopped green pepper
1 tablespoon vegetable oil
1 (14½-ounce) can stewed tomatoes
1 tablespoon cornstarch
1 teaspoon Creole seasoning
¼ teaspoon hot sauce
4 (6-ounce) skinless grouper fillets about
    ¾ inch thick
2 teaspoons lemon juice

Combine garlic, onion, green pepper, and oil in a 2-quart bowl. Microwave mixture at HIGH for 2½ to 3 minutes, stirring once.

Drain tomatoes, reserving juice. Combine tomato juice and cornstarch, stirring until dissolved. Add cornstarch mixture, tomatoes, Creole seasoning, and hot sauce to onion mixture, stirring well. Microwave at HIGH 3 to 4 minutes or until thick, stirring once. Set sauce aside.

Line a 12- x 8- x 2-inch baking dish with 2 layers of paper towels. Arrange fish on paper towels with thickest portions to outside of dish, overlapping thin portions at center of dish. Cover with 2 layers of paper towels, and microwave at HIGH 6 to 8 minutes, rearranging fish after 3 minutes. Cook until fish turns opaque. Let stand covered 3 to 5 minutes.

Arrange fillets on serving plate; drizzle with lemon juice. Pour sauce over fish. Yield: 4 servings.

GREEK-STYLE MONKFISH

¼ cup butter or margarine
1 clove garlic, minced
¼ cup thinly sliced green onions
½ teaspoon dried whole oregano
½ teaspoon salt
¼ teaspoon pepper
2 tablespoons lemon juice
2 pounds monkfish or pompano, cut into
    4 servings
Lemon wedges (optional)
Parsley (optional)

Place butter in a 1-cup glass measure. Microwave at HIGH for 55 seconds or until melted. Stir in garlic and green onions; microwave at HIGH for 30 seconds or until onion is crisp-tender. Add oregano, salt, pepper, and lemon juice; mix well. Set aside.

Line a 12- x 8- x 2-inch baking dish with 2 layers of paper towels. Arrange fish with thickest portion to the outside of dish, overlapping thin portions in center of dish. Cover with 2 layers of paper towels. Microwave at HIGH for 8 to 10 minutes, rotating dish after 3 minutes, or until fish is opaque. Let stand covered 3 to 5 minutes.

Transfer fish to a serving platter. Pour sauce over fish; garnish with lemon wedges and parsley, if desired. Yield: 4 servings.

DRESSED OYSTERS
ON THE HALF SHELL

3 slices bacon
½ cup round buttery cracker crumbs
¼ cup mayonnaise
1 tablespoon minced green onions
1 tablespoon lemon juice
½ teaspoon hot sauce
½ teaspoon Worcestershire sauce
¼ teaspoon Dijon mustard
1 dozen medium oysters

Place bacon on a rack in a 12- x 8- x 2-inch baking dish; cover with paper towels. Microwave at HIGH 3 to 4 minutes or until bacon is crisp; drain. Crumble bacon, and set aside.

Combine cracker crumbs, mayonnaise, onions, lemon juice, hot sauce, Worcestershire sauce, and mustard; stir well, and set aside.

Wash and rinse oysters thoroughly in cold water. To shuck oysters, place them on a large round plate with hinges toward inside. Microwave on WARM (30% power) 2 to 3 minutes or until shells open slightly, turning plate once. Shuck oysters, reserving deep half of shells; drain oysters in colander.

Place oysters in half shells. Spread

1½ teaspoons mayonnaise mixture over each oyster; top with crumbled bacon. Microwave at HIGH for 1½ to 2 minutes or until oysters curl, turning once. Yield: 1 dozen.

Note: To shuck and cook the oysters at the same time, microwave at HIGH 3 to 4 minutes or until shells open and oysters curl.

From Our Kitchen To Yours

Exceptional in taste appeal, low in calories, and high in nutritional value, fish is a wise choice when planning your menus. Besides being easy to prepare, it adds variety and interest to meals.

Whether you choose lean or fat fish, a wide variety in both types is available. Lean fish designates the species with oil content less than 5%. Speckled sea trout, pompano, grouper, sole, flounder, snapper, tilefish, black sea bass, scamp, shark, triggerfish, cod, crappie, croaker, monkfish, orange roughy, halibut, ocean perch, white sea trout, and whiting are classifed as lean fish. Fat fish includes species with an oil content of more than 5%. The oil is distributed throughout the flesh, causing fat fish to be darker in color. The exact oil percentage depends on the species, season of the year, and water depth from which the fish was taken. Spanish mackerel, salmon, tuna, king mackerel, mullet, rainbow trout, lake trout, amberjack, carp, and freshwater catfish are in this category.

Market Forms

Fish is marketed as whole, drawn, dressed, steaks, and fillets. When buying, allow 1 pound whole fish, ½ pound dressed fish, and ⅓ pound steaks or fillets per person.

Whole fish, fresh from the water, must be scaled and eviscerated (entrails removed) before cooking.

Drawn fish is already eviscerated. Scales, head, tail, and fins need to be removed before cooking.

Dressed or pan-dressed means the fish without the scales, entrails, head, tail, and fins.

Steaks are cross-section slices (¾ to 1 inch thick) of large dressed fish.

Fillets are lengthwise cuts from the sides of fish. They may be skinned or not, but they are free of bones.

Selecting Fish

Fresh fish is firm and elastic with no traces of browning or drying out. Fillets and steaks have a moist fresh-cut appearance and a fresh, mild aroma.

A whole fish is fresh when the eyes are bright, full, and protruding from the head, and the pinkish-red gills are free from slime. When gently pressed, the iridescent skin should spring back.

Frozen fish should be solid with no discoloration or freezer burn. Aroma, if any, will be slight. Wrapping should be moistureproof and vaporproof, with little or no air space and the package clearly labeled and free from damage.

Storing, Freezing, And Thawing Fish

Proper handling and correct storage of fish are crucial to preserving quality and taste. After purchasing fresh fish, immediately store it in the coldest part of your refrigerator in its original leak-proof wrapper. Be sure to cook the fish within two days.

Date commercially packaged frozen fish before placing in your freezer. Generally, fish with a high oil content will keep up to three months, and lean fish keeps up to one year.

If you want to freeze fresh-caught or store-bought fish, it is best to do this as soon as possible to preserve the quality. To freeze by glazing, place the fish on a tray, cover with aluminum foil, and freeze. Remove the foil, and dip the frozen fish in ice water to form a glaze. Return to freezer. Repeat this procedure two or three times until the fish is completely glazed. Package in aluminum foil or freezer paper; eliminate air pockets. Label, date, and freeze.

Fish may also be frozen in block form in waxed cartons or plastic containers. Fill each carton half full of water, place fish in carton, and fill with water to within 1 inch of the top. Staple the carton; label, date, and freeze.

Plan to cook fish soon after thawing. Do not store thawed products more than one day before cooking. Thaw fish in the refrigerator, allowing 18 to 24 hours for a 1-pound package. For a quicker method, place frozen fish under cold running water. Never thaw fish at room temperature or in warm water, and don't refreeze.

Cooking Fish

Simple cooking methods seem to enhance the natural flavor of fish. The preferred methods are baking, broiling, microwaving, poaching, smoking, steaming, and grilling.

Cooking times will vary according to the thickness and size of the fish. To prevent overcooking, test the fish halfway through the recommended cooking time and afterward until the fish becomes opaque and flakes easily when tested with a fork.

Tips

As a general rule, fat fish have more flavor. Lean fish may be substituted, but more frequent basting is required because of the lower oil content.

If recipe preparation requires frequent handling of fish, as is the case with chowders or soups, a firm-textured fish, such as grouper, will retain its shape, giving a better appearance.

Appetizers And Salads For Two

If you have a small family and don't want leftovers, these appetizers and salads are for you. Created on a smaller scale, they provide as much variety and eye appeal as regular recipes, but without any waste.

Pepper-Cheese Stacks fit nicely into a menu as a salad or as an appetizer, and they make quite a conversation piece. A mixture of blue cheese and cream cheese is stuffed into a green pepper and then chilled. When the pepper is sliced, there's a solid cheese center trimmed with a green border.

Quick Orange Salad is also easy. Fresh orange sections are topped with a cream cheese mixture thinned to a drizzling consistency using honey and orange juice. Serve it on a bed of lettuce for a dimensional effect.

QUICK ORANGE SALAD

3 oranges, peeled and sectioned
Lettuce leaves
¼ cup whipped cream cheese
1 tablespoon honey
1 tablespoon orange juice

Arrange orange sections on lettuce-lined plates; cover and chill.

Combine remaining ingredients; stir until smooth. Pour dressing over orange sections, and serve immediately. Yield: 2 servings.   *Linda Lee Duke,*
Corpus Christi, Texas.

PEPPER-CHEESE STACKS

1 medium-size green pepper
2 ounces blue cheese, softened
4 ounces cream cheese, softened
1 large tomato
Lettuce leaves
Paprika (optional)

Cut and discard top and bottom from green pepper. Remove and discard seeds. Wash pepper, and drain well.

Combine cheeses; stir well. Place green pepper on a sheet of plastic wrap; fill with cheese mixture. Wrap and chill 2 hours.

Cut tomato into 4 slices. Cut green pepper into 4 slices. Place 2 tomato slices on each of 2 lettuce-lined plates. Place pepper slices on top of tomato slices. Garnish with paprika, if desired. Yield: 2 servings.   *Sarah Diuguid,*
Ghent, Kentucky.

ASPARAGUS-HORSERADISH SALAD

1 (10-ounce) package frozen asparagus
   spears
Lettuce leaves
¼ cup commercial sour cream
1 tablespoon mayonnaise
2 teaspoons prepared horseradish
1 hard-cooked egg yolk, sieved

Cook asparagus according to package directions for 3 minutes; drain and chill.

Arrange the asparagus on lettuce-lined plates. Combine sour cream, mayonnaise, and horseradish; stir well. Spoon over asparagus; sprinkle with egg yolk. Yield: 2 to 3 servings.
Mrs. Roy Carlisle,
Columbus, Georgia.

BANANA SALAD

½ cup finely chopped pecans
½ cup flaked coconut
¼ cup commercial sour cream
1 tablespoon lemon juice
1 tablespoon honey
2 small bananas, peeled and cut into
   1-inch slices
1 small red apple, unpeeled and thinly
   sliced
1 kiwifruit, peeled and thinly sliced
Lettuce leaves (optional)

Combine pecans and coconut in a shallow dish; set aside.

Combine sour cream, lemon juice, and honey in a small bowl; stir well.

Dip banana slices in sour cream mixture; roll in coconut-pecan mixture. Cover and chill 2 hours.

To serve, arrange apple, kiwifruit, and banana on lettuce-lined salad plates, if desired. Yield: 2 servings.
Margaret Kennard,
Starkville, Mississippi.

ONION-CHEESE SOUP

2 tablespoons butter or margarine
⅓ cup minced onion
1½ tablespoons all-purpose flour
2 cups milk
5 slices sharp process American cheese, torn into small pieces
¼ teaspoon salt
Dash of pepper
Chopped chives (optional)
Paprika (optional)

Melt butter in a saucepan; add onion, and cook until tender. Add flour, stirring until blended. Cook 1 minute, stirring constantly. Gradually add milk; bring to a boil over medium heat. Stir in cheese, salt, and pepper. Reduce heat to low; cook, stirring constantly, just until cheese melts. Serve immediately. Garnish with chives and paprika, if desired. Yield: 2½ cups.
Janice Pruitt,
North Wilkesboro, North Carolina.

Salad Dressings To Boast About

Commercial salad dressings offer variety and convenience, but when the salad needs to be special, you might want to make the dressing from scratch. It's not hard to do; these recipes take only minutes to prepare. And the results will have your family thinking you went to a lot of trouble.

SESAME SEED DRESSING

½ cup sesame oil
¼ cup honey
¼ cup vinegar
3 tablespoons sesame seeds, lightly toasted
2 tablespoons lemon juice
⅛ teaspoon garlic juice

Combine all ingredients in a jar; cover tightly, and shake vigorously. Chill. Shake well before serving. Serve dressing over salad greens or fruit. Yield: 1 cup.
Mrs. David Stearns,
Mobile, Alabama.

TANGY BLUE CHEESE DRESSING

½ cup vegetable oil
¼ cup cider vinegar
4 ounces blue cheese, crumbled
½ teaspoon salt
1½ teaspoons coarsely ground black pepper
½ teaspoon dry mustard
½ teaspoon paprika
1 teaspoon Worcestershire sauce
½ teaspoon prepared horseradish

Combine all ingredients in a jar. Cover tightly, and shake vigorously. Chill. Serve dressing over salad greens. Yield: 1 cup.
Jean Pashby,
Memphis, Tennessee.

HONEY FRENCH DRESSING

¾ cup vegetable oil
½ cup catsup
½ cup honey
½ cup cider vinegar
¾ teaspoon dry mustard
¾ teaspoon paprika
¾ teaspoon celery seeds
¼ teaspoon ground cloves

Combine all ingredients in a jar; cover tightly, and shake vigorously. Chill. Shake well before serving. Serve over salad greens or citrus fruit. Yield: 2 cups.
Linda Pierce,
Germantown, Tennessee.

DRESSING FOR FRUIT SALAD

½ cup mayonnaise or salad dressing
½ cup commercial sour cream
¼ cup orange juice
1 tablespoon sugar
1 tablespoon honey
1 teaspoon vanilla extract
¼ teaspoon grated lemon rind

Combine all ingredients in a small bowl; stir until well blended. Cover and chill. Serve over fruit. Yield: 1⅓ cups.
Paula Carol Griswold,
Hendersonville, North Carolina.

LIME-HONEY FRUIT SALAD DRESSING

¼ teaspoon grated lime rind
⅓ cup lime juice
⅓ cup honey
½ teaspoon seasoning salt
½ teaspoon paprika
¾ teaspoon prepared mustard
1 cup vegetable oil

Combine lime rind, lime juice, honey, seasoning salt, paprika, and mustard in container of an electric blender; process on medium speed a few seconds. While blender is still running, slowly pour oil into blender; continue to blend a few seconds. Cover and chill. Serve over fruit. Yield: 1½ cups.
Sarah Watson,
Knoxville, Tennessee.

Pork Pleasers For Two

Cooking for two can be a hassle if you have to modify recipes to yield fewer servings. But these recipes make things simple. They feature pork entrées scaled for only two servings.

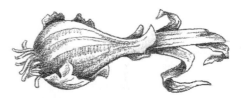

CIDER-SAUCED PORK CHOPS

2 shallots, finely chopped
1 tablespoon plus 1 teaspoon chopped fresh parsley
⅛ teaspoon salt
⅛ teaspoon white pepper
3 (½-inch-thick) pork chops (about 1 pound)
2 tablespoons butter or margarine, melted
½ cup apple cider

Combine shallots, parsley, salt, and pepper; stir well. Pat onto both sides of pork chops, and place chops in a lightly greased 9-inch square baking pan. Drizzle butter over chops; cover and bake at 325° for 30 minutes.

Remove from oven; uncover and drain drippings. Pour cider over chops; bake, uncovered, an additional 30 minutes or until done. Yield: 2 servings.
Hazel S. Stephenson,
Denison, Texas.

HAWAIIAN PORK CHOPS

⅓ cup all-purpose flour
½ teaspoon salt
¼ teaspoon pepper
4 (½-inch-thick) center-cut loin pork
  chops
3 tablespoons vegetable oil
1 (8-ounce) can crushed pineapple,
  undrained
2 tablespoons brown sugar
¼ teaspoon ground cinnamon
4 green pepper rings

Combine flour, salt, and pepper; dredge pork chops in flour mixture.

Heat oil in a large skillet over medium heat; brown pork chops on both sides. Drain off pan drippings.

Combine the crushed pineapple, brown sugar, and cinnamon; spoon the mixture evenly onto pork chops. Top each with a green pepper ring. Cover, reduce heat, and simmer 40 minutes or until the pork chops are tender. Yield: 2 servings. *Ruth Spitzer,*
Pinson, Alabama.

BACON SPAGHETTI

5 slices bacon, chopped
¼ cup chopped onion
¼ cup chopped green pepper
4 ounces uncooked spaghetti, broken
1 cup boiling water
1 (14½-ounce) can tomatoes, undrained
  and chopped
1 tablespoon Worcestershire sauce
2 tablespoons grated Parmesan cheese

Combine bacon, onion, and green pepper in a large skillet; sauté 5 minutes. Drain drippings. Add spaghetti, water, and tomatoes.

Cover and simmer 20 minutes or until spaghetti is tender, stirring occasionally. Stir in Worcestershire sauce. To serve, sprinkle each serving with cheese. Yield: 2 servings. *Mrs. C. W. Horton,*
Demopolis, Alabama.

STIR-FRY SAUSAGE AND VEGETABLES

6 green onions, chopped
1 cup (about 2 small) cubed yellow squash
2 cloves garlic, minced
2 tablespoons butter or margarine, melted
½ pound smoked sausage, cut into ¼-inch
  slices
8 cherry tomatoes, halved
2 teaspoons Worcestershire sauce
Chopped parsley (optional)

Sauté onions, squash, and garlic in butter in a heavy skillet for 2 minutes. Add sausage, tomatoes, and Worcestershire sauce; stir-fry until thoroughly heated. Garnish with chopped parsley, if desired. Yield: 2 servings.
Victoria J. Rousuck,
Port Aransas, Texas.

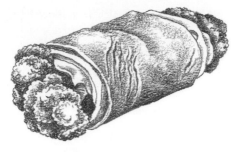

HAM-AND-BROCCOLI ROLLS

1 (10-ounce) package frozen broccoli
  spears
1½ teaspoons butter or margarine
1½ teaspoons all-purpose flour
¼ cup milk
⅛ teaspoon salt
1½ teaspoons prepared horseradish
1 teaspoon prepared mustard
¼ teaspoon Worcestershire sauce
¼ teaspoon grated onion
1 egg yolk, beaten
½ cup pineapple juice
6 (6- x 4-inch) slices cooked ham
2 (6- x 4-inch) slices Swiss cheese
2 pineapple slices (optional)
Paprika (optional)

Cook broccoli according to package directions; drain. Melt butter in a heavy saucepan over low heat; add flour, and cook 1 minute, stirring constantly. Gradually add milk; cook over medium heat until thickened. Stir in salt, horseradish, mustard, Worcestershire sauce, and onion. Combine egg yolk and pineapple juice; add to sauce, and stir until thickened.

Divide ham into 2 portions (3 slices each). Top ham with cheese. Arrange half of broccoli on each cheese slice; spoon about 1 tablespoon sauce over broccoli. Roll ham and cheese around broccoli; secure with wooden picks. Place in a 9-inch square baking dish; cover and bake at 350° for 15 to 20 minutes.

To serve, reheat remaining sauce; spoon over ham rolls. Garnish with pineapple slices, and sprinkle with paprika, if desired. Yield: 2 servings.
Brenda Russell,
Signal Mountain, Tennessee.

Use Your Canned Beans

Canned beans are especially useful when fresh vegetables are in short supply, but they're also great to have on hand when you need to whip up a meal in a hurry. These easy recipes featuring canned beans use ingredients you are likely to have in your pantry, so there's no last-minute running to the store.

For the best taste, Vegetable Soup needs to simmer about two hours. But most of the ingredients come from cans, so once you chop the carrots, celery, and garlic, it's merely a matter of adding the remaining ingredients to the soup pot.

Colorful Six-Bean Salad tastes best when chilled several hours to let the flavors blend. But the actual preparation takes only a few minutes.

If you've been trying to think of a new use for pork and beans, try Pork-'n'-Bean Salad. The beans, bacon, hard-cooked eggs, cheese, pickles, ham, tomato, and more may seem unusual for a salad, but it's a tasty combination that you just mix and chill.

COLORFUL SIX-BEAN SALAD

1 (16-ounce) can garbanzo beans, drained
1 (16-ounce) can red kidney beans,
  drained
1 (16-ounce) can Great Northern beans,
  drained
1 (16-ounce) can lima beans, drained
1 (16-ounce) can wax beans, drained
1 (16-ounce) can cut green beans, drained
1 cup chopped scallions
1 cup olive oil
1 egg yolk
⅓ cup red wine vinegar
2 tablespoons sugar
3 cloves garlic, minced
⅛ teaspoon freshly ground pepper
Leaf lettuce
3 hard-cooked eggs, quartered

Combine all beans and scallions in a large bowl; stir to mix.

Combine olive oil, egg yolk, vinegar, sugar, garlic, and pepper in container of an electric blender. Process at low speed until well blended. Pour over vegetables. Cover and chill 4 hours.

To serve, spoon bean salad onto lettuce-lined salad plates; garnish with quarters of hard-cooked eggs. Yield: 12 servings. *Fred Wells,*
Ayden, North Carolina.

PORK-'N'-BEAN SALAD

2 (16-ounce) cans pork and beans, drained
3 stalks celery, chopped
4 slices bacon, cooked and crumbled
2 hard-cooked eggs, chopped
1 cup (4 ounces) cubed Cheddar cheese
¾ cup chopped sweet pickles
2 (1-ounce) slices ham, chopped
1 large tomato, cubed
½ cup chopped onion
3 tablespoons mayonnaise
1 teaspoon prepared mustard

Rinse beans with cold water; drain well. Combine beans, celery, bacon, eggs, cheese, pickles, ham, tomato, and onion in a large bowl.

Combine mayonnaise and mustard; add to mixture. Cover; chill 1 hour. Yield: 6 to 8 servings.   *Pam Bryant, Monroe, Louisiana.*

VEGETABLE SOUP

3½ quarts water
1 smoked ham hock
3 cloves garlic, minced
5 stalks celery, finely chopped
4 large carrots, finely diced
1 (16-ounce) can tomatoes, undrained and chopped
1 (15-ounce) can tomato sauce
1 (10½-ounce) can beef broth
1 (8-ounce) can English peas, drained
1 (8-ounce) can whole kernel corn, drained
1 (8-ounce) can cut green beans, drained
1 (8-ounce) can lima beans, drained
4 ounces small bow egg noodles
¼ teaspoon pepper

Combine water, ham hock, and garlic in a Dutch oven. Bring to a boil; cover, reduce heat, and simmer 1½ hours. Remove ham hock; add celery, carrots, tomatoes, tomato sauce, and beef broth. Return to a boil, and cook 20 minutes. Add remaining ingredients, and simmer 25 minutes. Yield: 1 gallon.
Mavis E. Dallinga, Winter Park, Florida.

GREEN BEANS AND TOMATOES WITH MUSTARD

6 slices bacon
¾ cup chopped onion
½ cup chopped green pepper
2 tablespoons all-purpose flour
1 (16-ounce) can tomatoes, chopped
1 tablespoon Worcestershire sauce
½ teaspoon pepper
⅛ teaspoon dry mustard
1 (16-ounce) can cut green beans, drained

Cook bacon in a large skillet until crisp; remove bacon, reserving 2 tablespoons drippings. Crumble bacon, and set aside.

Sauté onion and green pepper in bacon drippings until tender. Stir in flour, and cook 1 minute, stirring constantly. Add tomatoes, Worcestershire sauce, pepper, and mustard; cook over medium heat until thickened. Stir in green beans, and cook until thoroughly heated. Transfer to serving bowl; sprinkle with crumbled bacon. Yield: 6 servings.   *Shirley Crowley, Hartsville, South Carolina.*

Oranges Add Tangy Flavor

From entrées to desserts, oranges make a tasty contribution. The juice, pulp, and orange rind all add to the refreshing flavors of these recipes.

When only the juice or pulp is used, grate the colored rind before cutting the orange, and freeze it for later use. Avoid using the white portion of the rind because it is bitter. Orange rind adds zest to baked items, sauces, meats, and soups. But use it sparingly; a teaspoon goes a long way.

Two recipes, Sweet Potato Delight and Citrus Salad Bowl, use oranges sliced to include the membrane that separates the sections. This membrane contains a lot of nutrients. And by slicing the fruit rather than sectioning it, very little juice is lost.

SWEET POTATO DELIGHT

8 medium-size sweet potatoes (about 4½ pounds)
3 oranges
¼ cup plus 1 tablespoon butter or margarine, melted
¾ cup firmly packed brown sugar
3 tablespoons cornstarch
½ teaspoon salt
2 cups orange juice
½ cup chopped pecans

Place sweet potatoes in a Dutch oven; cover with water. Bring to a boil over medium heat; cover, reduce heat, and simmer 10 to 12 minutes or until potatoes are fork-tender. Drain and let cool. Peel sweet potatoes, and cut into ½-inch slices; set aside.

Grate 2 tablespoons rind from oranges; set rind aside. Peel oranges and cut into ½-inch slices. Layer half each of sweet potato slices and orange slices in a lightly greased 13- x 9- x 2-inch baking dish. Repeat layers.

Combine butter, brown sugar, cornstarch, and salt in a heavy saucepan; blend well. Gradually add orange juice; cook over medium heat, stirring constantly, until mixture is thickened and bubbly. Stir in orange rind; pour over sweet potatoes and oranges. Sprinkle with chopped pecans. Bake at 350° for 30 minutes. Yield: 8 to 10 servings.
Rublelene Singleton, Scotts Hill, Tennessee.

CITRUS SALAD BOWL

2 oranges
1 grapefruit, peeled and sectioned
1 (20-ounce) can pineapple chunks, undrained
½ cup commercial sour cream
1 tablespoon brown sugar
¼ teaspoon ground ginger
Dash of ground nutmeg
Lettuce leaves
1 large avocado, peeled and thinly sliced
¼ cup chopped pecans, toasted

Grate 1 teaspoon rind from oranges; set rind aside. Peel oranges, and cut into ½-inch slices; quarter each slice. Combine orange slices, grapefruit sections, and pineapple chunks in a medium bowl; cover and chill.

Combine sour cream, brown sugar, 1 teaspoon orange rind, ginger, and nutmeg; set aside.

To serve, arrange lettuce leaves on individual salad plates. Place avocado slices on lettuce. Drain fruit mixture; spoon fruit over avocado slices. Top with dressing, and sprinkle with chopped pecans. Yield: 4 to 6 servings.   *Sara A. McCullough, Broaddus, Texas.*

ORANGE-CRANBERRY PORK CHOPS

6 (¾-inch-thick) pork chops
1 tablespoon vegetable shortening, melted
2 tablespoons water
1 teaspoon salt
¼ cup sugar
¼ cup light corn syrup
2 tablespoons grated orange rind
2 cups orange sections, including juice
2 cups fresh cranberries
Hot cooked rice

Trim fat from pork chops; brown chops in shortening in a large skillet. Drain, if necessary. Add water and salt; cover and cook over medium heat 45 to 50 minutes or until chops are done.

Add sugar, corn syrup, orange rind, orange sections, and cranberries, and cook an additional 5 minutes. Serve over rice. Yield: 6 servings.
Nancy Swinney,
Tallahassee, Florida.

ORANGE MERINGUE CAKE

2¼ cups sifted cake flour
1½ cups sugar
1 tablespoon baking powder
1 teaspoon salt
5 egg yolks
1 tablespoon grated orange rind
¾ cup orange juice
½ cup vegetable oil
7 egg whites
½ teaspoon cream of tartar
Orange Filling
Meringue Frosting

Combine flour, sugar, baking powder, and salt in a large bowl. Combine egg yolks, orange rind, orange juice, and oil; add mixture to dry ingredients, and beat at medium speed of an electric mixer until smooth.

Beat egg whites (at room temperature) until foamy; add cream of tartar, and beat until stiff. Fold egg yolk mixture gently into egg whites; blend well. Spoon batter into an ungreased 10-inch tube pan. Bake at 325° for 1 hour or until cake springs back when lightly touched with fingers. Invert pan on funnel or bottle; cool 1 hour or until completely cooled.

Remove cake from pan, and slice into 5 equal layers. Place bottom layer of cake on an ovenproof platter or wooden board; spread with one-fourth of Orange Filling. Repeat with remaining layers and filling, ending with cake on top. Spread top and sides with Meringue Frosting. Bake at 400° for 5 minutes or until lightly browned. Yield: one 10-inch tube cake.

Orange Filling:

1 cup sugar
½ cup cornstarch
1 teaspoon salt
3 cups orange juice
¼ cup lime juice
6 egg yolks, beaten
1 tablespoon grated orange rind

Combine sugar, cornstarch, and salt in a medium saucepan; gradually stir in orange and lime juices. Cook over medium heat, stirring constantly, until it thickens and boils.

Slowly stir a small amount of hot mixture into egg yolks; add to remaining hot mixture, stirring constantly. Boil 1 minute longer, stirring constantly. Remove from heat, and stir in orange rind; cool. Yield: 3½ cups.

Meringue Frosting:

5 egg whites
1 teaspoon cream of tartar
¾ cup sugar

Beat egg whites (at room temperature) and cream of tartar until foamy. Gradually add sugar, 1 tablespoon at a time, beating until stiff peaks form. Yield: enough for one 10-inch cake.
Sandra Russell,
Gainesville, Florida.

No-Frost Cakes

Grab a cup of coffee and a slicing knife because these cakes come out of the oven ready to eat. Orange Pound Cake is one you'll be proud to take to neighbors or serve at your own table. And you'll want to save a piece for breakfast, too.

Swiss Chocolate Chip Cake and Orange Liqueur Cake both use cake mixes for convenience. The glaze on Orange Liqueur Cake is made of orange juice, butter, and Triple Sec. If you just can't wait to sample, go ahead and cut into the cake. Make the glaze later to serve over it.

ORANGE POUND CAKE

1½ cups butter or margarine, softened
3 cups sugar
5 eggs
3½ cups all-purpose flour
1 teaspoon cream of tartar
1½ teaspoons baking powder
¼ teaspoon salt
¾ cup plus 2 tablespoons milk
¼ cup orange juice
1 teaspoon vanilla extract
1 teaspoon almond extract
2 tablespoons grated orange rind

Cream butter; gradually add sugar, beating at medium speed of an electric mixer until light and fluffy. Add eggs, one at a time, beating after each addition. Combine flour, cream of tartar, baking powder, and salt; add to creamed mixture alternately with milk and orange juice, beginning and ending with flour mixture. Mix just until blended after each addition. Stir in flavorings and orange rind.

Pour batter into a greased and floured 10-inch tube pan. Bake at 325° for 1 hour and 25 to 30 minutes or until a wooden pick inserted in center comes out clean. Cool cake in pan 10 minutes. Remove cake from pan, and cool completely on a wire rack. Yield: one 10-inch cake.
Ann Hall Harden,
Pleasant Garden, North Carolina.

ORANGE LIQUEUR CAKE

1 cup chopped pecans
1 (18.25-ounce) package yellow cake mix with pudding
3 eggs
½ cup vegetable oil
½ cup Triple Sec or other orange-flavored liqueur
2 teaspoons grated orange rind
¼ cup orange juice
¼ cup water
Glaze (recipe follows)

Sprinkle pecans in the bottom of a greased and floured 10-inch Bundt pan; set aside.

Combine remaining ingredients, except glaze, in a large mixing bowl. Beat 30 seconds at low speed of an electric mixer; then beat 2 minutes at medium speed. Pour into pan; bake at 325° for 1 hour or until a wooden pick inserted in center comes out clean. Cool in pan 10 minutes; remove from pan, and let cool completely on wire rack. Using a meat fork or wooden pick, pierce cake at 1-inch intervals. Spoon glaze over cake. Yield: one 10-inch cake.

Glaze:

½ cup butter or margarine
¼ cup orange juice
¾ cup sugar
1 teaspoon grated orange rind
½ cup Triple Sec or other orange-flavored
  liqueur

Melt butter in a heavy saucepan. Stir in orange juice and sugar; bring to a boil. Boil 5 minutes, stirring constantly. Remove from heat; stir in orange rind and Triple Sec. Yield: 1¼ cups.

Shirley S. Watson,
Spartanburg, South Carolina.

SWISS CHOCOLATE CHIP CAKE

1 cup raisins
1 tablespoon all-purpose flour
1 (18.5-ounce) package Swiss chocolate
  cake mix
4 eggs
1 (8-ounce) carton commercial sour cream
⅓ cup water
⅓ cup vegetable oil
1 teaspoon vanilla extract
1 cup semisweet chocolate morsels
1 cup chopped pecans
Powdered sugar

Dredge raisins with flour; set aside.

Combine cake mix, eggs, sour cream, water, oil, and vanilla in a large mixing bowl; beat 2 minutes on medium speed of an electric mixer. Add raisins, chocolate morsels, and pecans; stir until ingredients are combined.

Pour batter into a greased and floured 10-inch Bundt pan. Bake at 350° for 45 to 50 minutes or until a wooden pick inserted in center comes out clean. Cool cake in pan 10 minutes; remove from pan, and cool completely on a wire rack. Dust top of cake with powdered sugar. Yield: one 10-inch cake.

Beulah Smith,
Bay Saint Louis, Mississippi.

Fast-Rising Rolls

Cream Cheese Pinches are rich yet quick. The recipe contains a fast-rising type of yeast now available in most grocery stores. Dough rising time is cut in half because a more active strain of yeast is used. This rapid-rise yeast can be used in recipes calling for the regular kind. Just be sure to add this kind of yeast to dry ingredients.

CREAM CHEESE PINCHES

1 (8-ounce) package cream cheese,
  softened
1 egg, beaten
¼ cup sugar
½ teaspoon vanilla extract
1 cup water
½ cup shortening
5 cups all-purpose flour, divided
½ cup sugar
1 package rapid-rise yeast
¼ teaspoon salt
3 eggs
Melted butter or margarine
1½ cups sifted powdered sugar
2 to 3 tablespoons milk
⅓ cup finely chopped pecans

Beat cream cheese at medium speed of an electric mixer until smooth; add 1 egg, ¼ cup sugar, and vanilla, stirring well. Set aside. Combine water and shortening in a saucepan; heat until very warm (120° to 130°).

Combine 4 cups flour, ½ cup sugar, yeast, and salt in a large mixing bowl. Add shortening mixture, stirring well. Add eggs; beat at medium speed of an electric mixer until smooth. Gradually stir in enough remaining 1 cup flour to make a soft dough. Turn dough out onto a well-floured surface, and knead 5 minutes until smooth and elastic. Cover dough; let rest 10 minutes.

Roll dough to ¼-inch thickness; cut into 3½-inch squares; spoon 1½ teaspoons cream cheese mixture into center of each square. Pull corners of dough together, and pinch seams securely. Turn corners under to form a ball, and place seam side down in greased muffin pans.

Cover and let rise in a warm place (85°), free from drafts, 30 minutes or until doubled in bulk. Bake at 375° for 15 to 20 minutes or until golden brown, brushing with melted butter the last 5 minutes. Remove from pans.

Combine powdered sugar and milk, stirring well. Drizzle glaze over warm rolls. Sprinkle tops with pecans. Yield: 2 dozen.

Garlon Phillips,
Baton Rouge, Louisiana.

Luscious Whole-Grain Bread

Cynthia Neal of Marietta, Georgia, was right when she said her Whole Wheat-Oatmeal Bread was great. The whole-grain combination of oats and whole wheat flour not only makes the bread taste good but also provides dietary fiber. Bread flour gives the loaf a better structure, and honey lends a mild, slightly sweet taste without overpowering the nutty flavor of the grains.

WHOLE WHEAT-OATMEAL BREAD

2 cups boiling water
1 cup regular oats, uncooked
½ cup honey
2 teaspoons salt
1 tablespoon butter or margarine
1 package dry yeast
½ cup warm water (105° to 115°)
2½ cups whole wheat flour
2 cups bread flour

Combine boiling water and oats in a large mixing bowl; let stand 1 hour. Add honey, salt, and butter, stirring mixture well.

Dissolve yeast in warm water; let stand 5 minutes. Add to the oats mixture. Stir in the flours.

Place dough in a greased bowl, turning to coat top. Cover and let rise in a warm place (85°), free from drafts, 1 hour or until doubled in bulk.

Punch dough down; turn out onto a lightly floured surface, and knead until smooth and elastic. Divide dough in half; shape each half into a loaf. Place each loaf in a well-greased 8½- x 4½- x 2½-inch loafpan.

Cover and let rise in a warm place (85°), free from drafts, 40 minutes or until doubled in bulk. Bake at 350° for 50 minutes or until bread sounds hollow when tapped. Shield loaf loosely with an aluminum foil tent during last 10 to 15 minutes of baking, if necessary. Yield: 2 loaves.

Tip: To protect the natural flavor of whole wheat flour and ensure a long shelf life, store in a moisture-proof bag in the refrigerator or freezer.

Peanut Butter Eggs For Your Easter Basket

Making Peanut Butter Easter Eggs is a tradition at the home of Marian Parsons, in Hurricane, West Virginia. The eggs are gifts each year for her family and friends. Last Easter, she even turned them into a highly successful project for her church.

PEANUT BUTTER EASTER EGGS

1½ cups butter or margarine, softened
¾ cup crunchy peanut butter
1½ tablespoons light corn syrup
½ teaspoon vanilla extract
1½ to 2 (16-ounce) packages powdered sugar, sifted
½ (24-ounce) package chocolate-flavored candy coating
Decorator Frosting

Combine butter, peanut butter, corn syrup, and vanilla; mix at low speed of an electric mixer until mixture is smooth and well blended. Gradually add powdered sugar until mixture is no longer sticky and can be handled with hands; divide into six even portions. Shape each portion into an oval shape with a flat bottom; place oval-shaped portions on paper towels. Cover loosely, and let sit 12 hours at room temperature.

Place candy coating in top of a double boiler; bring water to a boil. Reduce heat to low; simmer until coating melts. Carefully dip bottom of each egg in coating, and place on wax paper. Refrigerate 15 minutes. Place eggs on wire rack over wax paper. Spoon coating over eggs, letting excess drip on wax paper. (Excess candy coating can be reused by melting over simmering water.) Place eggs in refrigerator about 15 minutes or until firm.

Prepare decorating bags. Decorate the Easter eggs with Decorator Frosting as desired. Yield: 6 (½-pound) eggs.

Note: If making small eggs, shape mixture into 18 ovals, and follow the preceding procedures.

Decorator Frosting:
¼ cup shortening
2 cups sifted powdered sugar
3 tablespoons milk
Paste food coloring (optional)

Cream shortening in a mixing bowl; gradually add powdered sugar alternately with milk until desired consistency. Color portions of frosting with paste food coloring, if desired. Yield: about 1 cup.

Get a jump on the Easter Bunny! Make Peanut Butter Easter Eggs for a delightful holiday surprise. Our recipe makes 6 large eggs or 18 small ones.

Step 1: *Shape peanut butter portions into ovals with flat bottoms; cover and let sit 12 hours. Dip egg bottoms into melted candy coating. Place on wax paper; refrigerate.*

Step 2: *Transfer chilled peanut butter eggs to a wire rack placed over wax paper; spoon melted candy coating over eggs to cover. Refrigerate eggs until firm.*

Step 3: *Decorate eggs with frosting as desired, using decorating bags. (Color portions of frosting with paste food coloring, if desired.)*

May

Cheese Served With Flair

The next time you need an easy way to entertain, consider setting up a cheese buffet. You can probably purchase all the cheese and accompaniments from your neighborhood supermarket, and you won't have any cooking or baking to do.

Our buffet looks more complicated than it is. We simply added a few frills to make the cheese in the buffet unique by carving it, piping it, and skewering it into kabobs. Then we provided plenty of crusty bread, crackers, fruit, and wine to round out the special cheese buffet menu.

Planning the Buffet

A cheese buffet takes just a little advance planning and then last-minute assembling. Plan the buffet so that it offers a range of textures, flavors, and shapes. Cheese varies in flavor from mild to sharp; textures range from very soft to hard. In the buffet, serve wedges or rounds of cheese in addition to the shaped offerings.

Keep in mind that 2 to 4 ounces per person should be plenty when you are serving cheese as an appetizer. Offer 4 to 6 ounces per person for a light lunch, and include plenty of fresh fruit and crusty bread. For dessert, serve 2 to 4 ounces, and choose mild-flavored cheeses and sweet cheese spreads. Little biscuits and not-too-sweet cookies make good dessert bases for the cheeses.

To be sure the cheese is fresh when you serve it, wait until the day of your party to slice it. Prepare as much as you can that morning; then cover the cheese with plastic wrap, and chill it.

As you arrange the buffet, keep the cheese covered with plastic wrap. Remove the covering just before your guests begin to arrive.

Shaping the Cheese

Cheddar Cutouts on a Pick: Slice a brick of Cheddar into ½-inch slices. Cut desired shapes, using canapé cutters. Cut slice from bottom of eggplant so that eggplant will stand upright. Arrange cutouts on wooden picks, and insert into eggplant. Garnish top with lettuce, if desired. Shred cheese scraps to use in cooking.

Swiss Appetizer Kabobs: Cut 1 pound of Swiss cheese into 24 cubes; place cheese, 24 pimiento-stuffed olives, and loosely folded, thinly sliced ham (about 1 pound) on wooden skewers.

Fruited Cream Cheese Cookies: Spread fruited cream cheese onto commercial ginger cookies. Top each with matching fruit, such as a strawberry on strawberry cream cheese.

Neufchâtel Cheese Balls: Cut 1 (8-ounce) package of Neufchâtel cheese into 4 equal slices. Roll each slice into a ball. (Do not soften cheese.) Roll each cheese ball in paprika, chopped fresh parsley, chopped nuts, or lemon-pepper seasoning.

Mozzarella Pinwheels: Place 1 (1-ounce) round slice salami (at room temperature) on work surface; top with 1 thin round slice mozzarella (at room temperature). Roll meat and cheese jellyroll fashion. Slice log into 1-inch pieces, and insert a decorative wooden pick through each.

Cream Cheese and Lox in Party Rye: Soften 1 (8-ounce) package cream cheese; beat it until fluffy, using an electric mixer (or use commercially whipped cream cheese, and omit beating). Spoon cream cheese into a decorating bag fitted with metal tip No. 15. Place one slice of an 8-ounce loaf of party rye bread on work surface. Pipe small amount of cream cheese on bread; top with a small slice of smoked salmon (½ pound per loaf of bread). Place another slice of bread atop first canapé, and pipe and top it. Repeat filling and stacking procedure; set stack on its side to resemble reassembled loaf. Makes about 36 canapés.

Commercial Cheese Spread: Many grocery stores and cheese shops sell cheese already blended into sweet and

Cream Cheese and Condiments offers an eye-catching new way to serve the versatile cheese. Your guests can spread cream cheese on endive, and then sprinkle with toppings.

savory spreads. To hold sweet spreads, scoop out an apple, and rub the cut surface with lemon juice; spoon in the spread. For savory spreads, slice away the top from a red or green pepper, and scoop out seeds. Spoon in the spread, or pipe it, using a large fluted tip.

Gouda Flower: Using a small, sharp paring knife, make 4 to 8 intersecting cuts across top of a round of Gouda, cutting through the rind, but not into the cheese. With the tip of a knife, gently peel back cut wedges to look like petals of a flower.

Cream Cheese and Condiments: Unmold 1 (8-ounce) tub of commercial whipped cream cheese on a large lettuce-lined serving platter. Pull a metal decorating comb across the top, if desired. Arrange Belgian endive leaves around cream cheese to look like the petals of a flower. Group assorted toppings, such as chopped red pepper, chopped chives, black caviar, chopped pecans, or crumbled bacon, in lettuce cups around flower. (See photograph on opposite page.)

Wedges of Brie: Cut a round of Brie into serving-size triangles. Stand triangles upright to add height and dimension to buffet.

Get Ready For Fresh Vegetables

Whether we harvest from the garden or shop at a roadside stand or supermarket, selecting fresh vegetables is one of the joys of summer. And with all the produce available, we always look for new recipes—or rediscover old ones. You will find both new and traditional vegetable favorites included here.

For the best flavor and nutrition, handle vegetables properly from the time they are harvested until you serve them at the table. Remember, as storage time lengthens, vitamins A and C are lost, and some vegetables begin to lose their sweet taste. Store them in a cool, dry place away from light, and cook or preserve them as soon as possible.

FRIED OKRA
(pictured on page 99)

1 pound okra
3 tablespoons all-purpose flour
2 egg whites
1½ cups soft breadcrumbs
Vegetable oil
Salt

Wash okra, and drain well. Remove tip and stem end; cut okra into ½-inch slices. Coat okra with flour.

Beat egg whites (at room temperature) until stiff peaks form; fold in okra. Stir in breadcrumbs, coating okra well.

Deep fry okra in hot oil (375°) until golden brown. Drain on paper towels. Sprinkle with salt. Yield: 4 servings.
Shirley Ryer,
Canton, Texas.

FRESH OKRA AND TOMATOES

1 clove garlic, minced
½ cup chopped onion
½ cup chopped green pepper
2 tablespoons butter or margarine, melted
2 cups sliced okra
3 cups peeled, chopped tomatoes
¼ teaspoon dried whole oregano
½ teaspoon salt
½ teaspoon pepper

Sauté garlic, onion, and green pepper in butter about 10 minutes or until the vegetables are tender. Add remaining ingredients, and cook 5 minutes, stirring frequently. Yield: 4 to 6 servings.
Janet McIntire,
Marietta, Georgia.

TOMATO-BASIL VINAIGRETTE
(pictured on page 99)

4 large tomatoes, sliced
¼ cup plus 2 tablespoons chopped fresh basil
¼ cup plus 2 tablespoons olive oil
2 tablespoons vinegar
½ teaspoon salt
⅛ teaspoon pepper

Place tomatoes in a shallow dish; sprinkle with basil. Combine olive oil, vinegar, salt, and pepper in a jar; cover tightly, and shake vigorously. Pour over tomatoes. Chill 3 hours. Yield: 8 servings.
Charles Walton,
Birmingham, Alabama.

MAQUE CHOU STUFFED TOMATOES

4 medium tomatoes
3½ cups corn cut from cob
½ cup chopped onion
½ cup chopped green pepper
2 tablespoons water
1 tablespoon vegetable oil
½ teaspoon sugar (optional)
½ teaspoon salt
⅛ teaspoon pepper
Pinch of red pepper

Cut tops from tomatoes; scoop out pulp, leaving shells intact. Reserve pulp. Place tomato shells upside down on paper towels to drain.

Combine corn, reserved tomato pulp, and remaining ingredients in a saucepan; bring to a boil. Cover, reduce heat, and simmer 45 minutes, stirring occasionally. (Add additional water, if necessary, to prevent corn from sticking to saucepan.)

Spoon corn mixture into tomato shells. Place tomato shells in a 9-inch square dish; bake at 350° for 10 minutes. Yield: 4 servings. *Janie Lavin,*
Signal Mountain, Tennessee.

FRESH SUMMER SALSA

2 slices bacon
2 medium onions, chopped
4 cups chopped tomatoes
1 small chile pepper, chopped
1 clove garlic, crushed
1 teaspoon sugar
½ teaspoon cumin seeds, crushed
1 tablespoon lemon juice
Green or yellow peppers, cored and seeded (optional)
Tortilla chips (optional)

Cook bacon in a large Dutch oven until crisp; remove bacon, reserving 2 tablespoons drippings in Dutch oven. Crumble bacon, and set aside.

Sauté onion in reserved drippings until tender. Stir in tomatoes, and simmer 15 minutes. Add chile pepper and next 4 ingredients. Spoon salsa into hollow peppers, if desired. Serve with tortilla chips, if desired. Yield: 3½ cups.
Patsy Bell Hobson,
Liberty, Missouri.

Tip: Use a stiff vegetable brush to scrub vegetables rather than peel them. Peeling is not necessary for many vegetables and causes a loss of vitamins found in and just under the skin.

HERB SALAD

4 tomatoes, cut into bite-size pieces
1 cucumber, thinly sliced
¾ to 1 cup chopped purple onion
2 teaspoons dried whole oregano
1 teaspoon dried whole basil
½ teaspoon salt
⅔ cup crumbled feta cheese
½ cup olive oil

Combine first 3 ingredients in a bowl; sprinkle with oregano, basil, and salt. Cover and chill at least 30 minutes. Add feta cheese and olive oil; toss lightly. Let stand 15 minutes before serving. Yield: 4 to 6 servings.
Mrs. Stanley N. Pichon, Jr.,
Slidell, Louisiana.

GREEN BEAN SALAD

1 pound fresh green beans
¾ cup boiling water
1 small onion, sliced and separated into rings
½ cup plain yogurt
1 tablespoon red wine vinegar
1 tablespoon lemon juice
1 tablespoon Dijon mustard
1 teaspoon honey
¼ to ½ teaspoon dried whole dillweed
1 clove garlic, minced
⅛ teaspoon pepper

Wash beans; trim ends, and remove strings. Combine beans and water; bring to a boil. Cover and cook 6 to 8 minutes or until crisp-tender; drain.
Combine beans and onion; set aside. Combine remaining ingredients; mix well. Pour over bean mixture; toss gently to coat beans. Chill several hours before serving. Yield: 4 to 6 servings.
Elaine Winters,
College Park, Maryland.

CHILLED ZUCCHINI SOUP

1 (14½-ounce) can chicken broth
3 large zucchini, sliced
   (about 2 pounds)
2 medium onions, chopped
1 clove garlic, minced
¼ teaspoon salt
1 cup milk
¼ to ½ cup mayonnaise
1 teaspoon lemon juice
¼ teaspoon ground nutmeg
Additional zucchini slices (optional)

Combine broth, zucchini, onions, garlic, and salt in a large saucepan; bring to a boil, reduce heat, and simmer 10 minutes or until vegetables are tender. Let cool.
Place half of zucchini mixture into container of an electric blender; blend until smooth. Remove from blender container. Repeat procedure with remaining zucchini mixture. Combine mixtures, milk, mayonnaise, lemon juice, and nutmeg; cover and chill. Garnish with additional zucchini slices, if desired. Yield: 5½ cups.
Theodora Mann,
Big Lake, Texas.

LEMON-CUCUMBER MOLD

1 (3-ounce) package lemon-flavored gelatin
1 envelope unflavored gelatin
⅔ cup boiling water
½ teaspoon salt
2 cups commercial sour cream
3 tablespoons cider vinegar
1¼ cups finely chopped, peeled cucumber
2 teaspoons finely chopped green onions

Dissolve gelatins in boiling water; stir in salt. Combine sour cream and vinegar; stir into gelatin mixture. Chill until consistency of unbeaten egg white.
Fold cucumber and green onions into gelatin. Pour into a lightly oiled 4-cup mold. Chill until firm. Yield: 8 servings.
Della Taylor,
Jonesborough, Tennessee.

SKILLET CORN FRITTATA

10 eggs, beaten
½ cup whipping cream
1 teaspoon dried whole basil
½ teaspoon salt
⅛ teaspoon pepper
¼ cup plus 2 tablespoons butter or margarine
1½ cups corn cut from cob
¼ cup chopped green onions
6 green pepper rings
6 tomato slices
1 cup (4 ounces) shredded Swiss cheese

Combine eggs, whipping cream, basil, salt, and pepper; mix well. Set aside.
Melt butter in a 10-inch nonstick skillet; add corn and green onions, and sauté 5 minutes or until tender. Pour into egg mixture, stirring constantly.

Return skillet to heat; add egg mixture. Cover, reduce heat, and cook 15 to 18 minutes or until center is almost set. Arrange green pepper and tomato over top, leaving space to cut 6 wedges. Sprinkle with cheese. Cover and cook 5 minutes. Cut into wedges, and serve immediately. Yield: 6 servings.
Kay Castleman Cooper,
Burke, Virginia.

GARDEN SAUTÉ

¼ pound cooked ham, cut into strips
2 tablespoons vegetable oil
1 large green pepper, chopped
2 to 3 green onions, cut into ½-inch pieces
1 clove garlic, minced
2 large tomatoes, chopped
1 medium zucchini, thinly sliced
1 yellow squash, thinly sliced
¼ teaspoon salt
3 tablespoons grated Parmesan cheese

Sauté ham in hot oil in a large skillet. Remove ham, and set aside. Add green pepper, green onions, and garlic to skillet; sauté about 3 minutes over low heat. Add tomatoes, zucchini, yellow squash, and salt. Cook over medium heat until vegetables are crisp-tender (about 3 minutes). Add ham, and cook an additional 2 minutes. Spoon into serving dish; sprinkle with cheese. Yield: 2 to 3 servings. *Judy Guilliams,*
Clarksville, Texas.

MARINATED ROASTED PEPPERS

6 green peppers
6 sweet red peppers
1½ teaspoons sugar
¼ cup olive oil
¼ cup vegetable oil
¼ teaspoon freshly ground pepper
¼ teaspoon salt
¼ teaspoon dried whole oregano
2 cloves garlic, minced

Wash and dry peppers; place on an aluminum foil-lined baking sheet. Bake at 425° for 45 minutes. Put peppers in a plastic bag; close tightly, and let stand 10 minutes to loosen skins. Peel peppers; remove core and seeds. Cut peppers into 1-inch pieces.
Combine remaining ingredients; mix well. Pour mixture over peppers; toss well. Cover and chill. Yield: 3¾ cups.
Barbara Carson,
Hollywood, Florida.

Try A Seafood Entrée For Two

When you're cooking for two, fresh seafood is a good choice. It's usually not prepackaged so that you can purchase just the quantity you need. Most seafood preparation is quick and simple. Shrimp Dijonnaise is marinated in a delectable lemon-mustard sauce and then broiled or baked.

Steaming fish is an easy method that helps retain flavor. It is best suited for delicate, lean fish, such as red snapper, grouper, halibut, and salmon. For specific instructions on steaming, check the recipe we've included for Halibut With Orange-Curry Sauce. It is important to reduce the heat immediately after the water begins to boil.

The ingredients for Stir-fry Shrimp and Vegetables are numerous, but it's like a one-dish dinner because of the abundance of vegetables.

HALIBUT WITH ORANGE-CURRY SAUCE

½ cup commercial sour cream
2 tablespoons grated orange rind
1 tablespoon chopped fresh parsley
¼ teaspoon onion powder
¼ teaspoon dry mustard
¼ teaspoon curry powder
2 (5½- to 6-ounce) halibut steaks

Combine first 6 ingredients; chill.
Lightly grease a vegetable steaming rack; place in a Dutch oven. Add water to just below steaming rack; bring water to a boil. Place halibut on rack. Cover, reduce heat, and simmer 8 to 10 minutes or until fish flakes easily when tested with a fork. Serve with sauce. Yield: 2 servings. *Hazel B. James, Hendersonville, North Carolina.*

SHRIMP DIJONNAISE

¾ pound unpeeled large fresh shrimp
½ cup lemon juice
¼ cup butter or margarine, melted
2 tablespoons vegetable oil
2 tablespoons Dijon mustard
1 tablespoon Worcestershire sauce
8 to 10 cloves garlic, minced

Peel shrimp, leaving tails intact; devein. Set aside.

Combine remaining ingredients in a shallow glass container. Add shrimp; cover and refrigerate 4 hours.
Place shrimp on a lightly greased broiler pan. Broil 4 inches from heat 4 minutes or until shrimp are done. Yield: 2 servings.
Note: Shrimp may be baked at 450° for 3 to 4 minutes instead of broiled.
Mrs. Rodger Giles, Augusta, Georgia.

SHRIMP-AND-GROUPER SAUTÉ

1 (½-pound) grouper fillet
1 tablespoon butter or margarine, melted
¼ cup dry white wine
1 teaspoon lime juice
2 tablespoons chopped celery leaves
1 small onion, thinly sliced
6 large fresh shrimp, peeled and deveined
4 lime slices (optional)

Sauté grouper in butter in a large skillet 1 to 2 minutes on each side. Add wine and lime juice. Arrange celery leaves and onion slices on top of grouper. Cover, reduce heat, and simmer 10 minutes. Add shrimp; cover, reduce heat, and simmer 3 to 5 minutes or until shrimp are done and fish flakes easily when tested with a fork. Garnish with lime slices, if desired. Yield: 2 servings. *Mrs. Robert L. Fetzer, Jacksonville, Florida.*

STIR-FRY SHRIMP AND VEGETABLES

¾ pound unpeeled medium-size fresh shrimp
3 tablespoons vegetable oil, divided
¼ pound fresh mushrooms, sliced
¼ pound fresh snow peas
2 cups (about ¼ pound) broccoli flowerets
2 stalks celery, diagonally sliced into ½-inch slices
½ medium-size red pepper, cut into ¼-inch strips
½ teaspoon chicken-flavored bouillon granules
½ cup hot water
¼ cup sliced water chestnuts, drained
3 green onions, cut into 1-inch pieces
1¾ teaspoons cornstarch
2 tablespoons cold water
3 tablespoons soy sauce

Peel and devein shrimp. Heat 1 tablespoon oil at 325° in a wok or heavy skillet. Add shrimp, and stir-fry 2 minutes or until done. Remove shrimp, and set aside.
Add 1 tablespoon oil, and stir-fry mushrooms 1 to 2 minutes. Remove mushrooms, and set aside.
Add remaining 1 tablespoon oil, and stir-fry snow peas, broccoli, celery, and red pepper 2 minutes. Dissolve bouillon granules in ½ cup water; add to skillet. Cover and cook 3 minutes.
Add water chestnuts and onions to wok. Dissolve cornstarch in 2 tablespoons water; stir in soy sauce. Add soy sauce mixture, shrimp, and mushrooms to wok, stirring constantly. Stir-fry 2 minutes or until thoroughly heated and sauce thickens. Yield: 2 servings.
Ashlyn Ritch, Athens, Georgia.

Scrumptious Picnic Fare

No matter what you're celebrating, a picnic makes the occasion special. Select from our recipes here to suit your taste. All of the food can be made ahead and will serve 8 to 10 people.

Herbed Fried Chicken is an easy variation of the Southern favorite. Biscuit mix and salad-dressing mix are blended together for a crispy fried chicken coating. The Cheese Loaf (recipe on next page) is similar to a quick bread—it has no yeast, and it's easy to mix and bake.

HERBED FRIED CHICKEN

2 cups biscuit mix
2 (.07-ounce) packages Italian salad-dressing mix
6 pounds chicken pieces
Vegetable oil

Combine biscuit mix and salad-dressing mix in a plastic bag; shake to mix. Place 2 or 3 pieces of chicken in bag; shake well. Repeat procedure with the remaining chicken.
Heat 1 inch of oil in a large skillet to 325°; add chicken, and fry 30 to 35 minutes or until golden brown, turning once. Drain chicken on paper towels. Yield: 8 servings. *Barbara Rogers, Cleveland, Tennessee.*

CHEESE LOAF

3 cups self-rising flour
¼ cup sugar
1 cup (4 ounces) shredded Cheddar cheese
½ teaspoon minced onion flakes
1 egg, slightly beaten
1½ cups milk
¼ cup vegetable oil

Combine first 4 ingredients; mix well. Add remaining ingredients; stir until dry ingredients are moistened. Grease the bottom of a 9- x 5- x 3-inch loafpan. Bake at 350° for 1 hour or until golden brown. Cool in pan for 10 minutes. Remove to a wire rack to cool completely. Yield: 1 loaf. *Ruthie Stooksbury, Lake City, Tennessee.*

HAM SALAD SPREAD

2 cups ground cooked ham (about 1 pound)
½ cup finely chopped celery
¼ cup sweet pickle relish, drained
½ cup mayonnaise
1 to 2 teaspoons prepared horseradish

Combine all ingredients; mix well. Cover and chill at least 2 hours. Yield: about 2¼ cups. *Cathy Darling, Grafton, West Virginia.*

MIXED BAKED BEANS

½ pound bacon
2 large onions, chopped
1 (16-ounce) can pork and beans, drained
1 (16-ounce) can red kidney beans, drained
1 (17-ounce) can baby lima beans, drained
⅓ cup firmly packed brown sugar
¼ cup vinegar
1 cup catsup
1 tablespoon dry mustard
1 tablespoon Worcestershire sauce

Cook bacon in a large skillet until crisp; remove bacon, reserving drippings in skillet. Crumble bacon, and set aside. Sauté onion in drippings until tender; drain.

Combine onion, bacon, beans, and remaining ingredients in a large bowl; stir until mixed. Spoon into a lightly greased 2-quart casserole; cover and bake at 350° for 45 minutes. Yield: 8 to 10 servings. *Cathy Williams, Vale, North Carolina.*

MACARONI SALAD

1½ cups uncooked elbow macaroni
2 tablespoons tarragon vinegar
2 tablespoons vegetable oil
¼ cup mayonnaise
½ cup shredded carrot
½ cup sliced black olives
¾ cup diced sweet red pepper
½ cup snow peas

Cook macaroni according to package directions; drain. Rinse with cold water; drain again.

Combine vinegar and oil; pour over macaroni in a large bowl, and toss lightly until well coated. Chill macaroni several hours.

Add mayonnaise, and toss lightly until well coated. Stir in remaining ingredients. Yield: 8 to 10 servings. *Mrs. Homer Baxter, Charleston, West Virginia.*

FIRE-AND-ICE TOMATOES

6 medium tomatoes, peeled and quartered
1 medium onion, sliced
1 medium-size green pepper, cut into strips
1 large cucumber, peeled and sliced
¾ cup cider vinegar
¼ cup water
1 tablespoon plus 2 teaspoons sugar
1½ teaspoons celery salt
1½ teaspoons mustard seeds
½ teaspoon salt
½ teaspoon red pepper
⅛ teaspoon pepper

Combine vegetables in a large bowl, and set aside.

Combine remaining ingredients in a small saucepan. Bring to a boil, and boil 1 minute. Pour mixture over vegetables. Cover and chill 8 hours. Serve with a slotted spoon. Yield: 10 servings. *Helen Porterfield, Hemphill, Texas.*

SALTED PEANUT COOKIES

1 cup shortening
2 cups firmly packed brown sugar
2 eggs
2 cups all-purpose flour
1 teaspoon baking powder
1 teaspoon baking soda
½ teaspoon salt
2 cups quick-cooking oats, uncooked
1 cup crispy rice cereal
1 cup salted peanuts

Cream shortening; gradually add brown sugar, beating well at medium speed of an electric mixer. Add eggs, and beat well.

Combine flour, baking powder, soda, and salt; add to creamed mixture, mixing well. Stir in oats, cereal, and peanuts. (Dough will be stiff.) Drop dough by rounded teaspoonfuls onto lightly greased cookie sheets. Bake at 375° for 10 to 12 minutes. Remove cookies to wire racks to cool. Yield: 7 dozen. *Lucille Carroll, Boca Raton, Florida.*

Celebrate With A Party

It's that time of year when parties abound to celebrate graduations, marriages, and the end of the school year. Or you may have another festive occasion in mind.

To treat your friends to something special, try one of these ideas. You'll find it easy to prepare one large dessert for an evening party after dinner. Almond Cream With Fresh Strawberries is a spectacular choice. As guests arrive, serve them champagne with Lemon-Cheese Canapés, savory cookies with a cheese topping. And don't forget coffee later on.

For a more casual affair, offer a combination of brownies, cookies, and punch. The Mocha Brownies are filled with toasted pecans, and Sherry Snaps are cut in various shapes. Cheese Bonbons and Traders' Punch are perfect choices to complete the party menu.

**Champagne
Lemon-Cheese Canapés
Almond Cream
With Fresh Strawberries
Coffee**

LEMON-CHEESE CANAPÉS

1½ cups all-purpose flour
½ teaspoon salt
½ cup shortening
1 egg, slightly beaten
½ teaspoon grated lemon rind
2 tablespoons lemon juice
1 tablespoon milk
¼ cup finely chopped pecans
1 (8-ounce) package cream cheese, softened
3 tablespoons cocktail sauce
¼ teaspoon seasoned salt
Radish slices
Pimiento-stuffed olive slices

Combine flour and salt; stir well. Cut in shortening with a pastry blender until mixture resembles coarse meal. Add egg, lemon rind, lemon juice, and milk; mix well. Stir in pecans. Shape into ¾-inch balls; place on ungreased baking sheets. Flatten with bottom of floured glass. Bake at 375° for 15 minutes. Cool on wire racks.

Beat cream cheese until fluffy. Add cocktail sauce and seasoned salt; mix well. Cover and chill.

Before serving, pipe 1 teaspoon cream cheese mixture on top of each wafer. Garnish each with radish slice or olive slice. Yield: 3 dozen.

Velma Kestner,
Berwind, West Virginia.

ALMOND CREAM WITH FRESH STRAWBERRIES

1 quart fresh strawberries
⅓ cup amaretto
⅔ cup water
2 to 2½ dozen ladyfingers
1 cup butter or margarine, softened
1 cup sugar
½ cup amaretto
¼ teaspoon almond extract
1⅓ cups finely chopped almonds, toasted
2 cups whipping cream
Strawberry sauce (recipe follows)

Wash and hull strawberries; drain well. Set aside.

Line bottom and sides of a 3-quart glass bowl or mold with wax paper. Combine ⅓ cup amaretto and ⅔ cup water in a small bowl; mix well. Brush over ladyfingers.

Cream butter and sugar until light and fluffy. Add ½ cup amaretto and almond extract, mixing well. Fold in chopped almonds.

Beat whipping cream at medium speed of an electric mixer until soft peaks form. Fold whipped cream into butter mixture.

Line bottom and sides of bowl or mold with ladyfingers. Arrange about 10 strawberries between the ladyfingers. Layer half each of whipped cream mixture, strawberries, and ladyfingers. Repeat layers. Cover bowl with wax paper. Place a plate over bowl; refrigerate overnight.

Unmold, remove wax paper, and serve with Strawberry Sauce. Yield: 12 servings.

Strawberry Sauce:

2 cups fresh strawberries
¼ to ⅓ cup sugar
1½ tablespoons kirsch
½ teaspoon lemon juice

Wash and drain strawberries; puree in blender. Add remaining ingredients; mix well. Yield: 1¾ cups.

Reynolds Shook,
Birmingham, Alabama.

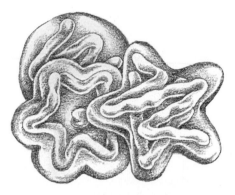

Cheese Bonbons
Mocha Brownies   Sherry Snaps
Traders' Punch

CHEESE BONBONS

2 (8-ounce) packages cream cheese, softened
¼ cup crumbled blue cheese
¼ teaspoon curry powder
3 tablespoons Madeira wine
Minced peanuts
Toasted sesame seeds

Combine cream cheese, blue cheese, curry powder, and wine in a medium mixing bowl; beat at medium speed of an electric mixer until well blended. Cover mixture and chill thoroughly.

Shape mixture into 36 (1-inch) balls. Roll balls in peanuts or sesame seeds. Serve with crackers. Yield: 3 dozen.

Eleanor K. Brandt,
Arlington, Texas.

MOCHA BROWNIES

¼ cup butter or margarine
2 cups finely chopped pecans
⅛ teaspoon salt
1 tablespoon instant coffee granules
½ cup plus 2 tablespoons butter or margarine
5 (1-ounce) squares unsweetened chocolate
4 eggs
½ teaspoon salt
2 cups sugar
1 teaspoon vanilla extract
¼ teaspoon almond extract
1 cup all-purpose flour

Place ¼ cup butter in a 9-inch square baking pan; bake at 350° for 3 minutes or until melted. Stir in pecans; bake 15 minutes, stirring twice. Drain on paper towels; sprinkle with ⅛ teaspoon salt. Set aside.

Grease a 15- x 10- x 1-inch jellyroll pan, and line with wax paper; grease and flour wax paper. Set aside.

Crush coffee granules with the back of a spoon; set aside.

Melt ½ cup plus 2 tablespoons butter in top of a double boiler. Add crushed coffee granules, and stir with a wire whisk until dissolved. Add chocolate; cook until melted, stirring often. Remove from heat; cool 10 minutes.

Combine eggs and ½ teaspoon salt in a large mixing bowl; beat at high speed of an electric mixer until foamy. Gradually add sugar, beating constantly. Beat an additional 10 minutes. Add chocolate mixture and flavorings; beat at low speed just until blended. Fold in flour and pecans. Pour mixture into jellyroll pan; place on lowest rack in a 450° oven. Immediately reduce heat to 400°; bake 20 to 25 minutes or until a wooden pick inserted in center comes out clean. (Do not overbake.)

Immediately invert onto a cookie sheet; peel off wax paper. Invert again onto another cookie sheet. Cool completely. Cut diagonally into 1-inch diamonds. Yield: 6 dozen. *Betty Smith,*
Gadsden, Alabama.

Tip: When preparing finger sandwiches in advance, keep them from drying out by placing them in a shallow container lined with a damp towel and wax paper. Separate sandwich layers with wax paper, and cover with another layer of wax paper and a damp towel; refrigerate.

SHERRY SNAPS

½ cup butter or margarine, softened
¼ cup shortening
½ cup sugar
1 egg
¼ cup cream sherry
2½ cups all-purpose flour
½ teaspoon salt
½ teaspoon ground cinnamon
½ teaspoon ground mace
Drizzle Glaze

Cream butter and shortening at medium speed of an electric mixer; gradually add sugar, beating until light and fluffy. Add egg; mix well. Add sherry; mix well.

Combine flour, salt, cinnamon, and mace; add to creamed mixture, mixing well. Form dough into a ball; cover and chill several hours.

Roll dough to ⅛-inch thickness on a lightly floured surface; cut with 2-inch cookie cutters. (Place unused dough in refrigerator.) Place cookies 1 inch apart on lightly greased cookie sheets. Bake at 350° for 12 to 15 minutes or until bottoms are lightly browned.

Remove cookies, and cool completely on wire racks. Repeat procedure with remaining cookie dough. Decorate cookies with Drizzle Glaze. Yield: 4 dozen (2-inch) cookies.

Drizzle Glaze:

2 cups sifted powdered sugar
¼ cup cream sherry
2 to 3 teaspoons milk
Food coloring

Combine sugar and sherry; mix well. Add milk for desired consistency. Divide glaze, and add desired food colorings; mix well. Insert No. 2 tip into a decorating bag. Spoon glaze into bag; close bag. Drizzle glaze over cookies. Let dry. Yield: ⅔ cup.

Margaret Brantley,
Montgomery, Alabama.

TRADERS' PUNCH

2 cups orange juice
2 cups lemon juice
1 cup grenadine syrup
½ cup light corn syrup
3 (33.8-ounce) bottles ginger ale, chilled

Combine orange juice, lemon juice, grenadine, and corn syrup, stirring until blended; chill well. Add ginger ale to fruit juice mixture just before serving. Yield: 1 gallon. *Nina Burch,*
Shreveport, Louisiana.

Appetizers From The Sea

Here's an easy tip for turning an ordinary meal into the extraordinary—serve a seafood appetizer. It's a good way to get any meal off to a great start. Our readers offer a scrumptious variety of seafood treats, some served cold, others served hot.

The recipe for Baked Clam Shells takes advantage of the convenience of canned minced clams. When combined with onion, celery, green pepper, Parmesan cheese, and Worcestershire sauce and piled into baking shells, they take on a rich and elegant character.

Tuna-Pecan Ball is seasoned with green pepper, onion, celery, olives, horseradish, and Worcestershire sauce. Pecans add a nice, crunchy texture. You'll especially enjoy this recipe when the appetizer needs to be made ahead of time.

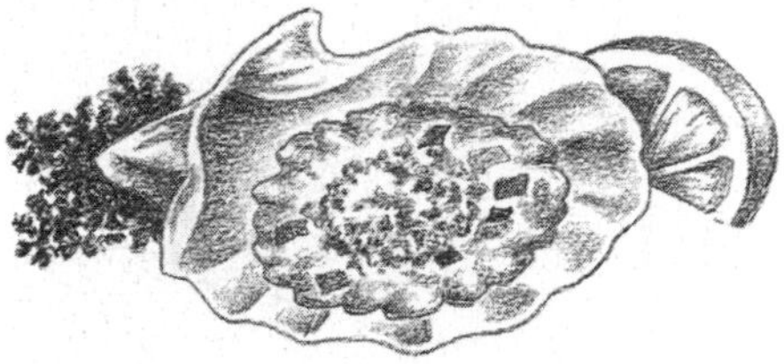

BAKED CLAM SHELLS

½ cup chopped onion
½ cup chopped celery
¼ cup chopped green pepper
¼ cup butter or margarine, melted
1 (6½-ounce) can minced clams, undrained
2 tablespoons all-purpose flour
1 tablespoon grated Parmesan cheese
⅛ teaspoon pepper
⅛ teaspoon Worcestershire sauce
⅛ teaspoon hot sauce
½ cup crushed round buttery crackers, divided
1 tablespoon butter or margarine, melted

Sauté onion, celery, and green pepper in ¼ cup butter in a small skillet until tender. Stir in clams, flour, cheese, pepper, Worcestershire sauce, and hot sauce. Add ¼ cup cracker crumbs; stir well. Cook over medium heat, stirring constantly, until thickened and bubbly. Spoon into individual baking shells.

Combine remaining ¼ cup cracker crumbs and 1 tablespoon butter; sprinkle over clam mixture. Bake at 350° for 15 minutes. Yield: 6 servings.

Rachel Teichelman,
Stamford, Texas.

TUNA-PECAN BALL

1 (8-ounce) package cream cheese, softened
1 (6½-ounce) can solid white tuna, drained and flaked
3 tablespoons diced green pepper
3 tablespoons diced onion
3 tablespoons diced celery
5 pimiento-stuffed olives, diced
2 teaspoons prepared horseradish
½ teaspoon hot sauce
½ teaspoon Worcestershire sauce
½ cup chopped pecans

Combine all ingredients except pecans; stir well. Shape mixture into a ball; cover and chill at least 1 hour. Roll in pecans; cover and chill. Serve ball with assorted crackers. Yield: about 2 cups. *Melinda Pipes,*
Hartford, Kentucky.

BACON-WRAPPED SCALLOPS

1 pound bay scallops
12 slices bacon, cut in half crosswise and lengthwise
1¼ teaspoons Greek seasoning
1 teaspoon freshly ground pepper
2 tablespoons lemon juice

Wrap each scallop with a piece of bacon; secure with a wooden pick. Sprinkle with seasonings and lemon juice. Place on a rack in a shallow roasting pan. Broil 5 inches from heat 8 minutes or until bacon is crisp, turning once. Serve immediately. Yield: 40 to 44 appetizers. *Pamela S. Mazaris,*
Charleston, South Carolina.

SHRIMP MOLD

3 cups water
1 pound unpeeled medium shrimp
1 envelope unflavored gelatin
¾ cup cold water
¼ cup Chablis or other dry white wine
1 cup mayonnaise
2 tablespoons diced onion
¼ cup lemon juice
1 teaspoon dry mustard
¼ teaspoon salt
¼ teaspoon white pepper
Dash of red pepper

Bring 3 cups water to a boil; add unpeeled shrimp, and cook for 3 to 5 minutes. Drain well, and rinse with cold water. Peel and devein shrimp. Set shrimp aside.

Soften gelatin in ¾ cup cold water; let stand 5 minutes. Heat wine in a small saucepan over low heat; add gelatin mixture, stirring until dissolved. Let mixture cool.

Place shrimp, gelatin mixture, and remaining ingredients in container of an electric blender; process until smooth. Pour into an oiled 3-cup mold; chill until firm. Unmold and serve with assorted crackers. Yield: 3 cups.

Linda Weaver,
Longwood, Florida.

SHERRIED AVOCADO-CRABMEAT COCKTAIL

½ cup catsup
¼ cup mayonnaise
2 tablespoons dry sherry
1 teaspoon lemon juice
Dash of red pepper
½ cup chopped celery
Shredded lettuce
1 medium avocado, diced
2½ cups fresh crabmeat, drained

Combine catsup, mayonnaise, sherry, lemon juice, and red pepper in a small bowl. Beat at medium speed of an electric mixer until well blended. Stir in celery. Cover and chill 1 hour.

To serve, line stemmed glasses with shredded lettuce. Arrange avocado and crabmeat over lettuce; top with dressing. Yield: 4 servings.

Eleanor K. Brandt,
Arlington, Texas.

Entrées Men Like To Cook

Many Tulsa, Oklahoma, folks label Jim Pemberton a gourmet cook. Spicy ethnic dishes are the ones Jim likes to cook best, and his Cajun Barbecued Shrimp fits that description to a tee. Tulsa Eggs is a rendition of huevos rancheros, but this version contains pork and potatoes as delicious additions. Italian Pot Roast calls for lots of different ingredients; be sure to include each of them. It's their special blend that gives the roast its unique flavor.

We've also included recipes from other men who like to cook.

ITALIAN POT ROAST

1 (3½-pound) arm roast, 2½ inches thick
½ cup all-purpose flour
½ cup olive oil, divided
1 large onion, diced
½ cup diced celery
1 carrot, diced
2 cloves garlic, minced
4 strips bacon, minced
½ cup Chablis or other dry white wine
½ teaspoon dried whole marjoram
1 teaspoon dried whole basil
1 cup beef broth
1 (16-ounce) can plum tomatoes, undrained
⅓ cup sliced pimiento-stuffed olives
⅓ cup sliced ripe olives
2 tablespoons chopped fresh parsley
2 teaspoons grated lemon rind
1 teaspoon lemon juice
Hot cooked fettuccine (optional)
Grated Parmesan cheese (optional)

Dredge roast with flour. Heat ¼ cup oil in a large Dutch oven; brown roast on both sides. Remove roast, and add remaining oil, onion, celery, carrot, garlic, and bacon; cook over medium heat 3 minutes, stirring constantly. Add wine; cook until wine is reduced.

Remove half of vegetable mixture; add roast, and return vegetable mixture to Dutch oven. Add marjoram, basil, broth, and tomatoes. Cover and simmer 2 hours or until tender. Add olives.

Combine parsley, lemon rind, and lemon juice; stir well. Serve with roast.

Serve roast, if desired, over fettuccine topped with freshly grated Parmesan cheese. Yield: 6 to 8 servings.

CAJUN BARBECUED SHRIMP

1 cup butter or margarine, divided
1 small onion, chopped
2 cloves garlic, minced
1 teaspoon red pepper
1 teaspoon black pepper
½ teaspoon white pepper
½ teaspoon crushed red pepper
½ teaspoon dried whole thyme
½ teaspoon dried whole rosemary, crushed
⅛ teaspoon dried whole oregano
1 teaspoon Worcestershire sauce
1 pound unpeeled jumbo shrimp
½ cup chicken broth
¼ cup beer
2 cups hot cooked rice
Fresh parsley sprigs (optional)
French bread

Melt ½ cup butter in a large skillet. Add onion and next 9 ingredients; cook 1 minute, stirring constantly. Add shrimp; cook 2 minutes, stirring constantly. Add remaining ½ cup butter and chicken broth; cook 2 minutes, stirring occasionally. Stir in beer, and cook 1 minute.

Remove from heat. Remove shrimp from skillet. Mound rice in center of skillet, and arrange shrimp around rice. Garnish with fresh parsley sprigs, if desired. Serve with French bread. Yield: 2 to 3 servings.

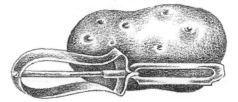

TULSA EGGS

1½ pounds pork shoulder steak, trimmed
1 teaspoon vegetable oil
1 medium potato, peeled and cubed
1 medium onion, chopped
1 clove garlic, minced
½ medium-size green pepper, cut into strips
1 (10-ounce) can tomatoes with green chiles, chopped
1 beef-flavored bouillon cube
½ teaspoon ground cumin
¼ teaspoon red pepper
¼ teaspoon black pepper
½ teaspoon salt
4 eggs
½ cup (2 ounces) shredded Cheddar cheese
4 crisp corn tortillas
Parsley
Sliced tomatoes (optional)

Cut pork steak into ½-inch cubes. Heat oil in a large skillet; sauté pork over medium heat about 1 minute. Add potatoes, onion, garlic, and green pepper; cook 3 to 4 minutes.

Add tomatoes, bouillon, cumin, red pepper, black pepper, and salt; stir well. Cover and cook over low heat 30 minutes or until potatoes are tender, stirring occasionally.

Make four indentations in cooked mixture with a knife; break an egg into each indentation.

Bake, uncovered, at 350° for 10 to 12 minutes. Remove from oven, and sprinkle Cheddar cheese over mixture. Cover and let stand 5 minutes.

Heat tortillas according to package directions. Spoon egg mixture over hot tortillas. Garnish each serving with parsley. Serve with sliced tomatoes, if desired. Yield: 4 servings.

■ **Donald F. Hupp** of Vienna, West Virginia, uses a unique combination of dry mustard, strong coffee, and sherry to give his Roast Leg of Lamb a delicious flavor.

ROAST LEG OF LAMB

1 (5½- to 6-pound) leg of lamb
½ teaspoon garlic salt
½ teaspoon salt
¼ teaspoon pepper
¼ teaspoon dry mustard
¼ cup all-purpose flour
½ cup hot water
¾ teaspoon instant coffee granules
½ cup milk
2 tablespoons dry sherry

Trim all visible fat from lamb; rub with garlic salt, salt, and pepper. Combine dry mustard and flour; stir well. Dredge lamb with flour mixture; place on a roasting rack.

Combine hot water and coffee granules; stir until coffee dissolves. Add milk and sherry, stirring well; set aside.

Bake at 425° for 1 hour; reduce heat to 325°, and bake an additional hour or until a meat thermometer registers 160°. Baste lamb with coffee mixture. Yield: 8 servings.

■ **Larry Miller** of Ashland, Kentucky, is $150 richer for his recipe for Kyoto Orange-Chicken Stir-fry. It won the grand prize in a local cooking contest.

KYOTO ORANGE-CHICKEN STIR-FRY

1 cup orange juice
½ cup soy sauce
¼ cup firmly packed brown sugar
1½ tablespoons cornstarch
3 tablespoons vegetable oil
3 pounds boneless chicken breasts, skinned and cut into 1-inch pieces
2 tablespoons grated orange rind
1 teaspoon ground ginger
¼ teaspoon hot sauce
4 green onions, cut into ¼-inch slices
1 (8-ounce) can sliced water chestnuts, drained
2 oranges, peeled, seeded, and sectioned
Hot cooked rice

Combine first 4 ingredients; stir until sugar and cornstarch dissolve. Set aside.

Pour oil into a preheated wok; heat to medium high (325°) for 2 minutes. Add chicken, and stir-fry 2 to 3 minutes. Add grated orange rind, ginger, and hot sauce; stir-fry 1½ minutes.

Add orange juice mixture, green onions, and water chestnuts; stir-fry 3 minutes or until thickened. Stir in orange sections. Serve over hot rice. Yield: 8 servings.

■ **Rob Rickerby,** a resident of Woodstock, Georgia, relaxes on weekends by cooking. One of his simple but elegant recipes is Seafood Brochette.

SEAFOOD BROCHETTE

1 pound grouper, cut into 1-inch cubes
½ pound sea scallops
½ pound medium shrimp, peeled and deveined
4 slices bacon, quartered
8 medium-size fresh mushroom caps
1 large green pepper, cut into 1-inch pieces
1 medium-size purple onion, quartered
Sherry Sauce
Sunshine Sauce

Alternate grouper, scallops, shrimp, bacon, mushroom caps, green pepper, and onion on five 14-inch skewers. Grill 15 minutes over medium-hot coals or broil in oven, turning to brown all sides. Baste frequently with Sherry Sauce or Sunshine Sauce. Yield: 4 to 6 servings.

Sherry Sauce:

1 tablespoon cornstarch
2 tablespoons water
¼ cup butter or margarine
½ cup sherry
¼ cup chicken broth

Dissolve cornstarch in water. Melt butter in a saucepan; add sherry, broth, and cornstarch mixture to saucepan. Cook, stirring constantly, until mixture boils. Yield: 1 cup.

Sunshine Sauce:

¼ cup butter or margarine
¼ cup pineapple juice
1 tablespoon Dijon mustard
1 tablespoon lemon juice
½ teaspoon ginger
Pepper to taste

Melt butter; stir in remaining ingredients. Yield: ½ cup.

■ **Dick Meeker** of Amarillo, Texas, gives new meaning to country-fried steak with his Beer-Braised Steaks.

BEER-BRAISED STEAKS

2 (12-ounce) top sirloin steaks, ½ inch thick
3 tablespoons vegetable oil
1 large onion, thinly sliced
2 cloves garlic, minced
3 tablespoons butter or margarine, melted
3 tablespoons all-purpose flour
1 cup beef broth
1 cup beer
1 (4-ounce) can mushroom stems and pieces, undrained
¼ cup tomato juice
1 bay leaf
½ teaspoon salt
¼ teaspoon pepper
Hot cooked noodles

Brown steaks in oil in a Dutch oven. Remove steaks from Dutch oven; set aside. Drain pan drippings.

Sauté onion and garlic in butter in Dutch oven until crisp-tender. Add flour, stirring well; cook 1 minute. Add beef broth and next 6 ingredients; stir until blended. Return steaks to Dutch oven; cover, reduce heat, and simmer 1 hour. Remove bay leaf. Serve over noodles. Yield: 4 servings.

MICROWAVE COOKERY

Quick And Easy Cakes

If it's hard to imagine baking a cake in just 10 minutes, then try baking one in the microwave oven. But keep in mind that the microwave version will differ from a heat-baked cake in several ways: The batter varies in ingredients, the cake doesn't brown or form a crust, and it doesn't follow the conventional tests for doneness.

If you compare the ingredients in batters for conventional and microwave cakes, you'll often find less flour and fewer eggs in the microwave version. These protein-rich ingredients cause toughening in foods that are baked in the microwave oven. In our recipe for

Our Fruit and Spice Cake starts with a mix and microwaves in just 5 minutes.

Place cake on cake platter; arrange fruit slices on top and around sides of cake. Place jelly in a 1-cup glass measure; microwave at HIGH for 45 seconds to 1 minute or until melted. Stir well. Drizzle melted jelly over fruit. Yield: one 1-layer cake.

NO-EGG CHOCOLATE MARSHMALLOW CAKE

1¼ cups all-purpose flour
1 teaspoon baking soda
½ teaspoon salt
1½ cups sugar
⅓ cup cocoa
1 cup buttermilk
½ cup vegetable oil
1½ teaspoons instant coffee powder
¾ cup water
1 cup marshmallow creme
Chocolate frosting (recipe follows)
½ cup chopped pecans

Combine first 5 ingredients. Add buttermilk and oil, stirring until smooth. Combine coffee powder and water in a 1-cup glass measure; microwave at HIGH for 2 minutes or until boiling. Stir into chocolate mixture just until blended; batter will be thin.

Grease bottom, but not sides, of a 12- x 8- x 2-inch baking dish. Pour batter into prepared dish. Microwave, uncovered, at MEDIUM (50% power) for 15 minutes, rotating dish twice. Microwave at HIGH for 6 to 7 minutes or until cake top is no longer doughy, rotating dish once; cake will still appear very moist. Spoon small mounds of marshmallow creme evenly over cake; do not spread. Let stand directly on countertop 5 minutes. Gently spread marshmallow creme evenly over cake.

Spread chocolate frosting over marshmallow creme, creating a marbled effect. Sprinkle with pecans. Cut into squares to serve. Yield: 12 servings.

Chocolate Frosting:

1 (1-ounce) square unsweetened chocolate
3 tablespoons milk
2 tablespoons butter or margarine
2 cups sifted powdered sugar
½ teaspoon vanilla extract

Combine chocolate, milk, and butter in microwave-safe bowl or glass measure; microwave at MEDIUM (50% power) for 1½ to 2 minutes or until softened and blended, stirring after 1 minute. Stir in remaining ingredients; beat with wooden spoon until mixture is smooth. Yield: enough for top of one 12- x 8- x 2-inch cake.

No-Egg Chocolate Marshmallow Cake, eggs are eliminated, and chocolate is the binding agent. The batter is also thinner than most conventional ones.

Dark spices or chocolate used in microwave cakes will make the lack of a browned crust less noticeable. Frostings, glazes, and toppings will also make the cake look more normal.

A microwaved cake is done when the top looks moist but not wet, and a wooden pick inserted in the center comes out clean. Unlike conventional cakes, if the sides of a microwaved cake have pulled away from the pan, it's usually overbaked.

Standing time after baking is critical with a microwave cake. After you remove it from the microwave, it needs to stand directly on the countertop, rather than on a cooling rack, to complete cooking. If the cake is still not done after the standing time, microwave it at MEDIUM (50% power) for 1 minute at a time until done.

If you like using cake mixes, you'll enjoy our recipe for Fruit and Spice Cake. Use one egg white rather than following package directions that call for two.

FRUIT AND SPICE CAKE

1 (9-ounce) package white cake mix
½ teaspoon ground cinnamon
¼ teaspoon ground allspice
¼ cup butter or margarine
1 egg white
¼ cup water
1 cup sliced fresh strawberries
2 kiwifruit, peeled and sliced
¼ cup strawberry or cherry jelly

Combine cake mix, cinnamon, and allspice in a medium mixing bowl; set mixture aside. Place butter in a microwave-safe mixing bowl; microwave at HIGH for 55 seconds or until melted. Add cake-mix mixture, egg white, and water, beating at medium speed of an electric mixer 2 minutes.

Grease bottom, but not sides, of an 8-inch round microwave-safe cakepan. Line with wax paper, and grease the wax paper. Pour batter into cakepan. Microwave, uncovered, at HIGH for 4½ to 5 minutes or until top is no longer doughy, giving pan a quarter-turn every 2 minutes. Cake will still appear very moist. Let cake stand directly on countertop 5 minutes. Remove from pan, and let cool completely.

Basil-Cheese Tart

The flavor of fresh basil and the texture of soft cheesecake make Herb-Cheese Tart a distinctive luncheon or brunch entrée. Tomatoes' affinity for basil makes them a natural garnish or side dish to accompany this dish that's similar to quiche. Cream cheese and ricotta cheese create its smooth texture. Serve a crunchy, green salad and a slice of fruit to complete the menu.

Cut into thin slices, Herb-Cheese Tart also serves nicely as an appetizer and goes well with white wine.

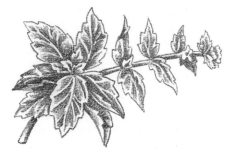

HERB-CHEESE TART

1 cup all-purpose flour
¼ teaspoon salt
⅛ teaspoon garlic salt
⅓ cup plus 1 tablespoon shortening
3 to 4 tablespoons cold water
1 (8-ounce) package cream cheese, softened
⅓ cup ricotta cheese
¼ cup butter or margarine, softened
2 eggs
2 tablespoons all-purpose flour
½ teaspoon salt
¼ teaspoon pepper
2 tablespoons chopped fresh basil
Cherry tomatoes, cut into wedges (optional)
Fresh basil sprigs (optional)

Combine 1 cup flour, ¼ teaspoon salt, and garlic salt; cut in shortening with pastry blender until mixture resembles coarse meal. Sprinkle cold water (1 tablespoon at a time) evenly over surface; stir with a fork until dry ingredients are moistened. Shape into a ball, and chill.

Roll dough to ⅛-inch thickness on a lightly floured surface. Trim dough into an 11-inch circle; place in bottom and 1½-inches up sides of an 8-inch springform pan. Prick with a fork; cover and chill 30 minutes.

Place a piece of aluminum foil over pastry; gently press into pastry shell. Cover foil with a layer of dried peas or pastry weights. Bake at 450° for 8 minutes; remove peas and foil. (If pastry sides have pulled away from pan, press back against pan sides with the back of a spoon.) Bake an additional 5 minutes or until lightly browned. Remove from oven; cool.

Combine cheeses and butter; beat at medium speed of an electric mixer 1 to 2 minutes or until light and fluffy. Add eggs, one at a time, beating well after each addition. Add 2 tablespoons flour and next 3 ingredients; beat just until blended. Pour into pastry shell; bake at 350° for 35 to 40 minutes or until set. Remove from oven; serve hot or at room temperature. Garnish with tomato wedges and basil sprigs, if desired. Yield: one 8-inch tart. *Alice Hawes, Dallas, Texas.*

Surprise Her With Breakfast

Moms are special folks who deserve a treat. With these recipes, children can surprise mom with a breakfast tray delivered to her room. We've planned a continental breakfast of Fruit Soup, Sour Cream-Bran Muffins, and coffee or tea.

The soup is easy to make because there's no cooking or pureeing. Applesauce is combined with juice and canned fruits. Sour Cream-Bran Muffins are moist and full of raisins.

These recipes also make enough to feed the rest of the family, or any leftovers can be saved for breakfast the next day. The soup is best served icy cold, so make it the night before. Leftover soup may be frozen.

FRUIT SOUP

1 (16-ounce) can applesauce
1 (6-ounce) can unsweetened pineapple juice
1 (8½-ounce) can pear halves, undrained and chopped
1 (8-ounce) can pineapple tidbits, undrained
1 cup frozen unsweetened sliced peaches, thawed and chopped
2 to 3 tablespoons brandy (optional)
1 teaspoon ground cinnamon
1 cup sliced fresh strawberries

Combine all ingredients except strawberries; stir gently. Cover and chill several hours. Stir in strawberries just before serving. Yield: about 5 cups.

Note: All ingredients may be combined and frozen. Remove soup mixture from freezer; let stand for 30 minutes. Serve soup while still slushy.

Minnie Young, Montgomery, Alabama.

SOUR CREAM-BRAN MUFFINS

½ cup butter or margarine, softened
¼ cup firmly packed brown sugar
1 egg, beaten
1 cup commercial sour cream
¼ cup molasses
1½ cups raisins
1 cup all-purpose flour
1 teaspoon baking soda
¼ teaspoon salt
1 cup shreds of wheat bran cereal

Cream butter; gradually add sugar, beating well at medium speed of an electric mixer. Add egg, sour cream, and molasses; mix well. Stir in raisins.

Combine flour, soda, salt, and cereal; add to creamed mixture, stirring just until moistened. Spoon mixture into greased muffin pans, filling three-fourths full. Bake at 400° for 15 minutes or until done. Yield: 16 muffins.

Nancy Young, Leitchfield, Kentucky.

Right: *There's nothing that says summer quite like fresh vegetables straight from the garden. Fried Okra and Tomato-Basil Vinaigrette are two of our recipes that make use of a variety of vegetables. (Recipes begin on page 89.)*

Pages 100 and 101: *Served alfresco in elegant style, Beef Tenderloin With Mushrooms and Vegetable Kabobs are grilled. Potato Croquettes and Easy Caesar Salad complement the entrée. Cheesecake With Raspberry Sauce is the delectable dessert. (Recipes begin on page 115.)*

Page 102: *A piquant tarragon vinaigrette helps season Herb-Roasted Chicken and the potato-and-celery stuffing (page 155).*

Put A Salad On The Menu

Crisp vegetables and a combination of canned and fresh fruits make salads easy to include on your menu. If your taste is for something simple, yet a little different, try Fresh Broccoli Salad. Helen Sands sent us this recipe, which our home economists raved about.

Citrus Salad combines grapefruit with oranges, avocado, mushrooms, purple onion, and lettuce. Commercial French dressing is the base for an easy dressing.

FRESH BROCCOLI SALAD

1 bunch fresh broccoli, cut into flowerets (about 1½ pounds)
1 cup thinly sliced carrots
1 cup (4 ounces) shredded Cheddar cheese
8 slices bacon, cooked and crumbled
½ cup mayonnaise
2 to 3 tablespoons sugar
1½ tablespoons red wine vinegar
Lettuce leaves (optional)

Place broccoli in a colander, and plunge into boiling water 10 seconds. Drain and dip into ice water. Combine broccoli, carrots, cheese, and bacon; gently toss. Combine mayonnaise, sugar, and vinegar; mix well. Add mayonnaise mixture to broccoli mixture, and toss well. Chill. Serve on lettuce leaves, if desired. Yield: 10 to 12 servings.
Helen Sands,
Columbia, South Carolina.

GREEK SALAD

4 cups torn romaine lettuce
6 cups torn iceberg lettuce
2 tomatoes, cut into wedges
1 large unpeeled cucumber, sliced
1 cup pitted black olives
½ cup olive oil
3 tablespoons red wine vinegar
1 teaspoon dried whole oregano
½ teaspoon freshly ground pepper
1 cup crumbled feta cheese

Combine lettuce greens, tomatoes, cucumber, and olives in a large bowl; toss well. Combine olive oil, vinegar, oregano, and pepper in a jar; cover tightly, and shake vigorously. Toss salad with olive oil mixture just before serving; sprinkle crumbled feta cheese over salad. Yield: 8 to 10 servings.
Madeline Gibbons,
Little Rock, Arkansas.

ZUCCHINI SALAD

1 medium zucchini, sliced
½ pound fresh mushrooms, sliced
1 tomato, chopped
½ cup chopped green onions
¼ cup vegetable oil
¼ cup vinegar
1 teaspoon sugar
1 teaspoon paprika
⅛ teaspoon salt
⅛ teaspoon pepper

Combine zucchini, mushrooms, tomato, and green onions in a mixing bowl; set aside.
Combine oil and remaining ingredients, mixing well; pour over vegetables, tossing lightly. Cover and chill before serving. Yield: 6 servings.
Janie Wallace,
Seguin, Texas.

APPLE SALAD WITH BLUE CHEESE DRESSING

4 cups unpeeled, diced red apples
2½ cups cantaloupe balls (about 1 small cantaloupe)
2 cups sliced celery
½ cup commercial sour cream
⅓ cup mayonnaise
2 ounces blue cheese, crumbled
Lettuce leaves

Combine apples, cantaloupe, and celery in a large bowl. Combine sour cream, mayonnaise, and blue cheese in a small mixing bowl; add to apple mixture, and toss lightly. Serve on lettuce leaves. Yield: 8 to 10 servings.
Virginia Martin,
Raytown, Missouri.

CITRUS SALAD

2 oranges, peeled and sectioned
1 grapefruit, peeled and sectioned
1 avocado, peeled and sliced
1 small purple onion, sliced and separated into rings
1 cup fresh mushrooms, sliced
3 cups torn romaine lettuce
3 cups torn iceberg lettuce
½ cup orange-flavored yogurt
½ cup commercial French salad dressing, chilled

Combine oranges, grapefruit, avocado, onion, and mushrooms; toss gently. Combine salad greens, and arrange onto individual salad plates; set aside. Spoon citrus mixture on salad greens. Combine yogurt and salad dressing; mix well and serve with salad. Yield: 6 to 8 servings.
Dolly G. Northcutt,
Fairfield, Alabama.

A New Twist For Chicken

Folks are eating more chicken these days, so there's a never-ending search for new ways to cook it. This recipe for Chicken Andalusia from Allen English of Jonesborough, Tennessee, combines some flavors you might not think of serving together—with delicious results.

CHICKEN ANDALUSIA

¼ cup dry sherry
2 tablespoons golden raisins
2 tablespoons orange juice
1½ teaspoons chopped fresh parsley
1 clove garlic, crushed
6 chicken breast halves, skinned and boned
½ cup all-purpose flour
1 teaspoon salt
½ teaspoon freshly ground pepper
½ cup olive oil
¼ cup butter or margarine
2 tablespoons sliced almonds
1 (3-ounce) jar pimiento-stuffed olives, drained
Orange slices
Parsley sprigs

Combine sherry and raisins; set aside. Combine orange juice, parsley, and garlic; brush mixture on chicken.
Combine flour, salt, and pepper; dredge chicken in flour mixture. Heat olive oil in a large nonstick skillet; add chicken, and sauté for 5 minutes on each side or until browned. Remove chicken; discard oil.
Melt butter in skillet over medium heat; add sherry-raisin mixture, almonds, and olives. Return chicken to skillet; cover and cook 10 minutes or until done. Transfer chicken to a serving platter, and pour glaze mixture over chicken. Garnish with orange slices and parsley. Yield: 6 servings.

Take A New Look At Sandwiches

The Earl of Sandwich may have come up with the idea of putting meat between two slices of bread, but sandwich ingenuity didn't stop there. The Danes went on to perfect the open-faced sandwich by placing a filling on top of a single slice of bread, and a sandwich with half the bread calories was born. Our low-calorie sandwiches go a step further to suggest a variety of fillings and some less-common bases on which to build your creations.

Those who diet repeatedly know that many fad diets exclude bread from the plan, so sandwiches are totally out of the question. These diets imply that bread and other carbohydrate foods are fattening, but nothing could be further from the truth. In recent years, nutritionists have encouraged us to eat more complex carbohydrates, and bread is a good source. It contains lots of B vitamins and also has dietary fiber when made with whole grains and/or whole grain flours.

Flatbreads, crisp breads, cracker breads, and matzos contain little or no fat, are low in calories, and are interesting alternatives to loaf bread. Or try rice cakes, pita bread, Holland rusks, hard rolls, melba toast, or English muffin halves as your base. Each offers a different flavor and texture that gives new meaning to the word sandwich.

Many of these bases are now available in whole grain or high-fiber versions. If you're unfamiliar with some of these breads, refer to the photo and chart with calorie analysis on the next page. The rest is as simple (or complex) as deciding which filling to try on which bread. There are enough combinations to have a different sandwich for many days to come.

Try Open-Faced Crab Sandwiches (recipe, page 106) on toasted English muffin halves, rice cakes, or Holland rusks. Crabmeat is seasoned with lemon juice, green pepper, chives, Parmesan cheese, and reduced-calorie mayonnaise. The mixture is piled onto the bread of choice and then heated.

Chopped hard-cooked eggs are mixed with diced tofu in Vegetable-Egg Spread (page 106) to yield more filling with less cholesterol than if all eggs had been used. Celery, onion, green peas, and a hint of dillweed add flavor.

Even on a low-calorie diet, you can enjoy the pleasure and convenience of sandwiches. These calorie-trimmed breads provide the perfect bases for a variety of light yet tasty fillings. (For identification of breads, see sketch and chart at right.)

Experiment serving this sandwich filling on flatbreads, crisp breads, cracker breads, or hard rolls.

Open-Faced Garden Sandwiches are a vegetarian's delight. A mixture of almonds and two types of cheese provides the protein to make this a main-dish treat. We use dark pumpernickel bread with this tasty combination.

Whole wheat pita bread rounds provide the perfect base for Lamb Pockets With Dilled Cucumber Topping. Any type of filling that is crumbly and hard to handle is a good choice for this type of bread. Keep in mind that if the sandwich filling is moist, you can line the pita pocket with a lettuce leaf to prevent soggy bread.

LAMB POCKETS WITH DILLED CUCUMBER TOPPING

1 cup grated unpeeled cucumber, drained well
¼ teaspoon dried whole dillweed
¼ teaspoon seasoned salt
½ cup plain low-fat yogurt
1 pound extra lean ground lamb
¼ cup chopped onion
1 clove garlic, minced
¼ teaspoon salt
¼ teaspoon pepper
1½ cups chopped tomatoes
½ cup sliced green onions
4 (6-inch) whole wheat pita bread rounds, halved
8 lettuce leaves

Combine first 4 ingredients in a small bowl; stir well. Cover and chill.

Cook lamb, onion, and garlic in a non-stick skillet over medium heat, until browned, stirring to crumble meat. Drain meat mixture in a colander, and pat dry with paper towels. Stir in salt and pepper.

Combine tomatoes and green onions; set aside. Line each pita half with a lettuce leaf; spoon ¼ cup meat mixture into bread pockets. Top each sandwich with 2 tablespoons of cucumber mixture and ¼ cup tomato mixture. Serve immediately. Yield: 8 servings.

☐ *137 calories, 14.1 grams protein, 3.8 grams fat, 10.6 grams carbohydrate, 43 milligrams cholesterol, 183 milligrams sodium, and 56 milligrams calcium per sandwich.* Cindi Adams,
St. Peters, Missouri.

ALTERNATIVE BASES FOR SLENDER SANDWICHES

Product	Serving Size	Calories
1. Multigrain rice cakes	1 cake	35
2. Dark pumpernickel bread	1 slice	80
3. Whole wheat pita bread rounds	½ of a 6″ round	46
4. Holland rusks	1 rusk	40
5. Whole grain Finnish, dark, thin crisp bread	1 slice	19
6. English snack bread	1 slice	20
7. Whole grain melba toast	1 slice	17
8. Norwegian whole grain thick-style crisp bread	1 wafer	35
9. French cracker bread	1 slice	16
10. English whole rye crisp bread	1 slice	16
11. Swedish fiber-plus crisp bread	1 slice	35
12. English muffins	½ muffin	65
13. Norwegian rye-bran flatbread	1 wafer	15
14. Whole wheat matzos	½ of a matzo	55
15. Norwegian thin-style crisp bread	1 wafer	20
16. Italian spices-flavored brown rice 'n' sesame squared rice cakes	1 cake	20
17. Swedish whole grain crisp bread	1 slice	30
18. French-style crackle bread	1 slice	19
19. Natural-flavored brown rice 'n' sesame squared rice cakes	1 cake	20
20. Hard rolls	1 roll (3″ diameter)	156
21. Vegetable toast	1 slice	16

Note:
The variety of breads shown in the photograph and named above can be purchased in delicatessens, gourmet food shops, large supermarkets, and some health food stores.

OPEN-FACED GARDEN SANDWICHES

4 cups chopped fresh spinach
¼ cup sliced almonds, toasted
⅛ teaspoon garlic powder
½ cup plus 2 tablespoons plain low-fat yogurt
4 slices pumpernickel bread
½ cup (2 ounces) shredded part-skim mozzarella cheese
½ cup (2 ounces) shredded 40% less-fat Cheddar cheese
½ cup sliced fresh mushrooms
⅓ cup unpeeled, scored, thinly sliced cucumber
½ cup alfalfa sprouts

Wash and drain chopped spinach well, and blot dry with paper towels. Combine spinach, sliced almonds, garlic powder, and yogurt in a large mixing bowl; set aside.

Place bread on an ungreased baking sheet. Combine cheeses; toss gently. Sprinkle cheese evenly over each bread slice. Bake at 400° for 2 to 3 minutes or until cheese melts.

Spread spinach mixture over cheese, and top with mushrooms, cucumber, and alfalfa sprouts. Serve immediately. Yield: 4 servings.

☐ *222 calories, 15 grams protein, 9 grams fat, 22.9 grams carbohydrate, 23.3 milligrams cholesterol, 396.8 milligrams sodium, and 358 milligrams calcium per sandwich.*

OPEN-FACED CRAB SANDWICHES

½ pound lump crabmeat, drained
1 tablespoon lemon juice
¼ cup chopped green pepper
1 (2-ounce) jar diced pimiento, drained
2 tablespoons chopped chives
2 tablespoons grated Parmesan cheese
¼ cup reduced-calorie mayonnaise
3 drops of hot sauce
Lemon slices (optional)

Combine crabmeat and lemon juice; toss gently. Add green pepper, pimiento, chives, cheese, mayonnaise, and hot sauce; stir well. Spread about ½ cup crabmeat mixture on bread of your choice. Bake at 350° for 5 minutes or until mixture is thoroughly heated. Garnish with lemon, if desired; serve immediately. Yield: 4 servings.

Note: Suggested bases for sandwich filling include toasted English muffin halves, rice cakes, and Holland rusks.

☐ *113 calories, 11.1 grams protein, 5.9 grams fat, 3.5 grams carbohydrate, 64 milligrams cholesterol, 257 milligrams sodium, and 62 milligrams calcium per ½ cup crabmeat mixture.*

Connie Tidwell,
San Antonio, Texas.

SHRIMP SALAD FILLING

4 cups water
1 pound unpeeled, fresh medium shrimp
2¼ cups finely shredded cabbage
½ cup shredded carrots
½ cup diced tomatoes, drained
¼ cup sliced green onions
1 (8-ounce) can water chestnuts, drained and chopped
½ cup reduced-calorie mayonnaise
¼ cup lemon juice
¼ teaspoon ground red pepper

Bring water to a boil; add shrimp, and cook 3 to 5 minutes. Drain well; rinse with cold water. Peel, devein, and coarsely chop shrimp.

Combine shrimp, cabbage, carrots, tomatoes, green onions, and water chestnuts in a large bowl; toss gently. Set aside.

Combine remaining ingredients in a small bowl; stir well. Add mayonnaise mixture to shrimp mixture; toss gently. Yield: 7 servings.

Note: Suggested bases for Shrimp Salad Filling include flatbreads, crisp breads, cracker breads, rice cakes, and pita bread.

☐ *136 calories, 13.8 grams protein, 5.2 grams fat, 8.3 grams carbohydrate, 113.7 milligrams cholesterol, 206.7 milligrams sodium, and 61.3 milligrams calcium per ¾ cup shrimp mixture.*

Suzanne M. Heath,
Sulphur, Louisiana.

CHICKEN SALAD FILLING

3 cups chopped cooked chicken breast (cooked without skin or salt)
1 cup fresh bean sprouts
1 cup diced celery
½ cup diced green pepper
½ cup diced onion
⅓ cup reduced-calorie mayonnaise
3 tablespoons lemon juice
1 teaspoon freshly ground pepper
¾ teaspoon dry mustard
½ teaspoon seasoned salt

Combine chicken, bean sprouts, celery, green pepper, and onion in a bowl; toss gently. Combine remaining ingredients; stir well. Add to chicken mixture; toss gently to mix. Yield: 9 servings.

Note: Suggested bases include flatbreads, crisp breads, cracker breads, and pita bread.

☐ *113 calories, 14.2 grams protein, 4.5 grams fat, 3.5 grams carbohydrate, 40 milligrams cholesterol, 211 milligrams sodium, and 18 milligrams calcium per ½ cup chicken mixture.*

Jan Thompson,
Highland, Maryland.

HAWAIIAN HAM SPREAD

1¼ cups lean cooked ground ham
1 (8-ounce) can unsweetened crushed pineapple, drained
½ teaspoon brown sugar
⅛ teaspoon ground cloves
2 tablespoons reduced-calorie mayonnaise

Combine all ingredients; stir well. Yield: 3 servings.

Note: Suggested bases for Hawaiian Ham Spread filling include flatbreads, crisp breads, cracker breads, hard rolls, and rice cakes.

☐ *160 calories, 15 grams protein, 6.6 grams fat, 9.8 grams carbohydrate, 41 milligrams cholesterol, 909.7 milligrams sodium, and 14.7 milligrams calcium per ½ cup ham mixture.*

Mrs. J. P. Weber,
Corpus Christi, Texas.

VEGETABLE-EGG SPREAD

3 hard-cooked eggs, peeled and chopped
2 ounces medium-firm tofu, drained and diced
½ cup thinly sliced celery
¼ cup chopped onion
1 tablespoon chopped fresh parsley
¼ teaspoon dried whole dillweed or 1 tablespoon chopped fresh dillweed
¼ teaspoon freshly ground pepper
½ teaspoon Worcestershire sauce
3 tablespoons reduced-calorie mayonnaise
2 tablespoons plain low-fat yogurt
½ cup frozen green peas, thawed and drained

Combine all ingredients except peas in a medium bowl; stir well. Add peas; toss gently. Cover and chill. Yield: 3 servings.

Note: Suggested bases for sandwich filling include flatbreads, crisp breads, cracker breads, and hard rolls.

☐ *167 calories, 9.7 grams protein, 10.6 grams fat, 8.1 grams carbohydrate, 279.7 milligrams cholesterol, 215.3 milligrams sodium, and 91 milligrams calcium per ⅔ cup egg mixture.*

OPEN-FACED VEGETARIAN MELT

1 cup thinly sliced unpeeled cucumber
½ cup grated carrot
¼ cup sliced green onions
3 tablespoons reduced-calorie Italian salad dressing
6 ounces Camembert cheese
2 English muffins, halved and toasted
½ cup alfalfa sprouts

Combine first 4 ingredients; toss gently, and set aside. Slice cheese into 4 equal pieces, and place on muffin halves. Broil 1 to 2 minutes or until cheese melts. Spoon vegetable mixture over cheese; garnish with alfalfa sprouts. Serve immediately. Yield: 4 servings.

Note: Rice cakes or Holland rusks may be substituted for English muffin halves. Do not toast.

□ *238 calories, 11.4 grams protein, 13 grams fat, 18.9 grams carbohydrate, 38.3 milligrams cholesterol, 637.4 milligrams sodium, and 235.5 milligrams calcium per sandwich (using English muffin as sandwich base).* Angela Falkner, Corpus Christi, Texas.

COTTAGE CHEESE SPREAD

1 (12-ounce) container 1% low-fat cottage cheese
1 teaspoon dried whole summer savory
½ cup diced tomato, drained
⅓ cup shredded carrot
⅓ cup chopped unpeeled cucumber
⅓ cup chopped green pepper
¼ cup sliced green onions
1 tablespoon red wine vinegar

Combine cottage cheese and savory; stir well. Add remaining ingredients; toss gently. Cover and chill. Yield: 4 servings.

Note: Suggested bases for sandwich filling include flatbreads, crisp breads, cracker breads, and rice cakes.

□ *77 calories, 11.1 grams protein, 1.03 grams fat, 5.9 grams carbohydrate, 3.5 milligrams cholesterol, 351.5 milligrams sodium, and 68.8 milligrams calcium per ¾ cup cottage cheese mixture.*

Get A Crush On Mint

All over the South, smart cooks crush fresh mint leaves to flavor meat, vegetables, fruit, desserts, and beverages. The herb is easily grown in gardens and window boxes, or it can be bought at the market. Choose the small, tender leaves at the top of the plants for the best flavor. Mint will last a week or more if stems are wrapped in damp paper towels, sealed in a plastic bag, and placed in a refrigerator.

Fresh mint has a stronger flavor than commercial mint and offers a fresher, greener color as well. Although mint is seldom paired with other herbs because of its distinctive taste, it will complement parsley, as it does in Middle Eastern Salad, a variation of tabbouleh. In Avocado-Chicken Salad, the herb is combined with chopped chicken, avocado, and fresh, ripe tomatoes.

AVOCADO-CHICKEN SALAD

¼ pound fresh mushrooms, sliced
1 tablespoon butter or margarine, melted
1 (10¾-ounce) can cream of celery soup, undiluted
¼ cup mayonnaise
3 tablespoons lemon juice
2 teaspoons Dijon mustard
4 mint sprigs, finely chopped
Dash of salt
Dash of pepper
3 teaspoons sugar (optional)
5 cups chopped cooked chicken
1 medium avocado, peeled and sliced
Lemon juice
Lettuce leaves
2 tomatoes, cut into wedges
Mint sprigs

Sauté mushrooms in butter until tender; set aside.

Combine soup and next 6 ingredients; add sugar, if desired, and mix well. Stir in mushrooms and chicken. Chill.

Dip avocado slices in lemon juice; chill. To serve, arrange chicken mixture on lettuce leaves. Garnish with avocado slices, tomato wedges, and mint sprigs. Yield: 6 to 8 servings.

Vivienne Johnson,
Durham, North Carolina.

MIDDLE EASTERN SALAD

2 slices whole wheat bread
2 cups chopped tomato
½ cup chopped cucumber
2 tablespoons dried chives
2 tablespoons chopped parsley
3 tablespoons chopped fresh mint
2 tablespoons vegetable oil
2 tablespoons lemon juice
½ teaspoon salt
⅛ teaspoon freshly ground pepper
Lettuce leaves
2 ounces Cheddar cheese, cut into cubes

Cut bread into ½-inch cubes; toast until lightly browned. Let cool. Combine tomato, cucumber, chives, parsley, and mint in a medium bowl; set aside.

Combine oil, lemon juice, salt, and pepper; pour over vegetables, and gently toss. Cover and chill.

Arrange lettuce leaves on serving plates. Spoon vegetable mixture on lettuce leaves; top with cheese and croutons. Yield: 4 to 6 servings.

Cheryl Keener,
Lenoir, North Carolina.

MINT TEA

7 tea bags
7 mint sprigs
1 cup sugar
1 quart boiling water
3¼ cups water
2¼ cups pineapple juice
1 (6-ounce) can frozen lemonade concentrate, thawed and undiluted
Mint sprigs (optional)

Combine first 3 ingredients. Pour boiling water over tea mixture; cover and let stand 30 minutes.

Remove tea bags and mint sprigs; discard. Transfer tea to a large pitcher, and add water, pineapple juice, and lemonade concentrate; stir well. Serve over ice. Garnish with mint sprigs, if desired. Yield: 2½ quarts.

Bonnie Taylor,
Jackson, Tennessee.

MINTED DELIGHT

1 (6-ounce) can frozen limeade concentrate, thawed and undiluted
¾ cup vodka
½ cup fresh mint leaves
Ice cubes

Combine first 3 ingredients in container of an electric blender; cover and blend at high speed 1 to 2 minutes or until mint is finely chopped. With blender running at high speed, remove cover of small opening. Add enough ice cubes to fill blender to 4 cups; blend until frothy. Serve immediately. Yield: 4¼ cups.

Judi Burns,
Monroeville, Alabama.

Look What's Happening With Pasta

Macaroni and cheese, spaghetti with meat sauce, and lasagna are weekly specials for many families as a way to stretch the food dollar. This desire to feed more people for less money has also stretched our readers' imaginations and transformed our standard pasta dinner into something special.

From the standpoint of nutrition, pasta is an excellent source of complex carbohydrates that supply energy. It appears frequently in many health-conscious diets, and many athletes favor a pasta dinner before competition.

Linguine Carbonara's buttery cheese sauce and the tomato sauce for Shrimp and Feta Cheese on Vermicelli work best with rod-shaped members of the spaghetti family, such as vermicelli and linguine.

Twisted and curved pastas trap the chunky meat and vegetables as in Chicken and Tomato With Rotelle. Large shells or broad noodles can be paired with broccoli, sausage, and ham chunks. Lasagna noodles are convenient for casseroles.

LINGUINE CARBONARA

½ pound bacon
¼ cup olive oil
1 onion, chopped
1 bunch fresh parsley, chopped
4 ounces Fontina cheese, cubed
3 ounces prosciutto, cut into ¼-inch strips
4 egg yolks, slightly beaten
½ cup half-and-half
1 pound uncooked linguine
Salt and freshly ground pepper to taste
1 cup grated Parmesan cheese, divided

Cut bacon into 1-inch lengths, and cook in a large skillet until crisp. Drain well on paper towels. Pour off drippings, and add olive oil and chopped onion to skillet; sauté onion until tender. Set aside.

Combine parsley, Fontina cheese, and prosciutto in a small bowl; set aside. Combine egg yolks and half-and-half; set aside.

Prepare linguine in a Dutch oven according to package directions; drain. Return linguine to Dutch oven; add bacon, onion, parsley mixture, egg mixture, seasonings, and ½ cup Parmesan cheese. Cook over low heat, stirring constantly, until thoroughly mixed and heated; transfer to serving dish. Sprinkle with remaining ½ cup Parmesan cheese. Serve immediately. Yield: 6 to 8 servings.
Carolyn Rosen,
Nashville, Tennessee.

SHRIMP AND FETA CHEESE ON VERMICELLI

8 ounces uncooked vermicelli
1 pound medium shrimp, peeled and deveined
Pinch of crushed red pepper flakes
¼ cup olive oil, divided
⅔ cup (4 ounces) crumbled feta cheese
½ teaspoon crushed garlic
1 (14½-ounce) can tomato wedges, undrained
¼ cup dry white wine
¾ teaspoon dried whole basil
½ teaspoon dried whole oregano
¼ teaspoon salt
¼ teaspoon pepper
Fresh basil (optional)

Cook vermicelli according to the package directions. Drain, set aside, and keep warm.

Sauté shrimp and red pepper flakes in 2 tablespoons olive oil in a large skillet 1 to 2 minutes or until shrimp are slightly pink. Arrange shrimp in a 10- x 6- x 2-inch baking dish; sprinkle with feta cheese, and set aside.

Add remaining oil to skillet; sauté garlic over low heat. Add tomatoes and juice; cook 1 minute. Stir in wine, basil, oregano, salt, and pepper; simmer, uncovered, 10 minutes. Spoon tomato mixture over shrimp. Bake, uncovered, at 400° for 10 minutes. Serve over vermicelli. Garnish with fresh basil, if desired. Yield: 3 to 4 servings.
Heather Riggins,
Nashville, Tennessee.

CHICKEN AND TOMATO WITH ROTELLE

4 chicken breast halves, skinned, boned, and cut into 1-inch strips
3 tablespoons butter or margarine, melted
1 cup chopped onion
1 clove garlic, minced
1 cup chopped canned tomatoes
1 cup chicken broth
1 (4-ounce) can sliced mushrooms, drained
1 teaspoon ground ginger
1½ teaspoons paprika
¼ teaspoon chili powder
¼ teaspoon salt
⅛ teaspoon pepper
8 ounces uncooked rotelle noodles
2 tablespoons cornstarch
1 cup whipping cream
Parsley sprigs (optional)

Brown chicken on all sides in butter in a large skillet. Remove chicken from skillet, and sauté onion and garlic. Stir in tomatoes and next 7 ingredients. Arrange chicken strips over tomato mixture and simmer, uncovered, 40 minutes.

Cook noodles according to package directions; drain. Spoon noodles onto warm serving platter. Place chicken breast halves on top of noodles, reserving tomato mixture.

Combine cornstarch and whipping cream; add to tomato mixture. Cook, stirring constantly, until sauce is thickened and bubbly, about 3 to 5 minutes. Pour over chicken; garnish with parsley, if desired. Yield: 4 servings.
Sandra Hyche,
Jasper, Alabama.

HAM AND SWISS ON NOODLES

16 ounces uncooked egg noodles
¼ cup sliced green onions
½ cup butter or margarine, divided
1 (4-ounce) can sliced mushrooms, drained
1 (10-ounce) package frozen English peas, thawed and drained
¼ cup all-purpose flour
3 cups milk
½ teaspoon salt
½ teaspoon white pepper
2 cups (8 ounces) shredded Swiss cheese
2 cups cubed cooked ham
1 cup chopped canned tomatoes, drained

Cook noodles according to package directions. Drain, set aside, and keep noodles warm.

Sauté green onions in 2 tablespoons butter in a large heavy saucepan 3 minutes; add mushrooms and peas, and cook until heated. Remove from saucepan, and set vegetables aside.

Melt remaining butter in saucepan; add flour, stirring until smooth. Cook 1 minute, stirring constantly. Gradually add milk; cook over medium heat, stirring constantly, until mixture is thickened and bubbly. Stir in salt and pepper. Add cheese, and stir until mixture is smooth.

Add vegetables, ham, and tomatoes; mix well. Cook until thoroughly heated. Serve over noodles. Yield: 8 servings.

Mrs. Hoyt C. Taylor,
Palm City, Florida.

SEAFOOD CASSEROLE

6 uncooked lasagna noodles
3 tablespoons vegetable oil, divided
6 cups water
1 pound unpeeled fresh shrimp
1 large onion, chopped
1 (3-ounce) package cream cheese, softened
1 cup cottage cheese
1 egg, beaten
1 teaspoon Italian seasoning
Dash of ground nutmeg
⅛ teaspoon salt-free herb-and-spice blend
Salt to taste
Coarsely ground pepper to taste
1 (10-ounce) package frozen chopped spinach, thawed and drained
1 (10¾-ounce) can cream of celery soup, undiluted
⅓ cup evaporated skim milk
4 flounder fillets (about 1 pound), cut into 1- to 1½-inch pieces
1 pound crabmeat or seafood mix
2 tablespoons lemon juice
3 tablespoons grated Parmesan cheese
3 tablespoons seasoned, dry breadcrumbs
2 tablespoons butter or margarine, melted
⅓ cup (1.33 ounces) shredded Cheddar cheese

Cook noodles according to package directions, adding 1 tablespoon vegetable oil to boiling water; drain. Arrange noodles in bottom of a 13- x 9- x 2-inch baking dish. Set aside.

Bring 6 cups water to a boil; add shrimp, and partially cook 1 minute. Drain well; rinse with cold water. Peel and devein shrimp.

Sauté onion until translucent in remaining 2 tablespoons oil in a large skillet. Add cream cheese, cottage cheese, egg, and seasonings, and cook at medium-low heat until cheese is blended. Stir in spinach. Spoon mixture over lasagna noodles.

Combine soup, milk, shrimp, fish, and crabmeat; add lemon juice, and stir

well. Spoon over spinach and cheese mixture.

Combine Parmesan cheese, breadcrumbs, and butter; sprinkle mixture over casserole.

Bake at 350° for 45 minutes. Sprinkle with Cheddar cheese, and bake an additional 5 minutes or until cheese melts. Remove from oven, and let stand 15 minutes before cutting. Yield: 8 servings.

Marie M. Woodard,
Charlotte, North Carolina.

PASTA WITH BROCCOLI AND SAUSAGE

3 cups broccoli flowerets
1 cup sliced fresh mushrooms
1 clove garlic, minced
2 tablespoons butter or margarine, melted
1 pound hot Italian sausage, thinly sliced
6 ounces uncooked egg noodles
3 eggs, beaten
⅓ cup whipping cream
1 cup grated Romano or Parmesan cheese
⅛ teaspoon pepper

Steam broccoli 10 minutes or until crisp-tender; drain on paper towels. Set aside; keep warm.

Sauté mushrooms and garlic in butter in a heavy skillet until tender; set aside.

Cook sausage until browned, stirring often; drain and keep warm.

Cook noodles in a Dutch oven according to package directions; drain and return to Dutch oven.

Combine eggs, whipping cream, cheese, and pepper; stir until mixture is smooth. Add to noodles with mushroom mixture. Cook over low heat, stirring constantly, until thoroughly heated. Transfer to warm platter. Arrange broccoli and sausage on top. Yield: 4 servings.

Sue Fleming,
Charleston, South Carolina.

Desserts From The Freezer

For desserts made in advance, it's hard to beat these recipes featuring ice cream or sherbet. Just mix and freeze, and they're ready when you are.

Almost no cooking is required for these recipes. However, the crumb crusts for recipes such as Toffee Ice Cream Dessert (recipe, next page) and

Layered Sherbet Dessert will be firmer and won't crumble as easily if you bake them before adding the filling. To serve ice cream desserts with a crumb crust, dip the bottom of the dish or pieplate in warm water to loosen the crust and make it easier to serve.

Our recipe for Fruity Ice Cream Cake (recipe, next page) offers a twist. Pieces of angel food cake, strawberries, pineapple, and pecans are stirred into softened ice cream. The mixture is then frozen in a tube pan. To loosen the cake from the mold after freezing, run a hot knife around the edge of the pan, and transfer the dessert to a chilled plate.

Ice cream or sherbet used in frozen desserts usually needs to be softened, particularly if you're mixing it with other ingredients. But it should be softened only enough to mix; refreezing ice cream or sherbet that's too soft will result in large ice crystals. To soften, place ice cream or sherbet in the refrigerator 30 minutes, and it should reach the right consistency for mixing. For a quick method, microwave sherbet or ice cream on HIGH—15 seconds for a pint, 30 seconds for a quart.

LAYERED SHERBET DESSERT

1 cup vanilla wafer crumbs (about 30 wafers)
½ cup flaked coconut
1 (2-ounce) package slivered almonds, toasted and chopped
¼ cup plus 2 tablespoons butter or margarine, melted
1 quart raspberry sherbet, softened
1 quart pineapple sherbet, softened
1 quart lime sherbet, softened
Whipped cream (optional)

Combine first 4 ingredients, mixing well. Press mixture firmly in bottom of a 10-inch tube pan with removable bottom or a 9-inch springform pan. Bake at 375° for 15 minutes or until lightly browned. Cool.

Spread raspberry sherbet evenly over crust; freeze 30 minutes. Repeat with pineapple and lime sherbets, freezing 30 minutes between layers. Cover and freeze several hours or until firm.

If using a tube pan, run a hot knife around edges of pan to loosen; remove sides of pan. Remove center section of pan, if desired. If using a springform pan, remove sides of pan.

Let frozen dessert stand at room temperature 10 minutes before slicing. Garnish with whipped cream, if desired. Yield: 12 servings.

Mildred Bickley,
Bristol, Virginia.

TOFFEE ICE CREAM DESSERT

3 cups crushed cream-filled chocolate
   sandwich cookies
2 tablespoons butter or margarine, melted
½ gallon vanilla ice cream, softened
1 (6-ounce) package bits of brickle
Whipped cream
Commercial fudge sauce, warmed
Maraschino cherries

Combine chocolate cookie crumbs
and butter, mixing well. Press into a
lightly greased 13- x 9- x 2-inch dish.
Bake at 350° for 5 minutes. Cool.

Spread half of ice cream over crust;
sprinkle with half of bits of brickle. Repeat layers. Cover and freeze several
hours or until firm.

Cut dessert into squares to serve. Top
each serving with whipped cream, warm
fudge sauce, and a cherry. Yield: 15 to
18 servings.   *Peggy Faircloth,*
Birmingham, Alabama.

FRUITY ICE CREAM CAKE

½ gallon vanilla ice cream, softened
1 (16-ounce) angel food cake, torn into
   bite-size pieces
1 (10-ounce) package frozen strawberries,
   thawed
1 (8¼-ounce) can crushed pineapple,
   undrained
¾ cup chopped pecans
1 cup whipping cream, whipped

Combine all ingredients except
whipped cream in a large mixing bowl;
mix well. Fold in whipped cream.
Spoon mixture into an ungreased 10-
inch tube pan. Cover and freeze cake
several hours or until firm. Remove
cake from pan, and slice with a warm
knife. Yield: 12 servings.
   Mrs. T. J. McCaughan,
Santa Anna, Texas.

Grind, Chop, Or Slice Meat In The Processor

Whether it's red meat, poultry, or
seafood, you can grind it, chop it, or
slice it in the food processor. You know
that this appliance helps save time and
cleanup, but when it comes to meat, it
can save you money as well.

Grinding meat for casseroles, burgers,
and meat loaf is easy to do with any
kind or cut of meat. You save money
by taking advantage of roast or steak
sales and grinding the meat yourself,
using the knife blade. Just package it
for the freezer if you don't plan to use
it right away.

The processor is a must for folks who
want to trim fat from meat. You can
control how lean the ground meat is by
controlling the amount of fat you add to
it. Making Quick Processor Meatballs is
one way to enjoy the flavor of beef,
pork, and veal combined with as much
fat as you want to use.

When it comes to **slicing meat,** the
processor is a great help in achieving
beautiful, thin slices of rare roast beef.
It also produces the right-size slices of
meat and poultry for your favorite stir-
fry recipes.

The pulse button is the key to controlling the size of pieces when you're
chopping meat. To keep it coarse, as for
our Double-Crust Chicken Pie, one or
two pulses is sufficient. The texture of
raw meat is softer than that of cooked
meat, so it's easier to overprocess it. If
you want more uniform slices, partially
freeze raw meat or chicken until it is
firm but not solid. Chill cooked meat
before chopping or slicing; this makes
the meat firmer.

Use the techniques and tips listed
below for making the best use of your
food processor and meat selections.

—To slice uncooked red meat, cut a
roast or steak into large pieces that will
just fit into the bottom of the processor
food chute. Cut pieces with the grain
running lengthwise so the meat will be
sliced against the grain. The snugger the
meat fits in the food chute, the more
attractive the slices will be.

—Roll uncooked boneless chicken
breasts (whole or halves) lengthwise, or
fold in half to slice. Insert the chicken
into the bottom of the food chute. If
the chicken breasts are small, fit two
into the food chute.

—Cut red meat or poultry into 1-inch
pieces before chopping or grinding.
Using the knife blade, pulse until meat
reaches desired consistency. Leave
pieces coarsely chopped for pot pies,
salads, soups, and casseroles. It's best
to finely chop meat for spreads, terrines, and mousses.

—When grinding red meat for
burgers, meat loaf, and meatballs, leave
at least a small amount of fat on the
meat. The fat adds flavor and moisture.

—One pound of meat or poultry will
generally yield approximately 3 cups of
chopped meat.

—Slice luncheon meats into julienne
strips for salads, using square slices for
best results. Fold the entire stack of
slices from an 8-ounce package in half,
and insert vertically into the food chute.
Slice, using light pressure.

—To slice pepperoni, remove the casing. Cut into equal lengths 1 inch
shorter than the height of the food
chute. Arrange pepperoni pieces vertically in food chute for a snug fit. Slice
the pepperoni, using medium to firm
pressure. The firmer the pressure used,
the thicker the slices.

—To chop pepperoni, remove the
casing, and cut into ½-inch pieces. Insert the knife blade in processor, and
drop pepperoni through the food chute
with the machine running.

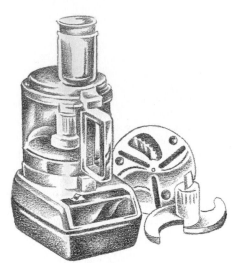

ZIPPY CHILI

2 cloves garlic
1 medium-size green pepper, quartered
1 medium onion, quartered
1 pound boneless beef chuck roast, cut
   into 1-inch cubes
½ teaspoon salt
2 tablespoons chili powder
1½ teaspoons paprika
½ teaspoon ground coriander
½ teaspoon dried whole cilantro
½ teaspoon ground cumin
½ teaspoon dried whole oregano
⅛ teaspoon pepper
1½ tablespoons all-purpose flour
1 (28-ounce) can tomatoes, undrained and
   chopped
½ cup beef broth
1 (16-ounce) can pinto beans, undrained
Hot cooked rice (optional)

Position knife blade in food processor
bowl; top with cover. Drop garlic
through food chute with processor running; process 3 to 5 seconds or until

garlic is minced. Add green pepper and onion to processor bowl; process just until coarsely chopped. Remove from processor bowl.

Add meat to processor bowl; pulse 4 or 5 times or until meat is cut into ¼-inch pieces. Combine meat and chopped vegetables in a Dutch oven. Sauté until meat is browned; drain.

Return meat mixture to Dutch oven; add salt, chili powder, paprika, coriander, cilantro, cumin, oregano, pepper, flour, tomatoes, and broth. Simmer, uncovered, 1 hour, stirring often. Add beans; cook until thoroughly heated. Serve chili over rice, if desired. Yield: about 2 quarts.

Mrs. F. C. Baldwin, Jr.,
Richmond, Virginia.

QUICK PROCESSOR MEATBALLS

2 cloves garlic
4 sprigs fresh parsley
4 slices white bread
1 small onion, quartered
½ teaspoon salt
⅛ teaspoon pepper
¼ teaspoon dried whole oregano
½ pound boneless round steak, trimmed
¼ pound boneless pork, trimmed
¼ pound veal, trimmed
1 egg
½ cup olive oil

Position knife blade in food processor bowl; top with cover. Drop garlic through food chute with processor running; process 3 to 5 seconds or until garlic is minced. Add parsley to processor; pulse until chopped. Remove crusts from bread slices, and tear into quarters. Add bread, onion, and seasonings to processor bowl; process until onion and bread are finely chopped. Remove bread mixture from processor bowl, and set aside.

Cut meat into 1-inch cubes. Position knife blade in processor bowl; add half of meat. Process 1½ minutes or until finely chopped. Set chopped meat aside, and repeat with remaining meat.

Combine chopped meat, bread mixture, and egg in processor bowl. Mix well, scraping sides of processor bowl occasionally.

Shape mixture into 12 (2-inch) meatballs. Cook in hot olive oil over medium heat 10 to 15 minutes or until browned. Drain meatballs well on paper towels. Yield: 4 servings.

Alice McNamara,
Eucha, Oklahoma.

SOMBRERO SPREAD

12 ounces Monterey Jack cheese
4 green onions, cut into 1-inch pieces
1 large onion, quartered
1½ pounds boneless round steak, cut into 1-inch pieces
1 (16-ounce) can refried beans
1 (4-ounce) can chopped green chiles, undrained
1 (8-ounce) jar taco sauce
1 (2¼-ounce) can sliced ripe olives, drained

Position shredding disc in food processor bowl; top with cover. Cut cheese to fit food chute; place cheese in chute. Shred using medium pressure with food pusher. Set cheese aside.

Position knife blade in processor bowl; add green onions. Process until chopped. Set aside.

Add onion quarters to processor bowl; pulse 2 or 3 times or until coarsely chopped. Add meat to processor bowl; process until meat is chopped. Transfer meat mixture to skillet; cook over medium heat until meat is browned, stirring to crumble.

Spread beans in a 12- x 8- x 2-inch baking dish. Layer meat mixture, green chiles, cheese, taco sauce, green onions, and olives evenly over beans. Bake at 400° for 20 minutes. Serve spread with corn chips. Yield: 6 cups.

Sherry Marr,
Burke, Virginia.

SHRIMP SPREAD

1½ cups water
½ pound medium unpeeled shrimp
½ cup butter or margarine, softened
1 teaspoon prepared horseradish
Dash of garlic powder
Dash of salt
Dash of hot sauce
Paprika

Bring water to a boil; add shrimp, and cook 3 to 5 minutes. Drain well; rinse with cold water. Chill. Peel and devein shrimp.

Position knife blade in food processor bowl; add shrimp. Top with cover; process until finely chopped. Add butter, horseradish, garlic powder, salt, and hot sauce; process until smooth.

Spoon shrimp mixture into a serving dish; sprinkle with paprika. Serve spread with assorted crackers. Yield: 1¼ cups.

Shirley A. Toche,
Ocean Springs, Mississippi.

DOUBLE-CRUST CHICKEN PIE

4 chicken breast halves (about 2½ pounds)
4 cups water
½ teaspoon salt
1 medium carrot, scraped and quartered
1 medium onion, halved
5 mushrooms
½ cup frozen English peas, thawed
2 tablespoons cornstarch
2 tablespoons water
¼ teaspoon salt
¼ teaspoon pepper
Pastry for double-crust 9-inch pie

Combine chicken, 4 cups water, and ½ teaspoon salt in a Dutch oven; cover and bring to a boil. Reduce heat, and simmer 45 minutes or until tender. Drain, reserving 2 cups broth. Cool chicken, and remove from bone; cut into large pieces.

Position knife blade in food processor bowl; add half of chicken. Top with cover; pulse 1 or 2 times or until chicken is coarsely chopped. Remove chicken from bowl; set aside. Repeat procedure with remaining chicken.

Position slicing disc in processor bowl; top with cover. Place carrot pieces snugly in food chute; slice using light pressure. Repeat procedure with onion halves. Cook carrot and onion in reserved 2 cups broth. Arrange mushrooms in food chute, and slice using light pressure. Add mushrooms and peas to broth.

Dissolve cornstarch in 2 tablespoons water; add to vegetable mixture, stirring constantly. Cook over medium heat, stirring constantly, until bubbly. Boil 1 minute. Stir in chopped chicken, ¼ teaspoon salt, and pepper.

Spoon chicken mixture into a pastry-lined 9-inch deep-dish pieplate. Top with pastry. Turn pastry edges under, and press firmly to rim of pieplate. Cut slits in top of pastry to allow steam to escape. Bake at 450° for 30 minutes or until crust is golden brown. Let stand 10 minutes before serving. Yield: one 9-inch pie.

Joanie Meyer,
Okarche, Oklahoma.

Tip: Learn to judge food labels carefully and take advantage of products with nutrient information on the label. Nutrition labels indicate the number of calories and the amount of protein, carbohydrates, and fat in a serving of the product. They also give an indication of major vitamins and minerals present in the product.

Hot Stuffing For Shrimp

If you're looking for an appetizer your guests will remember, try Shrimp With Herbed Jalapeño Cheese from Joanne Gross of Lufkin, Texas. "I prefer highly seasoned food," says Joanne. So she adapted the cream cheese stuffing from another recipe.

The recipe is a good one to make in advance. Pipe stuffing onto shrimp, and chill until serving time.

SHRIMP WITH HERBED JALAPEÑO CHEESE

2 pounds unpeeled large fresh shrimp
6 cups water
½ teaspoon salt
1 (8-ounce) package cream cheese, softened
1 clove garlic, minced
2 pickled jalapeño peppers, seeded and finely chopped
2 teaspoons dried cilantro
Salt and pepper to taste

Peel shrimp, leaving tail and the first joint of the shell intact; cut a deep slit down the length of the outside curve of each shrimp, and devein.

Combine water and ½ teaspoon salt in a large saucepan. Bring to a boil; add shrimp, and cook 3 to 5 minutes. Drain shrimp well; rinse with cold water. Pat dry. Chill.

Combine cream cheese and remaining ingredients; beat well. Fill a decorating bag fitted with metal tip No. 21 with the cream cheese mixture. Pipe filling lengthwise into the slits in the shrimp. Yield: 16 to 18 appetizer servings.

From Our Kitchen To Yours

Sunshine, gentle breezes, and the scent of fresh flowers accompany spring cleaning. While you're putting your house in order, don't forget to clean the freezer and make space for a fresh supply of fruits and vegetables. Here are some tips on cleaning your freezer and organizing its contents.

What is the proper method for cleaning the freezer? Consult freezer care booklet. General instructions recommend unplugging the cord and removing food items. Place paper under and over food, and cover with a clean blanket to prevent thawing. Wash inside of freezer, using a solution of 1 tablespoon baking soda to 1 quart water. (Do not use soap.) Rinse and wipe freezer dry, leaving door open long enough to air. Plug in cord; and replace food when temperature is near 0° F.

If defrosting is necessary, carefully scrape frost from sides with a dull-edge plastic scraper. Scoop up frost, and wipe up moisture. For quicker defrosting, pour cold water on the inside, using clean towels to absorb water.

What is the best way to organize the freezer? When cleaning your freezer, arrange food items by categories, using baskets, shelves, and dividers. Stack meats, bakery items, cooked foods, and fruit and vegetables in separate sections. Remember to leave space near the walls and away from the already frozen items for storing unfrozen foods. When placing foods in the freezer, allow space for air circulation to ensure rapid and uniform freezing. (Foods should freeze within 12 to 24 hours.)

You'll save time throughout the year if you make an inventory of the freezer's contents, checking each package label for the product's name, the preparation for freezing, the number of servings, and the date frozen. Place this list near the freezer.

What is the length of time fruits and vegetables can be frozen? When frozen too long, the quality, flavor, and texture of fruits and vegetables are affected. Fruits, except citrus, may be frozen up to one year; citrus fruits may be frozen three to four months. Freezer storage for vegetables is up to one year, with the exception of onions (three to four months) and cooked potatoes (three months).

How much food should be stored in the freezer? Two to three pounds of unfrozen food for every cubic foot of storage space is the general rule. Using foods continuously and replacing them with seasonal ones will keep your stock changed two to three times a year. If you keep the freezer two-thirds full, space will be available for taking advantage of special buys.

How can leftovers be safely frozen? Foods cooled immediately after cooking may be frozen; the cooling stops the cooking action, helping retain color, texture, and flavor. Home freezers don't have the fast heat-removal capability of commercial freezing equipment. Leftovers and similar small food quantities may be stored directly in the freezer. However, large quantities of food should be cooled first, allowing the food to be quickly frozen when it is placed in the freezer.

Why do frozen foods develop "off" flavors? Properly wrapping foods, using materials that are airtight and moisture- and vapor-proof, prevents smells from transferring from one food to another. Some fatty foods, such as pork, become rancid when exposed to freezer air.

Tips

—To easily remove wax paper or aluminum foil from frozen food, place package in 300° oven for 5 minutes.

—To prevent sogginess, sprinkle cracker or crumb toppings on thawed casseroles just before baking.

—Casseroles that have meat or pasta on top should be covered with sauce before freezing. This keeps ingredients from drying out.

—Line casseroles with aluminum foil, leaving a long overhang. Prepare casserole as directed; seal foil over food, and freeze. When it is frozen, remove wrapped casserole from dish; label and store in freezer. Heat in same dish.

Piping the filling gives a ruffled look to Shrimp With Herbed Jalapeño Cheese.

June

Pretty To Look At, Good To Eat

When you arrange these garnishes on dinner plates, you can bet they won't be there after the meal. Made from crunchy fresh vegetables, they're marinated in your choice of flavors and are intended to be eaten.

Select a marinade and a vegetable garnish that will complement your entrée in terms of flavor and color. These marinades and garnishes were planned to be interchangeable. So mix and match them to suit your menu.

Any small, sharp paring knife will work for carving the vegetables. Those who do a lot of work with fresh vegetables may appreciate having a relatively new gadget called a garnish knife. It looks like a regular knife, but the blade is very short and allows you more control. Garnish knives are available from many kitchen specialty shops and mail-order companies.

After the vegetables are cut, place them in the smallest container that will hold them so that the marinade will touch them. Double the marinade if you make more than four to six garnishes, and baste the vegetables occasionally if the marinade doesn't cover them well.

Don't think of these garnishes as too time-consuming to make. Shape them the day before you plan to serve them, and let them marinate overnight. They probably won't take any more time to prepare than another cooked vegetable you'd serve on the side.

Onion rose: For each rose, select a small sweet onion, and peel. Slice off stem end so that it will sit flat. Hold onion in one hand, and use a garnish knife or sharp paring knife to cut the outer layer of onion into petals, leaving petals connected at the bottom. Open the petals to expose the second layer of onion. Slice the second layer into petals, making petals alternate with petals of the first layer. Continue opening cut petals and cutting the next layer as many times as possible. Cut remaining center portion of onion in a crisscross pattern. Place onion rose in an airtight container; pour desired marinade over top. Cover and chill at least 8 hours. Drain and place on a lettuce leaf, if desired.

Squash buttercup: Select yellow squash with rounded bases and narrow necks. One squash makes two buttercups. Cut neck from squash, reserving for other uses; trim ½ inch from other end. Cut a 2-inch slice from each end of

Carve a small sweet onion into a pretty rose, and place it on a lettuce leaf if your dinner plates are light in color.

Nestle three squash buttercups, sporting cherry tomato centers, on a lettuce leaf when the menu is not very colorful.

A zucchini fan, trimmed with a sprig of fresh mint, will help to fill the plate when you're serving a one-dish meal.

Spoon marinated pasta into a tomato flower. When teamed with the dill marinade, it complements seafood.

the remaining squash base. (Reserve any remaining center part for other uses.) The narrow end of each piece of squash will be the base for buttercup.

Starting at the wider top end, cut squash into four or five petals using a garnish knife or sharp paring knife. Scoop out the center portion of each squash; place a small cherry tomato half in each center portion. Place squash buttercups in an airtight container; pour desired marinade over top. Cover and chill at least 8 hours. Drain and place on a lettuce leaf, if desired.

Zucchini fan: Select one small to medium zucchini for each fan. Place zucchini on cutting surface, and slice lengthwise into ¼-inch strips, leaving stem end of zucchini intact. Place zucchini fan in an airtight container, laying zucchini flat, and fanning out slices. Pour desired marinade over zucchini; cover and chill at least 8 hours. Drain zucchini. Gently fan out zucchini slices. Raise the top slice; twist and tuck under the rest of the zucchini. Place a sprig of mint or other fresh herb in the stem end of zucchini fan.

Marinated pasta in tomato flower: For each tomato flower, cook 1 ounce of pasta according to package directions, omitting salt. Rinse pasta, and place in desired marinade; cover and chill at least 8 hours.

Select one medium tomato for each flower. Hold tomato in one hand. Starting at top, cut a pointed petal through the skin about 1/16 inch into the tomato, using the tip of a garnish knife or small paring knife. Continue to cut petals at equal spaces around tomato. With tip of knife, peel petals away from top of tomato, but leave intact from center to bottom of tomato. Hollow out tomato, leaving bottom intact. (Reserve pulp for other uses.) Fold petals outward. Drain pasta; spoon into tomato.

Broccoli bouquet: Trim off large leaves of broccoli and tough ends of lower stalks. Wash broccoli thoroughly, and cut into spears, leaving stalks about 4 inches long. Arrange spears in a single layer in a shallow dish. Pour desired marinade over broccoli; cover and chill at least 8 hours. Drain broccoli; arrange several spears on each dinner plate as a bouquet. Place two pimiento strips over each bouquet. One pound of broccoli will make four to six bouquets.

GARLIC-AND-OREGANO MARINADE

¾ cup vegetable oil
½ cup vinegar
3 tablespoons minced fresh oregano or 1 tablespoon dried whole oregano
¼ teaspoon salt
¼ teaspoon pepper
2 cloves garlic, minced

Combine all ingredients, stirring well. Pour over desired cut vegetables; cover and chill at least 8 hours. Drain before serving. Yield: about 1⅓ cups.

DILL MARINADE

⅔ cup vegetable oil
3 tablespoons wine vinegar
3 tablespoons dry sherry
2 tablespoons lemon juice
¾ teaspoon dry mustard
½ teaspoon salt
½ teaspoon pepper
1½ tablespoons minced fresh dillweed or 1½ teaspoons dried whole dillweed

Combine all ingredients, stirring well. Pour over desired cut vegetables; cover and chill at least 8 hours. Drain before serving. Yield: 1¼ cups.

SWEET-AND-SOUR MARINADE

½ to ¾ cup sugar
¾ cup vinegar
½ cup vegetable oil
1 teaspoon pepper
½ teaspoon salt
½ teaspoon dry mustard

Combine all ingredients, stirring until sugar dissolves. Pour over desired cut vegetables; cover and chill at least 8 hours. Drain before serving. Yield: about 1⅔ cups.

Come For Dinner!

Set the dining room table with your finest china, or clean the patio furniture for an evening of dining. We've designed two menus to suit your preference. Advance preparation and careful planning of last-minute details are the keys to entertaining with ease.

Outdoor Dining

Our menu designed for outdoor dining is company fare you can prepare in advance. The entrée is beef tenderloin filled with mushroom stuffing and a hint of blue cheese; it's assembled the day before to marinate. Skewer sweet red peppers and zucchini to also marinate, and then cook them with the tenderloin during the last few minutes. After the tenderloin is on the grill, finish last-minute steps in the kitchen. While baking Potato Croquettes, finish the Easy Caesar Salad. Except for coddling the eggs and tossing the greens with the dressing, all steps for the salad are done a day in advance. Heat Bran Yeast Rolls for 5 minutes.

The Cheesecake With Raspberry Sauce is rich and firm. Like most cheesecakes, it is best made in advance and refrigerated overnight. Keep the topping separate to spoon on the cheesecake an hour before serving.

Beef Tenderloin With Mushrooms
Vegetable Kabobs   Potato Croquettes
Easy Caesar Salad
Bran Yeast Rolls
Cheesecake With Raspberry Sauce
Red Wine   Coffee

BEEF TENDERLOIN WITH MUSHROOMS
(pictured on pages 100 and 101)

1 pound fresh mushrooms, sliced
1 cup chopped green onions
¼ cup butter or margarine, melted
¼ cup chopped fresh parsley
1 (6- to 7-pound) beef tenderloin
½ teaspoon seasoned salt
¼ teaspoon lemon-pepper seasoning
1 (4-ounce) package crumbled blue cheese
1 (8-ounce) bottle red wine vinegar and oil dressing
Crushed peppercorns
Mushrooms (optional)
Watercress (optional)

Sauté sliced mushrooms and green onions in butter in a large skillet until tender; drain. Stir in parsley, and set mixture aside.

Trim excess fat from beef tenderloin. Cut tenderloin lengthwise to within ¼ inch of other edge, leaving one long side connected. Sprinkle with seasoned salt and lemon-pepper seasoning. Spoon mushroom mixture into opening of tenderloin; sprinkle with blue cheese. Fold top side over stuffing. Tie tenderloin securely with heavy string at 2-inch intervals. Place tenderloin in a large, shallow dish. Pour dressing over tenderloin; cover and refrigerate 8 hours, basting with marinade occasionally.

Remove tenderloin from marinade. Press crushed peppercorns onto each side of tenderloin. Grill over medium-hot coals, covered or tented, 35 minutes or until meat thermometer registers 140° (rare) to 160° (medium). Transfer to platter, remove string, and slice to serve. Garnish with whole mushrooms and watercress, if desired. Yield: 8 to 10 servings.

Note: Tenderloin may be baked at 350° for 40 minutes or until meat thermometer registers 140° to 160°.

Ann Renfrow,
Gadsden, Alabama.

VEGETABLE KABOBS
(pictured on pages 100 and 101)

2 sweet red peppers, cut into ½-inch
   strips
2 small zucchini, cut into ½-inch slices
¼ cup vegetable oil
2 tablespoons lemon juice
2 tablespoons vinegar
2 teaspoons Worcestershire sauce
1 teaspoon Italian seasoning
½ teaspoon salt

Thread peppers and zucchini onto 8
(6-inch) bamboo skewers, and place in a
shallow dish. Set aside. Combine oil
and remaining ingredients, mixing well;
pour over kabobs. Cover; refrigerate 8
hours, turning once.

Grill kabobs over medium-hot coals
10 to 15 minutes, turning and brushing
occasionally with the marinade. Yield: 8
servings.
   Margie Williams,
   Birmingham, Alabama.

POTATO CROQUETTES
(pictured on pages 100 and 101)

4 cups cooked mashed potatoes
2 eggs, beaten
2 to 4 tablespoons buttermilk
3 tablespoons chopped fresh chives
1 teaspoon salt
¼ teaspoon white pepper
1½ cups crushed round buttery cracker
   crumbs (about 40 crackers)
¼ cup butter or margarine, melted
½ teaspoon paprika
Chives (optional)

Combine first 6 ingredients; mix well.
Divide mixture into 8 portions, and
shape into croquettes; roll in cracker
crumbs. Place on a lightly greased 15- x
10- x 1-inch jellyroll pan; cover and refrigerate up to 24 hours.

Combine butter and paprika; drizzle
over croquettes. Bake at 375° for 20 to
25 minutes or until golden. Garnish croquettes with chives, if desired. Yield: 8
servings.

Note: Potato Croquettes may be frozen. To bake, place frozen croquettes
on a greased baking sheet. Combine
butter and paprika; drizzle over croquettes. Bake at 375° for 35 minutes or
until golden.

EASY CAESAR SALAD
(pictured on pages 100 and 101)

2 heads romaine lettuce
¾ cup olive oil
¼ cup vegetable oil
4 cloves garlic, halved
1 cup (¼-inch-square) white bread cubes
2 eggs
Juice of 1 large lemon
¼ teaspoon Worcestershire sauce
½ teaspoon salt
½ teaspoon freshly ground pepper
¼ cup freshly grated Parmesan cheese

Wash romaine; trim core, and separate stalk into leaves. Discard wilted or
discolored portion. Wash and drain.
Place romaine on a dry towel, roll
gently, and place in a plastic bag. Chill
lettuce 8 hours or overnight.

Combine olive oil, vegetable oil, and
garlic in a jar with a tight-fitting lid. Let
stand several hours.

Place bread cubes in a 15- x 10- x
1-inch jellyroll pan. Sprinkle about 3
tablespoons of oil mixture over cubes;
toss gently to coat. Bake at 250° for 15
minutes or until dry and crisp; cool.
Store in an airtight container.

Before combining salad, coddle eggs
by bringing water to a boil in a small
saucepan; turn heat off. Carefully lower
eggs into water, using a slotted spoon;
let stand 1 minute. Remove eggs from
water; set aside to cool.

Cut coarse ribs from large leaves of
romaine; tear leaves into bite-size
pieces, and place in a large salad bowl.
Discard garlic slices from olive oil mixture. Add eggs, lemon juice, Worcestershire sauce, salt, and pepper to oil.
Cover and shake vigorously. Pour over
romaine lettuce, and toss to coat. Sprinkle with grated Parmesan cheese, and
top with croutons. Serve immediately.
Yield: 8 servings.
   Rick Paler,
   Decatur, Alabama.

BRAN YEAST ROLLS

½ cup shortening
¼ cup plus 2 tablespoons sugar
¾ teaspoon salt
½ cup boiling water
½ cup shreds of wheat bran cereal
1 egg, beaten
1 package dry yeast
½ cup warm water (105° to 115°)
2¼ to 2½ cups all-purpose flour, divided
½ cup butter or margarine, softened

Cream shortening, sugar, and salt at
medium speed of an electric mixer until

well blended. Add ½ cup boiling water;
mix well. Add bran cereal and egg, mixing well.

Dissolve yeast in warm water; add to
shortening mixture, stirring well. Stir in
1 cup flour. Gradually add enough remaining flour to make a soft dough.

Place in a greased bowl, turning to
grease top. Cover and let rise in a warm
place (85°), free from drafts, 1 hour or
until doubled in bulk.

Punch dough down. Cover and refrigerate 8 hours or up to 3 days.

Divide dough in half. Roll dough into
a 12- x 6-inch rectangle (about ¼ inch
thick). Brush with butter. Cut dough
lengthwise into 1-inch strips. Stack 6
strips of dough, buttered side up, on
top of each other. Cut each stack into
1-inch sections. Place each stack, cut
side down, into greased muffin pans.
Continue same procedure with remaining dough and butter.

Cover and let rise in a warm place
(85°), free from drafts, 1 hour or until
doubled in bulk. Bake at 400° for 8
minutes. Yield: 4 dozen.

Note: To make a day ahead, bake
rolls as directed; cool. Store in an airtight container. To serve, place on a
baking sheet; bake at 350° for 5 minutes
or until hot.
   Betty Rabe,
   Plano, Texas.

CHEESECAKE
WITH RASPBERRY SAUCE
(pictured on pages 100 and 101)

1¾ cups graham cracker crumbs
¼ cup sugar
½ cup butter or margarine, melted
5 (8-ounce) packages cream cheese,
   softened
1¾ cups sugar
5 eggs
2 egg yolks
3 tablespoons all-purpose flour
¼ teaspoon salt
½ teaspoon grated orange rind
½ teaspoon grated lemon rind
¼ teaspoon vanilla extract
¼ cup commercial sour cream
Raspberry Sauce
Fresh raspberries (optional)
Mint leaves (optional)

Combine graham cracker crumbs, ¼
cup sugar, and butter, mixing well.
Press into bottom and up sides of a
10-inch springform pan. Bake at 350°
for 8 minutes; cool.

Beat cream cheese at medium speed
of an electric mixer until light and

fluffy. Gradually add 1¾ cups sugar, mixing well. Add eggs, one at a time, beating well after each addition. Add egg yolks, flour, salt, orange rind, lemon rind, and vanilla, mixing well. Stir in sour cream; pour into prepared pan. Bake at 350° for 45 minutes. Turn off oven, and let cheesecake remain in closed oven 45 minutes. Open door of oven, and leave cheesecake in oven an additional 45 minutes. Remove from oven, and cool to room temperature; cover and chill overnight.

Remove side of springform pan. Drizzle cheesecake with Raspberry Sauce, and serve remaining sauce on individual pieces. Garnish cheesecake with whole raspberries and mint leaves, if desired. Let cake stand at room temperature 1 hour before slicing. Yield: one 10-inch cheesecake.

Raspberry Sauce:

1 (10-ounce) package frozen raspberries, thawed
1 tablespoon cornstarch
1 tablespoon kirsch

Press raspberries through a sieve to puree and strain seeds; discard seeds. Combine puree, cornstarch, and kirsch in a small saucepan. Cook over medium heat, stirring constantly, until mixture thickens; cool. Yield: about ¾ cup.

Marilyn Darby,
Tunica, Mississippi.

You'll receive many compliments for this dinner: (front to back) Chicken Rolls Jubilee, Green Bean Bundles, Brown Rice Casserole, Brie Cheese Bake, Toffee Meringue Torte, and Bran Yeast Rolls.

Indoor Dining

This second menu is planned for indoor dining. Buffet service is popular, but sometimes it's nice to treat guests to a seated dinner complete with table service. This is a good idea when buffet space or serving pieces are limited. Ask one of the guests to help you with serving the meal.

Even the appetizer, Brie Cheese Bake, is served at the table with a knife and fork. It's best to bake it about 45 minutes before your guests arrive, to allow it to stand before slicing. Meanwhile, you can prepare the pineapple sauce for Chicken Rolls Jubilee.

After the Brie Cheese Bake comes out of the oven, reduce the temperature to 350°. About 45 minutes before dinnertime, place Chicken Rolls Jubilee in the oven, and set the timer for 15 minutes. The timer's buzz is your cue to put Brown Rice Casserole in the oven; reset the timer for 20 minutes.

This is a good time to seat everyone and serve Brie Cheese Bake. As you clear the appetizer dishes, check on the chicken and rice, and place Green Bean Bundles in the oven for 10 minutes. Reheat the pineapple sauce over low heat. Bran Yeast Rolls may be baked early in the day and warmed just before you serve dinner.

As you arrange food on the plates, let one of your guests take them to the table. Place rolls in a basket, and join your guests.

For dessert, you may wish to adjourn to the living room for coffee and Toffee Meringue Torte.

Brie Cheese Bake
Chicken Rolls Jubilee
Green Bean Bundles
Brown Rice Casserole
Bran Yeast Rolls
(recipe on page 116)
Toffee Meringue Torte
White Wine   Coffee

BRIE CHEESE BAKE

1 (8-inch) round loaf sourdough bread (about 1 pound)
1 (5-inch) round Brie cheese (about 1 pound)
1 pint strawberries, sliced

Slice off about ½ inch from top of sourdough bread loaf, using a large serrated knife. Reserve top of loaf for other uses.

Place Brie on top of bread; trace around outer edge of Brie. Set Brie aside. Cut on traced mark 1-inch deep or deep enough to hold Brie. Hollow out bread loaf, reserving bread pieces for other uses. Place Brie in hollowed-out bread loaf. Wrap loaf in foil. Refrigerate up to 24 hours.

Bake Brie-filled bread loaf at 350° for 20 to 30 minutes. Let stand 30 minutes before serving.

Place sliced strawberries on top. Cut into wedges. Yield: 10 to 12 servings.

Ouida Hamilton,
Birmingham, Alabama.

CHICKEN ROLLS JUBILEE

8 large chicken breast halves, boned and skinned
¼ teaspoon salt
¼ teaspoon freshly ground pepper
1 (15-ounce) can crushed pineapple
1 cup diced cooked ham
¼ teaspoon ground ginger
18 stone-ground wheat crackers, crushed
1 teaspoon paprika
2 tablespoons butter or margarine, melted
1 tablespoon plus 1 teaspoon cornstarch
1 teaspoon chicken-flavored bouillon granules
2 tablespoons white wine

Place each chicken breast half on a sheet of wax paper. Flatten chicken to ¼-inch thickness, using a meat mallet or rolling pin. Sprinkle chicken breast halves with salt and pepper.

Drain pineapple, reserving half the pineapple and all pineapple juice for the sauce. Combine remaining pineapple, ham, and ginger in a small mixing bowl; top each chicken breast half with an equal amount of pineapple mixture. Roll up each chicken breast half, and secure with a wooden pick.

Combine cracker crumbs and paprika; toss to mix. Brush chicken rolls with butter; roll in crumb mixture. Place chicken in a lightly greased 13- x 9- x 2-inch baking dish; cover and refrigerate up to 24 hours.

Remove chicken from refrigerator; let stand at room temperature 30 minutes. Bake, uncovered, at 350° for 45 minutes or until chicken is done. Slice to serve, if desired.

To prepare the sauce, add water, if necessary, to the reserved pineapple juice to make 1 cup. Combine cornstarch and bouillon granules in a small saucepan; add reserved pineapple juice, and stir to dissolve cornstarch.

Add reserved pineapple. Cook, stirring constantly, until mixture begins to boil; boil 1 minute. Stir in white wine. Serve sauce with chicken rolls. Yield: 8 servings. *Nita Pierce, Hopkinsville, Kentucky.*

Tip: Have your oven thermostat professionally checked at least once a year. Another way to occasionally check oven temperature is to prepare a cake mix according to package directions; the cake should cook the entire recommended time and test done. (A wooden pick inserted in the center should come out clean.)

GREEN BEAN BUNDLES

2 pounds small fresh green beans
1 quart water
2 small red or yellow sweet peppers
½ cup coarsely chopped cashews
½ cup butter, melted
½ teaspoon grated lemon rind
2 teaspoons lemon juice
2 tablespoons sliced green onions
2 tablespoons chopped parsley
Whole cashews (optional)

Wash beans; trim ends, and remove strings. Bring water to a boil; add green beans, and cook, uncovered, 4 to 5 minutes or just until crisp-tender. Drain beans, and plunge them into cold water; then drain again.

Divide green beans into 8 bundles. Slice sweet peppers into 8 (¼-inch) rings. Secure each bundle with a pepper slice. Arrange on a baking sheet. Cover and refrigerate at least 8 hours.

Cook cashews in butter, stirring constantly, until cashews are toasted and butter is lightly browned. Remove from heat; add lemon rind and juice, green onions, and parsley. Cover and refrigerate up to 24 hours.

Remove cashew butter and beans from refrigerator 30 minutes before serving. Spoon cashew butter over beans. Cover and bake at 350° for 10 minutes or until beans are hot. Spoon pan drippings over green beans. Garnish with whole cashews, if desired. Yield: 8 servings. *Beppy Hassey, Montgomery, Alabama.*

BROWN RICE CASSEROLE

1 bunch green onions, chopped
3 medium carrots, scraped and chopped
½ cup butter or margarine, divided
2 cups uncooked brown rice
4½ cups chicken broth
½ cup dry white wine
2 cloves garlic, minced
½ pound fresh mushrooms, sliced
¾ cup chopped fresh parsley
¼ teaspoon freshly ground black pepper
1 cup freshly grated Parmesan cheese
2 eggs, beaten
1 cup half-and-half
⅛ teaspoon ground nutmeg
Green onion slices (optional)

Sauté green onions and carrots in ¼ cup butter in a large skillet 5 minutes. Add rice, and cook 1 minute, stirring constantly. Add chicken broth and wine. Bring to a boil; cover, reduce heat, and simmer 45 minutes or until liquid is absorbed and rice is tender.

Sauté garlic in remaining ¼ cup butter 1 minute; add mushroom slices, and cook 5 minutes. Drain. Stir in parsley and pepper.

Layer half of rice mixture in a lightly greased 12- x 8- x 2-inch baking dish. Spoon mushroom mixture over rice; top with half of Parmesan cheese. Spread remaining rice mixture on top. Sprinkle with remaining Parmesan cheese.

Combine eggs, half-and-half, and nutmeg, mixing well. Pour over rice. Cover and refrigerate up to 24 hours.

Remove rice from refrigerator, and let stand 30 minutes. Bake at 350° for 30 minutes or until thoroughly heated. Garnish with green onion slices, if desired. Yield: 8 servings.
Harriett Phillips, Gadsden, Alabama.

TOFFEE MERINGUE TORTE

4 egg whites
1 teaspoon vinegar
1 cup sugar
1 teaspoon vanilla extract
6 (1.1 ounces) English toffee-flavored candy bars, frozen, and crushed
2 cups whipping cream, whipped
Chocolate curls (optional)

Grease bottoms of two 8-inch round cakepans, line with brown paper, and grease paper. Beat egg whites (at room temperature) at high speed of an electric mixer until foamy. Add vinegar; continue beating until soft peaks form. Gradually add sugar, 1 tablespoon at a time, beating until stiff peaks form. Stir in vanilla. Spoon meringue into prepared pans. Bake at 275° for 2 hours. Remove layers from pans and paper from layers. Cool on wire racks.

Gently fold crushed candy into whipped cream. Spread whipped cream frosting between layers and on top and sides of meringue layers. Cover loosely, and chill 8 hours or overnight. Garnish with chocolate curls, if desired. Yield: 8 to 10 servings. *Alice McNamara, Eucha, Oklahoma.*

Expect The Unexpected In New Southwestern Cuisine

It's spicy, earthy, gutsy, robust, fresh, colorful, adventuresome, and revolutionary, say food critics nationwide of the new Southwestern cuisine. The young chefs promoting this curious blend of Texas flavors have raised some eyebrows, but Texans, and now others, have welcomed it.

This latest regional craze is an unusual blend of tradition and modern innovation. In a sense, it mirrors the unique cultural melting pot of Texas.

The first glance at a menu featuring Southwestern cuisine makes Texans warm to the recognition of familiar ingredients—black beans, tortillas, chiles, cilantro, and the like. But a second glance may evoke puzzled looks. While the ingredients are traditional, the unusual combinations have elevated the down-home fare to a new level. It's a Texas version of new American cuisine.

What makes new Southwestern cuisine more a trend than a passing fad is the serious approach the chefs take to each recipe. Each chef has a background in classical cooking techniques from culinary schools or training under renowned chefs. By transferring these techniques to old-time basic recipes with new ingredients, the chefs claim the cuisine has a solid, longer lasting foundation. The chefs also draw from the desires of a health-conscious public and preparation techniques of representative ethnic cuisines of Texas.

Southwestern chefs Dean Fearing, Stephan Pyles, George Geary, and Robert Del Grande share some of their Texas recipes. They've added classical preparation steps to a few favorite specialties to create unexpected combinations. Besides representing combined cultural traditions, displaying artistic food presentation, and leaning toward healthier recipes, they claim that flavor is their first concern.

Read each recipe carefully; most of them offer a challenge. You'll find the salsas, relishes, and sauces complement some of your own entrées, and they are fairly quick to prepare.

If you aren't familiar with the typical Texan ingredients included in these recipes, check the glossary below. We also suggest some substitutions in case specialty produce dealers in your area can't get the listed ingredients for you.

GLOSSARY OF SOUTHWESTERN INGREDIENTS

Anaheim or California green chile: Slender green chile about 6 to 8 inches long with rounded tip; mild flavored; substitute: canned green chiles

Ancho (ahn-cho) chile: Dried form of poblano chile; substitute: ½ teaspoon chili powder for each ancho chile

Chorizo (cho-ree-soh): Spicy Mexican smoked-pork sausage; substitute: any seasoned bulk-pork sausage

Cilantro: Leafy green herb similar in appearance to parsley; is actually fresh coriander and also called Chinese parsley; has a distinct lemon flavor

Epazote (eh-pah-soh-teh): Leafy green herb sometimes known as "pigweed" that grows abundantly in Texas though it isn't cultivated; difficult to get fresh outside Southwest region. A mail-order source for the dried and fresh versions is Herb Valley, 204 John McCain Road, Colleyville, Texas 76034; or call (817) 498-6362. (The fresh herb can be obtained during the summer; there is no substitute.)

Jalapeño (ha-la-pain-yoh) pepper: Small green or red cigar-shaped chile about 2½ inches long; very hot

Jicama (hé-kah-mah): A brown-skinned vegetable about the size of a grapefruit; flesh is slightly sweet and similar in texture to a turnip or radish; eaten raw or cooked

Poblano chile: Large dark green chile that resembles an elongated bell pepper; difficult to find outside of Texas and Southwestern states; ranges from mild to hot; substitute: sweet green pepper

Serrano chile: Dark green to red chile 1 to 2 inches long; hot to very hot; substitute: jalapeño pepper

Sweet green pepper: Bell-shaped pepper available in green, yellow, or red; sweet flavored; often roasted over open fire or broiler and peeled for Southwestern recipes

Tomatillos (toh-ma-tee-yos): Tiny green tomatoes with a thin, papery husk; tart lemony flavor

Peppers

Tomatillos

Ancho chiles

Jicama

Robert Del Grande of Café Annie in Houston was looking for a diversion after he completed his Ph.D. in biochemistry. His diversion is now a full-time career where he uses both his creativity and science background.

BLACK BEAN TERRINE WITH GOAT CHEESE

3 cups dried black beans
3 small cloves garlic
1 bunch epazote
½ pound pork fatback, cut in pieces
6 slices bacon
1½ pounds chorizo
5 ancho chiles
1 cup butter or margarine
1½ teaspoons coarse salt
1½ teaspoons hot sauce
2 (11-ounce) logs goat cheese
Tomato Salsa
Corn Relish
Fresh cilantro

Sort and wash beans; place in a large Dutch oven. Cover with water 2 inches above beans; soak overnight.

Drain beans; cover with 1½ quarts water. Add garlic and epazote; cover and simmer 3 to 4 hours or until beans are tender. Remove cover; cook to reduce excess liquid. Set aside one-fourth of cooked beans.

Position knife blade in food processor bowl; add one-fourth of remaining cooked beans. Top with cover; process 1 minute or until beans are smooth, scraping sides of processor bowl occasionally. Remove beans to large bowl. Repeat procedure with remaining beans. Mix bean puree with reserved whole cooked beans. Set aside.

Position knife blade in food processor bowl; add fatback and bacon. Top with cover; pulse 3 or 4 times until fatback is chopped. Cook fatback and bacon in a large skillet until the fat is rendered. Add chorizo, and cook, stirring to crumble meat, until browned. Drain and set aside.

Place ancho chiles in a bowl, and cover with hot water. Let soak 30 minutes; drain. Remove seeds from chiles. Position knife blade in processor bowl; add chiles. Top with cover; pulse 3 or 4 times until smooth.

Add chile puree to chorizo mixture; cook 3 minutes, stirring constantly. Combine chorizo mixture and bean mixture in a large Dutch oven, stirring to blend. Cook over medium heat until liquid evaporates. (Mixture should be very thick and pull away from the sides of the pan. This is a crucial step. If the mixture is not thick enough, it will not set firmly in the terrines.) Cool.

Cut butter or margarine into 1-inch pieces. Work butter into bean mixture, one piece at a time, until well mixed. Stir in the salt and hot sauce, mixing until well blended.

Line two 8½- x 4½- x 2½-inch loafpans with plastic wrap. Fill each pan three-fourths full of black bean mixture. Place a log of goat cheese into the center of each terrine; cover with remaining black bean mixture. Cover with plastic wrap.

Chill several hours or overnight.

To serve terrine, invert onto a platter. Cut into ½-inch-thick slices. Sauté slices quickly in a lightly greased skillet. Place each slice in the center of a dinner plate. Serve with Tomato Salsa and Corn Relish. Garnish with cilantro. Yield: 2 (8-inch) loaves.

Tomato Salsa:

2 tomatoes, chopped
⅓ cup chopped purple onion
1 serrano pepper, seeded and chopped
3 tablespoons lime juice
½ cup chopped cilantro
Salt and pepper to taste

Combine tomatoes, onion, and pepper. Stir in remaining ingredients, tossing well. Yield: 1⅔ cups.

Corn Relish:

2 large ears fresh corn
½ cup chorizo
½ cup diced sweet red pepper
½ cup diced green pepper
2 green onions, chopped
1 ancho chile, seeded and chopped
½ cup chopped cilantro
1½ tablespoons fresh lime juice
1 tablespoon maple syrup

Remove corn from cob. Place skillet over high heat until hot. Add corn and chorizo, and cook, stirring frequently, until chorizo is browned and corn is crisp-tender. Add remaining ingredients, stirring until well mixed. Do not overcook. Yield: 2 cups.

GRILLED SCALLOPS TOSTADA

4 (6-inch) corn tortillas
¼ cup vegetable oil
1½ pounds sea scallops
Cabbage Salad
Avocado Relish
Tomato Salsa
Fresh cilantro leaves

Fry tortillas, one at a time, in hot oil until crisp; drain well on paper towels.

Place scallops on skewers; grill over hot coals 10 minutes or until done, turning occasionally.

Layer one-fourth each of Cabbage Salad, Avocado Relish, and scallops over each tortilla. Top with Tomato Salsa and cilantro leaves. Serve immediately. Yield: 4 servings.

Cabbage Salad:

¼ cup commercial sour cream
1 tablespoon lime juice
1 small serrano chile, finely chopped
¼ teaspoon salt
⅛ teaspoon pepper
¼ medium head cabbage, shredded

Combine all ingredients except cabbage; mix well. Pour over cabbage; stir gently. Yield: 2 cups.

Avocado Relish:

2 ripe avocados, peeled and mashed
¼ to ½ cup finely chopped sweet red pepper
1 cup finely chopped purple onion
2 serrano chiles, minced
¾ cup chopped fresh cilantro
2 tablespoons lime juice
1 tablespoon hazelnut oil
1 teaspoon salt
⅛ teaspoon pepper

Combine all ingredients in a mixing bowl; mix well. Yield: 2¼ cups.

Tomato Salsa:

1 pound Italian tomatoes, coarsely chopped
¼ to ½ cup minced purple onion
¾ cup chopped fresh cilantro
1 serrano chile, minced
2 tablespoons lime juice
1 teaspoon salt
⅛ teaspoon pepper

Combine all ingredients; mix well. Yield: 2¼ cups.

Tip: When purchasing scallops, count on 40 to the pound. Since they are highly perishable, cook scallops within two days of purchase. Always wash scallops well before cooking to remove sand and grit.

Stephan Pyles, chef and part owner of Dallas's Routh Street Cafe, is known for the Texas style he gives to game and for his food artistry. Customers flock to his restaurant for his unusual specialties, such as the following recipes.

SMOKED DUCK ENCHILADAS WITH RED PEPPER-SOUR CREAM

1 poblano pepper or sweet green pepper
2 sweet red peppers
½ cup commercial sour cream
1½ pounds tomatillos, chopped
5 cloves garlic, minced
3 serrano chiles, seeded and chopped
1 small onion, chopped
1 cup chicken broth
½ cup fresh cilantro leaves, loosely packed
¼ teaspoon salt
1 cup peanut oil
8 (6-inch) corn tortillas
Smoked Duck Breasts (recipe follows)
Black Bean-Tomatillo Relish

Wash and dry poblano pepper and red peppers; place on a baking sheet. Broil 3 to 4 inches from heat, turning often with tongs, until blistered on all sides. Immediately place peppers in a plastic bag; seal and let stand 10 minutes to loosen skins.

Peel peppers; remove core and seeds. Chop poblano pepper, and set aside. Chop red peppers, and place in container of an electric blender; process until smooth. Whisk the red pepper puree into sour cream. Refrigerate mixture about 1 hour.

Combine chopped poblano, tomatillos, garlic, serrano chiles, onion, and chicken broth in a saucepan; cook over medium-high heat 10 to 12 minutes, stirring frequently. Pour mixture into container of an electric blender; add cilantro, and process mixture until smooth. Stir in salt; set tomatillo sauce mixture aside.

Heat oil in skillet to 300°. Fry tortillas, one at a time, for 1 second on each side or just until tortillas are softened. Drain on paper towels.

For each tortilla, place about one-eighth of smoked duck slices down center of tortilla. Top with 2 tablespoons tomatillo sauce. Roll up, and place seam side down in a lightly greased 13- x 9- x 2-inch baking dish. Repeat procedure with remaining ingredients. Cover and bake at 400° for 8 to 10 minutes or until heated. Place 2 enchiladas on each dinner plate; spoon tomatillo sauce lengthwise down the center of each enchilada. Spoon red pepper-sour cream mixture across each enchilada. Serve with Black Bean-Tomatillo Relish. Yield: 4 servings.

Smoked Duck Breasts:

2 cups water
¼ cup plus 1 tablespoon coarse salt
2 tablespoons dark brown sugar
½ teaspoon fresh thyme, chopped
1 bay leaf
2 black peppercorns
1 whole clove
2 whole duck breasts (about 1½ pounds each)

Combine all ingredients except duck in a saucepan. Bring to a boil; reduce heat, and simmer 5 minutes. Cool.

Place duck in nonmetallic container; cover with brine. Cover and refrigerate 12 hours. Drain; pat dry.

Prepare charcoal fire in meat smoker; let fire burn 15 to 20 minutes. Soak hickory chips in water 15 minutes, and place chips on coals. Place water pan in smoker; fill pan with water.

Place ducks on lightly oiled rack. Insert meat thermometer in breast so it doesn't touch bone or fat. Cover with smoker lid; cook 20 to 25 minutes or until breast meat is firm but springs back when squeezed (or until thermometer registers 190°). Slice thinly. Yield: 2 whole smoked duck breasts.

Black Bean-Tomatillo Relish:

1 ear fresh corn
1 cup cooked black beans
2 to 3 tomatillos, diced
1 serrano chile, seeded and minced
¼ cup diced papaya
2 green onions, thinly sliced
2 teaspoons chopped fresh cilantro
1 small clove garlic, minced
2 tablespoons vinaigrette
2 teaspoons white wine
2 teaspoons lime juice
½ teaspoon salt
Tomatillo husks

Remove husks and silks from corn just before cooking. Grill corn over medium coals 20 minutes, turning several times. Cool. Cut corn from cob.

Combine corn and remaining ingredients except tomatillo husks in a bowl. Cover and refrigerate at least 1 hour. Spoon into tomatillo husks to serve. Yield: about 2 cups.

GRILLED CORN SOUP

4 ears fresh corn
2 cloves garlic
½ cup chopped carrot
½ cup chopped onion
¼ cup chopped celery
½ to 1 small jalapeño pepper, seeded and chopped
⅛ teaspoon salt
1½ cups chicken stock
1 cup half-and-half
Cilantro Cream
Ancho Chile Cream

Grill corn and garlic over low coals for 20 minutes, turning often. Let cool.

Combine carrot, onion, celery, jalapeño pepper, and salt in a medium saucepan; bring to a boil, and cook, covered, for 5 minutes. Cut corn from the cobs; add corn and garlic to vegetable mixture, and cook 10 minutes.

Pour corn mixture into container of an electric blender; process until mixture is smooth. Pour mixture into a saucepan; add half-and-half, and simmer 5 minutes. Spoon mixture into bowls; add Cilantro Cream and Ancho Chile Cream over soup mixture. Draw a knife through the soup to make a swirl design over top. Yield: 2 cups.

Cilantro Cream:

2 cups water
5 fresh spinach leaves, stems removed
1 cup fresh cilantro leaves, loosely packed
3 tablespoons half-and-half
2 tablespoons commercial sour cream

Bring water to a boil in a small saucepan; add spinach, and cook 1 minute. Drain spinach. Place leaves in ice water for 1 minute (to set color in leaves). Drain spinach leaves.

Combine cilantro, spinach, and half-and-half in a container of an electric blender; process until smooth. Spoon mixture into a small bowl; whisk in sour cream. Yield: ½ cup.

Ancho Chile Cream:

1 small ancho chile
3 tablespoons half-and-half
2 tablespoons commercial sour cream

Slice chile in half; remove seeds and stem. Place chile halves on a baking sheet, and bake at 400° for 1 minute. Cover chile with hot water; let stand 10 minutes. Drain.

Combine chile and half-and-half in a container of an electric blender; process until mixture is smooth. Sieve mixture into a small bowl; whisk in sour cream. Yield: ⅓ cup.

Executive Chef Dean Fearing of Dallas says robust flavor and lots of color characterize his creations, such as Medallions of Beef With Ancho Chile Sauce.

A childhood diet of down-home Southern food still inspires Chef **Dean Fearing** at The Mansion on Turtle Creek in Dallas. He's been dazzling his customers with sophisticated Texas fare since the early 1980s.

MEDALLION OF BEEF WITH ANCHO CHILE SAUCE

1 tablespoon peanut oil
1 cup diced jicama
1 small sweet red pepper, diced
1 small sweet yellow pepper, diced
½ cup cooked black beans, drained
8 (3-ounce) beef tenderloin steaks
½ teaspoon salt
¼ teaspoon pepper
3 tablespoons peanut oil
Ancho Chile Sauce
Cilantro leaves

Place a medium saucepan over medium-high heat; add 1 tablespoon oil, and heat thoroughly. Add jicama, red and yellow peppers, and beans; sauté 2 minutes. Remove and keep warm.

Sprinkle tenderloin steaks with salt and pepper. Heat a large skillet over medium heat; add 3 tablespoons oil, and heat thoroughly. Add steaks, and cook until desired degree of doneness; turn once. If desired, place steaks on a grill over hot coals to sear.

Pour enough Ancho Chile Sauce to cover bottom of a warm dinner plate. Place 2 steaks over sauce. Sprinkle bean mixture around meat; garnish with cilantro leaves. Yield: 4 servings.

Ancho Chile Sauce:

4 ancho chiles
1 teaspoon beef-flavored bouillon granules
1 cup hot water
2 tablespoons butter or margarine
3 tablespoons all-purpose flour
½ teaspoon salt
Dash of pepper
1 large yellow onion, diced
1 tablespoon peanut oil
3 shallots, chopped
2 cloves garlic, chopped
1 jalapeño, seeded and chopped
1 cup chicken broth
12 cilantro stems, chopped
1 cup half-and-half
1 teaspoon lime juice

Place chiles in a bowl, and add hot water to cover. Let soak 30 minutes; drain. Combine bouillon granules and 1 cup hot water, stirring until dissolved; set aside.

Melt butter in a heavy saucepan; add flour, stirring until smooth. Cook over low heat, stirring constantly, until bubbly. Gradually stir in bouillon; cook 5 minutes, stirring constantly. Stir in salt and pepper; remove mixture from heat, and set aside.

Sauté onion in oil 2 minutes in a medium saucepan. Add shallots, garlic, and jalapeño; sauté 2 minutes. Add chiles, chicken broth, and cilantro stems; simmer 10 minutes. Add reserved brown sauce; cook over medium heat 10 minutes, stirring often. Stir in half-and-half; bring to a boil, stirring often. Cool slightly.

Pour mixture into container of an electric blender; add lime juice. Process until smooth. Yield: about 3½ cups.

WARM LOBSTER TACO WITH YELLOW TOMATO SALSA AND JICAMA SALAD

3 tablespoons vegetable oil
4 (½-pound) fresh lobster tails, split, cleaned, and coarsely chopped
6 (8-inch) flour tortillas
1 cup (4 ounces) shredded Monterey Jack cheese with jalapeño peppers
1 cup shredded fresh spinach
Yellow Tomato Salsa
Jicama Salad

Place a large skillet over medium-high heat; add oil, and heat thoroughly. Add lobster, and sauté about 4 minutes. Drain.

Heat tortillas in another hot skillet (without oil) over medium-high heat for 1 second on each side. Spoon lobster evenly in the center of each tortilla. Sprinkle evenly with cheese and spinach. Roll up tortillas, jellyroll fashion. Spoon about ½ cup Yellow Tomato Salsa on a dinner plate. Place lobster taco on sauce, and garnish with Jicama Salad. Repeat procedure with remaining salsa, tacos, and salad. Serve immediately. Yield: 6 servings.

Yellow Tomato Salsa:

2 pints yellow cherry tomatoes
1 large shallot, finely chopped
1 clove garlic, minced
2 tablespoons finely chopped fresh cilantro
1 to 2 serrano chiles, finely chopped
⅓ cup lime juice
3 tablespoons white wine vinegar
¼ teaspoon salt

Position knife blade in food processor bowl; add cherry tomatoes. Top with cover; process until coarsely chopped (about 10 to 15 seconds). Spoon into bowl; add remaining ingredients, stirring to blend. Cover and refrigerate about 2 hours. Yield: 4 cups.

Jicama Salad:

1 small zucchini
1 small jicama (about 1½ pounds), cut in julienne strips
1 small sweet red pepper, cut in julienne strips
1 small sweet yellow pepper, cut in julienne strips
1 carrot, cut in julienne strips
¼ cup plus 2 tablespoons peanut oil
3 tablespoons lime juice
¼ teaspoon salt
Pinch of red pepper

Peel zucchini; cut zucchini peeling into julienne strips. Reserve zucchini for other uses.

Combine zucchini strips, jicama, peppers, and carrots in a large bowl. Combine remaining ingredients; pour over jicama mixture, tossing well to coat. Yield: 6 cups.

George Geary, executive chef at The Tutwiler hotel in Birmingham, was the first of the Texas chefs to take Southwestern recipes outside the state. He is now finding ways to incorporate Alabama ingredients into his recipes and still offer a Texas twist.

MARINATED BREAST OF CHICKEN

4 chicken breast halves, boned and skinned
2 tablespoons vegetable oil
2½ cups water
½ cup soy sauce
4 bay leaves
4 sprigs fresh thyme
2 tablespoons chopped shallots
1½ tablespoons chopped gingerroot
6 small cloves garlic, chopped
Saucy Potato Salad

Sauté chicken in oil just until golden brown on each side. Remove and set aside. Combine water, soy sauce, and bay leaves in a saucepan; bring to a boil. Boil mixture until reduced to 1 cup liquid. Remove bay leaves; cool.

Place chicken breast halves in a shallow dish; top with thyme, shallots, gingerroot, and garlic. Pour soy sauce marinade over chicken; cover and refrigerate 24 hours.

Remove chicken from marinade, discarding marinade. Grill chicken 7 minutes on each side over hot coals. To serve, thinly slice chicken, and arrange on individual plates with Saucy Potato Salad. Yield: 4 servings.

Saucy Potato Salad:

1½ pounds new potatoes, unpeeled
1 cup mayonnaise
1 cup coarse-grain mustard
½ cup balsamic vinegar
3 large green onions, chopped
⅓ cup chopped purple onion
Salt and pepper to taste

Cook unpeeled potatoes in boiling water to cover 20 minutes or until tender. Drain well, and let cool. Cut potatoes into 1½-inch cubes.

Combine mayonnaise, coarse-grain mustard, balsamic vinegar, green onions, purple onion, salt, and pepper; add potatoes, stirring gently to coat. Yield: 4 servings.

SOUTHWESTERN SCALLOP BROTH WITH BLACK BEANS AND CILANTRO

¼ cup dried black beans
10 cups fish stock, divided
¼ cup olive oil
2 cloves garlic, minced
1 medium jicama, chopped
1 stalk celery, chopped
1 medium onion, chopped
1 carrot, chopped
1 bay leaf
1½ pounds bay scallops
8 tomatillos, ground
2 teaspoons chopped fresh cilantro
1 tablespoon tequila
½ teaspoon salt
¼ teaspoon pepper
Corn tortillas (optional)

Sort and wash beans. Cover beans with water; soak overnight. Drain

beans. Bring 5 cups fish stock to a boil; add beans, cover, and simmer 2 to 3 hours or until desired degree of doneness. Remove from heat. Cool beans in fish stock; set aside.

Heat olive oil in a large Dutch oven over medium-high heat. Add garlic, jicama, celery, onion, carrot, bay leaf, and scallops, and sauté until vegetables are transparent. Add tomatillos, cilantro, and remaining 5 cups fish stock; bring to a boil.

Strain and rinse black beans; discard stock. Drain and add to vegetable-broth mixture. Bring to a boil; add tequila, salt, and pepper. Remove bay leaf. Yield: 12 cups.

Note: If desired, broth can be garnished with corn tortillas cut into ⅛-inch strips and deep-fried until crisp.

Make Extra Soup, And Freeze It

Betty Nelson of Dothan, Alabama, enjoys the taste of summer all year long. She packs plenty of fresh produce into her Vegetable Soup and freezes it. In the winter, she pulls it from her freezer and adds ground beef.

The soup is a great way to stock the freezer, and use up a bumper crop of produce as well.

VEGETABLE SOUP

8 medium ears fresh corn
5½ pounds (about 19 medium) tomatoes, peeled and chopped
3 medium onions, chopped
2 medium-size green peppers, chopped
2 cups water
1 cup fresh baby lima beans
1 cup sliced fresh okra
1 hot pepper
¼ cup vinegar
¼ cup sugar
2 tablespoons salt

Cut corn from cob. Combine corn and remaining ingredients in a large Dutch oven; cover and bring to a boil. Cover, reduce heat, and simmer 1 hour.

To freeze, cool completely. Spoon mixture into 1-pint freezer containers. Label and freeze. Thaw and heat soup before serving. Yield: 7½ pints.

Quick Cooking For Summer

Cooking meals in the microwave oven can help you beat the heat in your kitchen. And if you're trying to juggle a work schedule and family activities, microwave meals can save you time. These one-dish meals are easy and quick to prepare. Just add a salad or French bread to complete your menu.

Cheese-Sauced Tuna Salad is especially simple to prepare. The microwave is used to cook the bacon and a cheese sauce. Stir the other ingredients together, and serve on tomato wedges.

In our test kitchens, we found that rice takes about as long to cook in the microwave as it does on a cook surface, so we cook it both ways, depending on the recipe. Because rice and pork chops require about the same amount of cooking time, they are microwaved together for Pineapple Pork Chops. With Quick Chicken Toss, however, the microwave time for the chicken is much shorter, so the rice is started on a cook surface even before the chicken is put into the microwave.

Most egg dishes made in the microwave have a lighter, fluffier texture than those cooked conventionally. Our Olé Omelet takes only 11 minutes to make and is stuffed with bean sprouts, mushrooms, ham, and Monterey Jack cheese. It's a winner for any meal of the day.

PINEAPPLE PORK CHOPS

1 (8-ounce) can unsweetened pineapple slices
2 cups water
1 cup uncooked long-grain rice
½ cup raisins
4 (½-inch-thick) pork chops
¼ teaspoon salt
1 medium-size green pepper, cut into rings
1 small onion, cut into rings and separated
⅔ cup unsweetened orange or apple juice
2 teaspoons cornstarch
¼ teaspoon curry powder

Drain pineapple, reserving ⅓ cup juice; set aside.

Combine water, rice, and raisins in a lightly greased 2½-quart shallow casserole; cover with heavy-duty plastic wrap. Microwave at HIGH for 5 minutes; stir.

Arrange pork chops over rice mixture; sprinkle with salt. Cover and microwave at MEDIUM (50% power) for 10 minutes, giving dish a quarter-turn after 5 minutes.

Arrange green pepper, onion rings, and pineapple slices over pork chops. Cover and microwave at MEDIUM for 20 to 25 minutes, giving dish a quarter-turn at 5-minute intervals. Let stand covered 10 minutes.

Combine reserved pineapple juice, orange juice, cornstarch, and curry powder in a 2-cup glass measure; stir until cornstarch dissolves. Cover with wax paper, and microwave at HIGH for 2½ to 3 minutes or until mixture is thickened and bubbly. Serve with pork chop-rice mixture. Yield: 4 servings.

QUICK CHICKEN TOSS

¼ cup butter or margarine
2 tablespoons lemon juice
1 teaspoon dried whole basil
1 teaspoon dried whole oregano
½ teaspoon dried whole thyme
1 pound boneless chicken breasts, cut into bite-size pieces
1 medium yellow squash, cut into julienne strips
1 medium zucchini, cut into julienne strips
1 small sweet red pepper, cut into julienne strips
1 small green pepper, cut into julienne strips
½ cup chopped pecans
¼ teaspoon salt
⅛ teaspoon pepper
Hot cooked rice (optional)

Combine butter, lemon juice, basil, oregano, and thyme in a 1-cup glass measure. Microwave at HIGH for 1 to 2 minutes or until butter is melted.

Place chicken in a shallow 1½-quart casserole. Brush with half of butter mixture. Cover with heavy-duty plastic wrap, and microwave at HIGH for 4 to 5 minutes, turning casserole once.

Add squash, zucchini, red pepper, green pepper, pecans, salt, and pepper; pour remainder of butter mixture over vegetables. Cover with heavy-duty plastic wrap, and microwave at HIGH for 4 additional minutes or until vegetables are crisp-tender, turning casserole once. Stir and let stand 5 minutes before serving. Serve chicken over rice, if desired. Yield: 4 servings.

CHEESE-SAUCED TUNA SALAD

6 slices bacon
1 (12½-ounce) can tuna, drained and flaked
1 (11¾-ounce) carton deli coleslaw
⅛ teaspoon white pepper
4 large tomatoes
2 tablespoons butter or margarine
2 tablespoons all-purpose flour
2 teaspoons dry minced onion
⅛ teaspoon dry mustard
¼ teaspoon salt
1 cup milk
¾ cup (3 ounces) shredded sharp Cheddar cheese
Paprika
Parsley (optional)

Place bacon on a rack in a 12- x 8- x 2-inch baking dish; cover with paper towels. Microwave at HIGH for 4 to 6 minutes or until bacon is crisp. Drain bacon; crumble and set aside.

Combine tuna, coleslaw, and pepper; stir well. Core tomatoes; cut to, but not through, the base of each tomato. Place on individual salad plates. Spread wedges slightly apart, and fill each tomato with tuna mixture.

Place butter in a 2-cup glass measure; microwave at HIGH for 45 seconds or until melted. Add flour, onion, mustard, and salt; stir well. Microwave at HIGH for 1 to 1½ minutes; stir well. Add milk; microwave at HIGH for 2½ to 3 minutes until thickened, stirring at 1-minute intervals. Add cheese, stirring until melted. Spoon cheese sauce over each tuna salad. Top with bacon; sprinkle with paprika. Garnish with parsley, if desired. Yield: 4 servings.

OLÉ OMELET

1 tablespoon butter or margarine
½ cup cubed cooked ham (about ¼ pound)
¼ cup sliced mushrooms
3 eggs, separated
2 tablespoons commercial sour cream
2 tablespoons mayonnaise
Dash of salt
Dash of red pepper
Vegetable cooking spray
½ cup (2 ounces) cubed Monterey Jack cheese
⅓ cup bean sprouts
Picante sauce

Combine butter, ham, and mushrooms in a 1-quart casserole; cover with heavy-duty plastic wrap, and microwave at HIGH for 3 to 3½ minutes, stirring after 2 minutes. Drain; set aside.

Beat egg whites (at room temperature) until stiff peaks form. Combine egg yolks, sour cream, mayonnaise, salt, and red pepper; beat well. Gently fold egg whites into yolk mixture.

Pour egg mixture into a 9-inch pieplate coated with cooking spray. Microwave at MEDIUM (50% power) for 8 to 9 minutes or until center is almost set, turning pieplate once. Top with cheese; microwave at MEDIUM for 30 to 40 seconds or until cheese melts. Remove from oven. Spread ham mixture over half of omelet. Top with bean sprouts. Loosen omelet with spatula, and fold in half. Gently slide omelet onto a serving plate. Serve with picante sauce. Yield: 2 servings.

COOKING LIGHT®

It's Yogurt— Not Ice Cream

Make it easier to bypass the ice cream shop next time by keeping your freezer full of homemade frozen yogurt. Lots of people are giving up ice cream to discover the unique and refreshing flavor of frozen yogurt.

Some make the switch because it's a healthier choice. Ice cream has over 7½ times the amount of fat and cholesterol as low-fat frozen yogurt. Others have made the change simply because frozen yogurt tastes so good, and we agree.

Our frozen yogurt contains plain low-fat yogurt, skim milk, and unflavored gelatin. And even though the recipe calls for sugar, our version saves you 56 calories per serving over regular ice cream. And there's more good nutrition news. Frozen yogurt contains about 1¼ times as much calcium as ice cream.

Enjoy frozen yogurt plain, or doll it up in a sundae, using one of our tasty, light fruit toppings. They have been calorie trimmed by using a combination of fruit, fruit juice, flavorings or spices, and a bit of cornstarch for thickening.

VANILLA FROZEN YOGURT

1 cup sugar
2 envelopes unflavored gelatin
Dash of salt
2 cups skim milk
5 cups plain low-fat yogurt
1 tablespoon plus 1 teaspoon vanilla extract

Combine sugar, gelatin, and salt in a medium saucepan; add milk, and let stand 1 minute. Cook over low heat, stirring constantly, 5 minutes or until gelatin and sugar dissolve; let cool. Stir in yogurt and vanilla; chill.

Pour mixture into freezer can of a 1-gallon hand-turned or electric freezer; freeze according to manufacturer's instructions. Serve immediately, or let ripen 1 hour. Yield: 10½ cups.

□ *84 calories, 4.2 grams protein, 0.9 gram fat, 14.7 grams carbohydrate, 4 milligrams cholesterol, 58 milligrams sodium, and 128 milligrams calcium per ½-cup serving.*

SPICY APPLE TOPPING

2 cups unsweetened apple juice, divided
1½ cups peeled and chopped apple
1 tablespoon dark brown sugar
¼ teaspoon apple pie spice
2 tablespoons cornstarch

Combine 1¾ cups apple juice and next 3 ingredients in a heavy saucepan; bring to a boil. Reduce heat, and simmer 5 to 8 minutes or until the apples are partially tender.

Dissolve cornstarch in remaining ¼ cup apple juice; stir into hot mixture. Cook over medium heat, stirring constantly, until smooth and thickened. Remove from heat; let cool. Serve over Vanilla Frozen Yogurt. Yield: 2½ cups.

□ *10 calories, 0 grams protein, 0 grams fat, 2.6 grams carbohydrate, 0 milligrams cholesterol, 0 milligrams sodium, and 1 milligram calcium per tablespoon.*

BLUEBERRY TOPPING

1½ cups unsweetened grape juice, divided
2 cups fresh blueberries, divided
1 tablespoon frozen unsweetened orange juice concentrate, thawed and undiluted
⅛ teaspoon ground cinnamon
⅛ teaspoon ground ginger
1 tablespoon plus 2 teaspoons cornstarch

Combine 1 cup grape juice, 1 cup blueberries, orange juice concentrate, cinnamon, and ginger in a saucepan. Bring to a boil; reduce heat, and simmer about 3 minutes or until blueberries pop. Combine cornstarch and remaining ½ cup grape juice; stir into fruit mixture. Bring to a boil, and cook 1 minute; stir constantly. Cool; stir in remaining blueberries. Serve over yogurt. Yield: 2½ cups.

□ *12 calories, 0.1 gram protein, 0 grams fat, 3 grams carbohydrate, 0 milligrams cholesterol, 1 milligram sodium, and 2 milligrams calcium per tablespoon.*

STRAWBERRY-BANANA TOPPING

2 tablespoons cornstarch
⅛ to ¼ teaspoon ground coriander
2 cups unsweetened apple juice
1 tablespoon honey
1 cup sliced fresh strawberries
1 medium-size ripe banana, sliced

Combine cornstarch and coriander in a small saucepan; slowly stir in apple juice and honey. Cook over medium heat until thick, stirring constantly. Remove from heat; let cool. Fold in strawberries and banana just before serving. Serve over Vanilla Frozen Yogurt. Yield: 2½ cups.

□ *14 calories, 0.1 gram protein, 0 grams fat, 3.4 grams carbohydrate, 0 milligrams cholesterol, 0 milligrams sodium, and 2 milligrams calcium per tablespoon.*

CHUNKY PIÑA COLADA TOPPING

1 (8-ounce) can unsweetened crushed pineapple, undrained
1 medium-size ripe banana, chopped
⅛ teaspoon rum flavoring
⅛ teaspoon coconut flavoring
2 tablespoons flaked coconut

Combine pineapple, banana, and flavorings; chill well. Serve over Vanilla Frozen Yogurt; sprinkle with coconut. Yield: 1 cup.

□ *19 calories, 0.2 gram protein, 0.2 gram fat, 4.5 grams carbohydrate, 0 milligrams cholesterol, 0 milligrams sodium, and 3 milligrams calcium per tablespoon.*

CHERRY-PINEAPPLE TOPPING

1½ cups unsweetened pineapple juice
1 (8-ounce) can unsweetened pineapple tidbits, undrained
1 (16-ounce) can pitted sour cherries, drained
⅛ teaspoon ground mace
2 tablespoons cornstarch

Combine all ingredients in a heavy saucepan; bring mixture to a boil over medium heat. Cook mixture 1 minute, stirring constantly; let cool. Serve topping over Vanilla Frozen Yogurt. Yield: 3 cups.

☐ *11 calories, 0.1 gram protein, 0 grams fat, 2.6 grams carbohydrate, 0 milligrams cholesterol, 1 milligram sodium, and 3 milligrams calcium per tablespoon.*

RASPBERRY-PEACH TOPPING

1 (6-ounce) can frozen unsweetened apple juice concentrate, thawed and undiluted
1 cup water, divided
2 cups chopped fresh peaches
3 tablespoons cornstarch
¼ teaspoon almond extract
1 cup fresh raspberries

Combine apple juice concentrate, ⅔ cup water, and peaches in a heavy saucepan; cook over medium heat about 5 minutes or until peaches are tender. Combine remaining ⅓ cup water and cornstarch in a small mixing bowl; stir into peach mixture, and bring to a boil. Cook 1 minute, stirring constantly. Remove mixture from heat; stir in almond extract, and cool. Stir in raspberries before serving. Serve topping over Vanilla Frozen Yogurt. Yield: 3½ cups.

☐ *11 calories, 0.1 gram protein, 0 grams fat, 2.6 grams carbohydrate, 0 milligrams cholesterol, 1 milligram sodium, and 2 milligrams calcium per tablespoon.*

Tip: Make certain your refrigerator or freezer is cold enough. Refrigerator temperature should be maintained at 34°F to 40°F, and freezer temperature at 0°F or lower. To allow the cold air to circulate freely, make sure that foods are not overcrowded.

End The Meal With Crêpes

For an elegant dessert that's as pleasing to look at as it is to taste, Emily Tempel of Higginsville, Missouri, makes Raspberry Crêpes. The crêpes can be made ahead and then frozen, unfilled, until needed.

Almonds, cream cheese, and frozen raspberries are easy to keep on hand, so this special dessert can be prepared at a moment's notice. It's bound to make such an impression that you'll have a hard time convincing friends and neighbors you didn't spend half a day in the kitchen making this treat.

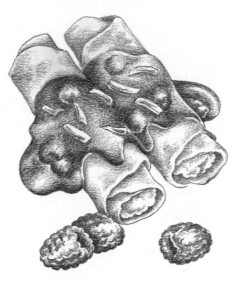

RASPBERRY CRÊPES

½ (8-ounce) container whipped cream cheese, softened
8 crêpes
⅓ cup slivered almonds, toasted and divided
1 (10-ounce) package frozen sweetened raspberries, thawed
⅓ cup sugar
2 tablespoons cornstarch
2 tablespoons butter or margarine
2 tablespoons lemon juice

Spread cream cheese evenly over crêpes. Sprinkle with half of almonds; roll up, jellyroll fashion. Place seam side down on serving dishes.

Drain raspberries, reserving ½ cup juice; set raspberries aside.

Combine sugar and cornstarch in a small saucepan; add reserved raspberry juice, stirring to blend. Cook over medium heat, stirring constantly, until mixture boils; cook 1 minute. Remove from heat; stir in butter, lemon juice, and

raspberries. Spoon raspberry sauce over crêpes; sprinkle with remaining almonds. Yield: 4 servings.

Crêpes:

1 cup all-purpose flour
2 tablespoons sugar
1½ cups milk
2 eggs
1 tablespoon vegetable oil
Vegetable oil

Combine flour, sugar, and milk, beating until smooth. Add eggs, and beat well; stir in oil. Refrigerate batter at least 2 hours. (This allows flour particles to swell and soften so that crêpes are light in texture.)

Brush bottom of a 6-inch crêpe pan or heavy skillet with oil; place over medium heat until just hot, not smoking.

Pour 2 tablespoons batter into pan; quickly tilt pan in all directions so batter covers pan in a thin film. Cook 1 minute or until lightly browned.

Lift edge of crêpe to test for doneness. Crêpe is ready for flipping when it can be shaken loose from pan. Flip crêpe, and cook about 30 seconds on other side. (This side is usually spotty brown and is the side on which filling is placed.)

Place crêpes on a towel to cool. Stack between layers of wax paper to prevent sticking. Repeat until all batter is used. Yield: 16 (6-inch) crêpes.

Note: Crêpes may be frozen, if desired. Thaw at room temperature; fill as directed.

Perk Up Vegetables With A Cream Sauce

If you're bored with plain boiled, steamed, or fried vegetables, you might want to try serving them in a cream sauce. Sour cream, half-and-half, or whipping cream, along with carefully selected seasonings added to the vegetables, gives any of them a rich and elegant touch to serve to family or guests.

Make good use of the season's bounty with Creamed Spring Vegetables. Carrots, pearl onions, new potatoes, and asparagus make this a colorful dish. The sauce contains half-and-half as well as liquid reserved from cooking the vegetables. This liquid gives the sauce more nutrients, because vitamins are leached into the water during preparation.

CREAMED SPRING VEGETABLES

1 pound carrots, scraped and sliced ½
   inch thick
½ pound pearl onions, peeled
½ pound new potatoes (about 6),
   scrubbed
1 teaspoon salt
5 cups water
½ pound fresh asparagus, cut into
   1½-inch pieces
¼ cup butter or margarine
¼ cup all-purpose flour
¾ cup half-and-half
1 teaspoon sugar
¼ teaspoon pepper

Combine carrots, pearl onions, potatoes, salt, and water in a large saucepan. Bring to a boil; cover, reduce heat,
and cook 15 minutes. Add asparagus to
vegetable mixture; cook an additional
10 minutes. Drain vegetables, reserving
¾ cup cooking liquid; set vegetables
aside, and keep warm.

Melt butter in a small heavy saucepan
over low heat; add flour, stirring until
smooth. Cook 1 minute, stirring constantly. Gradually add reserved vegetable liquid and half-and-half; cook over
medium heat, stirring constantly, until
mixture is thickened and bubbly. Stir in
sugar and pepper. Add to vegetables,
and toss gently. Yield: 6 servings.
Mrs. Raymond Warren,
Lake Village, Arkansas.

CREAMY BAKED MUSHROOMS

1 pound small fresh mushrooms
3½ tablespoons all-purpose flour
1½ teaspoons chicken-flavored bouillon
   granules
1 cup milk
Dash of hot sauce
2 tablespoons chopped chives, divided
⅓ cup commercial sour cream

Clean mushrooms with damp paper
towels. Place mushrooms in an ungreased 1½-quart casserole; set aside.

Combine flour and bouillon granules
in a small saucepan; gradually add milk,
stirring until smooth. Add hot sauce
and 1 tablespoon chives. Cook over medium heat, stirring constantly, until
thickened and bubbly. Pour mixture
over mushrooms.

Bake mushrooms at 350° for 25 minutes. Remove from oven; add sour
cream, and sprinkle top with remaining
1 tablespoon chives. Yield: 6 servings.
Cindi Rawlins,
Dunwoody, Georgia.

BROCCOLI
WITH SOUR CREAM SAUCE

1 pound fresh broccoli
1 (8-ounce) carton commercial sour cream
2 tablespoons brown sugar
2 tablespoons vinegar
½ teaspoon prepared mustard
¼ teaspoon salt

Trim off large leaves of broccoli; remove tough ends of lower stalks. Wash
broccoli thoroughly, and coarsely chop.
Place broccoli in vegetable steamer over
boiling water. Cover and steam 10 to 15
minutes or until broccoli is crisp-tender.

Combine sour cream and next 4 ingredients in a small saucepan. Cook
until thoroughly heated; do not boil.
Spoon over broccoli. Yield: 4 to 6
servings.
Betty Nelson,
Dothan, Alabama.

HOT-AND-CREAMY DUTCH SLAW

½ cup whipping cream
1 tablespoon sugar
1 tablespoon vinegar
Pinch of baking soda
2 tablespoons butter or margarine
1 small (1¼ pound) cabbage, finely
   shredded
½ teaspoon salt
½ teaspoon white pepper
Paprika

Combine first 4 ingredients in a small
bowl; stir well. Set aside.

Melt butter in a Dutch oven; add cabbage, salt, and pepper. Cover and simmer over medium heat about 5 minutes,
stirring occasionally. Drain cabbage
well. Pour whipping cream mixture over
cabbage; stir well. Sprinkle with paprika. Yield: 6 servings.
Clara Deal Dellinger,
Memphis, Tennessee.

Add A Chilled Sauce
To Meat

When there isn't time to prepare a
hot entrée, rely on deli meats or meats
you can cook ahead of time and serve
chilled. It may sound a bit boring at
first, but that thought will never enter
anyone's mind if you spruce up the
meat, poultry, or seafood with a delectable chilled sauce.

RAISIN SAUCE

¾ cup golden raisins
1 (8-ounce) carton commercial sour cream
2 teaspoons prepared horseradish
1 teaspoon lemon juice
Dash of salt

Cover raisins with hot water; let stand
5 minutes. Drain well, and blot dry with
paper towels. Combine raisins and remaining ingredients; stir well. Cover
and chill. Serve sauce with ham. Yield:
1¼ cups.
Kay Castleman Cooper,
Burke, Virginia.

SPICY CHILI SAUCE

1 cup chili sauce
½ cup chopped onion
1 teaspoon brown sugar
¼ teaspoon garlic salt
¼ teaspoon dry mustard
3 tablespoons lemon juice
1 tablespoon vegetable oil
2 teaspoons cider vinegar
½ teaspoon hot sauce

Combine all ingredients in a saucepan; stir. Bring to a boil; reduce heat,
and simmer 5 minutes. Cover and chill.
Serve sauce with shrimp or fish. Yield:
1⅓ cups.
Ruth Horomanski,
Satellite Beach, Florida.

HORSERADISH SAUCE

1 (8-ounce) carton commercial sour cream
2 tablespoons prepared horseradish
1 tablespoon spicy brown mustard

Combine all ingredients, stirring well.
Cover and chill. Serve sauce with roast
beef. Yield: 1¼ cups.
Mrs. Robert L. Fetzer,
Jacksonville, Florida.

QUICK TARTAR SAUCE

½ cup mayonnaise
1 tablespoon chopped dill pickle
1 tablespoon chopped pimiento-stuffed
 olives
1 tablespoon lemon juice
½ teaspoon grated onion
¼ teaspoon Worcestershire sauce

Combine all ingredients, stirring well. Cover and chill sauce mixture. Serve sauce with seafood. Yield: ½ cup.
Viola Williams,
Silsbee, Texas.

COCKTAIL SAUCE

3 tablespoons dark brown sugar
½ teaspoon cornstarch
⅛ teaspoon ground cinnamon
⅛ teaspoon ground cloves
⅛ teaspoon ground red pepper
1 (10¾-ounce) can tomato soup,
 undiluted
3 tablespoons prepared horseradish
2 tablespoons vinegar
2 tablespoons lemon juice

Combine brown sugar, cornstarch, cinnamon, cloves, and red pepper in a saucepan; stir well. Add remaining ingredients; stir well. Cook over medium heat, stirring constantly, until mixture is thickened. Remove from heat; cool. Cover and chill sauce mixture. Serve sauce with shrimp. Yield: 1½ cups.
Violet Moore,
Montezuma, Georgia.

This Menu Is For Two

Wouldn't you like to present a meal for two that looks and tastes special without spending your entire afternoon preparing it? Then try our tempting menu. All of the dishes are easy to make. Start by putting Baked Lemon Cups in the oven—they can be served warm or at room temperature.

You can prepare Fish-Asparagus Divan in 20 minutes. Sauté the fish, mix up the Parmesan sauce, and cook the asparagus. Boneless chicken breasts, ham slices, or shellfish can be substituted for the fish fillets. If you use chicken breasts, pound them slightly and dip in flour before you sauté them.

**Fish-Asparagus Divan
Tossed Bibb Salad
Glazed Carrots and Onions
Commercial Rolls
Baked Lemon Cups
Wine   Water**

FISH-ASPARAGUS DIVAN

2 fish fillets (¾ pound)
Salt and pepper to taste
¼ cup butter or margarine, divided
½ pound fresh asparagus
2 small green onions, thinly sliced
2 tablespoons all-purpose flour
1 cup milk
¼ cup freshly grated Parmesan cheese
¼ cup dry white wine
Additional Parmesan cheese

Sprinkle fillets with salt and pepper. Sauté fillets in 2 tablespoons butter until almost done and lightly browned.

Snap off tough ends of asparagus. Remove scales from stalks with a knife or vegetable peeler, if desired. Cook asparagus, covered, in a small amount of boiling water 5 minutes or until crisp-tender. Drain. Arrange spears in a shallow baking dish. Place fish on top of the asparagus. Set aside.

Sauté green onions in remaining 2 tablespoons butter in a heavy saucepan over low heat. Add flour, stirring until smooth. Cook 1 minute, stirring constantly. Gradually add milk; cook over medium heat, stirring constantly, until mixture is thickened and bubbly. Stir in ¼ cup Parmesan cheese and wine; continue cooking, stirring constantly, until mixture is thickened. Pour over fish in baking dish. Sprinkle with additional Parmesan cheese. Bake, uncovered, at 350° for 10 minutes or until bubbly. Yield: 2 servings.   *Marian E. Dils,*
Altamonte Springs, Florida.

TOSSED BIBB SALAD

2 tablespoons vegetable oil
1 tablespoon plus 1 teaspoon minced fresh
 parsley
1 tablespoon vinegar
2 teaspoons minced chives
½ teaspoon seasoned salt
½ teaspoon dried whole oregano
2 cups torn bibb lettuce
1 small tomato, chopped
⅓ cup croutons

Combine oil, parsley, vinegar, chives, salt, and oregano in a jar; cover tightly, and shake vigorously until well blended. Chill dressing mixture thoroughly.

Combine lettuce and tomato just before serving. Shake dressing well to mix. Pour over salad, and toss well. Sprinkle with croutons, and serve immediately. Yield: 2 servings.
Mrs. E. W. Hanley,
Palm Harbor, Florida.

GLAZED CARROTS AND ONIONS

3 medium carrots, scraped and cut into
 quarters
1 teaspoon chicken-flavored bouillon
 granules
4 small onions, peeled and halved
¼ cup butter or margarine
1 teaspoon sugar
1 tablespoon chopped fresh parsley

Combine carrots, bouillon granules, and water to cover in a saucepan. Bring to a boil; cover, reduce heat, and simmer 10 minutes. Add onions, and cook 6 minutes or until vegetables are tender. Drain well. Spoon vegetables into a serving dish.

Melt butter in a small saucepan; add sugar, stirring constantly, until golden brown. Pour over vegetables, and sprinkle with parsley. Yield: 2 servings.
Lona B. Shealy,
Leesville, South Carolina.

BAKED LEMON CUPS

¼ cup sugar
1 tablespoon all-purpose flour
Dash of salt
1½ teaspoons butter or margarine, melted
½ teaspoon grated lemon rind
1 tablespoon lemon juice
1 egg, separated
⅓ cup milk
Sweetened whipped cream
Lemon slices

Combine first 3 ingredients in a mixing bowl; stir in butter, lemon rind, and lemon juice. Beat egg yolk until thick and lemon colored. Add yolk and milk to lemon mixture; stir well. Beat egg white until stiff peaks form; fold into lemon mixture. Pour into 2 greased 6-ounce custard cups or ramekins.

Place the custard cups in a shallow baking pan; pour hot water into baking pan to depth of 1 inch. Bake at 350° for 25 to 30 minutes or until set. Cool. Garnish with sweetened whipped cream and lemon slices. Yield: 2 servings.

Mrs. J. A. Allard,
San Antonio, Texas.

It's Time To Pick Blackberries

You may have to fight a few brambles to enjoy blackberries, but they are well worth the effort.

Waiting until the dew evaporates is best because dry berries stay fresh longer than those that are picked wet. Use within two hours of picking, or store them, unwashed, in refrigerator. Washed berries that sit overnight may spoil, even if refrigerated.

Plump and juicy blackberries, with a sweet yet tart taste, are the dark pearls of summer.

FRUIT SALAD WITH HONEY DRESSING

1 (20-ounce) can pineapple chunks, drained
2 cups cubed cantaloupe
2 cups fresh strawberries
1 cup seedless green grapes
2 cups fresh blackberries
Honey Dressing

Combine pineapple, cantaloupe, strawberries, and grapes; cover and chill. Add blackberries just before serving, and gently toss. Serve with Honey Dressing. Yield: 8 servings.

Honey Dressing:

⅓ cup sugar
1 teaspoon dry mustard
1 teaspoon paprika
¼ teaspoon salt
⅓ cup honey
1 tablespoon lemon juice
¼ cup vinegar
1 cup vegetable oil
1 teaspoon grated onion
1 teaspoon celery seeds

Combine sugar, dry mustard, paprika, salt, honey, lemon juice, and vinegar in container of an electric blender. Cover and blend well. Slowly add oil, continuing to blend until thick.

Stir in onion and celery seeds; chill. Yield: 2 cups. *Marlana M. Mitchell, Frankfort, Kentucky.*

BLACKBERRIES-AND-CREAM PARFAIT

1 (3-ounce) package blackberry-flavored gelatin
1 cup boiling water
½ cup orange juice
1 (8-ounce) package cream cheese, softened
3 tablespoons sugar
1 (8-ounce) container frozen whipped topping, thawed
2 cups fresh blackberries

Dissolve gelatin in boiling water; stir in orange juice; set aside.

Combine cream cheese and sugar; beat at medium speed of electric mixer until smooth and fluffy. Gradually add gelatin, beating at low speed until mixture is smooth. Chill gelatin mixture until consistency of unbeaten egg white; fold in whipped topping.

Layer gelatin mixture and blackberries in individual parfaits or serving dishes; chill until serving time. Yield: 8 servings. *Janie Wallace, Seguin, Texas.*

Tip: When preparing a recipe, follow directions carefully. Avoid substituting items; for example, don't use soft margarine for butter or margarine, or whipped cream cheese for cream cheese.

BLACKBERRY-APPLE PIE

Pastry for double-crust 9-inch pie
3 cups fresh blackberries
1 cup peeled and thinly sliced apples
1 cup sugar
3 tablespoons quick-cooking tapioca
½ teaspoon ground cinnamon
2 tablespoons butter or margarine

Roll half of pastry to ⅛-inch thickness, and fit into a 9-inch pieplate.

Combine blackberries and apple slices; place in pastry shell. Combine sugar, tapioca, and cinnamon; stir well. Sprinkle sugar mixture over blackberries; dot with butter.

Roll out remaining pastry to ⅛-inch thickness, and place over filling. Trim pastry; seal and flute edges. Cut slits in top for steam to escape. Bake at 350° for 1 hour or until golden brown. Cool before serving. Yield: one 9-inch pie.

Doris F. Davis,
Narrows, Virginia.

BLACKBERRY BARS

1 cup all-purpose flour
¾ cup firmly packed brown sugar
¼ cup butter or margarine
½ cup commercial sour cream
1 egg, beaten
¾ teaspoon baking soda
¼ teaspoon salt
1 teaspoon ground cinnamon
½ teaspoon vanilla extract
1 cup fresh blackberries
Sifted powdered sugar

Combine flour and brown sugar; cut in butter with pastry blender until mixture resembles coarse meal. Press 1⅓ cups of mixture in bottom of an ungreased 8-inch square pan.

Combine remaining crumb mixture, sour cream, egg, baking soda, salt, cinnamon, and vanilla; blend well. Stir in blackberries. Spoon over crust, spreading evenly. Bake at 350° for 35 minutes. Cool; cut into 3- x 2½-inch bars. Sprinkle with powdered sugar. Yield: one dozen bars. *Mary Brooke Casad,*
Gainesville, Georgia.

From Our Kitchen To Yours

The appliances in our test kitchens must operate precisely. In preparing more than 100 recipes each week, we depend on our ovens, dishwashers, and refrigerators for efficiency and accuracy. Below are tips on use and care of these appliances.

When performance difficulties arise, we read the manufacturer's use and care manual. Being knowledgeable about the operation and maintenance of appliances helps avoid problems. To help understand your appliances better, check our tips and your manual; then maybe you can avoid a service call.

Dishwasher

For the best cleaning results, use hot (140° F) water and select the correct cleaning cycle. Proper loading ensures good water circulation and allows the spray arms to turn freely. Use the correct amount of *only* automatic dishwasher detergent, and after each cycle, clean the food-filter screen.

Unclean items, odor problems, spotting and filming, and discoloration of the dishwasher are caused by using too little detergent. Problems resulting from too much detergent are etching, undissolved detergent deposits, faded items, and strong chemical or perfume odors. Etching, the permanent corrosion of glass, is a complex problem involving many variables—water quality, water temperature, detergent concentration, insufficient rinsing, and the type of glassware.

Refrigerator

Incorrect refrigerator temperatures may be caused by wrong location, a worn gasket or a poor gasket fit, heavy family usage, warm food, dust and lint on condenser coils, or incorrect control settings.

Ideal compartment temperatures range from 34° to 40° F in the refrigerator section and 0° to 5° F for the freezer section. Be sure that your refrigerator is level, with spacing around the sides and back for venting heat. Stiff, cracked, or damaged door gaskets allow air seepage. Overloading and frequent door openings raise the temperature.

Adding too much warm food at once also raises the temperature of the air in the refrigerator. Frost buildup in the freezer compartment of ¼ inch or more acts as an insulator and interferes with cooling efficiency.

Microwave Oven

Infrequent cleaning can cause slower cooking times, poor door seal, and unpleasant odors. Clean your microwave after each use with a paper towel, soft cloth, or sponge that has been dipped in a mild detergent solution. Remove cooked-on foods by boiling 1 cup water in a 2-cup glass measure for several minutes; the moisture will help loosen food particles. Then you can wipe off the cooked-on foods with ease.

Erase stains with a baking soda-and-water paste, a special ceramic glass cleaner, or a mild cleanser. (Harsh cleansers and steel-wool pads cause surface scratches and possible rusting.) Eliminate odors by boiling ½ cup lemon juice and 1 cup water in a 4-cup glass measure for several minutes; let stand 5 minutes.

Oven

Uneven browning or baking may be caused by an inaccurate thermostat, improper pan size, improper ingredient proportions, unlevel range, dark baking pans, warped pans, or baking on preheating settings. Slow baking or underdone food can result from not preheating, placing too many pans in oven, or opening the door too often during baking.

An incorrectly calibrated thermostat causes improper baking. Use an oven thermometer to check the temperature. Refer to the manufacturer's manual to see if the thermostat can be recalibrated or to determine if a service technician should be called.

Using aluminum foil on racks in most ovens is not recommended. It reduces air circulation and radiation transfer of heat to the food, which slows cooking and causes uneven browning.

When using a self-cleaning oven, keep in mind that smoke can occur during the cleaning cycle, and dark deposits often remain. (Slight smoking is normal.) To remove the dark deposits, increase time on next cleaning cycle. To decrease excess smoke, wipe out any food spillage. Manually clean areas outside the oven door seal.

A continuous-cleaning oven is designed to be presentably clean—not spotless. The surface is covered with peaks and valleys that spread spills very thinly so that they gradually burn away at normal to high baking temperatures. It's important to use only cleaners specifically recommended by the manufacturer for heavy buildup. Keep in mind that vinegar water may help remove the residue.

July

Present Dessert In A Shell Of Chocolate

If you're a chocolate lover, chances are you cherish the flavorful confection for its versatility. You probably enjoy chocolate-filled pastries and chocolate-dipped candies, as well as desserts that are chocolaty throughout. But have you ever served from (and eaten!) a chocolate container? If not, then it's time to try these impressive works of art.

There are two techniques that work well for making chocolate containers. The simplest way is to paint the melted confection on the inside of miniature foil cups and gently peel away the cups after the chocolate has hardened.

In testing this type of technique, we found that first painting a thin layer of chocolate-flavored candy coating in the foil cup and then painting a thicker layer of real chocolate works best. The candy coating on the outside makes the little cups less messy to pick up, while the real chocolate on the inside leaves a prettier finish and richer flavor.

Fill these cups with your favorite liqueur for an after-dinner treat, or pipe Creamy Chocolate Mousse or Kahlúa Cream inside for a dainty dessert. You can use the same technique on 2½-inch foil baking cups to make individual-size dessert servings. Just be sure that you don't paint the chocolate too thick, or it will be difficult to cut with a fork.

Chocolate Lace Cups are a little trickier to make, but they're a spectacular presentation at a dinner party. The trick is in piping enough chocolate to make them sturdy enough to fill, but not more than is necessary or the cups will lose their delicate, lacy look.

For these containers, pipe melted chocolate into a lacy network on the outside of foil-covered, inverted custard cups. Chill the cups, and pipe a second lacy network of chocolate. Chill again; then remove the custard cups, and gently peel away the foil.

Use your imagination to make other shapes and sizes of chocolate containers using this same technique. Piping over a banana-split dish will give you a little larger oval shell. You can even use small serving bowls, but remember that the larger the container, the more fragile the chocolate network will be. See the note at the end of the recipe for Chocolate Lace Cups.

Chill both types of chocolate cups until you're ready to serve. Fill cups directly on the plate on which you'll serve them because they may tear if you try to transfer them after filling. Serve the chocolate cups immediately.

Whether or not you try these chocolate containers, don't overlook the Creamy Chocolate Mousse recipe. This classic dessert is bound to be a hit. It's one of our best!

MINIATURE CHOCOLATE CUPS

1 (6-ounce) package chocolate morsels
1 teaspoon shortening
3 (1-ounce) squares chocolate-flavored candy coating
½ pint fresh raspberries
Chambord or other raspberry-flavored liqueur

Combine chocolate morsels and shortening in top of a double boiler; bring water to a boil. Stir until chocolate melts and mixture is smooth. Spoon into a small bowl, and set aside.

Melt candy coating in top of double boiler, stirring until smooth. Paint a thin layer of coating on the inside of miniature foil cups, using a small artist brush. Chill 10 minutes.

Paint a thick layer of melted chocolate morsels over coating. Chill at least 1 hour. Carefully peel foil cups from chocolate. Store in an airtight container in refrigerator until ready to serve. To serve, place a raspberry and about 1½ teaspoons Chambord in each. Yield: 1½ to 2 dozen.

Note: This procedure will also work for 2½-inch foil baking cups. Fill them with ice cream or fruit.

If you want to dazzle your guests, use Miniature Chocolate Cups for after-dinner drinks of raspberry liqueur; place a raspberry in each cup for color and flavor.

Paint melted candy coating on inside of miniature foil cups; chill. Paint melted chocolate morsels over candy coating; chill.

After chocolate-morsel layer has chilled at least one hour, gently peel the foil cups from the molded chocolate cups.

chocolate container would be too delicate to hold a larger volume of filling.) Use metal tip No. 12 or 14 for piping, so that lace network will be stronger. Use these larger chocolate containers to serve Creamy Chocolate Mousse, whipped cream, Kahlúa Cream, or other firm but lightweight fillings. Do not use for thin fillings, as they could seep through lace network. Serve immediately after filling.

CHOCOLATE LACE CUPS

1 (12-ounce) package semisweet chocolate morsels

Invert six 6-ounce custard cups, and cover each cup with a piece of aluminum foil, molding it firmly over each cup and allowing foil to extend 1 to 2 inches beyond cup. Press foil tightly around the bottom of cup to make a definite edge.

Place chocolate morsels in top of a double boiler; bring water to a boil. Stir until chocolate melts; let stand about 10 minutes. Spoon chocolate into a decorating bag fitted with metal tip No. 4 or 5. Slowly and continuously drizzle chocolate in a lacy design over each custard cup, slightly extending chocolate over foil to make a small rim around edge. (If chocolate drizzles too fast, let cool a little longer. If it becomes too firm to pipe, remelt it.) Carefully transfer to a baking sheet, and chill 10 minutes.

Pipe a second layer of chocolate over cups. Chill at least 1 hour. Remove custard cups, and gently peel away foil. Store chocolate cups in an airtight container in refrigerator until ready to serve. Fill chocolate cups with fruit, mousse, or ice cream, and serve immediately. Yield: 6 chocolate cups.

Note: You can pipe a larger chocolate serving container using this same technique. Use no larger than a 3-cup serving container as a mold. (The lacy

CREAMY CHOCOLATE MOUSSE

3 eggs, separated
1½ teaspoons vanilla extract
½ teaspoon almond extract
4 (1-ounce) squares semisweet chocolate, melted and cooled slightly
½ teaspoon cream of tartar
½ cup sugar
1 cup whipping cream

Beat egg yolks lightly; add flavorings and chocolate to egg yolks, stirring well.

Beat egg whites (at room temperature) and cream of tartar at high speed of an electric mixer until frothy. Gradually add sugar, 1 tablespoon at a time, beating until stiff peaks form and sugar dissolves (2 to 4 minutes). Stir about one-fourth of meringue into chocolate mixture; fold remaining meringue into chocolate mixture.

Beat whipping cream at medium speed of an electric mixer until soft peaks form; fold cream into chocolate mixture. Cover and chill at least 2 hours. Yield: 5 cups.

Use small custard cups to mold Chocolate Lace Cups. Cover them with aluminum foil, molding firmly over each cup.

Drizzle chocolate in a lacy design over foil-covered cups; chill. Pipe a second layer of chocolate, and chill again.

After the second layer of chocolate has chilled at least one hour, gently peel the foil away, leaving the chocolate cups.

KAHLÚA CREAM

2 tablespoons Kahlúa
1 teaspoon instant coffee granules
1 teaspoon hot water
2 cups whipping cream
2 tablespoons powdered sugar
1 teaspoon vanilla extract

Combine Kahlúa, coffee granules, and water, stirring until mixture is smooth. Beat whipping cream, powdered sugar, and vanilla until foamy; add coffee mixture, beating until stiff peaks form. Yield: 4 cups.

Delicious Summer Gifts

Generosity overflows when the summer harvest is abundant. But why not make your garden gifts unusual? With these recipes, you can add some creativity to summer food gifts.

Raspberries are a delicacy anyone will appreciate. To enjoy that flavor longer, make our Raspberry-Lemon Vinegar. Select a beautiful vinegar bottle to put it in; add a bow and a copy of our recipe for Fresh Fruit Dressing.

One of the best things is that you can have most of these gifts sitting on the pantry shelf. Then when the need arises, just add a personal touch with a bow, a basket of extras, or just a friendly visit.

FRESH FRUIT DRESSING

¼ cup plus 2 tablespoons sugar
3 tablespoons lemon juice
2 tablespoons Raspberry-Lemon Vinegar
   (recipe, top of next column)
½ teaspoon dry mustard
½ teaspoon paprika
¼ teaspoon salt
½ cup vegetable oil

Combine sugar, lemon juice, Raspberry-Lemon Vinegar, mustard, paprika, and salt in a saucepan; cook over low heat, stirring constantly, until sugar dissolves. Let cool. Pour mixture into a container of an electric blender; gradually add oil in a stream, processing until smooth and thickened. Store in an airtight container, and refrigerate. Serve with fresh fruit. Yield: ¾ cup.

RASPBERRY-LEMON VINEGAR

3 cups fresh raspberries
1 lemon
4 cups white wine vinegar (5% acidity)
½ cup sugar

Rinse raspberries, and allow to air-dry on paper towels. Place berries in a 6-cup jar. With a vegetable peeler, remove rind of lemon in a long, single strip; add to jar of berries. Set aside.

Combine vinegar and sugar in a saucepan; bring almost to a boil over low heat, stirring constantly, until sugar melts. Pour hot vinegar over berries. Cover jar tightly; let stand at room temperature 48 hours.

Remove lemon rind; strain vinegar through several layers of cheesecloth to remove berries. Discard berries. Store vinegar in jars with airtight lids. Store jars in a cool, dark place up to 6 months. Serve vinegar mixture over salad greens. Yield: 5 cups.

GREEN TOMATO PICKLES

4 quarts sliced green tomatoes, loosely
   packed
1 quart sliced onion, loosely packed
1 cup pickling salt, divided
2 (1-pound) packages brown sugar
6 cups vinegar (5% acidity)
2 small red chile peppers
¼ cup plus 2 tablespoons whole mustard
   seeds
¼ cup celery seeds
1 teaspoon pepper
1 tablespoon whole allspice
1 tablespoon whole cloves

Place tomatoes and onion in separate bowls; sprinkle ¾ cup salt over tomatoes and ¼ cup salt over onion, mixing well. Cover both bowls and let stand at least 4 hours.

Place tomatoes in a cheesecloth bag, and squeeze gently to remove excess juice. Repeat this procedure for onion. Discard the salt liquid.

Combine tomatoes, onion, sugar, vinegar, chile peppers, mustard seeds, celery seeds, and pepper in a large Dutch oven. Tie allspice and cloves in a cheesecloth bag; add to tomato mixture. Bring mixture to a boil. Reduce heat, and cook, uncovered, over low heat 20 minutes or until tomatoes are tender.

Pack tomato mixture and liquid into hot sterilized jars, leaving ½ inch headspace; wipe jar rims. Cover at once with metal lids, and screw on bands. Process in a boiling-water bath 10 minutes. Yield: 2 quarts.

APPLE-MINT JELLY

1½ cups firmly packed mint leaves, finely
   chopped
4 cups apple juice
1 (1¾-ounce) package powdered fruit
   pectin
½ cup lemon juice
5 cups sugar

Combine mint and apple juice in a saucepan; bring to a boil. Remove from heat, cover, and let stand 10 minutes. Strain juice, and pour into a large heavy saucepan. Discard mint.

Stir pectin and lemon juice into apple juice, and bring to a boil over high heat, stirring constantly. Stir in sugar all at once. Stir and bring to a full rolling boil (a boil that cannot be stirred down), and boil hard for 1 minute, stirring constantly. Remove from heat. Skim off foam with a metal spoon.

Quickly pour jelly into hot sterilized jars, leaving ¼ inch headspace; wipe jar rims. Cover at once with metal lids, and screw on bands. Process in boiling-water bath 5 minutes. Yield: 7 half pints.

HERBED MUSTARD

⅓ cup dry mustard
¼ cup sugar
4 eggs
½ cup white wine vinegar
¼ cup dry white wine
2 teaspoons crushed thyme
2 teaspoons crushed oregano
   leaves

Combine mustard and sugar in a large saucepan. Add eggs, vinegar, and wine; mix well at medium speed of an electric mixer. Cook over low heat, beating constantly at high speed of an electric mixer 5 minutes or until thick. (Mixture will double in volume, and then fall.) Stir in crushed thyme and oregano leaves. Cool mixture to room temperature; stir well, and pour into jars. Cover and store mixture in refrigerator up to 1 month. Yield: 2 cups.

Right: *Save the bourbon for dessert; try our homemade Bourbon Ice Cream (page 139).*

Page 136: *Any occasion will be special when you feast on this luscious Blueberries 'n' Cream Cheesecake (page 140).*

summer Suppers.

Summertime Food And Fun

It's summertime, and the living is fun. Family reunions, picnics, cookouts, and lavish parties are just a few occasions where you can try some of the recipes and ideas that we've included in this special section.

At a neighborhood gathering, you can offer children our Chocolate Cookie Ice Cream Sandwiches, while adults savor Bourbon Ice Cream. We also present a variety of other desserts you can serve to guests when sitting on the porch or watching a late-night movie. Our entrée salads are good choices for a brunch or luncheon on the weekend. For dessert, Blueberries 'n' Cream Cheesecake is a good "Sunday best" selection.

And what's summertime without cookouts? The Marinated and Grilled Shrimp is sure to be a crowd-pleaser. An outdoor meal would be a good time to create a special atmosphere with candles (page 148) and flower arrangements (page 147).

Enjoy all the delicious food and good ideas we offer in this 11th annual "Summer Suppers" special section. But first come along with us to Louisiana for an elegant alfresco supper.

Let's Have a Veranda Supper

In Lafayette, Louisiana, the tradition of hospitality is as evident as magnolia blossoms. Jean and Pat Hurley's party is a fine example.

For a summer evening, Jean planned this lavish supper and doubled many of the recipes to serve the party of 16. She designed a menu that features Creole and Cajun cuisines.

Once guests arrive, they settle back in wicker chairs on the veranda, sipping lemonade, munching on Pepper Pecans, and chatting. Then while Jean is in the kitchen adding finishing touches to the dinner, the host is outside ladling Crab-and-Corn Bisque into coffee cups. Pat likes to use cups instead of bowls so that everyone can stand while enjoying the bisque.

When the dinner bell rings, guests serve themselves at the buffet table. Stuffed Snapper filled with crabmeat dressing and topped with a shrimp and mushroom sauce is the highlight of the menu. It's accompanied by Hearts-of-Palm Salad that's topped with a vinaigrette dressing. Creole Potatoes is a deliciously seasoned side dish. With their plates piled high, guests descend from the veranda to the courtyard, where tables are arranged around a gurgling fountain. Later they're served dessert—homemade Fig Ice Cream and Cajun Cake; both are rich and fruity.

Lemonade
Pepper Pecans
Crab-and-Corn Bisque
Stuffed Snapper
Creole Potatoes
Hearts-of-Palm Salad
Commercial French Bread
Cajun Cake
Fig Ice Cream
Wine

PEPPER PECANS

2 tablespoons butter or margarine, melted
¼ cup golden Worcestershire sauce
2 dashes of hot sauce
Dash of pepper
2 cups pecan halves

Combine butter, Worcestershire sauce, hot sauce, and pepper; stir in pecans. Let stand 30 minutes; drain.

Spread pecans evenly in a 13- x 9- x 2-inch pan; bake at 300° for 30 minutes, stirring frequently. Yield: 2 cups.

CRAB-AND-CORN BISQUE

½ cup chopped celery
½ cup chopped green onions
¼ cup chopped green pepper
½ cup butter or margarine, melted
2 (10¾-ounce) cans cream of potato soup, undiluted
1 (17-ounce) can cream-style corn
1½ cups half-and-half
1½ cups milk
2 bay leaves
1 teaspoon dried whole thyme
½ teaspoon garlic powder
¼ teaspoon white pepper
Dash of hot sauce
1 pound lump crabmeat
Chopped parsley (optional)
Lemon slices (optional)

Sauté celery, green onions, and green pepper in butter in a Dutch oven. Add soup, corn, half-and-half, milk, bay leaves, thyme, garlic powder, pepper, and hot sauce; cook until thoroughly heated. Gently stir in crabmeat, and heat thoroughly. Discard bay leaves. Garnish with parsley and lemon slices, if desired. Yield: 11 cups.

Tip: Rub hands with fresh parsley to remove any unpleasant odors.

STUFFED SNAPPER

6 green onions, sliced
2 stalks celery, chopped
¼ cup butter or margarine, melted
1 cup toasted fresh breadcrumbs
1 cup fresh crabmeat
¼ cup dry white wine
2 tablespoons chopped fresh parsley
½ teaspoon dried whole basil
½ teaspoon dried whole thyme
¼ teaspoon salt
⅛ teaspoon pepper
1 (3- to 4-pound) whole snapper, dressed
½ cup dry white wine
¼ cup water
½ cup chopped onion
Shrimp Sauce
Cooked shrimp, peeled and deveined
** (optional)**
Lump crabmeat (optional)
Lemon wedges (optional)
Paprika (optional)

Sauté green onions and celery in butter in a large skillet until tender. Stir in breadcrumbs, 1 cup crabmeat, ¼ cup wine, parsley, basil, thyme, salt, and pepper; stuff mixture into fish cavity. Place fish in a 15- x 10- x 1-inch jellyroll pan. Combine ½ cup wine, water, and onion; pour over fish. Bake, uncovered, at 350° for 30 minutes, basting occasionally. Drain pan juice, reserving ⅓ cup for Shrimp Sauce.

Pour Shrimp Sauce over fish. Bake, uncovered, at 350° an additional 30 minutes. Garnish top of snapper with shrimp, crabmeat, and lemon wedges dipped in paprika, if desired. Yield: 8 servings.

Shrimp Sauce:

¼ cup butter or margarine
1 tablespoon all-purpose flour
⅓ cup reserved pan juice
¼ cup water
¼ cup dry white wine
1 tablespoon lemon juice
1 egg, beaten
1 bay leaf
½ teaspoon sugar
½ teaspoon dried whole basil
¼ teaspoon salt
⅛ teaspoon pepper
8 to 10 medium uncooked fresh shrimp,
** peeled and deveined**
½ cup sliced mushrooms

Melt butter in a heavy saucepan over low heat; add flour, stirring until smooth. Cook 1 minute, stirring constantly. Gradually add pan juice, water, wine, and lemon juice, stirring until well blended. Gradually stir about one-fourth of hot mixture into egg; add to remaining hot mixture, stirring constantly. Add bay leaf, sugar, basil, salt, and pepper. Cook over low heat 8 to 10 minutes; remove from heat, and stir in shrimp and mushrooms. Remove bay leaf. Yield: about 1⅔ cups.

CREOLE POTATOES

16 small new potatoes (about 2 pounds)
1½ teaspoons Creole seasoning
¼ cup butter or margarine, melted
½ cup chopped parsley
Parsley sprigs (optional)

Cut potatoes into quarters; place in a steamer rack over boiling water. Cover and steam 12 to 15 minutes or until tender. Transfer potatoes to a bowl, and sprinkle with Creole seasoning. Add butter and chopped parsley; toss, coating potatoes thoroughly. Garnish with parsley sprigs, if desired. Yield: 8 servings.

HEARTS-OF-PALM SALAD

1 pound fresh green beans
4 cups torn leaf lettuce
1 (14-ounce) can hearts of palm, drained
** and cut into ½-inch slices**
½ cup sliced celery
½ cup sliced green onions
½ cup pimiento-stuffed olives
½ cup chopped fresh parsley
Leaf lettuce
2 tomatoes, sliced and quartered
Vinaigrette dressing (recipe follows)
Sweet red pepper (optional)

Wash beans; trim ends, and remove strings. Place green beans in a steamer basket over boiling water; cover and steam 10 minutes or until crisp-tender. Cool beans.

Combine green beans, lettuce, hearts of palm, celery, onions, olives, and parsley in a large bowl; toss gently. Arrange in a lettuce-lined bowl. Garnish with tomatoes. Serve vinaigrette dressing in a hollowed-out red pepper, if desired. Yield: 8 servings.

Vinaigrette Dressing:

⅓ cup vegetable oil
¼ cup cider vinegar
½ cup finely chopped green
** onions**
¼ cup sweet pickle relish
1 tablespoon sugar
1 tablespoon chopped fresh basil
1 tablespoon chopped pimiento
2 tablespoons tarragon vinegar
½ teaspoon coarse-grained mustard
** with white wine**
¼ teaspoon salt
⅛ teaspoon pepper

Combine all ingredients in a small bowl; stir well. Cover and chill 3 to 4 hours. Yield: 1¼ cups.

CAJUN CAKE

1 (15¼-ounce) can crushed pineapple
½ cup butter or margarine, softened
1½ cups sugar
2 eggs
2 cups all-purpose flour
2 teaspoons baking powder
½ teaspoon baking soda
¼ teaspoon salt
¼ cup butter or margarine
½ cup sugar
⅓ cup evaporated milk
½ cup flaked coconut
½ cup chopped pecans
½ teaspoon vanilla extract
Toasted flaked coconut (optional)
Pineapple slices (optional)
Fresh pineapple leaves (optional)

Drain pineapple, reserving ½ cup juice. Set aside.

Cream ½ cup softened butter; gradually add 1½ cups sugar, beating well at medium speed of an electric mixer. Add eggs, one at a time, beating well after each addition.

Combine flour, baking powder, soda, and salt; add to creamed mixture alternately with reserved juice, beginning and ending with flour mixture. Mix just until blended after each addition. Stir in crushed pineapple.

Pour batter into a greased and floured 10-inch Bundt pan. Bake at 350° for 50 to 55 minutes or until a wooden pick inserted in center comes out clean. Cool in pan 10 minutes; remove from pan, and place on serving plate.

Combine ¼ cup butter, ½ cup sugar, evaporated milk, coconut, and pecans in a small saucepan. Bring to a boil; reduce heat, and simmer 3 minutes. Stir in vanilla. Spoon on top of warm cake. Cool. Sprinkle with toasted coconut and garnish with pineapple slices and leaves, if desired. Yield: one 10-inch cake.

FIG ICE CREAM

2 (17-ounce) cans Kadota figs, drained
1 cup milk
1¾ cups sugar, divided
2 tablespoons lemon juice
1½ tablespoons crème de cacao
2 eggs, beaten
3 cups milk
2 cups whipping cream

Combine figs, 1 cup milk, 1 cup sugar, lemon juice, and crème de cacao in container of an electric blender. Process until mixture is pureed.

Combine eggs, fig puree, remaining ¾ cup sugar, 3 cups milk, and whipping cream in a large bowl; mix well. Pour into freezer can of a 4-quart, hand-turned or electric freezer. Freeze according to manufacturer's instructions. Let ice cream ripen about 1 hour. Yield: 3 quarts.

Tip: Make ice cubes for a party ahead of time and store them in plastic bags in the freezer. Count on 350 cubes for 50 people or about 7 cubes per person.

Hot Days Call For Cool Desserts

Anything cool is a welcome relief from summer heat. With this in mind, we offer some refreshing recipes to cap off the meal. Most of these desserts can be made ahead of time to help ease your schedule when you entertain.

LEMON CURD

5 eggs, beaten
2⅓ cups sugar
2 tablespoons grated lemon rind
½ cup lemon juice
½ cup butter or margarine

Combine all ingredients in top of a double boiler; mix well. Bring water to a boil; reduce heat, and cook over hot water, stirring constantly, until mixture thickens (about 15 minutes). Remove from heat; cool. Store in refrigerator. Serve with pound cake or gingerbread. Yield: 3 cups.
Mrs. Donald MacMillan,
Cartersville, Georgia.

SPECIAL-OCCASION BROWNIE DESSERT

4 (1-ounce) squares unsweetened chocolate
1 cup butter or margarine
1½ cups sugar
4 eggs, beaten
2 teaspoons vanilla extract
1 cup all-purpose flour
¼ teaspoon salt
1 cup chopped walnuts
Graham cracker crust (recipe follows)
2 cups frozen whipped topping, thawed
Finely chopped walnuts (optional)

Combine chocolate and butter in a heavy saucepan; place over low heat, stirring constantly, until melted. Add sugar, stirring until combined. Remove from heat, and cool 5 minutes. Stir in eggs and vanilla.

Combine flour and salt; add to creamed mixture, stirring well. Stir in 1 cup walnuts, and pour into prepared graham cracker crust. Bake at 325° for 45 to 50 minutes; cool and chill 8 hours. Remove from pan; spread with whipped topping, and if desired, sprinkle with finely chopped walnuts. Yield: 10 to 12 servings.

Graham Cracker Crust:

2 cups graham cracker crumbs
½ cup ground almonds
½ cup ground walnuts
¼ cup sugar
¾ cup butter or margarine, melted

Combine all ingredients, mixing well. Press into bottom and up sides of a 9-inch springform pan. Bake at 350° for 8 to 10 minutes; let cool. Yield: one 9-inch graham cracker crust.
Mary Kay Menees,
White Pine, Tennessee.

BOURBON ICE CREAM
(pictured on page 135)

4 eggs
¾ cup sugar
¼ cup bourbon
1 (14-ounce) can sweetened condensed milk
6 cups half-and-half
Fresh mint sprigs (optional)

Beat eggs on medium speed of an electric mixer; gradually add sugar. Add bourbon and condensed milk; mix well. Add half-and-half. Pour mixture into freezer can of a 1-gallon hand-turned or electric freezer. Freeze according to manufacturer's instructions. Let ice cream ripen at least 1 hour. Garnish each serving with mint sprigs, if desired. Yield: 3 quarts. *Jean Howard,*
Auburn, Alabama.

Blueberries At Their Best

Make the best of the berries with this array of blueberry delights. Blueberries 'n' Cream Cheesecake is a prizewinner that takes advantage of an abundance of fresh fruit; pureed blueberries are swirled in the cheesecake, while whole berries are mixed in the glaze. Another hit dessert is Blueberry Pinwheel Cobbler, served warm with ice cream.

BLUEBERRIES 'N' CREAM CHEESECAKE
(pictured on page 136)

2½ cups fresh blueberries
1 tablespoon cornstarch
3 (8-ounce) packages cream cheese, softened
1 cup sugar
5 eggs
2 tablespoons cornstarch
¼ teaspoon salt
1½ cups commercial sour cream
2 tablespoons sugar
½ teaspoon vanilla extract
¼ cup sugar
¼ cup water
1 cup fresh blueberries

Combine 2½ cups blueberries and 1 tablespoon cornstarch in container of electric blender; blend until smooth. Cook puree in saucepan over medium-high heat about 15 minutes or until slightly thickened, stirring constantly. Set mixture aside to cool. Reserve ½ cup puree for glaze.

Beat cream cheese with an electric mixer until light and fluffy. Gradually add 1 cup sugar, mixing well. Add eggs, one at a time, beating well after each addition. Stir in 2 tablespoons cornstarch and salt. Pour batter into a greased 9-inch springform pan. Pour puree over cheesecake batter; gently swirl with a knife. Bake at 325° for 45 minutes or until set. Remove from oven; cool on wire rack 20 minutes.

Combine sour cream, 2 tablespoons sugar, and vanilla in a small bowl; mix well. Spread sour cream mixture over cheesecake. Bake at 325° an additional 10 minutes. Cool cheesecake on wire rack. Cover and chill 8 hours.

Combine reserved ½ cup puree, ¼ cup sugar, and water in a small saucepan; cook over medium heat, stirring constantly, until thickened. Gently fold in 1 cup blueberries; let cool.

Remove sides of springform pan. Spoon blueberry glaze on cheesecake. Yield: 10 to 12 servings.

Judith Baldwin,
Decatur, Georgia.

BLUEBERRY PINWHEEL COBBLER

2 cups sugar
2 cups water
1 teaspoon vanilla extract
½ teaspoon lemon juice
½ cup butter-flavored shortening
1½ cups self-rising flour
⅓ cup milk
2 cups fresh blueberries
½ cup butter or margarine
Vanilla ice cream or frozen whipped topping, thawed

Combine sugar and water in a saucepan; stir well. Cook over medium heat, stirring constantly, until sugar dissolves; stir in vanilla and lemon juice. Set mixture aside.

Cut shortening into flour until mixture resembles coarse meal; add milk, stirring just until dry ingredients are moistened. Turn dough out onto a lightly floured surface, and knead lightly 4 or 5 times.

Roll dough to a 12- x 9-inch rectangle. Spread blueberries over dough; roll up, jellyroll fashion, beginning with long side. Set aside.

Melt butter in a 13- x 9- x 2-inch baking dish. Cut dough into 12 (1-inch) slices; place slices, cut side down, in butter. Pour sugar syrup around slices; bake at 350° for 55 to 60 minutes or until golden. Serve warm with vanilla ice cream or whipped topping. Yield: 8 to 10 servings.

Willie Mae Hogan,
Birmingham, Alabama.

BLUEBERRY-ORANGE BREAD

2 tablespoons butter or margarine
¼ cup boiling water
1 tablespoon grated orange rind
½ cup orange juice
1 egg
1 cup sugar
2 cups all-purpose flour
1 teaspoon baking powder
¼ teaspoon baking soda
½ teaspoon salt
1 cup fresh blueberries
1 teaspoon grated orange rind
2 tablespoons fresh orange juice
2 tablespoons honey

Combine butter and boiling water in a small bowl; add 1 tablespoon grated orange rind and ½ cup orange juice. Set mixture aside.

Beat egg and sugar with an electric mixer until light and fluffy. Combine the flour, baking powder, soda, and salt; add to egg mixture alternately with orange juice mixture, beginning and ending with flour mixture.

Fold in blueberries. Spoon batter into a greased and floured 9- x 5- x 3-inch loafpan. Bake at 350° for 55 minutes. Cool bread in pan 10 minutes; remove to wire rack.

Combine 1 teaspoon orange rind, 2 tablespoons orange juice, and 2 tablespoons honey, mixing well. Spoon over hot bread; let cool. Yield: 1 loaf.

Martha Johnston,
Birmingham, Alabama.

Grilled Meats For Lazy Evenings

Grilling outdoors is as much a part of the season as softball, lemonade, and summer camp. If you're in charge of meals at your house, you know what a challenge it is to satisfy a hungry family or dinner guests after a day in the sun.

Turn to recipes such as Chicken Kabobs or Flank Steak Pinwheels to make summer grilling easy. The flank steak is cut into strips, rolled up, and then secured with a wooden pick. For Chicken Kabobs, the vegetables are already skewered on the kabob alongside the meat. All you add is rice and a green salad to round out the menu.

FLANK STEAK PINWHEELS

2 (1- to 1¼-pound) flank steaks
2 cups chopped onion
1 cup vegetable oil
⅔ cup vinegar
4 cloves garlic, minced
2 teaspoons salt
½ teaspoon dried whole thyme
½ teaspoon dried whole marjoram
Dash of pepper

Cut flank steaks diagonally across grain into ¼-inch-thick slices; roll up slices, and secure with wooden picks. Place pinwheels in a 13- x 9- x 2-inch baking dish; sprinkle onion over pinwheels. Combine remaining ingredients; stir well. Pour over onion and pinwheels; cover and chill 8 hours.

Remove pinwheels from marinade; grill over medium-hot coals 14 to 16 minutes or until desired degree of doneness, turning often. Yield: 8 to 10 servings.   *Ken Johnson,*
Wynne, Arkansas.

PATIO STEAK

½ cup dry red wine
¼ cup vegetable oil
3 tablespoons lime juice
2 tablespoons vinegar
2 tablespoons instant minced onion
1 bay leaf, crushed
2 teaspoons dried whole thyme
1 teaspoon dried whole marjoram
1 (3-pound) boneless chuck roast (2 inches thick)

Combine wine, oil, lime juice, vinegar, minced onion, bay leaf, thyme, and marjoram in a shallow dish, and mix well. Place roast in dish, turning once in marinade. Cover and refrigerate 8 hours, occasionally turning the meat.

Remove roast from refrigerator, and let stand 1 hour. Drain roast, reserving marinade. Grill roast about 6 inches from medium-hot coals for 30 minutes on each side or until a meat thermometer registers 140° (rare) or 150° (medium rare); baste frequently with reserved marinade. Yield: 6 to 8 servings.
Pat Boschen,
Ashland, Virginia.

MARINATED AND GRILLED SHRIMP

⅓ cup sherry
⅓ cup sesame seed oil
⅓ cup soy sauce
½ teaspoon sugar
¼ teaspoon garlic powder
¼ teaspoon ground ginger
2 pounds large fresh shrimp, peeled and deveined

Combine all ingredients except shrimp in a shallow dish, and mix well. Add shrimp, tossing gently to coat. Cover and chill for 2 to 3 hours, stirring occasionally.

Drain shrimp, reserving marinade. Place shrimp on six 14-inch skewers. Grill over medium-hot coals 3 to 4 minutes on each side, basting frequently with marinade. Yield: 4 to 6 servings.
Connie Burgess,
Knoxville, Tennessee.

CHICKEN KABOBS

8 slices bacon, cut in half
4 chicken breast halves, skinned and boned
1 (15¼-ounce) can unsweetened pineapple chunks
1 large onion, cut into 16 pieces
2 large green peppers, cut into 16 pieces
16 cherry tomatoes
½ cup white wine
3 tablespoons Worcestershire sauce
⅛ teaspoon pepper

Cook bacon for 1 to 3 minutes or until transparent; drain and set aside.

Cut each chicken breast into 4 strips. Drain pineapple, reserving juice. Combine chicken, pineapple chunks, bacon, onion, green pepper, and cherry tomatoes in a shallow dish.

Combine ½ cup reserved pineapple juice and remaining ingredients, and stir well. Pour the marinade over chicken mixture; cover and chill for 8 hours, stirring occasionally.

Drain and reserve marinade. Wrap a piece of bacon around each piece of chicken; alternate with vegetables on skewers. Grill about 6 inches from medium-hot coals for 20 minutes or until done, turning and basting often with reserved marinade. Yield: 4 servings.   *J. Gordon Coleman, Jr.,*
Waco, Texas.

Grilling Tips

—Be sure to follow the manufacturer's instructions when lighting the outdoor grill.

—Lightly coat the grilling rack with vegetable cooking spray before placing it over the fire; less meat will stick to it, making cleanup easier.

—To reduce excessive flaring, place a foil pan under the food to catch drippings. Place the pan directly on the briquets in a gas grill; make a well in the center of charcoal briquets.

—Remember that the wind and outside temperature will affect the cooking temperature of the grill and may alter cooking times.

—Use a meat thermometer to determine the degree of doneness for large cuts of meat, and let the meat stand about 15 minutes before carving.

—Choose tongs rather than a fork to turn thin pieces of meat, such as steaks and chicken; forks pierce the meat and allow juices to escape.

GRILLED CUMIN CHICKEN

2 (2½- to 3-pound) broiler-fryers,
   quartered
Juice of 3 lemons
2 tablespoons vegetable oil
2 tablespoons ground cumin
1 tablespoon salt
1 tablespoon coarsely ground pepper
2½ teaspoons celery salt
¼ teaspoon red pepper

Place chicken in a large shallow dish;
pour lemon juice over chicken. Cover
and chill 2 to 3 hours, turning once.
Remove chicken from lemon juice; rub
with oil.

Combine remaining ingredients; stir
well. Sprinkle seasoning over chicken.

Place chicken, skin side up, on grill;
cook over medium-hot coals 30 to 35
minutes or until done, turning once.
Yield: 8 servings. *Marlene Gaither,*
Albertville, Alabama.

COOKING LIGHT®

Spirited Main Dishes

For an easy way to transform common main dishes into something glam-
orous, add a splash of spirits. But isn't
alcohol fattening, you may ask. It does
contain an appreciable amount of calories—7 per gram. That's more than protein or carbohydrate (4 calories per
gram), but slightly less than the number
of calories in fat (9 calories per gram).
But when heated to simmering temperatures, alcohol evaporates, leaving behind few calories and a flavor to
complement other ingredients.

Alcohol used in cookery is best used
in moderation. Like any other ingredient, too much can overpower a dish.

SPIRITED BEEF KABOBS

1 pound lean boneless sirloin steak
¼ cup reduced-sodium soy sauce
¼ cup whiskey
2 tablespoons vegetable oil
2 tablespoons lemon juice
1 clove garlic, crushed
½ teaspoon pepper
16 cherry tomatoes
1 large green pepper, cut into 16 (1-inch)
   pieces
16 medium-size fresh mushrooms (about
   12 ounces)
1 large onion, cut into 16 (1-inch) pieces
Vegetable cooking spray

Trim excess fat from steak; cut meat
into 1-inch cubes. Place meat in a shallow container; set aside.

Combine soy sauce, whiskey, oil,
lemon juice, garlic, and pepper; pour
over meat. Cover and chill 4 hours, stirring occasionally. Remove meat from
marinade, reserving marinade.

Alternate meat and vegetables on
skewers; brush with marinade. Coat
grill rack with cooking spray. Grill
kabobs over medium-hot coals 15 minutes or until desired degree of doneness, turning and basting frequently
with marinade. Yield: 4 servings.

☐ *287 calories, 31.4 grams protein, 11*
grams fat, 16.2 grams carbohydrate, 79.5
milligrams cholesterol, 368.8 milligrams
sodium, and 44.8 milligrams of calcium
per serving. Jan Thompson,
Highland, Maryland.

VEAL PICATTA WITH CAPERS

6 (4-ounce) veal cutlets
2 tablespoons lemon juice
½ teaspoon paprika
⅛ teaspoon pepper
1 tablespoon vegetable oil
2 tablespoons drained capers
⅓ cup Chablis or other dry white wine
1 bay leaf
¼ cup evaporated skim milk

Drizzle veal cutlets with 2 tablespoons
lemon juice; sprinkle with paprika and
pepper, and set aside.

Heat oil in a heavy skillet. Add veal
and capers; cook 2 to 3 minutes on each
side or until veal is done. Remove veal
to serving platter, reserving drippings;
keep warm.

Add wine and bay leaf to skillet; stir
well. Bring to a boil; reduce heat, and
simmer 3 minutes. Remove bay leaf,
and discard. Add milk; return to a boil,
stirring constantly. Remove wine mixture from heat; spoon over warm veal.
Yield: 6 servings.

☐ *166 calories, 17.8 grams protein, 9.1*
grams fat, 2.5 grams carbohydrate, 60.8
milligrams cholesterol, 312.8 milligrams
sodium, and 42.3 milligrams calcium per
3-ounce serving. Karen G. Edwards,
Greenville, South Carolina.

BEER-BROILED SHRIMP

2 pounds large unpeeled shrimp
¾ cup light beer
2 tablespoons vegetable oil
1 tablespoon plus 1 teaspoon
   Worcestershire sauce
2 tablespoons chopped fresh parsley
1 clove garlic, minced
⅛ teaspoon salt
¼ teaspoon pepper
⅛ teaspoon hot sauce
Vegetable cooking spray

Peel shrimp, leaving tails on; devein
and set aside.

Combine beer, oil, Worcestershire
sauce, parsley, garlic, salt, pepper, and
hot sauce in a large shallow dish. Add
shrimp; toss well to coat. Cover and
chill 2 to 3 hours, stirring occasionally.

Coat broiler rack with cooking spray;
thread shrimp on skewers, and place on
broiler rack.

Broil about 4 inches from heat 3 to 4
minutes; turn and broil 1 to 2 minutes
or until done. Yield: 6 servings.

☐ *144 calories, 24 grams protein, 3.4*
grams fat, 2.7 grams carbohydrate, 198
milligrams cholesterol, 226 milligrams
sodium, and 87 milligrams calcium per
serving. June H. Johnson,
Mocksville, North Carolina.

SCALLOP-VEGETABLE VERMICELLI

2 cloves garlic, minced
1 cup julienne-cut carrots
2 cups diagonally sliced celery
2 tablespoons olive oil
1½ cups peeled and chopped tomatoes
½ cup sliced green onions
1 cup sliced fresh mushrooms
1½ pounds scallops
2 teaspoons grated fresh gingerroot
¼ teaspoon salt
¼ teaspoon white pepper
½ cup Sauterne wine
3 cups hot cooked vermicelli (cooked without salt or fat)

Sauté garlic, carrots, and celery in olive oil in a skillet 5 minutes, stirring often. Add tomatoes, onions, mushrooms, scallops, gingerroot, salt, and pepper; cook 5 minutes, stirring often. Add wine, and cook an additional 3 minutes. Serve over vermicelli. Yield: 6 servings.

☐ *169 calories, 21 grams protein, 5.9 grams fat, 7.8 grams carbohydrate, 40 milligrams cholesterol, 370.4 milligrams sodium, and 130.9 milligrams calcium per 1 cup serving scallop mixture plus 96 calories, 3.2 grams protein, 0.3 gram fat, 19.6 grams carbohydrate, 0 milligrams cholesterol, 1 milligram sodium, and 7 milligrams calcium per ½ cup vermicelli. Sarah Barberio, Jupiter, Florida.*

SHERRIED CHICKEN WITH ARTICHOKES

6 (4-ounce) skinned and boned chicken breast halves
½ teaspoon pepper
1 teaspoon paprika
Vegetable cooking spray
1 (14-ounce) can artichoke hearts, drained
1⅓ cups sliced fresh mushrooms
3 tablespoons thinly sliced green onions
1 tablespoon cornstarch
1 teaspoon chicken-flavored bouillon granules
⅔ cup water
¼ cup dry sherry
½ teaspoon dried whole rosemary, crushed

Sprinkle chicken with pepper and paprika; set aside. Coat a large nonstick skillet with cooking spray; heat skillet. Add chicken, and cook 5 minutes or until browned, turning once.

Place chicken in a 13- x 9- x 2-inch baking dish coated with cooking spray. Arrange artichoke hearts around chicken; set aside.

Combine mushrooms and green onions in a skillet; cook 5 minutes or until vegetables are tender. Combine cornstarch and remaining ingredients; stir well. Pour into skillet, and bring to a boil; boil 1 minute, stirring constantly. Pour over chicken mixture. Cover and bake at 375° for 30 minutes. Yield: 6 servings.

☐ *132 calories, 21.1 grams protein, 1.7 grams fat, 7.6 grams carbohydrate, 50 milligrams cholesterol, 166 milligrams sodium, and 32 milligrams calcium per 3 ounces chicken with artichokes.*
Thayer Wilson, Augusta, Georgia.

Easy Ways With Dinner Breads

These breads are for times when you want to bypass mixing, rising, and kneading. They begin with convenience products—either French bread loaves or rolls, or refrigerated dough.

Cheese adds flavor to all of these breads. For Brie Bread, remove the rind from the cheese by sliding a knife under it; then peel it away. Do this when the Brie is cold, and save the rind for snacking.

BRIE BREAD

1 (14-ounce) loaf unsliced French bread
¼ cup butter or margarine, melted
1 (1-pound) round, fully ripened Brie
½ cup diced onion
Paprika

Diagonally slice French bread into ½-inch slices, not quite cutting through bottom crust. Drizzle butter over the bread; set aside.

Remove rind from cheese. Combine cheese and onion in top of a double boiler; cook until melted. Spread cheese mixture on top and between bread slices; sprinkle with paprika. Broil 6 inches from heat until thoroughly heated. Yield: 1 loaf. *Brooks Carlson, Memphis, Tennessee.*

HERB-AND-CHEESE PULL APARTS

1 (8-ounce) package cream cheese, softened
1 teaspoon dried parsley flakes
1 teaspoon dried whole basil
1 teaspoon chopped chives
½ teaspoon dillseeds
⅛ teaspoon garlic powder
1 (8-ounce) can refrigerated crescent dinner rolls
1 egg, slightly beaten
½ teaspoon poppy seeds

Combine cream cheese, parsley flakes, basil, chives, dillseeds, and garlic powder in a small mixing bowl; stir well. Set aside.

Unroll crescent rolls into two rectangles; connect ends to make one long rectangle. Press perforations to seal. Spread cream cheese mixture over crescent rolls to within ½ inch of edge. Roll, starting at long side, jellyroll fashion. Pinch edge to seal.

Place on a lightly greased baking sheet. Using kitchen shears, cut ½-inch slices alternating from right to left side of dough, being careful not to cut completely through the dough. Pull out alternating sides, exposing jellyroll pattern. Brush with egg; sprinkle with poppy seeds. Bake at 375° for 12 to 15 minutes. Yield: 6 to 8 servings.
Jayne Chesnut, Augusta, Georgia.

ROMANO SESAME ROLLS

3 tablespoons butter or margarine
1 tablespoon sesame seeds
1 tablespoon dried parsley flakes
¼ teaspoon garlic powder
2 (8-ounce) cans refrigerated crescent
   dinner rolls
½ cup grated Romano cheese

Melt butter in an 8-inch round cake-pan in a 350° oven. Sprinkle sesame seeds, parsley flakes, and garlic powder over melted butter.

Remove rolls from package; do not unroll dough. Cut dough into 6 slices; cut each slice into 4 equal pieces.

Place cheese in a plastic bag. Add 6 pieces of dough to bag, and shake gently until coated; place pieces in pre-pared pan. Repeat process with remain-ing dough. Sprinkle the remaining cheese over rolls. Bake at 350° for 35 minutes or until done. Invert the pan onto a serving plate. Yield: 8 servings.
Charlene Albrecht,
Pembroke Pines, Florida.

SPINACH BREAD

1 (10-ounce) package frozen chopped
   spinach, thawed
1 (10-ounce) package French rolls
¼ cup butter or margarine, softened
1 medium onion, chopped
¼ cup butter or margarine, melted
1 (6-ounce) roll process cheese food with
   garlic
1 teaspoon Worcestershire sauce
⅛ teaspoon pepper
2 cups (8 ounces) shredded mozzarella
   cheese

Drain spinach, and squeeze dry with paper towels; set aside.

Cut rolls in half lengthwise; spread halves with ¼ cup butter. Sauté onion in remaining ¼ cup butter; add garlic cheese, stirring until cheese melts. Re-move from heat; add spinach, Worces-tershire sauce, and pepper, stirring well. Spread spinach mixture on bread; sprin-kle with mozzarella cheese. Bake at 350° for 8 minutes or until cheese melts. Serve immediately. Yield: 12 servings.
Karen Caston,
Covington, Louisiana.

When The Entrée Is A Salad

When you're planning menus, be sure to include a main-dish salad for one or more meals. Protein-rich foods, such as chicken, tuna, salmon, and cheese, tossed with crisp greens turn salads into substantial lunch or supper entrées. You may even want to plan a salad bar, using several of these recipes.

CURRIED CHICKEN-AND-ORANGE SALAD

1¼ quarts water
½ teaspoon salt
6 chicken breast halves
1 (2.2-ounce) can sliced ripe olives,
   drained
1 (2-ounce) package slivered almonds,
   toasted
½ cup chopped purple onion
1 (11-ounce) can mandarin oranges,
   undrained
½ cup plus 2 tablespoons mayonnaise
1 tablespoon lemon juice
1 teaspoon curry powder
Lettuce leaves

Combine water and salt in a Dutch oven; bring to a boil. Add chicken. Re-turn to a boil; cover, reduce heat, and simmer 25 to 30 minutes. Remove from heat; cool chicken in broth. Drain. Skin, bone, and cut chicken in ½-inch pieces. Combine chicken, ripe olives, al-monds, and onion in a bowl; toss mix-ture gently.

Drain mandarin oranges, reserving 2 tablespoons juice. Set aside juice and 8 orange sections. Combine the reserved juice, mayonnaise, lemon juice, and curry powder in a small bowl; mix well. Pour over chicken mixture; toss gently until chicken is coated. Add orange sec-tions, and toss gently.

Cover and chill at least 1 hour. To serve, spoon into a lettuce-lined bowl, and garnish with reserved orange sec-tions. Yield: 6 to 8 servings.
Jeanne S. Hotaling,
Augusta, Georgia.

POULET RÉMOULADE

1½ quarts water
1 teaspoon salt
8 chicken breast halves (about 4½ pounds)
1 cup shredded carrots
½ cup chopped celery
1 tablespoon minced fresh parsley
1 tablespoon chopped green onions
1 cup mayonnaise
1 tablespoon dry mustard
1 tablespoon vinegar
2 tablespoons olive oil
1 teaspoon paprika
1½ teaspoons prepared horseradish
½ teaspoon Worcestershire sauce
Dash of hot sauce
Carrot strips (optional)
Carrot flower (optional)

Combine water and salt in a Dutch oven; bring to a boil. Add chicken. Re-turn to a boil; cover, reduce heat, and simmer 25 to 30 minutes. Remove from heat; cool chicken in broth. Drain. Skin, bone, and cut chicken into bite-size pieces.

Combine chicken, shredded carrots, celery, parsley, and green onions in a large bowl; set aside.

Combine mayonnaise, mustard, vine-gar, oil, paprika, horseradish, Worces-tershire sauce, and hot sauce; mix well. Add to chicken mixture; toss gently. Cover and chill at least 3 hours. To serve, garnish with carrot strips and a carrot flower, if desired. Yield: 6 to 8 servings.
Joanne C. Champagne,
Covington, Louisiana.

BLT CHICKEN SALAD

½ cup mayonnaise
¼ cup commercial barbecue sauce
1 tablespoon finely chopped onion
1 tablespoon lemon juice
½ teaspoon pepper
8 cups shredded lettuce
2 large tomatoes, chopped
2 cups chopped cooked chicken
8 slices bacon, cooked, drained, and
   crumbled
2 hard-cooked eggs, sliced

Combine mayonnaise, barbecue sauce, onion, lemon juice, and pepper in a bowl; mix well, cover, and chill.

Combine lettuce, tomatoes, and chicken; toss to mix. Just before serving, place salad on individual salad plates. Spoon dressing over salad, and sprinkle with bacon. Garnish with egg slices. Yield: 4 to 6 servings.

Mary H. Windell,
Fort Mill, South Carolina.

DELIGHTFUL CRAB SALAD

1 pound fresh crabmeat
¼ cup chopped celery
8 ripe olives, chopped
1 tablespoon chopped onion
¼ cup mayonnaise
1 to 1½ teaspoons prepared mustard
⅛ teaspoon salt
⅛ teaspoon white pepper
Toasted bread or lettuce leaves

Combine crabmeat, celery, olives, onion, mayonnaise, mustard, salt, and pepper; toss to mix. Cover and chill until serving time. Spread on toasted bread, or serve on lettuce leaves. Yield: 6 to 8 servings.

Zoe S. Miles,
Monroe, Virginia.

SALMON-SPINACH SALAD

1½ cups water
1 chicken bouillon cube
½ cup Chablis or other dry white wine
2 (1-inch-thick) salmon steaks
½ cup mayonnaise
½ cup commercial sour cream
¾ teaspoon fresh dillweed
½ pound small fresh green beans
6 to 8 cups torn spinach leaves
1 medium cucumber, scored and sliced
⅓ cup water chestnuts, drained
1 medium tomato, cut into thin wedges
Fresh dillweed (optional)

Combine water, bouillon cube, and wine in a fish poacher or skillet; bring to a boil, and add salmon. Cover, reduce heat, and simmer 8 to 10 minutes or until fish flakes easily when tested with a fork. Remove fish from liquid; cover and chill. Reserve 1 tablespoon poaching liquid. Combine liquid with mayonnaise, sour cream, and ¾ teaspoon dillweed; stir mixture well. Cover and chill 2 to 3 hours.

Wash beans; trim ends, and remove strings. Bring water to a boil; add beans, and cook, uncovered, 5 minutes or until crisp-tender. Drain beans, and plunge into cold water; drain again.

Break salmon into small chunks. Line individual salad plates with spinach leaves. Arrange salmon, beans, cucumber, water chestnuts, and tomato on spinach. Serve with dill dressing. Garnish salad with fresh dillweed, if desired. Yield: 4 servings.

TUNA-TACO SALAD

2 (6½-ounce) cans solid white tuna, drained and flaked
½ cup (2 ounces) shredded Cheddar cheese
½ cup sliced pimiento-stuffed olives
3 tablespoons finely chopped onion
½ cup commercial sour cream
¼ teaspoon garlic powder
¾ teaspoon chili powder
Lettuce leaves
1 large avocado, peeled and sliced
2 medium tomatoes, cut into wedges
Paprika
Tortilla chips

Combine tuna, cheese, olives, and onion in a medium bowl. Combine sour cream, garlic powder, and chili powder in a small bowl. Add sour cream mixture to tuna mixture, and toss. Place lettuce leaves on individual salad plates.

Spoon tuna mixture on lettuce; arrange avocado and tomato wedges around tuna. Sprinkle with paprika. Serve salad with tortilla chips. Yield: 4 servings.

Sara A. McCullough,
Broaddus, Texas.

MANDARIN HAM-AND-RICE SALAD

1 cup uncooked regular rice
2½ cups chicken broth
3 cups (¼-inch strips) cooked ham
½ cup diced green pepper
2 tablespoons diced onion
½ to ¾ cup commercial French salad dressing
1 tablespoon soy sauce
1 teaspoon sugar
1 (11-ounce) can mandarin oranges, drained

Combine rice and chicken broth in a saucepan over medium-high heat; bring to a boil. Cover, reduce heat, and simmer 20 minutes or until rice is done. Let cool.

Combine rice, ham strips, diced green pepper, and diced onion. Add French salad dressing, soy sauce, and sugar; toss gently to mix. Add mandarin oranges to salad mixture, and toss gently. Cover and chill. Yield: 6 servings.

Dr. W. H. Pinkston,
Knoxville, Tennessee.

ITALIAN SALAD

1 (12-ounce) package spiral pasta
2 (6-ounce) jars marinated artichokes, undrained
1¼ cups pitted ripe olives, sliced
1 cup chopped green pepper
¼ pound hard salami, cut into ¼-inch strips
½ cup grated Parmesan cheese
¼ cup chopped onion
¼ cup chopped fresh parsley
1 (0.7-ounce) package Italian salad dressing mix

Cook pasta according to package directions. Drain and cool. Drain artichokes, reserving ¼ cup liquid; set aside. Cut artichokes into fourths. Set artichokes aside.

Combine pasta, artichokes, reserved artichoke liquid, and remaining ingredients in a large bowl; toss gently. Cover and chill. Yield: 6 servings.

Judy Mogridge,
Tacoma, Washington.

Appetizers For Summer

Around the pool or on the patio, these appetizers are sure to win compliments. Whipping cream, powdered sugar, and crème de menthe are the basic ingredients in Mint Dip With Fresh Fruit. Serve the dip from cantaloupe shells. Connect the shells with a wooden skewer, using one as the base and the other for the dip. Line the shell for dip in plastic wrap.

SEAFOOD SPREAD

1 (4¼-ounce) can tiny shrimp
1 envelope unflavored gelatin
2 tablespoons water
1 (10¾-ounce) can cream of tomato soup, undiluted
1 (3-ounce) package cream cheese, softened
½ cup mayonnaise
⅓ cup diced onion
¾ cup diced celery
¾ cup diced green pepper
¼ cup chopped olives
¼ cup chopped pecans
1 (6-ounce) can white crabmeat, drained
1 (6½-ounce) can clams, drained
⅛ teaspoon garlic powder
⅛ teaspoon pepper
½ teaspoon lemon juice
3 to 5 drops hot sauce
Vegetable cooking spray

Drain shrimp; rinse and let stand in ice water 20 minutes. Drain and set shrimp aside.
Sprinkle gelatin over water; set aside. Combine soup and cream cheese in a medium saucepan, and stir over low heat until well blended. Add mayonnaise, and stir until blended. Remove from heat. Add dissolved gelatin, shrimp, and remaining ingredients, stirring well.
Pour into a 5-cup mold, coated with cooking spray. Cover and chill 8 hours. Yield: 4½ cups.   *Janice Romero,*
Kaplan, Louisiana.

SHRIMP MINIQUICHES

1 (4¼-ounce) can medium shrimp
1 (8-ounce) can crescent dinner rolls
1 (4-ounce) can crescent dinner rolls
1 egg, beaten
½ cup half-and-half
1 tablespoon brandy
½ teaspoon salt
Dash of pepper
½ cup (2 ounces) shredded Gruyère cheese

Drain shrimp. Rinse and let stand in ice water 20 minutes. Drain and set shrimp aside.
Separate rolls into triangles. Cut each triangle in half; roll out each portion on a lightly floured surface until large enough to cut a circle with a 2-inch biscuit cutter. Press the 24 dough circles into lightly greased 1¾-inch muffin pans. Divide shrimp equally into each pastry shell; set aside.
Combine egg, half-and-half, brandy, salt, and pepper; mix well. Fill pastry shells equally with mixture; bake at 375° for 15 minutes. Sprinkle quiche with cheese; bake an additional 5 minutes. Yield: 2 dozen appetizer servings.
Betty Rabe,
Plano, Texas.

SALMON-AND-HORSERADISH SPREAD

1 (15½-ounce) can pink salmon
1 (8-ounce) package cream cheese, softened
¼ cup commercial sour cream
¼ cup prepared horseradish
1 tablespoon pickle relish
¼ teaspoon salt
⅛ teaspoon garlic powder
Lettuce leaves
Paprika

Drain and flake salmon; remove and discard bones and skin, if desired. Add cream cheese, sour cream, horseradish, pickle relish, salt, and garlic powder; stir well. Chill several hours.
Spoon mixture on lettuce leaves, and sprinkle with paprika. Serve with assorted crackers. Yield: about 3 cups.
Nancy J. Holmberg,
Pinehurst, North Carolina.

MINT DIP WITH FRESH FRUIT

1 cup whipping cream
¼ cup sifted powdered sugar
1 tablespoon plus 1 teaspoon green crème de menthe
1 large cantaloupe
30 strawberries (1 to 2 pints)
1 fresh pineapple, cut into 30 bite-size pieces
1 fresh pineapple (optional)
1 strawberry fan (optional)

Beat whipping cream at medium speed of an electric mixer until soft peaks form. Add powdered sugar and green crème de menthe; continue beating until stiff peaks form. Chill.
Cut cantaloupe in half, and remove seeds; scoop out 30 melon balls. Scallop edges of the cantaloupe shells, if desired; set aside.
Arrange cantaloupe balls, strawberries, and pineapple pieces on 6-inch wooden skewers; insert skewers into whole pineapple, if desired.
Spoon dip into one cantaloupe shell, and garnish with strawberry fan, if desired. (To make a strawberry fan, slice a strawberry, and arrange slices in the shape of a fan.) Use other cantaloupe shell as base. Yield: about 30 appetizer servings.   *Laura Inge,*
New Orleans, Louisiana.

Beverages On Ice

Ease the summer heat with cold beverages that are brimming with fruit juices. Tea Party Punch, a lemonade drink with a hint of orange and loaded with fresh mint, captures the essence of refreshing summer flavors.
Steeped tea is another refreshing beverage often used as a base for party punches. Teaberry Sangria is tea spiked with red wine. Pureed strawberries are added for fruity flavor and sweetness. For zest and fizz, the carbonated beverage should be added just before serving.
Red Roosters, a slushy frozen delight, boasts the tangy tartness of cranberry and orange juices.

TEABERRY SANGRIA

2 cups water
¾ cup sugar
1 orange, sliced
1 lemon, sliced
1 lime, sliced
4 regular tea bags
2 cups red wine
1 (10-ounce) package frozen sliced
   strawberries, thawed and pureed
2 cups lemon-lime carbonated beverage

Combine water and sugar in a saucepan; bring to a boil, stirring to dissolve sugar. Add fruit slices; boil 1 minute. Remove from heat; add tea bags. Cover and let stand 5 minutes. Remove tea bags; cool. Combine tea mixture, wine, and strawberries in a pitcher; chill.

Add lemon-lime beverage, and gently stir. Serve immediately. Yield: 2 quarts.
Beth McClain,
Grand Prairie, Texas.

TEA PARTY PUNCH

Juice of 6 lemons, reserving rinds
Juice of 3 oranges, reserving rinds
1 cup sugar
1 cup loosely packed mint leaves
2 cups water
Fresh mint sprigs

Combine lemon and orange juices; set aside.

Combine sugar, mint leaves, and water in a Dutch oven. Bring to a boil, stirring to dissolve sugar. Add reserved rinds, and boil 15 minutes. Discard rinds and mint, reserving liquid; add water to make 2 quarts.

Add juices, stir well. Pour into a 13- x 9- x 2-inch pan; cover and freeze about 3 hours, stirring occasionally, to make a slushy mixture. Serve in punch cups or tall glasses. Garnish with fresh mint sprigs. Yield: about 3 quarts.
Anne Butler Hamilton,
St. Francisville, Louisiana.

Tip: Use muffin pans to make extra large ice cubes for punch.

RED ROOSTERS

1 (32-ounce) jar cranberry juice cocktail
1 (12-ounce) can frozen orange juice
   concentrate, thawed
4½ cups water
2 cups vodka

Combine all ingredients; mix well. Freeze.

To serve, remove from freezer; let stand 15 minutes. Spoon about 4 cups mixture into container of electric blender; process until mixture reaches desired consistency. Repeat with the remaining mixture. Yield: 3 quarts.
Judi Burns,
Monroeville, Alabama.

Yummy Ice Cream Sandwiches

When the temperature rises and you want to cool down, reach for an ice cream treat. Our recipe features a creamy filling, sandwiched between rich chocolate cookies. The sandwiches will delight everyone, because they can be made in advance and stored in the freezer.

CHOCOLATE COOKIE ICE CREAM SANDWICHES

1 cup shortening
1 cup sugar
½ cup firmly packed brown sugar
2 eggs
1¾ cups all-purpose flour
½ cup cocoa
1 teaspoon baking soda
½ teaspoon salt
1 cup semisweet chocolate mini-morsels
1 teaspoon vanilla extract
½ gallon vanilla or chocolate-mint ice
   cream

Cream shortening; gradually add sugars, beating well. Add eggs, one at a time, beating well after each addition.

Combine flour, cocoa, soda, and salt; add to creamed mixture. Stir in mini-morsels and vanilla.

Shape dough into 1½-inch balls, and place on ungreased cookie sheets. Flatten each with palm of hand to a 2½-inch circle, about ¼ inch thick.

Bake at 375° for 8 minutes or until done. Cool 1 minute on cookie sheets; then place on wire racks to cool completely. Remove ice cream from freezer 5 minutes before assembling the sandwiches. Place one large scoop (about ½ cup) on bottom side of one cookie. Spread ice cream with spatula. Cover with another cookie; press sandwich together gently.

Serve immediately or store tightly covered in freezer until ready to serve. Yield: about 20 sandwiches.
Erma Jackson,
Huntsville, Alabama.

Put Together A Summer Bouquet

Making a flower arrangement is somewhat like assembling a puzzle. When all the pieces are in place, the picture is complete. We asked Arline Walter, a Birmingham, Alabama, floral designer, to use summer flowers to make a simple arrangement—one that we could photograph in progress. Our idea was to uncover some of the principles and thought processes that might be second nature to an experienced flower arranger but a mystery to those who haven't had much practice or formal training.

"First you should decide where the arrangement is going to be placed," says Arline, "and then choose your container. Since this bouquet was for a garden table, I thought a basket would be appropriate."

The second step is to choose the flowers and their colors. Arline recommends using a mixture of round flowers and buds, graceful blossoms, large blooms for a focal point, and spiked blossoms and branches of foliage to give the arrangement lines.

Our summer bouquet includes Transvaal daisies (gerberas), wild liatris, zinnias, cosmos, and bachelor's-buttons. A base of florist foam supports the colorful flowers. The foam is first soaked in water; then it is covered with chicken wire and firmly taped into a shallow bowl that fits inside the basket.

In assembling the bouquet, Arline put the long spikes of wild liatris in first— they formed the outline. "This controls the height and width of the arrangement," she says, "and no stems should be the same height. Then fill in the outline with flowers, letting some spill over the rim of the basket."

Arline saved the largest, best, and brightest colored flowers for the center, recessing them to give depth to the arrangement. She turned a few flowers to the side and set a few facing each other. Finally, she hid any exposed foam with flowers or greenery.

Set The Mood With Candles

Outdoor entertaining calls for soft lights, so why not light up the night with candles? You can have as many as you want with minimal expense. There is wide variety in the materials the candles are made of, and they do not have to be made totally weatherproof like permanent electric fixtures.

Shown here is a sampling of some of the varieties that are available. Some of these examples, such as the citronella pots, are common enough to be found in your local grocery store. The floating candles can be purchased at a party goods store, and the lanterns can be found in hardware stores as well as in casual-furniture stores. Mail-order catalogs that carry products for outdoor entertaining also carry an interesting array of hurricane lamps.

Most of these products can occasionally get wet with no adverse effects; however, citronella candles lose their effectiveness if left out in the rain. Many materials may hold water and crack if you leave them out in freezing temperatures, so bring them in after the outdoor entertaining season. Select items that are easy to store until next year.

Safety should be a consideration when you plan your lighting. Make sure the candles are placed so that they cannot be easily knocked over or will not be dangerously close to clothing or foliage. You may also want to look for containers that will protect the flame from blowing out if there's a breeze.

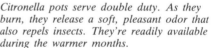

Citronella pots serve double duty. As they burn, they release a soft, pleasant odor that also repels insects. They're readily available during the warmer months.

Arranging a bouquet like this requires just a few simple steps. First prepare a base of water-soaked florist foam to hold spikes of wild liatris, which will form the outline. Once the outline is formed, fill in with flowers, adding the larger ones as focal points. The finished bouquet, combining florist and garden flowers, makes a colorful centerpiece.

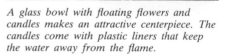

A glass bowl with floating flowers and candles makes an attractive centerpiece. The candles come with plastic liners that keep the water away from the flame.

Pickles: The Quick Way

If your schedule doesn't permit the weeks of tender, loving attention folks once spent making homemade pickles, then you'll like these recipes for pickles and relishes you can make in a day. Just follow the information below.

All of the following recipes use the **fresh-pack** or **quick-process** method, which means that vegetables are covered with a boiling vinegar-and-spice mixture, processed, and allowed to stand. Although you can eat these pickles and relishes right away, the flavor is best if they sit in the jars for three to four weeks after processing.

If this article inspires you to pull out your own treasured recipes, read on to see if you need to update them to the latest preservation safety standards. You may notice **lime** or **alum** listed as an ingredient in some older recipes. These additives were once used to ensure crisp pickles but are no longer recommended by the U.S. Department of Agriculture because they tend to cause digestive problems in some people. If you follow up-to-date methods for pickling and start with good quality ingredients, pickles will be crisp.

Processing pickles and relishes in a water bath is an important safety precaution, which may not be part of handed-down recipes. This step is necessary to destroy yeasts, molds, and bacteria that cause spoilage. It also inactivates enzymes that can change color, flavor, and texture.

Most **fresh-pack pickles** and **relishes** use this standard water-bath method: Place jars into the canner filled with simmering water. The water should cover the jar tops by 1 to 2 inches. Start to count processing time when the water returns to a boil. If no processing time is given in a recipe, process 10 minutes for both pints and quarts. Relishes and pickles made from vegetables other than cucumbers may require longer processing times.

For **fresh-pack dill pickles**, use a slightly different water-bath processing procedure: Fill the canner with boiling water. Begin to count processing time as soon as the pickles are placed in the water. Process pints and quarts 10 minutes if no time is given.

For pickles and relishes processed less than 15 minutes, the canning jars must be sterilized before adding the vegetables. Simply place the empty jars in boiling water, and boil 15 minutes.

Here are some additional points to keep in mind for the best fresh-packed pickles and relishes.

—For cucumber pickles, select a pickling variety. Your local Extension office can help you determine the one most available in your area.

—Always use just-ripe produce that has no blemishes or deformities. It's best to pickle produce within 24 hours after harvest. If you can't start pickling right away, store unwashed vegetables in the refrigerator, or spread them in a cool, ventilated area.

—Always use vinegar between 4% and 6% acidity (it's listed on the label) for preservation safety.

—Never reduce the amount of sugar in a pickle recipe. Sugar helps plump pickles and keeps them crisp.

—Use fresh, whole spices because the ground versions may darken the pickles and make the liquid cloudy.

—To ensure a proper seal, it's important to wipe jar rims after filling jars with pickles or relishes.

—To screw the bands onto jars, twist on with your fingertips until tight; then give another turn, just until snug. If the band is too tight, the lid may collapse and leave a weak seal. If it's too loose, large amounts of liquid will be lost in processing, leaving a weak seal.

For solutions to pickling problems, see "From Our Kitchen to Yours," page 150. More pickling information can be found in "Putting Up Pickles," *Southern Living 1985 Annual Recipes,* page 174.

LAZY WIFE DILLS

21 (5- to 6-inch-long) cucumbers (about 4 pounds)
4 slices onion, divided
1 tablespoon plus 1 teaspoon pickling spices, divided
1 teaspoon celery seeds, divided
4 large sprigs fresh dillweed or ¼ cup dillseeds, divided
1 quart water
4 cups sugar
4 cups white vinegar (5% acidity)
½ cup pickling salt

Wash cucumbers; remove ¼ inch from ends. Cut each cucumber lengthwise into 8 strips. Pack cucumber strips into hot, sterilized quart jars, leaving ½ inch headspace. Add 1 onion slice, 1 teaspoon pickling spices, ¼ teaspoon celery seeds, and 1 sprig of dillweed or 1 tablespoon dillseeds to each quart jar.

Combine water, sugar, vinegar, and pickling salt in a saucepan; bring to a boil. Remove from heat; pour hot vinegar mixture over cucumbers, leaving ½ inch headspace. Wipe jar rims.

Cover at once with metal lids, and screw on bands. Place jars on a rack in a canner of boiling water. Water should cover jars by 1 to 2 inches. Begin counting processing time as soon as jars are placed in water. Process quart jars in water bath 10 minutes. For best flavor, do not use for at least one month. Yield: 4 quarts.

Note: Water-bath procedure in this recipe is specifically for dill pickles.

Cathy Williams,
Vale, North Carolina.

QUICK SWEET PICKLES

6 pounds medium-size cucumbers, unpeeled
1 large sweet red pepper, cut in strips
1 small onion, sliced
2 cloves garlic
1½ cups pickling salt
2 quarts crushed ice
3 cups sugar
1 quart white vinegar (5% acidity)
2 tablespoons mustard seeds

Wash cucumbers; remove ¼ inch from ends. Cut into ¼-inch slices. Combine cucumbers, red pepper, onion, and garlic in a large bowl; add salt, and stir well. Pack ice over cucumbers; cover and let stand 3 hours. Remove garlic; rinse and drain.

Combine remaining ingredients in a large Dutch oven; bring to a boil. Add vegetables, and reduce heat; simmer, uncovered, 5 minutes. Pack cucumber mixture into hot, sterilized pint jars, leaving ½ inch headspace. Wipe jar rims. Cover at once with metal lids, and screw on bands. Process in boiling water bath 10 minutes. Yield: 7 pints.

H. F. Bowman,
Lake Worth, Florida.

CHOWCHOW

2 cups thinly sliced cucumbers
2 cups chopped green pepper
2 cups chopped cabbage
2 cups sliced onion
2 cups chopped green tomatoes
1½ cups salt
2 quarts water
2 cups fresh baby lima beans
2 cups cut fresh green beans
2 cups sliced carrots
2 cups water
1 quart white vinegar (5% acidity)
4 cups sugar
2 cups water
¼ cup mustard seeds
2 tablespoons celery seeds
1 tablespoon plus 1 teaspoon ground
   turmeric

Combine cucumbers, green pepper, cabbage, onion, and tomatoes in a large nonmetal container. Dissolve salt in 2 quarts water; pour over vegetables. Cover and let stand 8 to 10 hours. Drain well.

Cook lima beans, green beans, and carrots in 2 cups water 20 minutes or until crisp-tender; drain. Combine all vegetables and remaining ingredients in a Dutch oven; boil 10 minutes.

Pack vegetables into hot pint jars, leaving ½ inch headspace. Pour hot vinegar mixture over vegetables, leaving ¼ inch headspace. Wipe jar rims. Cover at once with metal lids, and screw on bands. Process in boiling water bath 15 minutes. Yield: 4 pints.

SQUASH PICKLES

8 cups sliced squash (about 2¼ pounds)
2 large onions, sliced (about 1¼ pounds)
4 cups chopped green pepper
2 cups sliced cauliflower
1¼ cups sliced carrots
1½ cups sliced celery
1 (2-ounce) jar sliced pimiento, drained
½ cup salt
4½ cups sugar
3 cups white vinegar (5% acidity)
3 tablespoons pickling salt
1 tablespoon celery seeds
1 tablespoon mustard seeds
1½ teaspoons ground turmeric

Combine squash, onions, green pepper, cauliflower, carrots, celery, and pimiento in a large glass bowl; sprinkle with ½ cup salt. Cover and let stand about 2 hours. Drain and rinse in cold water. Drain well. Pack vegetables in hot pint jars, leaving ½ inch headspace.

Combine sugar, vinegar, pickling salt, celery seeds, mustard seeds, and turmeric in a saucepan, stirring well. Bring mixture to a boil, and cook 1 minute. Pour hot vinegar mixture over vegetables, leaving ½ inch headspace. Wipe jar rims.

Cover at once with metal lids, and screw on bands. Process in boiling water bath 15 minutes. Yield: 5 pints.

Carolyn Webb,
Jackson, Mississippi.

From Our Kitchen To Yours

Pickling transforms summer's bounty into conveniently stored, inexpensive, and flavorful condiments. The crispy, crunchy bites add zest to meals and make welcome gifts. "Pickles—The Quick Way" on page 149 offers recipes that skillfully blend spices, sugar, and vinegar with fresh vegetables.

When serving your homemade pickles, always be on the alert for signs of spoilage. Before opening the pickles, closely examine the jar. Leakage or a bulging lid means contaminated contents. After opening the jar, check for mold, disagreeable odor, change in color, spurting liquid, or an unusual softness. If there is the slightest indication of spoilage, do not taste the contents; dispose of the food.

Spoilage is the most serious problem. Unsterilized or unsealed jars, old lids, incorrect processing time, weak vinegar, and inaccurate measuring create danger. Water in the water-bath canner must be kept at a full boil through processing time and must be 1 to 2 inches above the jar tops.

Soft or **slippery** pickles result from improper processing, using hard water, not removing the blossom ends, or using vinegar of too-low acidity.

Hollowness in pickles is caused by using cucumbers that are too large. During washing, these cucumbers float to the top and should be reserved for other uses.

Shriveling may result from using a heavy syrup or too strong a vinegar. Dry weather during cucumber growth produces shriveled pickles, as does overprocessing.

Hard water, iodized salt, and ground spices **discolor** vegetables. Leaving spices in pickles and using brass, iron, copper, or zinc utensils will also cause discoloration.

Excessive exposure to light and poor vegetable quality promote **spotted, dull, or faded color.** The vegetables change colors if they are not processed long enough to destroy the enzymes that affect color or if the liquid in the jars does not cover contents.

Salt substitutes and too strong a vinegar create a **strong, bitter taste.** Using too many spices or cooking the spices too long in the vinegar can also cause bitterness.

White sediment in the bottom of jars is a telltale sign that table salt has been substituted for pickling salt.

MICROWAVE COOKERY

Quick-Cooking Garden Fare

Garden-fresh vegetables are one of the most welcome signs of summer. Microwaving makes them a flavorful, nutritious, and easy part of a meal. Because many vegetables have a naturally high moisture content, only a small amount of water is needed; microwave energy converts the moisture to steam that cooks the vegetables. Minimal use of water and short cooking time allow vegetables to retain nutrients as well as their fresh-picked color and flavor.

Microwaved vegetables are especially tasty because none of the flavor is lost in cooking water. Spicy Corn on the Cob is one of the best examples. Seasoned butter is spread on the corn to smother each kernel as it cooks. Then each ear is individually wrapped in heavy-duty plastic wrap, and natural moisture steams the corn.

Fresh corn cut from the cob cooks evenly because of the uniform kernels. Our recipe for Okra, Corn, and Peppers is a flavorful and colorful vegetable trio.

Grains of salt sprinkled on uncooked vegetables cause dark, dried-out spots to develop as they are microwaved. You can salt vegetables after they are done, or dissolve salt in cooking liquid before adding the vegetables. This technique is used in Crisp Squash-and-Pepper Toss. And for Seasoned New Potatoes, salt, lemon juice, and chicken bouillon granules are added to the cooking liquid before microwaving the potatoes; the seasonings penetrate the potatoes rather than just coat them.

In Asparagus With Lemon Butter, lemon accents the flavor of fresh asparagus. When you microwave asparagus or any other vegetable with stalks, proper placement in the cooking dish is important. The thick stalks require longer cooking time and should be placed toward the outside of the dish where they will receive more microwave energy.

ASPARAGUS WITH LEMON BUTTER

¼ cup sliced almonds
2 tablespoons butter or margarine
¼ cup water
¼ teaspoon salt
1½ pounds fresh asparagus spears
¼ cup butter
½ teaspoon grated lemon rind
2 tablespoons lemon juice

Combine sliced almonds and 2 tablespoons butter in a pieplate. Microwave at HIGH for 3 to 3½ minutes or until almonds are lightly toasted, stirring once. Drain and set aside.

Combine water and salt in a 12- x 8- x 2-inch casserole. Snap off tough ends of asparagus. Remove scales from stalks with a knife or vegetable peeler, if desired. Arrange asparagus in casserole with thick stem ends toward the outside. Cover with heavy-duty plastic wrap; microwave at HIGH for 6 to 7 minutes or until crisp-tender, giving dish a half-turn after 3 minutes. Let asparagus stand 3 minutes.

Place ¼ cup butter in a 1-cup glass measure. Microwave at HIGH for 1 minute or until melted. Add lemon rind and juice. Microwave at HIGH for 50 seconds or until hot.

Drain asparagus. Arrange in serving dish. Pour butter mixture over asparagus; sprinkle with toasted almonds. Yield: 6 servings.

SPICY CORN ON THE COB

4 ears fresh corn
¼ cup butter or margarine
1 teaspoon seasoned salt
⅛ teaspoon pepper
¼ teaspoon hot sauce

Remove the husks and silks from corn; set aside.

Place butter in a 1-cup glass measure. Microwave at HIGH for 55 seconds or until melted. Stir in seasoned salt, pepper, and hot sauce.

Brush corn generously with butter mixture, and wrap each ear in heavy-duty plastic wrap. Place corn in an 8-inch square baking dish; microwave at HIGH for 8 to 9 minutes, giving dish a quarter-turn after 4 minutes. Yield: 4 servings.

OKRA, CORN, AND PEPPERS

¼ cup butter or margarine
2 sweet red peppers, coarsely chopped
½ cup sliced green onions
1½ cups sliced okra
1½ cups fresh corn (about 4 ears)
¼ cup hot water
½ teaspoon salt
⅛ teaspoon pepper

Place butter in a 2-quart casserole. Microwave at HIGH for 55 seconds or until melted. Add sweet red peppers and green onions; cover tightly with heavy-duty plastic wrap. Microwave at HIGH for 1½ to 2 minutes or until vegetables are crisp tender. Add okra, corn, water, salt, and pepper; cover tightly with heavy-duty plastic wrap. Microwave at HIGH for 3 minutes; stir well. Cover and microwave at HIGH for 7 to 9 minutes or until corn is tender. Yield: 6 servings.

SEASONED NEW POTATOES

2 tablespoons water
¼ teaspoon chicken-flavored bouillon granules
½ teaspoon seasoned salt
2 tablespoons lemon juice
12 medium-size new potatoes (about 2½ pounds)
3 tablespoons butter or margarine
¼ cup chopped fresh parsley

Place water in a 2-quart shallow casserole; microwave at HIGH for 12 to 15 seconds. Add bouillon granules; stir until the granules are dissolved. Stir in seasoned salt and lemon juice.

Scrub potatoes, and cut into ½-inch slices; place in seasoned liquid in casserole. Cover with heavy-duty plastic wrap; microwave at HIGH for 14 to 16 minutes or until potatoes are tender, stirring after every 4 minutes. Add butter; cover and microwave at HIGH for 1 minute. Gently stir in parsley. Yield: 4 to 6 servings.

GREEN BEANS

1 pound fresh green beans
1 tablespoon sliced red chile pepper
½ cup water
1 cup chicken broth
1 tablespoon cornstarch
1 teaspoon Dijon mustard
Grated Parmesan cheese
2 tablespoons sesame seeds, toasted

Wash green beans; trim ends, and remove strings. Cut into 1½-inch pieces. Place beans and sliced red chile pepper in a 2-quart baking dish; add water. Cover with heavy-duty plastic wrap; microwave at HIGH for 12 to 14 minutes or until beans are tender, stirring twice. Let stand, covered, 3 to 4 minutes.

Combine broth and cornstarch in a 2-cup glass measure, stirring until smooth. Microwave at HIGH for 3 to 4 minutes or until mixture is thickened and bubbly, stirring at 1-minute intervals. Stir in mustard.

Drain beans; pour sauce over beans. Sprinkle with cheese and sesame seeds. Yield: 4 servings.

EASY EGGPLANT

6 slices bacon
1 medium eggplant, peeled and diced (about 1¼ pounds)
1 small green pepper, chopped
1 cup thinly sliced celery
1 small onion, chopped
2 tablespoons water
2 medium tomatoes, chopped
1 tablespoon brown sugar
½ teaspoon salt
⅛ teaspoon pepper
¼ cup grated Parmesan cheese

Place bacon in a 2½-quart shallow baking dish. Cover with wax paper; microwave at HIGH for 5 to 7 minutes or until crisp. Remove bacon, reserving drippings. Crumble bacon; set aside.

Add eggplant, green pepper, celery, onion, and water; stir well. Cover with heavy-duty plastic wrap (do not vent). Microwave vegetables at HIGH for 6 minutes, giving dish a quarter-turn at 2-minute intervals.

Let stand 5 minutes; drain. Add tomatoes, brown sugar, salt, and pepper to eggplant mixture. Stir well. Cover with heavy-duty plastic wrap; microwave at HIGH for 4 minutes, stirring after 2 minutes. Let stand 5 minutes. Sprinkle with Parmesan cheese and bacon. Yield: 6 to 8 servings.

Evelyn Letson,
Anniston, Alabama.

CRISP SQUASH-AND-PEPPER TOSS

¼ teaspoon dried whole basil
¼ teaspoon dried whole oregano
¼ teaspoon dried whole thyme
½ teaspoon salt
¼ teaspoon pepper
1 tablespoon red wine vinegar
2 tablespoons water
2 pounds yellow squash, cut into ½-inch slices
1 large onion, chopped
1 clove garlic, minced
1 sweet red pepper, cut into ½-inch strips
2 tablespoons olive oil
¼ pound kielbasa (Polish sausage), cut into ¼-inch slices

Combine basil, oregano, thyme, salt, pepper, vinegar, and water in a shallow 2½-quart casserole; add squash. Cover with heavy-duty plastic wrap; microwave at HIGH for 3 to 4 minutes. Let stand, covered, 3 to 4 minutes. Add onion, garlic, sweet red pepper, and olive oil; toss gently. Cover and microwave at HIGH for 2 to 4 minutes. Add sausage, and toss gently; cover and microwave at HIGH for 1 to 2 minutes. Yield: 6 to 8 servings.

COOKING LIGHT®

Cool, Crisp Salads To Beat The Heat

Most people plan menus starting with the main dish. And it's not uncommon that by the time a salad is chosen, creativity dwindles to plain green salad with an ordinary dressing. But we've got some ideas to help change all that. Each of our salads and dressings gives you the most flavor, variety, and nutrition at little caloric cost.

You'll notice that several of our dressing recipes call for rice vinegar, and there's a definite reason for this. Most oil-and-vinegar-based salad dressings use a 2 to 1 or greater ratio of oil to vinegar, making the dressing very high in calories. But our recipes using rice vinegar allow a 2 to 1 or greater ratio of vinegar to oil because of the mild and slightly sweeter taste it has compared to other salad vinegars. Rice vinegar can be purchased in most large grocery stores, gourmet food or kitchen shops, and Oriental food markets.

Oriental Salad Bowl goes well with grilled chicken or broiled flank steak. The recipe calls for a number of ingredients; make sure you include each one. Water chestnuts, snow peas, celery, bean sprouts, miniature whole corn, and chow mein noodles provide plenty of crunch. The base consists of fresh spinach leaves and Chinese cabbage, which has a taste similar to a cross between iceberg lettuce and cabbage. Top it with Soy-Sesame Dressing with only 15 calories per tablespoon.

MARINATED BEAN-AND-RICE SALAD

½ pound fresh green beans
2 cups hot cooked brown rice (cooked without salt or fat)
½ cup diagonally sliced celery
½ cup sliced green onions
1 (15-ounce) can garbanzo beans, drained
1 clove garlic, minced
1 teaspoon dried whole oregano or 1 tablespoon fresh oregano leaves, minced
⅛ teaspoon white pepper
½ teaspoon dry mustard
½ teaspoon grated lemon rind
2 tablespoons lemon juice
⅓ cup cider vinegar
⅓ cup olive oil
12 radicchio leaves
1 tablespoon chopped ripe olives
¼ cup minced fresh parsley

Wash green beans; trim ends, and remove strings. Cut beans into 1-inch pieces. Place beans in a vegetable steamer. Place steamer over boiling water; cover and steam 8 minutes or until beans are crisp-tender. Combine green beans, rice, celery, green onions, garbanzo beans, and garlic in a large bowl; set aside.

Combine oregano, white pepper, mustard, lemon rind, lemon juice, vinegar, and olive oil; stir well. Pour over vegetable mixture; stir well. Cover and chill 8 hours, stirring occasionally.

To serve, line a serving platter with radicchio leaves. Spoon vegetable mixture onto platter. Combine olives and parsley; sprinkle over salad. Yield: 12 servings.

☐ *125 calories, 2.6 grams protein, 6.9 grams fat, 14.3 grams carbohydrate, 0 milligrams cholesterol, 102 milligrams sodium, and 29.2 milligrams calcium per ½ cup serving.* Mrs. L. R. Givens, Lubbock, Texas.

CRISP VEGETABLE ASPIC WITH HORSERADISH DRESSING

2 envelopes unflavored gelatin
4 cups tomato juice, divided
⅓ cup sliced green onions
¼ cup chopped green pepper
1 tablespoon brown sugar
2 bay leaves
4 whole cloves
1 (2-inch) stick cinnamon
3 tablespoons lemon juice
⅛ teaspoon hot sauce
1 cup shredded cabbage
½ cup diced green pepper
Vegetable cooking spray
3 cups shredded cabbage
Horseradish Dressing

Sprinkle gelatin over 1 cup tomato juice; set aside. Combine 2 cups tomato juice, green onions, ¼ cup green pepper, brown sugar, bay leaves, cloves, and cinnamon in a heavy saucepan. Bring to a boil; reduce heat, and simmer, uncovered, 5 minutes. Strain mixture, reserving juice.

Add gelatin mixture to hot tomato juice, stirring until gelatin dissolves. Add remaining 1 cup tomato juice, lemon juice, and hot sauce; stir well. Chill until mixture is consistency of unbeaten egg white.

Stir in 1 cup cabbage and ½ cup green pepper. Pour into a 5-cup mold coated with cooking spray. Cover; chill until firm. Unmold on 3 cups cabbage; serve with Horseradish Dressing. Yield: 10 servings.

☐ *33 calories, 2.5 grams protein, 0.2 gram fat, 6.5 grams carbohydrate, 0 milligrams cholesterol, 358 milligrams sodium, and 17 milligrams calcium per ½ cup serving plus 9 calories, 0.8 gram protein, 0.2 gram fat, 1.1 grams carbohydrate, 1 milligram cholesterol, 11 milligrams sodium, and 26 milligrams calcium per tablespoon dressing.*

Horseradish Dressing:

1 cup plain low-fat yogurt
2 teaspoons prepared horseradish
⅛ teaspoon white pepper

Combine all ingredients; stir well. Cover and chill. Yield: 1 cup.

Tip: Add marinated vegetable salads to your next dinner party. They can be prepared in advance and chilled until serving time—an important bonus for the busy cook.

SUMMER GARDEN SALAD

1 cup peeled julienne-cut cucumber
1 cup sliced yellow banana peppers
¼ cup vegetable oil
½ cup rice vinegar
1 teaspoon sugar
¼ teaspoon dried whole Italian
  seasoning
⅛ teaspoon garlic powder
⅛ teaspoon salt
⅛ teaspoon white pepper
4 cups shredded lettuce

Combine cucumber and banana peppers in a medium bowl; set aside. Combine oil, vinegar, sugar, Italian seasoning, garlic powder, salt, and white pepper in a jar. Cover tightly, and shake. Pour marinade mixture over cucumber mixture; chill 3 hours. Drain mixture; reserve marinade.

Combine cucumber mixture, lettuce, and 1 tablespoon reserved marinade; toss gently. Yield: 5 servings.

☐ 65 calories, 0.8 gram protein, 5.6 grams fat, 3.8 grams carbohydrate, 0 milligrams cholesterol, 34 milligrams sodium, and 15 milligrams calcium per 1 cup serving.

ORIENTAL SALAD BOWL

3 cups torn fresh spinach leaves
3 cups coarsely chopped Chinese cabbage
½ cup diagonally sliced celery
½ cup coarsely shredded carrots
1 cup fresh bean sprouts
⅓ cup thinly sliced green onions
35 snow peas, trimmed (about 3 ounces)
1 (8-ounce) can sliced water chestnuts, drained
1 (15-ounce) can miniature corn, drained
¾ cup chow mein noodles
Soy-Sesame Dressing

Combine spinach, cabbage, celery, carrots, bean sprouts, green onions, snow peas, water chestnuts, and corn in a large bowl; toss gently. Garnish salad mixture with chow mein noodles, and serve with Soy-Sesame Dressing. Yield: 6 servings.

☐ 107 calories, 4.5 grams protein, 2.7 grams fat, 19.1 grams carbohydrate, 0 milligrams cholesterol, 115.7 milligrams sodium, and 84 milligrams calcium per 2 cups salad plus 15 calories, 0.4 gram protein, 0.8 gram fat, 1.6 grams carbohydrate, 0 milligrams cholesterol, 146 milligrams sodium, and 4 milligrams calcium per tablespoon dressing.

Soy-Sesame Dressing:

1 tablespoon sugar
¾ teaspoon chicken-flavored, no-salt-added
  bouillon granules
1 tablespoon cornstarch
⅛ teaspoon red pepper flakes
⅛ teaspoon ground ginger
1 large clove garlic, minced
1 cup water
¼ cup plus 2 tablespoons rice vinegar
1½ teaspoons dry sherry
1 tablespoon sesame oil
¼ cup plus 2 tablespoons reduced-sodium
  soy sauce
1 tablespoon sesame seeds, toasted

Combine all ingredients except sesame seeds in a medium saucepan; cook over medium heat, stirring constantly, until mixture begins to bubble. Boil 1 minute, stirring constantly. Remove from heat; stir in sesame seeds. Cover and chill. Yield: 1½ cups.

CRIMSON GREENS

5 cups loosely packed Boston lettuce
  leaves (about ½ pound)
3 cups loosely packed watercress
2 cups orange sections
Raspberry Dressing
1 tablespoon plus 1 teaspoon sliced
  almonds, toasted

Arrange lettuce leaves on 6 salad plates; arrange watercress and orange sections over lettuce. Spoon Raspberry Dressing over salad; sprinkle with almonds. Yield: 6 servings.

☐ 40 calories, 1.6 grams protein, 0.8 gram fat, 7.8 grams carbohydrate, 0 milligrams cholesterol, 9 milligrams sodium, and 45 milligrams calcium per salad plus 23 calories, 0.1 gram protein, 0.9 gram fat, 3.7 grams carbohydrate, 0 milligrams cholesterol, 0 milligrams sodium, and 1 milligram calcium per tablespoon dressing.

Raspberry Dressing:

¾ cup fresh raspberries
3 tablespoons sugar
1 tablespoon cornstarch
1 cup water
2 tablespoons lemon juice
2 tablespoons rice vinegar
1 tablespoon Chablis or other
  dry white wine
1 tablespoon vegetable oil

Combine all ingredients in a heavy saucepan. Bring to a boil over medium heat, stirring constantly; cook 1 minute, stirring constantly. Remove saucepan from heat, and pour mixture through a nonmetal strainer; discard seeds and pulp. Cover raspberry mixture and chill thoroughly. Yield: 1 cup.

MELON BALL BOWL
WITH CUCUMBER-MINT
DRESSING

1½ cups watermelon balls
1½ cups cantaloupe balls
1 cup honeydew melon balls
1 cup peeled julienne-cut jicama
1 cup fresh pineapple chunks
1 tablespoon pomegranate seeds
  (optional)
6 lettuce leaves
Cucumber-Mint Dressing

Combine melon balls, jicama, pineapple chunks, and, if desired, pomegranate seeds in a large bowl; toss gently. Spoon fruit mixture into individual compotes lined with lettuce leaves. Serve fruit mixture with Cucumber-Mint Dressing. Yield: 6 servings.

☐ 60 calories, 1.4 grams protein, 0.6 gram fat, 13.7 grams carbohydrate, 0 milligrams cholesterol, 11 milligrams sodium, and 20 milligrams calcium per 1 cup salad plus 13 calories, 0.5 gram protein, 0.9 gram fat, 0.8 gram carbohydrate, 1 milligram cholesterol, 27 milligrams sodium, and 15 milligrams calcium per tablespoon dressing.

Cucumber-Mint Dressing:

¾ cup plain low-fat yogurt
¼ cup reduced-calorie mayonnaise
½ cup unpeeled, diced cucumber
2 teaspoons minced fresh mint
⅛ teaspoon celery seeds
⅛ teaspoon white pepper

Combine all ingredients in a small bowl; stir well. Cover dressing mixture, and let chill thoroughly before serving. Yield: 1⅓ cups.

PEACHES IN A GARDEN NEST

8 lettuce leaves
1 (4-ounce) carton alfalfa sprouts
½ cup lemon low-fat yogurt, divided
2 large fresh peaches
2 teaspoons lemon juice
2 tablespoons dried banana chips, crushed
2 tablespoons raisins
2 tablespoons unsalted sunflower kernels
2 tablespoons coarsely shredded carrots

Place 2 lettuce leaves on each of 4 salad plates. Rinse alfalfa sprouts, and pat dry; divide alfalfa sprouts evenly, and place on lettuce, arranging into individual nests.

Spread 1 tablespoon yogurt in each sprout nest. Peel peaches, and slice into wedges; toss gently with lemon juice. Arrange peaches in sprout nests; top each with 1 tablespoon yogurt. Combine banana chips and remaining ingredients; sprinkle over yogurt. Serve immediately. Yield: 4 servings.

□ *109 calories, 4 grams protein, 2.9 grams fat, 19.5 grams carbohydrate, 1 milligram cholesterol, 24 milligrams sodium, and 56 milligrams calcium per serving.*

Casseroles For Potluck Dinners

These casseroles are tailor-made for family reunions, as well as church and community meals. Covered with foil and packed in a box or basket, they travel easily. And you're sure to be asked for the recipes.

RICE-AND-CHICKEN CASSEROLE

1 cup carrots, peeled and sliced diagonally
2 cups cooked rice
1 (10¾-ounce) can cream of chicken soup, undiluted
½ cup milk
2 (5-ounce) cans boned chicken, drained and chopped
1 (2½-ounce) can ripe olives, drained and chopped
1 (8-ounce) can sliced water chestnuts, drained

Boil carrots in a small amount of water over medium heat 10 to 15 minutes or until crisp-tender. Drain and set aside. Combine rice, soup, and milk in a heavy saucepan; stir well. Cook, stirring constantly, until thoroughly heated. Add carrots and remaining ingredients; stir well. Spoon into a greased 2-quart shallow casserole; bake at 350° for 25 to 30 minutes. Yield: 4 servings.

*Albert C. Noble,
Bristol, Tennessee.*

MACARONI CASSEROLE

1 (14-ounce) package deluxe macaroni and cheese dinner
1 (10¾-ounce) can cream of mushroom soup, undiluted
1 (4-ounce) jar diced pimiento, drained
¼ cup chopped green pepper
¼ cup chopped onion
½ cup milk
⅓ cup mayonnaise
½ cup (2 ounces) shredded sharp American cheese

Cook macaroni according to package directions, omitting salt; drain well. Add the pouch of cheese sauce from package, soup, pimiento, green pepper, onion, milk, and mayonnaise; mix well. Spoon into a lightly greased 2-quart casserole. Bake, uncovered, at 400° for 20 minutes. Sprinkle with cheese, and bake 5 more minutes. Yield: 6 servings.

*Betty J. Smith,
Fayetteville, North Carolina.*

ZUCCHINI CASSEROLE

1 bay leaf
6 medium zucchini, sliced
2 eggs, slightly beaten
1 cup commercial sour cream
1 cup (4 ounces) shredded Cheddar cheese
1 teaspoon dried whole basil
½ teaspoon dried whole oregano
½ teaspoon garlic powder
¼ teaspoon salt
½ teaspoon pepper
2 tomatoes, chopped
6 slices bacon, cooked and crumbled
⅓ cup dry Italian seasoned breadcrumbs
2 tablespoons grated Parmesan cheese

Combine bay leaf and a small amount of water in a saucepan; boil. Arrange zucchini in a steaming rack or colander. Reduce heat, and place rack in saucepan. Cover and steam 8 minutes, or until zucchini is crisp-tender. Set aside.

Combine eggs, sour cream, Cheddar cheese, basil, oregano, garlic, salt, and pepper in a large bowl; stir to mix. Add zucchini, tomatoes, and bacon; stir gently to mix.

Spoon mixture into a lightly greased 12- x 8- x 2-inch baking dish. Combine breadcrumbs and Parmesan cheese; sprinkle over casserole. Bake at 350° for 30 minutes. Yield: about 8 servings.

*Christine Chamblin,
St. Petersburg, Florida.*

CURRY PEA CASSEROLE

1 (10¾-ounce) can cream of mushroom soup, undiluted
½ cup commercial sour cream
¼ teaspoon curry powder
½ teaspoon soy sauce
1 tablespoon Worcestershire sauce
2 (14.5-ounce) cans small English peas, drained
1 medium onion, chopped
¼ cup sliced almonds
¼ cup chopped pimiento, drained
¾ cup herb seasoned stuffing mix
½ cup (2 ounces) shredded Cheddar cheese

Combine soup, sour cream, curry, soy sauce, and Worcestershire sauce in a medium bowl; stir well. Stir in peas, onion, almonds, and pimiento. Spoon into a lightly greased 2-quart baking dish. Top with stuffing mix. Bake at 350° for 20 minutes. Sprinkle with cheese, and bake an additional 5 minutes or until cheese melts. Yield: 6 servings.

*Beth Cherry,
Belmont, North Carolina.*

MIXED-VEGETABLE CASSEROLE

2 cups water
1 cup broccoli flowerets
1 cup cauliflower flowerets
½ cup sliced celery
2 cups sliced yellow squash (about 3 medium)
1 (10¾-ounce) can cream of mushroom soup, undiluted
½ cup (2 ounces) shredded sharp Cheddar cheese
⅓ cup chopped onion
¼ teaspoon pepper
2 tablespoons crushed corn flakes

Bring water to a boil in a saucepan. Add broccoli, cauliflower, and celery; cover and cook 5 minutes. Add squash, and cook an additional 4 minutes or until vegetables are crisp-tender. Drain.

Combine mushroom soup, cheese, onion, and pepper. Add to vegetables; blend well. Spoon into a greased 1½-quart casserole; sprinkle top with crushed corn flakes. Bake at 350° for 20 to 30 minutes or until hot. Yield: 4 to 6 servings. *Mrs. Randy Throneberry, Shelbyville, Tennessee.*

Mighty Flavor From Tarragon

Reminiscent of anise, aromatic tarragon leaves flavor seafood, chicken, green salads, and tomatoes and are often used to season vinegar. The tiny leaves can easily overpower the food, so use them sparingly—just enough to enhance the natural flavors of your main ingredients.

ZESTY SHRIMP-AND-ORANGE RICE SALAD

1 cup uncooked regular rice
1 pound fresh asparagus
1 pound medium shrimp, peeled, deveined, and butterflied
2 slices bacon, cut into ½-inch pieces
1 shallot, chopped
2 tablespoons olive oil
¾ cup mayonnaise
¼ cup sliced green onions
1 tablespoon chopped fresh tarragon or 1 teaspoon dried whole tarragon
1 teaspoon capers
¼ teaspoon salt
⅛ teaspoon freshly ground pepper
2 teaspoons grated orange rind
2 oranges, peeled and sectioned

Cook rice according to package directions; cool. Set aside.

Snap off tough ends of asparagus. Remove scales from stalks with a knife or vegetable peeler, if desired. Place asparagus in steaming rack. Place over boiling water; steam 6 to 8 minutes or until crisp-tender. Cut asparagus into 1½-inch pieces. Set aside.

Sauté shrimp, bacon, and shallot in olive oil in a skillet 5 to 7 minutes or until shrimp turn pink. Drain.

Combine mayonnaise, green onions, tarragon, capers, salt, pepper, and orange rind in a large bowl; add orange sections, rice, asparagus, and shrimp mixture, tossing gently. Cover and chill. Yield: 6 servings. *Susan Todd, Shreveport, Louisiana.*

SALMON STEAKS WITH TARRAGON BUTTER

¼ cup butter or margarine, softened
1 shallot, minced
1 tablespoon chopped fresh tarragon
1 tablespoon chopped fresh chives
1½ teaspoons chopped fresh parsley
⅛ teaspoon freshly ground pepper
1 tablespoon Dijon mustard
4 (1½-inch-thick) salmon steaks

Combine butter, shallot, tarragon, chives, parsley, pepper, and mustard; mix well.

Brush salmon steaks with butter mixture, and grill over hot coals 8 minutes on each side or until fish flakes easily when tested with a fork, brushing frequently with the remaining butter mixture. Yield: 4 servings. *Rick Paler, Decatur, Alabama.*

HERB-ROASTED CHICKEN
(pictured on page 102)

2 tablespoons butter or margarine, melted
¼ cup plus 2 tablespoons vinegar
3 tablespoons lemon juice
3 tablespoons chopped fresh tarragon
2 tablespoons olive oil
1 clove garlic, minced
1 teaspoon salt
1 teaspoon freshly ground pepper
1 pound new potatoes, unpeeled
1 cup diagonally sliced celery
1 (2-ounce) jar sliced pimiento, drained
¼ cup chopped fresh parsley
1 (5- to 6-pound) stewing chicken
Fresh parsley (optional)
Fresh tarragon (optional)

Combine butter, vinegar, lemon juice, 3 tablespoons tarragon, oil, garlic, salt, and pepper, mixing well. Set aside.

Cover potatoes with water in saucepan; cook, covered, over medium heat 15 minutes or until tender. Drain potatoes; cool. Cut potatoes into bite-size pieces. Add celery, pimiento, and ¼ cup parsley, tossing gently. Add 2 tablespoons tarragon-oil mixture, tossing to coat. Set aside.

Remove giblets from cavity of chicken, and reserve for other uses. Rinse chicken with cold water, and pat dry. Fold neck skin over back; secure with a wooden pick. Lift wingtips up and over back, and tuck under chicken. Stuff cavity with potato mixture. Close cavity, and secure with wooden picks; truss chicken.

Place chicken, breast side up, on a roasting rack. Brush entire chicken with remaining tarragon-oil mixture.

Insert meat thermometer in breast or meaty part of thigh, making sure it does not touch bone. Bake at 375° until meat thermometer reads 185° (about 2 hours), basting frequently with tarragon-oil mixture. Let cool 10 to 15 minutes before slicing. Garnish with fresh tarragon and parsley, if desired. Yield: 4 servings. *Leslie Cosby, Gadsden, Alabama.*

TARRAGON PASTA-CHICKEN SALAD

1 (8-ounce) bottle commercial Italian salad dressing
¼ cup white wine vinegar
2 tablespoons chopped fresh tarragon
1 clove garlic, minced
4 chicken breast halves, skinned and boned
4 ounces seashell macaroni, uncooked
2 cups sliced celery
½ cup chopped sweet red pepper or green pepper
¼ cup chopped green onions
1 tablespoon chopped fresh parsley
½ cup mayonnaise

Combine salad dressing, vinegar, tarragon, and garlic in a jar, and cover tightly. Shake vigorously until well mixed. Place chicken in a 12- x 8- x 2-inch baking dish; pour ¾ cup dressing mixture over chicken, reserving remaining mixture. Cover and chill 8 hours. Remove from refrigerator; let stand 30 minutes at room temperature. Bake at 350° for 25 to 30 minutes or until done. Drain chicken, and cool slightly; coarsely chop.

Cook pasta according to package directions; drain and cool slightly. Combine chicken, reserved dressing mixture, pasta, and remaining ingredients in a large bowl; toss gently. Cover and chill. Yield: 4 to 6 servings. *Cheryl Midgley, Gadsden, Alabama.*

CHERRY TOMATO SALAD

1 pint cherry tomatoes, halved
1 large cucumber, sliced
1 small onion, sliced
2 tablespoons chopped fresh parsley
½ cup vegetable oil
¼ cup tarragon-flavored wine vinegar
1 tablespoon chopped fresh tarragon
½ teaspoon garlic salt
¼ teaspoon salt
¼ teaspoon ground savory
¼ teaspoon celery salt
¼ teaspoon pepper
⅛ teaspoon ground bay leaves

Layer tomatoes, cucumber, onion, and parsley in a shallow dish.

Combine vegetable oil and remaining ingredients in a jar. Cover tightly, and shake vigorously; pour dressing mixture over vegetables. Cover and chill at least 8 hours. Drain vegetables before serving. Yield: 6 servings.

Mrs. Clark Adams,
Clearwater, Florida.

A Southern Breakfast In Just Minutes

In High Point, North Carolina, Karen Cauble knows how to put a delicious prize-winning breakfast on the table. The menu that follows was the top winner in a contest that required the use of brown-and-serve sausage in a quick Southern breakfast.

Angel Heart Biscuits With Sausage
Scalloped Apples
Good Morning Grits
Coffee

ANGEL HEART BISCUITS WITH SAUSAGE

1 package dry yeast
2 cups warm water (105° to 115°), divided
1 egg, beaten
¼ cup sugar
¼ cup butter or margarine, melted
4 cups self-rising flour
2 teaspoons chopped chives
Melted butter or margarine
2 (8-ounce) packages brown-and-serve sausage patties

Dissolve yeast in ½ cup warm water in a large mixing bowl. Add egg, sugar, butter, and remaining 1½ cups water; stir until smooth. Gradually stir in flour and chives. Spoon into greased cast-iron, heart-shaped muffin pans or regular muffin pans; bake at 400° for 20 to 25 minutes or until golden. Brush with melted butter.

Cut sausage patties, using a 1½-inch, heart-shaped cookie cutter; cook in a large skillet until thoroughly heated, turning once. Split biscuits, and insert sausage. Serve immediately. Yield: 15 sausage-filled biscuits.

Note: Dough baked in regular muffin pans will look more like muffins than biscuits; spoon less batter in the pans so that they won't rise as high as muffins.

SCALLOPED APPLES

4 medium Rome apples
1 (15-ounce) jar scalloped apples

Remove a slice from stem end of apples. Scoop out pulp, leaving a ½-inch-thick shell; repeat procedure for remaining apples. Using a sharp paring knife, cut edges of apple cups into scallops, if desired.

Heat scalloped apples according to label directions; spoon into apple shells. Yield: 4 servings.

GOOD MORNING GRITS

3 cups boiling water
¾ cup quick-cooking grits
¼ cup butter or margarine
1 cup (4 ounces) shredded American cheese
Cheese cutouts
Parsley sprig

Cook grits according to package directions. Add butter and shredded cheese, stirring until cheese melts. Spoon into serving dish, and garnish with cheese cutouts and parsley sprig. Yield: 4 servings.

Try Warm-Weather Soups

If you think of soup as wintertime fare, these recipes are sure to change your mind. For something cold and sweet, serve Cold Fresh Fruit Soup. It's a delightful blend of cantaloupe, strawberries, grapes, and apple especially suited as an appetizer for a luncheon or light dinner. If the meal starts with a highly seasoned salad, serve the soup next, and then the entrée.

When fresh corn is available, use the juicy just-ripened kernels in our recipe for Corn Soup for real summertime flavor. Remember to scrape the corncobs with a knife after removing the kernels. You'll get even more sweet, creamy corn taste. Freeze some corn so that you can also make this recipe later.

CORN SOUP

2 cups corn cut from cob and cobs scraped
1 cup water
2 cups milk
1 teaspoon sugar
1 teaspoon salt
¼ teaspoon white pepper
2 tablespoons butter or margarine
6 slices bacon, cooked and crumbled
Chopped fresh parsley
Chopped green onions

Combine corn and water in a heavy saucepan. Bring to a boil; reduce heat, and simmer 10 minutes, stirring often. Add milk, sugar, salt, pepper, and butter. Heat thoroughly. Stir in bacon. Garnish each serving with fresh parsley and green onions. Yield: 5 cups.

Ann Elsie Schmetzer,
Madisonville, Kentucky.

CHARLESTON OKRA SOUP

1 large meaty beef shank bone
2½ quarts water
1 teaspoon salt
½ teaspoon pepper
1 bay leaf
8 cups sliced okra
2 cups chopped onion
8 large tomatoes, peeled and chopped
1 tablespoon beef-flavored bouillon granules
4 slices bacon, cooked and crumbled

Sour cream and strips of orange rind garnish this serving of Cold Fresh Fruit Soup.

Combine peaches, plums, sugar, cinnamon, 1¾ cups water, and wine in a Dutch oven. Bring to a boil; reduce heat, and simmer 10 minutes or until fruit is tender. Spoon 2 cups fruit mixture into container of an electric blender; process until smooth. Repeat with remaining mixture. Return fruit to Dutch oven; bring to a boil. Combine arrowroot and ¼ cup water; stir into soup, and boil 1 minute, stirring constantly. Garnish soup with whipped cream. Yield: 6 cups. *Louise Walker, Lexington, Tennessee.*

Party Spreads And Sandwich Fillings

These spreads are tailor-made for any occasion—from receptions to open houses. The flavors range from sweet to tangy, and some use cream cheese as a base, while others rely on chicken and shrimp.

Festive Chicken Spread is a special addition to any party menu. Depending on how you serve it, the spread can be a topping for crackers or a moist filling for finger sandwiches.

Simplicity is the key to all of these spreads—and you can make them even more attractive with a few simple serving ideas. Consider serving the spread from a green or red pepper cup or from a crystal bowl, surrounded by a variety of crackers. If you make finger sandwiches, stop by a bakery and pick up party breads in a variety of flavors and sizes. For something different, pair Honey-Nut Spread with gingersnaps, or spread it over hot biscuits for a mid-morning breakfast.

Combine beef bone, water, salt, pepper, and bay leaf in a stockpot; bring to a boil. Cover, reduce heat, and simmer 2 hours. Remove shank; cool. Remove fat and meat from bone; discard fat. Cut meat into ¼-inch cubes. Return beef to stock.

Add okra, onion, tomatoes, and bouillon granules to stock. Bring to a boil. Cover, reduce heat, and simmer 30 minutes. Stir in bacon; remove bay leaf. Yield: 1 gallon. *Mrs. John McMullen, Georgetown, Kentucky.*

Combine cantaloupe, strawberries, grapes, apple, sugar, water, and lemon juice in a large Dutch oven; bring to a boil. Reduce heat, and simmer, uncovered, 15 minutes. Pour half of fruit mixture into container of an electric blender. Cover and process until smooth. Repeat with remaining mixture. Add orange juice to fruit mixture; stir and chill.

Spoon into bowls; garnish each serving with a dollop of sour cream and orange rind. Yield: 7 cups.

Gayle Fleming, Northport, Alabama.

COLD FRESH FRUIT SOUP

2 cups coarsely chopped cantaloupe
2½ cups fresh strawberries
¼ cup seedless green grapes
3 cups coarsely chopped cooking apple
¼ cup sugar
2 cups water
¼ cup lemon juice
1¼ cups orange juice
Commercial sour cream
Orange rind strips

PEACH-PLUM SOUP

½ pound fresh peaches, peeled and sliced
½ pound fresh plums, peeled and sliced
1 cup plus 2 tablespoons sugar
1 (2-inch) stick cinnamon
1¾ cups water
2 cups Burgundy wine
1 teaspoon arrowroot
¼ cup water
½ cup whipping cream, whipped

HONEY-NUT SPREAD

1 (8-ounce) package cream cheese, softened
¼ cup commercial sour cream
2 tablespoons honey
¼ cup chopped pecans

Combine first 3 ingredients in a mixing bowl; beat at medium speed of an electric mixer until smooth. Stir in pecans; cover and chill. Serve with gingersnaps. Yield: 1⅓ cups.

Gynell V. Silcox, Jacksonville, Florida.

CURRIED SHRIMP SPREAD

2 (4½-ounce) cans shrimp
⅔ cup mayonnaise
1½ teaspoons curry powder
¼ cup diced green pepper
¼ cup diced celery

Rinse shrimp; soak in ice water 20 minutes. Drain well. Set aside.

Combine mayonnaise and curry powder; stir until blended. Fold in shrimp, green pepper, and celery. Chill. Yield: 1⅔ cups.

Betty Clinton,
Clearwater, Florida.

FESTIVE CHICKEN SPREAD

1 (8-ounce) package cream cheese, softened
3 tablespoons mayonnaise
1 tablespoon lemon juice
½ teaspoon salt
¼ teaspoon ground ginger
⅛ teaspoon pepper
4 drops hot sauce
2 cups diced cooked chicken
2 hard-cooked eggs, diced
¼ cup diced green onions
3 tablespoons chopped green pepper
Green pepper strips
2 tablespoons sesame seeds, toasted
3 tablespoons chopped black olives
3 tablespoons chopped sweet red pepper
5 slices cucumber, halved (optional)
Parsley sprigs (optional)

Combine cream cheese, mayonnaise, lemon juice, salt, ginger, pepper, and hot sauce; beat at medium speed of electric mixer until smooth. Add chicken, eggs, green onions, and chopped green pepper; stir well.

Line a 1-quart mixing bowl or mold with plastic wrap. Spoon mixture into bowl; press firmly with back of a spoon. Cover and chill at least 4 hours.

Invert bowl onto serving platter. Remove bowl, and peel off plastic wrap. Garnish mound with green pepper strips, sesame seeds, black olives, and sweet red pepper. Arrange cucumber slices and parsley sprigs around bottom of mound, if desired; serve with assorted crackers. Yield: 3 cups.

BariLynn Mitchell,
St. Peters, Missouri.

Tip: Pull a sharp fork down the length of a cucumber before slicing it to give the slices a fancy look.

HAWAIIAN CHEESE SPREAD

2 (8-ounce) packages cream cheese, softened
1 (8¼-ounce) can crushed pineapple, well drained
1 cup chopped pecans
¼ cup chopped green pepper
2 tablespoons diced onion
1 teaspoon celery salt
⅛ teaspoon garlic powder

Beat cream cheese at medium speed of electric mixer until fluffy; stir in remaining ingredients. Serve on crackers or bread. Yield: 3¼ cups.

Susan W. Puckett,
Burlington, North Carolina.

APRICOT-CREAM CHEESE SPREAD

1 cup chopped dried apricots
¾ cup water
2 (8-ounce) packages cream cheese, softened
¾ cup orange marmalade
2 tablespoons milk
1 cup chopped pecans

Combine apricots and water in a small saucepan. Bring to a boil; cover, reduce heat, and simmer 10 minutes. Drain well.

Beat cream cheese at medium speed of electric mixer until smooth and fluffy; stir in apricots and remaining ingredients. Serve on crackers or bread. Yield: about 3½ cups.   *Christie Jones,*
Birmingham, Alabama.

Kids Will Love These Snacks

Kids love peanut butter and jelly. That's why Peanut Butter Muffins, filled with grape jam or strawberry preserves, probably won't last long at your house.

Young children and adolescents need extra calories to fuel their rapidly growing bodies, so give them nutritious snacks and well-balanced meals. Remember to include milk, cheese, and raw fruits and vegetables.

Chewy Soft Pretzels have B vitamins and are less sweet than some other snacks. Rich Yummy Fudge Bars, combining candy-coated chocolate pieces and oats, are sure to be a hit.

PEANUT BUTTER MUFFINS

1 egg, beaten
1 cup milk
½ cup crunchy peanut butter
2 tablespoons vegetable oil
1½ cups crispy rice cereal squares
1 cup all-purpose flour
⅓ cup sugar
2 teaspoons baking powder
¼ teaspoon salt
¼ cup grape jam or strawberry preserves

Combine first 4 ingredients in a small mixing bowl; mix well. Stir in cereal; let stand 5 minutes.

Combine flour, sugar, baking powder, and salt. Add cereal mixture; stir just until dry ingredients are moistened. Fill greased muffin pans about half full, reserving remaining batter. Spoon 1 teaspoon jam on center of each muffin, and spoon remaining batter over jam, carefully covering jam. Bake at 400° for 25 to 30 minutes or until done. Let cool 10 minutes before serving. Yield: 1 dozen.   *Mary Andrew,*
Winston-Salem, North Carolina.

YUMMY FUDGE BARS

2 cups quick-cooking oats, uncooked
1½ cups all-purpose flour
1 cup chopped pecans
1 cup firmly-packed light brown sugar
1 teaspoon baking soda
¼ teaspoon salt
1 cup butter or margarine, melted
2 tablespoons vegetable oil
1½ cups candy-coated chocolate pieces, divided
1 (14-ounce) can sweetened condensed milk

Combine oats, flour, pecans, sugar, soda, and salt; mix well. Add butter, and mix until mixture resembles coarse crumbs.

Reserve 1½ cups crumb mixture; press remainder in a greased 15- x 10- x 1-inch jellyroll pan. Bake at 375° for 10 minutes. Remove from oven.

Heat 2 tablespoons oil in a heavy saucepan. Add 1 cup chocolate pieces; continue cooking at low heat, stirring constantly. Press chocolate pieces with back of a spoon to break up. (The candies will almost be melted with pieces of color coating still visible.) Remove from heat; stir in condensed milk, and mix well. Spread mixture over partially baked crust, leaving a ½-inch border on all sides.

Combine reserved 1½ cups crumb mixture and remaining ½ cup chocolate pieces; sprinkle evenly over chocolate mixture, and press lightly.

Bake at 350° for 20 minutes or until golden brown; cool. Cut into bars. Yield: 4 dozen. *Mrs. M. J. Keener, San Angelo, Texas.*

JAM-IT BARS

2 cups all-purpose flour
½ cup sugar
½ teaspoon vanilla extract
¼ teaspoon salt
⅛ teaspoon ground cinnamon
⅛ teaspoon ground nutmeg
¾ cup butter or margarine
1 cup chopped pecans, divided
1 (10-ounce) jar peach jam or preserves

Combine first 6 ingredients; cut in butter with pastry blender until mixture resembles coarse meal. Stir in ½ cup pecans. Remove ¾ cup of mixture, and set aside. Press remaining mixture evenly into a lightly greased 9-inch square pan. Spread peach jam over crumb mixture; sprinkle with remaining ½ cup pecans. Sprinkle reserved crumb mixture over pecans. Bake at 350° for 35 to 40 minutes; cool. Cut into bars. Yield: about 2 dozen. *Becky Duncan, Leming, Texas.*

CHEWY SOFT PRETZELS

3½ cups all-purpose flour
2 tablespoons sugar
1 teaspoon salt
1 package dry yeast
Dash of white pepper
1 egg yolk
1 tablespoon butter or margarine, melted
1 cup warm water (120° to 130°)
1 egg yolk
1 tablespoon water
Kosher salt

Combine first 8 ingredients in a large mixing bowl. Beat with dough hooks at medium speed of electric mixer until well blended. Form dough into a ball; place in a greased bowl, turning to grease top. Cover and let rise in a warm place (85°), free from drafts, 1 hour or until doubled in bulk.

Using kitchen shears dipped in flour, cut dough into 16 pieces; roll each into a ball. Roll each ball on a floured surface to form a rope 14 inches long. Twist each into a pretzel shape; place on a lightly greased baking sheet, about 1½ inches apart.

Combine remaining egg yolk and water; mix well. Brush each pretzel with egg yolk mixture; sprinkle with kosher salt. Bake at 375° for 15 to 20 minutes or until golden. Serve warm. Yield: 16 pretzels.

Note: Rock or table salt may be substituted for kosher salt.

Craig R. McNees, Sarasota, Florida.

Chicken With A Cajun Flair

If you like your entrée hot and spicy, Cajun-Style Drumsticks is for you. Mrs. Robert Cast of Miami, Florida, soaks chicken legs in buttermilk and then dredges them in a mixture of 11 different seasonings for just the right amount of punch and interest. Serve the drumsticks with mild-seasoned side dishes, such as mashed potatoes and buttered green beans, so that other flavors won't compete with this spicy main dish.

CAJUN-STYLE DRUMSTICKS

8 chicken drumsticks
2 cups buttermilk
½ cup butter or margarine, melted
¼ cup all-purpose flour
¼ cup cornmeal
1½ teaspoons garlic powder
1½ teaspoons onion powder
1½ teaspoons chili powder
1⅓ teaspoons dried whole thyme
1½ teaspoons dried whole oregano
1½ teaspoons paprika
1 teaspoon salt
¾ teaspoon ground cumin
½ teaspoon black pepper
½ teaspoon white pepper
½ teaspoon red pepper

Place chicken in a shallow dish; pour buttermilk over top. Cover and chill for 8 hours.

Place butter in a shallow dish; set aside. Combine flour, cornmeal, and

seasonings in a plastic bag. Drain chicken; roll in butter, and place in bag, 1 or 2 pieces at a time. Close bag securely, and shake until well coated.

Arrange chicken on a rack placed over a roasting pan; drizzle with any remaining butter. Bake at 400° for 15 minutes. Turn chicken; reduce heat to 350°, and bake for 30 to 35 minutes or until done. Yield: 4 servings.

Ice Cream Parlor Beverages

Top an icy-cold beverage with a scoop of ice cream or sherbet, add a long straw, and enjoy a float. On a hot summer day what could be more refreshing? These ice cream beverages are instant energizers, as nourishing as they are delicious.

FROSTY FRUIT FLOAT

1 cup milk
1 pint orange sherbet, divided
1 (8-ounce) can crushed pineapple, undrained
1 cup sliced strawberries

Combine milk, 1 cup sherbet, pineapple, and strawberries in container of an electric blender; process until smooth. Pour mixture into three 12-ounce glasses, and top each serving with a scoop of orange sherbet. Yield: 3 servings. *Julie Earhart, St. Louis, Missouri.*

TAHITIAN FLOWER

1 cup apricot nectar
1 cup unsweetened pineapple juice
1 cup orange juice
2 tablespoons grenadine syrup
Ice cubes
4 scoops orange sherbet (about 1 pint)

Combine apricot nectar, pineapple juice, orange juice, and grenadine in container of an electric blender. Add enough ice cubes to fill blender to 4 cups; process until frothy. Pour mixture into four 10-ounce glasses, and top each serving with a scoop of sherbet. Yield: 4 servings. *Linda H. Sutton, Winston-Salem, North Carolina.*

BANANA SMOOTHIE

3 cups milk, divided
2 bananas, sliced
⅓ cup commercial chocolate syrup
3 tablespoons sugar
½ teaspoon vanilla extract
5 small scoops vanilla ice cream
  (about 1 pint)

Combine 2 cups milk, bananas, chocolate syrup, sugar, and vanilla in container of an electric blender; process until mixture is smooth. Add remaining 1 cup milk; process until smooth. Pour mixture into five 10-ounce glasses; top each serving with a scoop of ice cream. Yield: 5 servings.

Carolyn McCue,
Oklahoma City, Oklahoma.

STRAWBERRY-BANANA FLOAT

2 cups milk, divided
3 cups strawberry ice cream,
  divided
1 cup fresh strawberries, sliced
2 small bananas, sliced
¼ cup orange juice

Combine 1 cup milk, 1 cup strawberry ice cream, strawberries, and bananas in container of an electric blender; process until mixture is smooth. Add remaining 1 cup milk and orange juice; process until smooth. Pour mixture into five 10-ounce glasses, and top each serving with a scoop of strawberry ice cream. Yield: 5 servings.

Sarah Bondurant,
Hernando, Mississippi.

LIME COOLER

3 cups milk, divided
1 pint vanilla ice cream
1 (6-ounce) can frozen limeade
  concentrate, undiluted
5 small scoops lime sherbet
  (about 1 pint)

Combine 2 cups milk, vanilla ice cream, and limeade concentrate in container of an electric blender; process until mixture is smooth. Add remaining 1 cup milk; process until smooth. Pour mixture into five 10-ounce glasses, and top each serving with a scoop of lime sherbet. Yield: 5 servings.

Jeannie R. Atwell,
Durham, North Carolina.

Pineapple-Flavored Ham is a good choice for a summer dinner. The next day, slice it for sandwiches, use in an omelet, or bake in a casserole.

Baked Ham Stretches Summer Menus

Bake a ham in the heat of summer? Sure! Leave this ham in the oven, and head outdoors for the sunshine.

Mrs. Mack Pierce of Pikeville, North Carolina, has a recipe that's sure to please. She knows what makes a ham tasty—and pretty, too. Pineapple, honey, and brown sugar flavor this smoked pork shoulder. It's elegant enough for entertaining and yet practical as a family entrée.

PINEAPPLE-FLAVORED HAM

1 (6- to 7-pound) fully cooked picnic
  shoulder
1 (15¼-ounce) can pineapple slices
¼ cup firmly packed brown sugar
¼ cup honey
Maraschino cherries
Whole cloves
Escarole (optional)

Remove skin from ham; place ham, fat side up, on a baking rack or in a shallow pan. Cover ham loosely with aluminum foil. Insert meat thermometer, making sure it does not touch fat or bone. Bake at 325° for 25 to 30 minutes per pound or until meat thermometer registers 140°.

Drain pineapple, reserving ¼ cup juice. Combine ¼ cup juice, brown sugar, and honey in a heavy saucepan; cook over low heat until sugar dissolves, stirring often.

Remove foil; score fat in a diamond design. Brush ham with pineapple glaze. Arrange pineapple slices and cherries in desired pattern, securing with wooden picks; stud ham with cloves, and brush with glaze. Bake at 325° for an additional 25 to 30 minutes; baste with glaze. Place ham on serving platter; garnish with escarole, if desired. Yield: 10 to 15 servings.

Tip: Ham labeled "fully cooked" does not require further heating and may be eaten cold. However, if you prefer to heat it, an internal temperature of 140° brings out the most flavor.

August

Not Your Everyday Melon

Carving a huge melon into wedges on a picnic table may be the most typical way to serve this summer fruit, but we have some new thoughts on preparing melon for company.

You'll take advantage of the brilliant colors of cantaloupe and honeydew when you prepare Swirled Melon Soup. Flavor and whirl the fruits separately in a blender until smooth. Then measure about ½ cup of each melon mixture in separate measuring cups. With one measuring cup in each hand, pour the mixtures simultaneously into individual bowls; then gently swirl the soup with a spoon. If you prepare the melon mixtures a day ahead, it takes just minutes to serve.

Minted Melon Balls can double as an appetizer or salad. For an appetizer, just spoon the melon balls into a serving bowl, garnish with mint leaves, and offer the fruit with decorative wooden picks. When serving individual salads, place the melon balls on beds of lettuce.

Consider Grilled Cantaloupe Wedges next time you grill mild-flavored chicken. Just put the fruit on the grill after you remove the meat. This unusual side dish will take only about five minutes to cook.

Freeze Honeydew Granita to cleanse the palate between a spicy salad course and the entrée. The granita will be equally refreshing as a not-so-sweet dessert. Either way, spoon it into crystal champagne or sherbet glasses.

MINTED MELON BALLS
(pictured on page 169)

1 cup sugar
⅓ cup water
½ cup loosely packed fresh mint leaves
4 cups watermelon balls
Fresh mint leaves

Combine sugar and water in a small saucepan; bring to a boil, stirring occasionally. Remove from heat.

Combine sugar mixture and mint leaves in container of an electric blender; process until leaves are finely chopped. Toss watermelon balls with mint mixture, and chill at least 2 hours.

Serve melon balls, using a slotted spoon. Garnish melon balls with fresh mint leaves. Yield: 4 cups.

SWIRLED MELON SOUP
(pictured on page 169)

6½ cups coarsely chopped cantaloupe (about 1 large)
¼ cup sugar, divided
¼ cup dry sherry, divided
¼ cup orange juice, divided
6½ cups coarsely chopped honeydew (about 1 medium)
Fresh mint sprigs

Place cantaloupe in container of an electric blender or food processor; add half each of sugar, sherry, and orange juice. Process until very smooth. Spoon mixture into an airtight container, and chill at least 3 hours.

Place honeydew in container of an electric blender or food processor; add remaining sugar, sherry, and orange juice. Process until very smooth. Spoon mixture into an airtight container, and chill at least 3 hours.

For each serving, pour equal amounts of both mixtures into individual bowls, pouring both at the same time. Swirl soup gently with a spoon, and garnish with a mint sprig. Yield: 9 cups.

HONEYDEW GRANITA

½ cup sugar
3 tablespoons dark rum
1¼ cups water
2½ cups chopped honeydew
1 tablespoon lemon juice

Combine sugar, rum, and water in a saucepan; bring mixture to a boil, and boil until sugar dissolves. Boil an additional 3 minutes. Let syrup cool.

Combine honeydew, syrup, and lemon juice in container of an electric blender; puree until smooth. Pour mixture into an airtight container, and chill 2 hours or until very cold. (Honeydew mixture may be chilled overnight at this point, if desired.)

About 2 to 3 hours before serving, stir honeydew mixture well, and pour into a 13- x 9- x 2-inch pan. Freeze mixture 2 to 3 hours or until frozen but not solid, stirring every 30 minutes. Scrape granita with a fork to separate crystals, and serve in chilled containers. Yield: 3½ cups.

GRILLED CANTALOUPE WEDGES

¼ cup vegetable oil
3 tablespoons vinegar
1 tablespoon minced onion
2 teaspoons minced fresh or ¾ teaspoon dried whole thyme
Dash of white pepper
1 large cantaloupe, peeled and cut into 12 wedges

Combine oil, vinegar, onion, thyme, and pepper, stirring well. Thread 3 or 4 cantaloupe wedges onto 2 skewers, piercing skewers through ends of wedges so that skewers hold cantaloupe securely. Repeat with remaining cantaloupe and additional skewers. Grill over hot coals 2 to 3 minutes on each side or until thoroughly heated, basting often with marinade. Serve immediately. Yield: 6 servings.

COOKING LIGHT®

Traditional Southern Foods Go Light

Remember when you weren't trying to diet and looked forward to meals that included Southern specialties, such as fried chicken, okra and tomatoes, cornbread, and blackberry cobbler? We've come up with some recipes that make these down-home delicacies fit your diet.

Crunchy Oven-Fried Chicken and Southern Oven-Fried Catfish are baked to save calories, but you won't miss flavor. We've added herbs and other seasonings to make them delicious. Another plus is that you won't have the cleanup associated with frying foods.

Mock Country-Fried Steak contains no added fat. Lean steak is browned in a nonstick skillet coated with vegetable cooking spray. And the gravy is made from unsalted beef bouillon granules, water, and cornstarch rather than whole milk and flour that is often found in cream gravies.

Instead of adding bacon, fatback, and ham hocks for flavoring vegetable dishes, our recipes rely on herbs, spices, and other seasonings that are lower in fat and sodium.

Dieter's Cornbread (page 164) is different from most cornbread because there's no added fat. Cultured nonfat buttermilk gives it the proper texture.

And for dessert, there's fresh summer fruit to enjoy. In both New-Fashioned Blackberry Cobbler and Spiced Peaches With Nutty Dumplings (recipes, page 164), we used unsweetened fruit juices in combination with a number of complementary spices so that we could sweeten the dish with less sugar.

SOUTHERN OVEN-FRIED CATFISH

2 egg whites
¼ cup malt vinegar
1 cup crushed crispy wheat cereal squares
¼ teaspoon dried whole dillweed
¼ teaspoon seasoned salt
2 pounds fresh catfish fillets
Vegetable cooking spray
Lemon wedges (optional)

Combine egg whites and vinegar; stir well, and set aside. Combine cereal, dillweed, and seasoned salt; toss to mix. Dip fillets into egg white mixture; lightly coat with cereal mixture. Place fillets on a broiler pan lightly coated with cooking spray. Bake at 400° for 15 minutes or until fish flakes easily when tested with a fork. Garnish with lemon wedges, if desired. Yield: 8 servings.

☐ *144 calories, 21.3 grams protein, 3.6 grams fat, 5.3 grams carbohydrate, 62 milligrams cholesterol, 181 milligrams sodium, and 30 milligrams calcium per 3-ounce serving.*

MOCK COUNTRY-FRIED STEAK

4 (4-ounce) slices lean, cubed sirloin steak
½ teaspoon lemon-pepper seasoning
Vegetable cooking spray
4 (¼-inch) slices onion
1 teaspoon no-salt-added, beef-flavored bouillon granules
1 cup hot water
1 tablespoon cornstarch
¼ cup water
2 cups hot cooked rice (cooked without salt or fat)
Parsley sprigs (optional)

Sprinkle steak with lemon-pepper seasoning; set aside.
Coat a nonstick skillet with cooking spray; place over medium heat until hot. Add steak; cook over medium heat until browned, turning once. Place an onion slice on top of each piece of steak. Combine bouillon granules and hot water, stirring well; add bouillon mixture to skillet. Bring to a boil; reduce heat, and simmer, uncovered, 10 minutes. Remove steak to serving platter; keep warm.
Combine cornstarch and water; stir into bouillon mixture in skillet. Cook over medium heat, stirring constantly, until mixture is thickened and bubbly. Serve steak and gravy over rice. Garnish steak with parsley sprigs, if desired. Yield: 4 servings.

☐ *176 calories, 27.2 grams protein, 4.7 grams fat, 3.5 grams carbohydrate, 55 milligrams cholesterol, 199.5 milligrams sodium, and 15 milligrams calcium per 3 ounces steak with gravy plus 118 calories, 2.2 grams protein, 0.1 gram fat, 25.9 grams carbohydrate, 0 milligrams cholesterol, 1 milligram sodium, and 8 milligrams calcium per ½ cup rice.*
Kay Suber Vann,
Thomasville, Georgia.

CRUNCHY OVEN-FRIED CHICKEN

1 cup nutlike cereal nuggets
2 tablespoons chopped fresh parsley
½ teaspoon Creole seasoning
½ teaspoon poultry seasoning
¼ teaspoon lemon-pepper seasoning
4 (6-ounce) chicken breast halves, skinned
¼ cup plain lowfat yogurt
Vegetable cooking spray
Parsley sprigs (optional)

Combine cereal, chopped parsley, Creole seasoning, poultry seasoning, and lemon-pepper seasoning in a shallow dish. Brush chicken with yogurt, and roll in cereal mixture. Place chicken on a broiler pan coated with cooking spray. Bake, uncovered, at 400° for 45 minutes or until done. Garnish chicken with parsley sprigs, if desired. Yield: 4 servings.

☐ *260 calories, 30.2 grams protein, 4.3 grams fat, 24.5 grams carbohydrate, 73 milligrams cholesterol, 567 milligrams sodium, and 54 milligrams calcium per chicken breast half.*

PICKLED BEETS

1¼ pounds fresh beets
2 teaspoons mixed pickling spices
1 (3-inch) stick cinnamon, broken
½ cup cider vinegar
1 teaspoon sugar

Leave root and 1 inch of stem on beets; scrub well with vegetable brush. Place beets in a saucepan, and add water to cover. Bring to a boil; cover, reduce heat, and cook 35 to 40 minutes or until tender. Drain, reserving ½ cup liquid. Pour cold water over beets, and drain again. Let cool. Trim off beet stems and roots, and rub off skins. Slice beets, and reserve 2 cups. Place beets in a shallow 1-quart dish; set aside.
Tie spices in a cheesecloth bag. Combine spice bag, reserved cooking liquid, vinegar, and sugar in a small saucepan; bring to a boil. Pour over beets. Cover and chill 8 hours. Use a slotted spoon to serve. Yield: 4 servings.

☐ *48 calories, 1 gram protein, 0 grams fat, 11.5 grams carbohydrate, 0 milligrams cholesterol, 49.3 milligrams sodium, and 11.3 milligrams calcium per ½-cup serving.*

SQUASH CASSEROLE

1 pound yellow squash, sliced
⅓ cup chopped onion
3 tablespoons chopped green pepper
1 (2-ounce) jar diced pimiento, drained
⅓ cup (1.3 ounces) shredded 40% less-fat Cheddar cheese
1 egg, beaten
¼ teaspoon salt
⅛ teaspoon pepper
Vegetable cooking spray
1½ tablespoons dry breadcrumbs
1 tablespoon chopped fresh parsley
Dash of paprika

Place squash and onion in a vegetable steamer over boiling water; cover and steam 12 to 15 minutes or until crisp-tender. Combine squash mixture, green pepper, pimiento, cheese, egg, salt, and pepper; stir gently. Spoon into a 1-quart baking dish coated with cooking spray.
Combine breadcrumbs, parsley, and paprika; stir well. Sprinkle over squash mixture; bake at 350° for 25 to 30 minutes or until thoroughly heated. Yield: 5 servings.

☐ *72 calories, 4.7 grams protein, 3 grams fat, 7.3 grams carbohydrate, 62.3 milligrams cholesterol, 195.4 milligrams sodium, and 94.2 milligrams calcium per ½-cup serving.*

GREEN BEANS
WITH NEW POTATOES

1½ pounds fresh green beans
6 small new potatoes (about 12 ounces)
1 cup water
1 teaspoon beef-flavored bouillon granules
¾ teaspoon dried whole summer savory
Dash of ground nutmeg
Dash of pepper

Wash beans; trim ends, and remove strings. Cut beans into 1½-inch pieces. Combine beans and remaining ingredients in a Dutch oven. Bring to a boil; cover, reduce heat, and simmer 25 minutes or until beans are crisp-tender and potatoes are done. Yield: 6 servings.

□ *78 calories, 3.3 grams protein, 0.3 gram fat, 17.4 grams carbohydrate, 0 milligrams cholesterol, 124 milligrams sodium, and 46 milligrams calcium per ½ cup beans and 1 potato.*

TOMATOES AND OKRA

Vegetable cooking spray
1 teaspoon vegetable oil
1 cup chopped onion
¾ cup chopped green pepper
3 medium tomatoes, peeled and quartered
2 cups sliced fresh okra
¼ teaspoon salt
¼ teaspoon pepper

Coat a large skillet with cooking spray; add oil, and sauté onion and green pepper until tender. Add remaining ingredients; cover and cook 5 minutes, stirring occasionally. Yield: 7 servings.

□ *53 calories, 1.5 grams protein, 2.3 grams fat, 7.5 grams carbohydrate, 0 milligrams cholesterol, 92 milligrams sodium, and 35 milligrams calcium per ½-cup serving.*   Mrs. W. H. Kolter,
Houston, Texas.

DIETER'S CORNBREAD

1½ cups stone-ground yellow cornmeal
½ cup all-purpose flour
1 teaspoon baking powder
1 teaspoon baking soda
1 egg, beaten
2 cups cultured nonfat buttermilk
Vegetable cooking spray

Combine cornmeal, flour, baking powder, and soda in a medium bowl,
and stir well. Add beaten egg and buttermilk; stir until smooth.

Pour batter into a 9-inch square pan coated with cooking spray. Bake at 400° for 35 minutes or until cornbread is golden. Yield: 9 servings.

□ *120 calories, 5 grams protein, 2 grams fat, 19.6 grams carbohydrate, 33 milligrams cholesterol, 199 milligrams sodium, and 114 milligrams calcium per 3-inch square.*

NEW-FASHIONED
BLACKBERRY COBBLER
(pictured on page 170)

2 tablespoons cornstarch
½ cup unsweetened orange juice, divided
8 cups fresh blackberries
⅔ cup sugar
¼ teaspoon ground cinnamon
¼ teaspoon ground nutmeg
¼ teaspoon ground cloves
Vegetable cooking spray
1 cup all-purpose flour
¼ teaspoon salt
2 tablespoons plus 2 teaspoons vegetable oil
2 to 3 tablespoons cold water

Combine cornstarch and ¼ cup orange juice; set aside.

Combine remaining ¼ cup orange juice, blackberries, sugar, cinnamon, nutmeg, and cloves in a heavy saucepan; stir well. Bring to a boil; reduce heat, and simmer 8 minutes, stirring occasionally. Stir in cornstarch mixture. Return to a boil, and cook 1 minute, stirring constantly, until mixture is thickened and bubbly. Remove from heat; pour into a 10- x 6- x 2-inch baking dish coated with cooking spray, and set aside.

Combine flour and salt in a small bowl; stir well. Combine oil and water in a small bowl; stir well. Pour oil mixture into flour mixture; stir with a fork until dry ingredients are moistened. Shape into a ball; cover and chill.

Roll dough to ⅛-inch thickness on a lightly floured surface. Cut into ½-inch strips; arrange over blackberry mixture in a lattice fashion. Bake at 425° for 30 to 35 minutes. Yield: 8 servings.

□ *203 calories, 1.9 grams protein, 3 grams fat, 44.3 grams carbohydrate, 0 milligrams cholesterol, 37.3 milligrams sodium, and 50.4 milligrams calcium per ½-cup serving.*

SPICED PEACHES
WITH NUTTY DUMPLINGS
(pictured on page 170)

½ cup all-purpose flour
1 teaspoon baking powder
¼ teaspoon salt
¼ cup sugar, divided
2 tablespoons chopped pecans, toasted
¼ cup skim milk
⅛ teaspoon butter flavoring
2 cups sliced fresh peaches (about 1½ pounds)
⅔ cup unsweetened white grape juice
¼ teaspoon apple pie spice

Combine flour, baking powder, salt, 2 tablespoons sugar, and pecans; stir well. Stir in milk and butter flavoring; set mixture aside.

Combine peaches, grape juice, remaining 2 tablespoons sugar, and apple pie spice in a saucepan; stir well. Bring to a boil. Drop one-fourth of batter at a time into boiling peach mixture.

Cover and cook over medium heat 10 to 12 minutes or until dumplings are done. Yield: 4 servings.

□ *193 calories, 3 grams protein, 2.8 grams fat, 40.4 grams carbohydrate, 0 milligrams cholesterol, 254 milligrams sodium, and 89 milligrams calcium per ½ cup peaches and 1 dumpling.*

MICROWAVE COOKERY

Dessert Is Easy
With Fruit Sauces

These fruit sauces can turn a scoop of ice cream or a slice of pound cake into a sumptuous dessert in just a few minutes. When you use a microwave oven to cook the fruit, it will have a firmer texture and brighter color than if it were cooked conventionally.

For some sauces, fruit is stirred in after the sauce base is cooked, preserving the fresh flavor. We've used fresh fruit for these recipes, but you can substitute frozen if fresh is not in season.

When fruit is at its peak of sweetness, it's best to keep the sauce flavors simple to allow the natural fruit taste to be most prominent. However, the addition of nuts, raisins, or liqueurs enhances the flavor rather than overpowers it. Apple Dessert Sauce is simply seasoned with cinnamon, but you may want to stir in some raisins or toasted pecans.

APPLE DESSERT SAUCE

¾ cup chopped apple
1 tablespoon water
1 cup firmly packed brown sugar
1 cup commercial sour cream
¼ teaspoon ground cinnamon

Combine apple and water in a 3-cup glass bowl. Cover and microwave at HIGH for 1 minute. Add remaining ingredients, stirring well. Microwave at MEDIUM (50% power) 1 to 2 minutes or until brown sugar melts, stirring once. Serve warm over ice cream or cake. Yield: 1¾ cups.

PEACH-BERRY SAUCE

2 tablespoons sugar
1½ tablespoons cornstarch
2 fresh peaches, peeled and sliced
½ cup red currant jelly
½ cup fresh blueberries
½ cup fresh raspberries

Combine sugar and cornstarch in a 1½-quart casserole. Add peach slices and jelly. Microwave at HIGH for 4 to 5 minutes, stirring every minute, until mixture is thickened and bubbly. Stir in berries. Serve warm over pound cake or ice cream. Yield: 2⅔ cups.

Our Peach-Berry Sauce features peach slices, raspberries, and blueberries for an easy summer dessert. You may substitute other berries, if you wish.

CHOCOLATE CHERRY SAUCE

¼ cup butter or margarine
1½ cups firmly packed brown sugar
¼ cup cocoa
3 tablespoons all-purpose flour
¾ cup light corn syrup
1 (5-ounce) can evaporated milk
¾ cup pitted fresh cherries, halved
2 tablespoons kirsch or other
  cherry-flavored liqueur

Place butter in a 3-cup glass bowl. Microwave at HIGH for 55 seconds or until melted. Combine sugar, cocoa, and flour; mix well. Add to butter, stirring well. Stir in corn syrup and milk. Microwave at HIGH for 2 to 3 minutes, stirring once or until mixture is hot and sugar dissolves. Stir in cherries and kirsch. Serve warm over ice cream or cake. Yield: 2½ cups.

Tip: For a great dessert, pour cream sherry over chilled grapefruit.

AMARETTO-STRAWBERRY SAUCE

½ cup slivered almonds, chopped
¼ cup butter or margarine, divided
⅔ cup firmly packed brown sugar
¼ cup half-and-half
2 tablespoons light corn syrup
2 tablespoons amaretto
¾ cup sliced fresh strawberries

Combine almonds and 2 tablespoons butter in a glass pieplate. Microwave at HIGH for 3 to 3½ minutes or until lightly toasted, stirring once. Set aside.
Combine sugar, half-and-half, corn syrup, and remaining 2 tablespoons butter in a 1-quart glass bowl. Microwave at HIGH for 2 minutes; stir. Microwave at HIGH for 1 to 2 minutes or until mixture comes to a boil; cool. Stir in amaretto, toasted almonds, and sliced strawberries. Serve sauce over ice cream. Yield: 1⅔ cups.

LEMON DESSERT SAUCE

½ cup sugar
1½ tablespoons cornstarch
⅛ teaspoon salt
1 cup water
1½ teaspoons grated lemon rind
⅓ cup lemon juice
1 tablespoon butter or margarine

Combine sugar, cornstarch, and salt in a 4-cup glass measure; add water, and stir until sugar dissolves.
Microwave at HIGH for 2 minutes; stir well. Microwave at HIGH for 1½ to 2 minutes, stirring at 1-minute intervals until mixture is clear, thickened, and bubbly. Stir in lemon rind, lemon juice, and butter. Chill, if desired. Serve with fresh fruit, pound cake, or ice cream. Yield: 1½ cups.
Note: Lime rind and juice may be substituted for lemon rind and juice, if desired.

Add Eggplant To The Menu

Eggplant has been incorporated into the cuisines of regions all over the globe, and the South is no exception. Southerners love crispy fried foods, so our recipe for Fried Parmesan Eggplant fits in with tradition. Cut like French fries, these tasty morsels can be served just as you would serve the look-alike potato version.

Because of the delicately flavored flesh, eggplant ideally combines with a variety of seasonings or other food flavors. A regional favorite in Greece is moussaka, using lamb, eggplant, and a spicy tomato sauce. Ground lamb is available in markets today, but ground beef is a good substitute, if you prefer.

Caponata, another eggplant specialty with European roots, is traditionally a sweet-sour mixture of eggplant, capers, olives, and tomato sauce. The Italians serve it chilled as an appetizer.

Several varieties of eggplant are popping up at produce markets these days, but the bulbous purple version is still the most common. For the best flavor, select long, thin eggplants with glossy skins. The smaller ones are generally sweeter. Because the flesh darkens when exposed to air, you'll want to cut the eggplant just before cooking.

MOUSSAKA

1 large eggplant
Salt
Olive oil
1¼ pounds ground lamb or beef
2 medium onions, chopped
2 cloves garlic, minced
1 teaspoon salt
½ teaspoon dried whole thyme
½ teaspoon dried whole oregano
1 teaspoon dried whole basil
¼ teaspoon ground nutmeg
2½ tablespoons chopped fresh
   parsley
1 cup canned tomatoes, drained
½ cup dry vermouth
2 egg whites
½ cup fine breadcrumbs, divided
White sauce (recipe follows)
¼ cup (1 ounce) grated Parmesan
   cheese

Peel eggplant, and cut into ½-inch-thick slices. Sprinkle both sides of slices with salt; allow to sit 30 minutes. Rinse and pat dry. Arrange eggplant slices on a baking sheet; brush with olive oil, and broil 3 to 5 minutes or until lightly browned. Turn eggplant slices, and repeat procedure. Set aside.

Brown meat, onion, and garlic in a large skillet. Drain off pan drippings; stir in seasonings, tomatoes, and vermouth. Cover, reduce heat, and simmer 30 minutes, stirring occasionally. Remove from heat; cool.

Add unbeaten egg whites and ¼ cup breadcrumbs to meat mixture, stirring until blended.

Sprinkle remaining ¼ cup breadcrumbs in a greased 12- x 8- x 2-inch baking dish. Top with eggplant; cover with meat mixture. Top with white sauce. Bake at 350° for 40 minutes. Top with Parmesan cheese, and bake an additional 5 minutes. Yield: 6 servings.

White Sauce:

3 tablespoons butter or margarine
3 tablespoons all-purpose flour
1½ cups milk
2 egg yolks
½ teaspoon salt

Melt butter in a heavy saucepan over low heat; add flour, stirring until smooth. Cook 1 minute, stirring constantly. Gradually add milk; cook over medium heat, stirring constantly, until mixture is thickened and bubbly.

Beat egg yolks until thick and lemon colored. Gradually stir about one-fourth of hot mixture into yolks; add to remaining hot mixture, stirring constantly. Stir in salt. Yield: about 2 cups.

Jenny Heinzmann,
Lothian, Maryland.

FRIED PARMESAN EGGPLANT

1 (1-pound) eggplant
1 teaspoon salt
¾ cup cornmeal
¼ teaspoon white pepper
⅛ teaspoon garlic powder
Vegetable oil
¼ cup grated Parmesan cheese

Peel eggplant, and cut into 2- x ¾-inch strips; sprinkle with salt, and let stand 30 minutes. Pat dry.

Combine cornmeal, pepper, and garlic powder. Dredge eggplant in cornmeal mixture, and fry in deep, hot oil (375°) until golden brown, cooking only a few at a time. Sprinkle with Parmesan cheese. Yield: 4 to 6 servings.

Marie B. Curry,
Chunchula, Alabama.

CAPONATA

1 eggplant, unpeeled and diced
1 medium onion, coarsely chopped
1 medium-size green pepper, chopped
½ cup chopped celery
2 cloves garlic, minced
¼ cup olive oil
1 (8-ounce) can tomato sauce
1 (6-ounce) can tomato paste
¾ cup pitted ripe olives, sliced
½ cup salad olives, chopped
2½ tablespoons sugar
2½ tablespoons vinegar
Dash of hot sauce
⅛ teaspoon dried whole oregano
Salt and pepper to taste

Sauté eggplant, onion, green pepper, celery, and garlic in oil in a large skillet. Add tomato sauce, tomato paste, ripe olives, salad olives, sugar, and vinegar; cover, reduce heat, and simmer 30 minutes, stirring frequently. Stir in hot sauce, oregano, and salt and pepper; chill 24 hours. Serve with crackers. Yield: 4½ cups.

Anne Trapp,
Bay City, Texas.

POTATO-EGGPLANT CASSEROLE

1 medium eggplant (about 1¼ pounds),
   peeled and sliced
2 large potatoes, peeled and sliced
1 large onion, sliced
1 green pepper, cut into rings
½ teaspoon garlic powder
½ teaspoon Italian seasoning
¾ teaspoon salt
¼ teaspoon pepper
1 (10¾-ounce) can cream of chicken soup,
   undiluted
⅔ cup milk
2 tablespoons grated Parmesan cheese
¼ cup fine dry breadcrumbs
2 tablespoons butter or margarine, melted

Divide vegetables in half. Layer half each of eggplant, potatoes, onion, and green pepper in a lightly greased 13- x 9- x 2-inch baking dish. Repeat layers with remaining vegetables.

Combine garlic powder, Italian seasoning, salt, and pepper; sprinkle over vegetables. Combine soup and milk; pour over vegetables. Sprinkle cheese over soup mixture. Combine breadcrumbs and butter; sprinkle over casserole. Cover and bake at 425° for 45 minutes; uncover and bake an additional 15 minutes. Yield: 8 servings.

Chris Blanton,
Madison, Tennessee.

Dinner's Ready In Less Than An Hour

When time is at a premium, try one of our less-than-an-hour dinner menus. The quick, practical recipes use ingredients you're likely to have on hand or can find easily at the grocery store.

We asked the home economists in our test kitchens to prepare each menu with a plan to make preparation smooth and easy. You can follow it, if you like, or you may want to substitute your own time-saving ideas.

Here are a few tips to make your meal preparation easier.

—Use a food processor to chop onions and green peppers. Shred cheese in the processor, and refrigerate it in an airtight container. Sliced tomatoes and carrots will keep refrigerated up to a week in an airtight plastic bag.

—Substitute dried herbs in the same way you would fresh.

—Rely on such convenience products as canned soups, dried soup mixes, or prepared desserts.

Saucy Chicken Breasts
Easy Zucchini
Parslied Rice
Tomato Slices With Lemon Dressing
Fresh Peach Sauce
Commercial pound cake

Plan: Prepare tomatoes and dressing. While tomatoes are marinating, begin chicken, and cook rice. Fix zucchini, and make peach sauce. Serve dinner when chicken is done.

SAUCY CHICKEN BREASTS

2 tablespoons butter or margarine
4 chicken breast halves, skinned
½ cup chopped onion
½ cup chopped green pepper
1 cup sliced mushrooms
1 (1.3-ounce) package golden onion soup mix or (1.25-ounce) package onion soup mix
1¼ cups water
¼ cup white wine Worcestershire sauce
1 tablespoon cornstarch
3 tablespoons water

Melt the butter in a large skillet. Add chicken, and brown on both sides. Remove chicken from skillet, reserving drippings in skillet. Add chopped onion, green pepper, and mushrooms to skillet; sauté until crisp-tender.

Return chicken to skillet. Combine soup mix, 1¼ cups water, and Worcestershire sauce in a small bowl. Pour over chicken. Cover, reduce heat, and simmer 20 minutes or until chicken is tender. Remove chicken to a serving platter. Combine cornstarch and 3 tablespoons water; add to sauce. Return to boil; boil 1 minute. Serve sauce over chicken. Yield: 4 servings.

Harriett Ransbottom,
Richmond, Texas.

EASY ZUCCHINI

2 medium zucchini
2 tablespoons butter or margarine, melted
1 tablespoon lemon juice
2 tablespoons grated Parmesan cheese

Cut zucchini in half crosswise; cut each piece into 6 sticks. Place zucchini in steaming rack. Place rack over boiling water; cover and steam 3 to 5 minutes or until crisp-tender.

Transfer zucchini to serving dish. Combine butter and lemon juice; pour over zucchini, and toss gently. Sprinkle with cheese. Yield: 4 servings.

PARSLIED RICE

2½ cups water
¼ teaspoon salt
1 teaspoon dried parsley flakes
2 tablespoons butter or margarine
1 cup uncooked long-grain rice

Combine water, salt, parsley, and butter in a medium saucepan; bring to a boil. Add rice, stirring well; cover, reduce heat, and simmer 20 minutes or until tender. Yield: 4 servings.

TOMATO SLICES WITH LEMON DRESSING

2 medium tomatoes, sliced
2 tablespoons lemon juice
⅓ cup vegetable oil
½ teaspoon seasoned salt
½ teaspoon sugar
½ teaspoon pepper
1 teaspoon fresh minced parsley

Arrange tomato slices in a shallow container. Combine remaining ingredients; mix well, and pour over tomatoes. Cover and marinate in refrigerator 45 minutes. Yield: 4 servings.

Clota Engleman,
Spur, Texas.

FRESH PEACH SAUCE

3 tablespoons sugar
2 teaspoons cornstarch
½ cup water
Pinch of ground nutmeg
2 large peaches, pared and sliced
¼ teaspoon almond extract

Combine sugar, cornstarch, water, and nutmeg in a small saucepan, stirring until smooth. Add peaches, and cook over medium heat, stirring constantly, until mixture boils. Boil 1 minute; remove from heat. Stir in almond extract. Serve warm over pound cake. Yield: 1⅓ cups.

Jean Hamilton,
Bolivar, Tennessee.

Spaghetti Carbonara
Nutty Green Salad
Easy Bread
Fudge Pie

Plan: Cook spaghetti; assemble salad ingredients. Brush seasonings on bread, and set aside. Make pie; toss salad. Finish carbonara, and broil bread.

SPAGHETTI CARBONARA

1 (8-ounce) package spaghetti
8 slices bacon, cut into 1-inch pieces
¼ cup butter or margarine
⅔ cup chopped green onions
1 (4-ounce) can sliced mushrooms, drained
3 egg yolks, beaten
1 cup (4 ounces) shredded Cheddar cheese
Dash of pepper

Cook spaghetti according to package directions; drain and set aside.

Cook bacon in skillet until crisp; drain and set aside. Add butter to skillet; sauté green onions and mushrooms over low heat 2 minutes. Add spaghetti, bacon, egg yolks, cheese, and pepper, tossing gently. Serve immediately. Yield: 4 servings.

Judy K. Sailer,
McAllen, Texas.

NUTTY GREEN SALAD

6 cups torn, mixed salad greens
1 medium zucchini, sliced
1 medium carrot, scraped and sliced
½ cup peanuts
⅓ cup commercial Italian salad dressing

Combine greens, zucchini, carrot, and peanuts; toss. Pour dressing over salad; toss. Yield: 4 servings.

EASY BREAD

¼ cup butter or margarine, melted
½ teaspoon parsley flakes
⅛ teaspoon garlic powder
2 (3-ounce) French rolls, cut in half horizontally
2 tablespoons grated Parmesan cheese
½ teaspoon poppy seeds

Combine butter, parsley, and garlic powder, stirring well. Brush on rolls. Sprinkle with Parmesan cheese and poppy seeds. Place bread on baking sheet, and broil until golden. Cut bread halves into 2 pieces. Yield: 4 servings.
Lynne Teal Weeks,
Columbus, Georgia.

FUDGE PIE

½ cup butter or margarine
1 (1-ounce) square unsweetened chocolate
2 eggs, beaten
1 cup sugar
1 teaspoon vanilla extract
½ cup all-purpose flour
Vanilla ice cream
Commercial fudge sauce (optional)

Combine butter and chocolate in a small saucepan; cook over low heat until melted. Set aside.

Combine eggs, sugar, and vanilla in a medium bowl, stirring well. Stir in chocolate mixture. Add flour; stir until blended.

Pour mixture into a greased 9-inch piepan. Bake at 325° for 25 minutes or until pie tests done (do not overbake). Serve with ice cream and fudge sauce, if desired. Yield: one 9-inch pie.
Anna Robinson,
Oak Ridge, Tennessee.

Tip: When melted, semisweet chocolate morsels and semisweet chocolate squares can be used interchangeably.

Treats From The Freezer

Time's running short, and the gang is coming over. What to fix? Hosting a crowd is easy when you can pull these tasty snacks from the freezer.

Pecan-Cheese Crispies are appropriate for casual gatherings or fancy parties. If you crave the taste of pizza, try our Pizza Squares. A new convenience crust is baked into squares and then served with commercial pizza sauce.

Fruit Pops are especially designed for kids. Children can have as much fun making them as they do eating them.

PIZZA SQUARES

1 (10-ounce) can refrigerated pizza dough
2 tablespoons butter or margarine, melted
2 tablespoons grated Parmesan cheese
1 tablespoon Italian seasoning
Commercial pizza sauce

Unroll pizza dough to a 12- x 9-inch rectangle on a lightly greased baking sheet. Brush with butter; sprinkle Parmesan cheese and Italian seasoning evenly over dough.

Cut dough into 2-inch squares with a pizza cutter. Bake squares at 425° for 15 minutes. Let squares cool on a wire rack. Heat pizza sauce. To serve, dip squares in pizza sauce.

To freeze, decrease baking time to 10 minutes. Let squares cool on a wire rack. Transfer squares to an airtight container, and freeze. To serve, place frozen squares on baking sheet, and heat at 425° for 5 minutes. Yield: 2 dozen.
Margaret Scott,
Marshall, North Carolina.

FRUIT POPS

2 cups sugar
3 cups water
1 (12-ounce) can frozen orange juice concentrate, undiluted
1 (15¼-ounce) can crushed pineapple, undrained
¼ cup lemon juice
6 bananas, thinly sliced

Combine sugar and water in a saucepan; boil 5 minutes, and remove from heat. Add orange juice concentrate, and stir until melted; cool. Add remaining

ingredients to orange juice mixture, mixing well. Pour mixture into 25 (3-ounce) or 15 (5-ounce) paper cups.

Partially freeze; insert a wooden stick into center of each cup, and freeze. To serve, let pops stand at room temperature 5 minutes; tear off cups. Yield: 15 or 25 servings.
Dorothy Burgess,
Huntsville, Texas.

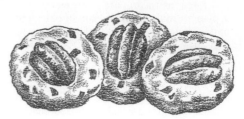

PECAN-CHEESE CRISPIES

2 cups (8 ounces) shredded sharp Cheddar cheese
1 cup butter or margarine, softened
¼ teaspoon hot sauce
½ teaspoon dry mustard
1 cup all-purpose flour
1 cup self-rising flour
2 cups crispy rice cereal
Pecan halves

Combine cheese and butter in a large mixing bowl; beat at medium speed of an electric mixer until blended. Add hot sauce and mustard; gradually add flours, mixing until blended. Stir in cereal. Shape dough into 1-inch balls; place on ungreased baking sheets, and flatten with a fork, making a crisscross design. Press a pecan half in the center of each cookie. Bake at 350° for 12 to 14 minutes; cool.

To freeze, let wafers cool completely on wire rack. Transfer to airtight container, and freeze. To serve, thaw wafers at room temperature for 1 hour. Yield: 5 dozen.
Melanie Smith,
Molena, Georgia.

Right: *Melons add refreshing flavor and vibrant color to a menu that includes Swirled Melon Soup and Minted Melon Balls (recipes, page 162).*

Page 170: *Desserts lower in calories? You bet! You can enjoy Spiced Peaches With Nutty Dumplings for only 193 calories per serving, or try New-Fashioned Blackberry Cobbler with only 203 calories per serving (recipes, page 164).*

It's Better With Fresh Basil

The clovelike flavor of basil works magic on food, especially summer vegetables, salads, and pasta. The recipes we offer here are a tasty incentive to plant your own herbs or search the local market for fresh ones. They have intense and distinctive flavors.

BASIL CHICKEN

½ cup dry white wine
¼ cup olive oil
¼ cup chopped fresh basil
2 cloves garlic, minced
Dash of hot sauce
4 chicken breast halves, skinned and boned

Combine wine, oil, basil, garlic, and hot sauce in an 8-inch square dish. Add chicken; cover and marinate in refrigerator for 8 hours, turning occasionally.

Drain and reserve marinade. Let chicken stand at room temperature 30 minutes before baking. Bake at 350° for 10 minutes; then turn chicken. Brush with reserved marinade, and bake an additional 10 minutes.

Note: Chicken may be grilled 5 inches from hot coals for 5 minutes. Turn chicken; brush with reserved marinade, and grill an additional 5 minutes. Yield: 4 servings. *Beth Hawes Watson, Dallas, Texas.*

HERBED POTATO SALAD

1 tablespoon chopped fresh basil
1½ teaspoons chopped fresh marjoram
1½ teaspoons chopped fresh savory
¾ cup mayonnaise
½ cup chopped onion
¼ cup cider vinegar
4 cups cubed cooked potatoes (about 2 pounds)
2 hard-cooked eggs, diced
1 teaspoon celery salt
½ teaspoon pepper

Combine basil, marjoram, savory, and mayonnaise in a small bowl; cover and refrigerate 2 hours.

Combine onion and vinegar; let stand 15 minutes. Drain.

Combine potatoes, eggs, celery salt, pepper, and onion; mix well. Add mayonnaise mixture; toss gently. Serve immediately or chill. Yield: 6 servings. *Ann Renfrow, Gadsden, Alabama.*

BASIL BUTTER

½ cup butter, softened
1 clove garlic, minced
¼ cup finely chopped fresh basil
2 tablespoons minced fresh parsley
1 teaspoon cracked black peppercorns

Combine all ingredients. Let stand at room temperature 1 hour. Store butter in refrigerator in an airtight container up to 1 week.

To freeze, chill mixture until slightly firm. Shape 1 tablespoon mixture into a ball. Repeat procedure with the remaining butter mixture.

Use to sauté vegetables, spread on bread, or season pasta and broiled or grilled chicken and fish. Yield: ½ cup plus 1 tablespoon. *Pam Lee, Gadsden, Alabama.*

FRESH TOMATO SAUCE

8 ripe tomatoes
2 cloves garlic, minced
¼ cup chopped fresh basil
½ cup sliced black olives
½ teaspoon salt
¼ teaspoon coarsely ground pepper
½ cup olive oil
1 (8-ounce) package vermicelli

Peel and seed tomatoes; cut into ½-inch strips. Combine tomatoes, garlic, basil, olives, salt, pepper, and oil in a large bowl; stir well. Cover and let stand at room temperature 2 hours.

Cook vermicelli according to package directions; drain well. Stir sauce; toss with cooked vermicelli. Serve at room temperature or chilled. Yield: 6 to 8 servings. *Barbara Carson, Hollywood, Florida.*

Cornbread Mix Offers Possibilities

The convenience of a mix is always appreciated by busy homemakers. And cornbread mix is one that offers a number of possibilities in addition to basic cornbread.

Although Cornbread-Sausage-Apple Pie may sound like a dessert, it's actually a breakfast or brunch main dish. Cooked sausage is stirred into the cornbread batter and baked. When the pie is done, apple pie filling is spread on top. Serve with scrambled eggs or cheese grits and a glass of orange juice for a complete morning meal.

Chile-Cheese Cornbread uses self-rising cornmeal mix. Cream-style corn, chopped green chiles, onion, and mayonnaise make the bread moist and delicious. And Cornbread Salad (recipe, next page) is a variation of layered salad. But instead of lettuce, cooked and crumbled cornbread is the base.

CORNBREAD-SAUSAGE-APPLE PIE

1 pound bulk pork sausage
1 tablespoon vegetable oil
1¾ cups cornbread mix
1 egg, beaten
1½ cups buttermilk
1 (21-ounce) can apple pie filling
1 tablespoon sugar
⅛ teaspoon ground cinnamon

Cook sausage over medium heat until browned, stirring to crumble; drain well, and set aside.

Place oil in a 10-inch cast-iron skillet; heat at 400° for 5 minutes or until very hot. Combine cornbread mix, egg, and buttermilk in a large mixing bowl; stir until smooth. Stir in sausage. Pour mixture into heated skillet; bake at 400° for 25 to 30 minutes.

Place pie filling, sugar, and cinnamon in a small saucepan; cook over low heat, stirring constantly, until thoroughly heated. Spread over cornbread. Serve hot. Yield: 8 servings. *Kay Castleman Cooper, Burke, Virginia.*

CHILE-CHEESE CORNBREAD

3 eggs, slightly beaten
1 (17-ounce) can cream-style corn
1 (4-ounce) can chopped green chiles, drained
½ cup mayonnaise
¾ cup diced onion
2 cups (8 ounces) shredded Cheddar cheese
2 cups buttermilk
3 cups self-rising cornmeal mix

Combine eggs, corn, chiles, mayonnaise, onion, cheese, and buttermilk in a large bowl; stir to blend. Add cornmeal mix, stirring just until moistened. Pour into a greased 13- x 9- x 2-inch pan. Bake at 375° for 40 to 45 minutes or until golden. Yield: 18 to 20 servings. *Glendora Waldrup, Euless, Texas.*

CORNBREAD SALAD

1 (8½-ounce) package cornbread mix
1 egg
⅓ cup milk
4 medium tomatoes, peeled and chopped
1 green pepper, chopped
1 medium onion, chopped
½ cup chopped sweet pickles
9 slices bacon, cooked and crumbled
1 cup mayonnaise
¼ cup sweet pickle juice

Combine cornbread mix, egg, and milk; stir well. Spoon cornbread mixture into a greased 8-inch square pan; bake at 400° for 15 to 20 minutes. Cool and crumble; set aside.

Combine tomatoes, green pepper, onion, pickles, and bacon; toss gently.

Combine mayonnaise and pickle juice; stir well, and set aside.

Layer half each of cornbread, tomato mixture, and mayonnaise mixture in a large glass bowl. Repeat layers. Cover and chill 2 hours. Yield: 8 servings.

Mrs. Roy L. Sweeney,
Louisville, Tennessee.

Feature Special Shrimp Creole, and serve with hot French bread and a tossed salad.

Shrimp, Wonderful Shrimp!

"Fresh Shrimp From the Coast." As soon as the words are seen on a sign, mouths begin to water. And with so many different ways to use the tasty seafood, it's no wonder. The recipes here offer plenty of variety.

SPECIAL SHRIMP CREOLE

1 medium onion, chopped
1 medium-size green pepper, chopped
½ cup sliced fresh mushrooms
2 to 3 cloves garlic, minced
2 tablespoons butter or margarine, melted
1 (16-ounce) can stewed tomatoes
1 (16-ounce) can tomato sauce
1 (6-ounce) can tomato paste
1½ teaspoons sugar
½ teaspoon Creole seasoning
⅛ teaspoon paprika
2 bay leaves
1½ pounds large fresh shrimp, peeled and deveined
½ cup frozen green peas
Hot cooked rice
Lemon slices (optional)
Parsley sprigs (optional)

Sauté onion, green pepper, mushrooms, and garlic in butter in a large skillet until tender. Stir in stewed tomatoes, tomato sauce, tomato paste, sugar, Creole seasoning, paprika, and bay leaves. Bring to a boil; reduce heat, and simmer, uncovered, 20 minutes. Add shrimp and peas; simmer an additional 10 to 12 minutes or until the shrimp are done, stirring occasionally. Discard bay leaves. Serve over rice; garnish with lemon slices and parsley, if desired. Yield: 6 servings.   *Marie B. Curry,*
Chunchula, Alabama.

FRIED SHRIMP WITH APRICOT SAUCE

1½ cups all-purpose flour
1 tablespoon paprika
1 teaspoon white pepper
½ teaspoon garlic powder
½ teaspoon Italian seasoning
1 (12-ounce) can beer
2 pounds medium-size fresh shrimp, peeled and deveined
Vegetable oil
Apricot sauce (recipe follows)

Combine flour, paprika, pepper, garlic powder, Italian seasoning, and beer in a medium bowl; stir until smooth. Set aside for 30 minutes.

Dip shrimp in batter, and fry in hot oil (375°) until golden. Serve with apricot sauce. Yield: 6 to 8 servings.

Apricot Sauce:

1 cup apricot preserves
1 (4-ounce) jar diced pimiento, drained
2½ tablespoons vinegar

Combine all ingredients in a saucepan. Bring to a boil over medium heat; reduce heat. Simmer 3 minutes. Cover; chill 2 hours. Yield: 1⅓ cups.

Barbara Carson,
Hollywood, Florida.

Tip: When buying seafood for two, use these amounts as a guideline: 1⅓ pounds of whole fish or ½ to ⅔ pound of fish fillets; ½ to 1 pound of shucked or shelled crab, lobsters, scallops, oysters, and shrimp.

ZESTY MARINATED SHRIMP

6 cups water
2 pounds medium-size fresh shrimp, unpeeled
1 lemon, thinly sliced
1 medium onion, thinly sliced
½ cup sliced ripe olives
1 (2-ounce) jar diced pimiento, drained
1 cup lemon juice
½ cup vegetable oil
2 tablespoons white wine vinegar
½ teaspoon salt
1 teaspoon white pepper
¼ teaspoon red pepper
¼ teaspoon dry mustard
1 bay leaf
Lettuce leaves

Bring water to a boil; add shrimp, and cook 3 to 5 minutes. Drain well; rinse with cold water. Chill. Peel and devein shrimp. Combine shrimp, lemon, onion, olives, and pimiento; toss gently.

Combine lemon juice, oil, vinegar, salt, white pepper, red pepper, dry mustard, and bay leaf in a jar. Cover tightly, and shake vigorously. Pour over shrimp; toss gently. Cover and chill 8 hours, tossing occasionally. Discard bay leaf. Use a slotted spoon to place shrimp on individual salad plates lined with lettuce leaves. Yield: 6 to 8 appetizer servings.   *Kitty Cromer,*
Anderson, South Carolina.

GRILLED MARINATED SHRIMP

2 cloves garlic, minced
1 medium onion, diced
½ cup vegetable oil
¼ cup soy sauce
¼ cup lemon juice
2 tablespoons chopped crystallized ginger
2 pounds fresh jumbo shrimp, peeled and deveined

Combine all ingredients except shrimp in a shallow dish; stir well. Add shrimp, tossing gently to coat. Cover and chill 2 to 3 hours.

Remove shrimp from marinade, reserving marinade. Thread shrimp onto six 14-inch skewers. Grill over medium-hot coals 3 to 4 minutes on each side, basting frequently with reserved marinade. Yield: 6 servings.

Alberta Pinkston,
Corryton, Tennessee.

These Appetizers Are Really Hot

Cooks in Louisiana and Texas are known for fiery-flavored dishes that can reduce the strongest man to tears. And it's hot sauce (sometimes called pepper sauce) that is the culinary culprit.

Check the ingredient list on the hot sauce bottle to determine whether the contents will be mildly hot or very hot. If cayenne pepper is one of the ingredients, the sauce will be milder than some. But if Tabasco peppers are used to make the sauce, you can be assured that it will be more powerful. Tabasco peppers are the most potent of all chiles. In fact, the peppers actually got their name from the famous hot sauce that has been made from them on Avery Island, Louisiana, since the end of the Civil War. This sauce is a patented mixture of vinegar, spices, and red, green, and yellow peppers grown in the salty island soil.

HOT PIMIENTO CHEESE

1 pound process American cheese, shredded
¼ cup tomato sauce
1 tablespoon hot sauce
½ cup mayonnaise
¾ cup diced pimiento, drained

Combine cheese, tomato sauce, hot sauce, and mayonnaise; stir well. Fold in pimiento. Cover and chill thoroughly. Yield: 3⅓ cups.   *Louise Holmes,*
Winchester, Tennessee.

CHILE-CHEESE DIP

1 pound process cheese, cubed
1 (4-ounce) can chopped green chiles, well drained
¼ cup minced onion
1 medium tomato, peeled, chopped, and drained
¼ cup picante sauce

Place cheese in top of a double boiler; bring water to a boil. Reduce heat to low; cook until cheese melts. Add remaining ingredients; cook until mixture is hot, stirring often.

Serve dip hot with tortilla chips. Yield: 3 cups.   *Sandra Moore,*
Ralls, Texas.

SAUCY COCKTAIL SAUSAGES

1 cup catsup
1 tablespoon prepared mustard
1 tablespoon vinegar
1½ tablespoons light brown sugar
¼ teaspoon Worcestershire sauce
½ to 1 teaspoon hot sauce
¼ cup dry red wine
1 (16-ounce) package smoked cocktail sausages

Combine all ingredients except sausages in a large saucepan; stir well. Simmer 2 to 3 minutes, stirring constantly. Add cocktail sausages; cook until sausages are thoroughly heated. Transfer sausages and sauce to a chafing dish, and serve hot. Yield: 15 to 18 servings.   *Weita Coleman,*
Hopkins, South Carolina.

SHRIMP COCKTAIL

2 quarts water
3 pounds unpeeled fresh shrimp
¼ teaspoon grated lime rind
¼ cup lime juice
¼ cup dry white wine
⅓ cup catsup
1 to 2 teaspoons hot sauce
Salt and pepper to taste

Bring water to a boil; add shrimp, and cook 3 to 5 minutes. Drain well; rinse with cold water. Chill. Peel and devein shrimp. Chill.

Combine remaining ingredients; mix well. Chill.

Combine shrimp and sauce; serve immediately. Yield: 6 to 8 appetizer servings.   *Katherine Shoemaker,*
Pensacola, Florida.

SPICY BLOODY MARYS

1 (46-ounce) can vegetable juice cocktail
¼ cup lemon juice
¼ cup Worcestershire sauce
¼ cup beef broth
2 tablespoons sugar
½ teaspoon salt
¼ teaspoon pepper
¼ teaspoon hot sauce
2 cups vodka

Combine all ingredients except vodka; cover and refrigerate at least 8 hours. Add vodka, stirring well. Serve over ice. Yield: about 2 quarts.

Krista L. Harden,
Savannah, Georgia.

Cooking Smart Means Cooking Healthy

Nothing brings color and vibrance to a menu like bright, freshly cooked vegetables. Fortunately, the same techniques that ensure good color and appeal are often the cooking techniques that also save valuable nutrients.

Vitamin C, a water-soluble vitamin that often dissolves in cooking water, is the vitamin most often saved by modifying or improving your cooking methods.

To save vitamin C and keep vegetables looking their best, cook vegetables whole or with their skins on whenever possible and only until they are crisp-tender. A vegetable that is done will pass the fork test: A fork will easily go in and out.

As Southerners, many of us grew up on tender, almost mushy vegetables that had been cooked all day. What we probably didn't know was that almost 80% of a vegetable's vitamin C could be lost when cooked for prolonged periods of time in too much water. With this in mind, try **boiling** vegetables in just enough water to cover. First, bring the water to a boil, add the vegetables, and then bring the water back to a slow boil. Covering with a lid keeps the steam in and speeds up cooking time.

There are some instances where you'll want to leave the lid off or cook with a little extra water. These exceptions are largely with green vegetables and the sulfur-containing vegetables, such as cabbage and cauliflower. If green vegetables are covered, acids stay inside the saucepan and turn the green chlorophyll to an olive color. To compensate, leave the lid off the first 5 to 7 minutes of cooking, and cover at the end. The sulfur vegetables develop a strong flavor as they cook. Add extra water, and cook them uncovered, also. In order to save nutrients, keep the cooking time short.

Canned vegetables need the same attention as fresh ones. Drain the canning liquid into a saucepan, and bring to a boil. Add vegetables, and reduce heat. By the time the vegetables come to a slow boil, they'll be ready to serve. Home-canned vegetables should boil 15 minutes in order to kill any harmful bacteria that might have developed during processing.

Steaming is one of the smartest ways to cook vegetables because the cooking liquid never touches the food. Steamed broccoli retains up to 80% of its vitamin

To save valuable nutrients, boil vegetables in a small amount of water over moderate heat, covering with a lid.

Steaming is one of the best vegetable cooking methods because the water never touches the vegetables.

To bake, dot vegetables with butter; cover, and bake in a hot oven until vegetables are fork-tender.

Pressure cooking is appropriate for dense vegetables, such as potatoes.

Only a few tablespoons of water are needed to microwave yellow squash.

Stir-frying uses a small amount of oil and high heat to cook vegetables quickly.

C, while boiled broccoli only retains up to 33%. To steam vegetables, bring water to a boil, and place the steaming rack in a medium saucepan. Put vegetables in rack, and cover. Most vegetables will steam in 10 minutes or less. If you don't have a steaming rack, you can substitute a colander or strainer.

Stir-frying is yet another nutritionally sound cooking method because vegetables are cooked in minutes over high heat. It's okay to use the high heat when stir-frying because the vegetables cook so quickly. To stir-fry, cut the vegetables on the diagonal so that the greatest amount of surface area will be exposed to heat. Heat a small amount of oil in a wok or skillet, add the vegetables, and stir constantly. Butter or margarine will smoke at high temperatures, so use peanut or vegetable oil.

Frying is certainly a higher calorie method of cooking because the vegetables are cooked in about ¼ inch of oil. However, an egg-and-flour coating seals nutrients into the vegetables. Dip slices of zucchini and other vegetables into beaten egg and then flour. Place in hot oil, brown on both sides, and drain on a paper towel. Serve immediately. Try experimenting with different coatings and seasoning mixtures for flavor variety.

Baking is a healthy method because vegetables cook in their own juices. Simply dot the vegetables with butter, or brush with a small amount of salad dressing. Cover and bake until vegetables are fork-tender.

Pressure cooking is a simple but less frequently used method. A small amount of water is quickly changed to steam, and the resulting heat is what actually cooks the food. It's easy to overcook vegetables in a pressure saucepan, so you may want to use this

Frying adds more calories, but the egg-and-flour coating seals in nutrients.

method mostly with large quantities or with dense vegetables, such as potatoes or acorn squash. Always refer to the manufacturer's time charts and instructions when using a pressure cooker. Be sure the rubber ring is inserted in the lid and that the lid is placed securely on the saucepan. When the weight at the top jiggles, reduce heat, and allow food to cook for the amount of time instructed. Cool quickly by running cold water over the saucepan. After the pressure has decreased, you may remove the weight.

Microwaving opens up all kinds of possibilities for vegetable cookery. Add a few tablespoons of water to vegetables in a microwave-safe dish. Cover the dish with heavy-duty plastic wrap, and vent it at one corner. Microwave at HIGH for the length of time the instruction manual directs. To finish cooking, let the dish stand a few minutes after removing from the oven.

Chicken—Fried Crisp And Delicious

Of all the ways to fix chicken, frying is probably the most traditional. The crisp, brown crust conceals tender, moist meat inside when chicken is cooked quickly in hot oil.

When deep-frying chicken or other foods, we recommend using peanut or vegetable oil. The smoke point (degree at which the fat bursts into flames) is higher for these fats than others. Remember that you can reuse the oil for frying, but the smoke point is lowered with each use. Be sure to strain it before storing. Keep in mind, too, that oil should be discarded if it foams heavily when food is added to it.

DEEP-FRIED WALNUT CHICKEN

4 boneless chicken breast halves (about 1¼ pounds)
1 tablespoon sherry
1 teaspoon salt
⅛ teaspoon pepper
2 egg whites
¼ cup cornstarch
2 to 2½ cups finely chopped walnuts
Vegetable oil
Gingered Plum Sauce

Cut chicken into bite-size pieces; sprinkle with sherry, salt, and pepper. Set aside.

Beat egg whites (at room temperature) at high speed of an electric mixer until foamy. Gradually add cornstarch to egg whites, beating until stiff peaks form. Gently fold in chicken. Roll each chicken piece in chopped walnuts; fry in 2 inches hot oil (350°) until golden brown. Drain on paper towels. Serve chicken with Gingered Plum Sauce. Yield: about 3 dozen appetizers.

Gingered Plum Sauce:

1 cup plum jam
1 tablespoon catsup
2 teaspoons grated lemon rind
1 tablespoon lemon juice
2 teaspoons vinegar
½ teaspoon ground ginger
½ teaspoon anise seeds, crushed
¼ teaspoon dry mustard
¼ teaspoon ground cinnamon
⅛ teaspoon ground cloves
⅛ teaspoon hot sauce

Heat plum jam in a small saucepan over medium heat until melted. Stir in remaining ingredients. Bring mixture to a boil; cook 1 minute, stirring constantly. Yield: 1¼ cups.

Mrs. T. W. Elliott,
Alexandria, Virginia.

BUTTERMILK DRUMSTICKS

8 chicken drumsticks (about 1¾ pounds)
⅔ cup buttermilk
¾ cup all-purpose flour
1½ teaspoons salt
1 teaspoon onion powder
¼ teaspoon pepper
Vegetable oil

Place chicken in a 9-inch square baking dish. Pour buttermilk over chicken; cover and chill 1 to 2 hours, turning occasionally. Drain.

Combine flour, salt, onion powder, and pepper in a plastic bag. Add chicken; close bag securely, and shake to coat chicken.

Heat 1 inch of oil in a large skillet to 325°; add chicken, and cook about 10 minutes, turning once. Cover, reduce heat, and cook 20 minutes, turning occasionally. Remove cover; cook 3 minutes, turning once. Drain chicken on paper towels. Yield: 4 servings.

Kitty Cromer,
Anderson, South Carolina.

HOT BUFFALO WINGS

2½ pounds chicken wings
1 teaspoon salt
¼ teaspoon pepper
Vegetable oil
¼ cup hot sauce
¼ cup water
¼ cup butter or margarine
1 tablespoon cider vinegar

Cut chicken wings in half at joint; cut off tips of wings, and discard. Sprinkle chicken with salt and pepper. Heat 2 inches of oil in a large skillet to 350°. Add chicken, and fry 10 minutes, frying about 1 dozen at a time. Drain on paper towels. Arrange fried chicken wings in a 13- x 9- x 2-inch dish.

Combine hot sauce and remaining ingredients in a small saucepan; cook over low heat until butter melts. Pour over fried chicken wings. Bake, uncovered, at 350° for 10 to 15 minutes or until hot. Yield: 3 dozen appetizers.

Janet McIntire,
Marietta, Georgia.

MEXICAN FRIED CHICKEN

1 (3-pound) broiler-fryer, cut up
1 egg, beaten
1 cup buttermilk
⅓ cup all-purpose flour
⅓ cup cornmeal
1 (1¾-ounce) package chili seasoning mix
Vegetable oil

Place chicken in a shallow pan. Combine beaten egg and buttermilk, stirring well; pour mixture over chicken. Cover and chill for 30 minutes.

Combine flour, cornmeal, and chili seasoning mix in a plastic bag; shake to mix. Place 2 pieces of chicken in bag, and shake to coat. Repeat procedure with remaining chicken. Place chicken in a shallow dish; cover and refrigerate 30 minutes.

Heat 1 inch of oil in a large skillet to 325°; add chicken, and fry 20 to 30 minutes or until done, turning once. Drain on paper towels. Yield: 4 servings.

Dr. W. H. Pinkston,
Knoxville, Tennessee.

Tip: When grilling chicken, place bony or rib-cage side of chicken down next to heat first. The bones act as an insulator and keep chicken from browning too fast.

Try Hot Salads For A Change

If your menus have become routine, you might try fixing a hot salad. These salads use familiar ingredients, such as potatoes, canned green beans, vinegar, chicken, bacon, and turkey, in creative, tasty ways.

HOT TURKEY SALAD

2 cups chopped cooked turkey
2 cups chopped celery
½ cup mayonnaise
½ cup chopped almonds, toasted
2 teaspoons minced onion
½ cup (2 ounces) shredded Cheddar cheese
½ cup crushed potato chips

Combine turkey, celery, mayonnaise, almonds, and onion in a bowl; mix well. Spoon into a greased shallow 1-quart casserole. Cover and bake at 350° for 15 minutes. Sprinkle with cheese and potato chips; bake an additional 5 minutes. Yield: 4 servings. *Jenny Peebles, Miami Shores, Florida.*

BAKED CHICKEN SALAD

2 cups diced cooked chicken
2 cups chopped celery
½ cup sliced water chestnuts
¼ cup plus 2 tablespoons lemon juice
3 tablespoons diced pimiento, drained
2 hard-cooked eggs, chopped
1 (10¾-ounce) can cream of chicken soup, undiluted
½ cup mayonnaise
1 cup herb-seasoned stuffing mix
¼ cup butter or margarine, melted

Combine chicken, celery, water chestnuts, lemon juice, pimiento, eggs, soup, and mayonnaise in a bowl; mix well. Spoon chicken mixture into a lightly greased shallow 2-quart casserole.

Combine stuffing mix and butter; mix well. Sprinkle over casserole. Bake at 350° for 30 minutes. Yield: 6 servings.

Mrs. Nels E. Johnson,
McLean, Virginia.

HOT GREEN BEAN SALAD

2 (16-ounce) cans French-cut green beans, drained
½ cup sugar
½ cup vinegar
½ cup vegetable oil
1 medium purple onion, thinly sliced
½ cup water chestnuts, sliced
1 (4-ounce) jar sliced pimiento, drained
4 slices bacon, cooked and crumbled
Lettuce leaves

Place beans in a shallow dish. Combine sugar, vinegar, and oil, and pour over beans; cover and chill 1 hour.

Drain beans. Add onion, water chestnuts, and sliced pimiento; toss gently. Spoon into a lightly greased 2-quart casserole, and sprinkle bacon over top. Bake at 350° for 30 minutes. Serve hot over lettuce leaves. Yield: 6 servings.

Dorsella Utter,
Louisville, Kentucky.

HOT DUTCH POTATO SALAD

10 slices bacon (about ½ pound)
2 tablespoons all-purpose flour
2 tablespoons sugar
1 teaspoon dry mustard
⅔ cup vinegar
⅔ cup water
1 teaspoon salt
¼ teaspoon pepper
3 large potatoes, cooked, peeled, and sliced
½ cup chopped celery
⅓ cup chopped green onions

Cook bacon in a large skillet until crisp; remove bacon, reserving 2 tablespoons drippings in skillet. Crumble bacon, and set aside.

Combine flour, sugar, and dry mustard; mix well. Add to drippings, stirring until smooth. Cook 1 minute, stirring constantly. Gradually add vinegar and water; cook over medium heat, stirring constantly, until mixture is thickened and bubbly. Stir in salt and pepper; remove mixture from heat, and set aside.

Layer half each of the potatoes, celery, green onions, and crumbled bacon in a lightly greased 12- x 8- x 2-inch baking dish. Pour half the sauce over the bacon. Repeat layers with the remaining ingredients. Cover and bake at 350° for 20 minutes. Uncover and bake an additional 10 minutes. Yield: 8 servings.

Carol Barclay,
Portland, Texas.

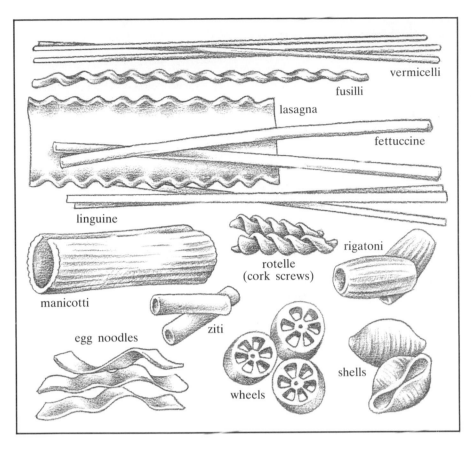

When cooked al dente, pasta can be reheated. To do this, drop cooked pasta in boiling water that has been removed from heat one to two minutes. To store cooked pasta, toss lightly with olive oil to prevent sticking together; cover and refrigerate until needed.

Uncooked pasta of similar sizes and shapes may be interchanged in recipes, but measure by weight and not by volume. When cooked, noodles swell slightly; spaghetti and macaroni double in size. Cooked pasta, however, can be substituted cup for cup. Allow 2 ounces of uncooked pasta and 1 to 1½ cups cooked pasta per person.

Measuring

Spaghetti that is uncooked is easily weighed but difficult to measure by cupfuls. If you don't have a scale, wrap a tape measure or marked piece of twine around a bundle:

4 ounces (3-inch bundle) = 2 to 2½ cups cooked

8 ounces (4½-inch bundle) = 4 to 5 cups cooked

12 ounces (5½-inch bundle) = 6½ to 7½ cups cooked

1 pound (6½-inch bundle) = 8 to 10 cups cooked

Elbow macaroni and other small shapes can be measured by cupfuls:

8 ounces elbow macaroni (2 cups) = 4½ cups cooked

8 ounces fine egg noodles (4 cups) = 4 cups cooked

8 ounces medium egg noodles (6 cups) = 4 cups cooked

Storing

Low-moisture content enables uncooked packaged pasta to have a long shelf life. Store pasta in a cool, dry place free from dust and moisture for up to one year; store egg noodles for up to six months.

Cooked pasta can be stored in the refrigerator up to four days or in the freezer up to one month. Keep in mind that you can refrigerate pasta dishes one to two days, or freeze them for up to six months.

Tips

—Add a small amount of vegetable oil to boiling water to reduce splashing and prevent sticking.

—Do not substitute Oriental-style noodles (cellophane or rice sticks) for noodles in pasta recipes.

—Cooking pasta in a microwave oven is not a time-saving practice, but it does eliminate having to use a large pan of boiling water.

From Our Kitchen To Yours

Intriguing in its variety of shapes, styles, and colors, pasta blends with many foods. From the Italian word for paste, this bland nourishment is generally a mixture of hard wheat flour and water. Taste-tempting pasta fare can be prepared light and delicate, rich and creamy, or hearty and robust, depending upon its accompanying food.

Basic Categories

Spaghetti, solid rods in various thicknesses, can be purchased round, oval, straight, or wavy. Vermicelli, fusilli, and capellini are favorite forms.

Noodles are flat, ribbonlike forms, sometimes curled on one or both edges and available in varying widths. Noodles contain eggs in addition to wheat flour and water. Lasagna, linguine, and fettuccine are classics.

Macaroni is cylindrical, hollow pasta that is available long or short, smooth or ridged, and curved or straight. Rigatoni, ziti, rotelle, manicotti, and elbows are some of the most popular ones listed in this category.

Specialty products include shells, pastina, bow ties, alphabets, fans, and wheels. The addition of special ingredients, such as spinach or tomato, gives color to some pasta.

Variety products, such as ravioli and tortellini that are filled with meat, cheese, or other ingredients, are also readily available.

Cooking

Cooking time varies with pasta's size, shape, and moisture content. Fresh pasta cooks in one to three minutes, while dried pasta requires four to fifteen minutes. Cook pasta until al dente (to the tooth); this means it's pliable but firm to the bite and no longer starchy.

Three quarts of rapidly boiling water for every 8 ounces of dried pasta provides enough water for individual pieces to float freely and cook evenly. To prevent the boil from subsiding, add pasta gradually in small amounts, and follow package directions for cooking times.

Drain pasta immediately, and transfer to a warmed serving bowl. No rinsing is necessary unless specifically stated in the recipe or unless preparing a cold pasta salad. Slightly undercook pasta that will be used as part of a recipe requiring further cooking.

Favorite Family Desserts

Family style is the only way to go with these basic, down-home desserts. Tailored to fit a busy schedule, each recipe uses tasty, easy-to-find ingredients in a variety of ways.

Peach-Caramel Cobbler is a quick variation on an old Southern favorite. This recipe uses canned fruit and commercial refrigerated rolls instead of pastry. It takes 15 minutes or less to prepare and about 20 minutes to bake. In a snap, you've got dessert for eight.

You won't want to miss Crunchy Ice Cream Treats. The crunch is found in a mixture of corn cereal, brown sugar, and peanut butter topped with fudge and vanilla ice cream. Let the children help with this treat—if they can get it into the freezer before eating it!

PEACH-CARAMEL COBBLER

1 (29-ounce) can sliced peaches
¼ cup all-purpose flour
¼ teaspoon salt
1 (11-ounce) package refrigerated
 caramel-Danish rolls with nuts
½ teaspoon grated lemon rind (optional)
¾ cup ginger ale
1 tablespoon butter or margarine

Drain peaches, reserving 1 cup syrup; set aside.

Combine flour, salt, commercial sugar-nut mixture from refrigerated rolls, and lemon rind, if desired, in a heavy saucepan. Stir in ginger ale and reserved peach syrup. Cook over medium heat, stirring constantly, until smooth and thickened. Stir in butter and peaches; bring to a boil. Pour hot peach mixture into a lightly greased 8-inch square baking dish. Separate caramel rolls, and arrange on top of mixture. Bake at 375° for 18 to 23 minutes or until rolls are golden brown. Yield: 8 servings.
Mrs. P. J. Davis,
Drexel, North Carolina.

APPLE-CRANBERRY CRUNCH

3 cups peeled diced apple
2 cups cranberries
½ cup sugar
¼ cup orange juice
¼ cup butter or margarine, melted
1 cup regular oats
½ cup firmly packed brown sugar
⅓ cup all-purpose flour
½ cup chopped pecans
Vanilla ice cream or whipped cream

Combine apple, cranberries, sugar, and orange juice; mix well. Spoon into a lightly greased 10- x 6- x 2-inch baking dish. Combine butter, oats, brown sugar, flour, and pecans; mix well. Spoon evenly over apple-cranberry mixture; bake, uncovered, at 350° for 40 to 45 minutes. Serve warm or cool with vanilla ice cream. Yield: 6 to 8 servings.
Lil Summerville,
Gastonia, North Carolina.

PLUM PUDDING-GELATIN MOLD

1 (3-ounce) package raspberry gelatin
1½ cups boiling water
½ cup golden raisins
¼ cup currants
½ teaspoon ground cinnamon
¼ teaspoon ground cloves
⅛ teaspoon ground ginger
⅛ teaspoon salt
1 (8-ounce) can crushed pineapple,
 drained
1 cup chopped pecans
¼ cup chopped mixed candied fruit
¼ cup chopped dates

Dissolve gelatin in boiling water; stir in raisins, currants, cinnamon, cloves, ginger, and salt. Chill until consistency of unbeaten egg white.

Fold remaining ingredients into gelatin mixture. Spoon into a lightly oiled 6-cup mold or 10 to 12 individual molds. Chill until firm. Unmold to serve. Yield: 10 to 12 servings.
Martha Short,
Jackson, Missouri.

CRUNCHY ICE CREAM TREATS

2¼ cups corn cereal squares, crushed
1 tablespoon butter or margarine
¼ cup crunchy peanut butter
1½ tablespoons brown sugar
1 quart vanilla ice cream, softened
¼ cup hot fudge topping or fruit
 preserves

Place crushed cereal in an 8-inch square pan; bake at 325° for 10 minutes or until toasted. Place 10 (5-ounce) paper cups in a 12-cup muffin pan for easy handling.

Combine crushed cereal, butter, peanut butter, and brown sugar; press 1 tablespoon mixture into the bottom and slightly up sides of each cup. Freeze 10 minutes. Spoon enough ice cream into cup to cover crumbs. Spoon a heaping teaspoon of fudge topping into each cup. Layer remaining ice cream into cups. Cover cups with one large piece of aluminum foil. Insert a popsicle stick into each cup through foil. Freeze 8 hours or until firm. Peel off cups to serve. Yield: 10 servings.
Helen H. Maurer,
Christmas, Florida.

CHOCO-MAPLE FROZEN DESSERT

1⅔ cups vanilla wafer crumbs
¼ cup butter or margarine, melted
½ cup butter or margarine, softened
1 cup sifted powdered sugar
3 eggs
3 (1-ounce) squares unsweetened chocolate,
 melted
¾ cup whipping cream
2 tablespoons maple syrup
1 cup miniature marshmallows
½ cup chopped pecans, divided

Combine vanilla wafer crumbs and ¼ cup melted butter. Press into a lightly greased 8-inch square dish.

Cream ½ cup butter and powdered sugar, beating well. Gradually add eggs and chocolate, beating well after each addition. Spread mixture evenly over crumbs; place in freezer.

Combine whipping cream and maple syrup; beat mixture until stiff peaks form. Fold in marshmallows and ¼ cup pecans. Spread evenly over chocolate layer. Sprinkle top with remaining ¼ cup pecans. Freeze 8 hours. Cut into squares to serve. Yield: 9 servings.
Daisy Cotton,
Karnes City, Texas.

Tip: Three tablespoons unsweetened cocoa powder plus 1 tablespoon shortening may be substituted for each 1-ounce square unsweetened chocolate called for in a recipe.

September

Picante Sauce Burns With Flavor

Picante sauce is a fiery red sauce that's bottled and sold internationally. Texans contend that the spicy blend, which resembles thick tomato sauce with crisp pieces of jalapeño and onion, tastes good on just about everything but ice cream.

Although picante sauce is of American origin, the ingredients are similar to those used in a familiar Tex-Mex version of pico de gallo, a fresh vegetable salsa served as you would serve picante sauce. In fact, this salsa is considered to be the homemade version of commercial picante sauce, even though the two differ in appearance and texture, according to Dr. Lou Rasplicka, president of the Texas Pepper Foundation. "Commercial picante sauce is traditionally made with crisp vegetables, has a rather thin sauce, and is cooked," Dr. Rasplicka explains. "The salsas tend to be soft vegetable bases with little sauce; they have more vegetable pieces."

Hilary Hylton Silva, one of our readers, came up with her own version of the fresh salsa, based on her extensive travels and study of Mexico. "I call it Salsa Cruda, which means 'raw sauce,' because that's actually what it is—a fresh, uncooked sauce," she says. Serrano chiles, which are hotter than jalapeños, are used in most fresh versions, along with lime and cilantro.

Hilary suggests using Salsa Cruda with any grilled food. "Another thing I use it for is avocado salad," she says. "Just take an avocado half, and serve the sauce in it. You'd want to be sure to leave the sauce kind of chunky for this. Or you may want to mix chunks of grilled fish or shrimp with it to serve in the avocado half."

For a homemade sauce more similar to the commercial kind, Hilary says she often purees leftover Salsa Cruda to use as a dip, a taco sauce, or a sauce base for ceviche (marinated raw fish) or huevos rancheros (a tortilla-and-egg dish), traditional Mexican favorites. If you don't use the puree right away, you can freeze it in ice-cube trays, remove it from the trays, and package for freezer storage.

While you can control the heat you put into the fresh sauce, this isn't the case with commercial sauces. If you've ever wondered why the "medium" picante sauce you just purchased is hotter than the last jar you bought, Dr. Rasplicka says it's because of the variable heat levels in jalapeños. If the sauce is too hot for your taste, the problem can be remedied. "I tell people to cut a few pieces of fresh tomato or fresh onion and add it to the sauce to make it milder," he says. To increase the heat of a sauce, just stir in a chopped jalapeño or serrano chile.

You'll find some traditional and creative ways to use picante sauce in the recipes that follow. The commercial sauce and the homemade version can be interchanged in each recipe.

SALSA CRUDA
(pictured on pages 204 and 205)

3 large ripe tomatoes, chopped
1 clove garlic, minced
4 sliced green onions
2 tablespoons diced purple onion
3 serrano or jalapeño chiles, diced
2 tablespoons minced fresh cilantro or fresh parsley
½ teaspoon salt
2 tablespoons lime juice

Combine all ingredients; stir well. Sauce may be served with grilled chicken or fish, or as a dip with tortilla chips. Yield: 4 cups.

Note: Sauce may be pureed in a food processor or blender and frozen up to 2 weeks. Drain if necessary.

Hilary Hylton Silva,
Austin, Texas.

FIESTA

1 pound ground beef
¼ cup chopped onion
1 (15-ounce) can ranch-style beans, undrained
1 (14½-ounce) can tomatoes, undrained and chopped
1 (8-ounce) can tomato sauce
1 (6-ounce) can tomato paste
½ cup water
1 teaspoon chili powder
¼ teaspoon garlic powder
1 (7-ounce) package instant rice
1 (8-ounce) package corn chips, crushed
1 cup (4 ounces) shredded Cheddar cheese
½ cup chopped onion
4 cups shredded iceberg lettuce
1 large tomato, chopped
½ cup chopped salad olives
½ cup chopped pecans
½ cup flaked coconut
1 (8-ounce) jar picante sauce

Cook ground beef and ¼ cup onion in a Dutch oven until browned, stirring to crumble beef. Drain well.

Combine ground beef mixture, beans, and next 6 ingredients. Bring mixture to a boil over medium heat; reduce heat, and simmer 1 hour.

Cook rice according to package directions; set aside.

Spread a layer of corn chips on each serving plate. Top with rice and meat mixture, and serve with cheese, onion, lettuce, chopped tomato, olives, chopped pecans, and coconut as condiments. Serve with picante sauce. Yield: 4 to 6 servings. *Mary Bell Williams, Goldthwaite, Texas.*

GARLIC-GRILLED CHICKEN
(pictured on pages 204 and 205)

4 chicken breast halves, skinned and boned
1 cup picante sauce
2 tablespoons vegetable oil
1 tablespoon lime juice
2 cloves garlic, minced
½ teaspoon ground cumin
½ teaspoon dried whole oregano, crushed
¼ teaspoon salt
Additional picante sauce

Place each chicken breast between 2 pieces of plastic wrap. Flatten chicken to ¼-inch thickness, using a meat mallet or rolling pin; cut into 1-inch-wide strips. Place in a shallow container.

Combine next 7 ingredients, mixing well. Pour over chicken; cover and chill 1 to 2 hours.

Thread chicken onto skewers; cook over hot coals 6 to 8 minutes or until done, turning occasionally and basting with remaining marinade. Serve with picante sauce. Yield: 4 servings.

MIGAS
(pictured on pages 204 and 205)

6 eggs, beaten
⅛ teaspoon salt
⅛ teaspoon pepper
¾ cup chopped onion
2 cloves garlic, minced
2 tablespoons vegetable oil
2 (6-inch) corn tortillas, torn into bite-size pieces
1 (4-ounce) can chopped green chiles, drained
1 cup (4 ounces) shredded Monterey Jack cheese
2 medium tomatoes, peeled and chopped
6 (8-inch) flour tortillas
Alfalfa sprouts
Picante sauce

Combine eggs, salt, and pepper; beat with a wire whisk. Set aside.

Sauté onion and garlic in oil in a large skillet until tender. Stir in corn tortillas and green chiles. Pour egg mixture into skillet; cook over medium heat, stirring often, until eggs are firm but still moist. Stir in cheese and tomatoes. Spoon about ½ cup egg mixture onto each flour tortilla; fold opposite sides over. Line serving platter with alfalfa sprouts; place filled tortillas, seam side down, over sprouts. Serve with picante sauce. Yield: 6 servings.

Rosemary Vaughn,
Austin, Texas.

CHINESE BURRITOS

½ cup diced onion
2 tablespoons butter or margarine, melted
2 pounds lean ground beef
⅛ teaspoon onion powder
⅛ teaspoon garlic powder
1½ teaspoons pepper
1½ teaspoons ground cumin
1 (16-ounce) can stewed tomatoes, undrained
1 (10-ounce) can tomatoes with green chiles, undrained
1 (11-ounce) can Cheddar cheese soup, undiluted
½ cup picante sauce
1 (16-ounce) package fresh or frozen egg roll wrappers
Vegetable oil
Picante sauce
Commercial sweet-and-sour sauce
Commercial hot mustard

Sauté onion in butter in a Dutch oven until tender. Add ground beef, and cook until browned, stirring to crumble meat; drain. Add onion powder and next 5 ingredients; simmer, uncovered, about 1 hour, stirring frequently. Add cheese soup and ½ cup picante sauce; stir well. Cook 45 minutes or until thickened, stirring frequently. Let cool slightly.

Spoon about 2 heaping tablespoonfuls of meat mixture in center of each egg roll wrapper. Fold top corner of wrapper over filling; then fold left and right corners over filling. Lightly brush the open corner of wrapper with water. Tightly roll the filled end of the wrapper toward the open corner; gently press to seal roll.

Heat about 3 inches of oil to 375° in a Dutch oven. Place 3 egg rolls in hot oil, and fry about 45 seconds on each side or until golden brown; drain on paper towels. Repeat with remaining egg rolls. Serve hot with picante sauce, sweet-and-sour sauce, or hot mustard. Yield: 16 egg rolls.

Judy K. Hollifield,
Lampasas, Texas.

GUACAMOLE SALAD

2 ripe avocados, peeled, seeded, and coarsely chopped
3 tablespoons picante sauce
¼ teaspoon salt
⅛ teaspoon pepper
1 small tomato, peeled, finely chopped, and drained
2 tablespoons chopped onion
4 cups shredded iceberg lettuce

Position knife blade in food processor bowl; add avocado, picante sauce, salt, and pepper. Top with cover; process until avocado is pureed. Spoon mixture into a mixing bowl; gently stir in tomato and onion.

Arrange shredded lettuce on each of six individual salad plates; top with about ⅓ cup avocado mixture. Yield: 6 servings.

M. Espinoza,
San Marcos, Texas.

Not The Same Old Pizza

There's a pizza revolution quickly spreading throughout the South. Neighborhood pizza parlors didn't start it, but casual supper establishments with progressive menus did, and the idea has captured much interest.

These new pizzas sport the familiar crispy crust, but you'll see less of the traditional red sauce, and more unusual toppings, such as pesto, clams, chicken, and artichokes. You'll also see vegetarian pizzas for those who are cutting back on meat consumption.

All of these pizzas use our Crispy Pizza Crust. It is crispiest when baked on a pizza brick sprinkled with cornmeal, but it will also work well on a regular pizza pan or baking sheet sprinkled with cornmeal. The cornmeal helps make the crust crisper on the bottom. If you're serious about pizza-making and would like to try a pizza brick, you can usually find them at kitchen specialty shops or large department stores. They're relatively inexpensive.

CRISPY PIZZA CRUST

1 cup warm water (105° to 115°)
1 tablespoon olive or vegetable oil
1 teaspoon salt
1 package dry yeast
3 to 3¼ cups all-purpose flour, divided
1 to 2 teaspoons yellow cornmeal

Combine water, oil, and salt in a large mixing bowl; sprinkle yeast over water mixture, stirring to dissolve. Add 1½ cups flour; beat at medium speed of an electric mixer until blended. Gradually add enough remaining flour to make a firm dough, mixing well.

Turn dough out onto a lightly floured surface; knead until smooth and elastic (about 5 minutes). Shape into a ball, and place in a well-greased bowl, turning to grease all sides. Cover and let rise in a warm place (85°), free from drafts, 1 hour or until doubled in bulk.

Punch dough down, and divide in half. Roll one half to a 12-inch circle on a lightly floured surface. Transfer dough to an ungreased pizza brick or pizza pan sprinkled with cornmeal. Fold over edges of dough, and pinch to form crust. Repeat with remaining dough. Bake at 450° for 10 minutes. Fill and bake as desired. Yield: two 12-inch pizza crusts.

Note: Dough for second pizza may be greased on all sides, wrapped securely in plastic wrap, put into a plastic bag, and stored in refrigerator up to 3 days. Punch dough down daily. (Dough may also be frozen up to one month.) Let dough come almost to room temperature before shaping crust.

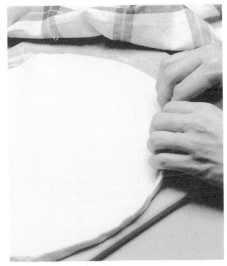

Transfer rolled dough to a pizza brick sprinkled with cornmeal. Pinch dough edges to form crust.

GRUYÈRE-CHICKEN PIZZA

1½ cups chopped cooked chicken
1 (8-ounce) carton commercial sour cream
1½ cups (6 ounces) shredded Gruyère
   cheese, divided
¼ teaspoon ground cumin
⅛ teaspoon hot sauce
1 clove garlic, minced
½ recipe, Crispy Pizza Crust
⅓ cup sliced ripe olives
¼ cup chopped green onions
2 tablespoons grated Parmesan cheese

Combine chicken, sour cream, 1 cup Gruyère cheese, cumin, hot sauce, and garlic; stir well, and spread over Crispy Pizza Crust.

Top with olives, green onions, remaining ½ cup Gruyère cheese, and Parmesan cheese. Bake at 450° for 5 minutes or until cheese melts. Yield: one 12-inch pizza.

BABY CLAM PIZZA

1 medium onion, sliced and separated into
   rings
1 clove garlic, minced
1 tablespoon vegetable oil
2 cups (8 ounces) shredded mozzarella
   cheese
½ recipe Crispy Pizza Crust
8 (2- x ¼-inch) strips pimiento
1 (10-ounce) can whole baby clams,
   drained
2 to 3 tablespoons chopped fresh parsley

Sauté onion and garlic in hot oil until onion is tender; set aside.

Sprinkle cheese over Crispy Pizza Crust; top with onion mixture. Arrange pimiento strips in a sunburst design over cheese. Bake at 425° for 5 minutes.

Arrange clams between pimiento strips; sprinkle chopped parsley in center and around edge of pizza. Bake an additional 3 to 5 minutes. Yield: one 12-inch pizza.

PESTO PIZZA

1 cup packed fresh basil, parsley,
   or coarsely chopped spinach
¼ cup walnut pieces
1 large clove garlic, cut in half
⅛ teaspoon salt
⅛ teaspoon freshly ground pepper
¼ cup olive oil
¼ cup grated Parmesan cheese
½ recipe Crispy Pizza Crust
2 ounces fontina or mozzarella cheese

Remove stems from fresh basil. Wash basil leaves thoroughly in warm water, and drain.

Position knife blade in food processor bowl; add basil, walnuts, garlic, salt, and pepper. Top with cover. Process until mixure is smooth. With processor running, pour olive oil through food chute in a slow, steady stream, processing until oil is blended into mixture. Stir in Parmesan cheese.

Spread pesto over Crispy Pizza Crust. From fontina, cut 1 small star for center of pizza; cut remaining fontina into thin strips. Arrange fontina strips over the pizza in a sunburst design. Place star in center of pizza. Bake at 450° for 5 minutes or until cheese melts. Yield: one 12-inch pizza.

PIZZA WITH ARTICHOKE
AND PROSCIUTTO
(pictured on page 203)

Italian-Style Tomato Sauce
½ recipe Crispy Pizza Crust
1 (6-ounce) jar marinated artichoke
   hearts, drained and chopped
¾ cup (3 ounces) finely shredded
   mozzarella cheese
¼ cup grated Parmesan cheese
1 (3-ounce) package thinly sliced
   prosciutto, coarsely chopped
6 small green pepper rings

Spread Italian-Style Tomato Sauce on Crispy Pizza Crust. Sprinkle sauce with chopped artichokes. Combine cheeses in a small bowl; sprinkle evenly over artichokes. Arrange chopped prosciutto in 6 groupings near edge of pizza. Top each prosciutto grouping with a green pepper ring. Bake pizza at 450° for 7 minutes or until heated. Yield: one 12-inch pizza.

Italian-Style Tomato Sauce:

1 (16-ounce) can Italian plum tomatoes,
   well drained
¼ cup tomato paste
1 teaspoon dried whole oregano
¾ teaspoon dried whole basil
½ teaspoon fennel seeds
¼ teaspoon salt

Position knife blade in food processor bowl; add all ingredients. Top with cover, and process until the sauce mixture is blended and plum tomatoes are finely chopped.

Pour into a small saucepan, and bring to a boil over medium heat. Reduce heat, and simmer, uncovered, 10 minutes. Yield: 1½ cups.

ORIGINAL ITALIAN-STYLE PIZZA

½ recipe unbaked Crispy Pizza Crust
2 tablespoons olive oil
3 large cloves garlic, pressed
¼ cup grated Parmesan cheese (optional)
¾ teaspoon dried whole oregano
¼ teaspoon coarsely ground or kosher salt

Brush shaped Crispy Pizza Crust with olive oil; spread garlic over crust. Sprinkle with Parmesan cheese, if desired, and oregano and salt. Bake pizza at 400° for 15 to 20 minutes on lower rack of oven. Break crust into small pieces, or cut into wedges to serve. Yield: one 12-inch pizza.

SALAD PIZZA

1 cup small broccoli flowerets
¼ cup sliced black olives
1 sweet red pepper, cut into 1½-inch
   strips
½ cup commercial Italian dressing
2 cups shredded iceberg lettuce
1 recipe Original Italian-Style Pizza,
   omitting salt
3 small tomatoes, cut into 8 wedges
½ (3½-ounce) package sliced pepperoni
   (optional)
½ cup (2 ounces) shredded mozzarella
   cheese
½ avocado, cut into 8 wedges
1 teaspoon lemon juice

Combine broccoli, olives, red pepper, and dressing; toss well. Cover and chill 2 hours. Just before serving, spread lettuce over Original Italian-Style Pizza. Arrange tomato wedges around edge of pizza. Arrange pepperoni, if desired, around inside edge of tomatoes.

After draining marinated vegetables with a slotted spoon, spread in center of pizza. Drizzle remaining marinade over tomatoes. Sprinkle cheese over pizza. Coat avocado wedges with lemon juice, and arrange wedges in center of pizza. Cut into wedges to serve. Yield: one 12-inch pizza.

Pecans And Peanuts, Plain And Fancy

Our love for peanuts and pecans has spanned generations. Maybe it's the memories that make them special—climbing Grandpa's forbidden pecan tree, helping shell nuts for cakes and pies, eating peanut butter and jelly sandwiches, or munching on roasted peanuts from little brown bags at ball games or the circus.

We rely on these flavorful nuts for some of the South's most prized traditions from the kitchen. Favorite recipes from our readers attest to the widespread appeal of peanuts and pecans in scrumptious cakes and pies. Dot McLendon, for example, uses ground pecans in place of flour to create an impressive Pecan Roulade and tops it with Raspberry Sauce.

For snacking, serve roasted peanuts and pecans instead of conventional sweets. Both nuts are chock-full of protein and other nutrients.

Storing Peanuts and Pecans

Fall is the time to harvest peanuts and pecans and stow them away for a year's worth of good eating. Each year, we order about 150 pounds of nuts for our test kitchens. We use the following guidelines to preserve their goodness all year long.

Select the freshest nuts possible. Nuts in the shell resist aging longer than those that have been shelled. However, shelling them before storage means that the nuts take up less space and are handier to use.

Left in the shell, **peanuts** stay fresh about four months in a dry place, nine months if refrigerated, and two years or longer if frozen. Shelled peanuts keep about six months in the refrigerator and one year when frozen in an airtight container. One pound shelled peanuts yields 3 cups nutmeats.

Unshelled **pecans** stay fresh about six months. Shelled pecans are at their best for two months at room temperature, nine months if refrigerated, and up to two years if frozen. One pound shelled pecans yields 4 cups nutmeats.

Roasting and Toasting Nuts

For **roasting** or **parching peanuts in the shell,** spread the nuts, one or two layers deep, in a large shallow pan, and roast at 300° for 45 minutes to 1 hour. Test the peanuts for doneness after 45 minutes. For **shelled peanuts,** roast at 300° for 30 to 45 minutes.

The skins should slip off easily, and the nuts should be beige. If you prefer darker nuts, cook them a bit longer. But remember that the nuts continue to darken and crisp after they are taken from the oven. To remove the red skins from peanuts, use pot holders, and carefully shake the pan so that the peanuts bump each other and the loosened skins rub off. Or using a cook's mitt, lightly rub the peanuts to help remove the skins. Salt the peanuts after roasting, if desired.

Roasted pecans are an old-time Southern favorite, too. Spread 1 cup pecan halves or pieces in a shallow pan. Pour 2 tablespoons melted butter over pecans, and stir well. Bake at 300° for 30 to 45 minutes, stirring every 15 minutes. Add salt to taste. When **toasting,** place pecans in a shallow baking pan; bake at 350° for 10 to 15 minutes, stirring occasionally. Cool.

SPECIAL CHICKEN SALAD

1½ quarts water
1 teaspoon salt
5 large chicken breast halves (about 3 pounds)
2 cups chopped celery
1 (4.5-ounce) jar whole mushrooms, drained
4 slices bacon, cooked and crumbled
½ cup pecan halves, toasted
1 (8-ounce) carton commercial sour cream
¼ cup mayonnaise
2 teaspoons lemon juice
½ teaspoon salt
Lettuce leaves
Celery leaves (optional)
Pecan halves (optional)

Combine water and salt in a Dutch oven; bring to a boil. Add chicken. Return to a boil; cover, reduce heat, and simmer 25 to 30 minutes. Remove from heat; cool chicken in broth. Drain. Skin, bone, and cut chicken into bite-size pieces.

Combine chicken, celery, mushrooms, bacon, and ½ cup toasted pecans in a large bowl; set aside. Combine sour cream, mayonnaise, lemon juice, and salt; stir well. Pour sour cream mixture over chicken mixture, tossing until well coated. Cover and chill 1 to 2 hours.

Arrange lettuce leaves on a serving platter; spoon chicken salad on top. Garnish with celery leaves and pecan halves, if desired. Yield: 6 to 8 servings.

Susan Todd,
Shreveport, Louisiana.

PECAN ROULADE

6 eggs, separated
¾ cup sugar
1 tablespoon baking powder
1½ cups coarsely ground pecans
2 tablespoons powdered sugar
3 cups whipping cream
1½ tablespoons amaretto
¾ cup sifted powdered sugar
Toasted pecan halves (optional)
Raspberry Sauce

Grease a 15- x 10- x 1-inch jellyroll pan with vegetable oil, and line with wax paper. Grease wax paper; set jellyroll pan aside.

Beat egg whites (at room temperature) at high speed of an electric mixer in a large bowl until peaks are stiff but not dry.

Beat egg yolks at high speed of an electric mixer in a large bowl until thick. Gradually add ¾ cup sugar, beating until yolks are lemon colored; stir in baking powder and pecans. Fold egg whites into yolk mixture. Spread batter evenly in prepared pan. Bake at 350° for 18 to 20 minutes. Let cool in pan on wire rack 10 minutes.

Sift 2 tablespoons powdered sugar in a 15- x 10-inch rectangle on a towel. Loosen cake from sides of pan, and turn out onto sugar. Peel off wax paper. Starting at short side, roll up cake and towel together; cool on a wire rack, seam side down.

Beat whipping cream and amaretto until foamy; gradually add ¾ cup powdered sugar, beating until peaks hold their shape.

Unroll cake, and remove towel. Spread cake with half of whipped cream mixture, and reroll. Spread remaining whipped cream mixture over top and sides of cake roll. Garnish with toasted pecan halves, if desired. Serve cake roll with Raspberry Sauce. Yield: one 10-inch cake roll.

Raspberry Sauce:

1 (10-ounce) package frozen sweetened raspberries, thawed
2 teaspoons cornstarch
1 tablespoon Triple Sec or other orange-flavored liqueur

Place raspberries in container of electric blender, and puree; strain, discarding seeds. Pour puree into a small saucepan; stir in cornstarch. Cook over low heat, stirring constantly, until smooth and bubbly. Cook 1 minute, stirring constantly. Remove from heat; stir in Triple Sec. Cover and chill 1 to 2 hours. Yield: 1 cup.

Dorothy McLendon,
Atlanta, Georgia.

CUSTARD PECAN PIE

3 eggs, separated
⅛ teaspoon salt
¼ cup plus 2 tablespoons sugar
½ teaspoon vanilla extract
1 cup sugar
2 tablespoons cornstarch
1 cup milk
1 cup chopped pecans, toasted
¼ cup butter or margarine
1 (9-inch) baked pastry shell
Sliced pecans (optional)

Combine egg whites (at room temperature) and salt in a mixing bowl; beat until foamy. Gradually add ¼ cup plus 2 tablespoons sugar, 1 tablespoon at a time, and vanilla, beating until stiff peaks form. Set aside.

Combine 1 cup sugar and cornstarch in a heavy saucepan. Beat egg yolks lightly in a small bowl; add milk. Add yolk mixture to sugar mixture in saucepan; stir well. Cook over medium heat, stirring constantly, until mixture comes to a boil. Boil 1 minute, stirring constantly. Remove from heat; stir in toasted pecans and butter. Pour into pastry shell. Spread meringue over warm filling, sealing to edge of pastry. Bake at 400° for 8 minutes or until lightly browned. Garnish with sliced pecans, if desired. Cool before serving. Yield: one 9-inch pie.

Bunnie George,
Birmingham, Alabama.

PEANUT BREAD

1¾ cups all-purpose flour
2½ teaspoons baking powder
½ teaspoon salt
½ cup sugar
½ cup creamy peanut butter
2 eggs, slightly beaten
¾ cup milk
2 tablespoons vegetable oil
½ cup chopped dry roasted peanuts

Combine flour, baking powder, salt, and sugar in a large mixing bowl. Cut peanut butter into flour mixture with a pastry blender until mixture resembles coarse meal. Set aside.

Combine eggs, milk, and oil in a small bowl; mix well. Add to flour mixture, stirring just until moistened. Fold in peanuts.

Spoon mixture into a greased and floured 9- x 5- x 3-inch loafpan. Bake at 350° for 40 minutes or until a wooden pick inserted in center comes out clean. Cool in pan 10 minutes; remove from pan, and cool completely on a wire rack. Yield: 1 loaf. *Jodie McCoy,*
Tulsa, Oklahoma.

PEANUT SOUP

¼ cup finely chopped onion
1 tablespoon unsalted butter, melted
½ cup creamy peanut butter
1 (10¾-ounce) can cream of chicken soup, undiluted
2¼ cups milk
¼ cup roasted salted peanuts
Green onions (optional)
Peanuts (optional)

Sauté onion in butter until tender. Add peanut butter; cook over low heat, stirring constantly, until melted. Add soup and milk; stir with a wire whisk until smooth. Add ¼ cup roasted peanuts, and cook until thoroughly heated. Garnish with green onions and peanuts, if desired. Yield: 1 quart.

Kay Castleman Cooper,
Burke, Virginia.

CHOCOLATE-PEANUT CLUSTER CAKE

¾ cup butter or margarine, softened
1 cup creamy peanut butter
2¼ cups sugar
3 eggs
3 (1-ounce) squares unsweetened chocolate, melted
1½ teaspoons vanilla extract
3 cups all-purpose flour
1½ teaspoons baking soda
¾ teaspoon salt
1½ cups ice water
Peanut Butter-Fudge Frosting
¼ cup finely chopped roasted peanuts
Peanut clusters (recipe follows)

Grease three 9-inch round cakepans, and line with wax paper; grease wax paper. Cream butter and peanut butter; gradually add sugar, beating at medium speed of an electric mixer. Add eggs, one at a time, beating well after each addition. Add chocolate and vanilla; beat well.

Combine flour, soda, and salt; add to creamed mixture alternately with ice water, beginning and ending with flour mixture. Mix just until blended after each addition.

Pour batter into prepared pans. Bake at 350° for 25 to 27 minutes or until cake starts to leave edges of pans. Do not overbake. Cool in pans 10 minutes; remove from pans, and cool completely on wire racks. Prepare Peanut Butter-Fudge Frosting. Place 2 cups of frosting in a small bowl; add chopped peanuts, stirring well. Spread between layers, and spread remaining frosting on top and sides of cake. Garnish with peanut clusters. Yield: one 3-layer cake.

Peanut Butter-Fudge Frosting:

3 cups sugar
3 (1-ounce) squares unsweetened chocolate
¼ teaspoon salt
1 cup milk
¾ cup shortening
½ cup creamy peanut butter
1 teaspoon vanilla extract

Combine sugar, chocolate, salt, milk, and shortening in a heavy saucepan. Bring to a boil, stirring constantly; boil 3 minutes, stirring constantly. Remove from heat. Pour into a large mixing bowl. Add peanut butter and vanilla; beat at high speed of an electric mixer 7 minutes. Yield: 3¾ cups.

Peanut Clusters:

2 ounces chocolate-flavored candy coating
½ cup plus 2 tablespoons roasted peanuts, divided

Melt candy coating in top of a double boiler; remove from heat, and stir until smooth. Stir in ½ cup peanuts. Drop by teaspoonfuls onto wax paper. Garnish each with 3 peanut halves. Chill until firm. Yield: 10 clusters. *Betsy Owens,*
Rocky Mount, North Carolina.

BRITTLE WITH CRUSHED PEANUTS

12 ounces shelled raw peanuts
2 cups sugar

To roast peanuts, bake at 400° for 10 minutes, stirring after 5 minutes; cool. Remove skins from peanuts. Place peanuts in a heavy plastic bag. To crush peanuts, roll over bag with a rolling pin. Transfer peanuts to a colander, and sift to separate coarsely chopped from finely chopped peanuts. Set aside coarsely chopped peanuts.

Cover a baking sheet with aluminum foil. Sprinkle half of finely chopped peanuts on foil. Set aside.

Place sugar in a 10-inch cast-iron skillet; cook over medium heat until caramelized (sugar melts and turns golden brown), stirring constantly with a wooden spoon. Remove skillet from heat; add coarsely chopped peanuts, stirring constantly. Immediately pour caramelized sugar-peanut mixture over finely chopped peanuts on baking sheet. Sprinkle remaining finely chopped peanuts on top. Using a rolling pin, quickly roll candy to a very thin sheet. Mark candy into squares with a knife. Cool and break into squares. Store in an airtight container. *Jennie Lee Hyde,*
Senatobia, Mississippi.

POPCORN SCRAMBLE

6 cups freshly popped popcorn, unsalted
2 cups bite-size crispy rice cereal squares
2 cups toasted oat cereal
2 cups roasted salted peanuts
½ cup butter or margarine
1 cup firmly packed light brown sugar
¼ cup light corn syrup
½ teaspoon baking soda
1 teaspoon vanilla extract

Combine first 4 ingredients in a large roasting pan; toss gently. Set aside.

Melt butter in a saucepan; stir in brown sugar and corn syrup. Bring to a boil over low heat, stirring constantly; cook, without stirring, 5 minutes. Remove from heat; stir in soda and vanilla. Pour over popcorn mixture; stir until coated. Bake at 250° for 1 hour, stirring every 15 minutes; cool. Store in an airtight container. Yield: 12 cups.

Mrs. Ben Killion,
Fayetteville, Arkansas.

Perk Up Your Burgers

Backyard gourmets and inventive cooks often overlook grilled burgers when they want to make something special. The recipes we present here are proof that with the addition of some seasonings and ingredients, burgers can be just as flavorful and exciting as any other entrée.

Burgers au Poivre Blanc translated from the French means "burgers with white pepper." Crushed white peppercorns are pressed into the sides of the patties. Each side is then browned and flavored with wine and cognac. It's a fancy burger dish that's quite appropriate for a special occasion. (See page 186 for the recipe.)

A dollop of sour cream and a sprinkling of crunchy walnuts top Nutty Burgers.

Combine first 6 ingredients; mix well. Shape into 4 patties; grill over hot coals 8 to 10 minutes on each side or until desired degree of doneness. Transfer patties to serving platter. Top each with a dollop of sour cream; sprinkle 1 tablespoon walnuts evenly over patties. Yield: 4 servings.

Frieda Wolf,
Leesville, Louisiana.

Combine beef and sausage; mix well. Shape into 8 patties. Place in a skillet, and cook over medium heat 4 to 5 minutes on each side or until browned. Remove patties; drain off pan drippings. Return patties to skillet; add pizza sauce. Sprinkle with Parmesan cheese, and top with onion; cover and simmer 10 minutes. Remove from heat; top each patty with a slice of mozzarella. Cover burgers, and let stand 5 minutes. Serve on a bun, if desired. Yield: 8 servings.

Carolyn Baker,
Kingsport, Tennessee.

NUTTY BURGERS

1 pound ground chuck
½ cup finely chopped walnuts
2 tablespoons finely chopped green onions
1 egg, beaten
2 tablespoons soy sauce
¼ teaspoon pepper
¼ cup commercial sour cream
1 tablespoon chopped walnuts

PIZZA BURGER

1 pound ground chuck
1 pound bulk pork sausage
1 (15-ounce) jar pizza sauce
⅓ cup grated Parmesan cheese
1 medium onion, cut into 8 slices
1 (6-ounce) package mozzarella slices, halved
8 hamburger buns (optional)

Tip: For a delicious aroma and flavor, add some red wine to the skillet while frying hamburgers.

BURGERS AU POIVRE BLANC

2 pounds ground sirloin
½ teaspoon salt
2 tablespoons crushed white peppercorns
Vegetable cooking spray
2 tablespoons diced shallots
2 tablespoons cognac
¼ cup red wine
¼ cup water
¼ teaspoon chicken-flavored bouillon granules
1 tablespoon butter or margarine

Shape ground sirloin into 6 patties about ¾ inch thick. Sprinkle with salt, and press crushed peppercorns into meat. Heat a large nonstick skillet that has been sprayed with cooking spray. Place patties in skillet, and cook 4 minutes over medium-high heat; turn and cook 5 minutes or to desired degree of doneness. Remove patties from skillet; keep patties warm.

Discard drippings from skillet; add shallots, and cook over low heat 1 to 2 minutes, stirring often. Add cognac and wine; cook over medium heat until mixture is reduced by about half. Combine water and bouillon granules; add to skillet, and cook until mixture is reduced to about ⅓ cup. Add butter, and stir until melted. Serve sauce over patties. Yield: 6 servings.
Kathie Paul,
Casselberry, Florida.

STEAK-HOUSE BURGERS

1½ pounds ground beef
¼ cup grated onion
2 tablespoons commercial steak sauce
1 tablespoon minced fresh parsley
1 teaspoon salt
¼ teaspoon pepper
1 teaspoon grated lemon rind
Romaine lettuce
6 Kaiser rolls or hamburger buns, sliced in half
1 large tomato, cut into 6 slices
Mushroom Sauce
2 tablespoons chopped chives

Combine beef, onion, steak sauce, parsley, salt, pepper, and lemon rind; mix well. Shape into 6 patties about ¾ inch thick. Grill patties over medium-hot coals 8 to 10 minutes on each side or to desired degree of doneness, turning once. Remove patties from grill.

Place lettuce on bottom half of each roll; top with patty, tomato slice, Mushroom Sauce, and chives. Cover with top, and serve immediately. Yield: 6 servings.

Mushroom Sauce:

½ pound fresh mushrooms, sliced
3 tablespoons butter or margarine, melted
2 teaspoons Dijon mustard

Sauté mushrooms in butter in a skillet until tender and liquid is evaporated. Add Dijon mustard, stirring well. Yield: about ¾ cup.
Mrs. Iris Brenner,
Fort McCoy, Florida.

COOKING LIGHT®

Color Is The Key To Vitamins

Vitamins—pills of assorted shapes and sizes or colorful and delicious food? Although we spend $2 billion on vitamin supplements each year, most nutritionists still agree that eating a variety from the four basic food groups is still the preferred way to meet most people's vitamin needs.

Selecting Food With Vitamins

Let color be a guide when choosing foods for their vitamin content. A rainbow of hues—green, gold, orange, red, yellow, and brown—are all indicative of vitamin content, and a deeper color usually means a higher concentration. For example, yellow crookneck squash contains vitamin A, but acorn squash, with a darker golden flesh, contains much more of the vitamin.

Vegetables and fruit are not the only foods that contain a substantial amount of vitamins. Whole grain and enriched breads and cereals, dairy products, meat, fish, and poultry are also rich sources (refer to the chart on page 187). You will find each of these types of foods in the recipes featured here.

Retaining Vitamins in Food

Vitamins are nutrients essential for nearly all chemical reactions in the body. Vitamins are of two basic types: water soluble (the nine B-complex vitamins and vitamin C) and fat soluble (A, D, E, and K). Most vitamins break down when heated. Others, such as riboflavin, are unstable in light. Water-soluble vitamins are easily leached into cooking liquids, while vitamin C and those that are fat soluble are sensitive to heat and air.

To minimize vitamin loss in foods, always cover food items that need to be refrigerated. Also, when freezing foods, use vapor/moistureproof packaging, keep freezer temperature below 0° F, and avoid prolonged storage.

Peeling, slicing, and soaking foods increase vitamin loss, so prepare them just before cooking and serving. When possible, leave skins on fruit and vegetables. Try eating raw fruit and vegetables, or cook them only until crisp-tender. Choose a quick-cook method of preparation that uses little water, such as steaming, stir-frying, or microwaving. And when possible, use the packing liquid of canned fruit and vegetables and defatted broth and juice that cooks out of foods.

STRAWBERRY-ORANGE BREAKFAST SHAKE

2 cups fresh strawberries, divided
1 cup unsweetened orange juice, chilled
1 cup skim milk
1 (8-ounce) carton lemon low-fat yogurt

Reserve 5 strawberries for garnish. Rinse and cap remaining strawberries; place in container of an electric blender. Add orange juice and milk; cover and process on high speed until smooth. Add yogurt; process on low speed until blended. Pour into chilled glasses; garnish with reserved strawberries. Yield: 5 servings.

☐ *97 calories, 4.5 grams protein, 1.1 grams fat, 18.3 grams carbohydrate, 3 milligrams cholesterol, 76 milligrams sodium, and 143 milligrams calcium per 1-cup serving.*

Tip: Hull strawberries after washing so that they won't become mushy.

Beef-and-Broccoli Salad has vitamins A and C, B vitamins, and folic acid.

BEEF-AND-BROCCOLI SALAD

7 cups coarsely chopped fresh broccoli
1 medium-size sweet red pepper, cut into strips
⅓ cup sliced green onions
¾ pound deli-style roast beef, cut into thin strips
¼ cup rice vinegar
3 tablespoons reduced-sodium soy sauce
1 tablespoon water
1 tablespoon vegetable oil
1 clove garlic, minced
¼ to ½ teaspoon fresh grated gingerroot
⅛ teaspoon red pepper flakes
8 lettuce leaves

Arrange broccoli in vegetable steamer. Place over boiling water; cover and steam 5 minutes. Drain and chill. Combine broccoli, red pepper, green onions, and roast beef; set aside.

Combine vinegar and next 6 ingredients; stir well. Pour over broccoli mixture; toss gently. Cover and chill 2 hours, stirring occasionally. To serve, drain mixture, and arrange on lettuce. Yield: 4 servings.

☐ *288 calories, 29.4 grams protein, 14.2 grams fat, 12.8 grams carbohydrate, 69 milligrams cholesterol, 332 milligrams sodium, and 105 milligrams calcium per 2-cup serving.*

Vitamin	Food Sources
A	liver, dark green leafy vegetables, yellow and orange vegetables and fruit, fortified milk, egg yolks
D	fatty fish (herring, mackerel, salmon, sardines, tuna), fortified milk and margarine, liver*
E	vegetable oil, margarine, most nuts, sunflower kernels, wheat germ
K	green leafy vegetables, beef liver, asparagus, cheese, pork, oats, cauliflower, egg yolk**
B-1 (thiamine)	lean pork, sunflower kernels, whole grain and enriched breads and cereals, peanuts, wheat bran, beans, peas, legumes
B-2 (riboflavin)	organ meats, enriched breads and cereals, almonds, cheese, eggs, lean meat, milk, wheat bran
B-3 (niacin)	liver, lean meat, poultry, fish, nuts, peanut butter, enriched breads and cereals
B-6 (pyridoxine)	wheat bran, sunflower kernels, avocado, bananas, yellow corn, fish, lean meat, liver, nuts, poultry, brown rice, whole grains
B-12 (cobalamin)	organ meats, lean meats, fish, shellfish, eggs, milk, cheese
C	citrus fruits, green leafy vegetables, green pepper, strawberries, cauliflower, cantaloupe
folic acid (folacin)	liver, garbanzo beans, avocado, beans, beets, celery, eggs, fish, green leafy vegetables, nuts, oranges, whole wheat products
biotin	process cheese, liver, cauliflower, egg yolk, mushrooms, nuts, peanut butter, sardines, salmon, wheat bran
pantothenic acid	organ meats, wheat bran, nuts, mushrooms, salmon, blue cheese, eggs, brown rice, peanuts, whole grains (except wheat)

*People who get sun on their skin usually don't need food sources of vitamin D because it can be formed in the skin by the sun's ultraviolet rays.

**Vitamin K is also formed by certain bacteria in the intestine.

SPINACH SALAD WITH ORANGE DRESSING

7 cups torn fresh spinach
1 medium-size red apple, unpeeled and chopped
⅓ cup coarsely chopped walnuts, toasted
Orange-Poppy Seed Dressing

Combine spinach, apple, and walnuts in a large bowl; toss gently. Cover and chill until serving time. Serve salad with Orange-Poppy Seed Dressing. Yield: 8 servings.

Orange-Poppy Seed Dressing:

1 cup unsweetened orange juice
1 tablespoon cornstarch
2 teaspoons vegetable oil
Dash of ground nutmeg
Dash of ground cardamom
½ teaspoon poppy seeds

Combine orange juice, cornstarch, vegetable oil, nutmeg, and cardamom in a saucepan; cook over medium heat, stirring constantly, until mixture is smooth and bubbly.

Let mixture cool. Stir in poppy seeds. Cover and chill. Yield: ¾ cup plus 1 tablespoon.

☐ *53 calories, 2.1 grams protein, 3.3 grams fat, 5.3 grams carbohydrate, 0 milligrams cholesterol, 39 milligrams sodium, and 54 milligrams calcium per 1 cup salad plus 18 calories, 0.2 gram protein, 0.8 gram fat, 2.7 grams carbohydrate, 0 milligrams cholesterol, 0 milligrams sodium, and 3 milligrams calcium per tablespoon dressing.*

TUNA-MAC IN TOMATOES

1⅓ cups uncooked elbow macaroni
1 (6½-ounce) can water-packed tuna,
    drained and flaked
1 cup diced, unpeeled cucumber
½ cup diced green pepper
½ cup sliced green onions
¼ cup minced fresh parsley
⅓ cup reduced-calorie mayonnaise
2 teaspoons dry Italian salad dressing mix
1 tablespoon lemon juice
6 medium tomatoes
Parsley (optional)

Cook macaroni according to package directions, omitting salt. Drain and chill thoroughly.

Combine macaroni, tuna, cucumber, pepper, green onions, and parsley; toss gently. Combine mayonnaise, salad dressing mix, and lemon juice; stir well. Add to macaroni mixture; toss gently.

Core tomatoes. Cut each into 6 wedges, cutting to, but not through, base of tomato. Spread wedges slightly apart. Spoon tuna mixture into tomatoes. Garnish with parsley, if desired. Yield: 6 servings.

□ *207 calories, 11.3 grams protein, 4.4 grams fat, 31.1 grams carbohydrate, 18 milligrams cholesterol, 446.5 milligrams sodium, and 32 milligrams calcium per 1 cup salad with tomato.*

Mrs. R. E. Bunker,
Temple, Texas.

BANANA-OAT MUFFINS

½ cup regular oats, uncooked
⅓ cup plus 1 tablespoon skim milk
1 egg, slightly beaten
2 tablespoons molasses
2 tablespoons vegetable oil
¼ teaspoon vanilla extract
⅔ cup mashed ripe banana
½ cup all-purpose flour
½ cup whole wheat flour
1½ teaspoons baking powder
¼ teaspoon salt
¼ teaspoon ground cinnamon
Vegetable cooking spray

Combine oats and milk; let stand 5 minutes. Add egg, molasses, oil, vanilla, and banana; stir well.

Combine flours, baking powder, salt, and cinnamon. Make a well in center of mixture; add oat mixture to dry ingredients. Stir just until moistened.

Spoon batter into muffin pans coated with cooking spray, filling two-thirds full. Bake at 400° for 12 minutes or until done. Yield: 10 muffins.

□ *118 calories, 3.1 grams protein, 4.1 grams fat, 18.1 grams carbohydrate, 28 milligrams cholesterol, 91 milligrams sodium, and 39 milligrams calcium per muffin.*

MICROWAVE COOKERY

Try Your Hand At Adapting Recipes

Many of you have asked us how you can convert your favorite recipes for use in the microwave oven. In planning this story, we tried to come up with fail-safe methods and surefire results. As in most instances, not one quick answer covers everything. But we have found that many recipes can be adapted successfully. Just follow the guidelines included here, and we think you'll be pleased with the results.

Use these recipes as a guide for converting other recipes. All are readers' conventional recipes, which we've adapted in our test kitchens.

First, look for a published microwave recipe similar to the one you want to adapt. Look in your manufacturer's cookbook, our monthly "Microwave Cookery" feature, or in other microwave sources. Check the amount of food cooked, the cooking times, and any special techniques that might ensure the success of your recipe. If you can't find a similar recipe, the following tips will be especially helpful.

—Choose naturally moist foods, such as chicken, seafood, vegetables, and saucy casseroles, that will adapt well to microwave cookery. Because cakes and other baked products are more complex, it's best to rely on published recipes for those foods.

—Look at how much water or liquid is in a recipe. Because microwave dishes are covered and not cooked by dry heat, less water is lost during microwaving than during baking or boiling. You may need to decrease the amount of water for a microwave adaptation.

—Can you decrease the amount of fat used or eliminate it altogether? Sometimes it is not necessary to use fat in microwave recipes. For example, cooking carrots in the microwave requires only a small amount of water; butter would be added only for flavor. To sauté in a skillet, however, you need butter or oil to keep the carrots moist and to prevent sticking.

—Most microwave recipes cook in a shorter amount of time than the conventional versions. Usually you can decrease the cooking time by one-fourth to one-third that of the conventional recipe. Begin to check the food for doneness when you've cooked it half the time recommended conventionally. Then continue cooking in one- or two-minute intervals until the food tests done. Standing time helps finish cooking; in fact, most dense dishes, such as casseroles, need at least 10 minutes of standing time.

ZESTY LASAGNA

1 pound ground beef
2 to 3 cloves garlic, minced
3 (6-ounce) cans tomato paste
1¾ cups water
1 (4-ounce) can sliced mushrooms, drained
2 bay leaves
¼ teaspoon salt
¼ teaspoon pepper
1 teaspoon Italian seasoning
¼ teaspoon dried whole oregano
6 lasagna noodles
1 (12-ounce) carton small-curd cottage
    cheese
1 (8-ounce) carton sour cream
2½ cups (10 ounces) mozzarella cheese,
    divided

Cook beef and garlic in a heavy skillet over medium heat until meat is browned, stirring to crumble meat; drain. Stir in tomato paste, water, mushrooms, bay leaves, salt, pepper, Italian seasoning, and oregano. Cover, reduce heat, and simmer 30 minutes, stirring occasionally. Remove the bay leaves.

Cook noodles according to package directions, omitting salt. Drain. Combine cottage cheese and sour cream in a medium bowl; stir well.

Layer half each of noodles, meat sauce, and cottage cheese mixture in a greased 12- x 8- x 2-inch baking dish. Sprinkle with ¾ cup mozzarella cheese. Repeat layers of noodles, meat sauce, and cottage cheese mixture. Cover and bake at 350° for 40 minutes. Top with remaining mozzarella cheese; bake an additional 5 minutes or until cheese melts. Let stand 10 minutes before serving. Yield: 6 servings.

Microwave Directions:

Crumble beef into a 2-quart casserole; add garlic. Cover with wax paper; microwave at HIGH 5 to 6 minutes or until meat is done, stirring twice. Drain. Stir in tomato paste, water, mushrooms, bay leaves, salt, pepper, Italian seasoning, and oregano. Cover with heavy-duty plastic wrap; microwave at HIGH for 4 to 5 minutes or until mixture is thoroughly heated, stirring once. Remove bay leaves; set aside.

Place lasagna noodles in a 12- x 8- x 2-inch baking dish; cover with water. Cover with heavy-duty plastic wrap. Microwave at HIGH for 12 to 13 minutes, rearranging noodles after 7 minutes. Drain well.

Combine cottage cheese and sour cream; stir well.

Layer half each of noodles, meat sauce, and cottage cheese mixture in a greased 12- x 8- x 2-inch baking dish. Sprinkle with ¾ cup mozzarella cheese. Repeat layers of noodles, meat sauce, and cottage cheese mixture. Top with remaining mozzarella cheese. Cover and microwave at MEDIUM HIGH (70% power) for 10 to 12 minutes or until thoroughly heated, rotating dish once. Let stand at least 10 minutes before serving.   *Patsy Litz,*
Prattville, Alabama.

ONION-SMOTHERED STEAK

1½ pounds round steak
¼ cup all-purpose flour
¾ teaspoon salt
⅛ teaspoon pepper
2 to 3 tablespoons vegetable oil
¼ teaspoon dried whole thyme
2 medium onions, sliced
1 cup water
1 tablespoon vinegar
1 clove garlic, crushed
1 bay leaf

Pound steak to ½-inch thickness; cut into ¾-inch-wide strips. Combine flour, salt, and pepper. Dredge steak in flour mixture; brown in hot oil in a large skillet.

Add remaining ingredients. Bring mixture to a boil; cover, reduce heat, and simmer 1 hour or until steak is tender. Remove bay leaf before serving. Yield: 6 servings.

Microwave Directions:

Pound steak to ½-inch thickness; cut into ¾-inch-wide strips. Combine flour, salt, and pepper. Dredge steak in flour.

Preheat a 10-inch browning dish at HIGH for 8 to 9 minutes. Add oil and then steak; stir until sizzling stops. Microwave at HIGH for 3 minutes or until browned, stirring once. Add remaining ingredients; stir. Cover with lid or wax paper, and microwave at MEDIUM (50% power) for 30 to 35 minutes, stirring at 10-minute intervals. Remove bay leaf before serving.   *Cheryl Keener,*
Lenoir, North Carolina.

EASY SAUSAGE CASSEROLE

1 pound bulk pork sausage
1 small onion, chopped
1 cup chopped green pepper
2½ cups water
1 (10¾-ounce) can cream of chicken soup, undiluted
½ teaspoon salt
1 cup uncooked long-grain rice

Combine sausage, onion, and green pepper in a skillet; cook over medium heat until sausage is browned, stirring to crumble meat. Drain well; set aside.

Combine water, soup, and salt in a large saucepan; bring to a boil. Add rice; cover, reduce heat, and simmer 7 minutes. Add sausage mixture. Spoon into a 2½-quart casserole. Cover and bake at 375° for 35 minutes. Yield: 4 to 6 servings.

Microwave Directions:

Crumble sausage into a 2½-quart casserole. Add onion and green pepper; stir well. Cover and microwave at HIGH for 7 to 8 minutes or until sausage is browned, stirring once. Drain well; set aside.

Combine water, soup, salt, and rice in a glass bowl; stir well. Microwave at HIGH for 5 minutes, stirring once. Spoon into sausage mixture. Cover and microwave at HIGH for 20 mintues, stirring once. Let stand 10 minutes before serving.   *Mary Phillips,*
Jacksonville, Florida.

Vegetables You Can Rely On

The fall harvest brings us an abundance of vegetables that we often depend on for months. Cabbage, potatoes, and turnips are a challenge to serve in new and different ways. Our readers have presented us with several recipes that definitely have a tasty twist.

SWEET-AND-SOUR CABBAGE

2 tablespoons vinegar
1½ teaspoons sugar
Pinch of red pepper
2 tablespoons bacon drippings
5 cups coarsely chopped cabbage
1 medium onion, coarsely chopped
1 teaspoon salt
Dash of ground nutmeg

Combine vinegar, sugar, and red pepper; set aside.

Heat bacon drippings in a large skillet over medium-high heat. Add cabbage, onion, salt, and nutmeg; cook 5 minutes. Add vinegar mixture; simmer 1 to 2 minutes. Yield: 4 servings.
Virginia Laux,
Toney, Alabama.

CREOLE CABBAGE

1 cup chopped green pepper
1 cup chopped celery
½ cup chopped onion
2 tablespoons butter or margarine, melted
4 cups coarsely shredded cabbage
1 (16-ounce) can tomatoes, undrained and chopped
2 teaspoons beef-flavored bouillon granules
1 teaspoon sugar
¼ teaspoon white pepper

Sauté green pepper, celery, and onion in butter in a large skillet. Add remaining ingredients; cover and cook over medium heat 10 minutes. Yield: 6 servings.   *Nora Hendrix,*
Augusta, Georgia.

Tip: Cooking vegetables with the least amount of water possible will preserve vitamins and maintain flavor.

POTATOES LORRAINE

2 eggs, beaten
¼ cup breadcrumbs
½ teaspoon salt
⅛ teaspoon pepper
2 large potatoes, unpeeled
   and cooked
2 tablespoons minced onion
1 cup (4 ounces) shredded Cheddar
   cheese, divided
4 slices cooked bacon, crumbled
   and divided
Paprika

Combine eggs, breadcrumbs, salt, and pepper. Grate potatoes, and measure 3 cups; stir grated potatoes into egg mixture. Add onion, half of cheese, and half of bacon. Spoon mixture into a lightly greased 1½-quart casserole. Sprinkle top with paprika. Bake at 350° for 25 minutes. Sprinkle top with remaining cheese and bacon; bake casserole an additional 5 minutes. Yield: 4 servings.
Angie White,
Quitman, Texas.

SOUTHERN TURNIPS

2 pounds turnips, peeled and cubed
2 medium-size new potatoes, unpeeled and
   cubed
1 bay leaf
4 cups water
1 medium onion, chopped
2 tablespoons bacon drippings
½ teaspoon salt
½ teaspoon pepper
⅛ teaspoon red pepper
2 tablespoons minced fresh parsley

Combine turnips, potatoes, bay leaf, and water in a Dutch oven. Bring to a boil; cover, reduce heat, and simmer 20 minutes or until vegetables are tender. Drain; remove bay leaf.
Sauté onion in bacon drippings until tender. Add turnips, potatoes, salt, pepper, and red pepper; toss gently. Spoon into serving dish; sprinkle with parsley. Yield: 6 to 8 servings.
Evelyn Snellings,
Richmond, Virginia.

Stir In Flavor With Cottage Cheese

Many people enjoy the tangy, slightly acidic taste of cottage cheese eaten right from the carton, but the flavor is mild enough to be compatible with every kind of recipe from appetizers to desserts. These recipes offer examples of how it combines with a range of sweet as well as savory foods.

HOT SHRIMP DIP

1 (15-ounce) can small shrimp, drained
½ pound fresh mushrooms, finely chopped
2 tablespoons butter or margarine, melted
1½ cups cream-style cottage cheese
¼ cup mayonnaise
¼ cup commercial sour cream
½ teaspoon garlic salt
¼ teaspoon soy sauce

Rinse shrimp with cold water; drain well. Set aside.
Sauté mushrooms in butter until tender. Add cottage cheese, mayonnaise, sour cream, garlic salt, and soy sauce; stir over low heat until mixture is hot. (Do not boil.) Stir in shrimp. Serve hot with crackers. Yield: about 4 cups.
Shirley Mecca,
Manchester, Missouri.

CORN MOUSSAKA

1 (17-ounce) can whole kernel corn,
   drained
1½ pounds ground beef
1 tablespoon all-purpose flour
1 (8-ounce) can tomato sauce
½ teaspoon garlic salt
¼ teaspoon ground cinnamon
2 eggs, slightly beaten
1½ cups cream-style cottage cheese,
   drained
1 tablespoon chopped chives
1 cup (4 ounces) shredded mozzarella
   cheese
¼ cup grated Parmesan cheese
2 tablespoons slivered almonds, toasted

Place corn in an ungreased 10- x 6- x 2-inch baking dish.
Cook beef in a large skillet until meat is browned, stirring to crumble. Drain beef well. Add flour; cook and stir 1 minute. Add tomato sauce, garlic salt, and cinnamon, mixing well. Pour beef mixture over corn. Bake at 350° for 15 minutes.

Combine eggs, cottage cheese, and chives, mixing well; spread on beef layer. Bake at 350° for 15 minutes. Top with cheeses; sprinkle slivered almonds on top, and bake an additional 5 minutes. Yield: 6 servings.
Mary Belle Purvis,
Greeneville, Tennessee.

POTATO CASSEROLE

6 medium potatoes, peeled, cooked,
   and mashed
1 (12-ounce) carton small-curd cottage
   cheese
⅓ cup commercial sour cream
2 tablespoons minced onion
1 teaspoon salt
1 teaspoon butter, melted
¼ cup slivered almonds,
   toasted

Combine potatoes, cottage cheese, sour cream, onion, and salt. Spoon into a lightly greased 2-quart casserole. Drizzle with butter; sprinkle almonds on top. Bake, uncovered, at 350° for 30 minutes or until thoroughly heated. Yield: 6 to 8 servings.   *Claudia Reich,*
Anniston, Alabama.

COTTAGE CHEESE-SPINACH CUPS

1½ cups low-fat cottage cheese
2 (10-ounce) packages frozen chopped
   spinach, thawed
4 eggs, beaten
1 teaspoon salt
¼ teaspoon pepper
¼ teaspoon ground nutmeg
Miniature Cream Cheese Pastry Shells

Drain cottage cheese well using a strainer; set aside.
Drain chopped spinach well, and press between layers of paper towels to remove excess moisture.
Combine cottage cheese, spinach, eggs, salt, pepper, and nutmeg in a medium bowl; stir well. Spoon 2 teaspoons mixture into each pastry shell; bake at 350° for 25 to 30 minutes or until set. Yield: about 6 dozen.

Miniature Cream Cheese Pastry Shells:

3 cups all-purpose flour
¼ teaspoon salt
1 (8-ounce) package cream cheese,
   softened
1 cup butter or margarine

Combine flour and salt. Cut in softened cream cheese and butter until mixture resembles coarse crumbs. Press mixture together with hands until it forms a dough.

Shape dough into 72 (1-inch) balls. Place each into an ungreased 1¾-inch muffin pan; press dough onto bottom and sides to form miniature shells. Yield: 6 dozen. *Sue Gatlin, Toney, Alabama.*

For The Love Of Potatoes

Potatoes are highly regarded for their delicious taste, low cost, and availability, as well as for their food value. But most of all, potatoes are so versatile—they can be baked, stuffed, mashed, fried, boiled, scalloped, or prepared many other ways.

CREAMY COTTAGE CHEESE DESSERT

1 cup graham cracker crumbs
¼ cup butter or margarine, melted
3 eggs
1 (12-ounce) carton cream-style cottage cheese
⅓ cup sugar
Dash of salt
⅛ teaspoon ground cinnamon
⅛ teaspoon vanilla extract
⅛ teaspoon maple flavoring
1 (16-ounce) carton commercial sour cream
3 tablespoons sugar
½ teaspoon almond extract
2 tablespoons orange marmalade

Combine graham cracker crumbs and butter, stirring well. Press into bottom of a 9-inch springform pan. Bake at 350° for 10 minutes.

Combine eggs, cottage cheese, ⅓ cup sugar, salt, cinnamon, vanilla, and maple flavoring, beating well with electric mixer. Pour mixture into prepared pan; bake at 350° for 30 minutes.

Combine sour cream, 3 tablespoons sugar, and almond extract; spoon over cottage cheese mixture. Bake at 475° for 5 minutes. Let cool to room temperature on a wire rack; refrigerate for several hours. Remove sides of springform pan; spread top with orange marmalade. Yield: 8 servings. *Sarah Watson, Knoxville, Tennessee.*

Tip: During the week, keep a shopping list handy to write down items as you need them. This will eliminate unnecessary trips to the store. Before your weekly shopping trip, make a complete shopping list. If the list is arranged according to the layout of the store, you will save time and steps.

CREAMY POTATOES WITH HAM BITS

1 large potato, peeled and cubed
1 tablespoon butter or margarine
1 tablespoon all-purpose flour
1 cup milk
½ cup (2 ounces) shredded Swiss cheese
½ cup cubed cooked ham
1 tablespoon chopped parsley
1 teaspoon lemon juice
¼ teaspoon salt
⅛ teaspoon ground nutmeg
⅛ teaspoon pepper

Place cubed potato in a medium saucepan; add water to cover. Bring to a boil; cover, reduce heat, and simmer 15 to 20 minutes or until tender. Drain.

Melt butter in a heavy saucepan over low heat; add flour, stirring until smooth. Cook 1 minute, stirring constantly. Gradually add milk; cook over medium heat, stirring constantly, until mixture is thickened and bubbly. Add cheese, stirring until cheese melts. Stir in potatoes and remaining ingredients. Spoon mixture into a lightly greased 1-quart casserole. Bake at 350° for 15 minutes or until bubbly. Yield: 4 servings. *Mary Boden, Stuart, Florida.*

PARTY SCALLOPED POTATOES

6 medium potatoes
¼ cup chopped onion
¼ cup chopped green pepper
2 tablespoons butter or margarine, melted
1 tablespoon all-purpose flour
½ teaspoon salt
⅛ teaspoon pepper
1¼ cups milk
1 (8-ounce) carton Neufchâtel cheese dip with bacon and horseradish
1 (4-ounce) jar diced pimiento, drained
½ cup breadcrumbs
1 tablespoon chopped fresh parsley
1 teaspoon sesame seeds
2 tablespoons butter or margarine, melted

Cover potatoes with water, and bring to a boil; reduce heat, and cook about 30 minutes or until potatoes are tender. Cool slightly. Peel and cube potatoes; set aside.

Sauté onion and green pepper in 2 tablespoons butter in a large skillet until vegetables are tender. Stir in flour, salt, and pepper; cook 1 minute. Gradually add milk; cook over medium heat, stirring constantly, until mixture is thickened and bubbly. Stir in cheese dip.

Layer half each of cooked potatoes and pimiento in an ungreased 2-quart casserole; repeat layers. Pour cheese mixture over top.

Combine breadcrumbs and remaining ingredients; sprinkle mixture over casserole. Bake at 350° for 30 to 35 minutes or until hot and bubbly. Yield: 6 servings. *Grace Bravos, Timonium, Maryland.*

MUSHROOM SCALLOPED POTATOES

1 (10¾-ounce) can cream of mushroom soup, undiluted
1 (4-ounce) can mushroom stems and pieces, drained
¾ cup (3 ounces) shredded American cheese, divided
¼ cup diced pimiento, drained
½ teaspoon salt
⅔ cup evaporated milk
3 large potatoes (about 2¼ pounds)
Paprika

Combine soup, mushrooms, ½ cup cheese, pimiento, and salt in a large bowl; mix well. Stir in milk.

Peel potatoes, and cut into ¼-inch slices to measure 5 cups. Add potatoes to soup mixture. Spoon mixture into a greased 2-quart baking dish. Bake, uncovered, at 350° for 55 minutes or until potatoes are tender. Sprinkle remaining ¼ cup cheese over potatoes; bake an additional 5 minutes. Sprinkle top with paprika. Yield: 6 servings. *Kitty Cromer, Anderson, South Carolina.*

POTATOES
WITH SWEET RED PEPPERS

3 medium potatoes, unpeeled and cut into
½-inch slices
2 medium onions, cut into ½-inch slices
2 medium-size sweet red peppers, cut into
½-inch rings
1 (3-ounce) package prosciutto, shredded,
or 3 ounces thinly sliced ham,
shredded
½ teaspoon salt
¼ teaspoon pepper
½ teaspoon dried whole rosemary
¼ cup olive oil

Combine all ingredients except oil in
a 13- x 9- x 2-inch baking dish. Pour oil
over mixture; toss to coat well.

Cover and bake at 350° for 45 minutes or until potatoes are tender. Stir
occasionally. Yield: 6 to 8 servings.

Barbara Carson,
Hollywood, Florida.

JAZZY MASHED POTATOES

4 large potatoes (3 pounds), peeled and
cubed
½ teaspoon salt
¼ cup butter or margarine
½ cup milk
½ cup commercial sour cream
2 tablespoons frozen chives
¼ cup grated Parmesan cheese
Paprika

Cook potatoes in boiling water with
salt about 30 minutes or until tender.
Drain potatoes, and mash. Add butter,
milk, sour cream, and chives; mix well.
Spoon mixture into a lightly greased
1½-quart casserole.

Bake at 350° for 25 minutes; sprinkle
with cheese and paprika. Bake an additional 5 minutes, and serve immediately. Yield: 4 to 6 servings.

Mrs. Joseph H. Thompson,
Colquitt, Georgia.

STUFFED POTATOES
WITH CHEESE SAUCE

4 large baking potatoes
Vegetable oil
¼ cup butter or margarine, softened
½ cup (2 ounces) shredded sharp
American cheese
½ cup commercial sour cream
1 tablespoon chopped green onions

Scrub potatoes, and rub skins with
oil; bake at 400° for 1 hour or until
potatoes are done.

Combine butter, cheese, and sour
cream, stirring well with a fork to
blend. Split tops of potatoes lengthwise,
and fluff pulp with a fork. Spoon cheese
topping over potatoes; sprinkle green
onions over topping. Yield: 4 servings.

Linda Keller,
Jonesboro, Arkansas.

Add Pasta
To These Entrées

Pasta has increased in popularity over
the past few years; as a result, there is
an endless selection of shapes, sizes,
and even flavors from which to choose.
These recipes offer some suggestions for
stirring it into a variety of entrées, all
selected for convenience.

You can use any type of pasta in
these recipes. But if you plan to substitute one for another, remember to in-
terchange with a similar size.

QUICK CRAB BAKE

2¼ cups uncooked seashell macaroni
1 (8-ounce) package cream cheese,
softened
1 (8-ounce) carton commercial sour cream
1 cup cottage cheese
½ cup chopped green onions
½ cup chopped fresh parsley
2 (6-ounce) cans crabmeat, drained and
flaked
2 medium tomatoes, peeled and sliced
1½ cups (6 ounces) shredded Monterey
Jack or sharp Cheddar cheese

Cook macaroni according to package
directions, omitting salt; drain.

Combine cream cheese, sour cream,
cottage cheese, green onions, and parsley; mix well.

Layer half each of macaroni, cheese
mixture, and crabmeat in a lightly
greased 2-quart baking dish. Repeat
procedure, and top with tomato slices.
Bake at 350° for 25 minutes; sprinkle
with shredded cheese, and bake an additional 5 minutes. Yield: 6 servings.

Cynthia Brame,
North Wilkesboro, North Carolina.

PASTA AND GARDEN
VEGETABLES

2 tablespoons butter or margarine
1 tablespoon olive oil
1 pound boneless chicken breasts (about 4
breast halves), cut into strips
1½ cups chopped leeks
3 carrots, scraped and sliced
1 medium red pepper, cut into 1-inch
pieces
½ cup chopped onion
¼ cup chopped fresh parsley
2 teaspoons chopped fresh basil
3 small zucchini, diagonally sliced
2 large tomatoes, diced
½ cup chicken broth
½ teaspoon garlic salt
¼ teaspoon pepper
3 cups uncooked rotini
2 tablespoons freshly grated Parmesan
cheese
2 tablespoons freshly grated Romano
cheese

Heat butter and olive oil in a large
skillet. Add chicken, leeks, carrots, red
pepper, onion, parsley, and basil; cover
and simmer 10 minutes. Add zucchini,
tomatoes, broth, garlic salt, and pepper.
Cover and cook 10 minutes or until zucchini is crisp-tender.

Cook rotini according to package directions; drain well. Combine pasta and
cheeses in a large bowl; stir well to
coat. Add vegetables, stirring to blend.
Serve immediately. Yield: 6 servings.

Jane Honeyman,
Round Rock, Texas.

MEXICAN LUNCHEON

2 cups uncooked elbow macaroni
1 pound hot bulk pork sausage
1 cup chopped green pepper
1 cup chopped onion
1 (16-ounce) can tomatoes, undrained
and chopped
1 cup commercial sour cream
½ cup milk
1 tablespoon chili powder
⅔ cup (2.6 ounces) shredded Cheddar
cheese

Cook macaroni according to package
directions; drain well, and set aside.

Combine sausage, green pepper, and onion in a large skillet; cook over medium heat until sausage is browned and vegetables are tender, stirring to crumble meat. Drain off pan drippings. Stir in macaroni, tomatoes, sour cream, milk, and chili powder. Continue to cook until heated. Sprinkle with cheese; cover, reduce heat, and cook 3 minutes or until cheese melts. Yield: 4 to 6 servings.
Deloris Breidall,
Enfield, North Carolina.

ROTINI ROMANO

1 green pepper, cut into strips
1 medium onion, chopped
2 cups sliced fresh mushrooms
2 ounces pepperoni, sliced
½ cup white wine
2 tablespoons olive oil
2 teaspoons Italian seasoning
1 (12-ounce) package uncooked rotini
1½ cups (6 ounces) shredded mozzarella cheese
1 (32-ounce) jar commercial spaghetti sauce
¼ cup (1 ounce) freshly grated Romano cheese

Combine green pepper, onion, mushrooms, and pepperoni in a large bowl. Add wine, olive oil, and Italian seasoning, tossing gently. Marinate mixture at room temperature 1 hour.

Cook rotini according to package directions, omitting salt; drain. Add to marinated vegetable mixture; stir in mozzarella cheese, tossing gently.

Spoon pasta mixture into a lightly greased 13- x 9- x 2-inch baking dish. Pour spaghetti sauce over pasta, completely covering it. Cover and bake at 350° for 25 minutes. Sprinkle with Romano cheese; bake an additional 5 minutes. Yield: 6 servings.

Note: May substitute ¼ cup (1 ounce) shredded mozzarella cheese for Romano, if desired. *Michelle Marsh,*
Birmingham, Alabama.

Entrées To Bake Or Broil

Choose entrées carefully, and you'll find more than one way to save time when you cook. The ones we feature here are all baked or broiled. There are recipes that take merely minutes to prepare or some no-fuss versions that don't need any attention after you place them in the oven to bake. You can choose according to your amount of time.

If you have at least 45 minutes to prepare the meal, consider an oven entrée like Mrs. W. H. Colley's Turkey Parmigiana. After assembly, it bakes in 30 minutes. This leaves enough time to prepare the rest of the menu while the main dish cooks. The recipe originally featured veal, but Mrs. Colley substituted fresh turkey breast slices and came up with a winner.

TURKEY PARMIGIANA

1 medium onion, chopped
3 cloves garlic, minced
3 tablespoons olive oil, divided
1 (8-ounce) can tomato sauce
1 (28-ounce) can whole tomatoes, undrained and chopped
¼ teaspoon dried whole thyme
¼ teaspoon pepper
½ cup fine dry breadcrumbs
¼ cup grated Parmesan cheese
1 egg, beaten
1 tablespoon water
1 pound fresh turkey breast slices (about 6)
2 cups (8 ounces) shredded mozzarella cheese
⅔ cup grated Parmesan cheese
Hot cooked spaghetti (optional)

Sauté onion and garlic in 1 tablespoon olive oil in a saucepan over medium heat 3 to 5 minutes, stirring occasionally. Remove from heat. Add tomato sauce, tomatoes, thyme, and pepper; stir well, and set aside.

Combine breadcrumbs and ¼ cup Parmesan cheese; toss to mix, and set mixture aside.

Combine egg and water. Dip turkey slices in egg mixture, and dredge in breadcrumbs. Heat remaining 2 tablespoons olive oil in a large skillet; sauté turkey over medium heat until browned. Place in a lightly greased 13- x 9- x 2-inch baking dish. Spoon two-thirds of tomato sauce mixture over turkey; sprinkle with mozzarella cheese, and top with remaining sauce.

Bake, uncovered, at 350° for 25 minutes. Sprinkle evenly with ⅔ cup Parmesan cheese, and bake an additional 5 minutes. Serve over spaghetti, if desired. Yield: 6 servings.
Mrs. W. H. Colley,
Donelson, Tennessee.

HOT-AND-SPICY KABOBS

1 (2-pound) boneless sirloin steak
4 jalapeño peppers, seeded and chopped
2 tablespoons water
1½ cups red wine vinegar
1 cup water
2 teaspoons salt
½ teaspoon pepper
2 cloves garlic, crushed
1 teaspoon dried whole oregano
1 teaspoon ground cumin
1 teaspoon paprika

Trim all visible fat from steak; cut into 1½-inch cubes. Set aside.

Combine jalapeño peppers and 2 tablespoons water in container of an electric blender; process at high speed until pureed, stopping to scrape sides as needed. Combine pepper mixture, red wine vinegar, and remaining ingredients except steak in a large mixing bowl; stir well. Add steak; stir gently. Cover and chill 8 hours.

Drain steak, reserving marinade. Place steak cubes on skewers, and place skewers on a rack in a shallow baking pan. Broil 8 inches from heat 10 minutes on each side or until desired degree of doneness, basting with reserved marinade. Yield: 6 servings.

Note: If desired, grill kabobs over hot coals 10 minutes on each side or until desired degree of doneness.

Susan May,
San Antonio, Texas.

KIWI ORANGE ROUGHY

½ teaspoon salt
¼ teaspoon garlic powder
¼ teapoon pepper
¼ teaspoon dried whole oregano
4 orange roughy fillets (1½ pounds)
2 tablespoons vegetable oil
¼ cup butter or margarine, melted
¼ cup lime juice
1 (3½-ounce) jar macadamia nuts, chopped
2 kiwifruit, peeled and sliced

Combine salt, garlic powder, pepper, and oregano; sprinkle over fillets. Place fillets in a 12- x 8- x 2-inch baking dish coated with vegetable oil. Drizzle fillets with melted butter and lime juice. Cover and bake at 350° for 20 minutes or until fish flakes easily when tested with a fork. Transfer fillets to a serving platter; garnish with macadamia nuts and kiwifruit slices. Yield: 4 servings.
Ray M. Jackson,
Birmingham, Alabama.

Flavor The Entrée With Fruit

If you have meat in the refrigerator and fruit in the pantry, these recipes deserve your attention.

Chinese Meatballs may take a little longer to prepare than the other two recipes, but it's certainly worth the effort. Ground toasted almonds and pineapple set this recipe apart from the sweet-and-sour meatballs you may have eaten before. With bread and a salad, it's a dish you can offer company.

Our recipes for Fruited Pork Chops and Savory Pork Chops require fewer ingredients and can be prepared in 30 to 45 minutes. Try one of these flavorful recipes when you're in a hurry.

With a tangy sweet-and-sour sauce, Chinese Meatballs is special enough to serve company.

FRUITED PORK CHOPS

2 tablespoons shortening
4 (½- to ¾-inch-thick) pork chops
4 slices onion
2 tablespoons lemon juice
1 teaspoon Worcestershire sauce
½ teaspoon dry mustard
3 whole cloves
1 teaspoon salt
¾ cup hot water
¾ cup whole pitted prunes

Heat shortening in a heavy skillet over medium-high heat; brown chops quickly on both sides. Arrange onion slices on pork chops. Combine lemon juice, Worcestershire sauce, mustard, cloves, salt, and water; pour over chops. Cover, reduce heat, and simmer 20 minutes. Add prunes; cover and simmer 20 minutes or until chops are tender. Yield: 4 servings.

Mrs. Otis Jones,
Bude, Mississippi.

SAVORY PORK CHOPS

4 (½-inch-thick) center-cut pork chops
½ teaspoon salt
¼ teaspoon pepper
2 tablespoons butter or margarine
1 large Granny Smith apple, peeled and sliced
¼ cup golden raisins
1 teaspoon grated lemon rind
½ cup apple juice

Sprinkle pork chops with salt and pepper. Melt butter in a heavy skillet over medium heat; brown chops on both sides. Top with apple, raisins, and lemon rind. Add apple juice; cover, reduce heat, and simmer 30 minutes or until tender. Yield: 4 servings.

Patsy Hill,
San Antonio, Texas.

CHINESE MEATBALLS

1 pound ground beef
2 eggs, beaten
¾ cup minced celery
½ cup ground toasted almonds
½ cup breadcrumbs
1 clove garlic, crushed
1 tablespoon soy sauce
½ teaspoon salt
⅓ cup cornstarch
2 tablespoons vegetable oil
1 (15¼-ounce) can pineapple chunks, undrained
½ cup sugar
3 tablespoons cornstarch
1 cup chicken broth
½ cup vinegar
2 tablespoons soy sauce
1 medium-size green pepper, cut into thin strips
Hot cooked rice

Combine beef, eggs, celery, almonds, breadcrumbs, garlic, soy sauce, and salt; shape into 1-inch balls. Dredge in ⅓ cup cornstarch. Pour oil into a 13- x 9- x 2-inch pan; add meatballs, and bake at 350° for 35 to 40 minutes. Drain and set aside.

Drain pineapple, reserving ½ cup juice; set pineapple aside.

Combine sugar and 3 tablespoons cornstarch in a large saucepan; mix well. Combine chicken broth, reserved pineapple juice, vinegar, and 2 tablespoons soy sauce; gradually add to sugar mixture. Cook over medium heat, stirring constantly, until thickened and smooth. Add meatballs, pineapple, and green pepper; stir gently. Cook over medium heat, stirring often, until thoroughly heated. Serve over rice. Yield: 6 servings.

Norma Zeigler,
Huntsville, Alabama.

Tip: Grills or pans with a nonstick finish may become scratched or lose their finish with use. Spray the damaged surface with a nonstick vegetable spray to prevent food from sticking.

Eggs Benedict With A Twist

In the 1920's a creative chef developed eggs Benedict when a couple requested a new and different breakfast item. Today, eggs Benedict is an internationally famous recipe that traditionally consists of English muffins topped with ham or Canadian bacon, poached eggs, and hollandaise sauce. The creation was named after Mr. and Mrs. Benedict, who ordered this novel breakfast entrée.

Another inventive cook, Phyllis Rodesney of Midwest City, Oklahoma, adds her special touch to this traditional favorite. Phyllis substitutes crisp bacon for the ham and adds fried tomato slices to her Bacon-and-Tomato Eggs Benedict. We've included step-by-step photographs and directions for preparing the poached eggs in advance and holding them overnight. This simplifies the last-minute preparation and makes the dish a good choice for entertaining.

BACON-AND-TOMATO EGGS BENEDICT

8 eggs
8 cups water
½ cup vinegar
2 teaspoons salt
2 large ripe tomatoes
¼ cup all-purpose flour
Vegetable oil
½ teaspoon salt
½ teaspoon pepper
4 English muffins, split, buttered, and toasted
Hollandaise sauce (recipe follows)
8 slices bacon, cooked and crumbled

Break 1 egg into a custard cup; set aside. Combine water, vinegar, and 2 teaspoons salt in a large Dutch oven; bring to a boil. Swirl boiling water with a spoon to form a deep whirlpool in center of pan; slip egg into center of whirlpool, and reduce heat to simmer. Do not stir. As egg spins, it will form an oval shape with the white completely surrounding the yolk. Cook 2 minutes or until egg floats to top of water. Immediately place in a bowl of ice water, and refrigerate until serving time. Repeat procedure with remaining eggs.

Cut tomatoes into 8 slices, approximately ½ inch thick. Dredge in flour; fry in oil about 5 minutes or until tomatoes are lightly browned. Sprinkle with ½ teaspoon salt and pepper.

Place a fried tomato slice on each muffin half. Place poached egg in boiling water for 45 seconds; drain. Place poached egg on top of tomato slice; top with hollandaise sauce, and sprinkle with crumbled bacon. Repeat procedure with remaining eggs. Yield: 4 servings.

Hollandaise Sauce:

5 egg yolks
3 tablespoons lemon juice
⅛ teaspoon hot sauce
½ teaspoon salt
½ to ¾ teaspoon white pepper
¾ cup butter or margarine, melted

Combine egg yolks, lemon juice, hot sauce, salt, and pepper in container of electric blender; blend until mixture is thick and lemon colored. Turn blender to low speed; add butter in a slow, steady stream. Turn blender to high speed, and process until mixture is thick. Yield: 1¼ cups.

Note: Eggs may be poached and served immediately instead of placing in ice water and reheating.

Kick Off With Snacks

Excitement over the first football games of the season is sure to bring people together for plenty of socializing, cheering, food, and beverages. Be ready with our tasty dips and spreads. Just add assorted crackers, chips, and raw vegetables with drinks. You're bound to score points with your guests.

Fiery Tomato-Cheese Spread is spicy and hot enough to keep your taste buds interested, but not overwhelmed. (Recipe is on the next page.)

Another savory snack is Hotshot Bean Dip, which uses items you may have on hand—onion, garlic, bacon drippings, and kidney beans. This dip goes great with tortilla chips.

HOTSHOT BEAN DIP

1 medium onion, chopped
1 clove garlic, minced
2 tablespoons bacon drippings
1 (16-ounce) can red kidney beans, undrained and mashed
2 canned jalapeño peppers, minced
¾ cup (3 ounces) shredded Longhorn cheese, divided

Sauté onion and garlic in bacon drippings in a medium skillet 1 minute. Add kidney beans and cook, stirring constantly, until mixture is thickened. Add peppers and ½ cup cheese; stir until cheese melts. Spoon mixture into a serving dish; sprinkle remaining ¼ cup cheese on top. Serve dip warm with tortilla chips. Yield: 1½ cups.

Nita Shipp,
Madison, Missouri.

Step 1: *Swirl boiling water with a spoon. Then slip the egg into the water; the spinning action wraps the white around the yolk as the egg cooks in an oval shape.*

Step 2: *When the egg floats to the top, it is done. Serve immediately, or transfer to a bowl of ice water and refrigerate. At serving time, reheat in boiling water.*

Step 3: *For more attractive eggs, trim the uneven edges. (Follow these 3 steps for Bacon-and-Tomato Eggs Benedict or traditional eggs Benedict.)*

FIERY TOMATO-CHEESE SPREAD

2 cups (8 ounces) shredded sharp Cheddar
  cheese
2 (3-ounce) packages cream cheese,
  softened
1 (7½-ounce) can jalapeño relish
1 to 1½ teaspoons ground cumin
¾ teaspoon garlic powder

Position knife blade in food processor
bowl; add all ingredients. Top with
cover; process 1½ minutes or until mixture is smooth, scraping sides of bowl
occasionally. Serve spread with assorted
crackers. Yield: 2¼ cups.
Janet M. Filer,
Arlington, Virginia.

SHRIMP MOUSSE

2 (4¼-ounce) cans tiny shrimp
1 envelope plus 1 teaspoon unflavored
  gelatin
½ cup boiling water
1 (10¾-ounce) can tomato soup,
  undiluted
1 (8-ounce) package cream cheese,
  softened
¾ cup finely chopped onion
¾ cup finely chopped celery
1 cup mayonnaise
Lettuce leaves (optional)

Rinse shrimp well; drain. Coarsely
chop shrimp; set aside.
Dissolve gelatin in ½ cup boiling
water. Combine tomato soup and cream
cheese in a heavy saucepan. Cook over
low heat, stirring constantly, until
smooth and creamy. Remove from heat,
and stir in gelatin; mix well. Let mixture cool.
Combine shrimp, chopped onion,
chopped celery, and mayonnaise. Mix
well with soup mixture. Pour into a
lightly oiled 6-cup mold. Cover and chill
at least 8 hours. Unmold onto lettuce
leaves, if desired. Serve with assorted
unsalted crackers. Yield: 5¼ cups.
Kathy Hunt,
Dallas, Texas.

Tip: Onions offer outstanding nutritive
value. They are a good source of cal-
cium and vitamins A and C. They con-
tain iron, riboflavin, thiamine, and
niacin; have a high percentage of
water; and supply essential bulk. They
are low in calories and have only a
trace of fat.

CORNED BEEF SPREAD

1 (4-pound) corned beef brisket,
  trimmed
5 cups water
1 large onion, coarsely chopped
1 (16-ounce) can shredded sauerkraut,
  drained
1⅓ cups sliced dill pickles
½ cup mayonnaise

Place corned beef brisket in a Dutch
oven; add water. Bring to a boil; cover,
reduce heat, and simmer 4 hours or
until brisket is tender. Remove from
heat; let cool. Drain brisket; cut into
1-inch cubes.
Position knife blade in food processor
bowl; add half each of brisket cubes,
onion, sauerkraut, and pickles. Top
with cover, and pulse 5 or 6 times or
until coarsely ground. Remove to a
large mixing bowl. Repeat procedure
with remaining beef cubes, onion, sauerkraut, and pickles. Stir in mayonnaise. Serve spread with bread or
crackers. Yield: 6½ cups.
Anita McLemore,
Knoxville, Tennessee.

CHEESY BEER SPREAD

2 cups (8 ounces) shredded Cheddar
  cheese
1 (3-ounce) package cream cheese,
  softened
⅓ cup beer
2 tablespoons minced fresh parsley
1 small clove garlic, crushed
⅛ teaspoon red pepper

Combine all ingredients; stir well.
Cover and chill. Serve with crackers.
Yield: 1½ cups. *Laura Morris,*
Bunnell, Florida.

TANGY VEGETABLE DIP

1 (16-ounce) carton commercial sour
  cream
2 tablespoons mayonnaise
2 cloves garlic, crushed
1½ teaspoons seasoned salt
½ teaspoon freshly ground pepper
½ teaspoon dillweed
½ teaspoon prepared mustard

Combine all ingredients; stir well.
Cover and chill 1 hour; serve with as-
sorted raw vegetables. Yield: 2 cups.
Jackie Broome,
Greenville, South Carolina.

Fry This Appetizer

It's not often that you find a recipe
calling for the Mexican flavors of chili
powder and refried beans combined
with the Oriental flair of wonton skins.
But that's just what you get when you
make delicious Tex-Mex Wontons.

TEX-MEX WONTONS

½ pound ground beef
¼ cup chopped onion
2 tablespoons chopped green pepper
¾ cup refried beans
¼ cup (1 ounce) shredded Cheddar cheese
1 tablespoon catsup
1½ teaspoons chili powder
4 dozen wonton skins
Vegetable oil
Commercial taco sauce

Combine beef, onion, and green pepper in a large skillet; cook until meat is
browned, stirring to crumble meat.
Drain off pan drippings; discard. Add
beans, cheese, catsup, and chili powder;
stir well.
Place 1 teaspoon beef mixture in center of each wonton skin. Fold top corner over filling, fold side corners over,
then roll up jellyroll fashion. Moisten
edges with water to seal.
Heat 1½ inches oil to 375° in wok or
large skillet. Place 6 wontons in hot oil,
and fry 30 seconds on each side or until
golden brown; drain on paper towels.
Repeat with remaining wontons. Serve
with taco sauce. Yield: 4 dozen.
Marsha Littrell,
Sheffield, Alabama

Tex-Mex Dip Starts The Party

For a colorful, no-bake appetizer to
feed a crowd, Marideanne Blomgren of
Raleigh, North Carolina, says that
Chilled Mexican Appetizer is a hit with
her party guests. She tops a layer of
bean dip, tomato paste, and green
chiles with chopped fresh vegetables, a
spicy spread, and cheese. This dish
needs to chill well to make it easier to
dip with chips; while it chills, you have
plenty of time to tend to all the last-
minute details of your party.

CHILLED MEXICAN APPETIZER

1 (9-ounce) can commercial bean dip
1 (6-ounce) can tomato paste
1 (4-ounce) can chopped green chiles,
　　drained
2 avocados, peeled and coarsely chopped
2 small tomatoes, coarsely chopped
2 teaspoons lemon juice
½ cup commercial sour cream
½ cup mayonnaise
1 (1¼-ounce) package taco seasoning mix
1 small green pepper, coarsely chopped
1 bunch green onions, coarsely chopped
1 (2-ounce) jar diced pimiento, drained
1 (4¼-ounce) can chopped ripe olives,
　　drained
2 cups (8 ounces) shredded extra-sharp
　　Cheddar cheese
5 cherry tomatoes, quartered
Additional chopped green onions

Combine bean dip, tomato paste, and chiles; spread mixture in a 12-inch round platter with sides. Combine chopped avocados, chopped tomatoes, and lemon juice; toss and arrange evenly over bean mixture. Set aside.

Combine sour cream and next two ingredients; spoon over avocado mixture. Combine green pepper, green onions, pimiento, and olives; sprinkle over sour cream mixture. Top with cheese. Garnish with cherry tomatoes and additional green onions. Cover; chill 1 to 2 hours. Serve with tortilla chips. Yield: about 12 cups.

Celebrate Victory With A Buffet

Celebrate football victories past and present with a buffet at your house. This menu doubles as a pregame brunch or a postgame supper.

Some of the food can be made ahead of time. Sweet-and-Sour Beans, for instance, marinates for 8 hours. And the Chicken à la King will hold overnight in the refrigerator.

For dessert, serve commercial pound cake topped with Strawberry Sauce.

**Chicken à la King
Cornbread
Sweet-and-Sour Beans
Baked Tomatoes
Strawberry Sauce　　Cake**

CHICKEN À LA KING

6 chicken breast halves
8 mushroom caps, sliced
1 green pepper, chopped
2 tablespoons butter or margarine, melted
¼ cup plus 1 tablespoon butter or
　　margarine
¼ cup plus 1 tablespoon all-purpose flour
4½ cups half-and-half
¼ cup sherry
4 egg yolks
½ cup half-and-half
2 tablespoons sherry
1 tablespoon diced pimiento
1 teaspoon salt
¼ teaspoon white pepper
Diced pimiento (optional)

Place chicken in a Dutch oven; cover with water. Bring to a boil. Cover, reduce heat, and simmer 20 to 25 minutes or until tender. Remove chicken from broth; use broth for other recipes. Cool, bone, and chop chicken; set aside.

Sauté mushrooms and green pepper in 2 tablespoons butter in a skillet until crisp-tender. Drain and set aside.

Melt ¼ cup plus 1 tablespoon butter in a Dutch oven over low heat; add flour, stirring until smooth. Cook 1 minute, stirring constantly. Gradually add 4½ cups half-and-half and ¼ cup sherry; cook over medium heat, stirring constantly, until mixture is thickened and bubbly.

Beat egg yolks until thick and lemon colored; add ½ cup half-and-half. Gradually stir about one-fourth hot mixture into yolk mixture; add to remaining hot mixture, stirring constantly. Add chopped chicken, sautéed vegetables, 2 tablespoons sherry, and next 3 ingredients. Cook over medium heat, stirring constantly, until mixture is bubbly. Sprinkle additional diced pimiento over top, if desired. Serve over Cornbread. Yield: 8 servings.

CORNBREAD

1 cup all-purpose flour
1 tablespoon plus 1 teaspoon baking
　　powder
½ teaspoon salt
1 cup cornmeal
2 tablespoons sugar
2 eggs, beaten
1 cup milk
⅓ cup vegetable oil
1½ tablespoons vegetable oil

Combine flour, baking powder, salt, cornmeal, and sugar in a large bowl.

Combine eggs, milk, and ⅓ cup oil in a small bowl; add to cornmeal mixture. Stir until dry ingredients are moistened.

Spoon batter into a 10-inch cast-iron skillet coated with 1½ tablespoons oil and preheated. Bake at 400° for 20 minutes or until lightly browned. Yield: 8 servings.　　*Beverly Verdery,
Waco, Texas.*

SWEET-AND-SOUR BEANS

2 (16-ounce) cans whole green beans,
　　drained
2 small purple onions, thinly sliced
⅔ cup vegetable oil
1 cup cider vinegar
1 teaspoon summer savory
1 teaspoon dried whole marjoram
1 teaspoon sugar
Lettuce leaves

Combine beans and onions in a shallow dish; toss gently.

Combine oil, vinegar, savory, marjoram, and sugar in a jar. Cover tightly, and shake vigorously. Pour marinade over vegetables, and toss gently. Cover and chill 8 hours. Drain well. To serve, spoon beans into a lettuce-lined bowl. Yield: 8 servings.　　*Eleanor K. Brandt,
Arlington, Texas.*

BAKED TOMATOES

4 medium-size tomatoes, halved
⅛ teaspoon salt
1 tablespoon Dijon mustard
2 tablespoons diced green pepper
2 tablespoons diced celery
1 tablespoon diced onion
2 tablespoons butter, melted

Place tomato halves in a lightly greased 13- x 9- x 2-inch baking dish; sprinkle with salt. Spread with mustard. Combine green pepper, celery, and onion; spoon over cut surface of tomato halves. Drizzle with butter. Bake at 400° for 10 minutes or until tomatoes are heated. Yield: 8 servings.
*Jeanne S. Hotaling,
Augusta, Georgia.*

STRAWBERRY SAUCE

1 (10-ounce) package frozen strawberries, thawed
1½ tablespoons cornstarch
1 tablespoon lemon juice

Place strawberries in a liquid measuring cup; add enough water to measure 2 cups. Combine cornstarch and lemon juice in a saucepan; stir well. Add strawberries; cook over low heat, stirring constantly, until thickened and smooth. Chill. Serve over ice cream or pound cake. Yield: 2 cups.

Invite Friends For Dainties

These Almond Cream Confections are easy to make. Jean Carriger, a resident of Lakeland, Florida, has dazzled guests for years with these mouth-watering treats. Now we can all enjoy them.

ALMOND CREAM CONFECTIONS

½ cup butter
¼ cup sugar
2 tablespoons cocoa
2 teaspoons vanilla extract
¼ teaspoon salt
1 egg, slightly beaten
1 cup slivered almonds, toasted and chopped
1¾ cups vanilla wafer crumbs
½ cup flaked coconut
Cream Filling
2 (1-ounce) squares semisweet chocolate

Combine butter, sugar, cocoa, vanilla, salt, and egg in a heavy saucepan; cook over low heat, stirring constantly, until butter melts and mixture begins to thicken. Remove from heat; add almonds and next two ingredients, stirring well. Press firmly into an ungreased 9-inch square pan; cover and chill.

Spread Cream Filling over almond mixture; cover and chill. Cut into squares. Remove from pan, and place about ½ inch apart on a baking sheet; set aside.

Place chocolate in a zip-top heavy-duty plastic bag; seal. Submerge in hot water until chocolate melts. Using scissors, snip a tiny hole in end of bag; drizzle chocolate over Cream Filling. Yield: 3 dozen.

Cream Filling:

⅓ cup butter, softened
1 egg
½ teaspoon vanilla extract
2½ to 3 cups sifted powdered sugar

Cream butter, beating at high speed of an electric mixer. Add egg and vanilla; mix well. Slowly add sugar, mixing until smooth. Yield: about 2 cups.

You Can't Resist Brownies

Whether you prefer chewy fudge brownies or the kind with a light, cake-like texture, you'll be sure to find a recipe here to please your taste. For snacks, picnics, and lunchbox treats, it's best to choose a fudgelike version, such as Crunch-Crust Brownies. This brownie is unfrosted and won't break apart easily when packed to travel. For a dainty party tray, you can cut them into tiny squares or diamond shapes.

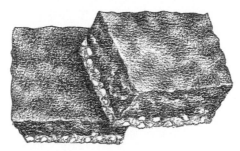

CRUNCH-CRUST BROWNIES

½ cup graham cracker crumbs
¼ cup firmly packed brown sugar
¼ cup chopped pecans
¼ cup butter or margarine, melted
1 (19.8-ounce) package fudge brownie mix
¼ cup hot water
¼ cup vegetable oil
1 egg

Combine first 4 ingredients in a small bowl; mix well. Press mixture into a greased 9-inch square pan. Set aside.

Combine brownie mix, hot water, oil, and egg in a large mixing bowl; mix with a wooden spoon until blended. Spoon over crumb mixture. Bake at 350° for 25 to 30 minutes. Cool and cut into 3- x 1½-inch bars. Yield: 18 bars.

Lisa Brown,
Jackson, Missouri.

CHOCO-MALLOW BROWNIES

½ cup butter or margarine, softened
1 cup sugar
2 eggs
¾ cup all-purpose flour
½ teaspoon baking powder
Pinch of salt
3 tablespoons cocoa
1 teaspoon vanilla extract
½ cup chopped pecans
2 cups miniature marshmallows
Chocolate frosting (recipe follows)

Cream butter in a large mixing bowl; gradually add sugar, beating until fluffy. Add eggs, one at a time, beating at medium speed of an electric mixer. Set mixture aside.

Combine flour, baking powder, salt, and cocoa; add to creamed mixture, stirring well. Stir in vanilla and pecans.

Spoon batter into a greased 9-inch square pan. Bake at 350° for 18 to 20 minutes. Remove from oven; sprinkle with marshmallows. Cover with foil, and allow to stand 5 minutes to melt marshmallows; remove foil.

Spread chocolate frosting on top of warm brownies. Cool and cut into squares. Yield: 3 dozen.

Chocolate Frosting:

¼ cup butter or margarine, melted
2 cups powdered sugar, sifted
3 tablespoons cocoa
3 to 4 tablespoons half-and-half

Combine butter, sugar, and cocoa in a mixing bowl. Gradually add half-and-half, beating at medium speed of an electric mixer until mixture reaches spreading consistency. Yield: enough for a 9-inch square pan of brownies.

Doris Ramsey,
Martinsville, Virginia.

BUTTERMILK CAKE BROWNIES

1 cup water
½ cup butter or margarine
½ cup cocoa
½ cup vegetable oil
2 cups all-purpose flour
2 cups sugar
¼ teaspoon salt
½ cup buttermilk
2 eggs, beaten
1 teaspoon baking soda
1 teaspoon vanilla extract
Chocolate frosting (recipe follows)

Combine water, butter, and cocoa in a small saucepan; cook over medium heat, stirring frequently, until mixture comes to a boil. Remove from heat. Stir in vegetable oil.

Combine flour, sugar, and salt in a large mixing bowl; add cocoa mixture, stirring well. Stir in buttermilk, eggs, soda, and vanilla. Pour batter into a greased and floured 13- x 9- x 2-inch pan. Bake at 350° for 30 minutes. Spread with chocolate frosting while warm. Cool and cut into squares. Yield: 15 to 18 servings.

Chocolate Frosting:
½ cup butter or margarine, softened
½ cup cocoa
¼ cup plus 2 tablespoons hot water
1 teaspoon vanilla extract
1 (16-ounce) package powdered sugar, sifted
1 cup chopped pecans (optional)

Combine first 4 ingredients; blend until smooth. Gradually add powdered sugar, mixing well. Stir in chopped pecans, if desired. Yield: enough frosting for a 13- x 9- x 2-inch pan of brownies. *Grace Coffman, Lebanon, Tennessee.*

OATMEAL BROWNIES

½ cup butter or margarine, melted
½ cup sugar
⅓ cup firmly packed brown sugar
1 teaspoon vanilla extract
2 eggs, slightly beaten
⅔ cup all-purpose flour
½ teaspoon baking powder
¼ cup cocoa
⅓ cup chopped pecans
3 tablespoons quick-cooking oats, uncooked

Grease an 8-inch square pan, and line with wax paper; set aside.

Combine butter, sugars, and vanilla; stir well. Add eggs; stir well. Combine flour, baking powder, and cocoa in a small bowl; add to creamed mixture, stirring well. Stir in pecans and oats.

Pour batter into prepared pan. Bake at 350° for 18 minutes. (Center will be soft.) Cool in pan 10 minutes; remove from pan, and remove wax paper. Cut into squares. Yield: 2 dozen.
Mrs. Paul Raper, Burgaw, North Carolina.

Tip: Stale cake or cookies can be made into crumbs in a blender. Sprinkle over ice cream for a delicious topping.

PEANUT BUTTER BROWNIES

½ cup shortening
½ cup peanut butter
1½ cups sugar
3 eggs
1 cup self-rising flour
1 teaspoon vanilla extract
1 (6-ounce) package semisweet chocolate morsels
1 cup chopped pecans

Cream shortening and peanut butter; gradually add sugar, beating at medium speed of an electric mixer until light and fluffy. Add eggs, one at a time, beating after each addition. Stir in flour, blending well. Stir in vanilla, chocolate morsels, and chopped pecans.

Spoon batter into a greased 13- x 9- x 2-inch pan. Bake at 350° for 30 minutes or until lightly browned. Cool. Cut into 2- x 1½-inch bars. Yield: 3 dozen.
Betty A. Bates, Elkton, Tennessee.

Energizing Blender Beverages

Whether you're starting the day or ending a workout, a nutritious fruit shake is refreshing. In these recipes, fruit juice, milk, yogurt, and an assortment of fruits are mixed and matched to suit a variety of preferences. Whirl these ingredients in a blender for a cool and quick energizing beverage. The shakes are packed with nutrients and are ideal for breakfast on the go.

If you want a beverage that's like an ice-cream shake, freeze the liquids until slushy, and use frozen fruit without thawing. In three of these recipes, for example, frozen banana slices work nicely in providing a thicker consistency for the beverages.

BANANA-STRAWBERRY FROST

1 ripe banana, sliced
1 cup frozen unsweetened strawberries, drained
1½ cups unsweetened apple juice

Combine all ingredients in container of an electric blender; process until smooth. Serve chilled or over ice. Yield: 3 cups. *Robin Silva, Orlando, Florida.*

THREE-FRUIT DRINK

1 banana, sliced
½ cup grapefruit juice, chilled
1½ cups orange juice, chilled
1 cup milk
2 tablespoons honey

Combine all ingredients in container of an electric blender; process until frothy. Serve chilled. Yield: 4 cups.
Dolly Northcutt, Fairfield, Alabama.

STRAWBERRY-YOGURT SHAKE

1 (8-ounce) container plain yogurt
1 (10-ounce) package frozen strawberries, thawed and drained
½ cup milk
½ cup crushed ice
1 to 1½ tablespoons honey

Combine first 4 ingredients plus 1 tablespoon honey in container of electric blender; process until smooth and thick. Add more honey, if desired. Serve immediately. Yield: 2⅔ cups.
Nora Henshaw, Castle, Oklahoma.

PINEAPPLE MILKSHAKE

1 cup pineapple juice, chilled
2 tablespoons orange juice
1 teaspoon lemon juice
3 tablespoons sugar
⅓ cup finely crushed ice
2 cups milk

Combine pineapple juice, orange juice, lemon juice, and sugar in container of an electric blender; process until sugar dissolves. Add crushed ice and milk; process until blended. Yield: 5 cups. *Lorene Hubbard, Russellville, Alabama.*

BREAKFAST EYE-OPENER

1 cup orange juice, chilled
1 egg
3 tablespoons wheat germ
1 tablespoon honey
½ cup frozen sliced peaches
½ cup plain yogurt

Combine first 5 ingredients in container of an electric blender; process until mixture is frothy. Stir in yogurt. Yield: 2¼ cups. *Susan Clapp, Nashville, Tennessee.*

TROPICAL SHAKE

1 quart orange juice, chilled
½ cup instant nonfat dry milk
  powder
1 teaspoon sugar
1 teaspoon coconut extract
1 (8¼-ounce) can pineapple tidbits,
  undrained
2 ripe bananas, sliced

Combine half of all ingredients in container of an electric blender. Process until smooth. Repeat procedure with remaining ingredients. Yield: 5½ cups.

Lori Moss,
Cocoa, Florida.

Carrot Dishes That Satisfy

Looking for a colorful and nutritious vegetable to round out the menu? Make carrots your first choice. It's hard to beat their high vitamin A content and their versatility. Use them in a bread, such as our Carrot Puffs, or as an appetizer in Dill-Spiced Carrots.

Serve Creamy Marinated Carrots as a side dish or salad. Either way, you're sure to enjoy the refreshing dish.

CARROT PUFFS

4 or 5 large carrots, scraped and sliced
1 cup all-purpose flour
1 teaspoon baking powder
¼ teaspoon salt
⅛ teaspoon white pepper
Pinch of ground nutmeg
1 egg, slightly beaten
1 tablespoon fresh minced parsley
Peanut oil
Powdered sugar (optional)

Cook carrots, covered, in a small portion of boiling salted water 15 minutes or until tender; drain. Mash carrots, and let cool.

Combine 1 cup mashed carrots and next 7 ingredients; stir well. Heat 1 inch of oil in a large skillet to 325°. Drop carrot mixture by tablespoonfuls into hot oil, and cook until golden, turning once. Drain on paper towels. Sprinkle with powdered sugar, if desired. Serve immediately. Yield: 1½ dozen.

Patricia Pashby,
Memphis, Tennessee.

DILL-SPICED CARROTS

1 pound carrots
1 cup dill pickle juice
1 (8-ounce) carton commercial sour cream
2 tablespoons chopped fresh dillweed
1 tablespoon minced fresh chives

Scrape carrots; cut lengthwise into quarters. Cut quarters in half crosswise. Combine carrots and pickle juice in a saucepan; cover and cook over low heat 20 to 25 minutes or until crisp-tender. Cool. Cover and chill 8 hours.

Combine sour cream, dillweed, and chives; cover and chill. Drain carrots; serve with sour cream mixture. Yield: 8 appetizer servings.

Daisy Cook,
Tyler, Texas.

GLAZED CARROTS WITH BACON AND ONION

1 pound carrots, scraped and sliced
  diagonally
3 slices bacon
1 small onion, chopped
3 tablespoons brown sugar
⅛ teaspoon pepper

Cook carrots, covered, in a small amount of boiling water 15 minutes or until crisp-tender; drain.

Cook bacon in a skillet until crisp; drain, reserving 1 tablespoon drippings in skillet. Crumble bacon, and set aside.

Sauté onion in reserved drippings until tender. Add brown sugar, pepper, and carrots; cook until thoroughly heated. Sprinkle with bacon. Yield: 4 servings.

Ann Rabito,
Webster, Texas.

CREAMY MARINATED CARROTS

2 pounds carrots
½ cup commercial buttermilk-style salad
  dressing
⅓ cup commercial Italian salad dressing
¼ cup finely chopped onion
1 tablespoon chopped fresh parsley
¼ teaspoon dried whole dillweed
Dash of white pepper

Scrape carrots, and cut into 1- x ¼-inch sticks. Cook carrots, covered, in a small amount of boiling water 5 to 10 minutes or until crisp-tender; drain. Place in shallow container; set aside.

Combine remaining ingredients; stir well. Pour over carrots; toss gently to coat. Cover and chill; stir occasionally. Yield: 8 servings.

Lynda Ramage,
Lilburn, Georgia.

A Relish You'll Rave About

Melissa Weber of Three Rivers, Texas, shared a smart way to use up summer's leftover zucchini. She makes a relish that's just as good on pinto beans as it is on hot dogs, hamburgers, or with good old-fashioned cornbread.

Zucchini Relish will keep for five days in an airtight container. Store it in the refrigerator.

ZUCCHINI RELISH

1½ cups chopped onion (about 1 large)
2 cloves garlic, minced
2 teaspoons olive oil
2 cups chopped zucchini (about 1 large)
½ cup chopped green pepper
½ cup chopped sweet red pepper
¼ cup chicken broth
¼ cup cider vinegar
1 bay leaf
¼ teaspoon ground allspice
⅛ teaspoon crushed red pepper

Sauté onion and garlic in oil in a medium saucepan until tender. Add zucchini and peppers; cook 3 minutes over medium heat. Stir in remaining ingredients; cover and simmer 10 minutes. Discard bay leaf. Store relish in airtight containers in refrigerator up to 5 days. Yield: 3 cups.

Tuna Salads To Rave About

When you have some canned tuna on the pantry shelf, you are assured that a good meal is always close at hand. And what better way to enjoy this economical, nutritious food than served in a main-dish tuna salad?

Company Tuna Salad won't remind you of any tuna salad you've had between two slices of bread; it's much too fancy for that. Green beans, potatoes, artichoke hearts, avocado, and ripe olives are only the beginning of this chunky creation. It's then stuffed into tomato cups and garnished with hard-cooked egg slices and anchovy fillets. French dressing gives the salad color.

Water chestnuts, cauliflower flowerets, celery, and slivered almonds combine to give Crunchy Tuna Salad its name. Heat up some rolls to serve with this cold dish for an appetizing contrast in temperature.

Curried Tuna Salad With Grapes is as colorful as it is delicious. Green grapes, celery, carrot, and purple onion adorn this salad.

CURRIED TUNA SALAD WITH GRAPES

2 (6½-ounce) cans white tuna in water,
   drained and flaked
1½ cups seedless green grapes, halved
1½ cups chopped celery
¾ cup shredded carrot
¾ cup chopped green onions
¼ cup chopped purple onion
¾ cup mayonnaise
½ teaspoon curry powder
Lettuce leaves
¼ cup shredded carrot (optional)

Combine tuna, grapes, celery, ¾ cup carrot, green onions, and purple onion. Combine mayonnaise and curry powder; add to tuna mixture, and toss gently to mix. Cover and chill. Spoon salad into a lettuce-lined serving dish, sprinkle with ¼ cup carrot, if desired. Yield: 6 servings. *Lynn Rollins, Mechanicsville, Virginia.*

CRUNCHY TUNA SALAD

2 (6½-ounce) cans white tuna in water,
   drained and flaked
1 (8-ounce) can sliced water chestnuts,
   drained
1 cup cauliflower flowerets
1 cup chopped celery
½ cup slivered almonds, toasted
½ cup mayonnaise
¼ cup diced onion
1 tablespoon sweet pickle relish
1 tablespoon lemon juice
½ teaspoon prepared mustard
¼ teaspoon curry powder
Lettuce leaves (optional)

Combine first 5 ingredients; stir well, and set aside. Combine mayonnaise, onion, relish, lemon juice, mustard, and curry powder; add to tuna mixture, stirring well. Cover and chill.
Serve on lettuce leaves, if desired. Yield: 6 servings. *Jane Klopfenstein, Delray Beach, Florida.*

Serve crackers and a dry white wine with Company Tuna Salad for a scrumptious dinner.

COMPANY TUNA SALAD

4 medium potatoes
   (about 2½ pounds)
2 cups fresh green beans
1 (14-ounce) can artichoke hearts,
   drained and halved
1 ripe avocado, peeled and cubed
1 (12½-ounce) can tuna, drained
1 cup whole pitted ripe olives
1 (8-ounce) bottle commercial French
   dressing
6 ripe tomatoes
6 lettuce leaves
6 hard-cooked eggs, sliced
2 (2-ounce) cans anchovy fillets,
   drained
6 fresh parsley sprigs
Freshly ground pepper

Cook potatoes in boiling water 15 to 20 minutes or until tender. Drain and cool. Peel potatoes, and cut into ½-inch cubes; set aside.

Wash and trim beans; cut in 2-inch pieces. Steam 5 minutes. Combine potatoes, beans, artichokes, avocado, tuna, olives, and dressing; toss gently. Cover and chill 2 hours.

To serve, cut each tomato into 6 wedges, cutting to, but not through, base of tomato. Carefully spread wedges to form a cup. Spoon tuna mixture into tomatoes, and place on lettuce-lined plates. Garnish each with hard-cooked egg slices, anchovy fillets, and parsley. Sprinkle with pepper. Yield: 6 servings. *Louise Walker, Lexington, Tennessee.*

TUNA-RICE SALAD

2 cups cooked long-grain rice
1 (6½-ounce) can white tuna, drained
½ cup chopped sweet red pepper
¼ cup sliced black olives
2 tablespoons thinly sliced green onions
2 tablespoons chopped fresh parsley
¾ cup mayonnaise
2 tablespoons white wine vinegar
½ teaspoon dried whole tarragon
⅛ teaspoon pepper
Lettuce leaves
Red pepper strips (optional)

Combine first 6 ingredients; stir well. Combine mayonnaise, vinegar, tarragon, and pepper; add to tuna mixture, and stir well. Spoon into a lightly oiled 3½-cup mold; let stand 5 minutes. Invert onto a lettuce-lined platter. Cover and chill. Garnish with pepper strips, if desired. Yield: 4 servings.

Cathy Williams,
Vale, North Carolina.

Stuff A Pita With Flavor

If you're ready for a sandwich that's different, why not try serving it on something besides buns or whole grain breads? Split a pita bread round to create a pocket sandwich. We borrowed our readers' best salad and sandwich ideas to come up with the pita sandwiches featured here.

For a satisfying lunch, serve Spinach-Walnut Pitas with gazpacho or a creamed vegetable soup. Pair Tuna-in-a-Pita Pocket with a fruit cup or yogurt. Or come up with a favorite combination all your own; the result will be a tasty, nutritious meal.

TUNA-IN-A-PITA POCKET

1 (6½-ounce) can tuna, drained
   and flaked
½ cup chopped celery
¼ cup chopped onion
½ cup process cheese spread
½ small head iceberg lettuce,
   shredded
¾ cup chopped cucumber
4 (6-inch) pita bread rounds,
   cut in half
1¼ cups chopped tomato

Combine tuna, celery, onion, and cheese spread; stir well. Layer lettuce, cucumber, and tuna mixture in pita halves. Top each with tomato; serve immediately. Yield: 4 servings.

Carolyn Gower,
Columbia, South Carolina.

HAM-AND-CHEESE PITA SANDWICHES

1 cup chopped, cooked ham
½ cup (2 ounces) shredded Swiss cheese
½ cup (2 ounces) shredded Cheddar
   cheese
¼ cup chopped onion
2 tomatoes, chopped
½ cup torn lettuce leaves
Salt and pepper to taste
3 to 4 tablespoons mayonnaise
3 (6-inch) pita bread rounds, cut in half
Lettuce leaves (optional)

Combine ham, cheeses, onion, tomatoes, lettuce, salt, pepper, and mayonnaise; toss gently. Line pita bread halves with lettuce, if desired; fill with ham mixture. Yield: 3 servings.

Jaquie Waller,
Oklahoma City, Oklahoma.

SPINACH-WALNUT PITAS

4 cups torn spinach, lightly packed
1 cup chopped iceberg lettuce
1 small zucchini, thinly sliced
1 (6-ounce) jar marinated artichoke
   hearts, drained and chopped
2 green onions, sliced
1 avocado, coarsely chopped
¼ cup toasted chopped walnuts
2 tablespoons toasted sesame seeds
Piquant French Dressing
4 (6-inch) pita bread rounds, cut in half

Combine spinach, lettuce, zucchini, artichoke, green onions, avocado, walnuts, and sesame seeds in a large bowl. Toss with Piquant French Dressing. Spoon into pita bread halves. Serve immediately. Yield: 4 servings.

Piquant French Dressing:

2 tablespoons sugar
½ teaspoon salt
½ teaspoon paprika
½ teaspoon dry mustard
⅛ teaspoon pepper
½ teaspoon celery seeds
½ teaspoon grated onion
2 tablespoons lemon juice
¼ cup plus 2 tablespoons vegetable oil
1 clove garlic, cut crosswise

Combine sugar, salt, paprika, mustard, pepper, celery seeds, onion, and lemon juice in a small mixing bowl; beat at medium speed of electric mixer until blended. Add oil slowly while mixer is running. Continue beating until mixture thickens. Add garlic, and refrigerate 1 hour. Remove garlic. Stir well before serving. Yield: ½ cup.

Anita Cox,
Fort Worth, Texas.

TURKEY SALAD PITA SANDWICHES

2 tablespoons vinegar
2 teaspoons water
½ teaspoon salt
¼ teaspoon sugar
¾ pound turkey, cut into julienne
   strips
2 hard-cooked eggs, chopped
½ cup chopped celery
½ cup seedless red grapes, halved
½ cup mayonnaise
3 (6-inch) pita bread rounds,
   cut in half
Lettuce leaves
½ cup pimiento-stuffed olives, sliced

Combine vinegar, water, salt, and sugar; stir well. Pour mixture over turkey strips; toss lightly. Cover and chill 2 hours. Drain turkey.

Combine turkey, eggs, celery, grapes, and mayonnaise; toss gently to coat. Line each pita bread half with lettuce, and fill with turkey mixture. Sprinkle with olives. Yield: 3 servings.

Sarah Watson,
Knoxville, Tennessee.

Right: *Today pizzas sport bold new flavors, such as Pizza With Artichoke and Prosciutto (page 182).*

Pages 204 and 205: *Jalapeño peppers provide the heat in commercial picante sauce that is used for traditional breakfast Migas (back) and Garlic-Grilled Chicken. Serrano chiles (in foreground) add fire to Salsa Cruda, a homemade version of picante sauce. (Recipes are on page 180.)*

Page 206: *Welcome fall with (front to back) Raisin-Pecan Pie, Butternut Squash Pie, and Holiday Mincemeat Pie. (Recipes begin on page 212.)*

Making The Best Cream Pie

Even the most experienced cook knows how tricky cream pies can be. Combining milk, eggs, and cornstarch requires expertise—and maybe a little luck. Cooking procedures (and even humid weather) can affect the thickness of the filling and the appearance of a meringue.

Cornstarch is the most critical ingredient because it thickens the filling. To avoid lumps, mix the cornstarch with other dry ingredients, or stir a cool liquid, such as milk, into it before adding to a hot liquid. Take extra care with the egg yolks, too. In most of the recipes, one-fourth of the hot filling is added to the beaten yolks before stirring the egg yolks into the hot mixture.

Once all the ingredients are in your saucepan, stir the mixture until thickened, or boil one minute. Keep stirring, and let the mixture boil only as long as specified in the recipe.

BANANA CREAM PIE

⅔ cup sugar
Dash of salt
¼ cup cornstarch
3 egg yolks
1 cup half-and-half
2 cups milk, scalded
2 tablespoons butter
1 teaspoon vanilla extract
¼ teaspoon banana extract (optional)
1 baked 9-inch pastry shell
2 ripe bananas, thinly sliced
Meringue (recipe follows)

Combine sugar, salt, and cornstarch in a heavy saucepan. Beat egg yolks and half-and-half at medium speed of an electric mixer; add to sugar mixture. Pour hot milk slowly into egg mixture, stirring constantly. Cook over medium heat, stirring constantly, until thickened. Remove from heat; add butter, vanilla, and if desired, banana extract. Pour one-third of mixture into baked pastry shell, and layer with banana slices. Repeat layers, ending with filling. Cover with wax paper, and set aside; make meringue.

Remove wax paper; spread meringue over filling, sealing to edge of pastry. Bake at 350° for 12 to 15 minutes or until golden brown. Cool completely before serving. Yield: one 9-inch pie.

Meringue:

½ cup sugar, divided
1 tablespoon cornstarch
⅛ teaspoon salt
½ cup water
3 egg whites
½ teaspoon vanilla extract

Combine ¼ cup sugar, cornstarch, and salt in a saucepan; stirring constantly, add water, and cook over medium heat until mixture comes to a boil. Boil 1 minute; cool completely.

Beat egg whites (at room temperature) at high speed of an electric mixer until foamy. Gradually add remaining ¼ cup sugar, 1 tablespoon at a time, beating until soft peaks form. Add vanilla and cornstarch mixture; beat until stiff peaks form. Yield: meringue for one 9-inch pie.
Mrs. Harry Zimmer, El Paso, Texas.

BUTTERSCOTCH CREAM PIE

¾ cup firmly packed brown sugar
⅓ cup whipping cream
2 tablespoons butter or margarine
2 cups milk, divided
¼ cup cornstarch
2 eggs, separated
1 teaspoon vanilla extract
1 baked 9-inch pastry shell
¼ teaspoon cream of tartar
¼ cup sugar

Combine brown sugar, whipping cream, and butter in a heavy saucepan; cook over low heat until butter melts, stirring often. Add 1½ cups milk, and continue cooking until milk is hot. Combine cornstarch and remaining ½ cup milk; mix well, and set aside. Beat egg yolks until thick and lemon colored. Gradually stir about one-fourth of hot mixture into yolks. Add to remaining hot mixture. Add cornstarch mixture, and bring to a boil over medium heat, stirring constantly. Boil 1 minute. Remove from heat, and stir in vanilla. Pour into pastry shell.

Beat egg whites (at room temperature) and cream of tartar at high speed of an electric mixer until foamy. Gradually add ¼ cup sugar, 1 tablespoon at a time, beating until stiff peaks form and sugar dissolves (2 to 4 minutes). Spread meringue over hot filling, sealing to edge of pastry.

Bake at 350° for 12 to 15 minutes, or until golden brown. Cool. Yield: one 9-inch pie. *Ann Marie Heatwole, Denmark, South Carolina.*

COCONUT CREAM PIE

¾ cup sugar
¼ cup cornstarch
¼ teaspoon salt
2 cups milk
3 egg yolks
2 tablespoons butter or margarine
1 teaspoon vanilla extract
1 cup flaked coconut
1 baked 9-inch pastry shell
1 cup whipping cream
¼ cup sifted powdered sugar
2 tablespoons flaked coconut, toasted
  (optional)

Combine ¾ cup sugar, cornstarch, and salt in a heavy saucepan; gradually stir in milk. Cook over medium heat, stirring constantly, until thickened and bubbly. Cook 1 minute. Beat egg yolks; gradually stir about one-fourth of hot mixture into yolks; add to remaining hot mixture, stirring constantly. Cook, stirring constantly, 30 seconds. Remove from heat; stir in butter, vanilla, and 1 cup flaked coconut. Pour into baked pastry shell. Cool completely; cover and chill 1 to 2 hours.

Beat whipping cream at high speed of an electric mixer until foamy; gradually add powdered sugar, one tablespoon at a time, beating until stiff peaks form. Pipe or dollop onto pie. Sprinkle with toasted coconut, if desired. Yield: one 9-inch pie. *Debbie Dermid, Horse Shoe, North Carolina.*

Tip: Always measure accurately. Level dry ingredients in a cup with a knife edge or a spoon handle. Measure liquids in a cup so that the fluid is level with the top of the measuring line. Measure solid shortening by packing it firmly in a graduated measuring cup.

CHOCOLATE CREAM PIE

2 (1-ounce) squares semisweet
   chocolate
¼ cup plus 1 tablespoon cornstarch
3 cups milk, divided
3 eggs, separated
1 cup sugar
1 teaspoon vanilla extract
1 baked 9-inch pastry shell
¼ teaspoon plus ⅛ teaspoon cream
   of tartar
¼ cup plus 2 tablespoons sugar

Melt chocolate in top of a double boiler, and set aside.

Combine cornstarch and ½ cup milk in a small bowl; set aside.

Scald remaining 2½ cups milk in a medium saucepan. Beat egg yolks and 1 cup sugar in a mixing bowl; gradually stir about one-fourth of hot milk into yolks, stirring until well blended. Add to remaining hot milk; stir in cornstarch mixture and melted chocolate. Bring mixture to a boil, stirring constantly with a wire whisk. Boil 1 minute. Remove from heat; stir in vanilla. Pour filling mixture into pastry shell.

Beat egg whites (at room temperature) and cream of tartar at high speed of an electric mixer. Gradually add remaining sugar, 1 tablespoon at a time, beating until stiff peaks form and sugar dissolves (2 to 4 minutes). Spread meringue over hot filling, sealing to edge of pastry. Bake at 350° for 12 to 15 minutes or until golden brown. Let cool. Yield: one 9-inch pie.

Barbara Kintzele,
Wilson, North Carolina.

From Our Kitchen To Yours

Improper storage, inadequate cooking, and unsanitary conditions can cause food spoilage. Unfortunately, you cannot see, smell, or taste the culprits—*Salmonella, Staphylococcus aureus, Clostridium perfringens,* and *Botulinum.* Nonetheless, these bacteria can cause mild to severe intestinal flulike symptoms. Careful attention to food handling can prevent potential illnesses.

— Always wash hands before preparing food and after handling raw meat. If you have a cut or infection, wear gloves. Between preparation steps, wash hands, countertops, acrylic cutting boards, and utensils, using hot, soapy water—especially when working with raw meat and poultry.

— Clean wooden cutting boards with a mixture of 1 part bleach to 8 parts water; then rinse. Wash kitchen linens often, and discard dirty or mildewed sponges.

— Do not store food near household cleaners or leaky pipes. Store frozen foods below 0° F, perishable foods in the rcfrigerator, and canned foods in a dry place.

— The high temperatures used when boiling, baking, frying, and roasting kill most bacteria. Cook meat and poultry to the recommended temperature (pork 160°, poultry 185°), using a meat thermometer for accuracy. If not serving hot food immediately, keep it safe at a holding temperature of 140° to 165°; do not leave hot food at room temperature for more than two hours. Refrigerate leftovers immediately.

— Bacteria will not multiply as fast below 40° F. When shopping, select refrigerated and frozen items last, and quickly take them home. Read food labels for special storage requirements. Wrap and store meat items in the coldest part of the refrigerator one or two days; do not let meat juice drip onto other foods. Thaw frozen meat and poultry in the refrigerator overnight. For faster thawing, place the frozen package in a watertight plastic bag under cold water, changing the water often. You should not thaw any kind of meat and poultry under warm water or at room temperature.

Tips

—Germs are more common in foods handled often during preparation, such as stuffing, potato salad, meat salads, and cream pies. Remember to treat these foods with care.

—Marinate food in glass or plastic containers in the refrigerator. (Marinades contain acid, which reacts with some metals.)

—Before serving all home-canned vegetables, boil them in a covered saucepan 10 minutes, but boil spinach, corn, and meats for 20 minutes.

Bacteria	Susceptible Foods	Prevention
Salmonella	Meat, poultry, fish, eggs, milk	Thoroughly cook all kinds of meat, poultry, fish. Keep raw food separate from cooked food. Do not drink unpasteurized or raw milk.
Staphylococcus aureus	Meat, poultry, cheese, egg products, starchy salads, meat and poultry salads, custards, cream-filled desserts	Wash hands and utensils before preparation. Do not leave at room temperature over 2 hours.
Clostridium perfringens	Large portions of foods that cool slowly, chafing-dish foods not kept hot, poultry, gravies, stews, meat casseroles	Keep food hot (over 140° F). Keep food cold (under 40° F). Divide foods cooked in bulk into shallow containers to cool.
Botulinum	Home-canned foods and commercial canned foods	Use only reliable recipes. Don't use canned goods with cloudy liquids, loose lids, spurting liquid, or goods in cracked jars; avoid swollen or dented cans and lids.

October

Cooked Up In The Bayous

Gumbo and jambalaya evolved out of the necessity to feed large families and crowds of people attending various social gatherings. Both dishes took seasonings well and utilized rice (which in Louisiana is locally grown). The amount of meat used varied, based upon availability and the budget. All this is still true today, and there are as many recipes for gumbo and jambalaya as there are good cooks in Louisiana.

Original jambalaya recipes depended on ham or at least a ham bone. The term *jambalaya* originated from the French word for ham, *jambon,* or the Spanish word, *jamón.*

Gombo, the African word for okra, gave gumbo its name. This dish is thickened with okra or gumbo filé (fee-lay) powder. It's best to add gumbo filé during the last few minutes of cooking; it will give a stringy consistency if cooked too long or if reheated. If you're going to make a large amount, let guests add it to each bowl as it's served. Many cooks consider gumbo filé essential for authentic gumbo.

All cooks agree on one thing: To make gumbo, you first make a roux, a gravylike mixture made by slowly cooking oil and flour. A dark-colored roux gives gumbo its characteristic texture as well as a smoky taste. (For some tips on cooking roux, see next page.)

SEAFOOD GUMBO

½ cup bacon drippings
1 cup all-purpose flour
1 bunch green onions
1 green pepper, diced
1 large onion, diced
3 stalks celery, diced
2 cloves garlic, minced
1 large tomato, chopped
2 quarts water
1½ teaspoons salt
2 teaspoons pepper
½ teaspoon red pepper
¼ cup minced fresh parsley
2 cups water
1½ pounds unpeeled fresh medium shrimp
1 pint Standard oysters, undrained
1 (10-ounce) package frozen sliced okra, thawed
½ pound crabmeat
Gumbo filé
Hot cooked rice

Heat bacon drippings in a heavy skillet over medium heat; stir in 1 cup flour. Cook, stirring constantly, about 30 minutes or until roux is the color of chocolate.

Slice green onions, reserving green tops, and set aside. Cook sliced green onions, green pepper, onion, celery, garlic, and tomato in roux until vegetables are tender. Combine vegetables, 2 quarts water, salt, pepper, red pepper, and parsley in a large Dutch oven; stir well. Simmer, uncovered, for 2 hours. Add 2 cups water; bring to a boil.

Peel and devein shrimp. Add shrimp, oysters, okra, and green onion tops; simmer 10 minutes. Stir in crabmeat and gumbo filé; let stand 15 minutes. Add water, if necessary, for desired consistency. Serve over rice. Yield: 1 gallon.
Chuck Spacek,
Portsmouth, Virginia.

CREOLE JAMBALAYA

¾ cup chopped onion
½ cup chopped celery
¼ cup chopped green pepper
1 tablespoon minced fresh parsley
1 clove garlic, minced
2 tablespoons butter or margarine, melted
1 (28-ounce) can tomatoes, undrained and chopped
1 (10½-ounce) can beef broth, undiluted
1¼ cups water
1 teaspoon sugar
½ teaspoon dried whole thyme
½ teaspoon chili powder
¼ teaspoon pepper
2 cups cubed cooked ham
1 cup uncooked long-grain rice
1½ pounds unpeeled fresh medium shrimp

Sauté first 5 ingredients in butter in a Dutch oven until vegetables are tender. Stir in tomatoes, broth, water, sugar, thyme, chili powder, pepper, and ham. Bring to a boil; stir in rice. Cover, reduce heat, and simmer 25 minutes.

Peel and devein shrimp. Add to rice mixture; simmer, uncovered, 10 minutes. Yield: 6 servings.
Gwen Templeton,
Albertville, Alabama.

GUMBO YA YA

1 (4-pound) broiler-fryer
1 (1½- to 2-pound) wild duck, dressed
1½ teaspoons salt
½ teaspoon pepper
4 quarts water
1 cup bacon drippings
1 cup all-purpose flour
5 to 6 stalks celery, chopped
3 large onions, chopped
2 green peppers, chopped
1 cup finely chopped fresh parsley
1 clove garlic, minced
1 pound smoked sausage, cut into ½-inch slices
1 (10-ounce) can tomatoes with green chiles, undrained
1 teaspoon seasoned pepper
¼ teaspoon hot sauce
1 (16-ounce) package frozen sliced okra, thawed
Hot cooked rice
Gumbo filé (optional)
Chopped green onions or chives (optional)

Combine chicken, duck, salt, and ½ teaspoon pepper in a large Dutch oven; cover with water, and bring to a boil. Cover, reduce heat, and simmer 1 hour or until duck is tender. Remove chicken and duck from broth; reserve broth. Set meats and broth aside to cool. Skin and bone chicken and duck. Coarsely chop both meats.

Combine bacon drippings and flour in a large Dutch oven; cook over low heat 30 to 35 minutes, stirring constantly, until roux is the color of chocolate.

Add celery, onions, green peppers, parsley, garlic, and sausage; cook over medium heat until vegetables are tender. Gradually add cooled broth, stirring constantly. Add chicken, duck, tomatoes, seasoned pepper, and hot sauce. Bring mixture to a boil; reduce heat, and simmer 2½ to 3½ hours. Add okra; cook an additional 20 minutes. Cool. Cover and refrigerate 8 hours.

Remove fat from surface, and discard. Heat gumbo over medium heat, stirring occasionally. Serve gumbo over hot cooked rice. Sprinkle with gumbo filé, green onions, or chives, if desired. Serve gumbo immediately. Yield: about 5 quarts.
Rick Freeland,
Helena, Arkansas.

Tip: When buying garlic, select firm, plump bulbs that have dry, unbroken skins. Store in a cool, dry place that is well ventilated. The flavor will remain sharp up to four months.

JAMBALAYA DE COVINGTON

1 pound turkey necks, smoked
5 to 6 cups water
2 cups uncooked long-grain rice
½ pound andouille sausage or other
   smoked link sausage
¼ cup vegetable oil
¼ cup all-purpose flour
1 bunch green onions
1 cup chopped onion
1 cup chopped celery
½ cup chopped green pepper
1 tablespoon minced parsley
4 cloves garlic, minced
½ cup tomato sauce
1 teaspoon garlic salt
½ teaspoon pepper
½ teaspoon paprika
½ teaspoon dried whole thyme
¼ teaspoon red pepper
1⅓ cups diced smoked ham (½ pound)

Place turkey necks in a large saucepan; cover with water, and bring to a boil. Cover, reduce heat, and simmer about 1 hour. Drain, reserving broth. Remove meat from necks; set aside.

Cook rice according to package directions using reserved broth as liquid.

Place sausage in a shallow pan; bake at 350° for 20 minutes. Chop sausage, and set aside.

Combine oil and flour in a large Dutch oven; cook over medium heat, stirring constantly, until roux is the color of caramel. Slice green onions, reserving green tops; set green tops aside. Add sliced green onions, chopped onion, celery, green pepper, parsley, garlic, and tomato sauce to the roux.

Cook, stirring frequently, about 15 minutes. Add garlic salt and next 4 ingredients; stir well. Add turkey, sausage, and ham; stir well. Add rice and green onion tops; toss gently. Yield: 8 to 10 servings. *Joanne Champagne, Covington, Louisiana.*

From Our Kitchen To Yours

Remember eating that incredibly rich-tasting gumbo? In most cases, the secret behind its distinctive flavor lies in the roux, which is a blend of all-purpose flour and vegetable oil or bacon drippings. Roux enhances traditional gumbo with unique flavor, richness, and color. The success in preparing this favorite Cajun food depends on cooking the roux to the proper color needed.

The color of roux can range from light to dark brown, depending upon how long the mixture cooks. The recipes featured in "Cooked Up in the Bayous" on the facing page use two distinct yet frequently used color stages—a light brown, we term caramel, and a dark brown that we describe as the color of chocolate. The longer the roux cooks, the darker it turns; dark roux makes the thinnest gumbos.

Cooking time, temperature, ingredient amounts, and type of pan are all factors that affect the procedure for making a roux. In our test kitchens we usually prepare a roux over medium heat using a cast-iron skillet.

If you use a Dutch oven instead, the roux takes longer to reach the desired color. Differences in ingredient amounts and specified colors account for the time variations in our recipes.

During the 18th century, **roux,** the French word for red, was defined as flour cooked long enough to change color. Today roux can be prepared using the traditional procedure (see photographs below), or by the quicker microwave procedure or conventional oven procedure, which eliminates the fat from the roux.

To make an oven roux: Place ¼ cup all-purpose flour in an 8-inch square pan. Bake at 400° for 15 to 20 minutes, stirring every 4 minutes. Flour will be the color of caramel. (This yields enough roux for 12 cups gumbo.)

To make a microwave roux: Combine ¾ cup vegetable oil and ¾ cup all-purpose flour in a 4-cup glass measure, stirring until mixture is blended. Microwave at HIGH 6 minutes; stir and microwave at HIGH 2 minutes. Stir mixture, and continue microwaving at HIGH 1 to 3 minutes, stirring at 1-minute intervals until mixture turns the color of caramel or chocolate. (Roux continues to brown as it cools; do not overcook.)

Additional Tips

—Use a wire whisk to initially blend flour into the roux; change to a wooden

To make a roux, heat oil or bacon drippings; add flour, stirring until blended.

Cook roux mixture until desired color is reached; this color is caramel.

This roux cooked longer than the one shown at left and is the color of chocolate.

spoon for stirring during the actual cooking process.

—Stir the roux constantly to prevent burning when cooking conventionally.

—Visible black specks indicate burned flour; discard the entire mixture, and start over.

—Roux darkens as it cools; adding vegetables, such as onion, green pepper, or celery, stops the browning process and enhances the flavor.

—To reduce fat in roux, prepare it ahead, cool, and store in an airtight container in the refrigerator. Spoon off excess oil before reheating.

—When microwaving roux, handle the glass measure with care; the glass gets very hot.

Traditional Fall Pies

To many Southerners, autumn's bounty of vegetables and nuts brings a bumper crop of hot, sweet pies. While traditional flavors such as apple and pumpkin remain popular choices, our readers share recipes for some more unusual pies. One, for instance, calls for butternut squash.

Many accomplished cooks say the pastry is what makes a really good pie. For the recipes here, you can use your own pastry or sample one from a reader. If time is short, consider a ready-made, commercial pastry. For pies such as Butternut Squash Pie, Autumn Pumpkin Pie, and Raisin-Pecan Pie, you can use either the zigzag or sunburst pie crust borders. To make the braided border you need a double-crust 9-inch dough, but you will probably have some left over.

GRANDMOTHER'S APPLE PIE

6½ cups peeled and thinly sliced apples (about 5 apples)
1 cup water
¾ cup sugar
¼ to ½ teaspoon ground allspice
Pinch of salt
Pastry for double-crust 9-inch pie

Combine apples and water in a large saucepan; bring to a boil. Cover, reduce heat, and simmer 10 minutes or until apples are tender. Drain well. Return to saucepan. Mash slightly with a potato masher. Stir in sugar, allspice, and salt, mixing well.

Roll half of pastry to ⅛-inch thickness, and fit into a 9-inch pieplate. Spoon apple mixture into pieplate. Roll remaining pastry to ⅛-inch thickness. Cover pie with crust. Trim pastry; seal and flute edges. Cut slits to make an apple design in top crust for steam to escape. Use extra pastry to make a leaf-shaped cutout; add cutout to apple design. Bake at 375° for 45 minutes or until golden brown. Cover edges with foil to prevent overbrowning. Yield: one 9-inch pie. *Gladys Stout, Elizabethton, Tennessee.*

BUTTERNUT SQUASH PIE

(pictured on page 206)

1 (2-pound) butternut squash
¾ cup sugar
1 teaspoon ground cinnamon
½ teaspoon ground allspice
½ teaspoon ground nutmeg
¼ teaspoon ground cloves
¼ teaspoon salt
1 (12-ounce) can evaporated milk
2 eggs, beaten
Pastry (recipe follows)

Slice squash in half lengthwise, and remove seeds. Place cut side down in a shallow baking pan; add water to depth of ¾ inch. Bake, uncovered, at 350° for 45 minutes or until tender. Drain and cool. Peel squash; mash pulp thoroughly. Set aside 1¼ cups mashed squash; store remainder in refrigerator for other uses.

Combine pulp, sugar, spices, and salt; stir well. Gradually stir in milk and eggs. Pour into pastry shell; bake at 400° for 10 minutes. Reduce heat to 350°; bake an additional 40 minutes or until set. Cool. Yield: one 9-inch pie.

Pastry:

1½ cups all-purpose flour
½ teaspoon salt
½ cup shortening
4 to 5 tablespoons milk

Combine flour and salt; cut in shortening with pastry blender until mixture resembles coarse meal. Sprinkle milk, one tablespoon at a time, over surface; stir with a fork until all ingredients are moistened.

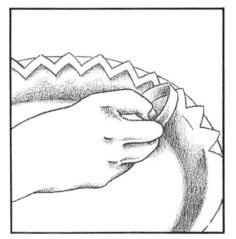

To make a sunburst edge, roll out pastry, and place in pieplate. Press one end of a diamond-shaped cookie cutter on pastry edge to make a pointed border around the pie. Repeat the procedure, using a smaller cookie cutter and making indentations underneath the first points.

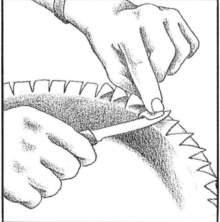

To make a zigzag edge, prepare pastry for a single-crust 9-inch pie. Roll out pastry, and place in pieplate. Cut vertical slits all around pastry edge at ½-inch intervals. Then fold each ½-inch piece of pastry diagonally, forming triangles all around the edge of the pieplate.

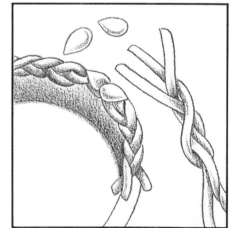

For braided edge, prepare pastry for a double-crust 9-inch pie, and place crust in pieplate. Roll other half into 14-inch strip; cut into nine ⅓-inch-wide strips. Braid 3 strips, and apply to moistened pastry edge. Repeat with rest of strips. Make leaf cutouts with rest of dough; set where braids join.

Shape dough into a ball, and place on a lightly floured surface; roll dough into a circle 2 inches larger than inverted 9-inch pieplate. Place in pieplate, and trim edges. Fold under to form standing rim; flute edges. Yield: one 9-inch pastry shell.   *Rudie Henn,*
Louisville, Kentucky.

RAISIN-PECAN PIE
(pictured on page 206)

Pastry for 9-inch pie
3 eggs, beaten
½ cup butter or margarine, melted
2 tablespoons vinegar
1½ cups sugar
½ teaspoon ground cinnamon
⅔ cup raisins
½ cup chopped pecans
1 teaspoon vanilla extract
Whipped cream (optional)

Roll pastry to ⅛-inch thickness on a lightly floured surface. Place in a 9-inch pieplate; trim off excess pastry along edges. Fold edges under, and flute. Prick bottom and sides of pastry with a fork. Bake at 450° for 3 to 5 minutes. Remove pastry from oven, and allow to cool completely.

Combine beaten eggs, melted butter, vinegar, sugar, and cinnamon, mixing well. Stir in raisins, chopped pecans, and vanilla. Pour into prepared pastry shell. Bake at 350° for 30 minutes or until pie is set. Garnish pie with whipped cream, if desired. Yield: one 9-inch pie.   *Barbara Sims,*
Union City, Tennessee.

AUTUMN PUMPKIN PIE

2 eggs, slightly beaten
3 cups mashed cooked pumpkin
1 (12-ounce) can evaporated milk
1 cup sugar
¼ cup all-purpose flour
1 teaspoon vanilla extract
½ teaspoon salt
½ teaspoon ground cinnamon
½ teaspoon ground ginger
½ teaspoon ground allspice
¼ teaspoon ground cloves
¼ teaspoon ground nutmeg
1 unbaked (10-inch) pastry shell
¼ cup butter or margarine, melted
½ cup all-purpose flour
½ cup firmly packed brown sugar
½ cup chopped pecans

Combine eggs, pumpkin, milk, 1 cup sugar, ¼ cup flour, vanilla, salt, and spices; blend well. Pour mixture into pastry shell. Bake at 400° for 10 minutes. Reduce heat to 350°, and bake an additional 35 minutes.

Combine butter, ½ cup flour, and ½ cup brown sugar; blend well. Stir in pecans; sprinkle mixture on pie. Bake at 350° for 10 minutes. Yield: one 10-inch pie.   *Helen H. Dosier,*
Sparta, North Carolina.

FRENCH PEAR PIE

6 cups peeled and sliced pears
2 tablespoons lemon juice
⅓ cup sugar
⅓ cup all-purpose flour
½ teaspoon ground ginger
⅓ cup light corn syrup
1 unbaked (9-inch) pastry shell
⅓ cup all-purpose flour
⅓ cup firmly packed brown sugar
2 tablespoons butter or margarine

Combine pears and lemon juice; toss gently. Combine sugar, ⅓ cup flour, and ginger; add sugar mixture and corn syrup to pears. Spoon mixture into pastry shell.

Combine ⅓ cup flour and brown sugar in a small bowl; blend well. Add butter; mix until crumbly. Sprinkle on pear mixture. Bake at 450° for 15 minutes. Reduce heat to 350°, and bake 30 minutes longer. Yield: one 9-inch pie.   *Ethel C. Jernegan,*
Savannah, Georgia.

HOLIDAY MINCEMEAT PIE
(pictured on page 206)

Pastry for double-crust 9-inch pie
1 (28-ounce) jar mincemeat
1 cup diced unpeeled apple
¼ cup brandy
Cheddar cheese slices (optional)

Roll half of pastry to ⅛-inch thickness on a lightly floured surface; fit into a 9-inch pieplate. Set aside. Chill the remaining pastry.

Combine mincemeat, apple, and brandy in a medium bowl; stir well. Spoon into pastry shell.

Roll remaining pastry to ⅛-inch thickness; cut pastry into ½-inch-wide strips. Twist each strip several times, and place on pie, lattice fashion. Trim edges; then seal and flute. Bake at 425° for 30 minutes or until golden. Serve with a slice of cheese over pie, if desired. Yield: one 9-inch pie.
Mrs. Fred M. Cloninger,
Atlanta, Georgia.

Treat Your Friends To A Halloween Buffet

Before the ghouls get you, host a Halloween buffet for the ghosts and goblins in your neighborhood. That special day can be as much fun for adults as it is for children.

Ask each guest to bring a small pumpkin to carve at the party. Set the carved pumpkins out on the front stoop with a candle inside to light the way for other partygoers. Or instead of serving Jack-O'-Lantern Cookies (next page) from the buffet, set up a table and let each guest decorate his or her own cookie.

Offer two beverages for different tastes. Orange Soda Punch (next page) is a frothy nonalcoholic treat, while Hot Mexican Cider is spiked with tequila.

We warn you. Satan's Wings (next page) are as hot as their name implies. Warn guests before they dip!

HOT MEXICAN CIDER

2 quarts apple cider
¼ cup lemon juice
1⅔ cups tequila
⅓ cup orange-flavored liqueur
Lemon slices

Combine apple cider and lemon juice in a Dutch oven; cook over medium heat until mixture simmers. Add tequila and orange liqueur; cook until heated.

To serve, pour into individual mugs, and garnish with lemon slices. Yield: 2½ quarts.   *Joanne Warner Gross,*
Lufkin, Texas.

ORANGE SODA PUNCH

4 egg whites
¼ cup sugar
1 quart orange juice, chilled
1 (10-ounce) bottle lemon-lime carbonated beverage, chilled
1 cup milk
¼ cup sugar
¼ teaspoon ground nutmeg
Ground nutmeg (optional)

Beat egg whites (at room temperature) at high speed of electric mixer 1 minute. Gradually add ¼ cup sugar, 1 tablespoon at a time, beating until stiff peaks form. Set aside.

Combine orange juice and next 4 ingredients in a large punch bowl; stir until sugar dissolves. Add egg whites; stir gently with a wire whisk just until blended. Sprinkle with additional ground nutmeg, if desired. Serve immediately. Yield: about 2½ quarts.

Dolly Northcutt,
Fairfield, Alabama.

SPINACH DIP

1 (10-ounce) package frozen chopped spinach, thawed
1 cup commercial sour cream
1 (8-ounce) can water chestnuts, drained and chopped
½ cup shredded carrot
1 tablespoon mayonnaise
1 tablespoon grated onion
1 (1-ounce) envelope buttermilk dressing mix
1 medium-size red cabbage

Drain spinach well, pressing between layers of paper towels; set aside.

Combine sour cream, water chestnuts, carrot, mayonnaise, onion, and buttermilk dressing mix; stir well. Stir in spinach. Chill.

Trim core end of medium-size cabbage to form a flat base. Cut a crosswise slice from top, making it wide enough to remove about a fourth of the head; lift out enough inner leaves from the cabbage to form a shell about 1 inch thick. (Reserve the slice and inner leaves of cabbage for other uses.)

Spoon dip into cavity of cabbage; serve with an assortment of fresh vegetables and crackers. Yield: 2½ cups.

Clairiece Gilbert Humphrey,
Charlottesville, Virginia.

SATAN'S WINGS

2 pounds chicken wings
½ cup all-purpose flour
1 teaspoon salt
½ teaspoon red pepper
¼ teaspoon black pepper
Vegetable oil
Sauce (recipe follows)

Split chicken wings at joints; discard tips. Combine flour and next 3 ingredients in a plastic 'bag; shake to mix. Place 3 or 4 pieces of chicken in plastic bag; shake well to coat. Repeat procedure with remaining chicken.

Heat 1 inch of oil in a large skillet to 325°; add chicken, and fry 20 minutes or until golden brown, turning once. Drain on paper towels. Serve with sauce. Yield: about 18 appetizer servings.

Sauce:

1 tablespoon red pepper flakes
2 tablespoons lemon juice
2 tablespoons hot sauce
¼ cup catsup
2 tablespoons vinegar
⅛ teaspoon salt
½ cup butter or margarine, melted

Place red pepper flakes in blender; blend on high speed 30 seconds. Add remaining ingredients except butter; blend on high speed 30 seconds.

Blend on low speed, adding butter in a slow, steady stream. Blend on high speed until thick. Yield: 1 cup.

Nancy Holmberg,
Pinehurst, North Carolina.

JACK-O'-LANTERN COOKIES

½ cup butter or margarine, softened
1 cup sugar
1 cup canned or mashed cooked pumpkin
1 tablespoon grated orange rind
2 cups all-purpose flour
1 teaspoon baking powder
1 teaspoon baking soda
¼ teaspoon salt
1 teaspoon ground cinnamon
½ cup raisins
½ cup chopped pecans
Frosting (recipe follows)
Decorative candies (optional)

Place the bowl of Orange Soda Punch in a grapevine wreath, and arrange treats, such as Jack-O'-Lantern Cookies, Satan's Wings, and Spinach Dip with vegetables around it. Serve the Hot Mexican Cider from mugs.

Combine butter, sugar, pumpkin, and orange rind in a large bowl; beat at medium speed of an electric mixer until light and fluffy.

Combine flour, baking powder, soda, salt, and cinnamon; beat at low speed of an electric mixer until blended. Stir in raisins and pecans.

Drop dough by heaping tablespoonfuls 4 inches apart onto lightly greased cookie sheets. Lightly press each cookie into a 3½-inch circle with fingertips dipped in flour. Bake at 375° for 16 to 18 minutes or until brown. Cool cookies completely on wire racks. Spread frosting on tops of cookies. Decorate with raisins, candy corn, chocolate morsels, and cinnamon candies, if desired. Yield: 1½ dozen cookies.

Frosting:

3 tablespoons butter or margarine,
   softened
3 cups sifted powdered sugar
3 to 4 tablespoons milk
1½ teaspoons vanilla extract
3 drops of red food coloring
3 drops of yellow food coloring

Combine butter, powdered sugar, and 3 tablespoons milk in a small bowl; beat at high speed of an electric mixer, adding more milk, if necessary, to make a spreading consistency. Add vanilla and food colorings; beat until well mixed. Yield: frosting for 1½ dozen cookies.

C. Gibson,
Brooksville, Florida.

Savory Pot Roasts

Pot roasts are weekly choices for many families, especially for Sunday dinner. These less expensive cuts of beef—chuck, round, and shoulder roasts—can be sumptuous if cooked properly.

The best method is braising, more commonly known as pot roasting. To cook, first slowly brown the meat on all sides over medium heat. This concentrates juices toward the center of the roast and adds color and flavor to the sauce. Then add seasonings and a small amount of liquid, and slowly simmer the roast until done.

For good flavor, tender meat, and rich sauce, try one of our recipes. They have a large array of seasonings and wine, rum, or brandy, to impart delectable flavor combinations.

Pot roast is best when prepared the day before serving. Its flavor improves when reheated, and leftovers freeze nicely. Chilling the meat facilitates slicing, and you can easily remove the fat from the pan drippings.

INDIAN POT ROAST

1 (3- to 4-pound) boneless chuck roast
½ teaspoon salt
2 tablespoons all-purpose flour
2 cloves garlic, crushed
2 tablespoons butter or margarine, melted
1 large onion, sliced
12 whole peppercorns
12 whole allspice
1 bay leaf, crumbled
1 tablespoon grated fresh horseradish
½ cup water
½ cup Burgundy or rum
6 carrots, scraped and quartered

Sprinkle roast with salt; dredge in flour. Set aside.

Sauté garlic in butter in a Dutch oven. Add roast; brown on all sides. Remove roast from pan. Place onion slices in pan; place roast on top. Add peppercorns, allspice, bay leaf, horseradish, water, and Burgundy; bring to a boil. Cover, reduce heat, and simmer 2 hours. Add carrots; cover and simmer 30 minutes or until tender. Transfer roast and carrots to platter. Remove peppercorns, allspice, and bay leaf with slotted spoon. Serve with pan drippings. Yield: 6 to 8 servings.

Esther Nethercutt,
Sherwood, Arkansas.

PEPPERED POT ROAST

1 (4- to 5-pound) boneless chuck roast
¾ teaspoon salt
¼ teaspoon pepper
3 tablespoons vegetable oil
1 cup dry red wine
1 cup beef bouillon
¼ cup chopped onion
2 tablespoons brown sugar
½ teaspoon garlic salt
Dash of ground nutmeg
Dash of dried whole thyme
2 tablespoons cornstarch
¼ cup water
2 tablespoons cracked peppercorns
¼ cup chopped fresh parsley

Sprinkle roast with salt and pepper. Brown roast on all sides in hot oil in a Dutch oven. Add wine, bouillon, onion, sugar, garlic salt, nutmeg, and thyme.

Cover and bake at 350° for 2½ hours. Remove meat from Dutch oven, reserving 2 cups cooking liquid. Slice meat thinly; place on serving platter. Set aside.

Combine cornstarch and water; blend well. Add cornstarch mixture to reserved cooking liquid. Add peppercorns. Cook over medium-high heat, stirring constantly, until mixture comes to a full boil. Boil 1 minute. Pour gravy over sliced roast. Sprinkle with parsley. Yield: 8 to 10 servings.

Beth R. McClain,
Grand Prairie, Texas.

POT ROAST IN RED SAUCE

1 (5-pound) boneless chuck roast
2 cloves garlic, thinly sliced
½ teaspoon salt
¼ teaspoon pepper
¼ cup all-purpose flour
¼ cup plus 2 tablespoons olive oil
1 (15-ounce) can tomato sauce, divided
1 cup Burgundy
2 cloves garlic, crushed
1 large onion, chopped
1 bay leaf
1 teaspoon dried whole rosemary
1 cup sliced ripe olives
½ cup cognac or other brandy
2 tablespoons minced fresh parsley

Make 8 to 10 lengthwise slits halfway through roast. Insert a garlic slice into each slit. Rub roast with salt and pepper; dredge in flour. Brown roast in hot oil in a Dutch oven. Add 1 cup tomato sauce, Burgundy, garlic, onion, bay leaf, and rosemary; cover, reduce heat, and simmer 2½ hours or until tender. Remove bay leaf.

Transfer roast to serving platter, reserving cooking liquid in Dutch oven. Add remaining tomato sauce, olives, and cognac; cook over medium heat 5 to 10 minutes. Sprinkle with parsley. Serve sauce with roast. Yield: 10 servings.

Gladys Tucker,
Vinton, Louisiana.

COUNTRY POT ROAST

1 (4-pound) boneless chuck roast
1 large clove garlic, crushed
¼ cup all-purpose flour
1 teaspoon freshly ground pepper
2 tablespoons vegetable oil
2 large cloves garlic, minced
2 large onions, thinly sliced
1 cup thinly sliced celery
2 medium carrots, thinly sliced
¼ cup white or red wine
1 (10½-ounce) can beef broth, undiluted
1 bay leaf, crumbled
2 whole cloves
6 peppercorns
1 teaspoon dried whole thyme
½ teaspoon dried whole oregano
12 baby carrots, scraped
12 small onions
12 small new potatoes, unpeeled
1 (10-ounce) package frozen English peas

Rub each side of roast with crushed garlic. Combine flour and pepper; dredge meat in flour mixture. Brown roast on all sides in hot oil in a Dutch oven. Remove roast from pan. Combine minced garlic, sliced onions, celery, and sliced carrots. Place half of vegetable mixture in Dutch oven. Place roast on top, and add remaining vegetable mixture. Cover and cook over medium heat 35 minutes. Add wine, broth, bay leaf, cloves, peppercorns, thyme, and oregano; cover, reduce heat, and simmer 2 hours. Remove roast, cover, and chill. Pour broth and vegetable mixture into a bowl; cover and chill.

Slice roast, and place in a large Dutch oven; add 12 baby carrots and remaining ingredients.

Skim off and discard any collected fat from chilled broth-vegetable mixture. Puree mixture in a food processor or blender; pour over vegetables. Cover; simmer over low heat about 45 minutes or until vegetables are tender.

Arrange meat on a large platter; group vegetables around meat. Serve with sauce. Yield: 8 servings.

Bill Shealy,
Columbia, South Carolina.

Tip: When selecting onions, consider all of the flavor possibilities. The large Spanish or Bermuda onion and the small white onion are usually mild in flavor, while Globe types, such as red, brown, and small yellow onions, are stronger flavored.

Meat Loaf, An Old Favorite

We've eaten it cold in a sandwich or hot with a plate of steaming vegetables. It reminds us of Grandma's house and the diner around the corner. Heralded today as a "comfort food" by restaurant critics, meat loaf is a simple dish that's been enjoyed for years. And even some fancy restaurants are featuring it on their menus.

Savory Meat Loaf is special enough for company. Ground pork and ground veal make the texture of this meat loaf firmer than others you've probably eaten. The old standby, catsup, covers the loaf with color, but you'll find an assortment of toppings in the recipes here. Barbecued Meat Loaf boasts a barbecue sauce you make yourself, and Mexican Meat Loaf has taco sauce topped with shredded cheese.

In our test kitchens, we cook meat loaf two ways. One is the traditional method, with the meat placed in a loaf-pan. The other way, we shape the meat into a loaf and bake it on a greased rack of a broiler pan. This method decreases calories because drippings fall into the broiler pan underneath rather than float in the loafpan.

SAVORY MEAT LOAF

1 pound ground beef
½ pound ground veal
½ pound ground pork
¾ cup cracker crumbs
½ cup diced celery
¼ cup diced onion
¼ cup minced parsley
¾ teaspoon salt
¼ teaspoon pepper
¾ cup milk
1 egg, slightly beaten
¼ cup catsup
3 green pepper rings
Parsley sprigs (optional)

Combine beef, veal, and pork; stir well. Add cracker crumbs and next 7 ingredients; stir well. Shape into a 9- x 6-inch loaf, and place on a lightly greased rack of a broiler pan. Spread top and sides with catsup.

Bake at 350° for 1 hour and 20 minutes. Top with green pepper rings; bake 10 minutes. Garnish with parsley, if desired. Yield: 8 servings.

Mae McClaugherty,
Marble Falls, Texas.

BARBECUED MEAT LOAF

1½ pounds lean ground beef
1 cup soft breadcrumbs
1 small onion, diced
1 egg, beaten
1 teaspoon salt
¼ teaspoon pepper
2 (8-ounce) cans tomato sauce, divided
3 tablespoons brown sugar
3 tablespoons vinegar
2 tablespoons prepared mustard
2 teaspoons Worcestershire sauce

Combine beef, breadcrumbs, onion, egg, salt, and pepper; add ½ cup tomato sauce, and stir well. Shape into a 12- x 7-inch loaf; place on a lightly greased rack of a broiler pan.

Combine remaining tomato sauce and remaining ingredients in a saucepan; stir well. Bring to a boil over medium heat. Reduce heat; simmer about 10 minutes, stirring occasionally. Set aside.

Bake meat loaf at 350° for 1½ hours, basting with barbecue sauce the last 30 minutes of baking. Serve with remaining sauce. Yield: about 6 servings.

Azine G. Rush,
Monroe, Louisiana.

GERMAN MEAT LOAF

2 cups soft rye breadcrumbs
1 (10-ounce) can sauerkraut, drained
2 eggs, beaten
½ cup milk
½ cup chopped onion
1 teaspoon caraway seeds
½ teaspoon pepper
2 pounds lean ground beef
Commercial mustard sauce (optional)

Combine breadcrumbs, sauerkraut, eggs, milk, onion, caraway seeds, and pepper, mixing well. Add ground beef, and mix well. Shape into a 9-inch loaf; place on a lightly greased rack of a broiler pan. Bake at 350° for 1½ hours. Let stand 10 minutes before slicing. Serve with mustard sauce, if desired. Yield: 8 servings.

Lenah Elliott,
Destin, Florida.

MEXICAN MEAT LOAF

2 eggs, beaten
½ cup taco sauce
2 to 3 jalapeño peppers, minced
⅓ cup wheat breadcrumbs
1 teaspoon salt
¼ cup chopped onion
1½ pounds ground beef
¼ cup taco sauce
⅓ cup (1.3 ounces) shredded Monterey
  Jack cheese

Combine eggs, taco sauce, peppers, breadcrumbs, salt, and onion in a large bowl; stir until blended. Add ground beef, and mix well. Shape into a 9- x 5-inch loaf; place on a lightly greased rack of a broiler pan. Spread ¼ cup taco sauce on top of loaf.

Bake, uncovered, at 325° for 1 hour. Sprinkle cheese on top of meat loaf; bake an additional 5 minutes or until cheese melts. Yield: 6 servings.
Doris Curls,
Anniston, Alabama.

Keep Chicken On The Menu

Chicken is a popular entrée choice for health and economic reasons. Perhaps no other meat lends itself so well to so many different flavor combinations and types of recipes. Chicken breasts are especially versatile.

Marie Bilbo's Crunchy Seasoned Chicken is brushed with a mixture of sour cream, lemon juice, Worcestershire sauce, and seasonings; it is then chilled several hours to absorb the flavors. Before the chicken breasts are baked, they are rolled in a seasoned coating to make them colorful and crunchy. You will think you're eating fried chicken, but with more flavor.

Poached Chicken With Black Beans and Salsa is a good, but unusual, combination of ingredients. The beans are pureed and then heated with a splash of balsamic vinegar and dash of red pepper to give them a pungent flavor. Balsamic vinegar has a rich burgundy color and a less robust vinegar flavor; it is made from grape juice and aged in wooden casks. Look for it in the supermarket in the gourmet section.

The pureed mixture is spooned on individual plates with the chicken breast served on top. Then salsa, a Mexican-flavored tomato sauce, is served over the chicken. The uncooked tomato sauce is flavored with hot chile pepper and cilantro, a variety of parsley with a distinctive mint flavor.

You can substitute regular parsley if cilantro is not available. It's an interesting contrast of hot and cold, and mild and spicy flavors.

CHICKEN, HAM, AND CHEESE BAKE

6 chicken breast halves, skinned and
  boned
¾ cup teriyaki sauce
¼ cup vegetable oil
⅛ teaspoon pepper
6 (1-ounce) slices smoked ham
2 medium tomatoes, peeled and sliced
1½ cups (6 ounces) shredded mozzarella
  cheese
1 tablespoon minced fresh parsley

Marinate chicken in teriyaki sauce in a shallow dish 1 hour in refrigerator, turning once. Remove chicken.

Sauté chicken in oil in a large skillet until golden brown on both sides. Arrange chicken in a 13- x 9- x 2-inch baking dish; sprinkle with pepper. Top each wtih a slice of ham and tomato. Bake, uncovered, at 350° for 25 minutes. Sprinkle with cheese and parsley; bake 5 minutes longer. Yield: 6 servings.
Deb Wakefield,
Tuscaloosa, Alabama.

CRUNCHY SEASONED CHICKEN

½ cup commercial sour cream
2 tablespoons lemon juice
1½ tablespoons Worcestershire sauce
1½ teaspoons celery salt
¼ teaspoon garlic powder
¼ teaspoon onion powder
⅛ teaspoon pepper
6 chicken breast halves, skinned
1¾ cups saltine cracker crumbs (about 40
  crackers)
1½ teaspoons paprika
2 tablespoons butter or margarine, melted
Lemon slices (optional)

Combine sour cream, lemon juice, Worcestershire sauce, celery salt, garlic powder, onion powder, and pepper in a small bowl; mix well. Brush on chicken breasts, coating well. Place chicken breasts in a 13- x 9- x 2-inch dish; cover and refrigerate overnight.

Combine cracker crumbs and paprika; roll chicken in cracker crumb mixture, coating well. Place chicken in a lightly greased 3-quart casserole. Drizzle with melted butter. Bake, uncovered, at 350° for 1 hour or until the chicken is tender. Garnish with lemon slices, if desired. Yield: 6 servings.
Marie Bilbo,
Meadville, Mississippi.

POACHED CHICKEN WITH BLACK BEANS AND SALSA

1 cup chicken broth
6 chicken breast halves, skinned and
  boned
¼ cup dry white wine
¼ teaspoon salt
¼ teaspoon pepper
1 (15-ounce) can black beans, undrained
2 teaspoons balsamic or red wine vinegar
Dash of red pepper
Salsa (recipe follows)

Bring chicken broth to a boil in a large skillet. Add chicken, wine, salt, and pepper; cover, reduce heat, and simmer mixture 15 to 20 minutes. Remove from heat.

Pour beans into a container of an electric blender; process until smooth. Combine beans, vinegar, and red pepper in a saucepan; heat thoroughly, stirring occasionally. Add 1 to 2 tablespoons broth from chicken if mixture is too thick. Divide bean mixture on individual serving plates; drain chicken, and arrange over bean puree. Top with salsa. Serve immediately. Yield: 6 servings.

Salsa:

1 large tomato, diced
1 serrano or other hot green chile pepper,
  minced
1 small onion, diced
1 clove garlic, minced
½ cup cilantro or parsley, finely chopped
¼ teaspoon salt
⅛ teaspoon pepper

Combine ingredients; refrigerate 2 to 3 hours. Yield: 1½ cups.
W. N. Cottrell II,
New Orleans, Louisiana.

SHERRY-CHICKEN SAUTÉ

4 chicken breast halves, skinned and
  boned
½ clove garlic, minced
¼ cup plus 2 tablespoons olive oil
¼ cup plus 2 tablespoons red wine
  vinegar
2 tablespoons chopped fresh parsley
1 teaspoon dried whole tarragon
½ cup sliced fresh mushrooms
½ cup dry sherry
¼ teaspoon salt
⅛ teaspoon pepper

Sauté chicken and garlic in oil 10
minutes. Add remaining ingredients;
cover, reduce heat, and simmer 20 minutes or until chicken is done. Yield: 4
servings.
Nancy B. Beasley,
Orlando, Florida.

MICROWAVE COOKERY

Timesaving Entrées

Most people spend more time preparing the entrée than any other single
item on a menu. But when you use the
microwave oven to make the main dish,
you can put the meal on the table much
faster.

If advance preparation is as important
to you as the time it takes just prior to
serving, try Tangy Beef Salad. Strips of
flank steak marinate two hours and are
ready to cook. The beef is served hot
on a bed of crisp lettuce, shredded carrot, and cherry tomatoes. To save time,
tear the lettuce and combine it with the
carrot in advance. Store the vegetables
in the refrigerator in a plastic bag until
ready to serve. Putting a damp paper
towel in the bag will keep the vegetables moist and crisp.

If you prefer having no advance preparation, try one of our other microwave
recipes. A bowl of soup and a slice of
Vegetable Quiche make a warming fall
meal. The quiche crust has a browned
appearance because it's made with
whole wheat flour. Baking the crust before adding the quiche filling keeps it
from becoming soggy on the bottom. To
keep the crust from puffing during pre-
baking, place wax paper or heavy-duty
plastic wrap over the crust, and fill the
pie shell with dried beans.

TANGY BEEF SALAD

½ cup vegetable oil
3 tablespoons vinegar
3 tablespoons red wine
2 tablespoons Worcestershire sauce
1 clove garlic, minced
1 teaspoon onion salt
1 (1- to 1½-pound) flank steak
1 small head iceberg lettuce, torn
1 pint cherry tomatoes, halved
1 cup shredded carrot
Dressing (recipe follows)

Combine oil, vinegar, wine, Worcestershire sauce, garlic, and onion salt in
a 12- x 8- x 2-inch microwave-safe baking dish.

Partially freeze steak; slice diagonally
across the grain into thin slices, and cut
into 2-inch lengths. Place steak in marinade; cover and marinate at least 2
hours in refrigerator. Cover with wax
paper, and microwave at MEDIUM
HIGH (70% power) 5 minutes; stir. Microwave at MEDIUM HIGH 3 to 5 additional minutes or to desired degree of
doneness, stirring after 2 minutes. Remove from oven; let stand 5 minutes.
Drain steak; discard marinade.

Combine lettuce, cherry tomatoes,
and carrot in a large bowl. Top with
steak. Pour hot dressing over salad.
Toss and serve immediately. Yield: 6
servings.

Dressing:

¾ cup vegetable oil
⅓ cup lemon juice
3 tablespoons sugar
1 teaspoon paprika
½ teaspoon celery seeds
1 teaspoon dry mustard
¼ teaspoon salt

Combine all ingredients in a 2-cup
glass measure; stir well. Microwave mixture at HIGH 1½ to 2 minutes; stir.
Yield: 1¼ cups.

CHICKEN DIVAN

1 pound fresh broccoli
½ cup water
4 chicken breast halves, boned and
  skinned
¼ cup dry white wine
½ teaspoon dried whole basil
1 tablespoon butter or margarine
¼ pound fresh mushrooms, sliced
1 (8-ounce) carton commercial sour cream
¼ teaspoon curry powder
⅓ cup grated Parmesan cheese

Trim off large leaves of broccoli. Remove tough ends of lower stalks, and
wash broccoli thoroughly. Divide into
equal-size spears, trimming stalks as
necessary. Pour water into a 12- x 8- x
2-inch baking dish; arrange broccoli
with flowerets facing center of dish.
Cover with plastic wrap, and microwave
at HIGH 8 to 10 minutes or until broccoli is tender, giving dish a half-turn
after 4 minutes. Drain. Rearrange broccoli in dish so flowerets face outside.

Cut chicken into 2- x ½-inch strips.
Place in a shallow baking dish without
overlapping pieces. Combine wine and
basil; pour over chicken. Cover with
wax paper, and microwave at ME-
DIUM (50% power) 7 to 9 minutes or
until chicken is no longer pink.

Combine butter and mushrooms in a
1-quart casserole. Cover and microwave
at HIGH 2 to 3 minutes. Drain.

Remove chicken from wine mixture,
reserving ¼ cup mixture; layer chicken
over broccoli in center of dish. Top with
mushrooms. Combine sour cream, curry
powder, and reserved wine mixture;
spread over mushrooms. Sprinkle with
cheese. Microwave, uncovered, at
HIGH 8 minutes or until heated, giving
dish a half-turn after 4 minutes. Yield: 4
servings.

OPEN-FACED SALMON PATTIES

¾ cup commercial sour cream
⅓ cup chopped tomato
⅓ cup chopped cucumber
½ teaspoon dried dillweed
⅛ teaspoon salt
⅛ teaspoon white pepper
1 (15½-ounce) can salmon, drained and
  flaked
2 eggs, beaten
⅓ cup fine dry breadcrumbs
¼ cup grated Parmesan cheese
¼ cup thinly sliced green onions
¼ teaspoon ground celery seeds
⅛ teaspoon dry mustard
2 English muffins, halved and toasted
Lettuce leaves

Combine sour cream, tomato, cucumber, dillweed, salt, and pepper; stir well. Let chill.

Combine salmon, eggs, breadcrumbs, cheese, green onions, celery seeds, and dry mustard; mix well. Shape into 4 patties, and place on a 12-inch glass plate. Microwave at MEDIUM HIGH (70% power) 5 to 6 minutes, turning once. Let stand 2 minutes.

Top each English muffin half with lettuce and a salmon patty. Spoon sauce over patties. Yield: 4 servings.

VEGETABLE QUICHE

1 cup whole wheat flour
1½ cups (6 ounces) shredded sharp Cheddar cheese, divided
¼ teaspoon paprika
¼ cup vegetable oil
1 cup thinly sliced zucchini
¼ cup sliced mushrooms
¼ cup black olives, sliced
¼ cup sliced green onions
2 tablespoons water
3 eggs, beaten
1½ cups half-and-half
1 tablespoon chopped fresh parsley
2 teaspoons dried whole oregano
¼ teaspoon salt
⅛ teaspoon pepper

Combine flour, ½ cup cheese, paprika, and oil; stir well. Press mixture into a 9-inch quiche dish. Microwave at HIGH 4 minutes; remove from oven, and set aside.

Combine zucchini and next 4 ingredients in a 1-quart casserole; cover with heavy-duty plastic wrap, and microwave at HIGH 3 to 4 minutes. Drain well on paper towels.

Sprinkle ½ cup cheese over crust; top with vegetable mixture. Combine eggs, half-and-half, and seasonings; stir until well blended. Pour mixture over vegetables, and microwave at MEDIUM HIGH (70% power) 12 to 15 minutes or until a knife inserted off center comes out clean. (Center will be slightly soft.) Sprinkle with remaining ½ cup cheese. Cover and let stand on the countertop 10 minutes before serving. Yield: one 9-inch quiche.

Tip: Remember—standing time is part of the cooking process in microwaving foods. It allows for the food to complete cooking.

Savor Veal

Make veal the highlight of your next company menu. The delectable flavor of veal makes it worth the extra cost as an impressive entrée.

Because veal is very young beef and has practically no fat to make it tender, you must add liquids, sauces, and fat to keep it moist. The most popular cuts of veal are the thin slices called scallops or cutlets that come from the rump and leg. Scallops are best when quickly sautéed or braised, as in Veal With Green Peppercorns (page 220) and Lemon Veal With Artichoke Hearts. Total cooking time for each recipe is about 6 minutes.

Although scallops are popular, don't forget the larger cuts of veal. Our Best Baked Veal Roast is coated with salt, pepper, tarragon, and mace, then spread with butter to keep it moist as it slowly cooks.

BEST BAKED VEAL ROAST

1 teaspoon salt
1 teaspoon pepper
1 teaspoon dried whole tarragon
1 teaspoon ground mace
1 (5-pound) rolled veal rump roast
½ cup butter or margarine, softened
10 small onions
5 medium carrots, scraped and sliced
1 bay leaf
¼ teaspoon beef bouillon granules
¼ cup boiling water
1 cup commercial sour cream
Fresh parsley sprigs

Combine salt, pepper, tarragon, and mace in a small bowl; mix well, and rub into roast. Place roast in a lightly greased 13- x 9- x 2-inch pan. Spread butter evenly on top and sides; bake, uncovered, at 450° for 30 minutes. Add onions, carrots, and bay leaf to pan; reduce heat to 325°, and bake, uncovered, 1 hour and 40 to 45 minutes or until a meat thermometer in veal registers 170°.

Transfer roast and vegetables to serving platter; keep warm. Discard bay leaf; reserve ¼ cup drippings.

Dissolve bouillon granules in water. Combine reserved drippings, bouillon, and sour cream; cook over medium heat, stirring constantly, until thoroughly heated. (Do not boil.) Serve with roast and vegetables. Garnish roast with parsley. Yield: 10 to 12 servings.
Alice McNamara,
Eucha, Oklahoma.

VEAL CORDON BLEU

1 (1-pound) veal round steak
4 (¾-ounce) slices cooked ham
4 (¾-ounce) slices Swiss cheese
2 tablespoons all-purpose flour
¼ teaspoon pepper
¼ teaspoon ground allspice
1 egg, beaten
½ cup dry breadcrumbs
3 tablespoons butter or margarine, melted
2 tablespoons water

Cut veal into 4 serving-size pieces. Place each piece between 2 sheets of wax paper; flatten to ¼-inch thickness, using a meat mallet. Place 1 slice of ham and 1 slice of cheese in center of each veal piece. Fold long sides of veal over cheese; tuck ends, and secure with wooden picks.

Combine flour, pepper, and allspice. Dredge veal in flour mixture; dip in egg, and roll in breadcrumbs.

Sauté veal in butter in a large skillet until lightly browned, turning once. Add water; cover and simmer 30 minutes or until tender. Yield: 4 servings.
Carolyn Brantley,
Greenville, Mississippi.

LEMON VEAL
WITH ARTICHOKE HEARTS

⅓ cup all-purpose flour
¼ teaspoon salt
1 pound veal scallops or cutlets, sliced ¼ inch thick
2 to 3 tablespoons butter or margarine
Juice of 2 lemons
2 tablespoons Worcestershire sauce
1 cup chicken broth
¼ cup dry vermouth
1 teaspoon dried whole marjoram
½ teaspoon minced garlic
1 bay leaf
1 (14-ounce) can artichoke hearts, drained
Hot cooked noodles
Lemon slices
Parsley

Combine flour and salt; dredge veal in flour mixture. Melt butter in a large skillet over medium heat. Add veal, and cook 1 minute on each side; remove and drain on paper towels. Add lemon juice, Worcestershire sauce, broth, vermouth, marjoram, garlic, and bay leaf to skillet. Bring to a boil, stirring often. Add veal and artichokes; cover, reduce heat, and simmer about 5 minutes. Discard bay leaf. Serve over noodles. Garnish with lemon and parsley. Yield: 4 servings.
Anna Beyer,
Springfield, Virginia.

VEAL
WITH GREEN PEPPERCORNS

1½ pounds veal scallops or cutlets, sliced
    ¼-inch thick
Salt and pepper
½ cup all-purpose flour
3½ tablespoons butter, divided
3½ tablespoons olive oil, divided
1 (8-ounce) package fresh mushrooms,
    sliced
1 cup dry white wine
1 cup whipping cream
1½ teaspoons Dijon mustard
1 tablespoon green peppercorns

Place veal between 2 sheets of wax paper, and flatten to ⅛-inch thickness, using a meat mallet or rolling pin. Sprinkle with salt and pepper, and dredge in flour. Set aside.

Heat half each of butter and olive oil in a large skillet; add mushrooms, and sauté until tender. Remove mushrooms from skillet, and set aside.

Add remaining butter and oil to skillet, and heat over medium high; add veal, and cook about 1 minute on each side or until lightly browned. Remove veal from skillet, and set aside.

Add wine to skillet, and cook to reduce liquid to ½ cup. Add remaining ingredients, and cook over medium heat, stirring constantly, until sauce is thickened. Return the veal and mushrooms to skillet. Cook 2 minutes or until thoroughly heated. Yield: 6 servings.
Rick Paler,
Decatur, Alabama.

APPLE VEAL CHOPS

¼ cup all-purpose flour
1½ teaspoons chopped fresh marjoram or
    ½ teaspoon dried whole marjoram
½ teaspoon salt
4 (1-inch-thick) veal chops (about 2
    pounds)
2 tablespoons butter or margarine
1 tablespoon olive oil
½ cup chopped onion
1 tablespoon all-purpose flour
½ cup chicken broth
¼ cup apple juice
2 Granny Smith apples, cut into ½-inch
    slices
4 sprigs fresh marjoram (optional)

Combine ¼ cup flour, marjoram, and salt in small bowl; mix well. Dredge veal chops in flour mixture; let chops stand 15 minutes.

Heat butter and olive oil in a large skillet; brown chops over medium-high

heat about 2 minutes on each side, turning once. Remove chops from skillet, and set aside. Drain off pan drippings, reserving about 1 teaspoon in skillet. Add onion, and sauté about 2 minutes. Add 1 tablespoon flour, and stir until blended and lightly browned. Gradually stir in chicken broth and apple juice. Place chops in skillet; top with apple slices and if desired, marjoram sprigs. Cover skillet, and cook over low heat 15 minutes. Yield: 4 servings.
Marilyn Johnson Robertson,
Huntsville, Alabama.

COOKING LIGHT®

Low In Cholesterol, Not In Flavor

Reducing fat in the diet isn't always synonymous with reducing dietary cholesterol; it's the type of fat you eat that makes the difference. But cholesterol stays low in these recipes because they contain few or no animal products, the only source of the substance.

You won't believe your eyes, or your taste buds, when you serve Orange Pound Cake. It looks and tastes like the real thing. But there's no cholesterol because we substitute vegetable oil and egg whites for the usual butter and whole eggs. And it's the egg yolk, rather than the egg white, that's loaded with cholesterol.

For Pumpkin-Pecan Bread, we made similar changes. Egg substitute, vegetable oil, and skim milk replace eggs, butter, and whole milk, but the bread is still moist and delicious. Pumpkin supplies vitamin A, an extra bonus.

When it comes to entrées, meat, fish, and poultry are popular choices. Of these, fish and poultry (without skin) are lower in fat than most meats. Fish also contains less cholesterol and fewer calories.

Another way to reduce dietary cholesterol is to use these foods in mixed dishes. Fish-and-Vegetable Stew is a good example. One pound of fish makes seven main-dish servings when nutritious vegetables are added.

FISH-AND-VEGETABLE STEW

Vegetable cooking spray
1 cup chopped onion
½ cup chopped celery
1 large clove garlic, minced
1 (16-ounce) can tomatoes, undrained and
    chopped
2 tablespoons malt vinegar
1 tablespoon reduced-sodium
    Worcestershire sauce
½ teaspoon dried whole basil
½ teaspoon pepper
⅛ teaspoon salt
⅔ cup water
1 cup sliced carrots
1 cup frozen whole kernel corn
1 cup frozen lima beans
1 pound orange roughy fillets or other
    lean white fish fillets, cut into bite-size
    pieces

Coat a Dutch oven with cooking spray; place over medium-high heat until hot. Add onion, celery, and garlic; sauté until tender. Stir in tomatoes, vinegar, Worcestershire sauce, basil, pepper, salt, and water; bring to a boil, and add remaining ingredients. Cover, reduce heat, and simmer 20 minutes, stirring occasionally. Yield: 7 cups.

☐ *145 calories, 16.3 grams protein, 1.1 grams fat, 18 grams carbohydrate, 36 milligrams cholesterol, 204 milligrams sodium, and 56 milligrams calcium per 1-cup serving.* *Mary P. Combs,*
Fairview, Tennessee.

EGGLESS QUICHE

1 cup all-purpose flour
3 tablespoons vegetable oil
¼ teaspoon salt
2½ to 3 tablespoons cold water
2 tablespoons imitation bacon bits
6 (⅔-ounce) slices reduced-calorie process
    Swiss cheese, diced
⅓ cup chopped onion
1 cup egg substitute
2 cups evaporated skim milk
¼ teaspoon dried whole basil
⅛ teaspoon white pepper
⅛ teaspoon ground marjoram
⅛ teaspoon ground red pepper

Combine flour, oil, and salt; stir until mixture resembles coarse meal. Sprinkle cold water (1 tablespoon at a time) evenly over surface; stir with a fork until dry ingredients are moistened. Shape dough into a ball.

Roll dough to ⅛-inch thickness on a lightly floured surface. Place in a 9-inch pieplate; trim off excess pastry along edges. Fold edges under, and flute. Place a piece of aluminum foil over pastry; gently press into pastry shell to keep sides of shell from collapsing.

Cover foil with a layer of dried beans or pastry weights. Bake at 400° for 10 minutes; remove weights and foil. Prick shell with a fork, and bake 3 to 5 minutes or until lightly browned. Cool.

Layer bacon bits, cheese, and onion in pastry shell. Combine egg substitute and remaining ingredients; stir well. Pour over onion mixture; bake, uncovered, at 425° for 15 minutes. Reduce heat to 300°; bake 40 to 45 minutes or until set. Remove from oven; let stand 10 minutes before serving. Yield: 6 servings.

□ *266 calories, 18.5 grams protein, 9 grams fat, 27.2 grams carbohydrate, 10 milligrams cholesterol, 546 milligrams sodium, and 407 milligrams calcium per wedge.* C. Gibson, Brooksville, Florida.

CHICKEN SPAGHETTI

Vegetable cooking spray
¼ cup plus 2 tablespoons diced onion
½ cup diced celery
¼ cup diced green pepper
1 clove garlic, minced
1 (16-ounce) can tomatoes, undrained and chopped
¼ teaspoon paprika
¼ teaspoon chili powder
¼ teaspoon ground cumin
¼ teaspoon black pepper
⅛ teaspoon red pepper
8 ounces skinned, boned, uncooked chicken breast, cut into bite-size pieces
1 cup hot cooked vermicelli (cooked without salt or fat)
Parsley sprigs (optional)

Coat a large skillet with cooking spray; place over medium-high heat until hot. Add diced onion, celery, green pepper, and minced garlic; sauté until tender. Stir in tomatoes, paprika, chili powder, cumin, pepper, and red pepper. Cover, reduce heat, and simmer 15 minutes. Add chicken; cover and simmer 15 minutes.

Serve chicken over hot vermicelli, and garnish with parsley sprigs, if desired. Yield: 2 servings.

□ *219 calories, 28.7 grams protein, 4.9 grams fat, 14.8 grams carbohydrate, 72 milligrams cholesterol, 392 milligrams*

sodium, and 111 milligrams calcium per 1 cup chicken mixture plus 96 calories, 3.2 grams protein, 0.3 gram fat, 19.6 grams carbohydrate, 0 milligrams cholesterol, 1 milligram sodium, and 7 milligrams calcium per ½ cup vermicelli. Mrs. C. E. Ferguson, Jr., San Antonio, Texas.

PUMPKIN-PECAN BREAD

1¾ cups all-purpose flour
1 teaspoon baking powder
½ teaspoon baking soda
¼ teaspoon salt
½ cup sugar
¾ teaspoon ground cinnamon
½ teaspoon ground nutmeg
¾ cup canned or cooked mashed pumpkin
⅓ cup skim milk
⅓ cup vegetable oil
½ cup egg substitute
½ cup chopped pecans
Vegetable cooking spray

Combine flour, baking powder, soda, salt, sugar, cinnamon, and nutmeg in a large bowl; make a well in center of mixture. Set aside.

Combine pumpkin, milk, oil, egg substitute, and pecans; add to dry ingredients, stirring just until moistened. Spoon into an 8½- x 4½- x 3-inch loafpan coated with cooking spray. Bake at 350° for 55 to 60 minutes or until a wooden pick inserted in center comes out clean.

Cool in pan 10 minutes; remove from pan, and cool completely on a wire rack. Yield: 16 servings.

□ *145 calories, 2.7 grams protein, 7.3 grams fat, 17.9 grams carbohydrate, 0 milligrams cholesterol, 96 milligrams sodium, and 34 milligrams calcium per ½-inch slice.* Mary E. McMahan, Greenback, Tennessee.

ORANGE POUND CAKE

Vegetable cooking spray
1¾ cups sifted cake flour
2 teaspoons baking powder
¼ teaspoon salt
¾ cup sugar
½ cup vegetable oil
½ cup unsweetened orange juice
1 teaspoon grated orange rind
4 egg whites, stiffly beaten

Coat the bottom of an 8½- x 4½- x 3-inch loafpan with cooking spray; dust with flour, and set aside.

Combine flour, baking powder, salt, and sugar in a large bowl. Add oil and orange juice; beat at medium speed of an electric mixer until batter is smooth (batter will be thick). Add orange rind and about one-third of egg whites, and stir gently; fold in remaining egg whites.

Pour batter into prepared pan. Bake at 350° for 45 minutes or until a wooden pick inserted in center comes out clean. Cool in pan 10 minutes; remove from pan, and cool on a wire rack. Yield: 16 servings.

□ *143 calories, 1.7 grams protein, 7 grams fat, 18.7 grams carbohydrate, 0 milligrams cholesterol, 87 milligrams sodium, and 28 milligrams calcium per ½-inch slice.* Barbara Kluding, Clearwater, Florida.

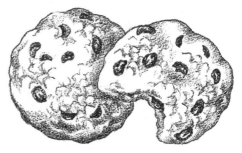

OATMEAL-RAISIN COOKIES

1 cup all-purpose flour
½ teaspoon baking powder
¼ teaspoon baking soda
½ teaspoon salt
½ cup sugar
½ teaspoon ground cinnamon
1 cup regular oats, uncooked
½ cup raisins
⅓ cup vegetable oil
¼ cup egg substitute
¼ cup water

Combine flour, baking powder, soda, salt, sugar, cinnamon, oats, and raisins in a large mixing bowl; stir well. Add remaining ingredients; stir well. Drop dough by teaspoonfuls onto an ungreased nonstick cookie sheet. Bake at 400° for 8 to 10 minutes or until done. Yield: 3½ dozen.

□ *48 calories, 0.8 gram protein, 1.9 grams fat, 7.1 grams carbohydrate, 0 milligrams cholesterol, 39 milligrams sodium, and 7 milligrams calcium per cookie.* Mrs. Augusta M. Gresham, Mobile, Alabama.

Sheet Cakes To Enjoy

Do you need a dessert for routine family meals, a covered-dish supper, or a sick friend? How about a sheet cake? They're easy to make and don't require a lot of time to frost and decorate. And best of all, you can serve these cakes straight from the pan.

Honey-Oatmeal Cake contains high-fiber oats and whole wheat flour. It's sweetened with honey and seasoned with cinnamon and nutmeg.

Ginger Cake is similar to gingerbread, but the texture is somewhat finer and softer because cake flour is used. Dark corn syrup stands in for molasses, and a mixture of cinnamon, ginger, and cloves helps give the cake a rich color and spiciness.

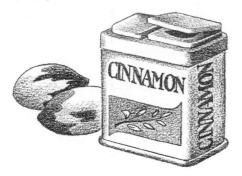

CINNAMON CAKE SQUARES

4 eggs
1 (16-ounce) package light brown sugar
1½ cups all-purpose flour
½ teaspoon salt
1 tablespoon ground cinnamon
1 cup chopped pecans
1 teaspoon vanilla extract
Frosting (recipe follows)

Beat eggs at medium speed of an electric mixer until frothy. Gradually add sugar, beating until thick. Add flour and next 4 ingredients, stirring well. Pour into a greased and floured 15- x 10- x 1-inch jellyroll pan. Bake at 350° for 25 minutes or until a wooden pick inserted in center comes out clean. Frost immediately. Cool. Cut into squares. Yield: 24 servings.

Frosting:

1 cup sifted powdered sugar
1 tablespoon milk
¼ cup butter or margarine, melted

Combine all ingredients; beat at medium speed of an electric mixer until mixture is smooth. Yield: ⅔ cup.
Linda Hilliard,
El Campo, Texas.

CHOCOLATE-SOUR CREAM CAKE

2 cups sugar
2 cups all-purpose flour
1 teaspoon baking soda
1 cup water
1 cup butter or margarine
¼ cup cocoa
2 eggs, beaten
½ cup commercial sour cream
Chocolate-Peanut Butter Frosting

Combine sugar, flour, and soda in a large bowl; mix well, and set aside.

Combine water, butter, and cocoa in a heavy saucepan; bring to a boil, stirring constantly. Gradually stir hot mixture into flour mixture; stir well. Stir in eggs and sour cream; mix well. Pour into a greased and floured 13- x 9- x 2-inch baking pan. Bake at 350° for 25 to 30 minutes or until a wooden pick inserted in center comes out clean. Cool. Frost with Chocolate-Peanut Butter Frosting. Yield: 15 to 18 servings.

Chocolate-Peanut Butter Frosting:

½ cup butter or margarine
¼ cup plus 2 tablespoons milk
¼ cup cocoa
1 (16-ounce) package powdered sugar, sifted
1 teaspoon vanilla extract
½ cup chopped peanuts
¼ cup peanut butter

Combine butter, milk, and cocoa in a heavy saucepan; bring to a boil, stirring constantly. Remove from heat. Add remaining ingredients; beat at medium speed of an electric mixer until mixture is smooth. Yield: 2¾ cups.
Mrs. Eugene Roach,
Winter Park, Florida.

GINGER CAKE

1 cup butter or margarine, softened
1 cup sugar
3 eggs, separated
1 cup dark corn syrup
3 cups sifted cake flour
1 teaspoon baking soda
1 teaspoon ground cinnamon
1 teaspoon ground ginger
1 teaspoon ground cloves
1 cup buttermilk
Powdered sugar

Cream butter; gradually add 1 cup sugar, beating at medium speed of an electric mixer until light and fluffy. Add egg yolks, one at a time, beating after each addition. Add corn syrup, beating well. Combine flour, soda, and spices.

Add flour mixture to creamed mixture alternately with buttermilk; begin and end with flour mixture.

Beat egg whites (at room temperature) until stiff peaks form; fold into cake batter.

Pour batter into a greased 13- x 9- x 2-inch baking pan. Bake at 350° for 50 to 55 minutes or until a wooden pick inserted in center comes out clean. Allow to cool. Dust top of cake with powdered sugar. Cut cake into squares. Yield: 15 to 18 servings.
Nola Thornton,
Florence, Alabama.

HONEY-OATMEAL CAKE

1¼ cups boiling water
1 cup uncooked regular oats
½ cup butter or margarine, softened
1½ cups honey
2 eggs
1 teaspoon vanilla extract
1¾ cups whole wheat flour
1 teaspoon baking soda
¾ teaspoon salt
1 teaspoon ground cinnamon
¼ teaspoon ground nutmeg
Commercial caramel-coconut frosting (optional)
Pecan halves (optional)

Combine boiling water, oats, and softened butter in a large bowl; stir well. Set aside for 20 minutes. Add honey, eggs, and vanilla; stir well.

Combine whole wheat flour, soda, salt, cinnamon, and nutmeg; gradually add to honey mixture. Pour into a greased and floured 13- x 9- x 2-inch baking pan. Bake at 350° for 30 to 40 minutes or until a wooden pick inserted in center comes out clean. Cool completely in pan. Frost top of cake with caramel-coconut frosting, and garnish with pecan halves, if desired. Cut cake into squares. Yield: 15 servings.
Nancy Cates,
Birmingham, Alabama.

Tip: When preparing sheet cake, cut enough servings for one meal; wrap and freeze the remainder. If cake is unfrosted, toppings or frostings can be varied with each serving.

LOADED-WITH-CHIPS COOKIES

½ cup butter or margarine,
  softened
½ cup shortening
1 cup firmly packed brown sugar
½ cup sugar
2 eggs
1 teaspoon vanilla extract
1½ cups regular oats, uncooked
1¾ cups all-purpose flour
1 teaspoon baking soda
½ teaspoon salt
1 (12-ounce) package semisweet
  chocolate morsels
¾ cup chopped pecans

Cream butter and shortening; gradually add sugars, beating at medium speed of an electric mixer until mixture is light and fluffy. Add eggs and vanilla, beating well.

Combine oats, flour, baking soda, and salt; add to creamed mixture, mixing well. Stir in chocolate morsels and pecans. Drop dough by heaping teaspoonfuls onto ungreased cookie sheets. Bake at 350° for 12 to 14 minutes or until brown. Remove to wire racks to cool. Yield: 6 dozen.

Peggy Wilson Witherow,
Pelham, Alabama.

Chocolate chips turn up everywhere—especially in Loaded-With-Chips Cookies and Honeyed Chocolate Mousse.

Sample A Chip Off The Old Chocolate Block

Cookies, pies, cakes, and mousse—all of these recipes are loaded with chocolate morsels. As for cookies, we think Peggy Wilson Witherow's Loaded-With-Chips Cookies are some of the best cookies you'll find anywhere. "My kids love chocolate chip cookies," Peggy says. "One day, we were making cookies, and we just kept adding and adding chocolate chips until the batter wouldn't hold any more. The kids like bunches and bunches, and of course, I do, too!" Peggy's even been known to add an extra 6-ounce package of chocolate chips to her recipe here.

Nancy Cates melted chocolate morsels to make her Honeyed Chocolate Mousse. If you make this recipe, prevent morsels from sticking or burning by melting them over low heat or hot, not boiling, water. For a special touch, you can add semisweet chocolate mini-morsels as a garnish.

CHOCOLATE-COCONUT ALMOND DROPS

1 cup sugar
1½ cups light corn syrup
½ cup water
1 (14-ounce) package flaked coconut
½ teaspoon vanilla or almond extract
2 (12-ounce) packages semisweet chocolate
  morsels
2 tablespoons shortening
Toasted slivered almonds

Combine sugar, corn syrup, and water in a large saucepan. Cook over medium heat, stirring constantly, until sugar dissolves. Cook, without stirring, to soft ball stage (236°). Remove from heat; add coconut and extract. Cool slightly; chill about 1 hour.

Shape chilled mixture into 1-inch balls; chill at least 1 hour.

Combine chocolate morsels and shortening in top of a double boiler; stir until chocolate melts. Dip each coconut ball into chocolate. Place on a wax paper-lined baking sheet. Top each candy with a slivered almond. Chill until firm. Store in refrigerator. Yield: about 6 dozen.

Marie A. Davis,
Morganton, North Carolina.

HONEYED CHOCOLATE MOUSSE

2 envelopes unflavored gelatin
½ cup honey
3 cups milk
1 (12-ounce) package semisweet chocolate
  morsels
1 teaspoon vanilla extract
1 cup whipping cream
Additional whipped cream for garnish
  (optional)
Semisweet chocolate mini-morsels
  (optional)

Combine gelatin and honey in a medium saucepan; mix well. Add milk and chocolate morsels; cook over low heat, stirring constantly, until gelatin dissolves and morsels melt (about 10 minutes). Add vanilla to chocolate mixture; stir until blended.

Chill mixture, stirring occasionally, until mixture mounds slightly. Beat 1 cup whipping cream until soft peaks form; fold into chocolate mixture. Spoon into parfait glasses. Chill until firm. Garnish mousse with additional whipped cream and mini-morsels, if desired. Yield: 8 to 10 servings.

Nancy Cates,
Birmingham, Alabama.

CHOCOLATE-ICE CREAM PIE

1 (6-ounce) package semisweet chocolate
  morsels
1 (5-ounce) can evaporated milk
2 cups miniature marshmallows
1 quart vanilla ice cream, softened
1 (9-inch) graham cracker crust

Combine chocolate morsels, evaporated milk, and marshmallows in a heavy saucepan. Cook over medium heat, stirring constantly, until marshmallows melt; cool.

Layer half each of vanilla ice cream and sauce in graham cracker crust; repeat layers.

Cover and freeze until pie is firm. Let stand at room temperature 5 minutes before serving, if necessary. Yield: one 9-inch pie.   *Diane Butts,*
Boone, North Carolina.

SPECIAL PECAN TARTS

3 eggs, beaten
1½ cups sugar
½ cup butter or margarine, melted
1 teaspoon cider vinegar
1 teaspoon cornmeal
1 teaspoon vanilla extract
½ cup flaked coconut
½ cup chopped pecans
½ cup semisweet chocolate mini-morsels
12 (3-inch) frozen pastry shells, thawed

Combine eggs and sugar; mix well. Gradually add butter, stirring well. Stir in vinegar, cornmeal, vanilla, coconut, and pecans. Sprinkle chocolate morsels evenly in pastry shells. Spoon about 3 tablespoons pecan mixture over chocolate morsels. Bake at 325° for 35 minutes. Yield: 12 (3-inch) tarts.
Mary Ann McGrath,
Lawrenceburg, Kentucky.

CHOCOLATE BROWNIE DELIGHT

6 (1-ounce) squares unsweetened chocolate
¾ cup butter or margarine
6 eggs, beaten
2 cups sugar
¼ teaspoon salt
2 teaspoons vanilla extract
1½ cups all-purpose flour
1 (6-ounce) package semisweet chocolate
  morsels
Mocha Frosting

Grease two 9-inch round cakepans, and line with wax paper; grease wax paper. Set aside.

Combine unsweetened chocolate and butter in a heavy saucepan; place over low heat, stirring constantly, until melted. Remove from heat, and cool.

Combine eggs, sugar, salt, and vanilla; add to chocolate mixture, stirring well. Stir in flour and chocolate morsels. Pour batter into prepared pans. Bake at 350° for 25 to 30 minutes. Cool in pans 10 minutes; remove from pans, and let cool completely on wire racks. Spread Mocha Frosting between layers and on top and sides of cake. Comb frosting, using a metal decorating comb, if desired. Yield: one 9-inch cake.

Mocha Frosting:

4 (1-ounce) squares unsweetened chocolate
⅓ cup honey
¼ cup water
1 tablespoon instant coffee granules
3 egg yolks, beaten
3 to 3½ cups sifted powdered sugar
¼ cup plus 2 tablespoons butter or
  margarine, softened

Combine chocolate, honey, water, and coffee granules in a saucepan. Cook over low heat, stirring constantly, until chocolate melts; cool. Add egg yolks, sugar, and butter; mix until smooth. Yield: 2¼ cups.

Jane Moore,
Norfolk, Virginia.

Pancakes And Waffles For Breakfast And More

Cooked until they're golden brown, slathered with butter, and topped with syrup, pancakes and waffles are versatile enough to use for many occasions. Serve them to overnight houseguests or after a child's pajama party. Or you might host a pancake/waffle buffet after a hayride.

Pancakes and waffles are easy to make. Use vegetable oil or shortening to grease your griddle, skillet, or waffle iron, and be sure to preheat the cooking surface. The griddle is adequately heated when a few added drops of water dance across the griddle before evaporating.

Freeze any leftovers. Place a piece of wax paper between pancakes or waffles; then wrap the stack in foil. Heat frozen leftovers in the toaster for a quick breakfast.

Pancake/Waffle Buffet

To do ahead: To set up a buffet, put out the griddle and/or waffle iron at end of table. Set plates and silverware nearby. Place beverages on a separate table or at the end of the buffet for easy access. Make toppings ahead of time, and refrigerate if necessary. A few hours before guests arrive, mix up the pancake or waffle batter. Cook bacon and sausage ahead, if desired.

Topping ideas: Mix and match any of the toppings included with the recipes here. You may want to add a few of your own, such as jams and jellies, peanut butter, or assorted flavors of syrup. For a dessert buffet, offer a sweet variety, such as ice cream, fruit, and chocolate or caramel toppings.

After guests arrive: Offer beverages while the cook surface preheats. When pancakes or waffles are done, let guests help themselves and create their own treat with the assorted toppings.

SPICY APPLE PANCAKES WITH CIDER SAUCE

2 cups biscuit mix
½ teaspoon ground cinnamon
1 egg, beaten
1⅓ cups milk
¾ cup shredded apple (about 1 medium)
Cider Sauce

Combine biscuit mix and cinnamon in a bowl. Combine egg and milk; stir into dry ingredients until smooth. Stir in shredded apple.

For each pancake, spoon about ¼ cup batter onto a hot lightly greased griddle. Turn pancakes when tops are covered with bubbles and edges are brown. Serve with Cider Sauce. Yield: 13 (4-inch) pancakes.

Cider Sauce:

½ cup sugar
1 tablespoon cornstarch
⅛ teaspoon ground cinnamon
⅛ teaspoon ground nutmeg
1 cup apple cider
1 tablespoon lemon juice
2 tablespoons butter or margarine

Combine first 4 ingredients in a heavy saucepan; gradually add apple cider and lemon juice. Cook over medium heat, stirring constantly, until mixture boils. Cook 1 minute, stirring constantly. Remove from heat; stir in butter. Yield: 1¼ cups.   *Marie Wiker,*
Pineville, Louisiana.

ISLAND PANCAKES

2 cups buttermilk
2 teaspoons baking soda
4 eggs, slightly beaten
2 tablespoons butter or margarine, melted
1 cup mashed ripe banana (about 2 bananas)
2 cups all-purpose flour
2 tablespoons sugar
½ teaspoon salt
Assorted toppings (recipes follow)

Combine buttermilk and soda; add eggs, butter, and banana; stir well.

Combine flour, sugar, and salt; add dry mixture to banana mixture. Stir just until moistened.

For each pancake, pour ¼ cup batter onto a hot lightly greased griddle. Turn pancakes when tops are covered with bubbles and edges are brown. Serve pancakes with toppings. Yield: 20 (4-inch) pancakes.

Assorted toppings:

■ For honey butter, beat ⅓ cup butter and ⅓ cup honey in a bowl until light and fluffy.
■ Top ½ cup commercial sour cream with ¼ teaspoon ground nutmeg.
■ ⅓ cup flaked coconut.

Mrs. W. J. Wallace,
Orlando, Florida.

ORANGE-YOGURT PANCAKES

1¼ cups biscuit mix
1 tablespoon sugar
¾ cup plain yogurt
⅓ cup orange juice
½ teaspoon grated orange rind
1 egg, slightly beaten
2 tablespoons melted butter or margarine
Fruit topping (recipe follows)
Whipped cream (recipe follows)

Combine biscuit mix and sugar in a large bowl; set aside. Combine yogurt and next 4 ingredients; add to dry mixture, stirring well.

For each pancake, pour ⅛ cup batter onto a preheated lightly oiled griddle or skillet. Turn when tops are covered with bubbles and edges are brown. Serve pancakes immediately with fruit topping and whipped cream. Yield: 16 (3-inch) pancakes.

Fruit Topping:

1 cup sliced strawberries
1 cup blueberries

Combine strawberries and blueberries in a bowl; toss lightly. Yield: 2 cups.

Whipped Cream:

½ cup whipping cream
2¼ teaspoons powdered sugar
¼ teaspoon vanilla extract

Beat whipping cream until foamy; gradually add powdered sugar, beating until soft peaks form. Fold in vanilla. Yield: 1 cup. *Mrs. Stanley Pichon, Jr.,*
Slidell, Louisiana.

SOUTHERN WAFFLES

1¼ cups self-rising flour
¾ cup self-rising cornmeal
½ teaspoon baking powder
1 tablespoon sugar
3 eggs, separated
1 cup buttermilk
¾ cup milk
¼ cup plus 2 tablespoons butter or margarine, melted

Combine flour, cornmeal, baking powder, and sugar; mix well. Combine egg yolks, buttermilk, milk, and butter; add to dry ingredients, stirring just until moistened.

Beat egg whites (at room temperature) at high speed of an electric mixer until stiff peaks form. Fold into batter.

Pour about one-fourth of batter into a preheated lightly oiled waffle iron. Cook 5 minutes or until steaming stops and waffles are done. Yield: 16 (4-inch) waffles.
Brenda Steedley,
Ozark, Alabama.

PECAN WAFFLES

1¾ cups all-purpose flour
2 teaspoons baking powder
½ teaspoon salt
2 eggs, separated
1¼ cups milk
½ cup vegetable oil
½ cup plus 1 tablespoon chopped pecans
Butter (optional)
Syrup (optional)

Combine flour, baking powder, and salt in a medium bowl; set mixture aside.

Beat egg yolks in a medium bowl; add milk and oil, mixing well. Stir mixture into dry ingredients.

Beat egg whites (at room temperature) at high speed of an electric mixer until stiff peaks form; fold into batter.

Pour one-third of batter into a preheated lightly oiled waffle iron. Sprinkle 3 tablespoons pecans evenly over batter. Cook about 5 minutes or until done. Repeat procedure with the remaining batter and pecans.

Serve with butter and syrup, if desired. Yield: 12 (4-inch) waffles.
Sandra G. Souther,
Gainesville, Georgia.

BEST EVER REFRIGERATOR WAFFLES

1 package dry yeast
¼ cup warm water (105° to 115°)
4 cups all-purpose flour
2 tablespoons baking powder
1 tablespoon baking soda
1 teaspoon salt
2 tablespoons sugar
4 cups buttermilk
6 eggs, beaten
1 cup half-and-half
¼ cup vegetable oil
2¼ cups frozen blueberries, thawed (optional)
Syrup (optional)

Dissolve yeast in warm water; let stand 5 minutes.

Combine flour, baking powder, soda, salt, and sugar in a large mixing bowl. Add buttermilk, stirring until smooth. Combine yeast, eggs, half-and-half, and oil. Add to buttermilk mixture, stirring well. (This batter will keep in refrigerator up to 7 days.)

Pour about 1 cup batter into a preheated lightly oiled waffle iron. Sprinkle ¼ cup blueberries evenly over batter, if desired.

Cook about 5 minutes or until steaming stops and waffles are done. Repeat procedure with remaining batter and blueberries. Serve with syrup, if desired. Yield: 36 (4-inch) waffles.

Note: For pancakes, spoon about ¼ cup batter onto a hot, lightly greased griddle. Sprinkle with 1 tablespoon blueberries, if desired. Turn pancakes when tops are covered with bubbles and edges are brown. Serve with syrup, if desired. Yield: 36 (4-inch) pancakes.
Geneva Alexander,
Frankston, Texas.

A Bread Made With Beer

Mrs. E. W. Hanley of Palm Harbor, Florida, eliminates much of the time-consuming mixing and measuring with her recipe for homemade bread. She begins with a commercial hot roll mix.

Take this loaf on a picnic, use it for a hostess gift, or share a loaf with friends. It's perfect for a gift basket stuffed with a bundle of pasta and the makings for a tangy sauce. Mrs. Hanley likes it best with spaghetti.

HEARTY BEER BREAD

1¼ cups beer
¼ cup butter or margarine
1 (16-ounce) package hot roll mix
½ cup nutlike cereal nuggets
2 tablespoons sugar
½ teaspoon salt
1 to 2 teaspoons milk

Combine beer and butter in a saucepan; cook over medium heat, stirring constantly, until butter melts. Cool to 105° to 115°. Add yeast packet from roll mix; stir until dissolved. Add roll mix, cereal nuggets, sugar, and salt; stir well.

Turn dough out onto a floured surface, and knead until smooth and elastic (about 5 minutes). Place in a well-greased bowl, turning to grease top. Cover and let rise in a warm place (85°), free from drafts, 1½ hours or until doubled in bulk.

Punch dough down; invert onto a floured surface. Cover and let stand 15 minutes. Shape into a 6-inch ball, and place on a lightly greased baking sheet. Cover and let rise in a warm place, free from drafts, 1 hour and 15 minutes or until dough is doubled in bulk. Gently brush dough with milk; bake bread at 375° for 25 to 30 minutes or until loaf sounds hollow when tapped. Yield: 1 (10-inch) round loaf.

Tip: Use an instant-registering thermometer to judge the liquid temperature used in bread baking. If the temperature is too low, the yeast will not dissolve and grow; if too high, the yeast will be killed and the bread will not rise.

The taste of this French Bread, sliced and buttered while it's still warm, will convince you it's worth every minute involved in baking it.

French Bread Baked Like The Pros

Baking French bread has an aura about it that frightens even the best of cooks. But not Estel Wilson. Years ago, he was challenged when he heard a friend was baking French bread. He said, "I can beat him."

Estel studied and learned some bakers' tricks. "Using bread flour is most important," he commented. We've used his suggestions as well as ideas from some of our other readers.

Most of us prefer French bread with a tender, moist interior, and this requires a very moist dough that's tricky to handle. If you add too much flour it will toughen the bread. Handling it with a pastry scraper (Step 1) for a few minutes develops the gluten to make the dough cohesive so that it can be formed into a ball. Kneading the dough (Step 2) helps develop the protein structure and strengthens the dough to produce loaves with higher volume.

According to Estel, "Keeping the humidity high during the rising and baking—that's the secret." Sufficient rising time is important for taste and texture to develop. Don't forget the second rising before shaping the loaves. The finger test can even be used on shaped loaves. Just punch a hole on an end where it won't be noticed.

Even after shaping, the dough will be too soft to hold its form without the support of long, half-cylindrical loafpans. Sprinkling the greased pans with cornmeal will yield a crispier crust.

The slashes on top of the loaves allow gases to escape, preventing the tops from splitting during baking, and they also enhance the texture.

Professional bakers have special humidified ovens that spray jets of steam; the moist atmosphere and steam delay drying and setting of the crusts so the loaves will expand more as they bake.

FRENCH BREAD

1 cup warm water (105° to 115°)
1 package dry yeast
1 teaspoon bread flour
1 teaspoon sugar
1 tablespoon vegetable oil
5½ to 6 cups bread flour, divided
1½ cups warm water (105° to 115°)
1 tablespoon plus 1 teaspoon sugar
1 tablespoon salt
1½ teaspoons vinegar
1 tablespoon olive or vegetable oil
About ¼ cup cornmeal

Combine 1 cup warm water, yeast, 1 teaspoon bread flour, and 1 teaspoon sugar; let stand 5 minutes. Stir in 1 tablespoon vegetable oil. Combine 1 cup bread flour, 1½ cups warm water, and next 3 ingredients in a large bowl; add yeast mixture, mixing well. Gradually stir in enough remaining flour to make a soft dough.

Turn dough out onto a floured surface, and knead until smooth and elastic (about 10 minutes). Brush a large bowl with olive oil; place dough in bowl, turning to grease top. Cover with plastic wrap, and let rise in a warm place (85°), free from drafts, 1 hour or until doubled in bulk.

Punch dough down. Cover again with plastic wrap, and let rise in a warm place (85°), free from drafts, 30 minutes or until doubled in bulk.

Grease 4 French bread loafpans; sprinkle with cornmeal, and set aside.

Punch dough down; divide into 4 portions. Let stand 5 minutes. On a lightly floured surface, flatten each portion into an oval. Fold dough over lengthwise, and flatten with open hand. Fold it again, and roll with palms of hands into a 15- x 2-inch rope, and place in prepared pans. Cover tightly with plastic wrap, and let rise in a warm place (85°) until doubled in bulk.

Place unglazed tiles on middle rack in oven, if desired. Place a pan of boiling water on lower rack. Preheat oven to 425°. Gently cut ¼-inch-deep slits crosswise at intervals on loaves with a razor blade or sharp knife. Place loaves in oven; spray loaves with water. Bake at 425° for 15 minutes, spraying every 3 minutes without removing loaves from oven. Bake an additional 10 to 15 minutes without spraying until loaves are golden and sound hollow when tapped. Yield: 4 loaves.

Note: For best results, the loaves should be baked on heated tiles to give the bread a fast start on the last bit of rising. The tiles absorb moisture from the bottom of the loaf to ensure a crunchy bottom crust.

Step 1: *To make French Bread, carefully follow recipe instructions for making bread dough. Then place dough on floured surface; turn it and fold it, using a pastry scraper. With floured hands, gather dough into a ball.*

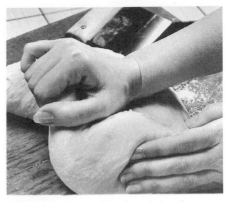

Step 2: *To knead, lift edge of dough farthest from you, and fold toward you. Press dough down and away from you with heels of both hands. Give dough a quarter turn, and repeat process until dough is smooth and elastic and loses its stickiness.*

Step 3: *Place dough in an oiled bowl; cover and let rise about an hour until doubled in bulk. To test for this, press finger ½ inch into dough. If indentation remains, the dough is ready; if dough springs back, let it rise longer. Punch dough down; cover and let rise again until doubled.*

Step 4: *Divide dough into 4 equal portions; flatten each portion of dough into an oval shape. Then fold dough over lengthwise, and flatten it with your open hand. Fold the dough again, and roll dough with the palms of your hands until it is almost the length of the pans.*

Step 5: *Place loaves in prepared pans, and cover tightly with plastic wrap. Let loaves rise until they are doubled in bulk; then gently cut ¼-inch-deep slits crosswise at intervals on loaves, using a razor blade or a sharp knife.*

Step 6: *Place unglazed tiles on middle rack in oven, leaving a 2-inch margin so that air can circulate. Place a pan of boiling water on lower rack to humidify oven. Spray loaves with water at 3-minute intervals during first 15 minutes of baking.*

Fresh-Baked Sugar Cake

Whiffs of cinnamon-spiced yeast dough baking in the brick ovens of Old Salem, North Carolina, produce more temptation than most tourists to the 19th-century village can stand. More than likely, folks lured into the bakery leave with several loaves of the famous Moravian sugar cake tucked under their arms.

The recipe here for Moravian Sugar Cake from Mildred Johnson of Pfafftown, North Carolina, is similar to the one you can purchase in Old Salem, where the Protestant denomination of Moravians settled in the early 1800's. Sweet yeast dough is made with mashed potatoes and baked with a brown sugar, butter, and cinnamon topping.

Traditionally, the cake was served for breakfast, but you'll find it difficult to resist sampling the hot, fresh bread right after it comes from the oven. Mildred's recipe yields two coffee cakes, so that you'll have one to serve and one to give away—or maybe one to serve and the other to hide and eat later!

MORAVIAN SUGAR CAKE

1 medium potato, peeled and diced
1 package dry yeast
½ cup warm water (105° to 115°)
1 egg, slightly beaten
⅓ cup butter, melted
⅓ cup sugar
½ teaspoon salt
2 to 2½ cups all-purpose flour
Softened butter
½ to ¾ cup firmly packed brown sugar
1 teaspoon ground cinnamon
⅓ cup butter or margarine, melted

Cook potato in a small amount of unsalted boiling water 10 to 15 minutes or until tender; drain. Mash potato, and measure ½ cup; set aside.

Dissolve yeast in warm water; let stand 5 minutes.

Combine potato, egg, ⅓ cup butter, sugar, and salt; mix well. Add yeast mixture and 1 cup flour, mixing well. Gradually stir in enough remaining flour to make a soft dough.

Turn dough out onto a floured surface, and knead until smooth (about 2 to 3 minutes). Place in a well-greased bowl, turning to grease top. Cover and let rise in a warm place (85°), free from drafts, 1½ hours or until dough is doubled in bulk.

Punch dough down, and divide in half; press each half in two well-greased 8-inch square pans. Brush with softened butter. Cover and let rise in a warm place (85°), free from drafts, 30 to 45 minutes or until doubled in bulk.

Punch holes, 2 inches apart, three-fourths through dough using the handle of a wooden spoon. Combine brown sugar and cinnamon; sift evenly over dough. Drizzle with ⅓ cup butter. Bake at 400° for 20 minutes. Cut into squares, and serve warm. Yield: two 8-inch coffee cakes.

Dried Fruit Is Always In Season

You don't have to go without the luscious flavor of peaches, plums, and apricots just because summer is over. Drying, as a form of preservation, makes these fruits and others available all year long. Eaten out of hand or used in one of our recipes, dried fruit makes a tasty and nutritious choice.

We use two dried fruits—apricots and prunes—for Baked Fruit Compote. To this combination, we add canned cherries and peaches, citrus juice, brown sugar, and cherry brandy. Serve it as a side dish for brunch or dinner. And be sure to include it on the menu when company comes. It makes enough to feed a small crowd.

BAKED FRUIT COMPOTE

1 (16-ounce) can pitted dark sweet cherries, undrained
½ cup firmly packed brown sugar
1 tablespoon cornstarch
2½ tablespoons lemon juice
¼ cup orange juice
1 (29-ounce) can sliced peaches, drained
1 (6-ounce) package dried apricots
½ (12-ounce) package pitted prunes, halved
1 tablespoon cherry brandy

Drain cherries, reserving 1 cup juice; set aside. Combine brown sugar and cornstarch. Gradually add reserved cherry juice, lemon juice, and orange juice; stir mixture well.

Combine cherries, peaches, apricots, and prunes in a 2-quart casserole. Pour brown sugar mixture over fruit. Sprinkle with cherry brandy. Cover and bake at 350° for 45 minutes or until apricots are tender. Serve warm or at room temperature. Yield: 10 to 12 servings.

Mary Alice Moore,
Ruston, Louisiana.

SPICED AUTUMN FRUIT SALAD

2 (3-ounce) packages lemon-flavored gelatin
2 cups boiling water
1½ cups ginger ale
1 (8-ounce) package mixed dried fruit, diced
½ cup golden raisins
½ cup chopped pecans, toasted
¼ teaspoon ground cloves
¼ teaspoon ground cinnamon
⅛ teaspoon ground allspice

Dissolve gelatin in boiling water; add ginger ale. Chill until consistency of unbeaten egg white. Stir in remaining ingredients. Pour into a lightly oiled 8-inch square dish. Cover and chill until firm. Yield: 9 servings.

Lynn McLendon,
Atlanta, Georgia.

FAVORITE STACK CAKE

½ cup butter or margarine, softened
1 cup sugar
½ cup buttermilk
1 egg
1 teaspoon vanilla extract
3½ cups all-purpose flour
1½ teaspoons baking powder
½ teaspoon baking soda
½ teaspoon salt
¼ cup butter or margarine, melted
Dried Apple Filling
Sifted powdered sugar (optional)

Cream butter; gradually add sugar, beating well at medium speed of an electric mixer. Add buttermilk, egg, and vanilla; mix well. Combine flour, baking powder, soda, and salt; gradually add to creamed mixture, mixing just until mixture is blended.

Divide dough into 6 equal portions; pat each into the bottom of a lightly greased 9-inch cakepan. Prick dough several times with a fork. Bake at 400° for 10 minutes or until lightly browned. Carefully remove layers to a wire rack; let cool.

Stack cake, spreading melted butter and Dried Apple Filling between each layer. Cover and chill 8 hours before serving. Sprinkle with powdered sugar, if desired. Yield: one 9-inch cake.

Dried Apple Filling:

2 (8-ounce) packages dried apples (about 5 cups)
4 cups water
¾ cup sugar
1 teaspoon ground cinnamon
½ teaspoon pumpkin pie spice

Combine apples and water in a large saucepan. Bring to a boil; cover, reduce heat, and simmer 30 minutes or until tender. Add sugar, cinnamon, and pie spice; stir well. Yield: about 3½ cups.
Mary Alice Cox,
Clinton, Tennessee.

Fruit And Spices Flavor Pork

Pork responds nicely to a world of seasonings—from barbecue sauce, fruits, and sweet spices, to tasty herb combinations.

For an elegant pork dinner, you'll appreciate the wonderful flavor of Pork Arlo. The butterfly chops are pounded thin to enclose slices of cheese and asparagus spears. The pork is seasoned with basil and oregano and topped with Tarragon Sauce.

PORK ARLO

4 boneless butterfly pork chops (about ½ pound each)
2 cloves garlic, minced
2 teaspoons olive oil
2 tablespoons all-purpose flour
½ teaspoon dried whole basil
½ teaspoon dried whole oregano
¼ teaspoon salt
Dash of pepper
4 slices provolone cheese
12 fresh asparagus spears, steamed
Rice pilaf (recipe follows)
Tarragon Sauce
Fresh tarragon (optional)

Pound pork chops to ¼-inch thickness. Sauté garlic in hot oil in a large skillet over medium heat. Remove garlic, reserving oil in skillet. Combine flour and next 4 ingredients; dredge chops in flour mixture. Brown in skillet, turning once. Place chops in a 13- x 9- x 2-inch baking dish. Place 1 slice cheese on each chop; top with 3 asparagus spears. Fold chops in half. Secure with wooden picks. Bake, uncovered, at 350° for 30 minutes or until done. Transfer to individual plates. Serve with rice pilaf and Tarragon Sauce. Garnish with tarragon, if desired. Yield: 4 servings.

Rice Pilaf:

2 tablespoons butter or margarine
½ cup chopped onion
⅔ cup fresh mushrooms, sliced
¼ cup chopped green pepper
¼ cup pine nuts
2 cups water
½ teaspoon salt
1 cup uncooked long-grain rice

Melt butter in a 2-quart saucepan over medium heat; sauté onion, mushrooms, green pepper, and pine nuts until lightly browned. Add water; bring to a boil; stir in salt and rice. Cover, reduce heat, and cook 20 minutes. Remove from heat; let stand 5 minutes. Yield: 4 servings.

Tarragon Sauce:

¼ cup butter or margarine
1 tablespoon cornstarch
1 cup half-and-half
2 teaspoons dry vermouth
½ teaspoon dried whole tarragon
¼ teaspoon salt
¼ teaspoon Worcestershire sauce
Dash of white pepper

Melt butter in a small saucepan over low heat; add cornstarch, stirring until smooth. Cook 1 minute. Remove from heat, and gradually stir in half-and-half until smooth. Return to heat; stir constantly, and bring to a boil. Cook 1 minute. Stir in remaining ingredients. Serve sauce over pork chops. Yield: about 1½ cups.
Karen Niegelsky,
Raleigh, North Carolina.

BARBECUED STUFFED CHOPS

½ cup chopped dry roasted peanuts
⅓ cup chopped celery
¼ cup chopped onion
⅓ cup raisins
¼ cup butter or margarine, divided
1 cup commercial barbecue sauce, divided
6 (1½-inch-thick) pork chops

Sauté first 4 ingredients in 2 tablespoons melted butter in a large skillet until vegetables are tender; stir often. Remove mixture to a bowl. Mix in 2 tablespoons barbecue sauce. Set aside.

Make pockets in pork chops, cutting from rib side just to beginning of fat edge of each chop. Add remaining 2 tablespoons butter to skillet; brown chops on both sides. Remove from skillet, and stuff pockets of chops with peanut mixture.

Place pork chops in an ungreased 13- x 9- x 2-inch baking dish. Spoon remaining barbecue sauce over pork chops. Cover and bake at 350° for 1 hour; remove cover, and bake an additional 30 minutes. Yield: 6 servings.
Louise Holmes,
Winchester, Tennessee

GLAZED PORK LOIN

½ cup sugar
1 cup boiling water
⅓ cup vinegar
1 teaspoon hickory-flavored smoked salt
1 (4- to 5-pound) boneless pork loin roast, rolled and tied

Sprinkle sugar in a heavy saucepan; place over medium heat. Cook, stirring constantly, until sugar melts and syrup is a deep golden brown. Stir in boiling water, vinegar, and hickory-flavored smoked salt. Boil until mixture thickens (about 10 minutes).

Place roast, fat side up, on a rack in a shallow roasting pan. Insert meat thermometer into thickest part of roast, making sure thermometer does not touch fat. Bake at 325° for 1½ hours. Brush with sugar-vinegar mixture. Continue baking for 30 minutes or until thermometer registers 160°. Yield: 10 to 12 servings.
Mrs. P. J. Davis,
Drexel, North Carolina.

SPICY APPLE PORK CHOPS

¼ cup all-purpose flour
½ teaspoon salt
½ teaspoon dry mustard
⅛ teaspoon pepper
⅛ teaspoon ground allspice
4 (1-inch-thick) pork chops
2 tablespoons butter
Vegetable cooking spray
2 tablespoons brown sugar
1½ cups apple cider
2 apples, peeled and sliced
⅓ cup raisins
½ teaspoon ground cinnamon
Caraway Buttered Noodles

Combine first 5 ingredients in a small bowl. Dredge pork chops with 2 tablespoons flour mixture, reserving remaining flour mixture. Melt butter in a large skillet; brown pork chops on both sides. Reserve meat drippings. Place pork chops in a 2-quart baking dish coated with cooking spray.

Add brown sugar and remaining 2 tablespoons flour mixture to meat drippings; stir until smooth. Cook 1 minute, stirring constantly. Gradually add apple cider; cook over medium heat, stirring constantly, until cider mixture is thickened and bubbly.

Arrange apple slices over chops; sprinkle with raisins. Pour sauce over chops. Sprinkle with cinnamon. Cover and bake at 350° for 1 hour or until chops are tender. Serve immediately with Caraway Buttered Noodles. Yield: 4 servings.

Caraway Buttered Noodles:

1 (8-ounce) package egg noodles
¼ cup butter or margarine
1 teaspoon caraway seeds

Cook noodles according to package directions; drain well. Melt butter in a small skillet; add caraway seeds.

Transfer noodles to a warmed serving platter; drizzle with caraway-butter mixture. Toss until noodles are coated. Yield: 4 servings.

Grace Bravos,
Timonium, Maryland.

Tip: Keep foods such as strawberries, pork chops, diced green pepper, and bacon from sticking together in the freezer by placing in a single layer on a baking sheet and freezing until firm. Remove from the baking sheet, store in freezer containers, and use as needed.

It's Ravioli, And It's Homemade!

With winter just around the corner, you'll undoubtedly be looking for warm and filling meals. Here's an entrée the whole family can get involved in making—Homemade Ravioli.

Adults can cook the meat mixture, and mix and roll the dough. Let children help by filling the dough with the cooled meat mixture and cutting the dough with a fluted pastry wheel into individual ravioli. It's a fun way to spend the better part of a day, and Marti Ledwidge, of Baton Rouge, Louisiana, knows the delicious rewards are well worth the effort.

Plan on 10 to 12 ravioli per serving, and top with your favorite commercial or homemade spaghetti sauce. Freeze the extra uncooked ravioli to enjoy at a later date.

Adults and children alike will love the flavor of Homemade Ravioli, especially when they can boast that they helped make the special treat.

HOMEMADE RAVIOLI

2 pounds ground round steak
½ cup chopped onion
2 cloves garlic, minced
1 tablespoon olive oil
1 (10-ounce) package frozen spinach,
    thawed and drained
1 cup freshly grated Romano cheese
½ cup soft breadcrumbs
2 tablespoons minced fresh parsley
½ teaspoon salt
¼ teaspoon pepper
1 egg, beaten
Homemade Ravioli Pasta
Water
2 tablespoons olive oil
½ teaspoon salt
Commercial spaghetti sauce
Freshly grated Romano cheese
Fresh basil sprigs (optional)

Cook ground meat, onion, and garlic in 1 tablespoon olive oil in a skillet until meat is browned and onion is tender, stirring to crumble meat; drain. Add spinach, 1 cup Romano cheese, breadcrumbs, parsley, ½ teaspoon salt, and pepper; stir well. Add egg, stirring well; set mixture aside.

Prepare Homemade Ravioli Pasta; divide dough into 8 equal portions. Pass each portion of dough through rollers of pasta machine. Continue moving width gauge to narrower setting, passing dough through rollers two times at each setting until dough is about 1/16-inch

Step 1: *Pass homemade ravioli dough through a pasta machine until it is 1/16-inch thick, dusting with flour as needed.*

Step 3: *Place meat mixture on dough between indentations; then moisten indentations with water to help seal edges when the additional strip of dough is placed on top.*

thick and 3 inches wide, dusting with flour as needed. Cut strip in half vertically. (Each piece should be about 24 inches long.)

Place 1 strip of dough on a lightly floured work surface. Roll dough with a ravioli rolling pin, using heavy pressure to make indentations. Spoon 1 scant teaspoon meat mixture in center of each rectangular pattern of dough. Brush water along lines of rectangle pattern on dough. Carefully align another layer of dough over indentations on bottom layer of dough; press edges to seal. Use a fluted pastry wheel to make individual ravioli, cutting through both layers of dough. Place ravioli on ungreased cookie sheet, and let air-dry 30 minutes; turn and continue to dry an additional 30 minutes. Repeat procedures with remaining dough and filling.

Combine 4 quarts water, 2 tablespoons olive oil, and ½ teaspoon salt in a large Dutch oven; bring to a boil.

Step 2: Lay one strip of dough on work surface. Use a ravioli rolling pin to make indentations.

Step 4: Lay an additional strip of dough over indentations; then carefully seal the edges of dough around indentations, and cut into individual ravioli, using a fluted pastry wheel.

Drop in about one-fourth of ravioli; reduce heat, and simmer 10 to 12 minutes. Drain. Repeat with remaining ravioli. Remove ravioli carefully from water with a slotted spoon; drain ravioli in colander.

Spoon a small amount of warm spaghetti sauce on a plate; place ravioli on sauce. Top with additional spaghetti sauce, and sprinkle with Romano cheese. Garnish with basil, if desired. Yield: about 11 dozen.

Homemade Ravioli Pasta:

3 eggs
6 to 7 cups all-purpose flour
1½ cups cold water

Beat eggs in a large mixing bowl, using a wire whisk. Add 1½ cups flour; beat with a wire whisk until blended. Add ¾ cup water, blending well. Work in remaining flour and water. Turn dough out onto a floured surface, and knead until stiff (about 10 minutes). Yield: enough to make 11 dozen ravioli.

Note: Ravioli may be frozen. To freeze, place uncooked ravioli in a single layer on a cookie sheet, and place in freezer until frozen. Transfer ravioli to a moisture/vaporproof plastic bag or container for storage. Thaw in refrigerator before using. Then follow directions for cooking and serving.

Cauliflower Is Best Now

Even though cauliflower is available all year in most markets, it's at the peak of flavor during fall and winter months. The mild flavor of cauliflower also makes it so compatible with other foods and seasonings that it's one of our most versatile vegetables. You'll find several ways to prepare it in these recipes.

If you like it best uncooked, you'll want to try Cauliflower-Pea Salad for one of your fall meals. It's a crunchy combination of fresh flowerets, lettuce, and English peas tossed in a creamy Parmesan dressing. Once the dressing is mixed with the vegetables, it must be served right away. To save preparation time at the last minute, you can combine the cauliflower, lettuce, and peas in advance, and then toss with the dressing just before serving.

Fried Cauliflower With Cheese Sauce can double as an appetizer or a side

dish. The coating on the cauliflower flowerets is a beer batter that makes each bite crisp and light.

Look for a white or creamy color when you purchase fresh cauliflower. Tight, firm flowerets are also a sign of quality. Once you purchase it, the vegetable will stay fresh up to a week in the refrigerator.

CAULIFLOWER-PEA SALAD

1 medium head cauliflower
1 medium head iceberg lettuce, torn
1 (10-ounce) package frozen English peas, thawed
¾ cup salad dressing or mayonnaise
2½ tablespoons grated Parmesan cheese
1 tablespoon sugar
8 slices bacon, cooked and crumbled

Wash cauliflower, and break into flowerets. Combine cauliflower, lettuce, and peas in a large salad bowl.

Combine salad dressing, cheese, and sugar; stir well. Spoon over vegetable mixture; sprinkle with bacon, and toss gently. Serve immediately. Yield: 6 to 8 servings. *Joyce Livesay, Lexington, Kentucky.*

FRIED CAULIFLOWER WITH CHEESE SAUCE

1 large head cauliflower
1 (12-ounce) can beer
1¼ cups all-purpose flour
Vegetable oil
2 tablespoons butter or margarine
2 tablespoons all-purpose flour
1 cup milk
1½ cups (6 ounces) shredded Cheddar cheese

Wash cauliflower, and break into flowerets. Cook, covered, in a small amount of boiling water 8 to 10 minutes or until crisp-tender; drain.

Combine beer (at room temperature) and 1¼ cups flour; beat well. Dip flowerets in batter. Deep-fry in hot oil (375°) until golden brown. Drain well on paper towels.

Melt butter in a heavy saucepan over low heat; add 2 tablespoons flour, stirring until smooth. Cook 1 minute, stirring constantly. Gradually add milk; cook over medium heat, stirring constantly, until thickened and bubbly. Remove from heat; add cheese, stirring until melted. Serve with cauliflower. Yield: 6 servings. *Pearle E. Evans, Myrtle Beach, South Carolina.*

FESTIVE CAULIFLOWER CASSEROLE

1 large head cauliflower
1 cup sliced fresh mushrooms
¼ cup diced green pepper
¼ cup diced sweet red pepper
¼ cup butter or margarine, melted
⅓ cup all-purpose flour
2 cups milk
1 teaspoon salt
1 cup (4 ounces) shredded Swiss cheese
Fresh parsley sprigs (optional)
Sweet red pepper strips (optional)

Wash cauliflower, and break into flowerets. Cook, covered, in a small amount of boiling water 8 to 10 minutes or until crisp-tender. Drain; set aside.

Sauté mushrooms, green pepper, and diced red pepper in butter until tender. Add flour, stirring until smooth. Cook 1 minute, stirring constantly. Gradually add milk; cook over medium heat, stirring constantly, until thickened and bubbly. Remove from heat. Add salt and cheese; stir until cheese melts and mixture is smooth.

Place half of cauliflower in a buttered 2-quart casserole. Spoon half of cheese sauce over cauliflower; repeat layers. Bake at 325° for 15 minutes or until thoroughly heated. Garnish with parsley sprigs and red pepper strips, if desired. Yield: 6 to 8 servings.

Mrs. John W. Stevens,
Lexington, Kentucky.

CAULIFLOWER WITH PIMIENTO SAUCE

1 large head cauliflower
2 tablespoons butter or margarine
2 tablespoons all-purpose flour
1 cup milk
½ cup (2 ounces) shredded Cheddar
  cheese
¼ cup mashed pimiento
1 teaspoon minced onion

Wash cauliflower; remove leaves, and cut out base. Cook, covered, in a small amount of boiling water 15 to 18 minutes or until tender; drain. Place cauliflower on a serving plate; keep warm.

Melt butter in a heavy saucepan over low heat; add flour, stirring until smooth. Cook for 1 minute, stirring constantly. Gradually add milk; cook over medium heat, stirring constantly, until thickened and bubbly. Add the remaining ingredients; stir until Cheddar cheese melts. Pour cheese mixture over cauliflower. Yield: 6 servings.

Clota Engleman,
Spur, Texas.

Spoon On Sauces For Flavor

If cooked vegetables sometimes seem too plain, drizzle them with one of these flavorful sauces just before serving. You'll be surprised at the difference a creamy sauce seasoned with a little lemon juice, onion, or mustard can make in ordinary vegetables.

Obvious vegetables to pair with Creamy Mustard Sauce include carrots, broccoli, and cauliflower, but the pretty yellow sauce would provide pleasing color and flavor contrasts to cooked pearl onions or artichokes as well. You'll find our other vegetable sauces equally versatile.

SHRIMP SAUCE

1 (3-ounce) package cream cheese,
  softened
½ cup milk
1 (10¾-ounce) can cream of shrimp soup,
  undiluted
1 teaspoon chopped chives
2 tablespoons lemon juice
2 tablespoons slivered almonds, toasted

Combine cream cheese and milk in a small saucepan; stir until blended. Add soup; cook over medium heat, stirring constantly, until mixture comes to a boil. Remove from heat. Stir in chives and lemon juice. Serve over broccoli, cauliflower, or other vegetables; sprinkle with almonds. Yield: 1½ cups.

Marge Killmon,
Annandale, Virginia.

COTTAGE CHEESE SAUCE

1 cup cottage cheese
1 tablespoon minced onion
1½ teaspoons Worcestershire sauce
½ teaspoon sugar
½ teaspoon paprika
¼ teaspoon white pepper
⅛ teaspoon salt
½ cup whipping cream, whipped

Combine all ingredients except whipped cream; stir well. Fold in whipped cream; cover and chill at least 2 hours. Serve on baked potatoes or other vegetables. Yield: about 2 cups.

Norma Cowden,
Shawnee, Oklahoma.

CREAMY MUSTARD SAUCE

2 tablespoons butter or margarine
1 tablespoon all-purpose flour
¾ cup milk
¼ teaspoon salt
⅛ teaspoon white pepper
2 tablespoons prepared mustard
1 egg yolk, beaten
2 teaspoons lemon juice

Melt butter in a heavy saucepan over low heat; add flour, stirring until smooth. Cook 1 minute, stirring constantly. Gradually add milk; cook over medium heat, stirring constantly, until mixture is thickened and bubbly. Stir in salt, pepper, and mustard. Gradually stir about one-fourth of hot mixture into egg yolk; add to remaining hot mixture, stirring constantly. Stir in lemon juice. Serve sauce over hot cooked carrots, cauliflower, or other vegetables. Yield: 1 cup.

Laura Plyler,
Lancaster, South Carolina.

ONION CREAM SAUCE

2 tablespoons butter or margarine
2 tablespoons all-purpose flour
1½ cups half-and-half
3 tablespoons minced onion
1 tablespoon chopped fresh parsley
½ teaspoon salt
Dash of white pepper
1 egg, well beaten

Melt butter in a heavy saucepan over low heat; add flour, stirring until smooth. Cook 1 minute, stirring constantly. Gradually add half-and-half; cook over medium heat, stirring constantly, until mixture is thickened and bubbly. Stir in minced onion, parsley, salt, and pepper.

Gradually stir about one-fourth of hot mixture into egg; add to remaining hot mixture, stirring constantly. Cook until mixture is thickened and bubbly. Serve over green peas, asparagus, or other vegetables. Yield: 1½ cups.

Rose Alleman,
Prairieville, Louisiana.

Celebrate Fall With A Salad

With fresh produce such as brussels sprouts, apples, pears, and cabbage available, fall salads are a natural addition to your menus. Cabbage Salad, with shredded cabbage, almonds, and Ramen noodles, is one you'll want to try. (You can find the Ramen noodles in the soup department in most grocery stores.)

In Mixed Fruit Cup, a pear, an apple, a banana, grapes, and oranges are combined with orange juice concentrate for a fall salad that's easy to fix.

BRUSSELS SPROUTS SALAD

1 pound fresh brussels sprouts
¼ cup vegetable oil
2 tablespoons vinegar
6 cherry tomatoes, cut in half
Lettuce leaves

Wash brussels sprouts thoroughly, and remove discolored leaves. Cut off stem ends, and slash bottom of each sprout with a shallow X. Place sprouts in a large saucepan; add water to cover, and bring to a boil. Cover, reduce heat, and simmer 5 minutes or until brussels sprouts are tender; drain. Place sprouts in a large bowl.

Combine oil and vinegar; pour over brussels sprouts. Cover and refrigerate 3 to 4 hours.

Add cherry tomatoes to brussels sprouts; toss gently. Serve salad on lettuce leaves. Yield: 4 servings.
Gwen Louer,
Roswell, Georgia.

CABBAGE SALAD

1 (3-ounce) package chicken-flavored Ramen noodles
6 cups shredded cabbage
4 green onions, chopped
½ cup toasted sunflower kernels
½ cup sliced almonds
½ cup vegetable oil
3 tablespoons vinegar
2 tablespoons sugar
½ teaspoon salt
½ teaspoon pepper

Remove seasoning packet from noodle package; set aside.

Crush noodles. Combine noodles, shredded cabbage, chopped green onions, sunflower kernels, and sliced almonds in a large bowl.

Combine seasoning packet and remaining ingredients; mix with a wire whisk. Pour dressing over the cabbage mixture; toss gently to coat. Cover and chill. Yield: 6 servings.
Ruby Eckard,
Mauldin, South Carolina.

APPLE SALAD

1 cup sugar
1 cup water
1 (8½-ounce) package red cinnamon candies
6 medium apples, peeled and cored
¼ cup plus 2 tablespoons chopped pecans
¼ cup plus 2 tablespoons chopped dates
1 tablespoon mayonnaise
Lettuce leaves

Combine sugar, water, and cinnamon candies in a large Dutch oven. Bring to a boil; add apples. Cover, reduce heat, and simmer 20 minutes or until apples are tender, turning occasionally. Drain apples, and chill.

Combine pecans, dates, and mayonnaise, mixing well. Fill each apple with about 2 tablespoons pecan mixture. Serve on lettuce leaves. Yield: 6 servings.
Louise Osborne,
Lexington, Kentucky.

MIXED FRUIT CUP

¼ cup frozen orange juice concentrate, thawed and undiluted
¼ cup water
1 cup seedless green grapes, halved
2 medium oranges or tangerines, sectioned
1 medium apple, cored and cubed
1 medium pear, cored and cubed
1 medium banana, sliced

Combine orange juice concentrate and water; stir well.

Combine all fruit, except banana. Add orange juice mixture; toss gently. Cover and chill 30 minutes. Add banana just before serving. Yield: 4 to 6 servings.
Bettye Cortner,
Cerulean, Kentucky.

What A Salad!

When Lou Baughman of Fort Walton Beach, Florida, prepares a recipe, she likes to add her own personal touch. You'll agree that she certainly has a special flair when you see her unique recipe for Salad Extravaganza. Guests sometimes choose from one large tray, or she may serve it on salad plates lined with spinach or romaine leaves.

SALAD EXTRAVAGANZA

1 pound fresh asparagus
1 (14-ounce) can artichoke hearts, drained
1 (14-ounce) can hearts of palm, drained and cut into thirds
1 (12½-ounce) jar baby carrots, drained
½ cup pitted black olives
1 cup fresh mushrooms
1 (0.7-ounce) envelope Italian salad dressing mix
1 small head romaine lettuce, separated
1 (10-ounce) package fresh spinach
1 avocado, sliced in wedges
Sour Cream Sauce
1 cup croutons
8 slices bacon, cooked and crumbled

Snap off tough ends of fresh asparagus. Remove scales with knife or vegetable peeler, if desired. Cook asparagus, covered, in a small amount of boiling water 6 to 8 minutes or until crisp-tender; drain.

Place asparagus and next 5 ingredients in a shallow dish. Prepare salad dressing mix according to package directions; pour over vegetables. Cover and refrigerate for 3 hours.

Drain vegetables; reserve marinade. Line a large platter with lettuce. Top with fresh spinach leaves. Arrange marinated vegetables and avocado on spinach. Drizzle the reserved marinade over salad arrangement. Serve with Sour Cream Sauce, croutons, and bacon. Yield: approximately 8 to 10 servings.

Sour Cream Sauce:

1 (8-ounce) carton commercial sour cream
½ cup mayonnaise
¾ tablespoon prepared horseradish
2 teaspoons chopped chives
2 teaspoons grated onion
1 teaspoon lemon juice
¼ teaspoon dry mustard

Combine all ingredients; stir well. Chill. Yield: 1½ cups.

Note: Frozen asparagus may be substituted for fresh asparagus, if desired.

Make A Soufflé To Brag About

James Sellers knows how easy it is to mix up Three-Egg Cheese Soufflé. He enjoyed his mother's version of the recipe as a boy growing up in the Florida Panhandle. Now, in Houston, Texas, James makes the sensational soufflé for brunch or dinner.

James uses the soufflé as a side dish or a main dish, depending on his menu. For brunch, he usually teams it with asparagus, link sausage, and whole wheat toast. For a variation on brunch, he sometimes pairs a soufflé with a refreshing watercress salad tossed in oil and vinegar.

When testing James's recipe, we greased only the bottom of the soufflé dish because the egg mixture clings to the ungreased sides and rises more readily. For the easiest cooking, grease the bottom of the dish and measure all the ingredients before you begin. If you don't have a soufflé dish, use a 1-quart casserole.

A white sauce—butter, flour, and milk—forms the base for the soufflé. Once the white sauce is thick and bubbly, cheese, seasonings, and egg yolks are added next. Beating the egg whites adds air and makes the soufflé light and fluffy. Beat the whites only until they're stiff and the tips of the peaks remain standing when the beaters are removed. Using a rubber spatula, gently *fold* the egg whites into the mixture to incorporate as much air as possible. The thick mixture will become light and airy.

Plan for the soufflé to come out of the oven after guests are seated. It'll be three cheers for you as you serve it hot, light, and golden. Remember, as the soufflé cools, it will "deflate." This is to be expected and doesn't affect the flavor one bit!

THREE-EGG CHEESE SOUFFLÉ

2 tablespoons butter or margarine
3 tablespoons all-purpose flour
1 cup milk
1 cup (4 ounces) shredded Cheddar
　cheese
⅛ teaspoon salt
¼ teaspoon paprika
3 eggs, separated

Lightly grease the bottom of a 1-quart soufflé dish; set aside.

Melt butter in a medium saucepan over low heat; add flour, stirring until smooth. Cook 1 minute, stirring constantly. Gradually add milk; cook over medium heat, stirring constantly, until mixture is thickened and bubbly. Remove from heat. Add cheese, salt, and paprika; stir until cheese melts. Cool. Beat egg yolks until thick and lemon colored; gradually stir yolks into the cheese mixture.

Beat egg whites (at room temperature) until stiff peaks form; stir one-third of beaten egg whites into cheese mixture. Fold in remaining egg whites. Spoon cheese mixture into prepared soufflé dish. Bake at 350° for 40 minutes or until soufflé is puffy and golden brown. Serve soufflé immediately. Yield: 2 to 4 servings.

One secret to making a light, airy soufflé is to incorporate as much air as possible when adding the egg whites. Quickly and gently fold the beaten whites into the cheese mixture. Then bake the soufflé until it's puffy and golden brown. Remove from the oven and serve immediately—you'll really have something to brag about.

November

Tangy, Crunchy Holiday Salads

With the holidays comes an abundance of foods, and smart meal planners will rely on salads for a colorful contrast to the many rich foods we savor this time of year. Whether your entrée is poultry, beef, or pork, our readers' offerings are as pretty as Raspberry Ribbon Salad or as traditional as Holiday Fruit Salad.

If the recipe calls for fresh produce, cut fruit with a sharp knife to prevent additional bruising. Apples and bananas won't turn dark if you dip them in lemon juice or salted water after slicing or peeling.

For a congealed salad, lightly coat the mold with vegetable oil. After the salad is firm, run a spatula around the edges of the mold to let air underneath. Wrap a hot, wet towel around the mold, and let it sit one or two minutes. Place a serving platter over the mold, and flip the salad onto it. Lift the mold off. If the salad doesn't unmold, repeat the process. Don't leave the towel on too long, or the salad will melt.

CHERRY FRUIT SALAD

1 (16-ounce) can pitted dark sweet
    cherries, undrained
1 (3-ounce) package black cherry-flavored
    gelatin
½ cup cream sherry
1 (16-ounce) can pear halves, drained
1 (3-ounce) package cream cheese, cut
    into small cubes
½ cup chopped pecans
Lettuce leaves

Drain cherries, reserving the syrup. Add enough water to cherry syrup to make 1½ cups liquid. Cut cherries in half, and set aside.

Combine gelatin and syrup mixture in a medium saucepan; cook over low heat until gelatin dissolves. Remove from heat, and stir in sherry. Chill until the consistency of unbeaten egg white.

Set aside 2 pear halves and chill; chop remaining pears. Fold chopped pears, cherries, cream cheese, and pecans into gelatin mixture. Spoon into an oiled 5-cup mold. Chill until firm. Unmold salad on a lettuce-lined plate. Slice reserved pear halves; garnish salad with pear slices. Yield: 8 servings.
June Miller,
Pensacola, Florida.

APRICOT NECTAR SALAD

1 (8-ounce) can crushed pineapple,
    undrained
1 cup apricot nectar
1 (3-ounce) package apricot-flavored
    gelatin
1 (8-ounce) package cream cheese, cubed
    and softened
1 cup shredded carrots
1 cup chopped pecans
1 cup frozen whipped topping, thawed

Combine pineapple and apricot nectar in a saucepan; bring to a boil. Add gelatin, stirring until gelatin dissolves. Add cream cheese; stir until melted. Chill until the consistency of unbeaten egg white. Fold in carrots, pecans, and whipped topping. Pour into an oiled 5-cup mold or 9-inch square dish. Chill until firm. Yield: 9 to 12 servings.
Johnnye Strawn,
Electra, Texas.

RASPBERRY RIBBON SALAD

2 (3-ounce) packages raspberry-flavored
    gelatin
1½ cups boiling water
2 (10-ounce) packages frozen raspberries
    in syrup, thawed and undrained
1 (15¼-ounce) can crushed pineapple,
    undrained
½ cup chopped pecans
2 cups commercial sour cream
Lettuce leaves

Tasty layers of sour cream form the white ribbons in Raspberry Ribbon Salad.

Dissolve gelatin in boiling water; stir in raspberries, pineapple, and chopped pecans. Blend well.

Spoon 1½ cups gelatin mixture into a lightly oiled 8-cup mold; chill until set. Spread 1 cup sour cream over raspberry layer. Spoon half of remaining raspberry mixture over sour cream layer. Chill until set. Spread 1 cup sour cream over raspberry layer. Spoon remaining raspberry mixture over sour cream. Chill until firm. Unmold on lettuce leaves. Yield: about 14 servings.
Alice Slaton Grant,
Concord, North Carolina.

HURRY-UP FRUIT SALAD

1 (15¼-ounce) can unsweetened pineapple
    chunks, undrained
2 medium bananas, sliced
2 (11-ounce) cans mandarin oranges,
    drained
¼ cup flaked coconut
¼ cup golden raisins
½ cup chopped walnuts

Drain pineapple, reserving juice; set pineapple aside. Combine bananas and pineapple juice; toss gently, and drain. Combine bananas, pineapple, oranges, and remaining ingredients in a medium bowl; toss gently. Yield: 8 servings.
Betty Czebotar,
Baltimore, Maryland.

HOLIDAY FRUIT SALAD

1 (15½-ounce) can crushed pineapple,
    drained
1 (8¾-ounce) can sliced peaches, drained
    and chopped
3 oranges, peeled and sectioned
1 large apple, unpeeled, cored, and
    chopped
1 banana, chopped
½ cup maraschino cherries, halved and
    drained
½ cup chopped pecans
1 egg yolk, beaten
1 tablespoon sugar
1 tablespoon vinegar
1 tablespoon butter or margarine
¾ cup miniature marshmallows
1 cup frozen whipped topping, thawed

Combine first 7 ingredients in a large bowl; set aside.

Combine egg yolk, sugar, vinegar, and butter in a small saucepan; cook over medium heat, stirring constantly, until mixture comes to a boil and thickens. Remove from heat; add marshmallows, stirring until melted. Cool. Stir in whipped topping. Pour dressing over fruit; toss gently until well coated. Yield: 8 servings.

Ruby Lee Johnson,
Fort Payne, Alabama.

Sausage— A Texas Tradition

In the midst of a section of the country where barbecue, chili, and cowboys are revered, there's another tradition that Texans hold close to their hearts. Fresh, smoked, and dried sausages are savored every meal of the day and in between, too.

In New Braunfels, as in many Texas towns, you'll find some of the most traditional samples of sausage, with most of the recipes handed down through generations from German, Czech, and Polish ancestors. But the Mexican influence found less than an hour away in San Antonio and the abundance of venison and beef in the hill country have spurred variations of the sausage recipes that make them unique to Texas.

For the real flavor of Texas sausage traditions, you just have to be there to sample the atmosphere and the sausage—smoky links right off the grill or home-cured sausage straight out of the crock. But if Texas is too far away, use these recipes from Texas readers to sample sausage favorites. (See "From Our Kitchen to Yours," page 238, for more sausage information.)

BREAKFAST TAQUITOS

½ pound fresh chorizo
6 slices bacon
2 tablespoons chopped onion
1 cup refried beans
2½ cups frozen hash brown potatoes
2 tablespoons vegetable oil
¼ teaspoon salt
2 tablespoons butter or margarine
6 eggs, beaten
¼ cup butter or margarine, softened
6 (8-inch) flour tortillas

Cook chorizo in a skillet over medium heat until browned, stirring to crumble. Drain and set chorizo aside.

Cook bacon in a skillet until crisp; remove bacon, reserving 2 tablespoons drippings in skillet. Crumble bacon, and set aside. Sauté onion in drippings until tender. Stir in refried beans, and cook over low heat until heated. Keep warm.

Cook potatoes in oil in a skillet over medium heat until browned, stirring occasionally. Sprinkle with salt. Remove to serving bowl; keep warm.

Melt 2 tablespoons butter in a skillet; add eggs. Cook over medium heat, stirring constantly, until set. Remove to bowl; keep warm.

Spread 1 teaspoon softened butter on each side of tortillas. Place tortillas one at a time, on hot griddle or skillet for 3 seconds on each side or until heated.

Spread half of each tortilla with desired fillings, and fold over as you would a taco. Serve immediately. Yield: 6 servings.

Note: Chorizo Substitute (next recipe) may be used for fresh chorizo, if desired.

Elaine Myers,
Willis, Texas.

The popularity of these sausages in Texas today hints at the cultural melting pot that is representative of the different ethnic groups that settled the state. **1.** Summer sausage rings (venison and pork) **2.** Summer sausage chub (venison and pork) **3.** Summer sausage (beef and pork) **4.** Smoked-beef sausage **5.** Blood sausage **6.** Fresh chorizo **7.** Smoked chorizo **8.** Knockwurst **9.** Bratwurst

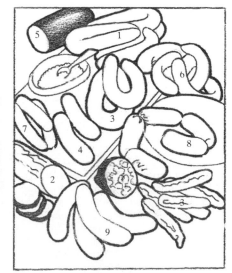

CHORIZO SUBSTITUTE

1 pound hot bulk pork sausage
1 tablespoon chopped fresh cilantro
2 tablespoons vinegar
2 teaspoons chili powder

Combine all ingredients; mix well. Yield: about 1⅛ pounds.

VENISON SAUSAGE STEW

2 pounds venison summer sausage,
    cut into ¼-inch slices
1 large onion, chopped
1 green pepper, chopped
2 tablespoons butter or margarine,
    melted
2 (14½-ounce) cans stewed tomatoes,
    undrained
2 cups diced carrots
2 cups cubed unpeeled potatoes
1 teaspoon dried whole thyme
1 teaspoon dried whole oregano
1 bay leaf
1 (17-ounce) can whole kernel corn,
    drained
1 tablespoon all-purpose flour
¼ cup water

Cook sausage, onion, and green pepper in butter in a large Dutch oven until sausage is browned; drain well. Return to Dutch oven; add tomatoes, carrots, potatoes, thyme, oregano, and bay leaf. Bring to a boil; cover, reduce heat, and simmer 30 minutes, stirring occasionally. Add corn; cook until thoroughly heated.

Combine flour and water in a small bowl; stir into sausage mixture. Cook until mixture is thickened, stirring constantly. Remove bay leaf before serving. Yield: 2½ quarts.

Note: Other types of summer sausage may be substituted for venison sausage.
Ann Temple Kuehler,
New Braunfels, Texas.

Tip: Fresh meat, poultry, and fish should be loosely wrapped and refrigerated; use in a few days. Loosely wrap fresh ground meat, liver, and kidneys; use in one or two days. Wieners, bacon, and sliced sandwich meats can be stored in original wrappings in the refrigerator. Store all meat in the coldest part of the refrigerator.

KRAUSE'S CAFE BRATWURST DINNER

3 (12-ounce) packages cooked bratwurst
3 tablespoons vegetable oil
8 new potatoes, peeled
2 tablespoons vegetable oil
¼ teaspoon salt
⅛ teaspoon pepper
1 (16-ounce) can sauerkraut, drained
Commercial spicy mustard

Sauté bratwurst in 3 tablespoons oil in a heavy skillet over medium heat 20 minutes. Set aside, and keep warm.

Cook potatoes in water to cover 15 minutes or until crisp-tender. Allow potatoes to cool, and finely chop. Sauté potatoes in 2 tablespoons oil in a skillet over high heat. Sprinkle with salt and pepper.

Cook sauerkraut until thoroughly heated. To serve, arrange 3 bratwurst, sauerkraut, and potatoes on each plate; serve with mustard. Yield: 4 servings.

From Our Kitchen To Yours

Labeled with intriguing names, the puzzling display of sausages in the meat department or at the delicatessen counter confuses many consumers. Basically, all sausages are mixtures of chopped or ground meat and seasonings. After the meat has been cured, smoked, cooked, and/or dried, unique tastes and textures emerge. Representing centuries of progress, sausage-making is a remarkable combination of old and new. Family traditions and personal flavor preferences have influenced the making of today's sausages.

Kinds of meats used, seasoning blends, and size and shape help identify sausage; we've included five different classifications according to how the sausages are prepared. (For more information and sausage recipes, turn back to "Sausage—A Texas Tradition," which starts on page 237.)

Fresh sausage is made from meat that is not cured or smoked. Pork sausage and bratwurst, which are highly seasoned all-pork or pork-and-veal mixtures, are well known. Bratwurst is sometimes served as a breakfast sausage but is traditionally served with sauerkraut, German potato salad or French fries, and spicy mustard as a lunch or dinner meat. Refrigerate these most perishable sausages up to three days, and cook thoroughly.

The most popular **uncooked, smoked** sausage is kielbasa or Polish sausage, which consists of coarsely ground lean pork and beef highly seasoned with garlic. Similar to fresh sausage, it's composed of uncooked meat that is cured and then smoked. Refrigerate up to three days, and cook thoroughly.

Generally made from fresh, uncured ground meat, **cooked** sausage is meat blended with spices and then cooked. Some kinds are smoked after cooking. Favorites in this group include braunschweiger (liverwurst), liver sausage, and blood sausage (a specialty item). Blood sausage is often fried and served for breakfast with scrambled eggs. However, these ready-to-eat sausages are usually served cold. They can be refrigerated up to six days.

Cooked, smoked sausage, such as knockwurst, smoked links, and Berliner style, is made from fresh meats that are smoked and fully cooked. Beerwurst, cotto salami, kosher salami, and cooked salami are in this group. Keep in mind that ready-to-eat cooked, smoked sausage is more flavorful when it is heated before serving; refrigerate this sausage up to five days.

Sausage that is air dried up to six months to remove approximately half the moisture, shrivel the casings, and harden the texture is classified as **dry** or **semidry** sausage. Hard salamis and chorizo, a highly spiced Spanish sausage of coarsely ground pork that is smoked after stuffing, are dry sausages. Semidry sausage, which is softer, includes a wide range of summer sausage or cervelats. Although it is not cooked, the manufacturing process makes it ready to eat. Usually served as a snack with cheese and crackers or sliced for sandwiches, dry and semidry sausages can be refrigerated up to three weeks.

Note: Fresh pork sausage, luncheon meats, frankfurters, and smoked sausage links and patties can be frozen up to two months. Freezing other sausages can lead to loss of quality because seasonings speed up changes in flavor during freezing.

Bring On The Holidays!

Our "Holiday Dinners" special section invites you to savor family holiday times with the very best of recipes from our readers and their families. We've included cheesy appetizers, beautiful entrées, classic side dishes, flavorful breads, and incredible cakes and pies. We've remembered party food for the health conscious, toasty beverages to warm you, and more.

Come feast with us. 'Tis the season for greeting friends and gathering with family. And what better way to celebrate than with food.

A Festive Georgia Gathering

In Atlanta, four spirited couples celebrate their friendship at an annual wild-game dinner. Begun in 1979, it's a traditional treat they never miss.

"The food is our favorite part," Joanie Michaels says. "In addition to shooting the game, the men are responsible for cooking it." They spend the afternoon of the dinner preparing the game according to their favorite recipes. The women do the table setting and prepare the side dishes and dessert.

It's a veritable feast enjoyed in a highly formal and festive setting. "We added formal attire about two years ago," Joanie adds.

This year the dinner is at the restored 1928 Tudor home of M. E. and Lilla Costello. "This is a party that *all* of us do," Lilla says. "We all prepare the food, and we all work to clean up." The other couples readily agree. Ed and Joanie Michaels, Barbara and Ernie Prickett, and Cord and Diane Middleton come to the Costello home laden with baskets of food.

Now the couples share their evening with us. Their lavish menu, along with all of their recipes, is featured here.

Hot Crab Canapés
Artichoke-Caviar Mold
Orange-Romaine Salad
Wild Goose With Currant Sauce
Duck Breasts With Raspberry Sauce
Pan-Roasted Doves
Georgia Quail With Gravy
Rice Mélange
Curried Fruit Bake
Mushroom-Artichoke Casserole
Bûche de Noël

HOT CRAB CANAPÉS

½ pound fresh crabmeat
1 cup (4 ounces) shredded Cheddar cheese
2 hard-cooked eggs, finely chopped
¼ cup mayonnaise
¼ teaspoon salt
⅛ teaspoon white pepper
⅛ teaspoon garlic powder
2 teaspoons grated onion
1 tablespoon minced parsley
20 slices sandwich bread

Combine all ingredients except bread; stir well, and set aside.

Trim crust from bread; cut each slice into 4 squares. Spread each square with crabmeat mixture, and place on ungreased baking sheets. Bake at 350° for 10 to 15 minutes or until lightly browned. Yield: 6½-dozen appetizer servings.

*Diane Middleton,
Atlanta, Georgia.*

ARTICHOKE-CAVIAR MOLD

2 (14-ounce) cans artichoke hearts
1 envelope unflavored gelatin
2 teaspoons dry Italian salad dressing mix
½ cup mayonnaise
1 (3½-ounce) jar black caviar, drained
Minced parsley
Pimiento rose

Drain artichokes, and reserve liquid; set artichokes aside. Sprinkle gelatin over ¼ cup reserved artichoke liquid in a heavy saucepan; let stand 1 minute. Stir over medium heat until gelatin is dissolved (about 1 minute).

Position knife blade in food processor bowl; add artichokes. Cover with top; process about 1 minute or until smooth, scraping sides of processor bowl occasionally. Add gelatin mixture and salad dressing mix; cover with top, and process until combined. Spoon mixture into a lightly oiled 2-quart bowl. Chill until mold is firm.

Unmold onto a serving tray. Spread with mayonnaise, covering mold completely. Lightly score mold into 6 wedges. Gently press caviar and minced parsley onto alternating wedges. Garnish top of mold with pimiento rose. Yield: one 3-cup mold.

*Barbara Prickett,
Atlanta, Georgia.*

ORANGE-ROMAINE SALAD

1 pound romaine lettuce, torn into
   bite-size pieces
8 scallions, sliced
2 oranges, peeled and sectioned
¼ cup pine nuts, toasted
Dressing (recipe follows)

Combine first 4 ingredients in a large bowl; toss well. Toss salad with dressing just before serving. Yield: 8 servings.

Dressing:

½ cup vegetable oil
2 tablespoons malt vinegar
2 tablespoons sugar
½ teaspoon salt
1 teaspoon Dijon mustard

Combine all ingredients in a jar. Cover tightly, and shake vigorously. Yield: ⅔ cup. *Diane Middleton,
Atlanta, Georgia.*

WILD GOOSE
WITH CURRANT SAUCE

1 cooking apple, cored and cut into
  wedges
1 large orange, unpeeled and cut into
  wedges
6 pitted dried prunes, chopped
2 (2½-pound) wild geese, dressed
2 (1.31-ounce) envelopes dry onion soup
  mix
2 cups dry red wine
2 cups water
Currant Sauce

Combine first 3 ingredients, stirring
well. Spoon into cavities of geese. Place
each goose, breast side up, in an oven
cooking bag. Combine soup mix, wine,
and water; pour half of mixture into
each bag. Seal bags; cut 6 small slits in
top of each bag to allow steam to escape. Place bags in a large shallow pan.
Bake at 350° for 3 to 3½ hours. Serve
with Currant Sauce. Yield: 4 servings.

Currant Sauce:

¼ cup red currant jelly
¼ cup catsup
¼ cup port wine
¼ cup Worcestershire sauce
2 tablespoons butter or margarine

Combine all ingredients in a small
saucepan. Cook over medium heat, stirring constantly, until thoroughly heated.
Yield: 1 cup.   *M. E. Costello,*
                       Atlanta, Georgia.

DUCK BREASTS
WITH RASPBERRY SAUCE

½ cup dry red wine
¼ cup soy sauce
¼ cup vegetable oil
¼ teaspoon freshly ground pepper
4 wild-duck breasts, skinned and boned
Sauce (recipe follows)

Combine wine, soy sauce, vegetable
oil, and pepper in a small bowl, stirring
well. Place duck breasts in a shallow

dish; pour marinade over meat. Cover
and refrigerate 2 to 2½ hours, turning
meat occasionally.

Remove duck breasts from marinade,
and place on broiler rack. Broil 5 inches
from heat 15 to 20 minutes, turning
once. To serve, thinly slice and serve
with sauce. Yield: 4 servings.

Sauce:

¼ cup seedless black raspberry preserves
¼ cup water
1½ tablespoons Dijon mustard
1 teaspoon lime juice
1 teaspoon soy sauce
½ teaspoon salt
½ teaspoon pepper
¼ teaspoon caraway seeds, crushed
½ teaspoon steak sauce

Combine all ingredients in a small
saucepan; cook over low heat until thoroughly heated. Yield: about ½ cup.
                       Ernie Prickett,
                       Atlanta, Georgia.

PAN-ROASTED DOVES

2 tablespoons all-purpose flour
½ teaspoon salt
1 teaspoon freshly ground black pepper
16 doves
2 tablespoons butter or margarine, melted
2 tablespoons bacon drippings
1 cup dry red wine, divided
1½ cups veal or chicken broth, divided
1 tablespoon red currant jelly
2 tablespoons all-purpose flour

Combine first 3 ingredients; dredge
doves in mixture. Brown doves on both
sides in butter and bacon drippings in a
large skillet. Gradually add ½ cup wine,
¾ cup broth, and jelly; cover and cook
over low heat 40 minutes.

Remove doves, and keep warm.
Combine 2 tablespoons flour, remaining
½ cup red wine, and remaining ¾ cup
broth, stirring until flour dissolves.
Gradually add flour mixture to the pan
drippings; cook over medium heat, stirring constantly, until mixture thickens.
Serve the gravy with doves. Yield: 4
servings.   *Cord Middleton,*
                       Atlanta, Georgia.

GEORGIA QUAIL WITH GRAVY

8 quail, dressed
½ teaspoon salt
¼ teaspoon pepper
¼ cup butter or margarine, melted
1 chicken- or beef-flavored boulllon cube
1 cup boiling water
2 tablespoons all-purpose flour
2 tablespoons water

Sprinkle quail with salt and pepper.
Brown quail on both sides in butter in a
large skillet over medium heat. Dissolve
bouillon cube in boiling water; add to
skillet. Cover, reduce heat, and simmer
40 minutes or until tender. Remove
quail from skillet; set aside.

Measure pan drippings; add water, if
necessary, to measure 1 cup. Combine
flour and 2 tablespoons water; gradually
add pan drippings. Cook over low heat,
stirring constantly, until thickened and
bubbly. Return quail to skillet; heat
thoroughly. Remove quail to a serving
platter, and serve with gravy. Yield: 4
servings.   *Ed Michaels,*
                       Atlanta, Georgia.

RICE MÉLANGE

1 (10½-ounce) can beef consommé,
  undiluted
1 (10½-ounce) can French onion soup,
  undiluted
¼ cup butter or margarine, melted
1½ cups uncooked long-grain rice
½ pound fresh mushrooms, sliced

Combine all ingredients; stir well.
Pour into a lightly greased 2-quart baking dish. Cover and bake at 325° for 1
hour and 10 minutes or until done.
Yield: 8 servings.   *Joanie Michaels,*
                       Atlanta, Georgia.

*Tip: When cooking for a crowd, plan
your menu so you can utilize several
cooking appliances rather than just
your oven. Don't forget to use the
stove top, microwave, electric skillet,
and toaster oven.*

CURRIED FRUIT BAKE

1 (29-ounce) can peach halves, drained
1 (29-ounce) can pear halves, drained
1 (20-ounce) can pineapple slices, drained
1 (15-ounce) can apricot halves, drained
¼ cup maraschino cherries, drained
¾ cup firmly packed brown sugar
⅓ cup butter or margarine, melted
2½ tablespoons curry powder

Combine first 5 ingredients in a 12- x 8- x 2-inch baking dish. Combine brown sugar, butter, and curry, stirring well; spoon over fruit. Cover and bake at 350° for 35 minutes or until thoroughly heated. Yield: 8 to 10 servings.

Barbara Prickett,
Atlanta, Georgia.

MUSHROOM-ARTICHOKE CASSEROLE

2 (9-ounce) packages frozen artichoke
    hearts
1 pound fresh mushrooms, sliced
¼ cup butter or margarine, melted
1 (10¾-ounce) can cream of mushroom
    soup, undiluted
3 tablespoons dry sherry
⅛ teaspoon pepper
¼ cup grated Parmesan cheese
Cherry tomato (optional)
Parsley sprig (optional)
Mushroom slices (optional)

Cook artichoke hearts according to package directions. Sauté 1 pound mushrooms in butter until tender; drain. Combine artichoke hearts, sautéed mushrooms, soup, sherry, and pepper in bowl; stir well, and spoon into an 8-inch square baking dish. Sprinkle with cheese, and bake at 350° for 20 minutes or until bubbly. Garnish with a cherry tomato stuffed with parsley and mushroom slices, if desired. Yield: 8 servings. *Joanie Michaels,*
Atlanta, Georgia.

BÛCHE DE NOËL

4 eggs, separated
⅔ cup sugar, divided
½ cup all-purpose flour
2 tablespoons cocoa
1 teaspoon baking powder
¼ teaspoon salt
1 to 2 tablespoons powdered
    sugar
Amaretto Filling
Creamy Chocolate Frosting
Red and green frosting
    (optional)

Grease a 15- x 10- x 1-inch jellyroll pan, and line with wax paper. Grease and flour wax paper.

Beat egg yolks in a large mixing bowl until thick and lemon colored; gradually add ⅓ cup sugar, beating well. Set mixture aside.

Beat egg whites (at room temperature) in a large mixing bowl until foamy; gradually add remaining ⅓ cup sugar, 1 tablespoon at a time, beating until stiff peaks form. Fold into egg yolk mixture.

Combine flour, cocoa, baking powder, and salt; mix well, and fold into egg mixture. Spread batter evenly in prepared pan. Bake at 375° for 8 to 10 minutes.

Sift 1 to 2 tablespoons powdered sugar in a 15- x 10-inch rectangle on a towel. When cake is done, immediately loosen from sides of pan, and turn out onto sugar-coated towel. Peel off wax paper. Starting at narrow end, roll up warm cake and towel together; allow the cake to cool completely on a wire rack, seam side down.

Unroll cake; remove towel. Spread with Amaretto Filling, and reroll. Frost cake with Creamy Chocolate Frosting. Pipe red and green frosting to make berries and leaves, if desired. Yield: 10 to 12 servings.

Amaretto Filling:

1 cup whipping cream
2 teaspoons Amaretto or ¼ teaspoon
    almond extract
2 tablespoons sugar

Beat 1 cup whipping cream until foamy; add Amaretto. Gradually add sugar, beating until soft peaks form. Yield: 2 cups.

Creamy Chocolate Frosting:

2 (1-ounce) squares unsweetened chocolate
½ cup butter or margarine, softened
2 teaspoons vanilla extract
2 cups sifted powdered sugar
2 tablespoons milk

Melt chocolate in top of a double boiler; set aside.

Cream butter until light and fluffy. Add chocolate, vanilla, and remaining ingredients; beat until spreading consistency. Yield: enough frosting for one cake roll. *Joanie Michaels,*
Atlanta, Georgia.

Sippers For The Holidays

Whether you like something laced with liquor or a drink that's hot and fruity, the recipes here will help you pour the best for your holiday guests. From this full selection of beverages, take your pick to suit the occasion.

For a quick hot drink, be sure to keep plenty of Fireside Coffee Mix on hand. You can stir up a cup in an instant, give the mix as a gift, or take it to a party.

FIRESIDE COFFEE MIX

2 cups non-dairy coffee creamer
1½ cups hot cocoa mix
1½ cups instant coffee granules
1½ cups sugar
1 teaspoon ground cinnamon
½ teaspoon ground nutmeg

Combine all ingredients, mixing well. Store mixture in an airtight container. Yield: 6½ cups mix.

Note: To make 1 cup, spoon 2 tablespoons plus 1 teaspoon of coffee mix in a cup. Add 1 cup boiling water; stir until well blended.

Mrs. Richard D. Conn,
Kansas City, Missouri.

CHRISTMAS EGGNOG

6 eggs, slightly beaten
2 cups sifted powdered sugar
2 tablespoons vanilla extract
2 (12-ounce) cans evaporated milk,
  undiluted
3 cups milk
1¼ cups dark rum
3 tablespoons brandy
Freshly ground nutmeg

Combine eggs, powdered sugar, and vanilla in a large bowl, stirring well. Stir in undiluted evaporated milk and milk. Add rum, a little at a time, stirring with a wire whisk. Allow to chill 24 hours. Stir in brandy; sprinkle eggnog with nutmeg. Serve chilled. Yield: 2½ quarts.   *Maggie Cates,*
Orlando, Florida.

RASPBERRY-ROSÉ PUNCH

3 (25.4-ounce) bottles rosé wine
2 (6-ounce) cans frozen lemonade
  concentrate, thawed and undiluted
2 quarts raspberry sherbet, divided
1 (28-ounce) bottle club soda, chilled

Combine wine, lemonade concentrate, and 1 quart sherbet; mix well. Let mixture chill.
To serve, combine wine mixture and club soda in punch bowl, stirring well; scoop remaining quart of sherbet on top. Yield: 1 gallon.
Elizabeth M. Watts,
Panama City, Florida.

HOT SPICED FRUIT TEA

1 teaspoon whole cloves
1 (2-inch) stick cinnamon
3 quarts boiling water
3 (1-quart) tea bags
1 to 1½ cups sugar
1 cup orange juice
¼ cup plus 2 tablespoons lemon
  juice

Tie cloves and cinnamon in a cheese-cloth bag; set aside.

Pour boiling water over tea bags; cover. Allow tea to stand 5 minutes. Discard tea bags.
Combine tea, sugar, juices, and spice bag in a large Dutch oven. Bring mixture to a boil; reduce heat, and simmer 15 to 20 minutes. Discard spice bag. Yield: about 3 quarts.   *Gladys Stout,*
Elizabethton, Tennessee.

KAHLÚA SMOOTHIE

1 pint vanilla ice cream
⅓ cup crème de cacao
⅓ cup Kahlúa

Combine all ingredients in container of an electric blender; process until smooth. Serve as an after-dinner drink. Yield: 2½ cups.   *Lisa Burns,*
Cape Girardeau, Missouri.

Entertaining: Casual And Easy

If the holidays bring more panic than good cheer to your kitchen, take a look at this casual menu. You can prepare most of it the night before and add finishing touches just prior to the arrival of your guests.
Here's a streamlined plan. A day in advance, make the pie and the salad. Prepare the bread, wrap it in foil, and refrigerate. Cut up carrots and apples for the cheese tray. Soak them in lightly salted water, and refrigerate.
Before guests arrive, assemble the cheese tray. Cook the chicken, and prepare the zucchini. While your guests enjoy the appetizers and cider (purchased and chilled or heated), arrange the prepared salad plates at table place settings, and bake the bread.
Set up the buffet, and allow guests to serve themselves. Remember to set the pie out at least 5 minutes before serving dessert so that it's easy to slice.

Festive cheese tray and cider
**Orange Chicken Breasts
With Parslied Rice
Baked Zucchini Fans
Marinated Vegetable Salad
Herbed French Loaf
Pumpkin Ice-Cream Pie
Coffee**

ORANGE CHICKEN BREASTS WITH PARSLIED RICE

¼ cup butter or margarine
6 chicken breast halves, skinned and
  boned
2 tablespoons all-purpose flour
½ teaspoon salt
2 tablespoons sugar
¼ teaspoon dry mustard
¼ teaspoon ground cinnamon
⅛ teaspoon ground ginger
1½ cups orange juice
1 tablespoon all-purpose flour
2 tablespoons water
Parslied Rice
1 orange, sliced (optional)
Parsley sprigs (optional)

Melt butter in a heavy skillet; add chicken, and brown on all sides. Remove chicken from skillet, reserving drippings in skillet; set chicken aside. Add 2 tablespoons flour and next 5 ingredients, stirring until smooth. Cook 1 minute, stirring constantly. Gradually add orange juice; cook over medium heat, stirring constantly, until mixture is thickened and bubbly.
Add chicken; cover and simmer 20 minutes or until chicken is tender. Remove chicken, keeping warm. Combine 1 tablespoon flour and water, mixing well. Gradually add flour mixture to pan juices; cook over low heat, stirring constantly, until mixture is thickened and bubbly. Serve chicken and sauce over Parslied Rice. Garnish with orange slices and parsley, if desired. Yield: 6 servings.

Parslied Rice:

3 cups water
1½ tablespoons butter or margarine
1 teaspoon salt
1½ cups uncooked long-grain rice
¼ cup chopped fresh parsley

Combine first 3 ingredients in a medium saucepan. Bring to a boil; add rice. Cover, reduce heat, and simmer 20 minutes or until tender. Stir in parsley. Yield: 6 servings. *Mrs. Otis Jones, Bude, Mississippi.*

BAKED ZUCCHINI FANS

6 small zucchini
¼ cup butter or margarine, melted
2 tablespoons lemon juice
2 tablespoons vinegar
1 teaspoon onion salt
½ teaspoon pepper
½ teaspoon dried whole thyme

Cut each zucchini lengthwise into ¼-inch-thick slices, taking care not to cut through the stem ends. Place zucchini fans in a lightly greased shallow pan.
Combine remaining ingredients, stirring well. Brush butter mixture over sliced zucchini; bake at 350° for 25 to 30 minutes or until tender, basting occasionally. Yield: 6 servings.

MARINATED VEGETABLE SALAD

½ cup mayonnaise
1 tablespoon chili sauce
1 tablespoon lemon juice
½ teaspoon dried whole dillweed
¼ teaspoon salt
5 cups cauliflower flowerets
5 cups broccoli flowerets
5 stalks celery, chopped
5 green onions, chopped
1 (8-ounce) bottle Italian salad dressing
Lettuce leaves
Cherry tomatoes

Combine first 5 ingredients in a small bowl, mixing well; cover and refrigerate 8 hours.

Combine cauliflower, broccoli, celery, green onions, and Italian salad dressing in a large bowl; toss gently. Cover and refrigerate 8 hours; drain. Add the mayonnaise mixture to vegetable mixture, stirring well. Serve on lettuce leaves, and garnish with cherry tomatoes. Yield: about 8 servings.
Mrs. Clifford B. Smith, Sr., White Hall, Maryland.

HERBED FRENCH LOAF

1 (1-pound) loaf unsliced French bread
½ cup butter or margarine, softened
¼ teaspoon salt
¼ teaspoon dry mustard
¼ teaspoon dried whole thyme
¼ teaspoon paprika
Dash of garlic powder

Slice French bread into ½-inch-thick slices. Combine remaining ingredients, mixing well. Spread butter mixture between bread slices. Wrap loaf in aluminum foil; bake at 400° for 15 minutes or until thoroughly heated. Yield: 1 loaf.
Virginia Granger, Montgomery, Alabama.

PUMPKIN-ICE CREAM PIE

1 cup canned or mashed cooked pumpkin
½ cup firmly packed brown sugar
¼ teaspoon ground nutmeg
½ teaspoon ground cinnamon
1 quart vanilla ice cream, softened
Graham cracker crust (recipe follows)
Whipped cream (optional)
Walnut halves (optional)

Combine pumpkin, brown sugar, nutmeg, and cinnamon in a large mixing bowl, stirring until sugar dissolves. Add ice cream; mix thoroughly. Spoon mixture into graham cracker crust; freeze 8 hours. Garnish with whipped cream and walnut halves, if desired. Allow pie to stand at room temperature 5 minutes before serving. Yield: one 9-inch pie.

Graham Cracker Crust:

1¼ cups graham cracker crumbs
3 tablespoons sugar
⅓ cup butter or margarine, melted

Combine graham cracker crumbs and sugar; stir in butter, mixing well. Press mixture firmly into a 9-inch pieplate. Bake at 350° for 8 minutes; cool before filling. Yield: one 9-inch crumb crust.
Rosa Lee Gay, Wilmington, North Carolina.

The Berries Of The Holidays

Thanksgiving and Christmas just wouldn't be the same without plump, red cranberries—whether they're strung on a tree or cooked in a sauce to enjoy with turkey and dressing.
Cranberries, appreciated for their tart and tangy flavor, can be used in a variety of ways. Our recipes include an hors d'oeuvre as well as bread and desserts.

FRESH CRANBERRY-APRICOT SAUCE

1 (12-ounce) package fresh cranberries
8 ounces dried apricots, chopped
1¼ cups sugar
2 cups orange juice
½ cup water

Combine all ingredients in a Dutch oven; cook over medium heat, stirring constantly, until sugar dissolves. Reduce heat, and simmer 30 minutes, stirring occasionally. Serve sauce warm or cold with poultry or pork. Yield: 4 cups.
Mrs. Thomas Byrd, Nashville, Tennessee.

CRANBERRY-AMARETTO CHUTNEY WITH CREAM CHEESE

2 (8-ounce) packages cream cheese, softened
2 cups cranberries
1 cup sugar
1 tablespoon plus 1 teaspoon lemon juice
½ teaspoon lemon rind
¼ cup amaretto
1 tablespoon orange marmalade

Line a 2-cup mold with damp cheesecloth, letting cloth hang over edges. Firmly press cream cheese, one spoonful at a time, into prepared mold. Fold cheesecloth over top; cover and chill 6 hours or until firm.

Combine cranberries, sugar, and lemon juice in a small saucepan. Cook over medium heat, stirring constantly, until mixture comes to a boil; reduce heat, and simmer 20 minutes. Remove from heat; add lemon rind, amaretto, and marmalade, stirring until blended. Cool mixture to room temperature.

Unmold cheese onto serving plate. Remove cheesecloth; spoon cranberry sauce over cheese. Serve with crackers. Yield: 20 appetizer servings.

Note: Sauce may be served hot or cold with meat. *Jan Fulghum, Statesville, North Carolina.*

CRANBERRY-ORANGE BREAD

2 cups all-purpose flour
1½ teaspoons baking powder
½ teaspoon baking soda
½ teaspoon salt
1 cup sugar
2 tablespoons shortening
¾ cup orange juice
1 egg, beaten
1 tablespoon grated orange rind
½ teaspoon almond extract
1½ cups cranberries, coarsely chopped

Combine first 5 ingredients in a medium bowl. Combine shortening, orange juice, egg, orange rind, and almond extract in a small bowl, stirring well. Add orange juice mixture to dry ingredients, stirring just until dry ingredients are moistened. Fold in cranberries.

Spoon batter into a greased and floured 8½- x 4½- x 3-inch loafpan. Bake at 350° for 1 hour or until a wooden pick inserted in center comes out clean. Cool in pan 10 minutes. Remove from pan, and cool on a wire rack. Yield: 1 loaf. *Michele Baker, Jackson, Tennessee.*

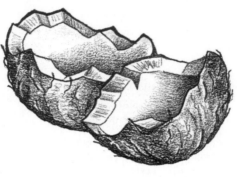

FRESH CRANBERRY TARTLETS

2 cups fresh cranberries
1 cup sugar
2 tablespoons cornstarch
⅓ cup water
1½ cups all-purpose flour
½ teaspoon salt
½ cup shortening
¼ cup grated coconut
3 to 4 tablespoons cold water
1 (3-ounce) package cream cheese, softened
¼ cup sugar
1 egg
1 tablespoon milk
1 teaspoon lemon juice
½ teaspoon vanilla extract
¼ cup grated coconut
Additional grated coconut (optional)

Combine first 4 ingredients in a heavy saucepan; stir well. Bring to a boil; cook 1 to 2 minutes or until cranberries pop and mixture thickens, stirring constantly. Remove from heat; cool. Cover and chill 2 to 3 hours.

Combine flour and salt; cut in shortening with pastry blender until mixture resembles coarse meal. Stir in ¼ cup coconut. Sprinkle cold water (1 tablespoon at a time) evenly over surface; stir with a fork just until dry ingredients are moistened. Shape into a ball; chill.

Roll dough to ⅛-inch thickness on a lightly floured surface. Cut into 6 (5-inch) circles; fit into a 3-inch fluted tart pan. Set aside.

Combine cream cheese and ¼ cup sugar; beat at medium speed of an electric mixer 1 minute or until smooth. Add egg, milk, lemon juice, and vanilla; beat until smooth. Spoon about 2½ tablespoons cream cheese mixture into each tart pan; bake at 350° for 25 minutes or until set. Cool.

Stir ¼ cup coconut into cranberry mixture; spoon evenly into tart shells. Sprinkle additional coconut on top, if desired. Yield: six 3-inch tarts.
Jana Dominguez, Navasota, Texas.

CRAN-RASPBERRY PIE

2¼ cups all-purpose flour
1 teaspoon salt
1 tablespoon sugar
¾ cup shortening
1 egg yolk, slightly beaten
2 teaspoons almond extract
¼ cup plus 2 tablespoons ice water
2 cups fresh cranberries
1 (10-ounce) package frozen, sweetened raspberries
1¼ cups sugar
¼ teaspoon salt
2 tablespoons quick-cooking tapioca
¼ teaspoon almond extract

Combine flour, 1 teaspoon salt, and 1 tablespoon sugar; cut in shortening with pastry blender until mixture resembles coarse meal. Combine egg yolk, 2 teaspoons almond extract, and water; sprinkle (1 tablespoon at a time) evenly over flour mixture; stir with a fork until all ingredients are moistened. Shape into 2 balls; chill 2 hours.

Roll half of dough to ⅛-inch thickness on a lightly floured surface. Place in a 9-inch pieplate; trim excess pastry around edges. Bake at 425° (with pie weights) for 5 minutes; remove weights, and bake an additional 5 minutes.

Combine cranberries and remaining ingredients in a heavy saucepan. Cook over medium heat 15 minutes, stirring often. Set aside, and cool slightly (about 10 minutes).

Spoon into prebaked pastry shell. Roll remaining pastry to ⅛-inch thickness on a lightly floured surface; cut 4 (10- x ½-inch) strips. Arrange in lattice fashion over berries; trim edges. Cut leaf designs from remaining pastry; arrange on pie and around edge of crust. Bake at 350° for 20 minutes or until golden. Shield edge of pastry shell with foil during last 10 minutes, if necessary. Yield: one 9-inch pie.

Mildred Sherrer,
Bay City, Texas.

Relishes And Chutneys Add Color, Flavor

Special occasions seem to bring on bowls full of rainbow-colored relishes and chutneys—just the something extra to complete a holiday table. These versatile side dishes are best made ahead, a great plus this time of year.

Commander's Chutney is a chutney that's a little different from most. It features mangoes (or you can substitute apples), raisins, and a tasty blend of sweet spices, a combination that would complement any main dish. Candied papaya and candied citron add a bright holiday touch. You can get these candied food products in most specialty grocery stores.

Corn Relish is a bit of a surprise for fall and winter. Bright flecks of red pepper and pimiento tossed with canned corn make a colorful side dish.

While relishes and chutneys can be processed in a boiling water bath to make them safe for shelf storage, the amounts these recipes make will be just right for use over the holidays. The mixtures are safe stored in the refrigerator and served chilled. Use them as gifts for friends, too. Just be sure to tell the receiver to store unprocessed jars in the refrigerator.

CORN RELISH
(pictured on page 272)

2 (17-ounce) cans whole kernel corn, drained
1 (4-ounce) jar diced pimiento, drained
1 small sweet red pepper, chopped
2 tablespoons vegetable oil
½ cup sugar
½ cup vinegar
2 teaspoons instant minced onion
¼ teaspoon celery seeds
⅛ teaspoon salt

Combine first 4 ingredients in a bowl, stirring well. Combine sugar and remaining ingredients in a small saucepan. Bring to a boil; cover, reduce heat, and simmer 2 minutes. Pour vinegar mixture over vegetables; toss gently. Cover and chill at least 2 hours. Yield: 4 cups.

Evelyn Hammond,
Camden, Arkansas.

COMMANDER'S CHUTNEY

4 cups peeled, chopped mangoes or cooking apples
1 cup chopped onion
1 cup raisins
¼ cup candied citron
¼ cup candied papaya
2 small cloves garlic, minced
½ cup firmly packed brown sugar
⅓ cup vinegar
⅔ cup water
2 teaspoons curry powder
1 teaspoon ground ginger
1 teaspoon salt
¼ teaspoon ground cinnamon
¼ teaspoon ground cloves

Combine all ingredients in a large Dutch oven. Bring to a boil, and cook, uncovered, over low heat 1 hour, stirring occasionally. Chill. Yield: 4 cups.

Al Noble,
Bristol, Tennessee.

CRANBERRY RELISH
(pictured on page 272)

1 (12-ounce) package fresh cranberries
1½ cups sugar
1½ tablespoons grated orange rind
¾ cup orange juice
1 teaspoon grated lemon rind
2½ tablespoons lemon juice

Combine all ingredients in a large saucepan. Bring to a boil; cook 3 minutes or until cranberry skins pop. Cool. Yield: 2½ cups.

Susan M. Davis,
Austin, Texas.

RHUBARB CHUTNEY

1 cup vinegar
1 cup firmly packed light brown sugar
1 pound rhubarb, chopped
½ cup chopped golden raisins
¼ cup chopped dried apricots
¼ cup chopped dried apples
3 tablespoons chopped candied red cherries
1 tablespoon chopped candied ginger
1 clove garlic, minced
¼ cup chopped onion
1 teaspoon grated orange rind
3 tablespoons chopped orange pulp
⅛ teaspoon red pepper
¼ cup sliced almonds, toasted

Combine all ingredients, except almonds, in a heavy 2-quart saucepan. Bring mixture to a boil; reduce heat, and simmer 2½ hours or until thickened, stirring occasionally. Stir in almonds. Yield: 2½ cups.

Margaret Ellen Holmes,
Jackson, Tennessee.

Tip: When squeezing fresh lemons or oranges for juice, first grate the rind by rubbing the washed fruit against surface of grater, taking care to remove only the outer colored portion of the rind. Wrap in plastic in teaspoon portions and freeze for future use.

Appetizers That Say Cheese

Mild, pungent, crumbly, or creamy, cheese is a favorite at any meal. This multifaceted delight takes on a Southern flavor when you combine it with shrimp in Seafood Tartlets or corn muffin mix in Cheese-and-Spinach Puffs.

The ingredients called for in Cheese-and-Spinach Puffs may sound unusual, but the flavor is divine. Corn muffin mix and spinach add texture to each bite. But Parmesan cheese, Cheddar cheese, and blue cheese dressing give a slightly pungent flavor.

PHYLLO-CHEESE TRIANGLES

4 cups (1 pound) shredded Muenster
  cheese
2 cups (8 ounces) shredded extra-sharp
  Cheddar cheese
½ cup chopped fresh parsley
2 eggs, beaten
Dash of red pepper
1 (16-ounce) package frozen phyllo pastry,
  thawed
¾ to 1 pound butter, melted

Combine cheeses and parsley in a large mixing bowl; add eggs and pepper, stirring well. Set aside.

Cut sheets of phyllo lengthwise into 3½-inch-wide strips. Working with one strip at a time, brush each with butter. Keep remaining strips covered with a damp cloth. Place 2 teaspoons cheese mixture at base of phyllo strip, folding the right bottom corner over it into a triangle. Continue folding back and forth into a triangle to end of strip. Repeat process with remaining phyllo and cheese mixture.

Place triangles, seam side down, on ungreased baking sheets. Brush tops with melted butter. Bake at 350° for 20 minutes or until lightly browned. Drain well on paper towels. Serve triangles warm. Yield: about 8 dozen.

Mig Sturr,
Kingsville, Maryland.

NUTTY FRUIT-AND-CHEESE SPREAD

1 cup boiling water
½ cup chopped dried apricots
4 cups (16 ounces) shredded Monterey
  Jack cheese
1 (8-ounce) package cream cheese,
  softened
½ teaspoon seasoned salt
⅓ cup milk
⅓ cup golden raisins
¼ cup chopped pitted dates
¾ cup chopped walnuts
Walnut halves (optional)

Pour boiling water over apricots; let stand 30 minutes. Drain well.

Combine Monterey Jack cheese, cream cheese, salt, and milk; beat at medium speed of electric mixer until smooth. Stir in apricots, golden raisins, dates, and chopped walnuts.

Line a 1-quart mold with plastic wrap. Spoon spread into mold, pressing firmly; cover and chill 3 to 4 hours. Unmold onto serving dish; remove plastic wrap, and garnish with walnut halves, if desired. Serve with assorted crackers. Yield: 4 cups.

Clairiece Gilbert Humphrey,
Charlottesville, Virginia.

CHEESE-AND-SPINACH PUFFS

1 (10-ounce) package frozen chopped
  spinach, thawed
½ cup chopped onion
½ cup water
2 eggs, slightly beaten
½ cup grated Parmesan cheese
½ cup (2 ounces) shredded Cheddar
  cheese
¼ cup plus 2 tablespoons commercial blue
  cheese dressing
⅛ teaspoon garlic powder
1 (8½-ounce) package corn muffin mix

Combine spinach, onion, and water in a saucepan; bring to a boil, and cook 10 minutes. Drain well, and squeeze to remove excess liquid. Combine mixture and remaining ingredients; stir well. Cover and chill 2 hours.

Shape mixture into 1-inch balls, and place 1½ inches apart on lightly greased baking sheets. Chill at least 30 minutes before baking.

Bake at 350° for 10 minutes; serve warm. Yield: 4 dozen.

Velma P. Kestner,
Berwind, West Virginia.

BITE-SIZE CHILES RELLENOS

1 cup all-purpose flour
½ teaspoon salt
¼ teaspoon garlic powder
1 cup beer
2 (4-ounce) cans whole green chiles,
  drained and seeded
4 ounces Monterey Jack cheese, cut into
  ½-inch cubes
Vegetable oil
Picante sauce (optional)

Combine first 3 ingredients; stir well. Gradually add 1 cup beer, stirring until smooth. Cover and let stand 1 hour.

Cut green chiles lengthwise into ¾-inch-wide strips. Roll each strip around a cheese cube, securing with a wooden pick. Cover and chill 1 hour.

Dip chile-cheese rolls in batter; allow excess to drip slightly. Deep-fry in hot oil (375°) about 15 seconds or until golden; drain on paper towels. Serve immediately with picante sauce, if desired. Yield: about 2 dozen.

Joanne Warner Gross,
Lufkin, Texas.

CHEESY-OLIVE APPETIZERS

1½ cups (6 ounces) shredded Cheddar
  cheese
1 cup chopped ripe olives
½ cup thinly sliced green onions
½ cup mayonnaise
½ teaspoon curry powder
6 English muffins, halved and toasted

Combine first 5 ingredients; stir well. Spread about 2 tablespoons cheese mixture on each muffin half. Broil 2 minutes or until cheese melts; cut each half into quarters. Serve warm. Yield: 48 appetizer servings. *Sharon McClatchey,*
Muskogee, Oklahoma.

CREAMY ORANGE DIP

1 (8-ounce) container soft cream cheese
1 (7-ounce) jar marshmallow cream
1 tablespoon grated orange rind
1 tablespoon frozen orange juice
  concentrate
1 tablespoon Grand Marnier or other
  orange-flavored liqueur

Combine cream cheese and marsh-mallow cream; beat until smooth. Stir in the remaining ingredients. Cover and chill for 1 to 2 hours; serve with assorted fresh fruit. Yield: 1¾ cups.

Matra T. Abbott,
Pewee Valley, Kentucky.

CHEESE AND CHUTNEY BALL

1 (8-ounce) package cream cheese,
  softened
1 (4-ounce) package blue cheese, crumbled
¼ cup commercial chutney
¾ cup chopped almonds, toasted

Combine first 3 ingredients; stir well. Cover and chill 1 hour.

Shape cheese mixture into a ball; roll in almonds. Cover and chill. Serve with crackers. Yield: one 4½-inch ball.

Grace Bravos,
Timonium, Maryland.

HERBED CHEESE SPREAD

1 (8-ounce) package cream cheese,
  softened
4 ounces process cheese
2 teaspoons Dijon mustard
1 teaspoon dried whole basil
¼ teaspoon onion powder
¼ teaspoon paprika
¼ teaspoon red pepper
¼ cup crumbled blue cheese

Combine cream cheese and process cheese in a mixing bowl; beat at medium speed of an electric mixer until smooth. Add mustard and next 4 ingredients, and mix well. Stir in blue cheese. Serve with apple and pear wedges or crackers. Yield: 2 cups.

Shirley L. Schlessmann,
Rockledge, Florida.

Parmesan and Swiss cheeses make a flavorful combination in Seafood Tartlets.

SEAFOOD TARTLETS

1 (1½-pound) loaf thin-sliced sandwich
  bread
⅓ cup butter or margarine, melted
1 (4¼-ounce) can tiny shrimp, drained
¾ cup mayonnaise
⅓ cup grated Parmesan cheese
⅓ cup (1.3 ounces) shredded Swiss cheese
¼ teaspoon Worcestershire sauce
⅛ teaspoon hot sauce
Paprika
Parsley sprigs (optional)

Roll each bread slice to ¼-inch thickness; cut with a 2½-inch daisy-shaped cutter. Lightly brush each side of bread with butter, and place in miniature tart shells. Bake at 400° for 8 to 10 minutes or until lightly browned.

Rinse shrimp; let stand in ice water 20 minutes. Drain well.

Combine shrimp, mayonnaise, cheeses, Worcestershire sauce, and hot sauce; stir well. Spoon shrimp mixture evenly into tart shells; sprinkle with paprika. Bake at 400° for 8 to 10 minutes or until bubbly. Garnish with parsley sprigs, if desired. Yield: 22 appetizers.

Susan Schroeder,
Woodbridge, Virginia.

Delicious Entrées To Carve

Holiday entrées will take on a whole new look with these recipes. Even the traditional turkey sports a unique squash-cheese dressing to make it different. If you like to stick to the ritual of carving the entrée at the table, sharpen your carving set. Each of these recipes makes a delicious presentation suitable for even the most formal affairs.

One of our favorite entrées is Stuffed Leg of Lamb. Although you can bone the leg easily with a sharp knife, cutting the meat closely along the bone, you may want to save some time by asking your butcher to do it for you.

No matter what type of meat you cook, remember that it will be easier to carve and slice if it is allowed to sit a few minutes after cooking before cutting. Be sure to use a meat thermometer to judge doneness by temperature. If the meat is not even in thickness, it will vary in degrees of doneness.

LOBSTER-STUFFED BEEF TENDERLOIN

3 (4-ounce) frozen lobster tails
1 (4- to 6-pound) beef tenderloin, trimmed
1 tablespoon butter or margarine, melted
1½ teaspoons lemon juice
Garlic salt
Freshly ground pepper
6 slices bacon
½ cup sliced green onions
½ cup butter or margarine, melted
½ cup dry white wine
⅛ teaspoon garlic salt

Place frozen lobster tails in boiling salted water to cover; simmer 5 minutes. Drain. Remove lobster in one piece from shells.

Trim excess fat from beef tenderloin. Remove 3 to 4 inches of small end; reserve for other uses. Cut tenderloin lengthwise to within ½ inch of other edge, leaving one long side connected. Place lobster tails end to end inside tenderloin (slice lobster tails lengthwise, if necessary, to extend entire length of tenderloin). Combine 1 tablespoon melted butter and lemon juice; drizzle over lobster. Fold top side of beef tenderloin over lobster.

Tie tenderloin securely with heavy string at 2- to 3-inch intervals. Sprinkle outside of meat evenly with garlic salt and freshly ground pepper; place on a rack in a shallow roasting pan. Bake at 425° for 35 to 40 minutes or until a meat thermometer registers 140° (rare) or 160° (medium).

Cook bacon just until transparent; drain and arrange crosswise on top of tenderloin. Bake 4 minutes or until the bacon is crisp. Remove to serving platter. Slice to serve.

Sauté green onions in ½ cup butter in a small saucepan until crisp-tender. Add wine and ⅛ teaspoon garlic salt; heat thoroughly. Serve with the sliced beef tenderloin. Yield: 10 to 12 servings.

Missy Wilson,
Birmingham, Alabama.

STUFFED LEG OF LAMB

3 to 5 slices bacon
1 small onion, chopped
¼ cup soft breadcrumbs
¼ cup milk
½ teaspoon grated lemon rind
2 tablespoons lemon juice
1 teaspoon chopped fresh parsley
½ teaspoon dried whole thyme or rosemary
¼ teaspoon salt
⅛ teaspoon pepper
1 (6-pound) leg of lamb, boned
Black pepper
½ cup chicken stock broth
½ cup dry red wine
Onion Sauce

Cook bacon in a large skillet until crisp; remove bacon, reserving 2 tablespoons drippings. Crumble bacon.

Combine bacon, onion, breadcrumbs, milk, lemon rind, lemon juice, parsley, thyme, salt, and pepper, stirring until blended. Stuff mixture in cavity of leg of lamb, and tie securely with heavy string at 2- to 3-inch intervals. Sprinkle with pepper over all sides.

Pour reserved bacon drippings into a shallow baking pan, and place lamb in pan. Bake at 350° for 2 hours or until a meat thermometer registers 160°. Let stand 20 minutes before carving.

Pour excess fat into a small saucepan. Add chicken broth and wine. Bring to a boil; reduce heat, and simmer until mixture is reduced by half. Serve wine sauce and Onion Sauce with lamb. Yield: 8 to 10 servings.

Onion Sauce:

2 large onions, thinly sliced
2 tablespoons butter or margarine, melted
1 tablespoon all-purpose flour
1 cup milk
¼ teaspoon salt
⅛ teaspoon pepper
⅛ teaspoon ground nutmeg
½ cup whipping cream

Sauté onions in butter until tender. Add flour, stirring until smooth. Cook 1 minute, stirring constantly. Reduce heat to medium; gradually add milk, and cook, stirring constantly, until mixture is thickened and bubbly. Stir in remaining ingredients. Yield: about 2 cups.

Patsy Hill,
San Antonio, Texas.

TURKEY WITH SQUASH DRESSING

1 (19-ounce) package cornbread mix
1 cup chopped onion
1 cup chopped celery
¼ cup butter or margarine, melted
2 tablespoons all-purpose flour
1½ teaspoons salt
½ teaspoon pepper
1 cup milk
2 cups (8 ounces) shredded American cheese
6 eggs, slightly beaten
4 (10-ounce) packages frozen yellow squash, cooked and drained
1 (12- to 14-pound) turkey
Salt
Vegetable oil

Prepare cornbread mix according to package directions. Cool on a wire rack.

Cut cornbread into ½-inch cubes. Let stand in a loosely covered bowl 8 hours.

Sauté onion and celery in butter until crisp-tender. Add flour, 1½ teaspoons salt, and pepper, stirring until smooth. Cook 1 minute, stirring constantly. Reduce heat to medium; gradually add milk. Cook, stirring constantly, until mixture is thickened and bubbly. Add cheese; stir until cheese melts. Gradually stir about one-fourth of hot mixture into eggs; add to remaining hot mixture, stirring constantly. Combine cornbread, squash, and cheese sauce in a large bowl; mix well. Set aside.

Remove giblets and neck from turkey. Rinse turkey with cold water; pat dry. Sprinkle cavity of turkey with salt. Lightly spoon ½ cup of dressing into the neck cavity. Pull neck skin to back of turkey; fasten securely with a small skewer. Lightly spoon half of remaining dressing into the body cavity; do not pack. Close cavity with skewers or wooden picks, and truss. Tie ends of legs to tail with cord; lift wingtips up and over back so that they are tucked under bird. Brush entire turkey with vegetable oil; place on a roasting rack, breast side up.

Insert meat thermometer in breast or meaty part of thigh, making sure it does not touch bone. Bake at 325° until meat thermometer reaches 185° (about 3 to 3½ hours). If turkey starts to brown too much, cover loosely with foil. When turkey is two-thirds done, cut the cord or band of skin holding the drumstick ends to the tail; this procedure will ensure that the insides of thighs are cooked. Turkey is done when drumsticks are easy to move up and down.

Remove to serving platter; let stand 20 to 30 minutes before carving.

Spoon remaining dressing in a lightly greased 12- x 8- x 2-inch baking dish. Bake at 350° for 25 to 30 minutes. Yield: 12 to 14 servings.

Mrs. M. L. Shannon,
Fairfield, Alabama.

Tip: Baste a roast with wine or wine vinegar for a distinctive flavor.

PORK ROAST WITH TOMATO SAUCE

1 (5-pound) pork loin
1 clove garlic, halved
½ teaspoon freshly ground pepper
Tomato sauce (recipe follows)

Trim excess fat from roast; rub with garlic and pepper. Place roast on a rack in a shallow roasting pan. Insert meat thermometer into pork, making sure thermometer does not touch bone or fat. Bake at 325° for 3 to 3½ hours or until meat thermometer registers 160°. Let roast stand 20 minutes before carving. Serve roast with tomato sauce. Yield: 8 servings.

Tomato Sauce:

⅓ cup chopped onion
1 tablespoon butter or margarine, melted
1 (8-ounce) can tomato sauce
3 tablespoons chopped sweet pickle
2 tablespoons chopped green pepper
2 tablespoons vinegar
1 tablespoon minced parsley
1 teaspoon sugar

Sauté onion in butter in a saucepan; add remaining ingredients, and simmer 10 minutes. Yield: 1½ cups.

Patricia Flint,
Staunton, Virginia.

Dinner Entrées For Two

If your holiday plans include a special dinner just for two, we offer these entrée suggestions. Chicken Florentine With Mushroom Sauce (recipe, next page) features a delicious sauce. After trying it, you'll depend on this recipe all through the year, even doubling and tripling it for more than just two servings.

What's Christmas or Thanksgiving dinner without cranberry sauce? One innovative cook places it atop the cheese and ham before rolling up in chicken pieces to give her Cranberry Chicken Kiev (recipe, next page) a festive flair.

If your dinner expectations include stuffing, Braised Stuffed Pork Chops provides a tasty substitute for the traditional stuffed bird.

BRAISED STUFFED PORK CHOPS

2 boneless butterfly pork chops (about ½ pound each)
1 tablespoon butter or margarine, melted
2 tablespoons diced onion
2 tablespoons diced celery
1 tablespoon butter or margarine, melted
½ cup commercial herb stuffing mix
1 teaspoon minced fresh parsley
¼ teaspoon paprika
⅛ teaspoon salt
⅛ teaspoon pepper
3 tablespoons milk
1 cup beef broth
1 tablespoon cornstarch

Lightly brown pork chops in 1 tablespoon butter, and set aside.

Sauté onion and celery in 1 tablespoon butter until vegetables are crisp-tender. Remove from heat. Add stuffing mix, parsley, paprika, salt, and pepper; mix well. Stir in milk. Stuff chops with stuffing mixture, and secure with wooden picks. Place chops in a lightly greased 8- x 8-inch baking dish. Pour beef broth over pork chops. Cover and bake at 350° for 1 hour or until done; baste occasionally. Transfer chops to serving dish. Add water to pan drippings to measure 1 cup; stir in cornstarch. Cook in a heavy saucepan over medium heat until mixture begins to bubble, and boil 1 minute, stirring constantly. Serve with pork chops. Yield: 2 servings. *Vera Hanley,*
Georgetown, South Carolina.

CRANBERRY CHICKEN KIEV

2 small whole chicken breasts, skinned
and boned
Salt and pepper
2 (1-ounce) slices boiled ham
2 (1-ounce) slices Swiss cheese
¼ cup jellied whole-berry cranberry sauce
1 egg, well beaten
½ cup all-purpose flour
2 tablespoons butter or margarine, melted
1 small onion, chopped
1 (4-ounce) can sliced mushrooms, drained
½ cup cream of chicken soup
2 tablespoons dry white wine

Place chicken between 2 sheets of
plastic wrap or wax paper. Using a meat
mallet or rolling pin, flatten chicken to
¼-inch thickness. Sprinkle chicken with
salt and pepper. Place 1 slice each of
ham and cheese on each chicken breast.
(If necessary, fold edge of ham or
cheese to fit chicken.) Place 2 tablespoons cranberry sauce on top of
cheese. Roll up each breast, and secure
with a wooden pick.

Dip each chicken breast in egg;
dredge in flour. Brown chicken in butter
in a skillet; add onion, mushrooms,
cream of chicken soup, and wine. Stir
to blend. Cover, reduce heat, and simmer 20 to 25 minutes. Yield: 2
servings.   *Peggy Blackburn,*
Winston-Salem, North Carolina.

CHICKEN FLORENTINE
WITH MUSHROOM SAUCE

2 chicken breast halves, skinned and
boned
¼ cup finely chopped onion
1 tablespoon butter or margarine, melted
1 (10-ounce) package frozen chopped
spinach, thawed and drained
½ cup (2 ounces) shredded Swiss cheese
⅛ teaspoon ground nutmeg
1⅓ cups sliced fresh mushrooms
1 tablespoon butter or margarine, melted
1½ teaspoons lemon juice
½ cup chicken broth
½ cup whipping cream
¼ cup dry white wine
Dash of white pepper
Tomato roses (optional)
Parsley sprigs (optional)

Place chicken between 2 sheets of
plastic wrap or wax paper; using a meat
mallet or rolling pin, flatten chicken to
¼-inch thickness. Set aside.

Sauté onion in 1 tablespoon butter.
Remove from heat; stir in spinach,
cheese, and nutmeg. Divide mixture in
half; shape each half into a mound, and
place in a lightly greased 10- x 6- x
2-inch baking dish. Place chicken breast
over each mound. Bake at 350° for 20
to 25 minutes or until chicken is done.

Sauté mushrooms in 1 tablespoon
butter until liquid evaporates. Add remaining ingredients; bring to a boil, and
cook 7 minutes. Stir constantly until liquid is reduced by two-thirds and is
slightly thickened. Spoon half of sauce
over each serving. Garnish with tomato
roses and parsley sprigs, if desired.
Yield: 2 servings.   *Edda Bickler,*
Lauderhill, Florida.

COOKING LIGHT®

It's Open House, And The Menu Is Light

When you plan this year's open house
menu, don't be tempted to veer from
your own dieting efforts. Offer these
delicious, low-calorie selections and
guests probably won't even notice the
difference. If they do, it's likely they
will appreciate your choices. Healthier
eating appeals to many.

There's an extra bonus for the host,
too. Tomato-Clam Cocktail, Marinated
Artichokes, Shrimp Mousse, and Mock
Pâté can be made ahead of time. Even
the dressing for Fruit Kabobs With Coconut Dressing and the spinach mixture
for Pesto-Cheese Pasta Bites can be
prepared in advance. Then just mix the
Holiday Punch, skewer the fresh fruit
kabobs, and fill the pasta shells the day
of the event.

What makes some of the dishes in
this low-calorie menu so special?
Shrimp Mousse keeps calories low with
plain low-fat yogurt and 1% low-fat cottage cheese.

Even those who dislike liver will
enjoy our Mock Pâté because there isn't
a bit of liver in the recipe. Instead, we
use lean deli-style roast beef as the
base. And unlike most high-fat pâtés,
ours contains only 2 tablespoons of
reduced-calorie mayonnaise, keeping
the light spread to a low 8 calories per
tablespoon.

Marinated Artichokes
Pesto-Cheese Pasta Bites
Shrimp Mousse or Mock Pâté
Plain crackers
Fruit Kabobs With Coconut Dressing
Tomato-Clam Cocktail
or
Holiday Punch

MARINATED ARTICHOKES
(pictured on page 271)

2 (14-ounce) cans artichoke bottoms,
undrained
3 tablespoons lemon juice
1 teaspoon sugar
¼ teaspoon dried whole oregano, crushed
¼ teaspoon dried whole tarragon, crushed
Dash of garlic powder
Radicchio leaves (optional)

Drain artichokes, reserving liquid;
quarter artichokes. Set aside.

Combine reserved liquid, lemon
juice, and next 4 ingredients; stir well.
Add artichokes; cover and chill 8 hours,
stirring occasionally.

To serve, drain artichokes, and place
on a bed of radicchio leaves, if desired.
Yield: 40 appetizer servings.

☐ *3 calories, 0.1 gram protein, 0 grams*
fat, 0.7 gram carbohydrate, 0 milligrams
cholesterol, 10.8 milligrams sodium, and
2 milligrams calcium per appetizer.
                              Patt Hancock,
Waverly, Tennessee.

PESTO-CHEESE PASTA BITES
(pictured on page 271)

48 medium-size shell macaroni, uncooked
½ cup firmly packed fresh spinach, drained well
½ cup firmly packed fresh basil, drained well
2 tablespoons grated Parmesan cheese
1 clove garlic, minced
¼ teaspoon white pepper
⅓ cup light process cream cheese product
1 (2-ounce) jar diced pimiento, drained

Cook pasta according to package directions, omitting salt; let cool.

Position knife blade in food processor bowl. Add spinach and next 4 ingredients. Top with cover; process 1 minute or until smooth. Set aside.

Place a small amount of cream cheese in each macaroni shell. Top with spinach mixture. Garnish with diced pimiento. Yield: 48 appetizer servings.

☐ *9 calories, 0.5 gram protein, 0.4 gram fat, 1.1 grams carbohydrate, 1.1 milligrams cholesterol, 14.8 milligrams sodium, and 13 milligrams calcium per filled macaroni shell.* Lorre Grimes, Hoover, Alabama.

SHRIMP MOUSSE
(pictured on page 271)

6 cups water
2 pounds medium-size unpeeled shrimp
1 envelope unflavored gelatin
¼ cup water
1 cup plain low-fat yogurt
1 cup 1% low-fat cottage cheese
¼ cup diced green pepper
¼ cup diced green onions
2 tablespoons lemon juice
¼ teaspoon hot sauce
⅛ teaspoon salt
1½ teaspoons Worcestershire sauce
¾ teaspoon paprika
Vegetable cooking spray
Parsley sprigs (optional)
Carrot curls (optional)

Bring 6 cups water to a boil; add shrimp, and cook 3 to 5 minutes. Drain well; rinse in cold water. Cover and chill. Peel, devein, and chop shrimp; set aside. Combine gelatin and ¼ cup water in a small saucepan; let stand 1 minute. Cook over low heat until the gelatin dissolves, stirring constantly; remove from heat.

Position knife blade in food processor bowl. Combine gelatin mixture, yogurt, and next 8 ingredients in processor bowl. Top with cover; process 1 minute or until mixture is smooth. Add shrimp, and stir well.

Pour shrimp mixture into a 5-cup mold coated with cooking spray. Chill 8 hours or until firm. Unmold mousse onto plate; garnish with parsley and carrot curls, if desired. Serve with crackers. Yield: 4½ cups.

☐ *18 calories, 3.2 grams protein, 0.2 gram fat, 0.6 gram carbohydrate, 21 milligrams cholesterol, 40 milligrams sodium, and 17 milligrams calcium per tablespoon.* Deborah F. Hamilton, Trenton, Tennessee.

MOCK PÂTÉ

1 envelope unflavored gelatin
½ cup cold water
½ teaspoon beef-flavored bouillon granules
1 cup boiling water
1 tablespoon cider vinegar
3 cups ground, deli-style lean roast beef
1 small onion, chopped
1 medium-size green pepper, chopped
2 tablespoons reduced-calorie mayonnaise
1 tablespoon catsup
1 tablespoon Worcestershire sauce
1 teaspoon celery seeds
⅛ teaspoon ground ginger
Pinch of pepper
Vegetable cooking spray
Pimiento strips (optional)

Dissolve gelatin in cold water; set aside. Dissolve bouillon granules in boiling water; add gelatin mixture to broth, stirring well.

Position knife blade in food processor bowl. Combine broth mixture, vinegar, and next 9 ingredients in processor bowl. Top with cover; process 30 seconds or until well blended. Spoon mixture into a 4-cup mold coated with cooking spray. Cover and chill 8 hours. Unmold onto serving plate, and garnish with pimiento strips, if desired. Serve with crackers. Yield: 4 cups.

☐ *18 calories, 2.5 grams protein, 0.6 gram fat, 0.3 gram carbohydrate, 6 milligrams cholesterol, 17 milligrams sodium, and 2 milligrams calcium per tablespoon.* Mrs. Malcolm Bowles, Mableton, Georgia.

FRUIT KABOBS
WITH COCONUT DRESSING

1 medium-size red apple, unpeeled
1 medium pear, unpeeled
1 tablespoon lemon juice
21 unsweetened pineapple chunks
21 seedless red or green grapes (about ¼ pound)
21 fresh strawberries, capped
Coconut Dressing

Cut apple and pear each into 21 bite-size pieces. Add lemon juice; toss gently.

Alternate apple, pineapple, grape, pear, and strawberry on a wooden skewer. Repeat with remaining fruit. Serve with Coconut Dressing. Yield: 21 appetizers.

Coconut Dressing:

1½ cups vanilla low-fat yogurt
1½ tablespoons flaked coconut
1½ tablespoons reduced-calorie orange marmalade

Combine all ingredients in a small bowl; stir well. Serve over kabobs. Yield: 1⅔ cups.

☐ *19 calories, 0.1 gram protein, 0.1 gram fat, 4.9 grams carbohydrate, 0 milligrams cholesterol, 0 milligrams sodium, and 5 milligrams calcium per kabob plus 13 calories, 0.6 gram protein, 0.2 gram fat, 2.2 grams carbohydrate, 1 milligram cholesterol, 9 milligrams sodium, and 22 milligrams calcium per tablespoon serving of dressing.*

TOMATO-CLAM COCKTAIL
(pictured on page 271)

1 (46-ounce) can no-salt-added tomato
  juice
2 (8-ounce) bottles clam juice
¼ teaspoon ground celery seeds
¼ teaspoon freshly ground pepper
¼ teaspoon dry mustard
⅛ teaspoon garlic powder
3 tablespoons lemon juice
Green onion fans (optional)

Combine all ingredients except green onions; stir well. Cover and chill. Garnish each serving with a green onion fan, if desired. Yield: 8 servings.

☐ *39 calories, 3.9 grams protein, 0.2 gram fat, 8.8 grams carbohydrate, 5 milligrams cholesterol, 329.5 milligrams sodium, and 16.6 milligrams calcium per 1-cup serving.*

HOLIDAY PUNCH

1 quart cranberry juice cocktail
1 quart unsweetened apple juice
¼ cup water
1 (6-ounce) can frozen unsweetened orange
  juice concentrate, thawed and
  undiluted
2 (3-inch) sticks cinnamon
6 whole cloves
Cinnamon sticks (optional)

Combine all ingredients except cinnamon sticks in a Dutch oven. Bring to a boil; reduce heat, and simmer 10 minutes. Discard spices. Serve warm, and garnish each serving with a cinnamon stick, if desired. Yield: 9 cups.

☐ *149 calories, 0.5 gram protein, 0.2 gram fat, 37.2 grams carbohydrate, 0 milligrams cholesterol, 8 milligrams sodium, and 17 milligrams calcium per 1-cup serving.*   A. A. Goodman,
                            Knoxville, Tennessee.

New Ideas For Side Dishes

Most folks lavish attention and extra time on entrées and desserts this time of year, but you can make the side dishes just as special for your holiday spread. These recipes give you ideas for adding flavor as well as garnishing touches to vegetables, such as sweet potatoes, broccoli, carrots, and more.

When time is a factor, Marinated Garden Vegetables is a real timesaver. A mixture of vegetables is marinated in an oil and vinegar dressing and chilled. Make it ahead of time, so that it's ready to serve when you are.

Carrots get a flavorful touch in a glaze of brandy, honey, and orange liqueur in our recipe for Brandied Carrots. The recipe uses baby carrots, but you can substitute carrot slices or julienne strips, if you wish. Just be sure to reduce the cooking time when you use the smaller pieces of carrot.

Holiday Broccoli With Rice combines two side dishes in one. Layer fresh steamed broccoli over rice and then top it with a pimiento cheese-flavored sauce. Just complete the meal with a salad, entrée, and bread, and you're ready to entertain.

HOLIDAY BROCCOLI WITH RICE

1 cup uncooked long-grain rice
1 (1½-pound) bunch fresh broccoli
1 medium onion, chopped
½ cup diced celery
¼ cup butter or margarine, melted
1 (10¾-ounce) can cream of chicken soup,
  undiluted
1 (4-ounce) jar pimiento cheese spread
1 teaspoon soy sauce
¼ teaspoon salt
Dash of ground nutmeg
Dash of red pepper
Pimiento strips (optional)

Cook rice according to package directions, omitting salt.

Trim off large leaves of broccoli. Remove tough ends of lower stalks, and wash broccoli thoroughly. Separate into spears. Arrange broccoli in steaming rack with stalks to center of rack. Place over boiling water; cover and steam 8 to 10 minutes. Set aside.

Sauté onion and celery in butter until tender. Add soup and next 5 ingredients, stirring well. Reserve ½ cup of sauce; combine remaining sauce and rice. Spoon rice mixture into a lightly greased 3-quart casserole. Arrange broccoli spears over rice. Spoon reserved ½ cup sauce over broccoli. Cover and bake at 350° for 35 to 40 minutes. Garnish with pimiento strips, if desired. Yield: 6 servings.   *Helen Dill,
                      Oklahoma City, Oklahoma.*

MARINATED GARDEN VEGETABLES

2 cups broccoli flowerets
2 cups cauliflower flowerets
2 cups sliced carrots
1 medium zucchini, sliced
1 medium cucumber, sliced
½ cup chopped sweet red pepper
½ cup chopped green pepper
½ cup sliced celery
½ cup sliced black olives
Dressing (recipe follows)
8 cherry tomatoes, halved
1 cup mushrooms, halved

Combine first 9 ingredients in a large bowl. Pour dressing over vegetables; toss gently. Cover. Chill at least 12 hours. Add tomatoes and mushrooms to marinated vegetables just before serving. Yield: 10 to 12 servings.

Dressing:

1¼ cups vegetable oil
⅔ cup vinegar
½ cup sugar
2 cloves garlic, crushed
1 teaspoon salt
1 teaspoon white pepper

Combine all ingredients in a jar. Cover tightly, and shake vigorously. Yield: about 1¾ cups.

                            *Kathy Hutton,
                        Blackwell, Oklahoma.*

MEXICAN RICE DRESSING

1¼ cups cornmeal
1 teaspoon salt
¾ teaspoon baking soda
1¼ cups milk
3 eggs, beaten
⅓ cup vegetable oil
2½ cups cooked rice
1 (17-ounce) can cream-style corn
1 (8-ounce) can cream-style corn
¾ cup chopped onion
3 tablespoons finely chopped jalapeño
   pepper
Additional cornmeal
2 cups (8 ounces) shredded Cheddar
   cheese

Combine 1¼ cups cornmeal, salt, and soda in a mixing bowl; mix well. Add milk and next 7 ingredients; stir until blended. Pour into a greased 13- x 9- x 2-inch pan sprinkled with additional cornmeal. Bake, uncovered, at 350° for 55 minutes. Sprinkle evenly with cheese, and bake an additional 5 minutes. Yield: 8 to 10 servings.

Kathleen Stone,
Houston, Texas.

BRUSSELS SPROUTS IN MUSTARD SAUCE

1 pound fresh brussels sprouts
½ cup whipping cream
¼ cup butter or margarine, melted
1 tablespoon Dijon mustard
¼ teaspoon salt
Dash of hot sauce

Wash brussels sprouts thoroughly, and remove discolored leaves. Cut off stem ends, and slash bottom of each with a shallow X. Place sprouts in a small amount of boiling water. Cover, reduce heat, and simmer 8 minutes or until brussels sprouts are tender; drain and set aside.

Combine remaining ingredients in a small saucepan; cook 5 minutes over medium heat, stirring until thickened. Pour mixture over brussels sprouts; toss well. Yield: 4 servings.

Virginia Mosely,
New Orleans, Louisiana.

BRANDIED CARROTS

24 baby carrots, scraped
¼ cup honey
¼ cup brandy
2 tablespoons Triple Sec or other orange-
   flavored liqueur
Juice of 1 lemon
Chopped fresh parsley

Combine all ingredients, except parsley, in a heavy skillet. Cover and cook 30 minutes or until carrots are tender. Sprinkle with parsley. Yield: 6 servings.

Mrs. H. Bennett,
Dunedin, Florida.

SEASONED POTATOES

3 large potatoes (about 2½ pounds),
   peeled and cubed
1 (8-ounce) carton commercial green
   onion dip
1 (3-ounce) package cream cheese,
   softened
¼ cup butter or margarine, melted
2 to 4 tablespoons milk
½ teaspoon garlic salt
Paprika (optional)

Cook potatoes in boiling water to cover 15 minutes or until tender. Drain and mash. Add green onion dip, cream cheese, butter, milk, and garlic salt, beating at medium speed of an electric mixer until smooth. Spoon potato mixture into a lightly greased 1½-quart baking dish; sprinkle with paprika, if desired. Bake at 350° for 30 minutes. Yield: 6 servings.

Mrs. Bill Duke,
Corpus Christi, Texas.

SWEET POTATO PUFFS

4 medium-size sweet potatoes
1 egg, beaten
1 teaspoon honey
¼ teaspoon ground cinnamon
1 tablespoon butter or margarine, melted
3 tablespoons finely chopped pecans
¼ cup firmly packed brown sugar
2 teaspoons cornstarch
½ cup water
½ cup raisins
½ teaspoon rum extract

Cook sweet potatoes in boiling water to cover 25 minutes or until tender. Let cool to touch; peel and mash. Combine sweet potatoes, egg, honey, and cinnamon, stirring well.

Spoon sweet potato mixture onto a lightly greased baking sheet, making 6 mounds; make an indentation in the center of each mound. Brush with melted butter, and sprinkle chopped pecans around outside of each indentation. Bake at 350° for 20 minutes.

Combine brown sugar, cornstarch, water, and raisins in a small saucepan. Cook over medium heat, stirring constantly, until thickened and bubbly. Stir in the rum extract, and spoon mixture into potato indentations. Yield: 6 servings.

Vivian Levine,
Oak Ridge, Tennessee.

BAKED FRUIT DRESSING

1 (15-ounce) can sliced peaches, drained
1 (16-ounce) can sliced pears, drained
1 (15¼-ounce) can pineapple chunks,
   drained
⅓ cup raisins
⅓ cup chopped walnuts
¾ cup firmly packed light brown sugar,
   divided
1 teaspoon vanilla extract
1 (15-ounce) can apricot halves, drained
5 slices white bread, toasted
¾ cup butter or margarine, melted

Combine peaches, pears, pineapple, raisins, walnuts, ½ cup brown sugar, and vanilla; stir gently. Spoon into a lightly oiled 13- x 9- x 2-inch baking dish; arrange apricot halves on top.

Cut bread slices into ½-inch cubes; sprinkle over fruit mixture. Combine butter and remaining ¼ cup brown sugar; pour over bread cubes. Bake at 325° for 25 to 30 minutes; serve warm. Yield: 8 to 10 servings.

Romanza Johnson,
Bowling Green, Kentucky.

More Flavor In These Breads

Even folks who don't like to bake make an extra effort this time of year to mix up some homemade bread. With these recipes, you'll be sure to find a bread that features some of your favorite flavors. Cheese, fruit, and spices are just a few of the ingredients that make them extra delicious.

Muffins are always a treat and one of the quickest breads to make. If you're entertaining overnight guests for the holidays, they're sure to enjoy some hot cinnamon-spiced Kiwifruit Muffins for breakfast.

If you prefer yeast breads, you'll love Light Wheat Rolls or a loaf of Cheese-Wine Bread seasoned with white wine and Monterey Jack cheese. The loaf bakes in a soufflé dish to give it a round shape. You can cut the bread into wedges to serve with dinner or try it with fresh fruit and a bottle of wine for a fireside snack.

CHEESE-WINE BREAD
(pictured on back cover)

½ cup dry white wine
½ cup butter or margarine
2 teaspoons sugar
1 teaspoon salt
3 cups all-purpose flour, divided
1 package dry yeast
3 eggs
1 cup (8 ounces) shredded Monterey Jack cheese

Combine first 4 ingredients in a small saucepan; cook over low heat until very warm (120° to 130°). Set aside.

Combine 1½ cups flour and yeast in a large mixing bowl. Add wine mixture and eggs; beat at medium speed of an electric mixer 2 minutes. Gradually stir in cheese and enough remaining flour to make a soft dough.

Turn dough out onto a floured surface, and knead until smooth and elastic (8 to 10 minutes). Place dough in a greased bowl, turning to grease top. Cover and let rise in a warm place

(85°), free from drafts, 1½ hours or until doubled in bulk.

Punch dough down; let rest 10 minutes. Place dough in a greased 1-quart soufflé dish or 9-inch pieplate. Cover and let rise in a warm place (85°), free from drafts, 40 minutes or until doubled in bulk. Bake at 375° for 20 minutes; cover with foil, and bake an additional 20 minutes. Yield: 1 loaf.

Joy Garcia,
Bartlett, Tennessee.

LIGHT WHEAT ROLLS
(pictured on back cover)

2 packages dry yeast
1¾ cups warm water (105° to 115°)
½ cup sugar
1 teaspoon salt
¼ cup butter or margarine
1 egg, slightly beaten
2¼ cups whole wheat flour
2¼ to 2¾ cups all-purpose flour
Melted butter

Dissolve yeast in warm water in a large mixing bowl; add sugar and salt to the yeast mixture.

Melt ¼ cup butter; cool to lukewarm. Add butter, egg, and whole wheat flour to yeast mixture, stirring well; gradually stir in enough all-purpose flour to make a soft dough.

Turn dough out onto a well-floured surface, and knead until smooth and elastic (about 5 minutes). Place in a well-greased bowl, turning to grease top. Cover and let rise in a warm place (85°), free from drafts, 1 hour or until doubled in bulk. Punch dough down, cover and let rise in a warm place (85°) until doubled in bulk.

Punch dough down, and divide into 2 equal portions. Roll each portion into a 14- x 6-inch rectangle. Cut dough into 12 (7- x 1-inch) strips. Roll each strip of dough into a spiral; place in well-greased muffin pans. Repeat process with remaining dough.

Brush with melted butter; let rise uncovered in a warm place (85°), free from drafts, 40 minutes or until doubled in bulk. (Buttering will prevent rolls

from drying out as they rise; rolls will stick to cloth or wax paper.) Bake at 400° for 12 to 15 minutes; brush again with melted butter. Yield: 2 dozen.

Note: Rolls can be prepared ahead of time and frozen. Bake at 400° for 8 minutes; let cool, and freeze. Let rolls thaw, and bake at 400° for 5 to 7 minutes.

Linda Keith,
Dallas, Texas.

PUMPKIN ROLLS

1 (16-ounce) package hot roll mix
⅓ cup warm water (105° to 115°)
1 cup canned or mashed cooked pumpkin
1 egg
2 tablespoons sugar
2 tablespoons butter or margarine, melted
½ cup sugar
1½ teaspoons pumpkin pie spice
⅓ cup raisins
1 cup sifted powdered sugar
1 tablespoon plus 1 teaspoon milk
¼ teaspoon vanilla extract

Dissolve yeast packet from hot roll mix package in warm water; let stand 5 minutes. Combine pumpkin, egg, and 2 tablespoons sugar; mix well. Add yeast; stir in flour packet from hot roll mix package to make a stiff dough. Place dough in a well-greased bowl, turning to grease top. Cover and let rise in a warm place (85°), free from drafts, 45 minutes or until doubled in bulk.

Turn dough out on a floured surface; knead 12 times. Roll dough into a 15- x 12-inch rectangle. Spread with melted butter. Combine ½ cup sugar and pumpkin pie spice; sprinkle over butter. Top with raisins. Beginning at long side, roll up jellyroll-fashion; press edges and ends together securely. Cut into 1-inch slices; place rolls, cut side down, in a greased 13- x 9- x 2-inch baking pan.

Cover and let rise in a warm place (85°), free from drafts, about 30 minutes or until doubled in bulk. Bake at 375° for 20 minutes or until golden.

Combine powdered sugar, milk, and vanilla; drizzle over warm rolls. Yield: 15 rolls.

Dina Walker,
Garland, Texas.

KIWIFRUIT MUFFINS

2 cups all-purpose flour
1 tablespoon baking powder
¾ teaspoon salt
⅓ cup sugar
¼ teaspoon ground cinnamon
1 egg, slightly beaten
1 cup milk
¼ cup vegetable oil
⅔ cup chopped kiwifruit

Combine first 5 ingredients in a large bowl. Set aside.

Combine egg, milk, and oil; add to dry mixture. Stir just until dry ingredients are moistened. Add chopped kiwifruit, and stir until blended.

Spoon batter evenly into greased muffin pans, filling three-fourths full. Bake at 400° for 20 minutes. Yield: 1 dozen.
Ethel Jernegan,
Savannah, Georgia.

PUMPKIN-COCONUT BREAD

2 eggs, beaten
1 cup sugar
¾ cup vegetable oil
1½ cups all-purpose flour
1 teaspoon baking powder
1 teaspoon baking soda
½ teaspoon salt
1 (3½-ounce) package coconut cream
   instant pudding mix
½ teaspoon ground nutmeg
½ teaspoon ground ginger
½ teaspoon ground cinnamon
1 cup canned or mashed cooked pumpkin
½ cup chopped pecans (optional)

Combine eggs, sugar, and oil in a large mixing bowl; beat at medium speed of an electric mixer until blended.

Combine flour and next 7 ingredients in a medium bowl; add to sugar mixture alternately with pumpkin, beginning and ending with flour mixture. Mix after each addition. Stir in pecans, if desired.

Pour batter into a greased and floured 9- x 5- x 3-inch loafpan. Bake at 350° for 1 hour or until a wooden pick inserted in center comes out clean. Cool in pan 10 minutes; remove loaf from pan, and let cool completely on a wire rack. Yield: one loaf. *Lazelle Kelley,*
Birmingham, Alabama.

ZUCCHINI-APPLE BREAD

4 cups all-purpose flour
1 tablespoon baking soda
¼ teaspoon baking powder
1½ teaspoons salt
1½ tablespoons ground cinnamon
½ teaspoon ground nutmeg
5 eggs
2 cups sugar
1 cup firmly packed brown sugar
1½ cups vegetable oil
1 tablespoon vanilla extract
2 cups shredded zucchini (about 3
   medium)
1 cup shredded apple (about 1 medium)
1½ cups chopped pecans

Combine first 6 ingredients; set aside. Combine eggs, sugars, oil, and vanilla in a large bowl; beat at medium speed of an electric mixer until well blended. Stir in zucchini, apple, and pecans. Add dry ingredients to zucchini-apple mixture, stirring just until moistened.

Spoon batter into 3 greased and floured 8¼- x 4½- x 3-inch loafpans. Bake at 350° for 50 to 55 minutes or until a wooden pick inserted in center comes out clean. Cool in pans 10 minutes; remove to wire rack, and cool completely. Yield: 3 loaves.
Joan I. Drinnen,
Savannah, Georgia.

Make Breads With Fruit And Nuts

These breads with their natural fruit goodness and crunchy nut texture are great for breakfast or snack time. Slice and serve with cream cheese and marmalade, or try toasted slices.

The aroma of Fresh Apple-Nut Bread will make your mouth water. Banana-Oat Tea Loaf has the healthful bonuses of bananas, oats, and raisins. (Both recipes are on page 256.) Prune-Nut Bread, flavored with cinnamon and orange rind and juice, takes advantage of fiber-packed prunes.

Who can resist home-baked bread? You'll be tempted to try these hot out of the oven, but the flavors of fruit and nut breads taste best if allowed to mellow about 12 hours. That makes them perfect to bake in advance.

If you are a novice baker, be careful not to overmix the batter after adding the dry ingredients; it will make the bread tough. And also avoid overbaking because the loaves dry out quickly in the oven and form a hard outer crust. But don't worry about a crack on top—it's typical.

PRUNE-NUT BREAD

1 cup dried prunes, chopped
2 teaspoons grated orange rind
1 cup orange juice
2 cups all-purpose flour
¾ cup sugar
1 tablespoon baking powder
½ teaspoon salt
½ teaspoon ground cinnamon
2 eggs, beaten
2 tablespoons vegetable oil
1 cup chopped pecans

Combine prunes, orange rind, and orange juice in a large bowl; stir gently. Let stand about 30 minutes.

Combine dry ingredients. Add eggs and oil to prune mixture; stir well. Add dry ingredients; stir until blended. Stir in pecans. Pour into a greased and floured 9- x 5- x 3-inch loafpan; bake at 350° for 55 to 60 minutes or until a wooden pick inserted in center comes out clean. Cool in pan 10 minutes. Remove from pan, and cool on a wire rack. Yield: 1 loaf.
Mrs. Russell T. Shay,
Murrells Inlet, South Carolina.

Tip: Cooking such vegetables as green peppers and cucumbers briefly in boiling water will make them more digestible than when raw.

FRESH APPLE-NUT BREAD

¼ cup butter or margarine, softened
1 cup firmly packed light brown sugar
2 eggs
2 cups all-purpose flour
1 teaspoon baking soda
¼ teaspoon salt
½ teaspoon grated lemon rind
1 teaspoon ground cinnamon
¼ teaspoon ground nutmeg
1 large apple, pared, cored, and grated
  (about 1 cup)
½ cup buttermilk
¾ cup chopped walnuts

Cream butter; add sugar, beating well at medium speed of an electric mixer. Add eggs, one at a time, beating well after each addition.

Combine flour, soda, salt, lemon rind, cinnamon, nutmeg, and apple; add to creamed mixture alternately with buttermilk, beginning and ending with flour mixture. Stir in walnuts.

Pour batter into a greased and floured 9- x 5- x 3-inch loafpan. Bake at 350° for 55 to 60 minutes or until a wooden pick inserted in center comes out clean. Cool bread in pan 10 minutes; remove and cool on a wire rack. Yield: 1 loaf.
Nancy B. Hall,
Calvert City, Kentucky.

PINEAPPLE-PECAN LOAF BREAD

¼ cup shortening
¾ cup firmly packed brown sugar
1 egg
2 cups all-purpose flour
1 teaspoon baking soda
½ teaspoon salt
⅓ cup frozen orange juice concentrate,
  thawed and undiluted
1 (8-ounce) can crushed pineapple,
  undrained
½ cup chopped pecans

Cream shortening; gradually add sugar, beating well at medium speed of an electric mixer. Add egg, beat well.

Combine flour, soda, and salt; add to creamed mixture alternately with orange juice concentrate, beginning and ending with flour mixture. Mix after each addition. Stir in pineapple and pecans.

Pour batter into a greased and floured 8½- x 4½- x 2½-inch loafpan. Bake at 350° for 50 to 55 minutes or until a wooden pick inserted in center comes out clean. Cool bread in pan 10 minutes; remove and allow to cool on wire rack. Yield: 1 loaf.
Eleanor K. Brandt,
Arlington, Texas.

LEMON BREAD

½ cup butter or margarine,
  softened
1 cup sugar
2 eggs
1¾ cups all-purpose flour
1 teaspoon baking powder
½ teaspoon salt
½ cup milk
½ cup toasted almonds
½ cup golden raisins
Grated rind of 1 lemon
½ cup powdered sugar
¼ cup lemon juice

Cream butter; add 1 cup sugar, beating well at medium speed of an electric mixer. Add eggs, one at a time, beating after each addition.

Combine flour, baking powder, and salt; add to creamed mixture alternately with milk, beginning and ending with flour mixture. Stir in almonds, raisins, and lemon rind.

Pour mixture into two well-greased 7- x 3- x 2-inch loafpans. Bake at 350° for 50 minutes.

Combine ½ cup powdered sugar and lemon juice, mixing well. Pour lemon glaze over hot bread. Cool bread in pans 10 minutes; remove from pans, and cool on wire racks. Yield: 2 loaves.
Jane Maloy,
Wilmington, North Carolina.

BANANA-OAT TEA LOAF

¾ cup butter or margarine, softened
1 cup firmly packed brown sugar
4 eggs
2 cups all-purpose flour
2 teaspoons baking soda
1½ teaspoons ground cinnamon
¼ teaspoon ground cloves
2 cups mashed banana
½ cup milk
2 cups uncooked regular oats
1¼ cups raisins
1½ cups chopped pecans

Cream butter; gradually add sugar, beating well at medium speed of an electric mixer. Add eggs, one at a time, beating well after each addition.

Combine flour, soda, cinnamon, and cloves; add to creamed mixture alternately with mashed banana and milk, beginning and ending with flour mixture. Fold in oats, raisins, and pecans. Spoon batter into two greased 8- x 5- x 3-inch loafpans. Bake at 350° for 55 minutes or until a wooden pick inserted in center comes out clean. Cool in pan 10 minutes. Remove from pan, and cool on a wire rack. Yield: 2 loaves.
Mrs. J. Russell Buchanan,
Cincinnati, Ohio.

Food Gifts To Mail

Playing Santa by mail is fun, especially when the goodies you send are homemade treats. If family members or friends are away from home this year, send them a package they're sure to remember. Chewy Molasses Cookies and Chocolate-Peanut Butter Fudge are just two of the tasty choices we offer.

For mailing, first choose a sturdy container. Cardboard shoe boxes, heavy-plastic containers, or snack-food packages work well for mailing most goods. Line the container with foil or plastic wrap, and pad the ends and sides with foil or crumpled napkins. You can even pop popcorn to make an inexpensive packing material.

For cookies, wrap four to six of the same size cookies together in foil, plastic wrap, or sandwich bags, and seal. Heavy items, such as fudge, should go in the bottom of your package. Layer wrapped cookies with crumpled napkins or wax paper.

If you send the food in a decorative tin, pack it inside a cardboard box, and cushion it with some of the packing materials already mentioned. Seal the lid with durable tape, and wrap in brown paper. With permanent ink, label "perishable food."

For a more elaborate gift to a nearby friend or family member, you may want to share a party basket filled with Party Mix, Christmas Lizzies, and an ornament for the tree.

PARTY MIX

1 (1-ounce) envelope ranch salad dressing mix
2 tablespoons dried whole dillweed
6 cups corn-and-rice cereal
1 (10-ounce) package oyster crackers
1 (6.5-ounce) package small pretzels
¾ cup vegetable oil

Combine salad dressing mix and dillweed in a large bowl; add cereal, oyster crackers, and pretzels, tossing well. Drizzle oil over mixture; stir well. Place mixture in a large paper bag; fold bag to close, and let stand 2 hours, shaking bag occasionally. Store mixture in an airtight container. Yield: 16 cups.

Laura Greene,
Greensboro, North Carolina.

Tip: Avoid using two strong-flavored herbs, such as a bay, rosemary, or sage, together as the flavors will fight each other. Instead, use a strong herb in combination with a milder one. The accent herbs are slightly milder than the strong herbs and include basil, tarragon, and oregano. Medium herbs are dill, marjoram, winter savory, fennel, mint, and lemon thyme. Delicate herbs include chervil, chives, parsley, and summer savory.

CHRISTMAS LIZZIES

½ pound candied green pineapple, chopped
1 pound candied red cherries, chopped
2 (8-ounce) packages chopped dates
2 cups chopped pecans
1½ cups all-purpose flour, divided
¼ cup butter or margarine, softened
½ cup sugar
2 eggs
½ teaspoon baking soda
1 teaspoon ground cinnamon
¼ teaspoon ground cloves
¼ teaspoon ground nutmeg
1½ tablespoons milk
3 tablespoons bourbon

Combine fruit and pecans; dredge in 1 cup flour, and set aside.

Cream butter; add sugar, beating at medium speed of an electric mixer. Add eggs, and beat well. Combine remaining ½ cup flour, soda, and spices; add to creamed mixture, mixing well. Stir in milk and bourbon. Add fruit mixture, and mix well. Batter will be stiff. Chill dough at least 1 hour.

Drop chilled dough by heaping teaspoonfuls onto lightly greased cookie sheets. Bake at 300° for 20 to 25 minutes or until lightly browned. Cool on wire racks. Yield: about 8 dozen.

Peggy McLeroy,
Dallas, Texas.

CHOCOLATE-PEANUT BUTTER FUDGE

2½ cups sugar
¼ cup cocoa
1 cup milk
1 tablespoon light corn syrup
½ cup butter or margarine, divided
½ cup peanut butter
1 cup chopped pecans
2 teaspoons vanilla extract

Combine sugar, cocoa, milk, and syrup in a large heavy saucepan; cook over medium heat, stirring constantly, until sugar dissolves. Add 2 tablespoons butter, and stir until melted; cover and boil mixture 3 minutes.

Remove cover, and continue to cook, without stirring, until mixture reaches soft ball stage (232°). Remove from heat, and add remaining butter, peanut butter, pecans, and vanilla (do not stir). Cool mixture 10 minutes.

Beat until butter, peanut butter, and pecans are blended into chocolate mixture. Pour immediately into a buttered 9-inch square pan. Cool and cut fudge into squares. Yield: 3 dozen.

Carolyn Webb,
Jackson, Mississippi.

CHEWY MOLASSES COOKIES

½ cup shortening
1 cup sugar
2 eggs
1 cup molasses
4 cups all-purpose flour
2 teaspoons baking soda
½ teaspoon salt
1 teaspoon ground ginger
1 teaspoon ground cinnamon
½ cup buttermilk

Cream shortening and sugar, beating well at medium speed of an electric mixer. Add eggs and molasses; mix well. Combine flour and next 4 ingredients; add to creamed mixture alternately with buttermilk, beginning and ending with flour mixture.

Drop dough by rounded teaspoonfuls 1½ inches apart on lightly greased cookie sheets. Bake at 350° for 10 to 12 minutes. Cool on wire racks. Yield: approximately 8 dozen cookies.

Ruth Chellis,
Easley, South Carolina.

Splurge With Cream-Filled Chocolates

There aren't many things more luxurious than cream-filled chocolates—the kind with the filling that oozes out just a little when you take a bite. Indulgers have long purchased chocolates of this kind rather than making them at home, perhaps thinking that making them would be too difficult. But it's not.

Professional chocolate-makers perform a special process, called tempering, that makes the candy firm, not sticky, on the outside. The process is not difficult to do at home if you'll take a little extra time when melting the chocolate. Then you can set up an assembly line and make batch after batch of Liqueur Cream-Filled Chocolates to serve guests during the holidays or to package as gifts.

Simply melting chocolate as you normally would works fine for baking and cooking, but using the tempering process is the only way to give coated candies the desired dark, shiny, firm surface once the chocolate hardens. Tempering monitors the temperature to which the chocolate is exposed, never letting the temperature get high enough to make the chocolate sticky after it hardens. The process works equally well when using white chocolate.

Directions for tempering are given in the recipe for Liqueur Cream-Filled Chocolates, and the step-by-step photographs guide you through the process. Just remember that designated temperatures are critical; if they're off even a little, you'll sacrifice color and firmness in the candy.

You'll need to have a double boiler, a general cooking thermometer, and plastic candy molds to make these candies. Molds of this type are available in most large department stores, kitchen specialty shops, or through mail-order sources. If you want to vary the liqueur used in your chocolates, select a mold with a different design for each liqueur you plan to use. Then you'll be able to tell the flavor of each candy at a glance.

Let Liqueur Cream-Filled Chocolates be the talk of your winter parties. You can tell the flavor of each candy if you use a different mold design for each liqueur variation.

LIQUEUR CREAM-FILLED CHOCOLATES

1 (14-ounce) can sweetened condensed milk
2 tablespoons butter or margarine
¼ cup amaretto, Chambord, or other liqueur
12 ounces semisweet chocolate squares or morsels or white chocolate

Combine condensed milk and butter in a small saucepan; cook over medium heat, stirring constantly, until mixture comes to a boil. Reduce heat, and simmer 5 minutes or until thickened, stirring constantly. Remove from heat, and stir in liqueur. Set aside to cool.

Grate or finely chop chocolate. Place two-thirds of grated chocolate in top of a double boiler, and heat, stirring constantly, over hot, not boiling, water until chocolate melts and temperature registers 115°. (Make sure water is below, not touching, top of double boiler.)

Remove top of double boiler from over hot water, and place on a dry towel. Add remaining one-third of grated chocolate to chocolate in double boiler, stirring constantly until grated chocolate melts.

Pour melted chocolate onto a marble or Formica surface. Using a spatula or pastry scraper, scrape and stir chocolate to smooth and cool it. When chocolate cools to 80° to 82°, return it to top of double boiler.

Place top of double boiler over hot, not boiling, water, and heat again, stirring constantly, until correct temperature is reached: 87° to 91° for semisweet chocolate and 83° to 88° for white chocolate. Remove top part of double boiler from over hot water.

Step 1: *To temper the chocolate, melt about two-thirds of grated chocolate in top of double boiler, stirring until the temperature registers 115°.*

Step 2: *Remove double boiler from over hot water, and place on a dry towel. Stir in remaining grated chocolate, stirring constantly until chocolate melts.*

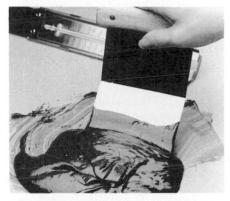

Step 3: *Pour melted chocolate onto marble or Formica surface, and scrape and stir until it cools to 80° to 82°; then reheat to designated temperature.*

Step 4: *Spoon about ½ teaspoon tempered chocolate into each candy mold, and spread to cover mold, using an art brush. Chill until firm.*

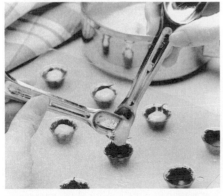

Step 5: *Carefully spoon about ½ teaspoon cream filling (made of sweetened condensed milk, butter, and liqueur) into each chocolate shell.*

Step 6: *Spoon about ½ teaspoon tempered chocolate over cream filling. Tap molds on counter, and chill until firm. Invert molds to remove candies.*

Spoon about ½ teaspoon tempered chocolate into each plastic candy mold (molds should be clean and dry). Spread chocolate to cover bottom and sides of mold, using an art brush or the back of a small spoon. Chill about 10 minutes or until firm.

Carefully spoon about ½ teaspoon cream filling into chocolate shell. Spoon about ½ teaspoon tempered chocolate over cream filling. Gently tap candy molds on counter to remove air bubbles. Chill 10 minutes or until firm. Invert molds, and remove candies. Yield: 5 dozen.

Baked Or Chilled, Pies Make Grand Finales

The holiday season usually calls for a traditional, full-fledged dessert, and pie fits the bill. Chances are, you'll want to serve several during the holidays. Here, we offer you a variety of choices ranging from traditional holiday favorites to colorful new pies.

WALNUT-CRANBERRY PIE

3½ cups fresh cranberries
½ cup raisins
¾ cup chopped walnuts
1½ cups sugar
3 tablespoons all-purpose flour
¼ cup light corn syrup
1 teaspoon grated orange rind
¼ teaspoon salt
1 tablespoon butter or margarine, softened
1 unbaked 9-inch pastry shell

Grind cranberries and raisins together. Stir in next 7 ingredients, mixing well. Spoon filling into pastry shell. Bake at 375° for 45 minutes. Yield: one 9-inch pie. *Kathryn Bibelhauser, Louisville, Kentucky.*

HOLIDAY APPLE PIE

5 cups peeled, thinly sliced apples
½ cup sugar
1 teaspoon ground cinnamon
1 unbaked 9-inch pastry shell
¼ cup sugar
¼ cup firmly packed brown sugar
¼ cup all-purpose flour
¼ cup wheat germ
¼ cup butter or margarine
¼ cup flaked coconut

Combine apples, ½ cup sugar, and cinnamon; toss gently. Spoon mixture evenly into pastry shell.

Combine ¼ cup sugar and next 3 ingredients; mix well. Cut butter into flour mixture with pastry blender until mixture resembles coarse meal. Stir in coconut; sprinkle over apple mixture. Bake at 375° for 45 minutes. Yield: one 9-inch pie.   *Beulah Turner,*
Strawberry Plains, Tennessee.

SOUTHERN SWEET POTATO CREAM PIE

2 cups mashed cooked sweet potatoes
¼ cup butter or margarine, softened
1 cup sugar
½ teaspoon salt
1 teaspoon ground cinnamon
1 teaspoon ground nutmeg
¼ teaspoon lemon extract (optional)
¼ teaspoon almond extract
2 teaspoons vanilla extract
3 eggs
1½ cups milk
1 unbaked 9-inch pastry shell
Pecan halves (optional)

Combine first 10 ingredients in a large mixing bowl; beat at medium speed of an electric mixer until smooth. Gradually add milk; beat until well blended.

Carefully pour filling into pastry shell. (Filling will come close to top of shell.)

Bake at 425° for 10 minutes; reduce heat to 375°, and bake an additional 60 to 65 minutes or until a knife inserted in center comes out clean. Let cool; garnish with pecan halves, if desired. Yield: one 9-inch pie.

Elizabeth M. Haney,
Dublin, Virginia.

ORANGE CHIFFON PIE

1 envelope unflavored gelatin
¼ cup water
4 eggs, separated
½ cup sugar
2 teaspoons grated orange rind
1 cup orange juice
1 tablespoon lemon juice
½ cup sugar
1 baked 9-inch pastry shell
1 cup whipping cream
3 tablespoons powdered sugar

Soften unflavored gelatin in water; let stand 5 minutes.

Beat egg yolks until thick and lemon colored. Add ½ cup sugar, orange rind, orange juice, and lemon juice; beat until smooth. Cook over medium heat 10 to 12 minutes, stirring constantly, until thickened. Remove from heat. Add gelatin; stir until dissolved. Chill until partially set.

Beat egg whites (at room temperature) until foamy. Gradually add ½ cup sugar, 1 tablespoon at a time, beating until stiff peaks form. Fold into chilled gelatin mixture; spoon into pastry shell. Chill until firm.

Beat whipping cream until foamy; gradually add powdered sugar, beating until soft peaks form. Spread on pie; chill until serving time. Yield: one 9-inch pie.   *Sandra Souther,*
Gainesville, Georgia.

COCONUT-CARAMEL PIES

¼ cup butter or margarine
1 (7-ounce) package flaked coconut
½ cup chopped pecans
1 (8-ounce) package cream cheese, softened
1 (14-ounce) can sweetened condensed milk
1 (16-ounce) container frozen whipped topping, thawed
2 baked 9-inch pastry shells
1 (12-ounce) jar caramel ice-cream topping

Melt butter in a large skillet. Add coconut and chopped pecans; cook until golden brown, stirring frequently. Set mixture aside.

Combine cream cheese and sweetened condensed milk; beat until smooth. Fold in whipped topping.

Layer one-fourth of cream cheese mixture in each pastry shell. Drizzle one-fourth of caramel topping on each pie. Sprinkle one-fourth of coconut mixture evenly over each pie. Repeat layers with remaining ingredients; cover and freeze until firm.

Let frozen pie stand at room temperature 5 minutes before slicing. Yield: two 9-inch pies.   *Deanna Ellis,*
Mount Pleasant, South Carolina.

PEPPERMINT CANDY-ICE CREAM PIE

1½ cups chocolate wafer crumbs
¼ cup plus 2 tablespoons butter or margarine, melted
1 pint peppermint ice cream
1 (8-ounce) container frozen whipped topping, partially thawed
3 tablespoons finely crushed peppermint candy
Additional peppermint candy for garnish (optional)

Combine crumbs and melted butter; press firmly into a 9-inch pieplate.

Combine ice cream and whipped topping; spoon into crumb crust. Sprinkle with 3 tablespoons candy; freeze until firm. Garnish with additional candy, if desired. Yield: one 9-inch pie.

Barbara L. Boyle,
Germantown, Maryland.

HEAVENLY CHOCOLATE PIE

4 egg whites
¼ teaspoon cream of tartar
1 cup sugar
1 (12-ounce) package semisweet chocolate morsels
2 eggs
3 egg yolks
1½ teaspoons rum
3 egg whites
1 cup whipping cream, whipped

Beat 4 egg whites (at room temperature) until foamy; add cream of tartar, beating slightly. Gradually add sugar, beating well after each addition; continue beating mixture until stiff and glossy. (Do not underbeat mixture.)

Spoon meringue into a well-greased 9-inch pieplate. Use a spoon to shape meringue into a pie shell, swirling sides high. Bake at 275° for 1 hour. Cool completely.

Place chocolate in top of a double boiler; bring water to a boil. Reduce heat to low; cook until chocolate melts. Remove from heat.

Beat 2 eggs. Gradually stir about one-fourth of melted chocolate into eggs; add to remaining chocolate, stirring constantly. Add 3 egg yolks, one at a time, beating well after each addition. Stir in rum.

Beat 3 egg whites (at room temperature) until stiff peaks form. Fold beaten egg whites and whipped cream into chocolate mixture. Pour filling into meringue shell, and spread evenly. Cover and refrigerate 8 hours. Yield: one 9-inch pie.
Mrs. R. P. Hotaling,
Augusta, Georgia.

FLUFFY NESSELRODE PIE

1 (8-ounce) package cream cheese, softened
1 cup milk, divided
2 tablespoons light rum
1 (3¾-ounce) package vanilla instant pudding mix
¾ cup finely chopped mixed candied fruit
1 (12-ounce) container frozen whipped topping, thawed and divided
Chocolate-Coconut Crust
Chocolate curls (optional)

Beat cream cheese in medium mixing bowl at low speed of an electric mixer until light and fluffy. Gradually add ½ cup milk, beating until smooth. Add remaining ½ cup milk, rum, and pudding mix; beat at low speed of electric mixer until thickened. Let stand 3 minutes. Fold in candied fruit and 3 cups whipped topping. Spoon into Chocolate-Coconut Crust. Chill at least 4 hours or until firm.

Garnish with remaining whipped topping; sprinkle with chocolate curls, if desired. Yield: one 9-inch pie.

Chocolate-Coconut Crust:

1 (4-ounce) package sweet baking chocolate
2 tablespoons butter or margarine
2 cups flaked coconut

Combine chocolate and butter in top of a double boiler; place over low heat, stirring occasionally, until chocolate melts. Remove from heat; stir in coconut. Press mixture onto bottom and sides of a greased 9-inch pieplate. Chill until firm. Yield: one 9-inch crust.
Sandie Bowlin,
Morristown, Tennessee.

Marvelous Marbled Desserts

Ribbons of chocolate, swirls of peanut butter, bits of chocolate, and lots of cream cheese make these marbled desserts the most tempting ever. Four recipes in all, they include a pie, a crumb cake, and two cheesecakes.

CALICO CRUMB CAKE

2½ cups all-purpose flour, divided
1 cup sugar
1 teaspoon baking soda
¼ teaspoon salt
1¼ cups buttermilk
½ cup shortening, melted
2 eggs, beaten
2 teaspoons vanilla extract
1 (6-ounce) package semisweet chocolate morsels, melted
½ cup firmly packed brown sugar
¼ cup butter or margarine
½ cup finely chopped pecans

Combine 2 cups flour and next 3 ingredients in a large bowl. Add buttermilk, shortening, eggs, and vanilla; beat at medium speed of an electric mixer until blended.

Combine ¾ cup batter and chocolate; set aside.

Spoon remaining batter into a greased and floured 13- x 9- x 2-inch pan. Spoon chocolate mixture over batter; gently swirl with a knife.

Combine remaining ½ cup flour and brown sugar; cut in butter with pastry blender until crumbly. Sprinkle mixture, then pecans over batter. Bake at 350° for 30 minutes. Cool and cut into squares. Yield: 15 servings.
Mrs. P. J. Davis,
Drexel, North Carolina.

MARBLED CHEESECAKE

12 ounces cream cheese, softened
½ cup sugar
1 teaspoon grated lemon rind
2 eggs
1½ cups commercial sour cream
⅔ cup (4 ounces) semisweet chocolate morsels, melted
Chocolate Crumb Crust

Combine cream cheese, sugar, and lemon rind in a medium bowl. Beat at medium speed of an electric mixer until mixture is smooth and well blended. Add eggs, one at a time, beating after each addition. Add sour cream, and beat until mixed.

Combine 1 cup cheesecake mixture and melted chocolate; mix well, and set aside. Pour remaining cheesecake mixture into prepared crust. Pour chocolate mixture over top of cheesecake mixture; gently swirl with a knife.

Bake cheesecake at 325° for 30 to 35 minutes. Allow to cool on a rack for 1 to 2 hours; chill at least 8 hours. Yield: one 8-inch cheesecake.

Chocolate Crumb Crust:

1½ cups chocolate chip cookie crumbs
½ teaspoon ground cinnamon
¼ cup butter or margarine, melted

Combine all ingredients. Press firmly into the bottom of a greased 8-inch springform pan, and chill. Yield: one 8-inch crumb crust.

Marietta Marx,
Louisville, Kentucky.

MOCHA SWIRL CHEESECAKE

2 (1-ounce) squares sweet chocolate
2 tablespoons instant coffee powder
1 tablespoon water
2 (8-ounce) packages cream cheese, softened
¾ cup sugar
2 eggs
2 teaspoons vanilla extract
Pastry shell (recipe follows)
Sweetened whipped cream (optional)

Combine first 3 ingredients in a heavy saucepan; cook over low heat, stirring often, until chocolate melts. Set aside.

Beat cream cheese at medium speed of an electric mixer until light and fluffy. Add sugar, eggs, and vanilla; beat until smooth. Stir 1 cup cream cheese mixture into chocolate mixture. Pour remaining cream cheese mixture into pastry shell. Spoon chocolate mixture on top; gently swirl with a knife.

Bake at 350° for 25 minutes; remove from oven. Let cool; cover and chill 8 hours. Serve cheesecake with sweetened whipped cream, if desired. Yield: one 9-inch cheesecake.

Pastry Shell:

⅓ cup shortening
1 cup self-rising flour
2 to 3 tablespoons cold water

Cut shortening into flour with pastry blender until mixture resembles coarse meal. Sprinkle cold water evenly over surface; stir with a fork until dry ingredients are moistened. Shape into a ball; chill 30 minutes.

Roll pastry to ⅛-inch thickness on a lightly floured surface. Place in a 9-inch pieplate; trim excess pastry along edges. Fold edges under, and flute. Prick pastry shell with a fork; bake at 475° for 8 to 10 minutes. Remove from oven; cool. Yield: one 9-inch pastry shell.

Mrs. Earl L. Faulkenberry,
Lancaster, South Carolina.

Tip: Pans used for pastry never need greasing. The pastry shell or crumb crust will not stick to the sides.

CHOCOLATE-PEANUT BUTTER SWIRL PIE

⅔ cup sugar
2 tablespoons all-purpose flour
1 tablespoon cornstarch
¼ teaspoon salt
2½ cups milk
3 egg yolks
½ cup creamy peanut butter
½ teaspoon vanilla extract
½ cup semisweet chocolate morsels
Chocolate Pastry Shell
½ cup whipping cream
1 tablespoon sifted powdered sugar
2 tablespoons dry-roasted peanuts, coarsely chopped

Combine ⅔ cup sugar, flour, cornstarch, and salt in a heavy saucepan. Gradually add milk; cook over medium heat, stirring constantly, until mixture is thickened and bubbly. Beat egg yolks. Gradually stir one-fourth of hot mixture into yolks; add to remaining hot mixture, stirring constantly. Cook, stirring constantly, until mixture thickens. Remove from heat, and add peanut butter and vanilla; stir until peanut butter melts. Stir in semisweet chocolate morsels until distributed, but not melted. Pour mixture into prepared Chocolate Pastry Shell. Let stand 3 minutes; gently swirl with a knife.

Beat whipping cream until foamy; gradually add powdered sugar, beating until soft peaks form. Pipe whipped cream around edge of pie; sprinkle with peanuts. Yield: one 9-inch pie.

Chocolate Pastry Shell:

1 cup all-purpose flour
¼ cup firmly packed brown sugar
2 tablespoons cocoa
¼ teaspoon salt
⅓ cup shortening
3 to 4 tablespoons cold water

Combine flour, brown sugar, cocoa, and salt; cut in shortening with pastry blender until mixture resembles coarse meal. Sprinkle cold water, 1 tablespoon at a time, evenly over surface; stir with a fork until all dry ingredients are moistened. Shape pastry mixture into a ball; chill 30 minutes.

Roll out pastry to ⅛-inch thickness on a lightly floured surface. Place in a

9-inch pieplate; trim excess pastry from edges and flute. Prick bottom and sides of pastry with a fork; bake at 450° for 8 minutes or until browned. Set aside to cool. Yield: one 9-inch pastry shell.

Grace Bravos,
Timonium, Maryland.

Make A Cake From Popcorn

Popcorn balls are nothing new, but have you heard of a popcorn cake? Mrs. Harry H. Lay, Jr., of Fairmount, Georgia, says her mother started their family tradition of making this cake many years ago. Her children devour the cake, and she admits it's equally popular with grown-ups.

For Christmas, Mrs. Lay tosses the popped corn with colorful gumdrops, and she varies it for other holidays. For Valentine's Day, the cake boasts red cinnamon candies, while an Easter cake might include multicolored jellybeans. For Halloween she substitutes either candy corn or black licorice and orange gumdrops.

When making the cake with gumdrops, consider adding some flowers made from additional gumdrops. The flowers are easy to make and are a playful garnish for this and other novelty desserts for children of all ages. Refer to the note at the end of the recipe for gumdrop flower directions.

POPCORN-GUMDROP CAKE

1 cup butter or margarine
1 pound marshmallows
5 quarts popped corn
½ pound roasted peanuts
1 pound small gumdrops
Gumdrop flowers (optional)

Combine butter and marshmallows in a large Dutch oven; cook over low heat, stirring constantly, until marshmallows

melt. Add popcorn, peanuts, and 1 pound gumdrops, stirring until blended. Press mixture into a well-greased 10-inch tube pan. Chill until firm. Invert cake onto serving plate, and garnish with gumdrop flowers, if desired (see note). Yield: one 10-inch cake.

Note: To make gumdrop flowers, use one large gumdrop for each flower. To make a rose, set a gumdrop upright on counter. Slice gumdrop into thirds vertically. Flatten each third into an oval by rolling with a rolling pin on a surface sprinkled with granulated sugar. Then roll the smallest piece into a cone, pinching at narrow end for stem. Roll remaining pieces around cone, pressing upper edges outward for a petal effect and pinching at bottom for stem end.

To make a daisy, set a gumdrop upright on counter. Using kitchen shears or a sharp knife, cut 8 equally spaced slits through rounded top of gumdrop, not quite cutting to bottom; sprinkle cut surfaces with sugar as necessary to eliminate stickiness. Pick gumdrop up, and squeeze bottom together slightly to make petals open. From a gumdrop of contrasting color, shape a ¼-inch ball; press gently into center of daisy.

Cakes And Pies For The Season

It's fun to serve a smashing new dessert along with the traditional fare; your family will welcome the variety. For old-fashioned favorites, try our flavorful variations. Or surprise family and guests with our readers' new ideas, such as White Chocolate-Coconut Cake.

WHITE CHOCOLATE-COCONUT CAKE
(pictured on page 310)

¼ pound white chocolate, coarsely chopped
½ cup water
1 cup butter, softened
1½ cups sugar
4 eggs, separated
2¼ cups sifted cake flour
1 teaspoon baking soda
1 cup buttermilk
¾ cup chopped almonds, lightly toasted
2 cups flaked coconut, divided
¼ cup sifted cake flour
¼ cup sugar
1 cup seedless raspberry jam
Whipped cream frosting (recipe follows)
1½ ounces (½ cup) grated white chocolate

Combine ¼ pound chopped chocolate and water in top of a double boiler; bring water to a boil. Reduce heat; cook, stirring constantly, until chocolate melts. Remove from heat; cool.

Cream butter; gradually add 1½ cups sugar, beating well at medium speed of an electric mixer. Add egg yolks, one at a time, beating well after each addition. Stir in white chocolate mixture.

Combine 2¼ cups flour and soda; add to creamed mixture alternately with buttermilk, beginning and ending with flour mixture. Mix after each addition.

Combine almonds and 1 cup coconut; dredge with ¼ cup flour, stirring to coat well. Stir into batter.

Beat egg whites (at room temperature) until soft peaks form; add ¼ cup sugar, 1 tablespoon at a time, and beat until stiff peaks form. Fold into batter.

Pour into 3 greased and floured 9-inch round cakepans. Bake at 350° for 20 to 25 minutes or until a wooden pick inserted in center comes out clean. Cool in pans 10 minutes; remove layers, and cool completely on wire racks.

Place 1 cake layer on cake platter; spread with ½ cup raspberry jam. Top with second layer of cake, and spread with remaining jam; top with third cake layer. Frost sides and top with whipped cream frosting. Sprinkle remaining 1 cup coconut on sides of cake; sprinkle grated chocolate on top of cake. Cover and chill. Yield: one 3-layer cake.

Whipped Cream Frosting:

2 cups whipping cream
2 tablespoons sifted powdered sugar

Beat whipping cream at medium speed of an electric mixer until foamy; add powdered sugar (1 tablespoon at a time), and beat until soft peaks form. Yield: 4 cups frosting. *Marie Berry, Louisville, Kentucky.*

MY FAVORITE APPLESAUCE CAKE

1½ cups chopped pecans
¼ cup chopped citron
½ cup all-purpose flour
½ cup butter, softened
¼ cup shortening
1 cup sugar
2 eggs
2½ cups all-purpose flour
2 teaspoons baking soda
½ teaspoon salt
1 teaspoon ground cinnamon
½ teaspoon ground cloves
½ teaspoon ground nutmeg
1 (16-ounce) can applesauce
1 teaspoon vanilla extract
1 teaspoon lemon juice
1 teaspoon brewed coffee
1½ cups raisins

Combine pecans and citron; dredge in ½ cup flour, stirring to coat evenly. Set mixture aside.

Cream butter and shortening; gradually add sugar, beating at medium speed of an electric mixer until light and fluffy. Add eggs, one at a time, beating after each addition. Combine 2½ cups flour and next 5 ingredients; add to creamed mixture alternately with applesauce, beginning and ending with flour mixture. Add vanilla, lemon juice, and coffee; mix until blended. Stir in pecan-citron mixture and raisins.

Pour batter into a greased and floured 10-inch tube pan. Bake at 350° for 1 hour and 15 minutes or until a wooden pick inserted in center comes out clean. Cool in pan 10 minutes; remove from pan, and cool on wire rack. Yield: one 10-inch cake.

Garland Phillips, Baton Rouge, Louisiana.

BOURBON-PECAN PUMPKIN PIE

3 eggs, slightly beaten
1 (16-ounce) can pumpkin
¾ cup firmly packed dark brown sugar
1½ cups half-and-half
3 tablespoons bourbon
1 teaspoon ground cinnamon
½ teaspoon ground ginger
¼ teaspoon salt
1 unbaked 9-inch pastry shell
2 tablespoons butter or margarine
¼ cup firmly packed dark brown sugar
1 cup pecan halves
¼ cup bourbon, divided

Combine first 8 ingredients; mix well. Pour mixture into pastry shell; bake at 425° for 10 minutes. Reduce heat to 350°; bake an additional 45 minutes or until set. Set aside to cool.

Combine butter and ¼ cup brown sugar in a saucepan; cook over medium heat, stirring until sugar dissolves. Add pecans and 2 tablespoons bourbon, stirring to coat. Spoon mixture over pie.

Heat remaining 2 tablespoons bourbon in a saucepan just long enough to produce fumes (do not boil); remove from heat, ignite, and pour over pie. Serve pie when flames die down. Yield: one 9-inch pie. *Glenda Marie Stokes, Florence, South Carolina.*

FIVE-FLAVOR POUND CAKE

1 cup butter, softened
½ cup shortening
3 cups sugar
5 eggs
3¼ cups sifted cake flour
½ teaspoon baking powder
½ teaspoon salt
1 cup milk
1 teaspoon vanilla extract
1 teaspoon lemon extract
1 teaspoon rum flavoring
1 teaspoon coconut flavoring
Glaze (recipe follows)

Cream softened butter and shortening; gradually add sugar to mixture, beating well at medium speed of an electric mixer. Add eggs, one at a time, beating after each addition.

Combine flour, baking powder, and salt; add to creamed mixture alternately with milk, beginning and ending with flour mixture. Mix after each addition. Stir in flavorings. Pour batter into a greased and floured 10-inch tube pan. Bake at 325° for 1 hour and 30 minutes or until a wooden pick inserted in center comes out clean. Cool cake in pan 10 minutes; remove from pan, and cool on wire rack.

Spoon hot glaze over warm cake. Let cake cool completely. Yield: one 10-inch cake.

Glaze:

½ cup sugar
⅓ cup water
½ teaspoon almond extract

Combine sugar and water in a small saucepan; bring to a boil. Remove from heat; add almond extract. Yield: about ½ cup. *Dolly O'Dell-Williams, Autaugaville, Alabama.*

CHOCOLATE MOUSSE CAKE
(pictured on page 310)

9 (1-ounce) squares semisweet chocolate
1 (8-ounce) package cream cheese, softened
1 (3-ounce) package cream cheese, softened
⅔ cup sugar
6 eggs
⅓ cup whipping cream
1 tablespoon plus 1 teaspoon vanilla extract
Chocolate Crust
Whipped cream topping (recipe follows)
Cocoa

Place chocolate in top of double boiler; bring water to a boil. Reduce heat to low; cook until chocolate melts. Remove from heat, and cool.

Combine cream cheese and sugar in a large mixing bowl; beat at medium speed of an electric mixer until light and fluffy. Add eggs, one at a time, beating after each addition. Add whipping cream, vanilla, and melted chocolate; mix at low speed of an electric mixer just until blended. Pour into Chocolate Crust. Bake at 375° for 30 to 35 minutes or until outside edges are firm and lightly browned and center is still soft. Cool to room temperature; cover and chill 8 hours.

Remove chilled cake from pan. Spread cake with whipped cream topping. Place paper doily on top, and sift cocoa over it. Carefully remove doily. Yield: 10 to 12 servings.

Chocolate Crust:

⅓ cup butter or margarine
2 (1-ounce) squares semisweet chocolate
1⅓ cups fine dry breadcrumbs
⅓ cup sugar

Combine butter and chocolate in top of double boiler; bring water to a boil. Reduce heat to low; cook until chocolate melts. Remove from heat.

Combine breadcrumbs and sugar; add to chocolate mixture, blending well. Press into bottom and 2 inches up sides of a 9-inch springform pan. Bake at 350° for 8 minutes. Refrigerate until well chilled.

Whipped Cream Topping:

1½ cups whipping cream
¼ cup sifted powdered sugar
½ teaspoon vanilla extract

Beat whipping cream until foamy; gradually add powdered sugar, beating until soft peaks form. Add vanilla; blend well. Yield: 3 cups.

Holly Leiser, Dunwoody, Georgia.

A Different Fruitcake

Traditions are for passing along, and that's exactly what Alda Brower's family of Fancy Farm, Kentucky, has done with the recipe for Layered Fruitcake. And no wonder—this special cake is different from the traditional fruitcake. This one is baked in three layers and covered with a caramel frosting.

"The recipe has been in my family for three generations," says Alda. "I remember when my mother used to make it. Now my sister, my daughter, and I make this fruitcake at Christmas."

LAYERED FRUITCAKE

½ cup butter or margarine, softened
1 cup sugar
5 eggs
2½ cups all-purpose flour
2 teaspoons baking powder
½ teaspoon salt
2 teaspoons cocoa
½ teaspoon ground cinnamon
½ teaspoon ground nutmeg
½ teaspoon ground allspice
½ teaspoon ground cloves
1 cup milk
1 cup chopped orange slice candy
1 cup chopped pecans
½ cup peach preserves
½ cup cherry preserves
½ cup red plum jam
½ teaspoon vanilla extract
½ teaspoon almond extract
½ teaspoon butter flavoring
½ teaspoon lemon extract
½ cup peach preserves
1 tablespoon water
Caramel frosting (recipe follows)
Chopped pecans
Pecan halves

Cream butter; gradually add sugar, beating well at medium speed of an electric mixer. Add eggs, one at a time, beating well after each addition.

Combine flour and next 7 ingredients, reserving 2 teaspoons to dredge chopped orange slice candy and 1 cup pecans. Add flour mixture to creamed mixture alternately with milk, beginning and ending with flour mixture.

Dredge orange candy and pecans in reserved 2 teaspoons flour mixture; add to cake batter. Stir in ½ cup peach preserves, cherry preserves, plum jam, and flavorings.

Pour batter into 3 greased and floured 8-inch round cakepans. Bake at 300° for 1 hour or until wooden pick inserted in center comes out clean. Cool in pans 10 minutes; remove from pans, and cool.

Combine ½ cup peach preserves and water. Spread between layers; spread top and sides with caramel frosting. Press chopped pecans on sides. Garnish top with pecan halves. Yield: one 3-layer cake.

Caramel Frosting:

2½ cups sugar, divided
1 cup whipping cream

Sprinkle ½ cup sugar in a heavy saucepan; place over medium heat. Cook, stirring constantly, until sugar melts and syrup is light golden brown.

Combine remaining 2 cups sugar and whipping cream in a medium saucepan; heat to boiling. Add caramelized sugar slowly to whipping cream mixture. (The mixture will tend to lump, becoming smooth with further cooking.) Cook over medium heat 15 to 20 minutes, stirring frequently, until mixture reaches soft ball stage (234°). Cool 5 minutes. Beat frosting mixture to almost spreading consistency, and spread on cooled cake. Yield: enough for top and sides of one 3-layer cake.

A Prize-Winning Cheesecake

At last! Here is a recipe for German Chocolate Cheesecake. Sweet baking chocolate, appreciated for its delicate flavor, is frequently used in German chocolate cakes that are finished with a yummy coconut-and-pecan topping. John Clayton Lanier of Jacksonville, Florida, combined these popular flavors to make a delectable cheesecake with a chocolate-wafer crust.

John eagerly shared his recipe after receiving honors in a local cooking contest. This was his first competition, and he was elated to be the second man in 17 years of the contest to receive the first-runner-up title. He warns, "Ladies, wait till next year!"

GERMAN CHOCOLATE CHEESECAKE

1 (8½-ounce) package chocolate wafers, crushed (about 1½ cups)
¼ cup plus 2 tablespoons butter or margarine, melted
3 (8-ounce) packages cream cheese, softened
1¼ cups sugar
3 tablespoons cake flour
¼ teaspoon salt
4 eggs
1 (4-ounce) package sweet baking chocolate, melted
¼ cup evaporated milk
1 teaspoon vanilla extract
Topping (recipe follows)
Toasted coconut (optional)
Pecan halves (optional)
Chocolate curl (optional)

Combine wafer crumbs and butter, mixing well. Press into bottom and 1¾ inches up sides of a 9-inch springform pan, and set aside.

Beat cream cheese at medium speed of an electric mixer until light and fluffy. Gradually add sugar, flour, and salt, mixing well. Add eggs, one at a time, beating well after each addition. Add chocolate, milk, and vanilla; mix well. Spoon into prepared pan; bake at 325° for 1 hour. Remove from oven; cool 15 minutes. Loosen sides from pan with spatula. Cool 30 minutes; remove sides of pan. Spread with topping, leaving about 1-inch of cheesecake showing around edge. Cover; chill 8 hours. Garnish with remaining ingredients, if desired. Yield: 10 to 12 servings.

Topping:

2 teaspoons cornstarch
¼ cup sugar
⅔ cup evaporated milk
¼ cup butter or margarine, melted
¾ cup chopped pecans
¾ cup flaked coconut
1 teaspoon vanilla extract

Combine cornstarch and sugar in a saucepan. Gradually add milk and butter. Cook over medium heat, stirring constantly, until mixture thickens and comes to a boil. Boil 1 minute, stirring constantly. Remove from heat; stir in pecans, coconut, and vanilla. Cool. Yield: 1⅓ cups.

When Dinner Is At Your House

Whether you're throwing a party for a few friends or an open house for the whole neighborhood, planning ahead will allow the event to be as much fun for you as for your guests. Here are a few tips that will make preparing for the function easier.

Preparation

■ Even if the dinner party is small, it will help to plan at least two items on the menu that can be made ahead of time. They may be a marinated salad and a frozen dessert, or you could even make yeast rolls a week before the party and freeze them.
■ If you'll be doing a lot of cooking over the holidays, save yourself some steps by preparing some of the most common ingredients all at once. For example, chop plenty of nuts, grate citrus rind, or shred fresh coconut for several recipes; then store for use during the next few weeks.
■ Plan in advance which serving dishes you'll be using for each recipe on the menu. Then if you need to borrow or purchase items, you can do so in plenty of time.
■ When refrigerator room is a problem, try using wire cooling racks between dishes to allow for more stacking room without damaging the food contents of the dish on bottom.

Serving

■ In a small house, space is at a premium, but with a well-planned strategy you can still entertain a large number of people. One option is to make the meal an open-house buffet and stagger the arrival times of the guests when you issue invitations.
■ If possible, direct guests to more than one area of the house. You might serve appetizers in the den, the main part of the meal in the dining room, beverages in the hallway, and dessert in the living room. This way, the main traffic areas won't be as crowded.
■ Make use of furniture you have for serving. Chests, coffee tables, desks, movable carts, folding tables, and makeshift buffets are possibilities.
■ Baskets, large wooden bread boards, marble pastry slabs, and other household items are handy for serving food. You can even cover metal baking sheets with metallic wrapping paper to use as an attractive tray. For an elegant look, garnish the tray with nonpoisonous leaves, such as grape or lemon leaves. (Order them from a local florist.)
■ Create a look of abundance in each area where the food is served. You can do this with garnishing techniques or a plentiful food centerpiece. If a bowl of vegetables looks skimpy on the buffet next to a generous-size turkey, place the vegetable bowl in the center of a large tray and arrange fresh vegetables around the bowl. Your centerpiece might consist of a container of beautiful apples and oranges or a mixture of fall nuts. Use leafy greens, especially this time of year, to surround a tray and add a festive touch.

Dining

■ If a large number of guests will be sitting down to dinner, arrange the seating at several small tables. You can rent tables or make your own by combining folding tables and particle board rounds.
■ For small spaces, a buffet is probably the best choice for entertaining. Because guests will most likely eat standing up or by balancing a plate on their laps, plan the meal so that only one utensil is needed. Meat should be tender enough to cut without a knife, or you may serve something like a bowl of chili with accompaniments for which guests will need only a spoon.

A Fresh Greeting For Guests

Though it's not quite time to hang the Yuletide wreath, you still want to welcome guests to your home in a special way. You can do this by decorating your entryway with fresh flowers. For a holiday party they don't have to last more than one evening.

An arrangement of cut flowers in a half basket or other hanging container can be used at just about any home. Although you could actually place the arrangement on the door, the continual opening and closing may leave the flowers in disarray. Instead, try hanging it beside the door, perhaps where your guests will see it as they reach for the doorbell. Making the arrangement is simple. Place moist florist foam in a jar or bowl, and arrange flowers. Set inside a decorative container, if desired. Chicken wire placed over the opening of the jar holds the flowers in place.

Flowering plants, such as poinsettias, offer an inexpensive and long-lasting alternative to cut flowers. Using potted plants is an ideal way to add color to the entry. Half baskets are useful for this type of decoration, too. Add a little greenery from your garden and the arrangement is complete. Other flowering plants to consider include chrysanthemums, cyclamen, Jerusalem cherry, and kalanchoe.

Perhaps the easiest idea of all is to simply tie a few blossoms to your door knocker. You can dress up the flowers even more by using brightly colored ribbon tied around the stems. Carnations are a good choice because they're durable enough to last all evening without water. Roses and lilies are other flowers to consider.

If you have a spacious porch or landing, place an arrangement on a small table or pedestal set outside for the evening. A candle or kerosene lamp will call attention to the flowers, while adding a welcoming glow. A vase of carnations or roses would be attractive. You could say goodnight by inviting guests to take a flower as they leave.

Entrées For Everyday

Whether you're cooking for the family or friends, you'll enjoy preparing recipes that are substantial enough to be meals in themselves. For any of these entrées, all you'll need to add is a salad and bread.

Royal Meatballs, a recipe on the next page, is a classic meal in itself. This type of dish is rarely teamed with anything but a leafy green salad and French bread. Thick 'n' Crusty Chicken Pot Pie contains so many vegetables, including potatoes, onions, and carrots, that you won't need any side dishes. However, you might want to include something else like a fresh fruit salad put together at the last minute or a congealed salad done in advance.

Because you won't have a lot of recipe preparation for this kind of easy menu, perhaps there'll be time enough left to prepare a luscious dessert to end the meal.

THICK 'N' CRUSTY CHICKEN POT PIE

1 (2½- to 3-pound) broiler-fryer
1 onion, quartered
1 stalk celery, cut into large pieces
1 teaspoon dried whole basil
1 teaspoon dried whole thyme
1 teaspoon dried whole rosemary leaves, crushed
1 teaspoon salt
1 bay leaf
1 cup finely chopped celery
1 cup finely chopped onion
1 cup finely chopped carrot
1 cup finely chopped potato
⅓ cup butter or margarine, melted
½ cup all-purpose flour
1½ cups half-and-half
½ teaspoon salt
¼ teaspoon pepper
Pastry (recipe follows)
1 egg
1 tablespoon milk

Combine first 8 ingredients in a Dutch oven. Cover with water, and bring to a boil; cover, reduce heat, and simmer 1 hour or until tender. Remove chicken from broth; strain broth, reserving 1½ cups. Cool chicken. Remove chicken from bone; chop meat.

Sauté 1 cup each of celery, onion, carrot, and potato in butter until crisp-tender. Add flour, stirring until smooth. Cook 1 minute, stirring constantly. Gradually add reserved 1½ cups broth and half-and-half; cook over medium heat, stirring constantly, until thickened and bubbly. Stir in ½ teaspoon salt, pepper, and the chopped chicken.

Roll half of pastry to ⅛-inch thickness on a lightly floured surface. Fit into a 9½-inch deep-dish pieplate. Spoon chicken mixture into prepared pastry.

Roll remaining pastry to ⅛-inch thickness, and place over chicken filling. Trim, seal, and flute edges. Roll out dough scraps, and cut into a chicken shape or other desired shape. Dampen with water, and arrange over pastry, if desired. Cut slits in top of pastry to allow steam to escape.

Combine egg and milk; blend well. Brush over pastry. Bake at 400° for 30 minutes or until golden brown. Yield: 6 servings.

Pastry:

3 cups all-purpose flour
1 teaspoon salt
1 cup shortening
1 egg, beaten
¼ cup plus 1 tablespoon ice water
1 tablespoon vinegar

Combine flour and salt; cut in shortening with pastry blender until mixture resembles coarse meal.

Combine egg, water, and vinegar; sprinkle evenly over surface, and stir with a fork until dry ingredients are moistened. Shape dough into a ball. Yield: enough for one double-crust 9-inch pie.   *Sally Murphy,*
Allen, Texas.

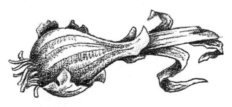

SPICY CHICKEN DISH

2½ pounds chicken breast halves
2 cups chopped onion
1 large green pepper, chopped
4 cloves garlic, minced
1 tablespoon olive oil
2 tablespoons all-purpose flour
2 (16-ounce) cans whole tomatoes, undrained and chopped
1 (6-ounce) can tomato paste
1½ tablespoons Worcestershire sauce
1¼ teaspoons salt
¾ teaspoon pepper
½ teaspoon chili powder
¼ teaspoon dried whole basil
1 bay leaf
4 cups hot cooked rice
⅓ cup chopped fresh parsley
Gumbo filé

Cook chicken in boiling salted water to cover 30 minutes. Drain, reserving 3 cups broth; let chicken cool. Skin, bone, and chop chicken; set aside.

Sauté onion, green pepper, and garlic in hot oil in a large Dutch oven until tender. Stir in flour; cook 1 minute, stirring constantly. Gradually add reserved broth. Add tomatoes and next 7 ingredients; stir well. Bring to a boil, stirring constantly; reduce heat, and simmer, uncovered, 1 hour, stirring occasionally. Add chicken; cook until thoroughly heated. Remove bay leaf.

Combine rice and parsley; stir well. Serve chicken mixture over rice; sprinkle with filé powder. Yield: 6 to 8 servings.   *Mrs. Phillip Rose,*
Harrisonburg, Virginia.

SWEET-AND-SOUR SHRIMP AND CHICKEN

¼ cup firmly packed brown sugar
2 tablespoons cornstarch
¾ teaspoon ground ginger
¼ teaspoon garlic powder
¼ teaspoon curry powder
1 tablespoon Worcestershire sauce
1½ cups pineapple juice
⅓ cup wine vinegar
¼ cup soy sauce
¼ cup catsup
1½ pounds unpeeled medium-size fresh shrimp
1 tablespoon butter or margarine, melted
1 tablespoon olive oil
2 cups cubed cooked chicken (about 3 breast halves)
1 cup unsalted cashew nuts
Hot cooked rice

Combine first 10 ingredients in a medium saucepan. Cook over medium heat 5 minutes or until thickened and clear, stirring frequently. Set aside.

Peel and devein shrimp. Sauté shrimp in butter and olive oil in a large skillet 3 minutes. Add chicken and cashew nuts; sauté an additional 2 minutes. Add sauce to shrimp mixture, and cook until thoroughly heated, stirring occasionally. Serve over rice. Yield: 6 servings.
           Beth R. McClain,
Grand Prairie, Texas.

Tip: To conserve energy, use pans with flat bottoms to absorb heat, and use covers that fit tightly. Food will continue to cook 3 to 5 minutes after you turn off the electrical unit.

TURKEY-OLIVE CASSEROLE

4 ounces uncooked egg noodles
1 (10¾-ounce) can cream of mushroom
   soup, undiluted
1 cup milk
2 cups chopped cooked turkey
½ cup sliced pimiento-stuffed olives
1 (2.8-ounce) can French-fried onion rings

Cook noodles according to package directions, omitting salt. Drain noodles and set aside.

Combine soup and milk in a large bowl; add turkey, olives, noodles, and half of onion rings; toss gently. Spoon mixture into a greased 10- x 6- x 2-inch baking dish; cover and bake at 350° for 20 minutes. Uncover and sprinkle with remaining onions. Bake, uncovered, an additional 10 minutes. Yield: 4 to 6 servings.
Linda Lefler,
Roxboro, North Carolina.

CAJUN CHICKEN OVER RICE

1½ pounds boneless chicken breast halves,
   cut into 1-inch pieces
⅛ teaspoon garlic powder
5 large tomatoes, peeled and chopped
2 large onions, chopped
1 large green pepper, chopped
¼ cup Worcestershire sauce
¼ cup soy sauce
1 to 2 teaspoons pepper
1 teaspoon dried whole basil
1 teaspoon dried whole marjoram
1 teaspoon dried whole oregano
Hot cooked rice

Sprinkle chicken with garlic powder; set aside.

Combine tomatoes and remaining ingredients except rice in a large Dutch oven. Bring to a boil; reduce heat, and simmer 15 minutes. Add chicken, and return to a boil. Cover, reduce heat, and simmer 30 minutes or until tender. Serve over rice. Yield: 6 servings.
K. Michelle Cobb,
Roxboro, North Carolina.

Tip: New cast-iron cookware should always be seasoned before using. Rub the interior of the utensil with oil or shortening, and place in a 250° or 300° oven for several hours. Wipe off oily film, and store. If scouring is necessary after using the utensil, reseason the surface immediately to prevent rusting.

CHILI BEAN ROAST

1 (3- to 3½-pound) beef round tip roast
1½ teaspoons spicy brown mustard
2 tablespoons brown sugar
1½ teaspoons chili powder
½ teaspoon salt
¼ teaspoon pepper
1 (15½-ounce) can Mexican-style chili
   beans, undrained
1 cup chopped onion

Trim excess fat from roast. Spread mustard on all sides of roast. Combine sugar, chili powder, salt, and pepper; rub on all sides of roast. Place roast in a Dutch oven; top with beans and onion. Cover and bake at 350° for 2½ hours or until done. Yield: 8 servings.
Dorothy Nieman,
Dunnellon, Florida.

ROYAL MEATBALLS

2 pounds ground beef
1 cup finely chopped onion
1½ teaspoons ground ginger
1½ teaspoons ground coriander
1 teaspoon chili powder
1 teaspoon paprika
1 teaspoon lemon-pepper seasoning
1 teaspoon salt
1 teaspoon chopped fresh parsley
1 (32-ounce) jar spaghetti sauce
2 cups finely chopped onion
2 cloves garlic, minced
1 tablespoon plus 1 teaspoon paprika
2 teaspoons chili powder
2 teaspoons grated fresh gingerroot
1½ teaspoons ground coriander
Hot cooked spaghetti

Combine first 9 ingredients; mix well. Shape mixture into 1½-inch balls; place meatballs on broiler pan, and bake at 300° for 20 minutes, turning after 10 minutes. Remove from oven, and drain meatballs on paper towels; set aside.

Combine spaghetti sauce, onion, garlic, and seasonings in a large Dutch oven. Cover and cook over medium heat 10 minutes. Add meatballs, and cook an additional 5 minutes. Serve over cooked spaghetti. Yield: 8 servings.
Sambhu N. Banik,
Bethesda, Maryland.

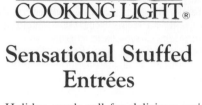

Sensational Stuffed Entrées

Holiday meals call for delicious main dishes as well as ones that are more elegant than everyday fare. But what entreé can we serve that appeals to almost everyone—even those concerned about losing weight, reducing dietary cholesterol, or practicing healthier eating habits? Our stuffed entrées make fine choices. Each recipe eliminates fatty broth, butter, and other high-fat, calorie-laden ingredients. Instead, a variety of fruits, vegetables, herbs, spices, and grains adds flavor and texture.

Making our Stuffed Turkey Breast is easier than it looks. (See page 270.) If you've never boned a turkey breast before, you may want the butcher to do it for you. It may cost a little more, but the time saved is worth it. In this recipe, wild rice, celery, onion, pecans, and currants make up the base for the stuffing. Unsweetened applesauce keeps it moist. Basting the turkey breast with an apple juice mixture keeps it from drying out during baking.

Ingredients for Stuffed Chicken Breasts Sardou are wrapped in heavy-duty plastic wrap, secured with string, and poached to keep them juicy. (You'll want to try this easy, fat-free cooking method with other foods, too.) Keep this recipe in mind when entertaining guests. You can prepare the stuffed chicken rolls ahead of time, keep the water on low heat, and cook the chicken once guests arrive.

Nestled inside Wine-Sauced Beef-and-Barley Rolls you'll find high-fiber barley, shallots, mushrooms, water chestnuts, and basil. A tasty mixture of red wine, bouillon granules, bay leaf, and browning-and-seasoning sauce serves as a basting mixture. After the beef rolls cook, skim the fat from the drippings, thicken the drippings with cornstarch, and serve as a low-calorie gravy.

WINE-SAUCED BEEF-AND-BARLEY ROLLS

6 (4-ounce) slices lean boneless sirloin
   tip roast
Vegetable cooking spray
½ cup sliced mushrooms
3 tablespoons minced shallots
1½ cups cooked pearl barley (cooked
   without salt or fat)
1 (8-ounce) can sliced water chestnuts,
   drained and chopped
2 tablespoons minced fresh parsley
½ teaspoon dried whole basil
¼ teaspoon salt
¼ teaspoon pepper
1 cup water
1 teaspoon beef-flavored bouillon
   granules
½ cup Burgundy or other dry
   red wine
1 bay leaf
2 teaspoons cornstarch
1 tablespoon water
¼ teaspoon browning-and-seasoning
   sauce

Place each piece of roast between two sheets of heavy-duty plastic wrap, and pound to ⅛-inch thickness using a meat mallet or rolling pin. Coat a skillet with cooking spray; heat until hot. Brown one side of each beef slice; set aside.

Coat skillet with cooking spray; place over medium-high heat until hot. Add mushrooms and shallots; sauté until tender. Remove from heat. Add barley and next 5 ingredients; stir well.

Spoon about ⅓ cup stuffing mixture on each beef slice. Roll each piece, jellyroll fashion, starting with the short side. Secure with wooden picks. Place in a 13- x 9- x 2-inch baking dish.

Combine 1 cup water, bouillon granules, wine, and bay leaf; pour wine mixture over beef rolls, and cover with aluminum foil.

Bake at 350° for 30 minutes, basting occasionally. Remove foil, and bake an additional 15 minutes, basting occasionally. Transfer beef rolls to serving platter; keep warm. Strain dripping mixture. Remove all fat from drippings; reserve 1 cup of fat-free drippings in a small saucepan. Heat to boiling. Combine cornstarch and 1 tablespoon water; gradually stir into drippings. Cook over medium heat, stirring constantly, until thickened and bubbly. Boil 1 minute. Stir in browning sauce. Spoon over beef rolls. Yield: 6 servings.

☐ *201 calories, 20 grams protein, 4.8 grams fat, 18.9 grams carbohydrate, 52 milligrams cholesterol, 256.3 milligrams sodium, and 17.7 milligrams calcium per beef roll with sauce.*

STUFFED CHICKEN BREASTS SARDOU
(pictured on page i)

8 (4-ounce) chicken breast halves, skinned
   and boned
Vegetable cooking spray
½ cup diced onion
1 cup diced fresh mushrooms
1 (10-ounce) package frozen chopped
   spinach, thawed
1 (14-ounce) can artichoke hearts, drained
   and chopped
2 tablespoons dry sherry
½ teaspoon dried whole thyme
½ teaspoon white pepper
Mock Mustard-Hollandaise Sauce
Parsley sprigs (optional)
Tomato roses (optional)

Place each piece of chicken between two sheets of heavy-duty plastic wrap, and flatten to ¼-inch thickness using a meat mallet or rolling pin; set aside.

Coat a skillet with cooking spray; place over medium-high heat until hot. Add onion and mushrooms; sauté until tender. Remove from heat.

Drain spinach well, pressing between layers of paper towels. Add spinach, artichokes, sherry, thyme, and pepper to mushroom mixture; stir.

Spread ¼ cup plus 1 tablespoon spinach mixture over each chicken breast; roll up, jellyroll fashion, starting with short side. Place on the end of a 12- x 8-inch piece of heavy-duty plastic wrap; roll up, and secure ends with string. Bring water to a boil in a large Dutch oven. Drop chicken rolls into boiling water; cover, reduce heat, and simmer 18 minutes or until done. Remove strings and plastic wrap; place chicken on serving plate. Slice crosswise into 5 pieces, and spoon sauce over chicken. Garnish with parsley and tomato roses, if desired. Yield: 8 servings.

Mock Mustard-Hollandaise Sauce:

Vegetable cooking spray
½ cup sliced fresh mushrooms
1 egg yolk, slightly beaten
¾ cup plain low-fat yogurt, divided
⅛ teaspoon salt
1 teaspoon Dijon mustard

Coat a skillet with cooking spray; place over medium-high heat until hot. Add sliced mushrooms, and sauté until tender. Remove mushrooms from heat, and set aside.

Combine egg yolk and ¼ cup yogurt in a small saucepan; cook over low heat, stirring constantly, until smooth and thickened. Stir in remaining ½ cup yogurt, salt, and mustard. Add mushrooms; stir well. Cook until thoroughly heated, stirring constantly. Do not boil. Yield: ¾ cup.

☐ *178 calories, 28.1 grams protein, 4.2 grams fat, 6.1 grams carbohydrate, 72 milligrams cholesterol, 149 milligrams sodium, and 69 milligrams calcium per stuffed chicken roll plus 16 calories, 1 gram protein, 0.8 gram fat, 1.2 grams carbohydrate, 24 milligrams cholesterol, 49 milligrams sodium, and 28 milligrams calcium per tablespoon sauce.*

Roll Stuffed Chicken Breasts Sardou in heavy-duty plastic wrap, and secure ends tightly with string.

Drop packages of chicken rolls into boiling water; cover, reduce heat, and simmer until chicken is done.

To make Stuffed Turkey Breast, slice through thickest part of each side to edge. Flip cut piece over to enlarge breast.

Spread stuffing mixture of rice, applesauce, pecans, and seasoning on turkey breast, and roll up, jellyroll fashion.

STUFFED TURKEY BREAST
(pictured on page 273)

1 (5-pound) whole turkey breast, boned
  and skinned
Vegetable cooking spray
½ cup diced onion
⅓ cup diced celery
2 cups cooked wild rice (cooked without
  salt or fat)
⅓ cup unsweetened chunky applesauce
¼ cup chopped pecans, toasted
¼ cup currants
2 tablespoons minced fresh parsley
½ teaspoon salt
¼ teaspoon pepper
¼ teaspoon ground cinnamon
¼ teaspoon apple pie spice
¼ teaspoon poultry seasoning
¾ teaspoon cornstarch
1 cup unsweetened apple juice
¼ teaspoon apple pie spice

Trim fat from turkey; remove tendons. Place outer side of turkey breast on heavy-duty plastic wrap with inside of breast facing up. Starting from the center, slice horizontally through the thickest part of each side of breast almost to, but not through, the outer edge. Flip cut piece over to enlarge breast. Place heavy-duty plastic wrap on turkey; pound to a more even thickness, using a meat mallet or rolling pin (place loose pieces of turkey over thinner portions). Set aside.

Coat a skillet with cooking spray; place over medium-high heat until hot. Add onion and celery; sauté until tender. Remove from heat. Add rice, applesauce, pecans, currants, parsley, salt, pepper, cinnamon, ¼ teaspoon pie spice, and poultry seasoning; stir well. Spread stuffing mixture in center of turkey breast within 2 inches of sides; roll up turkey breast, jellyroll fashion, starting with short side, to approximately an 11- x 6-inch roll. Secure at 2-inch intervals, using heavy string. Place, seam side down, on a rack in a shallow roasting pan coated with cooking spray.

Combine remaining ingredients in a small saucepan; cook over medium-high heat, stirring constantly, until hot and bubbly. Boil 1 minute; remove from heat. Brush mixture over turkey roll. Bake, uncovered, at 325° for 2 hours, basting often with apple juice mixture.

Transfer turkey roll to a serving platter. Let stand 15 minutes; remove string, and slice. Spoon remaining apple juice mixture over turkey. Yield: 13 servings.

☐ *181 calories, 27 grams protein, 2.7 grams fat, 11.3 grams carbohydrate, 72 milligrams cholesterol, 142 milligrams sodium, and 22 milligrams calcium per 3 ounces meat plus stuffing.*

FRUIT-STUFFED PORK TENDERLOINS

2 (¾-pound) pork tenderloins, well
  trimmed
Vegetable cooking spray
½ cup diced onion
⅓ cup diced celery
4 (1-ounce) slices cracked-wheat bread,
  torn into small pieces
¾ cup mixed dried fruit
½ teaspoon dried whole marjoram
¼ teaspoon ground coriander
¼ teaspoon white pepper
⅛ teaspoon ground cinnamon
3 tablespoons Chablis or other dry white
  wine
¼ cup frozen unsweetened orange juice
  concentrate, thawed and undiluted
¼ cup water
½ teaspoon browning-and-seasoning sauce

Cut a pocket lengthwise, almost to, but not through, the base of each tenderloin. Set aside.

Coat a medium skillet with cooking spray; place over medium heat until hot. Add onion and celery, and sauté until tender; remove from heat. Add bread, fruit, marjoram, coriander, pepper, cinnamon, and wine; stir well.

Spoon stuffing mixture into pocket of each tenderloin. Bring sides of meat together, and secure at 1-inch intervals, using heavy string. Place on a rack in a shallow roasting pan coated with cooking spray.

Combine remaining ingredients in a small bowl; stir well. Baste tenderloins with mixture. Loosely cover tenderloins with aluminum foil. Bake at 350° for 45 minutes, basting occasionally; uncover. Bake an additional 15 minutes or until done, basting occasionally.

Transfer tenderloins to a serving platter. Let stand 5 minutes; remove string, and slice. Spoon remaining orange juice mixture over pork. Yield: 6 servings.

☐ *247 calories, 26.7 grams protein, 4.8 grams fat, 23.9 grams carbohydrate, 79 milligrams cholesterol, 152.2 milligrams sodium, and 40 milligrams calcium per 3 ounces meat plus stuffing.*

Right: This colorful menu doesn't look low in calories, but it is. (Counterclockwise from back) Tomato-Clam Cocktail, Shrimp Mousse, Marinated Artichokes, and Pesto-Cheese Pasta Bites. (Recipes begin on page 250.)

Page 272: A lettuce-lined crystal bowl is an alternative to a relish tray for serving Corn Relish. In the background, an antique glass bowl is the perfect container for Cranberry Relish. (Recipes are on page 245.)

Page 273: No one will miss the cornbread dressing when you serve our Stuffed Turkey Breast (page 270) at this year's family gathering.

Page 273: These pastries combine the goodness of home cooking with the convenience of commercial frozen pastry: (from front) Little Phyllo Cheesecakes, Fruit Basket Strudel, and Apricot Pinwheels. (Recipes begin on page 275.)

Beautiful Pastries—Without The Trouble

Beautiful homemade pastries abound in the color photograph on page 274. Little Phyllo Cheesecakes and Fruit Basket Strudel begin with phyllo pastry, while Apricot Pinwheels are made from puff pastry.

Even if you're a novice when it comes to working with specialty doughs, you can make beautiful pastries that boast the crispness of phyllo pastry or the flakiness of puff pastry. You'll find these commercially prepared doughs in the freezer section of most supermarkets, ready to be made into an endless array of desserts.

Phyllo pastry, characterized by its extreme thinness, layers into treats such as Little Phyllo Cheesecakes and Fruit Basket Strudel (recipe, next page). In making both recipes, you brush melted butter over each sheet as you layer it so that it will crisp during baking. Once you examine the thin layers of phyllo, you'll be glad you can purchase it ready-made. Some people make their own phyllo pastry at home; however, rolling the dough thin enough is tedious for many people.

Apricot Pinwheels (page 276) and Coconut Puffs (page 277) show off the flaky layers of puff pastry. To make the dough for these pastries at home, a rolling, folding, and chilling process is repeated many times to layer butter and give the pastry its characteristic lightness. It's not difficult to make puff

pastry, but you'll save hours of work by using commercial dough.

The quality of these convenient doughs is very good if the doughs have been handled properly. Buy only from a reputable dealer who maintains proper freezer temperatures and doesn't waste time in getting these products from the distributor to the supermarket freezer. Frozen puff pastry will deteriorate each time it thaws and is refrozen. Most brands carry an expiration date to help you check for freshness. Frozen phyllo pastry's thin sheets are so brittle when frozen that they can crack if handled too roughly.

To ensure the highest quality for your pastries, follow the thawing instructions printed on the package. You can refreeze the unused portion of most brands of phyllo pastry, but it's not usually recommended to refreeze puff pastry. Sheets of puff pastry are individually wrapped so that you can thaw exactly the amount you need.

When using puff pastry, roll it on a lightly floured surface to the size and shape indicated in the recipe. Chill pastry on the baking sheet 10 minutes; then bake it immediately.

Working with phyllo pastry is a little trickier than using puff pastry. The thin sheets of phyllo dry out quickly and require extra care so that they won't tear. It is important to work with only one sheet at a time and to keep remaining sheets covered with a damp cloth towel. Use a damp towel as the work surface on which you assemble the layers, and be sure to brush each sheet of phyllo with melted butter to develop the characteristic crispness.

LITTLE PHYLLO CHEESECAKES
(pictured on page 274)

8 sheets commercial frozen phyllo pastry, thawed
½ cup butter or margarine, melted
3 (3-ounce) packages cream cheese, softened
½ cup sifted powdered sugar
1½ teaspoons grated orange rind
1 tablespoon orange juice
½ cup orange marmalade
2 teaspoons orange juice

Place 1 sheet of phyllo on a damp towel (keep remaining phyllo covered). Lightly brush phyllo with melted butter. Layer 3 more sheets phyllo on first sheet, brushing each with butter. Repeat to make another stack of 4 sheets phyllo. Cut each stack of phyllo into 3-inch squares, using kitchen shears.

Brush miniature muffin cups with melted butter. Place one square of layered phyllo into each muffin cup, pressing gently in center to form a pastry shell. Bake at 350° for 8 to 10 minutes or until golden. Gently remove from pan, and let cool on wire racks.

Combine cream cheese, powdered sugar, orange rind, and 1 tablespoon orange juice; beat at high speed of an electric mixer until blended and smooth. Spoon 1½ teaspoons mixture into each pastry shell.

Combine orange marmalade and 2 teaspoons orange juice; top each cheesecake with ½ teaspoon orange marmalade mixture. Yield: 40 pastries.

Note: Phyllo shells may be made up to 2 days in advance; store in an airtight container. Fill shells up to 4 hours before serving. Chill until ready to serve.

To make Little Phyllo Cheesecakes, place one sheet of phyllo pastry on a damp towel; lightly brush with melted butter. Layer phyllo as directed.

Cut layered and buttered phyllo pastry into 3-inch squares, using kitchen shears. Prepare miniature muffin pans, brushing muffin cups with melted butter.

Place one square of layered phyllo into each muffin cup, pressing gently in center to form a pastry shell. Bake, cool, and fill pastries as directed.

APRICOT PINWHEELS

(pictured on page 274)

1 (17¼-ounce) package frozen puff pastry, thawed
¼ cup plus 3 tablespoons apricot preserves
1 egg yolk, beaten
1 tablespoon water
1 cup sifted powdered sugar
1½ tablespoons water
½ cup finely chopped pistachios

Place 1 portion of pastry on top of other portion, and roll on a lightly floured surface into a 17½- x 15½-inch rectangle. Cut pastry into 20 (3½-inch) squares, using a sharp knife and leaving remaining strip of pastry uncut.

Cut each square of pastry diagonally from the corners to the center, leaving a 1-inch portion in center uncut.

Spoon about 1 teaspoon apricot preserves onto center of each square. Fold every other point of cut corners to the center to make a pinwheel. Press down firmly to seal seam of points.

Cut 20 (¾-inch) rounds from remaining pastry. Combine egg yolk and 1 tablespoon water. Brush 1 side of small round with egg yolk mixture. Place pastry round in center of each pinwheel, pressing gently to seal. Brush entire pinwheel with additional egg yolk mixture. Place on lightly greased baking sheets. Chill 10 minutes. Bake at 400° for 10 minutes or until golden brown. Let cool on wire racks.

Combine powdered sugar and 1½ tablespoons water, stirring until smooth. Drizzle over warm pastries, and sprinkle with pistachios. Serve warm or cool. Yield: 20 pastries.

FRUIT BASKET STRUDEL

(pictured on page 274)

½ cup chopped pitted prunes
½ cup chopped dried apricots
1 (8-ounce) can crushed pineapple, drained
⅓ cup sugar
1 tablespoon all-purpose flour
12 sheets commercial frozen phyllo pastry, thawed
½ cup butter or margarine, melted
½ cup plus 1 tablespoon fine dry breadcrumbs, divided
1 tablespoon butter or margarine, melted
Sifted powdered sugar

Cook prunes and apricots in a small amount of water, covered, for 5 to 10 minutes; drain. Combine fruit mixture, pineapple, ⅓ cup sugar, and flour, stirring until blended; set aside.

Place 1 sheet of phyllo on a damp towel (keep remaining phyllo covered). Lightly brush phyllo with melted butter. Repeat procedure with 5 more sheets of phyllo and melted butter. Sprinkle evenly with 3 tablespoons breadcrumbs, leaving a 1-inch border on narrow ends and on 1 wide end of phyllo; leave no border on other end. Layer 2 more sheets of phyllo, brushing each sheet with butter. Sprinkle with 3 tablespoons breadcrumbs. Repeat procedure 2 times with remaining phyllo, butter, and breadcrumbs, omitting breadcrumbs on last layer.

Spread fruit mixture over buttered phyllo, leaving a ¾-inch border on narrow ends and a 1-inch border on 1 wide end; leave no border on other end. Fold borders over fruit mixture. Roll up, jellyroll fashion, starting on the wide end without border, and place on a greased baking sheet, seam side down. Brush with 1 tablespoon melted butter.

Cut ¼-inch-deep slashes, about 1 inch apart, diagonally across top. Bake at 375° for 30 to 35 minutes or until pastry is golden brown. Sprinkle with powdered sugar. Cut strudel into slices to serve. Yield: 10 servings.

PUFFY APPLE TURNOVERS

1½ cups pared, cored, and chopped cooking apple (about 1 large apple)
¼ cup sugar
1 tablespoon all-purpose flour
1 teaspoon finely chopped crystallized ginger
½ teaspoon ground cinnamon
1 (17¼-ounce) package frozen puff pastry, thawed
Milk
Sugar

Combine apple, ¼ cup sugar, flour, ginger, and cinnamon; toss gently, and set aside. Roll each portion of pastry into a 10-inch square; cut each square into thirds vertically and horizontally to make 9 equal pieces from each square of pastry. Place 1 heaping tablespoon apple mixture in center of each square; fold 1 end diagonally over filling, and press gently to seal edges. Brush with milk, and sprinkle lightly with sugar. Place on lightly greased baking sheets. Chill 10 minutes. Bake at 400° for 20 minutes or until golden brown. Yield: 1½ dozen.

To make Apricot Pinwheels, roll puff pastry into a 17½- x 15½-inch rectangle; cut into 20 (3½-inch) squares, leaving remaining pastry strip uncut.

Cut each (3½-inch) square of pastry diagonally from the corners to the center of the square, leaving a 1-inch portion in center uncut.

Spoon preserves in center of each square. Fold every other point of cut corners to center. Cut rounds from remaining pastry, and place in centers.

COCONUT PUFFS

¾ cup flaked coconut
1 cup pecan pieces
¼ cup sugar
¼ teaspoon ground cinnamon
¼ teaspoon almond or vanilla extract
1 egg
1 (17¼-ounce) package frozen puff pastry, thawed
1 egg, beaten
1½ cups sifted powdered sugar
2 tablespoons hot water

Position knife blade in food processor bowl. Add coconut, pecans, ¼ cup sugar, cinnamon, almond extract, and 1 egg; process 1 minute or until finely ground. Set aside.

Working with 1 portion of pastry at a time, roll each of the 2 portions of pastry into a 15- x 9-inch rectangle on a lightly floured surface. Cut 12 (3-inch) squares from each portion of pastry. Cut 12 (¾-inch) rounds from each remaining portion of pastry.

Spoon about 2 teaspoons coconut mixture in center of each square of pastry. Brush beaten egg over edges of each square; fold corners to the middle, pinching edges to seal pastry. Brush 1 side of small rounds of pastry with beaten egg. Place 1 round on top of each filled pastry, egg side down; press gently to seal. Place on lightly greased baking sheets. Chill 10 minutes. Bake at 400° for 13 minutes or until golden brown. Let cool on wire racks.

Combine powdered sugar and water, stirring well; drizzle over warm pastries. Serve warm or cool. Yield: 2 dozen.

PINEAPPLE PHYLLO BUNDLES

1 (8-ounce) can crushed pineapple, undrained
3 tablespoons sugar
1 tablespoon cornstarch
2 teaspoons butter or margarine
½ teaspoon grated lemon rind
1½ teaspoons lemon juice
16 sheets commercial frozen phyllo pastry, thawed
1 cup butter or margarine, melted

Drain pineapple, reserving 2 tablespoons juice.

Combine sugar and cornstarch in a small saucepan; stir well. Add reserved pineapple juice; cook over medium heat, stirring constantly, until mixture boils. Boil 1 minute, and remove from heat. Add pineapple, 2 teaspoons butter, lemon rind, and lemon juice; stir until butter melts. Set aside.

Place 1 sheet of phyllo on a damp towel (keep remaining phyllo covered). Lightly brush phyllo with melted butter. Top with another sheet of phyllo, and brush with butter. Spoon about one-fourth of pineapple mixture in center of phyllo. Fold sides of phyllo over pineapple mixture, wrapping filling like a package. Wrap phyllo package in another sheet of buttered phyllo. Place package in center of another sheet of buttered phyllo. Draw corners of phyllo up and over package, twisting and squeezing together in center. Pull corners up and out to resemble a flower. Place on a lightly greased baking sheet; repeat 3 more times with remaining phyllo and filling. Brush all bundles with melted butter. Bake at 375° for 15 minutes or until golden brown. Serve warm. Yield: 4 servings.

PALMIERS

½ cup sugar, divided
1 (17¼-ounce) package frozen puff pastry, thawed
1 egg yolk, beaten
1 tablespoon water

Sprinkle 2 tablespoons sugar onto work surface. Roll one portion of pastry into a 13- x 11-inch rectangle. Sprinkle pastry with 2 tablespoons sugar. Roll up 2 shorter ends of pastry to meet in center. Combine egg yolk and water. Brush pastry with egg yolk mixture, and turn pastry over; brush with egg yolk mixture. Cut pastry into about ⅓-inch slices, using a sharp knife.

Place slices, cut side down, about 2 inches apart on lightly greased baking sheets. Chill 10 minutes. Bake at 375° for 10 minutes or until golden brown. Repeat entire procedure with remaining pastry, sugar, and egg yolk mixture. Yield: about 5 dozen.

NUTTY PHYLLO NESTS

1¼ cups slivered almonds, lightly toasted
⅔ cup sugar
2 eggs
1 tablespoon butter or margarine, softened
12 sheets commercial frozen phyllo pastry, thawed
½ cup butter or margarine, melted
⅓ cup sugar
⅓ cup water
3 tablespoons honey
1 teaspoon lemon juice

Position knife blade in food processor bowl. Add almonds; top with cover, and process 50 seconds or until finely ground. Remove and set aside 3 tablespoons ground almonds. Add ⅔ cup sugar, eggs, and 1 tablespoon butter to almonds remaining in processor bowl; process until blended. Set aside.

Place 1 sheet of phyllo on a damp towel (keep remaining phyllo covered). Lightly brush phyllo with melted butter; fold in half lengthwise. Brush again with butter, and spread about 1½ tablespoons ground almond mixture down length of phyllo, leaving a 2-inch border on 1 long side and a 1-inch border on other 3 sides. Fold all borders of pastry over filling. Roll phyllo jellyroll fashion, starting at side with 2-inch border. Wind strip loosely into a coil, and tuck end under coil. Place on a lightly greased baking sheet. Brush with melted butter. Repeat with remaining phyllo and almond mixture.

Bake at 375° for 16 minutes or until pastry is golden brown. Gently transfer to wire racks. As pastries bake, combine ⅓ cup sugar, water, honey, and lemon juice; bring to a boil, and boil 4 minutes. Let cool slightly.

Drizzle half of honey mixture over warm pastries; sprinkle with reserved 3 tablespoons ground almonds, and drizzle remaining honey mixture over almonds. Serve pastries warm or cool. Yield: 1 dozen.

Tip: Read labels to learn the weight, quality, and size of food products. Don't be afraid to experiment with new brands. Store brands can be equally good in quality and nutritional value, yet lower in price. Lower grades of canned fruit and vegetables are as nutritious as higher grades. Whenever possible, buy most foods by weight or cost per serving rather than by volume or package size.

Holiday Baking
In Minutes

Most folks don't think of using the microwave oven to make cookies or candy, but it is one way to speed up your holiday baking. You can turn out a batch of cookies in less than four minutes, and candies usually cook quicker and require less stirring when made in the microwave.

It's best to use recipes that are specifically intended for the microwave. Cookie doughs are stiffer and will not spread out as much as many conventional doughs. Also keep in mind that it's difficult to get a crisp cookie in microwave baking. The cookies will be soft, and you'll know they are done when they feel dry to the touch. To ensure even baking, it may be necessary to rotate the cookie sheet or plate.

Candies can be a little trickier to make than cookies because the cooking temperatures are so important. Be sure to use a candy thermometer specifically designed for microwave use.

You'll find that some candies, such as fudge, are less trouble when made in the microwave. Stirring every few minutes is sufficient. To prevent boilovers, be sure to use deep dishes for cooking candy mixtures, especially those containing milk or cream.

SPICE COOKIES

¾ cup butter or margarine, softened
⅔ cup sifted powdered sugar
1 egg
1 teaspoon vanilla extract
1⅔ cups all-purpose flour
½ teaspoon baking soda
¼ teaspoon salt
½ teaspoon cream of tartar
¼ teaspoon ground allspice
¼ teaspoon ground cinnamon
Powdered sugar
Small pecan halves
Candied cherry halves
1 tablespoon sugar
¼ teaspoon ground cinnamon

Cream butter; gradually add ⅔ cup powdered sugar, and beat at medium speed of an electric mixer until light and fluffy. Add egg and vanilla; beat well.

Combine flour and next 5 ingredients; add to butter mixture, beating until mixture forms a dough. Divide dough into 5 equal parts.

Shape 1 part of dough into a 9-inch-long cylinder; roll in powdered sugar. Place shaped dough on an 11- x 4-inch strip of wax paper. Transfer wax paper with dough to a microwave-safe cookie sheet or a 12- x 8- x 2-inch baking dish. Press 9 pecan halves or cherry halves in a row on top of dough; flatten dough evenly.

Microwave at MEDIUM (50% power) 3 to 4 minutes or until dough surface feels dry, giving cookie sheet a half-turn every minute. Slice diagonally between pecans or cherries. Combine 1 tablespoon sugar and ¼ teaspoon cinnamon; sprinkle the cinnamon-sugar mixture over cookies with pecans. Sprinkle powdered sugar over cookies with cherries. Repeat with remaining dough. Yield: 3½ dozen.

DOUBLE GOOD FUDGE

Vegetable cooking spray
1 (16-ounce) package powdered sugar, sifted
1 cup crunchy peanut butter
¼ cup plus 2 tablespoons milk
½ teaspoon vanilla extract
½ cup butter or margarine
1 (16-ounce) package powdered sugar, sifted
¼ cup milk
½ cup cocoa
½ cup chopped peanuts
1 teaspoon vanilla extract

Coat a 9-inch square pan with cooking spray. Line bottom of pan with wax paper, and coat with cooking spray. Set pan aside.

Combine 1 package powdered sugar, peanut butter, and ¼ cup plus 2 tablespoons milk in a large microwave-safe bowl; stir well. Stir in ½ teaspoon vanilla. Cover with wax paper, and microwave at HIGH 2 to 3 minutes. Spoon into pan.

Place butter in a microwave-safe bowl. Microwave at HIGH 1 minute or until melted. Stir in 1 package powdered sugar, ¼ cup milk, and cocoa. Cover with wax paper, and microwave at HIGH 2 to 3 minutes. Stir in peanuts and 1 teaspoon vanilla. Spoon chocolate mixture over peanut butter layer; cool and cut into squares. Store in airtight container. Yield: 3¼ pounds.

Ann Ruzic
Birmingham, Alabama.

PEANUT DIVINITY

2½ cups sugar
½ cup light corn syrup
½ cup water
⅛ teaspoon salt
2 egg whites
1 teaspoon vanilla extract
½ cup chopped, unsalted, roasted peanuts

Combine sugar, corn syrup, water, and salt in a 3-quart microwave-safe bowl; stir well. Microwave mixture at HIGH 5 to 6 minutes; stir well. Cover with heavy-duty plastic wrap; microwave at HIGH 2 minutes. Uncover and stir well. Microwave at HIGH, uncovered, 7 to 9 minutes or until mixture reaches hard ball stage (260°).

Beat egg whites (at room temperature) in a large mixing bowl until stiff peaks form. Pour hot sugar mixture in a very thin stream over egg whites while beating constantly at high speed of an electric mixer. Add vanilla, and continue beating 3 to 4 minutes until mixture holds its shape. Stir in peanuts.

Quickly drop mixture by heaping teaspoonfuls onto wax paper; cool. Yield: 3 dozen. *Jane Feagin*
Baton Rouge, Louisiana.

Hot Sandwiches
To Satisfy

Between dashing out for seasonal shopping and attending parties, there is hardly time to cook during holiday months. For a simple lunch or supper, consider making one of these hot sandwiches. Most of them are hearty enough to be the entire meal.

HOT CRAB-AND-CHEESE SANDWICHES

½ pound fresh crabmeat or 1 (6-ounce) package frozen crabmeat, thawed
1 small onion, chopped
½ cup chopped green pepper
2 cups (8 ounces) shredded Cheddar cheese
1 cup (4 ounces) shredded Monterey Jack cheese
⅔ cup cream of celery soup, undiluted
3 English muffins, split and toasted

Combine all ingredients except muffins; stir well. Spoon mixture onto cut side of each muffin; place on baking sheet. Bake at 350° for 15 to 20 minutes or until cheese melts. Yield: 6 servings.
Betty Burnside,
Newport, North Carolina.

AVOCADO, BACON, AND CHEESE SANDWICHES

1 avocado, peeled and chopped
3 tablespoons lime juice
1 small tomato, peeled and chopped
2 tablespoons chopped onion
1 clove garlic, minced
½ teaspoon ground cumin
Salt to taste
Dash of hot sauce
4 slices whole wheat bread, lightly toasted
4 slices bacon, cooked and crumbled
½ cup (2 ounces) shredded Swiss cheese

Combine avocado and lime juice; toss gently, and drain. Combine avocado, tomato, onion, garlic, cumin, salt, and hot sauce, tossing gently. Spoon mixture evenly over toast. Bake at 375° for 8 minutes or until mixture is thoroughly heated. Remove from oven; sprinkle each sandwich with bacon and cheese. Broil 6 inches from heat just until cheese melts. Yield: 4 servings.
Connie Burgess,
Knoxville, Tennessee.

SNACK BUNS

2 cups (8 ounces) shredded Cheddar cheese
3 tablespoons grated onion
¼ cup diced green pepper
½ cup tomato soup, undiluted
¼ teaspoon pepper
6 English muffins, split and lightly toasted
6 slices bacon, cooked and crumbled

Combine cheese, onion, green pepper, soup, and pepper; mix well. Spread about 2 tablespoons of cheese mixture over cut side of each muffin. Broil about 6 inches from heat 3 to 5 minutes or until cheese is hot and bubbly. Top with bacon. Yield: 12 servings.
Patricia Boschen,
Ashland, Virginia.

CREAMY BLUE CHEESE-HAM SANDWICHES

1 (8-ounce) package cream cheese, softened
1 (4-ounce) package crumbled blue cheese
¼ cup milk
1 tablespoon pickle relish
1 teaspoon instant minced onion
1 teaspoon prepared mustard
½ teaspoon Worcestershire sauce
¼ teaspoon pepper
⅛ teaspoon garlic powder
12 slices white bread
12 (1-ounce) slices thinly sliced ham
6 (1-ounce) slices Swiss cheese
¼ cup butter or margarine, melted

Combine cream cheese and blue cheese; beat until smooth. Add milk and next 6 ingredients; mix well. Chill 30 minutes.
Spread a very thin layer of cheese mixture over each slice of bread. Place 2 slices of ham and 1 slice of cheese on each of 6 slices of bread. Top sandwiches with remaining bread, cheese side down. Brush each side of sandwich with butter. Cook over medium heat in a skillet until golden brown, turning once. Yield: 6 servings.
Janis Moyer,
Farmersville, Texas.

OPEN-FACED SALAMI SANDWICHES

1 (1-pound) loaf Italian bread
¼ pound fresh mushrooms, sliced
¼ cup butter or margarine, melted
¼ cup all-purpose flour
1 cup half-and-half
½ cup dry white wine
¼ teaspoon white pepper
¼ teaspoon celery salt
12 slices salami (about 10 ounces)
12 (½-inch-thick) slices tomato
6 (¾-ounce) slices mozzarella cheese, cut diagonally

Cut loaf of bread in half lengthwise. Place cut side up on a baking sheet; bake at 425° for 10 minutes or until lightly browned. Remove from oven; keep warm.
Sauté mushrooms in butter in a heavy saucepan until mushrooms are tender. Add flour, and cook 1 minute, stirring constantly. Gradually add half-and-half; cook over medium heat, stirring constantly, until mixture is thickened and bubbly. Stir in wine, pepper, and celery salt; cook just until heated.
Spread sauce evenly over toasted side of each piece of bread. Layer salami slices, tomato slices, and cheese evenly on each; bake at 425° for 5 to 10 minutes or until cheese melts. Serve immediately. Yield: 4 to 6 servings.
Mary Kay Menees,
White Pine, Tennessee.

UPTOWN WELSH RAREBIT

1 (10-ounce) package frozen asparagus spears
¼ cup butter or margarine
3 cups (12 ounces) shredded Cheddar cheese
1 teaspoon Worcestershire sauce
½ teaspoon dry mustard
⅛ teaspoon red pepper
2 eggs, beaten
½ cup half-and-half
6 slices white bread
1 (6-ounce) can crabmeat, drained and flaked
3 hard-cooked eggs, sliced
Paprika

Cook asparagus spears according to package directions, and set aside.
Melt butter in top of a double boiler over medium heat; add cheese, and stir until melted. Add Worcestershire sauce, mustard, and red pepper; stir well. Combine eggs and half-and-half in a small bowl; stir well. Add egg mixture to cheese mixture; stir well. Cook, stirring often, about 12 minutes or until the mixture thickens.
Remove crust from bread; toast bread, and cut in half diagonally. Place toast points on individual serving plates; spoon a small amount of cheese sauce over toast points. Arrange asparagus spears over sauce, and top with crabmeat. Spoon additional sauce over crabmeat, and arrange egg slices on sauce. Sprinkle with paprika. Yield: 6 servings.
Lucy Adams,
Maitland, Florida.

Try These Sweet Potato Favorites

You'll find sweet potatoes in everyday meals as well as on the most elaborate holiday menus this time of year. The recipes here give you a good sampling of the wide variety of uses for the tasty fall vegetable.

Natural sugars just under the skins flavor the potatoes; thus, for any recipe that calls for mashed cooked sweet potatoes, be sure to cook whole potatoes in their jackets for the best flavor.

When you're selecting fresh sweet potatoes, look for those that are plump, medium sized, and tapered toward the ends. Store them in a cool place, but never in the refrigerator.

SWEET POTATO MUFFINS

½ cup butter or margarine, softened
1¼ cups sugar
2 eggs
1¼ cups mashed cooked sweet potatoes
¼ to ⅓ cup milk
1½ cups all-purpose flour
2 teaspoons baking powder
¼ teaspoon salt
1 teaspoon ground cinnamon
¼ teaspoon ground nutmeg
½ cup raisins
¼ cup chopped pecans
2 tablespoons sugar
¼ teaspoon ground cinnamon

Cream butter; gradually add 1¼ cups sugar, beating at medium speed of an electric mixer. Add eggs, one at a time, beating well after each addition. Stir in sweet potatoes and milk.

Combine flour, baking powder, salt, 1 teaspoon cinnamon, and nutmeg; add to creamed mixture, stirring just until moistened. Stir in raisins and pecans. Spoon into greased muffin pans, filling two-thirds full.

Combine 2 tablespoons sugar and ¼ teaspoon cinnamon; sprinkle over batter. Bake at 400° for 22 to 25 minutes. Yield: 2 dozen.

Mrs. Delbert R. Snyder,
Williamsburg, Virginia.

RASPBERRY SWEET POTATOES

8 medium-size sweet potatoes
1 teaspoon salt
¼ cup firmly packed brown sugar
¼ cup butter or margarine, softened
1 (10-ounce) package frozen raspberries, thawed and undrained

Cook sweet potatoes in boiling salted water 20 to 25 minutes or until tender. Drain and let cool to touch. Peel and cut in half lengthwise.

Arrange sweet potatoes in a lightly greased 13- x 9- x 2-inch casserole, cut side up. Combine brown sugar and butter in a small bowl, mixing well. Spread brown sugar mixture over cut surface of sweet potatoes.

Top with raspberries and juice. Bake, uncovered, at 350° for 25 minutes, spooning raspberries and juice over potatoes occasionally. Yield: 8 to 10 servings.
Hazel Sellers,
Albany, Georgia.

PEACH SWEET POTATO PUFFS

2 large sweet potatoes
2 tablespoons brown sugar
¼ teaspoon salt
Dash of ground cloves
1 teaspoon lemon juice
2 tablespoons butter, softened
1 (29-ounce) can peach halves, drained

Cook sweet potatoes in boiling water 25 to 30 minutes or until tender; drain. Let cool to touch. Peel, mash, and measure 2 cups potatoes. Combine potatoes, brown sugar, salt, cloves, lemon juice, and butter; stir until well mixed.

Pipe or spoon potato mixture onto peach halves. Bake at 400° for 15 minutes or until thoroughly heated. Yield: 6 to 8 servings.

Cheryl Richardson,
Fairfax Station, Virginia.

BOURBON SWEET POTATOES

6 medium-size sweet potatoes (about 4 pounds)
½ cup butter or margarine, melted
½ cup firmly packed brown sugar
⅓ cup orange juice
¼ cup bourbon
½ teaspoon salt
½ teaspoon pumpkin pie spice
½ cup chopped pecans

Cook sweet potatoes in boiling water for 20 to 25 minutes or until tender. Drain and let cool to touch. Peel potatoes, and mash pulp.

Combine potatoes, butter, brown sugar, juice, bourbon, salt, and pie spice, mixing well. Spoon mixture into a lightly greased 1½-quart baking dish. Sprinkle chopped pecans around edge of dish. Bake at 375° for 45 minutes. Yield: 8 to 10 servings.
Dorothy C. Taylor,
Palm City, Florida.

SWEET POTATO PANCAKES

1 cup all-purpose flour
1 teaspoon baking powder
2 tablespoons sugar
⅛ teaspoon ground cinnamon
Dash of ground cloves
⅔ cup mashed cooked sweet potatoes
1 tablespoon butter or margarine, melted
1 cup milk
1 egg, beaten

Combine first 5 ingredients; mix well. Combine mashed sweet potato and butter; stir well. Gradually stir in milk and egg. Add to dry ingredients, stirring just until moistened.

For each pancake, spoon about 2 tablespoons batter onto a hot, lightly greased griddle. Turn pancakes when tops are covered with bubbles and edges are brown. Serve pancakes with maple syrup. Yield: 1 dozen (4-inch) pancakes. *Elizabeth Thompson,*
Connelly Springs, North Carolina.

Serve Mushrooms Anytime

Fresh mushrooms were once a specialty item, but today they are standard in produce sections at most grocery stores. Because of the wide availability, mushrooms can be used for everyday recipes as well as for entertaining.

Jeanne Hotaling of Augusta, Georgia, prepares Heavenly Mushrooms for a rich-tasting side dish to serve at any meal. Sliced mushrooms are sautéed, then baked with sour cream and topped with Parmesan cheese and parsley.

In Memphis, one of Martha Feagin's favorite recipes, Toasted Mushroom Sandwiches, has been a hit with her guests for the past 12 years. "I have these whenever I have a group for lunch," she says. "I serve mushroom sandwiches, broccoli salad, and a dessert." The recipe is great for entertaining because it can be made ahead of time, Martha points out.

When selecting mushrooms for stuffing, use those with large caps for the best results. The mushrooms will shrink to less than half the original size after they are baked.

HEAVENLY MUSHROOMS

1 pound fresh mushrooms, sliced
1 tablespoon butter or margarine, melted
½ cup commercial sour cream
1 tablespoon all-purpose flour
⅛ teaspoon pepper
½ cup grated Parmesan cheese
2 tablespoons chopped fresh parsley

Sauté mushrooms in butter 2 to 3 minutes; drain. Combine sour cream, flour, and pepper in a small mixing bowl; stir well. Pour over mushrooms, stirring gently. Cook until thoroughly heated (do not boil).

Spoon into a lightly greased 1-quart casserole, and sprinkle with grated Parmesan cheese. Bake mushrooms at 425° for 10 to 15 minutes or until lightly browned. Remove from oven, and sprinkle with chopped fresh parsley. Yield: 4 servings. *Jeanne S. Hotaling, Augusta, Georgia.*

Serve Toasted Mushroom Sandwiches as an appetizer or as part of a luncheon menu. For entertaining ease, make them a day ahead of time and refrigerate.

STUFFED MUSHROOM DELIGHT

24 large fresh mushrooms
1 pound bulk pork sausage
½ cup chopped onion
2 tablespoons minced parsley
⅛ teaspoon salt
½ teaspoon pepper
1 (8-ounce) package cream cheese, softened

Clean mushrooms with damp paper towels. Remove mushroom stems; chop stems, and set caps aside.

Combine chopped stems and sausage in a large skillet; cook over medium heat, stirring to crumble, until meat is browned. Drain meat mixture into a colander, and pat dry with a paper towel. Return sausage mixture to skillet; add onion, parsley, salt, and pepper. Cook over low heat until mixture is thoroughly heated. Add cream cheese, stirring until blended. Remove mixture from heat.

Place mushroom caps on an ungreased baking sheet; spoon sausage mixture into mushroom caps. Broil 6 inches from heat 5 minutes or until browned. Yield: 2 dozen.

*Karen Caston,
Covington, Louisiana.*

TOASTED MUSHROOM SANDWICHES

½ pound fresh mushrooms, chopped
2 tablespoons butter or margarine, melted
1 (3-ounce) package cream cheese, softened
1 (10¾-ounce) can cream of mushroom soup, undiluted
1½ teaspoons Worcestershire sauce
1½ teaspoons prepared horseradish
Dash of garlic powder
⅓ cup slivered almonds, toasted
32 slices thin sandwich bread
Melted butter

Sauté mushrooms in 2 tablespoons butter; drain and set aside.

Combine cream cheese and mushroom soup in a small bowl; beat with an electric mixer until smooth. Add sautéed mushrooms, Worcestershire sauce, and next 3 ingredients; stir until blended. Set aside.

Trim crust from bread slices; roll each slice with a rolling pin to flatten. Place 1 tablespoon of filling diagonally across each slice; fold opposite corners of bread to overlap in the center, securing with a wooden pick. Place sandwiches on an ungreased baking sheet. Brush top of each sandwich lightly with melted butter. Bake at 450° for 7 minutes or until sandwiches are lightly browned. Yield: 32 sandwiches.

Note: Sandwiches can be refrigerated up to 24 hours before baking. Sandwiches may be frozen unbaked; thaw sandwiches before baking.

*Martha Feagin
Memphis, Tennessee.*

MUSHROOM SOUFFLÉS

¾ pound fresh mushrooms, chopped
1 tablespoon chopped onion
¼ cup plus 2 tablespoons butter or
    margarine, melted and divided
¼ cup plus 2 tablespoons all-purpose flour
2 cups milk
½ cup (2 ounces) shredded Cheddar
    cheese
¼ teaspoon salt
⅛ teaspoon pepper
⅛ teaspoon hot sauce
6 eggs, separated
Shrimp-and-Almond Sauce

Sauté mushrooms and onion in 3 tablespoons butter until tender; drain well, and set aside.

Combine remaining 3 tablespoons butter and flour in a saucepan; cook 1 minute, stirring constantly. Gradually add milk; cook over medium heat, stirring constantly, until thickened. Stir in Cheddar cheese, salt, pepper, and hot sauce; cool. Combine mushroom mixture and egg yolks; stir into cheese mixture, mixing well. Set aside.

Beat egg whites (at room temperature) until stiff peaks form; fold into mushroom mixture. Pour mushroom mixture into six lightly greased 10-ounce custard cups. Place cups in large shallow pan; pour water to depth of 1 inch in pan. Bake at 325° for 45 minutes or until knife inserted in center of soufflé comes out clean.

To serve, remove soufflés from custard cups, and invert onto individual plates or a serving platter. Top each soufflé with Shrimp-and-Almond Sauce. Yield: 6 servings.

Shrimp-and-Almond Sauce:

1 (10¾-ounce) can cream of shrimp soup,
    undiluted
1 (3-ounce) package cream cheese,
    softened
¾ cup milk
1 tablespoon lemon juice
1 (2-ounce) package sliced almonds,
    toasted

Combine cream of shrimp soup, cream cheese, milk, and lemon juice in a small saucepan; cook over low heat until thoroughly heated. Stir in almonds. Yield: 2 cups. *Kitty Chew, Birmingham, Alabama.*

Tip: Immediately before using fresh mushrooms, wipe them clean or quickly rinse them in a colander; never immerse mushrooms in water.

Warm Up With Dried-Bean Soup

As soon as the weather turns cold, thoughts turn to hot and satisfying soups, and dried-bean soups are a popular choice. This type of soup often simmers for an hour or more to tenderize the beans, and in the process, the soup develops a wonderful thick and rich-tasting broth. The tasty seasonings, vegetables, and meats often added pack the soup with flavor.

Because the beans for these soups are dried, they are very hard. You'll need to rehydrate and soften them by soaking before cooking.

BEEFY LENTIL SOUP

1 cup dried lentil beans
½ pound round steak, cut into 1-inch
    cubes
3 medium carrots, sliced
1 large onion, chopped
1 small hot pepper, chopped
1 teaspoon salt
1 teaspoon freshly ground pepper
2 tablespoons olive oil
2 bay leaves
Dash of dried whole basil
6½ cups water
1 (14½-ounce) can stewed tomatoes,
    undrained
1 (6-ounce) can tomato juice

Sort and wash beans; place in a Dutch oven. Cover with water 2 inches above beans; cover and let soak 8 hours. Drain beans, and return to Dutch oven.

Add round steak and next 9 ingredients to beans. Bring mixture to a boil; cover and simmer 1 hour, stirring occasionally. Add tomatoes and tomato juice; cover and simmer an additional 30 minutes. Remove bay leaves. Yield: 2 quarts. *Georgie D. O'Neill, Welaka, Florida.*

SAVORY NAVY BEAN SOUP

1 (16-ounce) package dried navy beans
    (2¼ cups)
6 cups water
2 slices bacon, chopped
½ cup diced onion
2 cloves garlic, minced
1 cup sliced carrots
1 cup sliced celery
1½ teaspoons salt
¼ teaspoon white pepper
¼ teaspoon red pepper
1 tablespoon dry sherry

Sort and wash beans; place in a Dutch oven. Add 6 cups water; cover and let soak 8 hours.

Bring mixture to a boil; reduce heat, and simmer 1½ hours, stirring occasionally. Remove from heat. Place about one-third of bean mixture in container of an electric blender; cover and process until smooth. Return to Dutch oven.

Sauté bacon, onion, and garlic until bacon is crisp; drain. Add bacon mixture and remaining ingredients to beans. Cover and simmer an additional 25 minutes. Yield: 7 cups.

Note: Additional water may be added if a thinner soup is desired.
Mrs. B. G. Knight, Sulphur Springs, Texas.

CHILL-CHASER SOUP

1 (16-ounce) package dried red beans
    (2½ cups)
2 cups water
3 or 4 slices bacon, cooked and crumbled
2 large onions, chopped
2 cloves garlic, chopped
2 cups dry white wine
2 tablespoons hot sauce
½ cup chopped fresh parsley
1 tablespoon Worcestershire sauce
1 to 2 pounds smoked sausage, sliced
About 1 cup water
Salt to taste
Hot cooked rice

Sort and wash beans; place in a large Dutch oven. Add 2 cups water; bring to a boil. Remove from heat; cover and let stand 1 hour.

Add bacon, onions, garlic, wine, hot sauce, parsley, and Worcestershire sauce; bring to a boil. Cover, reduce heat, and simmer 1 hour, stirring occasionally. Add sausage and 1 cup water, if necessary; cover and simmer 1½ hours or until beans are tender, stirring occasionally. Add salt to taste. Serve over rice. Yield: 3¾ quarts.
Mrs. Peter Rosato III, Memphis, Tennessee.

DRUNKEN BEAN SOUP

1 (16-ounce) package dried pinto beans
  (2½ cups)
3 cups water
1 slice bacon, cut into 1-inch pieces
2 teaspoons sugar
2 teaspoons salt
2 (12-ounce) cans beer
1 cup shredded cooked roast beef
2 teaspoons chili powder
1 teaspoon ground cumin
¼ teaspoon garlic powder
1 (10-ounce) can tomatoes and green
  chiles, undrained
Picante sauce or salsa (optional)
Shredded Cheddar cheese (optional)

Sort and wash beans; place in a Dutch oven. Cover with water 2 inches above beans; cover and let soak 8 hours. Drain beans, and return to Dutch oven.

Add 3 cups water to beans; bring to a boil. Add bacon, sugar, and salt; cover, reduce heat, and simmer 30 minutes. Stir in beer, beef, chili powder, cumin, and garlic powder; cover and simmer 1 hour, stirring occasionally. Stir in tomatoes and green chiles; cover and simmer an additional 30 minutes. Serve with picante sauce and cheese, if desired. Yield: 2 quarts.

Carole Drennan,
Abilene, Texas.

Serve Chicken Nuggets

Our recipe for Lemon-Chicken Nuggets makes fried chicken, a Southern favorite, even more versatile as an appetizer. Although you can buy bite-size fried chicken pieces almost everywhere now, you'll want to try this version for the tangy lemon flavor it offers.

Lockie Burge, a resident of Sulphur Rock, Arkansas, sends us the recipe and suggests that the tasty morsels be served with barbecue sauce or honey for dipping. For your fanciest parties, they make popular pick-up appetizers. You may want to place frilly wooden picks nearby for easier eating.

Of course, fried chicken suits even the most casual parties, too. Fry a batch of these appetizers to take along on picnics or tailgate get-togethers. They'll still be tasty even if they aren't piping hot. The nuggets are also great to include in an appetizer supper menu.

LEMON-CHICKEN NUGGETS

1 cup milk
¼ cup lemon juice
½ teaspoon salt
½ teaspoon paprika
¼ teaspoon pepper
4 chicken breast halves, skinned and
  boned
1 cup all-purpose flour
Vegetable oil
Honey (optional)
Barbecue sauce (optional)

Combine first 5 ingredients, mixing well. Cut chicken into 1-inch pieces; marinate in milk mixture 8 hours. Remove chicken from marinade, and dredge in flour.

Heat 1½ inches oil in a large heavy skillet to 350°. Fry chicken 1 minute on each side or until golden brown. Drain on paper towels. Serve chicken with honey or barbecue sauce, if desired. Yield: 8 appetizer servings.

Ground Beef Tastes Better Than Ever

Ground beef has been a staple in our diets for years—the number of recipes in our *Southern Living* reader files attest to that. But the way we're preparing it may be changing.

Karen Glisson uses frozen bread dough in Meat Loaf Wellington (recipe is on the next page). In this dish, the dough is wrapped around meat loaf like a Wellington pastry. The combination looks attractive and makes a nice dish for entertaining. The meat loaf is served with Mushroom Sauce.

STROMBOLI

½ pound ground beef
½ cup chopped onion
2 (16-ounce) loaves frozen bread dough,
  thawed and divided
2 tablespoons prepared mustard, divided
12 slices American cheese, divided
2 cups shredded mozzarella cheese,
  divided
½ pound pepperoni, sliced and divided
1 teaspoon Italian seasoning, divided
Vegetable oil
1 teaspoon Italian seasoning, divided

Combine ground beef and onion in a skillet; cook until beef is browned.

Roll 1 loaf of bread dough to a 15- x 12-inch rectangle on a lightly floured surface. Mark long sides of dough at 5-inch intervals, dividing dough into thirds.

Spread surface of dough with 1 tablespoon mustard. Layer 3 slices of American cheese, ½ cup mozzarella cheese, half of pepperoni, and half of beef mixture on center third of dough. Sprinkle with ½ teaspoon Italian seasoning. Top with ½ cup mozzarella cheese and 3 slices American cheese.

Fold each side of dough over meat and cheeses; press to seal sides and ends. Lay loaf on a greased baking sheet, seam side down. Brush top with vegetable oil, and sprinkle with ½ teaspoon Italian seasoning.

Repeat procedure with remaining bread dough, meat, cheese, and seasoning. Bake at 350° for 25 to 30 minutes or until loaves are golden. Yield: two 12-inch loaves.

Sheryl Shenk,
Victoria, Virginia.

GROUND BEEF GUMBO

1½ pounds ground beef
⅔ cup chopped onion
⅔ cup chopped celery
⅔ cup chopped green pepper
2 or 3 cloves garlic, minced
1 (15-ounce) can tomatoes, undrained
1 (15-ounce) can tomato sauce
2 (6-ounce) cans tomato paste
1 (6-ounce) jar sliced mushrooms, drained
2½ cups frozen okra, cut up
2 bay leaves
1½ tablespoons dried parsley flakes
2½ teaspoons Italian seasoning
1½ teaspoons dried whole basil
1 teaspoon dried whole oregano
1 teaspoon chili powder
1 teaspoon onion powder
½ teaspoon cumin powder
Salt and pepper to taste
½ cup water
2 tablespoons dry red wine
Hot cooked rice

Cook ground beef, chopped onion, celery, green pepper, and garlic in a heavy Dutch oven over medium heat until meat is browned; drain. Stir in undrained tomatoes and remaining ingredients except rice.

Simmer, uncovered, 1 hour. Remove bay leaves. Serve over hot cooked rice. Yield: 1¼ quarts.

Dee Buchfink,
Oologah, Oklahoma.

BEEF MADRAS

1 pound ground beef
¾ cup chopped onion
⅓ cup flaked coconut
1½ teaspoons curry powder
1 teaspoon garlic powder
¼ teaspoon ground cinnamon
2 cups water
2 beef-flavored bouillon cubes
1 cup water
2 tablespoons butter or margarine
Dash of salt
1 cup couscous
1 medium-size green pepper, cut into
   1-inch pieces
1½ tablespoons cornstarch
¼ cup water

Combine ground beef and onion in a large skillet; cook over medium heat until beef is browned, stirring to crumble meat. Drain. Stir in coconut, curry powder, garlic powder, cinnamon, 2 cups water, and bouillon cubes; bring to a boil. Cover, reduce heat, and simmer 20 minutes.

Combine 1 cup water, butter, and salt in a saucepan; bring to a boil. Stir in couscous; cover, remove from heat, and let stand 3 or 4 minutes.

Stir green pepper into beef mixture. Dissolve cornstarch in ¼ cup water; stir into beef mixture. Cook over medium heat, stirring constantly, until thickened and bubbly. Serve over hot couscous. Yield: 4 servings.   *Lynda Cable,*
Hixson, Tennessee.

MEAT LOAF WELLINGTON

1½ pounds ground beef
1 small onion, chopped
2 cups (8 ounces) shredded Swiss cheese
3 slices bread, crumbled
1 egg, slightly beaten
2 teaspoons dried parsley flakes
¼ teaspoon salt
⅛ teaspoon pepper
1 (16-ounce) loaf frozen bread dough,
   thawed
1 egg, beaten
Watercress
Mushroom Sauce

Cook ground beef and onion in a skillet over medium heat until beef is browned, stirring to crumble meat. Drain in a colander, and pat dry with a paper towel; cool. Combine meat, onion, cheese, bread, egg, parsley flakes, salt, and pepper. Set aside.

Roll two-thirds of bread dough to a 16- x 12-inch rectangle on a lightly floured surface. Line a greased 9- x 5- x 3-inch loafpan with dough. Spoon meat mixture into pan. Press with spoon to pack the meat tightly.

Roll out remaining bread dough to an 11- x 7-inch rectangle on a lightly floured surface. Reserve some dough to make pastry cutouts, if desired. Place on top of meat. Seal edges, and trim. Decorate with pastry cutouts, if desired. Cut slits to allow steam to escape. Brush with egg. Bake at 350° for 40 to 45 minutes or until golden. (Cover top with foil, if necessary, to prevent over-browning.) Garnish with watercress. Serve with Mushroom Sauce. Yield: 6 servings.

Mushroom Sauce:

1 pound fresh mushrooms, sliced
¼ cup butter or margarine, melted
1 teaspoon Worcestershire sauce
½ teaspoon soy sauce
⅛ teaspoon pepper

Sauté mushrooms in butter. Stir in remaining ingredients. Simmer 5 minutes. Yield: about 2 cups.
Karen E. Glisson,
Marietta, Georgia.

Casseroles
For Busy Days

Select a few vegetables from the pantry or the freezer. Combine them with canned soups or easy sauces, and you've got the casseroles we've offered here. The ingredient listings are short, and they're a snap to put together on a busy weeknight or when unexpected company arrives. They're sure to become favorites at supper clubs and church dinners, too.

BROCCOLI CASSEROLE

2 (10-ounce) packages frozen chopped
   broccoli, thawed
1 (10¾-ounce) can cream of mushroom
   soup, undiluted
1 cup (4 ounces) shredded sharp Cheddar
   cheese
¼ cup mayonnaise
2 eggs, beaten
1 teaspoon grated onion
¾ cup cheese-flavored cracker crumbs

Drain broccoli between paper towels. Combine uncooked broccoli and next 5 ingredients, mixing well. Spoon mixture into a lightly greased 2-quart casserole. Sprinkle with cracker crumbs. Bake, uncovered, at 350° for 30 minutes. Yield: 6 to 8 servings.   *Jan Bobbitt,*
Tarboro, North Carolina.

LIMA BEAN CASSEROLE

1 (16-ounce) package frozen lima beans
2 tablespoons butter or margarine
2 tablespoons all-purpose flour
1 cup milk
Salt and pepper to taste
1 tablespoon catsup
1 (4-ounce) jar chopped pimiento, drained
½ cup (2 ounces) shredded Cheddar
   cheese
¼ cup breadcrumbs
1 tablespoon butter or margarine, melted

Cook beans according to package directions; drain. Set aside.

Melt 2 tablespoons butter in a heavy saucepan over low heat; add flour, stirring until smooth. Cook 1 minute, stirring constantly. Gradually add milk; cook over medium heat, stirring constantly, until mixture is thickened and bubbly. Stir in salt and pepper. Add catsup, pimiento, and cheese. Stir until cheese melts, and set aside.

Spoon beans into a greased 1-quart casserole. Pour sauce over beans. Combine breadcrumbs and 1 tablespoon butter; sprinkle over casserole. Bake, uncovered, at 350° for 30 minutes. Yield: 4 to 6 servings.
Mrs. Thomas Byrd,
Nashville, Tennessee.

EASY GREEN BEAN CASSEROLE

2 (16-ounce) cans French-style green
   beans, drained
1 (10¾-ounce) can cream of celery soup,
   undiluted
½ cup (2 ounces) shredded Cheddar
   cheese
2 tablespoons minced onion
1 teaspoon caraway seeds
¼ cup round buttery cracker crumbs

Combine all ingredients except cracker crumbs; spoon into a lightly greased 1½-quart casserole. Sprinkle with cracker crumbs, and bake at 350° for 25 to 30 minutes or until bubbly. Yield: about 6 servings.
Mildred Matthews,
Bartlesville, Oklahoma.

CARROT CASSEROLE

4½ cups sliced carrots
¼ teaspoon salt
¼ teaspoon sugar
1½ cups water
1 cup diced celery
½ cup diced onion
½ cup mayonnaise
1 tablespoon prepared mustard

Combine carrots, salt, sugar, and water in a medium saucepan; bring to a boil over high heat. Reduce heat, cover, and simmer about 18 minutes or until tender; drain. Mash carrots. Add remaining ingredients; stir well. Spoon into a lightly greased 1-quart casserole. Bake at 350° for 30 minutes or until lightly browned. Yield: 6 servings.

Sonya H. Davis,
Huntington, West Virginia.

CAULIFLOWER 'N' CHILES CASSEROLE

1 (4-ounce) can whole green chiles, drained
1 medium cauliflower, cut into flowerets
2 cups (8 ounces) shredded Monterey Jack cheese
¼ cup all-purpose flour
1½ cups milk, divided
2 eggs, beaten

Cut green chiles in half lengthwise. Line the bottom of a lightly greased 10- x 6- x 2-inch baking dish with chiles. Set aside.

Arrange cauliflower on a steaming rack. Place over boiling water; cover. Steam 7 to 10 minutes or until crisp-tender. Drain. Place on chiles; sprinkle with cheese.

Combine flour and ½ cup milk, stirring until smooth. Add remaining milk and eggs, stirring well. Pour over cheese. Bake at 350° for 35 minutes or until mixture is set. Yield: 6 servings.

Mrs. Joe R. Haynes,
Knoxville, Tennessee.

Toss Turkey Into A Salad

If you find yourself with leftover turkey, toss tender chunks of the meat into one of these tasty salads. Both are served chilled with salad greens and lots of fruit, and they make a nice change of pace from heavy holiday feasting.

Lightly flavored with curry powder, Polynesian Turkey Salad resembles a traditional Waldorf Salad, while Turkey Salad With Hot Bacon Dressing is a meaty version of a familiar tossed green salad. Serve each with breadsticks or crackers for a light lunch or supper.

POLYNESIAN TURKEY SALAD

4 cups diced cooked turkey or chicken
1 cup diced unpeeled red Delicious apple
1 cup chopped pecans
1 (15¼-ounce) can pineapple tidbits, drained
1 cup mayonnaise
2 teaspoons lemon juice
½ teaspoon curry powder
1 (11-ounce) can mandarin oranges, drained
Lettuce leaves

Combine first 4 ingredients in a large bowl; mix well. Combine mayonnaise, lemon juice, and curry powder; stir into turkey mixture. Add mandarin oranges, and gently toss. Cover and chill. Serve on lettuce leaves. Yield: 6 to 8 servings.

Mrs. Robert A. Bailey
Knoxville, Tennessee.

TURKEY SALAD WITH HOT BACON DRESSING

1 (15½-ounce) can pineapple chunks, undrained
5 cups romaine lettuce, torn into bite-size pieces
2 cups cubed cooked turkey
½ cup sliced water chestnuts
2 green onions, sliced
2 slices bacon, coarsely chopped
2 tablespoons vinegar
1 teaspoon sugar
¼ teaspoon salt
⅛ teaspoon pepper

Drain pineapple, reserving 2 tablespoons juice for dressing; set aside.

Combine pineapple and next 4 ingredients in a large bowl.

Cook bacon in a small skillet until crisp; drain and set aside. Reserve 1½ teaspoons drippings in skillet. Stir in 2 tablespoons reserved pineapple juice, vinegar, sugar, salt, and pepper. Cook over low heat, stirring until sugar dissolves. Pour over salad, and toss well. Sprinkle with bacon. Serve immediately. Yield: 4 servings.

Kathleen Stone
Houston, Texas.

A Salad To Rave About

Smoked salmon is a delicacy and rare treat for many who find the price overwhelming. But Merle Dunson of Taylors, South Carolina, found an ingenious way to enjoy the fish without breaking the family budget. She uses it almost as an extensive garnish in Salmon-Potato Salad.

SALMON-POTATO SALAD

12 small new potatoes
½ cup olive oil
2 tablespoons red wine vinegar
1 tablespoon lemon juice
1 tablespoon Dijon mustard
1 teaspoon sugar
¼ teaspoon garlic powder
3 tablespoons minced green onions
1 green pepper, cut into strips
3 tablespoons chopped parsley
Radicchio or red-tipped leaf lettuce
⅓ pound thinly sliced smoked salmon, cut into thin strips
2 tablespoons chopped fresh chives

Scrub potatoes; cook in boiling salted water to cover 15 to 20 minutes or until tender. Drain. Let cool. Cut into ¼-inch slices; set aside.

Combine olive oil, vinegar, lemon juice, mustard, sugar, and garlic powder in a small bowl; stir well. Set aside.

Combine potatoes, green onions, green pepper, and parsley in a large bowl. Pour ½ cup dressing over top; toss gently. Cover and chill mixture 2 to 3 hours.

Line a serving plate with radicchio; top with potato mixture. Arrange salmon on top; drizzle with remaining dressing. Garnish salad with chives. Yield: 6 servings.

Chicken As An Elegant Entrée

If you've been looking for a special entrée to serve guests, try this one from Brenda Clark of Phenix City, Alabama. Her combination of chicken wrapped in phyllo pastry will serve six to eight guests for dinner.

In less than an hour, you can have Chicken in Phyllo ready to go into the oven. While it bakes, you can make the rest of the meal. We suggest an arranged fruit salad and steamed asparagus or broccoli to serve with it.

You'll find phyllo in the frozen-food section at the supermarket. Handle the sheets one at a time, and keep the sheets you aren't using moist with a damp towel. If a few sheets tear before you get the hang of it, don't despair. The package contains more than you'll need for this recipe. (For more recipes using phyllo pastry, see page 275.)

CHICKEN IN PHYLLO

16 sheets commercial frozen phyllo pastry
    (about 1 pound)
2 cups chopped celery
1½ cups chopped onion
2 tablespoons butter or margarine, melted
4 cups chopped cooked chicken
¼ cup chicken broth
1 tablespoon plus 1 teaspoon parsley
    flakes
1 teaspoon salt
1 teaspoon ground nutmeg
2 eggs, well beaten
½ cup butter or margarine, melted
Béchamel Sauce
Escarole (optional)
Radicchio (optional)
Lemon halves (optional)

Thaw phyllo in refrigerator 8 hours before using.

Cook celery and onion in 2 tablespoons butter until crisp-tender. Add chicken and broth; cook until all broth is absorbed. Stir in parsley flakes, salt, nutmeg, and eggs; set aside.

Place 1 sheet of phyllo on a flat surface. Cover remaining phyllo with a damp towel. Lightly brush phyllo sheet with melted butter. Layer phyllo sheets, brushing with ½ cup melted butter, to make 8 layers.

Spoon half of filling onto phyllo rectangle leaving a 1-inch border at bottom and 2 short sides of rectangle. Leave a 3-inch border at top long side of pastry.

Fold phyllo over chicken mixture 1 inch on 3 sides, and 3 inches on remaining side. Roll lengthwise, jellyroll fashion, starting at side with 1-inch fold. Place, seam side down, on a lightly greased baking sheet. Score top of roll diagonally (⅛-inch deep) into 4 portions. Brush with melted butter. Repeat procedure with remaining ingredients to make a second roll. Bake chicken rolls at 350° for 45 minutes. Serve with Béchamel Sauce. Garnish with escarole, radicchio, and lemon halves, if desired. Yield: 6 to 8 servings.

Béchamel Sauce:

¼ cup butter or margarine
¼ cup all-purpose flour
¼ teaspoon salt
2½ cups chicken broth
4 egg yolks
2 tablespoons plus 2 teaspoons lemon juice

Melt butter in a heavy saucepan over low heat; add flour and salt, stirring until smooth. Cook 1 minute, stirring constantly. Gradually add chicken broth; cook over medium heat, stirring until thickened and bubbly. Remove from heat. Beat yolks until thick and lemon colored. Gradually stir about one-fourth of hot mixture into yolks; add to remaining hot mixture, stirring constantly. Add lemon juice. Cook 2 minutes; stir constantly. Yield: 2½ cups.

Take A Look At These Sunday Suppers

If your Sunday afternoons lend themselves to relaxing or taking a nap rather than cooking, here are some recipes you'll appreciate. Most of them need only a green salad or bread to complete the meal.

Zippy Cheese Omelet is especially simple to prepare. Just blend eggs and sour cream together, and pour the mixture over picante sauce and shredded cheese. You can bake this in a pieplate if you don't have a quiche dish.

If you had ham for lunch, use the leftovers to make Creamy Ham and Eggs. It is served with buttered toast and takes about 30 minutes to fix. Enchilada Casserole will take a little more time because you have to brown the beef. But it takes advantage of several canned products you may have on hand, such as tomato sauce, Mexicorn, and enchilada sauce.

If you're in the mood for a less filling dish, try Chicken-and-Broccoli Pasta. Served with garlic bread, it makes a tasty, complete meal.

CHICKEN-AND-BROCCOLI PASTA

4 chicken breast halves
3 cups broccoli flowerets
8 ounces rotelle pasta
½ cup chopped walnuts,
    toasted
½ cup grated fresh Parmesan
    cheese
1 tablespoon lemon juice
1 teaspoon dried whole basil
¾ cup mayonnaise

Place chicken in a Dutch oven; add water to cover. Bring to a boil. Cover, reduce heat, and simmer 20 to 25 minutes or until chicken is tender. Remove chicken from broth; let chicken cool. Remove chicken from bone, and chop. Cover and chill.

Place broccoli in steaming rack; place over boiling water. Cover and steam 7 minutes or until crisp-tender. Let cool.

Cook rotelle pasta according to package directions, omitting salt. Drain and let cool.

Place chicken, broccoli, and pasta in a large bowl; add walnuts and remaining ingredients, and toss gently. Let chill. Yield: 4 to 6 servings.

Heather Riggins,
Nashville, Tennessee.

CREAMY HAM AND EGGS

3 tablespoons butter or margarine
3 tablespoons all-purpose flour
2 cups milk
½ teaspoon dry mustard
⅛ teaspoon white pepper
1 cup diced cooked ham
4 hard-cooked eggs, quartered
4 slices bread, toasted
Fresh parsley sprigs (optional)

Melt butter in a heavy saucepan over low heat; add flour, stirring until smooth. Cook 1 minute, stirring constantly. Gradually add milk; cook over medium heat, stirring constantly, until mixture is thickened and bubbly. Stir in mustard and pepper. Add ham and eggs; stir gently. Place toast on individual serving plates; spoon ham mixture over toast. Garnish with parsley, if desired. Yield: 4 servings.

Azine G. Rush,
Monroe, Louisiana.

COUNTRY HAM QUICHE

Pastry for 9-inch deep-dish pie
1 cup chopped cooked country ham
⅓ cup (1.34 ounces) shredded Gruyère cheese
⅓ cup (1.34 ounces) shredded Swiss cheese
4 eggs, beaten
1 cup whipping cream
½ cup milk
Dash of pepper
Pinch of ground nutmeg

Line a 9-inch quiche dish or deep-dish pieplate with pastry. Trim excess around edges. Prick bottom and sides of pastry with a fork; bake at 425° for 5 minutes. Let cool.

Sprinkle ham and cheeses evenly over pastry. Combine eggs and remaining ingredients; pour over ham and cheeses. Bake at 350° for 1 hour or until set. Let stand 10 minutes before serving. Yield: one 9-inch quiche.

ZIPPY CHEESE OMELET

½ cup picante sauce
1 cup (4 ounces) shredded Monterey Jack cheese
1 cup (4 ounces) shredded Cheddar cheese
6 eggs
1 (8-ounce) carton commercial sour cream
Picante sauce
Tomato wedges (optional)
Fresh parsley (optional)

Pour ½ cup picante sauce into a lightly greased 9-inch quiche dish or pieplate; sprinkle cheeses over sauce.

Place eggs in container of an electric blender; process until blended. Add sour cream, and process until well blended. Pour egg mixture over cheeses. Bake, uncovered, at 350° for 30 to 35 minutes or until set.

Serve omelet with additional picante sauce. Garnish omelet with tomato wedges and fresh parsley, if desired. Yield: 6 servings.

Mrs. Robert W. Meyer,
Seminole, Florida.

ENCHILADA CASSEROLE

2 pounds ground beef
1 medium onion, chopped
2 (8-ounce) cans tomato sauce
1 (12-ounce) can Mexicorn, drained
1 (10-ounce) can hot enchilada sauce
½ teaspoon chili powder
½ teaspoon pepper
¼ teaspoon salt
¼ teaspoon dried whole oregano
12 corn tortillas
2 cups (8 ounces) shredded Cheddar cheese, divided

Cook ground beef and onion in a large skillet until browned, stirring to crumble meat. Drain. Add tomato sauce and next 6 ingredients; mix well. Bring to a boil; reduce heat, and simmer 5 minutes.

Place half of tortillas in a 13- x 9- x 2-inch baking dish. Pour half of meat mixture over tortillas; sprinkle half of cheese over meat mixture. Repeat layers with tortillas and meat mixture. Bake at 350° for 20 minutes. Sprinkle with remaining cheese, and bake an additional 5 minutes. Yield: 8 servings.

Marie Threet,
Ruleville, Mississippi.

MEXICAN BURRITO PIE

1 (16-ounce) can refried beans with green chiles, onion, and garlic
1 cup biscuit mix
¼ cup water
1½ pounds ground beef
1 cup thick and chunky salsa
1 cup (4 ounces) shredded Monterey Jack cheese
½ cup commercial sour cream

Combine beans, biscuit mix, and water in a medium bowl; mix well. Spoon bean mixture into a lightly greased 9-inch pieplate to form a pie shell. Set pie shell aside.

Cook ground beef until browned, stirring occasionally to crumble; drain well. Spoon meat over bean mixture; top

with salsa. Bake at 375° for 25 minutes. Sprinkle with cheese, and bake an additional 5 minutes. Cut into wedges; serve immediately. Dollop with sour cream. Yield: 6 to 8 servings.

Linda Heath,
Roswell, Georgia.

SPICY TACO SALAD

1 pound process American cheese
1 (10-ounce) can diced tomatoes and green chiles
1 pound lean ground beef
1 large onion, chopped
1 green pepper, chopped
1 clove garlic, crushed
2 tablespoons chili powder
¼ teaspoon ground cumin
¼ teaspoon pepper
1 (11-ounce) bag corn chips, crushed
1 medium head lettuce, chopped
2 medium tomatoes, chopped

Combine first 2 ingredients in top of a double boiler; place over boiling water, and cook until cheese melts, stirring often. Set aside.

Combine ground beef, onion, green pepper, and garlic; cook over medium heat until the ground beef is browned, stirring to crumble. Drain well. Stir in seasonings and cheese mixture.

Layer half each of corn chips, meat mixture, chopped lettuce, and chopped tomatoes in a large salad bowl; repeat with remaining ingredients. Serve salad immediately. Yield: 6 servings.

Helen Goggans,
Kingsland, Arkansas.

GRILLED SOUR CREAM BURGERS

½ cup commercial sour cream-French onion dip
3 tablespoons fine dry breadcrumbs
¼ teaspoon salt
Dash of pepper
1 pound ground beef
4 hamburger buns, buttered and toasted
Commercial sour cream-French onion dip (optional)

Combine first 4 ingredients in a bowl; mix well. Add ground beef; stir until blended. Shape into 4 patties about ½-inch thick. Grill over medium coals 6 to 8 minutes on each side. Serve on buns with additional sour cream dip, if desired. Yield: 4 servings.

Jackie Bridges,
Leeds, Alabama.

Chicken Tortellini Salad boasts plenty of protein with chicken, cheese, and Canadian bacon.

Sauté chicken and garlic in 2 tablespoons oil until chicken is done; drain and set aside.

Cook tortellini according to package directions; drain well. Combine tortellini and 2 tablespoons oil in a large bowl, tossing gently. Add chicken, celery, red pepper, onion, and cheese.

Combine ¾ cup olive oil, vinegar, honey, and mustards in a jar. Cover tightly, and shake vigorously. Pour mixture over salad, and toss gently. Serve immediately or chill. Arrange on Bibb lettuce leaves, and top with Canadian bacon. Garnish with celery leaves, if desired. Yield: 6 servings.

BROCCOLI SOUP

1 pound fresh broccoli, chopped
1 medium onion, chopped
1 (10¾-ounce) can chicken broth,
    undiluted
1⅓ cups water
1½ cups commercial sour cream
½ to ¾ teaspoon Bouquet Garni
¼ teaspoon salt
¼ teaspoon pepper

Combine broccoli, onion, undiluted chicken broth, and water in a Dutch oven; cover and simmer 15 minutes or until broccoli is tender.

Remove from heat; pour half of broccoli mixture into container of an electric blender; process until smooth. Return pureed mixture to saucepan. Repeat procedure with remaining broccoli mixture. Add sour cream and remaining ingredients to mixture; heat thoroughly (do not boil). Yield: 7 cups.

Linda Askey,
Birmingham, Alabama.

Tip: Plan your menus for the week, but stay flexible enough to substitute good buys when you spot them. By planning ahead, you can use leftovers in another day's meal.

Wow! Pasta Salad

Fanciful pasta salads are the rage. Susan Todd of Shreveport, Louisiana, has an updated version that's sure to win compliments. She combines tortellini, sautéed chicken, crunchy vegetables, and even cheese and Canadian bacon. It's dressed with a delightful honey-mustard vinaigrette that seasons the ingredients without masking their striking taste combinations.

CHICKEN TORTELLINI SALAD

1 pound boneless chicken breasts, cut into
    strips
2 cloves garlic, minced
2 tablespoons olive oil
1 (8-ounce) package tortellini with
    Parmesan cheese
2 tablespoons olive oil
3 stalks celery, chopped
1 medium-size red pepper, cut into strips
⅓ cup chopped purple onion
5 ounces smoked Gouda cheese, cut into
    strips
¾ cup olive oil
¾ cup cider vinegar
2 tablespoons honey
2 tablespoons Dijon mustard
1 teaspoon dry mustard
Bibb lettuce leaves
5 slices Canadian bacon, cut into strips
Celery leaves (optional)

This Salad Is A Group Project

What's a good way to feed a crowd? Linda Myers of Muskogee, Oklahoma, serves Salad by Committee. "My real close friends and I decided this should be a group project. Everyone brings an ingredient, and we have a nice bottle of chilled wine and fun times making this salad." We think you'll enjoy the recipe as much as Linda's idea for preparing it. Served with hot French bread, the salad makes a complete meal.

SALAD BY COMMITTEE

2 (6-ounce) jars marinated artichoke
    hearts, undrained
1 cup vegetable oil
⅓ cup red wine vinegar
½ teaspoon garlic powder
½ teaspoon dry mustard
½ teaspoon salt
½ teaspoon pepper
1 teaspoon sugar
½ pound fresh mushrooms, sliced
3 medium heads iceberg lettuce, torn
1 pound cubed cooked chicken
1 pound cubed cooked roast beef
1 pound cubed cooked ham
1 pint cherry tomatoes
1 cup sliced radishes
1 cup sliced unpeeled cucumber
2 cups cauliflower flowerets
½ cup sliced ripe olives
1 small purple onion, sliced and separated
    into rings
2 avocados, chopped
3 hard-cooked eggs, quartered
1 pound bacon, cooked and crumbled

Drain artichokes, reserving marinade. Chop artichokes, and set aside. Combine marinade, oil, and next 6 ingredients in a bowl; stir well. Add artichokes and mushrooms; cover and chill 4 hours.

Combine lettuce, chicken, beef, ham, tomatoes, radishes, cucumber, cauliflower, olives, onion, and avocados in a large bowl; toss gently. Pour artichoke mixture over salad; toss gently. Arrange eggs around salad edge; sprinkle bacon over top. Yield: 18 servings.

Processor Crêpes And Fillings

By using the food processor and planning ahead, you can make elegant crêpes for your next brunch. Traditional crêpe batter—a mixture of eggs, flour, milk, and butter or oil—can be whirled for a few seconds in the processor or blender for a smooth creamy mixture. If lumps occur when the batter is hand mixed, the batter must be sieved. This problem isn't likely to occur using the processor.

Once the batter is mixed, it needs to sit 1 to 2 hours before it is cooked to allow the flour particles to expand and the air bubbles to collapse. It's easy to overprocess the batter; remember that 4 to 6 seconds should be sufficient time for mixing the batter.

The crêpe recipes we've included here are basic, but you can add your own touches. For example, you might add savory herbs to batter for crêpes that will wrap around meat or vegetables. Liqueurs and extracts give a flavor lift to dessert crêpes.

For the best results, use moderate heat to cook the crêpes. You'll know the pan is hot enough when a few drops

of water bounce and sizzle in the pan. Don't worry if you don't have a traditional crêpe pan—any low-sided pan with a 6- to 8-inch diameter cooking surface will do.

To save time when you entertain, make the crêpes ahead. They'll keep in the refrigerator up to 3 days and in the freezer for 4 months. To freeze, place wax paper between each crêpe, and wrap in aluminum foil. Then sandwich the stack between two paper plates, and wrap in foil. This will keep the edges of the crêpes from breaking off.

Save more cooking time by planning crêpe fillings that can be made in the processor. Or use your favorite recipes, looking for steps where the processor can help.

BASIC PROCESSOR CRÊPES

1½ cups all-purpose flour
¼ teaspoon salt
2 tablespoons butter or margarine, chilled
3 eggs
2 cups milk
Vegetable oil

Position knife blade in food processor bowl. Place flour, salt, and butter in processor bowl. Top with cover, and process until mixture resembles coarse meal. Add eggs through food chute, one at a time, processing just until blended. With processor running, pour milk through food chute and process until smooth. Refrigerate batter 1 to 2 hours. (This allows flour particles to swell and soften so that the crêpes will be light in texture.)

Brush bottom of a 6- or 8-inch crêpe pan or heavy skillet with oil; place the pan over medium heat just until hot, not smoking.

Pour 2 to 3 tablespoons batter into pan; quickly tilt pan in all directions so that batter covers pan in a thin film. Cook about 1 minute or until lightly browned. Lift edge of crêpe to test for doneness. Crêpe is ready for flipping when it can be shaken loose from pan. Flip crêpe, and cook about 30 seconds on other side. (This side is rarely more than spotty brown and is the side on which the filling is placed.) Repeat procedure until all batter is used.

Place crêpes on a towel to cool. Stack between layers of wax paper to prevent sticking. Yield: 24 (6-inch) crêpes or 18 (8-inch) crêpes.

MUSHROOM-CHEESE CRÊPES

2 small shallots, cut in half
½ pound fresh mushrooms
3 tablespoons butter or margarine, melted
1 (8-ounce) package cream cheese, softened
1 egg, beaten
Swiss Cheese Sauce
14 (6-inch) Basic Processor Crêpes
¼ cup (1 ounce) shredded Swiss cheese

Position knife blade in food processor bowl, and top with cover. With processor running, drop shallots through food chute, and process until minced. Remove knife blade, and leave shallots in processor bowl.

Position slicing disc in processor, and top with cover. Slice off one side of two mushroom caps. Arrange these mushrooms in food chute, cut side down. Stack remaining mushrooms sideways in chute, alternating stems and caps. Slice, using firm pressure.

Sauté shallots and mushrooms in butter in a heavy skillet about 3 minutes or until tender. Drain and set aside.

Position knife blade in processor bowl. Cut cream cheese into 1-inch pieces, and add to processor. Add egg to processor; top with cover, and process about 10 seconds or until smooth. Combine cream cheese mixture, vegetables, and 1¾ cups Swiss Cheese Sauce.

Spread ¼ cup mushroom filling in center of each crêpe; roll up, and place, seam side down, in a greased 13- x 9- x 2-inch baking dish. Spread remaining Swiss Cheese Sauce over crêpes, and sprinkle with cheese. Bake at 375° for 15 minutes. Yield: 7 servings.

Swiss Cheese Sauce:

¼ cup butter or margarine
¼ cup plus 1 tablespoon all-purpose flour
2¾ cups milk
¼ cup whipping cream
¾ cup (3 ounces) shredded Swiss cheese
⅛ teaspoon ground nutmeg
⅛ teaspoon pepper
Pinch of salt

Melt butter in a heavy saucepan over low heat; add flour, stirring with a whisk until smooth. Cook 1 minute, stirring constantly. Gradually add milk; cook over medium heat, stirring constantly, until mixture is thickened and bubbly. Stir in whipping cream and remaining ingredients; cook over low heat, stirring constantly, until cheese melts. Yield: about 3½ cups.

DESSERT CRÊPES

1½ cups all-purpose flour
1 tablespoon sugar
¼ teaspoon salt
½ teaspoon ground cinnamon (optional)
2 tablespoons butter or margarine, chilled
3 eggs
2 cups milk
1 teaspoon vanilla extract
Vegetable oil

Position knife blade in food processor bowl. Place flour, sugar, salt, and cinnamon, if desired, in processor bowl. Top with cover, and pulse 2 or 3 times to blend. Add butter; process until mixture resembles coarse meal.

Add eggs through food chute, one at a time, and process just until blended. Combine milk and vanilla. With processor running, pour milk mixture through food chute, and process until smooth. Refrigerate 1 to 2 hours. (This allows flour particles to swell and soften so the crêpes are light in texture.)

Brush the bottom of a 6-inch crêpe pan or heavy skillet with vegetable oil; place over medium heat just until hot.

Pour 2 tablespoons batter into pan; quickly tilt pan in all directions so that batter covers the pan in a thin film. Cook 1 minute or until lightly browned. Lift edge of crêpe to test for doneness.

Crêpe is ready for flipping when it can be shaken loose from pan. Flip crêpe, and cook about 30 seconds on other side. (This side is rarely more than spotty brown and is the side on which the filling is placed.) Repeat procedure until all batter is used.

Place crêpes on a towel to cool. Stack between layers of wax paper to prevent sticking. Yield: about 2 dozen crêpes.

STRAWBERRY ICE CREAM CRÊPES

¼ cup sugar
Rind of ½ lemon
1 (10-ounce) package frozen strawberries, partially thawed
¼ teaspoon vanilla extract
¾ cup whipping cream, chilled
6 (6-inch) Dessert Crêpes
Berry Sauce
Fresh strawberries (optional)

Position knife blade in food processor bowl. Add sugar and lemon rind; process until rind is finely chopped. Add partially thawed strawberries and vanilla; process 10 to 15 seconds or until strawberries are cut into small chunks. With machine running, pour chilled whipping cream through food chute,

The next time you entertain, serve elegant crêpes. The food processor makes it easy to prepare such dishes as Strawberry Ice Cream Crêpes.

and process 10 seconds or until mixture reaches a smooth, creamy consistency (some strawberry chunks may remain, if desired).

Immediately spoon about ⅓ cup ice cream in center of each crêpe; roll up, and place seam side down on individual serving plates. Top with Berry Sauce, and garnish with fresh strawberries, if desired. Serve immediately. Yield: 6 servings.

Berry Sauce:

1 (10-ounce) package frozen strawberries, thawed
1 tablespoon Kirsch or other cherry-flavored liqueur

Position knife blade in food processor bowl. Add strawberries and Kirsch to processor. Top with cover, and process until strawberries are pureed. Chill. Yield: about 1 cup.

December

Recipes For A Tree-Hunt Tradition

When Smith and Katie Broadbent host their annual Christmas tree-hunt party, their Cadiz, Kentucky, friends know what to expect. "The tree hunt means that you come and eat chili and hot dogs, and that we have just about the same food each time," says Katie.

Cookies are one of the biggest traditions at the family's party. "I make between 35 and 50 different kinds," Katie says. "And everybody has a favorite," adds Margaret, the Broadbents' daughter. "They all come in and try to hide at least a few of the ones they want."

Katie begins baking cookies months before the party. Her goal is always to start the first of October and be finished by Thanksgiving.

The cookie recipes as well as the others featured, have become standbys for the annual party and appeal to guests of all ages.

TREE-HUNT CHILI

1 pound ground beef
¾ cup chopped onion
1 clove garlic, minced
½ teaspoon salt
⅛ teaspoon pepper
3 tablespoons chili powder
1 (28-ounce) can tomatoes, undrained and chopped
1 (10¾-ounce) can tomato puree
1 (15-ounce) can chili beans, undrained
3 cups water

Combine ground beef, onion, and garlic in a Dutch oven; cook until beef is browned, stirring to crumble meat. Drain. Add remaining ingredients; cover, reduce heat, and simmer 1 hour, stirring frequently. Yield: 7 cups.

Tip: If power to your freezer is interrupted, do not open the door unnecessarily. Food in a full freezer will stay frozen 2 days, and food in a half-filled freezer about one day. If power is not resumed within this time, use dry ice to prevent spoilage, or move your food to a locker plant nearby.

SPICED CRANBERRY LEMONADE

4 to 8 whole cloves
1 (2-inch) stick cinnamon
3½ cups water
2 cups cranberry juice cocktail
⅓ cup sugar
1 (6-ounce) can frozen lemonade concentrate, thawed and undiluted
Orange slices

Combine cloves and cinnamon stick in a cheesecloth bag. Set aside.

Combine water, cranberry juice, and sugar in a Dutch oven; add spice bag. Bring mixture to a boil, stirring until sugar dissolves. Remove from heat; add lemonade, stirring well. Discard spice bag. Serve hot, and garnish with orange slices. Yield: 1½ quarts.

ORANGE PECANS

1 tablespoon grated orange rind
¼ cup orange juice
1 cup sugar
4 cups pecan halves

Combine grated orange rind, orange juice, and sugar in a heavy saucepan. Cook over medium heat until mixture comes to a full boil. Stir in pecans; continue to cook, stirring until pecans are coated and all syrup is absorbed. Remove from heat; stir just until pecans are separated. Spread onto wax paper to cool. Yield: 5½ cups.

ORANGE CHEESE SPREAD

1 (11-ounce) can mandarin oranges, undrained
2 (8-ounce) packages cream cheese, softened
2 tablespoons orange-flavored liqueur
¼ teaspoon orange extract

Drain oranges, reserving 15 sections for garnish. Chop remaining orange sections. Drain again.

Combine cream cheese, liqueur, and orange extract; beat at medium speed of an electric mixer until blended. Stir in chopped oranges. Spoon mixture into a 2½-cup mold lined with plastic wrap. Chill. Invert cheese onto serving plate; remove plastic wrap. Garnish with reserved orange sections. Serve with gingersnaps. Yield: 2¼ cups.

DATE-WALNUT SPREAD

1 (8-ounce) package cream cheese, softened
2½ tablespoons chopped walnuts
2½ tablespoons chopped dates
2 tablespoons rum
1 tablespoon powdered sugar
Walnut halves

Combine first 5 ingredients; beat at medium speed of an electric mixer until blended. Shape mixture into a ball; cover and chill. Garnish with walnut halves. Serve with gingersnaps. Yield: 1¼ cups.

ALMOND CHEESE SPREAD

1 (8-ounce) package cream cheese, softened
2 tablespoons amaretto
2 tablespoons chopped blanched almonds
Whole almonds

Combine cream cheese and amaretto; beat at medium speed of an electric mixer until blended. Stir in chopped almonds. Shape mixture as desired. Cover and chill. Garnish with whole almonds. Serve with gingersnaps. Yield: 1 cup.

CHOCOLATE CHEESE SPREAD

1 (8-ounce) package cream cheese or Neufchâtel cheese, softened
1 tablespoon powdered sugar
1½ teaspoons cocoa
2 tablespoons Kahlúa
Semisweet chocolate shavings

Combine cream cheese, powdered sugar, cocoa, and Kahlúa; beat at medium speed of an electric mixer until blended. Shape mixture as desired; cover and chill. Garnish with chocolate shavings. Serve with gingersnaps. Yield: 1 cup.

CHRISTMAS STRAWBERRIES

1 (8-ounce) package pitted whole dates
¼ cup flaked coconut
½ cup sugar
¼ cup butter or margarine
1 egg, slightly beaten
Dash of salt
1½ cups crispy rice cereal
½ cup chopped pecans
1 teaspoon vanilla extract
2 (2.25-ounce) jars red sugar crystals
1 (4.25-ounce) tube commercial green
   decorator frosting

Chop dates into small pieces. Combine dates, coconut, sugar, butter, egg, and salt in a large skillet. Cook over medium heat, stirring constantly, until mixture thickens and begins to boil (about 5 minutes). Remove from heat, and stir in cereal, chopped pecans, and vanilla. Let cool 10 minutes. Shape mixture to look like strawberries, using 2 teaspoons mixture for each. Roll in red sugar crystals, coating heavily. Pipe stems onto strawberries with green decorator frosting. Yield: 3 dozen.

VIENNESE SANDWICH COOKIES

1½ cups butter or margarine, softened
¾ cup sifted powdered sugar
3 cups all-purpose flour
1 tablespoon grated orange rind
1½ tablespoons orange juice
Sugar
Lemon filling (recipe follows)
Chocolate frosting (recipe follows)
Decorator candies

Cream butter; gradually add ¾ cup powdered sugar, beating at medium speed of an electric mixer until light and fluffy. Add flour, orange rind, and orange juice to creamed mixture, beating well. Cover and chill dough 2 hours.

Shape dough into 1-inch balls. Place about 2 inches apart on greased cookie sheets. Dip a flat-bottomed glass in sugar, and flatten each ball of dough to ⅛-inch thickness (about a 2-inch circle). Bake at 300° for 14 to 16 minutes or until lightly browned. Remove cookies to wire racks to cool.

Spoon about 1½ teaspoons lemon filling on half of cookies; spread evenly. Place a second cookie on top of filling. Spread top of each sandwich cookie with chocolate frosting. Sprinkle cookies with decorator candies. Yield: 3 dozen.

Lemon Filling:

½ cup butter or margarine, softened
2 cups sifted powdered sugar
2 to 4 tablespoons lemon juice

Cream butter, and gradually add powdered sugar. Add enough lemon juice to reach desired spreading consistency. Yield: 1¼ cups.

Chocolate Frosting:

3 (1-ounce) squares semisweet chocolate
1 tablespoon butter or margarine

Combine chocolate and butter in top of double boiler; bring water to a boil. Reduce heat to low; cook, stirring constantly, until melted. Yield: ¾ cup.

MINCEMEAT SWEETHEART COOKIES

½ cup butter, softened
1 (3-ounce) package cream cheese, softened
1¼ cups all-purpose flour
¼ teaspoon salt
2 tablespoons milk
About ½ cup commercial mincemeat
About 2 teaspoons powdered sugar

Cream butter and cream cheese. Add flour and salt; beat at low speed of an electric mixer until mixture is blended. Gradually stir in milk. Cover and chill dough 1 hour.

Roll dough to ¼-inch thickness on a lightly floured surface. Cut dough with a 1¾-inch heart-shaped cookie cutter; place on lightly greased cookie sheets. Bake at 400° for 6 to 8 minutes or until lightly browned. Remove cookies to wire racks to cool.

Spread about 1 teaspoon mincemeat onto bottom side of half of cookies; top each with another cookie, top side up. Sprinkle lightly with powdered sugar. Yield: 1½ dozen.

RIBBON COOKIES

1 cup butter or margarine, softened
1½ cups sugar
1 egg
1 teaspoon vanilla extract
2½ cups all-purpose flour
1½ teaspoons baking powder
½ teaspoon salt
¼ cup diced red candied cherries
⅓ cup semisweet chocolate morsels, melted
¼ cup chopped pecans
¼ cup diced green candied cherries

Line bottom and sides of a 9- x 5- x 3-inch loafpan with aluminum foil; set loafpan aside.

Cream butter; gradually add sugar, beating well at medium speed of an electric mixer. Add egg and vanilla; mix well. Combine flour, baking powder, and salt; gradually add to creamed mixture, mixing until blended. (Dough will be stiff.)

Divide dough into thirds (about 1 cup each). Add red cherries to one-third of dough; stir well. Press into prepared pan. Add chocolate and pecans to one-third of dough, and stir well. Press into pan over cherry layer. Add green cherries to remaining dough, and stir well. Press into pan over chocolate layer. Cover and chill dough at least 3 hours.

Invert pan, and remove dough. Cut dough in half lengthwise. Cut each section of dough crosswise into ⅛-inch slices. Place 1½ inches apart on ungreased cookie sheets. Bake at 350° for 10 to 12 minutes. Remove to wire racks to cool. Yield: 4½ dozen.

SWISS CINNAMON STARS

2 egg whites
1¼ cups sugar
1½ cups sliced unblanched almonds, ground
1½ tablespoons ground cinnamon
1 tablespoon lemon juice
2 tablespoons all-purpose flour
2 tablespoons sugar
1 cup sifted powdered sugar
2 tablespoons water

Beat egg whites (at room temperature) at high speed of an electric mixer 1 minute or until soft peaks form. Gradually add 1¼ cups sugar, 1 tablespoon at a time, beating until stiff peaks form and sugar dissolves (8 to 10 minutes).

Combine almonds, cinnamon, and lemon juice; stir well. Fold into egg whites; cover and chill at least 8 hours.

Combine flour and 2 tablespoons sugar; stir well. Sprinkle half of flour mixture over pastry cloth. Working with half of dough at a time (keep remaining dough chilled), roll each portion to ¼-inch thickness. Cut out with a 3-inch star-shaped cookie cutter, and place on lightly greased cookie sheets. Let cookies stand, uncovered, at room temperature 2 hours.

Combine 1 cup powdered sugar and 2 tablespoons water; stir until mixture is smooth. Set aside.

Bake cookies at 300° for 20 minutes; remove from oven. Brush top of each cookie gently with powdered sugar mixture; bake an additional 5 minutes. Remove to wire racks to cool. Store in an airtight container. Yield: 2 dozen.

A Fruit Wreath To Eat

You won't need a centerpiece on the buffet when you serve this recipe for Della Robbia Fruit Wreath from Waneta Tyler of Memphis, Tennessee. The fruit arrangement is attractive enough to serve as a side dish and adds a decorative touch to the table as well.

One of the biggest advantages to the recipe is that the ingredients are those you probably have on hand during the holiday season. "You don't have to go out and buy everything as you would for some recipes," says Waneta. She combines canned fruit, pecans, and green grapes and arranges them on a large tray to look like a Christmas wreath. Then it's served with commercial fruit dressing.

Waneta says she didn't realize what a hit her creation was until she served it several years ago at a holiday luncheon for her Memphis friends. "A lot of people asked me for the recipe, and then one friend asked me to fix it for a Christmas lunch she was having for out-of-town company," she says. "Since then I usually serve it sometime during the holidays each year."

DELLA ROBBIA FRUIT WREATH

¾ pound seedless green grapes
2 egg whites, slightly beaten
⅔ cup sugar
Curly endive
1 (15-ounce) can apricot halves, drained
1 (16-ounce) can peach halves, drained
1 (26-ounce) jar citrus salad, drained
1 (15¼-ounce) can pineapple slices, drained
1 cup pecan halves
10 maraschino cherries with stems
Commercial fruit salad dressing

Separate grapes into small clusters; place on a wire rack. Dip grapes in beaten egg whites. Sprinkle grapes with sugar, and allow to dry in a cool place. (Do not refrigerate.)

Place endive around rim of a large round serving plate; arrange grape clusters on endive. Arrange fruit between grape clusters. Place pecans and cherries evenly over fruit arrangement. Serve with salad dressing. Yield: 10 to 12 servings.

Holiday Baking Spices The Air

Many of us do a lot of baking all year long, but when December rolls around, the pace picks up and the rewards become pleasingly predictable. Recipes for cakes, pies, cookies, and sweet breads typically include such spices as cinnamon, ginger, cloves, and nutmeg, which fill the air with aromas as sweet as the desserts themselves. Chocolate and the grated rind and juice from citrus fruits also typify seasonal desserts and add to the sweet smells of Christmas.

Although any of these recipes can be baked year-round, several readers who submitted them wrote that they reserve them only for the holidays. "This is an old recipe carried down for generations in my family," explains Kathleen Stone of Houston about Spiced Christmas Cookies. "They have a wonderful flavor and delicious aroma when baking, and they make the whole house smell like Christmas."

Nancy Moore of Memphis is famous for her Eggnog Pie that she makes every year. She dresses it up with a wreath of whipped cream and sprinkles nutmeg and colorful candied fruit over the top. Her family knows it's Christmas when Nancy takes this selection from her recipe files.

If you're looking for some holiday-special sweets to prepare in the weeks ahead, try several of these recipes. We think you'll discover many favorites that may become part of your family's holiday traditions in the years to come.

CHOCOLATE-TIPPED LOG COOKIES

1 cup butter or margarine, softened
⅓ cup sugar
2 teaspoons brandy
2 teaspoons vanilla extract
¼ teaspoon salt
2 cups all-purpose flour
2 cups chopped pecans
Sifted powdered sugar
4 ounces chocolate-flavored candy coating, melted

Cream butter; gradually add sugar, beating until light and fluffy. Add brandy, vanilla, and salt, mixing well. Add flour, stirring until blended; stir in chopped pecans.

Shape dough into 1½- x ½-inch logs. Place 2 inches apart on ungreased cookie sheets. Bake at 325° for 15 to 20 minutes. Cookies should not brown. Remove to wire racks to cool.

Roll cookie logs lightly in powdered sugar while slightly warm. When cookies are completely cool, dip one end in melted candy coating. Let stand on wax paper until set. Yield: 4 dozen.

Grace Bravos,
Timonium, Maryland.

CRESCENT SUGAR COOKIES

1 cup butter or margarine
2 cups all-purpose flour
¾ cup commercial sour cream
1 egg yolk
¾ cup sugar
¾ cup chopped pecans
1 teaspoon ground cinnamon

Cut butter into flour with a pastry blender until mixture resembles coarse meal. Add sour cream and egg yolk, stirring until flour mixture is moistened. Cover and chill several hours.

Combine sugar, pecans, and cinnamon; set aside.

Divide dough into 5 equal portions. Roll each portion into an 8-inch circle; sprinkle with sugar mixture. Cut circle into eighths, using a sharp knife. Roll up each wedge, starting at wide end; seal points firmly. Place on ungreased cookie sheets, point side down. Bake at 350° for 25 minutes or until lightly browned. Remove to wire racks to cool. Yield: 40 cookies.

Beth Holcomb,
Charleston, West Virginia.

SPICED CHRISTMAS COOKIES
(pictured on cover)

¾ cup butter or margarine
1 cup firmly packed light brown sugar
1 cup sorghum or molasses
1 teaspoon ground allspice
1 teaspoon ground cinnamon
½ teaspoon ground cloves
½ teaspoon anise seeds
3⅔ cups all-purpose flour
1 teaspoon baking soda
½ teaspoon salt
Royal Icing
Decorator candies

Combine butter, brown sugar, sorghum, and spices in a large saucepan; bring to a boil. Remove from heat, and let cool. Cover and leave at room temperature 8 hours.

Combine flour, soda, and salt; stir flour mixture into syrup mixture. Chill several hours.

Divide dough into 4 portions. Work with 1 portion of dough at a time; cover and store remainder in refrigerator. Place dough on a lightly floured cookie sheet; roll to ⅛-inch thickness. Cut dough with a floured cookie cutter, leaving 1 to 2 inches between each cookie. Remove excess dough from cookie sheet.

Bake at 375° for 7 to 9 minutes. Remove to wire racks to cool. Repeat procedure with remaining dough. Decorate cookies as desired with Royal Icing and decorator candies. Yield: about 6 dozen 3-inch cookies.

Royal Icing:

3 egg whites
½ teaspoon cream of tartar
1 (16-ounce) package powdered sugar, sifted
½ teaspoon almond extract
Red and green paste food coloring (optional)

Combine egg whites (at room temperature) and cream of tartar in a large mixing bowl. Beat at medium speed of an electric mixer until frothy. Gradually add powdered sugar, mixing well. Add almond extract. Beat 5 to 7 minutes. Color icing with food coloring, if desired. (Icing dries very quickly; keep covered at all times with plastic wrap.) Yield: about 2 cups.

Note: Royal Icing dries very hard and is crunchy like candy.

Kathleen Stone,
Houston, Texas.

Pick either Eggnog Pie or Pumpkin Pie in Spiced Nut Crust to brighten your holiday dessert table.

EGGNOG PIE

1 envelope unflavored gelatin
¼ cup cold water
¾ cup sugar
1 tablespoon cornstarch
¼ teaspoon salt
2 eggs, separated
1½ cups milk
1 tablespoon plus 1 teaspoon vanilla extract
1 teaspoon ground nutmeg
1 baked 9-inch pastry shell
1 cup whipping cream, whipped
Diced candied fruit
Ground nutmeg

Soften gelatin in cold water; set aside.
Combine ¾ cup sugar, cornstarch, and salt in a heavy saucepan. Combine egg yolks and milk; beat well, and add to mixture in saucepan. Cook milk mixture over medium heat, stirring constantly, until mixture begins to boil; boil 1 minute. Remove from heat, and add

gelatin mixture; stir until gelatin granules dissolve. Stir in vanilla and 1 teaspoon nutmeg. Allow custard mixture to cool until the consistency of unbeaten egg white.

Beat egg whites (at room temperature) until soft peaks form; gradually add ¼ cup sugar, 1 tablespoon at a time, beating until stiff peaks form and sugar dissolves. Fold egg whites into custard. Pour filling into pastry shell; chill at least 8 hours.

Spoon whipped cream in a ring over pie. Arrange candied fruit on whipped cream; sprinkle lightly with nutmeg. Yield: one 9-inch pie. *Nancy Moore, Memphis, Tennessee.*

PUMPKIN PIE IN SPICED NUT CRUST
(pictured on cover)

1 (16-ounce) can pumpkin
1 (14-ounce) can sweetened condensed milk
2 eggs, beaten
1 teaspoon ground cinnamon
½ teaspoon ground ginger
½ teaspoon ground nutmeg
¼ teaspoon salt
Spiced Nut Crust

Combine all ingredients except Spiced Nut Crust; stir well. Pour into crust. Bake at 350° for 50 to 55 minutes or until set. Remove from oven; let cool. Yield: one 9-inch pie.

Spiced Nut Crust:

1 cup all-purpose flour
½ cup finely chopped pecans
¼ cup firmly packed light brown sugar
¼ cup plus 2 tablespoons butter or margarine, melted
½ teaspoon ground cinnamon
16 to 18 pecan halves

Combine all ingredients except pecan halves; stir well. Press onto bottom and sides of a 9-inch pieplate. Press pecan halves onto rim of crust at 1-inch intervals. Yield: one 9-inch pie shell.

Mrs. L. D. Howell,
Hendersonville, North Carolina.

Tip: Store spices in a cool place and away from any direct source of heat, as the heat will destroy their flavor. Red spices will maintain flavor and retain color longer if refrigerated.

COCONUT-SPICE CAKE

2½ cups all-purpose flour
1½ teaspoons baking soda
1 teaspoon salt
1½ cups sugar
1 teaspoon ground cinnamon
½ teaspoon ground allspice
½ teaspoon ground ginger
⅛ teaspoon ground nutmeg
1 cup chopped pecans
1 cup buttermilk
¾ cup butter or margarine,
   softened
3 eggs
2 tablespoons grated orange
   rind
½ cup orange juice
1 teaspoon orange extract
1 teaspoon vanilla extract
Seven-Minute Frosting
1 (3½-ounce) can flaked
   coconut
Pecan halves (optional)

Combine flour, soda, salt, sugar, cinnamon, allspice, ginger, nutmeg, and chopped pecans in a large mixing bowl; stir well. Make a well in center of mixture; add buttermilk, butter, eggs, orange rind, orange juice, and flavorings to dry ingredients. Beat mixture at low speed of an electric mixer about 30 seconds, scraping sides of bowl often. Beat mixture 3 minutes at high speed, scraping sides of bowl occasionally.

Pour batter into 3 greased and floured 9-inch round cakepans. Bake at 350° for 30 minutes or until a wooden pick inserted in center comes out clean. Cool in pans 10 minutes; remove layers from pans, and let cool completely on wire racks.

Spread Seven-Minute Frosting between layers and on top and sides of cake. Sprinkle top and sides with coconut; garnish with pecan halves, if desired. Yield: one 3-layer cake.

Seven-Minute Frosting:

1½ cups sugar
¼ cup plus 2 tablespoons water
2 egg whites
1 tablespoon light corn syrup
Dash of salt
1 teaspoon vanilla extract

Combine first 5 ingredients in top of a double boiler; beat at low speed of an electric mixer about 30 seconds or until blended. Place over boiling water; beat at high speed 7 minutes or until stiff peaks form. Remove from heat; add vanilla, and beat 1 minute or until frosting is thick enough to spread. Spread immediately on cooled cake. Yield: 5 cups.

Doris Curls,
Anniston, Alabama.

SPICED CARROT CAKE
(pictured on cover)

1 cup butter or margarine, softened
2 cups sugar
4 eggs
1½ cups finely grated carrots
⅔ cup chopped pecans
2½ cups all-purpose flour
1½ teaspoons baking soda
1 teaspoon baking powder
1 teaspoon ground cinnamon
1 teaspoon ground mace
½ teaspoon salt
⅓ cup water
½ cup commercial plum jam
Brown Sugar Frosting
Carrot curls (optional)
Pecan halves (optional)

Cream butter; gradually add sugar, beating well at medium speed of an electric mixer. Add eggs, one at a time, beating well after each addition. Stir in carrots and pecans.

Combine flour and next 5 ingredients; add to creamed mixture alternately with water, beginning and ending with flour mixture. Mix well after each addition.

Spoon batter into 3 greased and floured 9-inch round cakepans. Bake at 350° for 22 to 25 minutes or until a wooden pick inserted in center comes out clean. Cool in pans 10 minutes; remove layers from pans, and let cool completely on wire racks.

Spread jam between layers; spread Brown Sugar Frosting on top and sides of cake. Garnish with carrot curls and pecan halves, if desired. Yield: one 3-layer cake.

Brown Sugar Frosting:

1½ cups firmly packed brown sugar
½ cup water
⅛ teaspoon cream of tartar
3 egg whites
1 teaspoon vanilla extract
Pinch of salt

Combine first 3 ingredients in a medium-size heavy saucepan. Cook over medium heat, stirring frequently, until mixture comes to a boil and sugar dissolves. Continue cooking, stirring frequently, until mixture reaches soft ball stage (240°).

Beat egg whites (at room temperature) until foamy. While beating at medium speed of an electric mixer, slowly pour hot syrup in a thin stream over egg whites. Turn mixer to high speed, and continue beating until stiff peaks form and frosting is thick enough to spread. Add vanilla and salt; beat until blended. Yield: 6½ cups.

Mrs. Robert Bailey,
Knoxville, Tennessee.

CHOCOLATE POUND CAKE
WITH FUDGE FROSTING

1 cup butter, softened
½ cup shortening
3 cups sugar
5 eggs
3 cups sifted cake flour
¼ teaspoon baking powder
½ cup cocoa
1¼ cups milk
1 teaspoon vanilla extract
Fudge Frosting

Cream butter and shortening; gradually add sugar, beating well at medium speed of an electric mixer. Add eggs, one at a time, beating after each addition. Combine flour, baking powder, and cocoa; stir well. Add to creamed mixture alternately with milk, beginning and ending with flour mixture. Mix just until blended after each addition. Stir in vanilla.

Pour batter into a greased and floured 10-inch tube pan. Bake at 325° for 1 hour and 30 minutes or until a wooden pick inserted in center comes out clean. Cool in pan 10 minutes; remove from pan, and let cool completely on a wire rack. Spread Fudge Frosting on top and sides of cake. Yield: one 10-inch cake.

Fudge Frosting:

2 cups sugar
¼ cup cocoa
¼ teaspoon salt
⅔ cup milk
½ cup shortening
1 teaspoon vanilla extract

Combine all ingredients except vanilla in a heavy saucepan. Bring to a boil, stirring constantly; boil 2 minutes, stirring constantly. Remove from heat; pour into a small mixing bowl, and add vanilla. Beat at high speed of an electric mixer 5 minutes. Yield: 3 cups.

Mrs. James L. Twilley,
Macon, Georgia.

CHRISTMAS BREAD

2 cups boiling water
1 cup regular oats, uncooked
2 packages dry yeast
⅓ cup warm water (105° to 115°)
½ cup molasses
2 tablespoons butter or margarine,
   softened
2½ teaspoons salt
½ cup raisins
¼ cup chopped candied lemon peel
¼ cup chopped candied orange peel
5½ to 6 cups all-purpose flour

Pour 2 cups boiling water over oats in a large bowl; stir well. Set mixture aside 30 minutes.

Dissolve yeast in ⅓ cup warm water; let stand 5 minutes.

Add molasses, butter, salt, raisins, and candied peel to oats mixture. Stir in yeast mixture and 2 cups flour. Gradually stir in enough remaining flour to make a stiff dough.

Turn dough out onto a lightly floured surface, and knead until smooth and elastic (about 10 minutes); add extra flour as needed to keep dough from sticking. Place in a well-greased bowl, turning to coat top. Cover and let rise in a warm place (85°), free from drafts, 1½ hours or until doubled in bulk.

Punch dough down, and divide in half; place in two well-greased 8-inch cakepans or two 8½- x 4½- x 2½-inch loafpans. Cover and let rise in a warm place, free from drafts, 1 hour or until doubled in bulk.

Bake at 325° for 45 minutes or until loaves sound hollow when tapped. Cool on wire racks. Yield: 2 loaves.

Mrs. Delbert R. Snyder,
Williamsburg, Virginia.

FESTIVE BRAIDS
(pictured on cover)

2 packages dry yeast
½ cup warm water
   (105° to 115°)
1½ cups warm milk
   (105° to 115°)
1 cup sugar
2 teaspoons salt
2 teaspoons grated lemon rind
½ teaspoon ground mace
1 cup butter or margarine
8 cups all-purpose flour
2 eggs, beaten
1 cup raisins
½ cup slivered almonds, chopped
   and toasted
1 egg yolk
2 tablespoons water
1 cup sifted powdered sugar
2 tablespoons milk
Red and green candied cherries

Dissolve yeast in ½ cup warm water; let stand 5 minutes. Combine 1½ cups warm milk, sugar, salt, lemon rind, and mace; mix well.

Cut butter into flour with pastry blender in a large bowl until mixture resembles coarse meal.

Add yeast mixture and eggs to milk mixture, mixing well. Gradually stir into flour mixture, mixing well. Cover and let rise in a warm place (85°), free from drafts, 1 hour and 15 minutes or until doubled in bulk.

Punch dough down. Add raisins and almonds; knead until dough is smooth and elastic (about 8 to 10 minutes). Divide dough in half. Cover and set one half aside; divide other half into 4 portions. Roll each of 3 of the portions into 20-inch ropes, and place them side by side on a greased baking sheet; braid ropes. Tuck ends under to seal. Divide remaining fourth of dough in half; roll each half into a 15-inch rope. Twist ropes, and place lengthwise on top of braid, tucking ends under to seal. Repeat procedure with remaining half of dough. Cover and let rise in a warm place, free from drafts, 30 minutes or until doubled in bulk.

Beat egg yolk and 2 tablespoons water; gently brush over braids. Bake at 350° for 40 to 45 minutes or until braids sound hollow when tapped. Cool on wire racks. Combine powdered sugar and 2 tablespoons milk; stir well. Drizzle over braids; garnish with candied cherries. Yield: 2 braids.

Shirley Schlessmann,
Rockledge, Florida.

From Our Kitchen To Yours

Spices enhance the goodness of foods by lending fragrance, sweet or tangy flavor, and sometimes color. When skillfully added, spices complement and intensify flavor, providing an opportunity to reduce salt and sugar amounts.

Because personal tastes vary, use spices in small quantities so that you can become familiar with their flavors. When trying an unfamiliar one, use less than the specified amount; you can always add more. Try ¼ teaspoon for four servings (1 pound meat or 1 pint of sauce, soup, or vegetable).

As you plan menus, consider balance in seasonings. A little spice gives zest, but an excess is overpowering. If one recipe is heavily spiced, do not include the same seasoning or one of equal intensity in other foods.

Purchase and Store Properly

Once opened, spices begin to lose fragrance and sometimes color after three months. Purchase spices in small usable amounts; avoid buying spices displayed in open bins or bags.

Proper storage helps retain their flavor and aroma for up to six months. Protection from heat, moisture, and strong light is essential. Never display spices on open racks above or near cook tops, ovens, or dishwashers; heat dissipates their flavor. Store tightly sealed containers in a dark, cool, and dry place. In our test kitchens, infrequently used spices are kept in the freezer.

Check for Freshness

Check spices for freshness once a month, testing only three or four kinds at a time beginning with the more delicate scents. When you remove the lid from a spice container, a distinctive aroma should immediately be apparent. A change in color, a musty odor, or a faint aroma indicates that a spice is past its prime. Doubling the amount of a faint-hearted spice does not make it usable. (As a spice weakens, the character of the flavor changes.)

Grind Your Own

For maximum flavor and fragrance, purchase whole spices and grind them yourself. Crush small amounts using a spice mill, a mortar and pestle, a meat mallet, or a rolling pin. Grind large amounts in a coffee grinder, blender, or food processor. (Remember that a food processor is suitable only for spices that easily crumble.)

Tips

—Ground spices cloud liquids; for that reason, it's best to use whole spices in beverages and pickles.

—Tie whole spices in a small square of cheesecloth, or place in an aluminum tea ball so that they can easily be removed from soup, stew, or sauce.

—Substitute white pepper for black pepper in recipes in which black specks will mar the appearance of the food. Keep in mind that white pepper has a stronger aroma but less bite.

—Do not use a pepper mill for grinding other spices unless it is thoroughly washable.

—Ground spices immediately release flavor. Whole spices require a longer cooking time to release their full flavor and aroma.

—One whole nutmeg, grated, should yield about 1 tablespoon.

—One teaspoon ground ginger may be substituted for two tablespoons freshly grated gingerroot.

A tasty pineapple filling is hidden inside Christmas-Tree Coffee Cakes.

until doubled in bulk. Bake at 375° for 20 to 25 minutes. (Cover edges of rolls with aluminum foil to prevent over-browning, if necessary.)

Drizzle glaze over rolls while warm. Sprinkle with red and green sugar crystals. Garnish with candied cherries, if desired. Yield: 3 cakes.

Filling:

2 (8-ounce) cans crushed pineapple, drained
2 (8-ounce) packages cream cheese, softened
½ cup sugar
¼ teaspoon ground nutmeg
⅛ teaspoon salt

Place pineapple between paper towels to drain excess liquid. Combine cream cheese and remaining ingredients in a mixing bowl; beat at medium speed of an electric mixer until blended. Stir in pineapple. Yield: 3 cups.

Glaze:

2 cups sifted powdered sugar
3 tablespoons milk

Combine sugar and milk in a small bowl; beat at medium speed until blended. Yield: about 1 cup.

Coffee Cake For Christmas

Marian Parsons of Hurricane, West Virginia, decorates her Christmas-Tree Coffee Cakes with a sweet glaze, colored sugars, and candied cherries. Since the recipe makes three tree-shaped coffee cakes, you can bake one for yourself and give the others as gifts.

CHRISTMAS-TREE COFFEE CAKES

4 to 4½ cups all-purpose flour, divided
½ cup sugar
1½ teaspoons salt
2 packages dry yeast
¾ cup milk
½ cup water
½ cup butter or margarine
1 egg, slightly beaten
Filling (recipe follows)
Vegetable cooking spray
Glaze (recipe follows)
Red and green sugar crystals
Red and green candied cherries (optional)

Combine 2 cups flour, ½ cup sugar, salt, and yeast in a large mixing bowl; set mixture aside.

Combine milk, water, and butter in a small saucepan; heat to very warm. Add milk mixture to flour mixture; beat at medium speed of an electric mixer 2 minutes. Add egg and 1 cup remaining flour; beat at high speed 2 minutes, scraping bowl occasionally. Stir in enough flour to make a stiff batter. Cover bowl, and chill 8 hours.

Divide dough into 3 equal portions. Turn each portion out onto a lightly floured surface, and roll each into an 11- x 10-inch rectangle. Spread one-third of filling over each rectangle, leaving a ½-inch margin around edges. Carefully roll up, jellyroll fashion, beginning at long side. Cut each into 11 (1-inch) slices, using an electric knife. Arrange 10 slices on a greased baking sheet in a triangular shape. Center remaining slice at the base of triangle to complete Christmas-tree shape. Repeat procedure with remaining dough to make 2 additional cakes. Cover lightly with wax paper sprayed with vegetable cooking spray, and let rise in a warm place (85°), free from drafts, 1 hour or

Start With A Can Of Pie Filling

Our readers send us many recipes that use convenience products, and canned fruit pie filling is one ingredient that is frequently relied on for making simple desserts. You'll get a nice fruit flavor with this product, and there'll be no fresh fruit to peel and chop, and no fruit sauce to make. For these recipes, dessert's as simple as stirring up a few ingredients and opening a can.

PEACHY MELT-AWAY DESSERT

1 cup all-purpose flour
½ cup sugar
½ cup butter or margarine
1 teaspoon vanilla extract
2 (21-ounce) cans peach pie filling
4 egg whites
⅛ teaspoon cream of tartar
½ cup sugar
½ cup chopped pecans

Combine flour and ½ cup sugar; cut in butter with pastry blender until mixture resembles coarse meal. Stir in vanilla. Press mixture onto bottom of an ungreased 13- x 9- x 2-inch pan. Bake at 350° for 12 to 15 minutes. Cool.

Spread pie filling over crust. Beat egg whites (at room temperature) and cream of tartar until foamy. Gradually add ½ cup sugar, 1 tablespoon at a time, beating until stiff peaks form. Spread meringue over pie filling. Sprinkle with pecans. Bake at 350° for 30 minutes or until golden brown. Yield: 12 servings.
Cathy Darling,
Grafton, West Virginia.

CHOCOLATE-BLUEBERRY DESSERT SQUARES

1 (8½-ounce) package chocolate wafer cookies, crushed (about 2 cups)
½ cup butter or margarine, melted
2 egg whites
2 cups sifted powdered sugar
1 (8-ounce) package cream cheese, softened
1 (21-ounce) can blueberry pie filling
1 cup chopped pecans, divided
1½ cups whipping cream
3 tablespoons sugar
½ teaspoon vanilla extract
½ cup semisweet chocolate morsels
2 tablespoons milk

Combine cookie crumbs and butter, stirring well. Press mixture onto bottom of an ungreased 9-inch square pan. Bake at 350° for 10 minutes.

Beat egg whites (at room temperature) until foamy; gradually add powdered sugar, beating until blended. Add cream cheese; beat until smooth. Spread mixture over crust; top with pie filling, and sprinkle with ¾ cup pecans.

Beat whipping cream at high speed of an electric mixer until foamy; add sugar and vanilla, and beat until soft peaks form. Spread evenly over pie filling.

Combine chocolate morsels and milk in a small saucepan; cook over low heat until chocolate melts, stirring constantly. Drizzle chocolate mixture over whipped cream, and sprinkle with remaining ¼ cup pecans. Chill several hours. Yield: 9 servings.

Note: Cherry pie filling can be substituted for blueberry filling.
Joy Thomas,
Jackson, Mississippi.

Tip: Use baking soda on a damp cloth to shine up your kitchen appliances.

TART CRANBERRY-CHERRY PIE

1 (21-ounce) can cherry pie filling
1 (16-ounce) can whole-berry cranberry sauce
3 tablespoons quick-cooking tapioca
2 tablespoons sugar
1 teaspoon lemon juice
¼ teaspoon ground cinnamon
Double-crust pastry (recipe follows)
2 tablespoons butter or margarine
Milk

Combine pie filling, cranberry sauce, tapioca, sugar, lemon juice, and cinnamon; stir well. Let stand 15 minutes.

Roll 1 portion of double-crust pastry to ⅛-inch thickness on a lightly floured surface. Place in a 9-inch pieplate; trim off excess pastry along edges. Spoon cherry mixture into pastry shell. Dot with butter.

Roll remaining pastry to ⅛-inch thickness; cut into ½-inch strips. Arrange strips, lattice fashion, over cherry mixture. Trim strips even with edges; fold edges under, and flute. Brush pastry with milk. Bake at 400° for 40 to 45 minutes. Yield: one 9-inch pie.

Double-Crust Pastry:

2 cups all-purpose flour
½ teaspoon salt
½ cup shortening
4 to 5 tablespoons cold water

Combine flour and salt; cut in shortening with pastry blender until mixture resembles coarse meal. Sprinkle cold water (1 tablespoon at a time) evenly over surface; stir with a fork until dry ingredients are moistened. Divide dough in half; shape each half into a ball; chill. Yield: pastry for one double-crust pie.
Jana Dominguez,
Navasota, Texas.

HOT FRUIT DESSERT SAUCE

1 (20-ounce) can pineapple chunks, undrained
1 (21-ounce) can cherry pie filling
2 (11-ounce) cans mandarin oranges, drained
1 (6-ounce) package dried apricots
1 (12-ounce) package pitted prunes

Combine all ingredients; stir well. Spoon into a lightly greased 13- x 9- x 2-inch baking dish; cover with aluminum foil. Bake at 350° for 1 hour. Serve warm over ice cream or pound cake. Yield: 8 cups.
Paula Causey,
Byron, Georgia.

A Cheese-And-Date Delight

"The combination of cheese and dates is very nice," says Gloria Different of Harvey, Louisiana, when asked about her Nutty Date Dessert Cheese. A hint of rum and chopped dates adds just enough sweetness to end a holiday meal. Or it's perfect as a serve-yourself dessert for a cocktail buffet. You may want to complement the cheese with a glass of sherry for festive flair.

Though Gloria likes cheese-stuffed dates, her cheese spread combines the same delectable flavors, is easier to prepare, and is more versatile. It's also an excellent use for dates left over from holiday baking.

NUTTY DATE DESSERT CHEESE

⅔ cup walnuts
⅔ cup pitted dates
8 ounces sharp Cheddar cheese, cut into 1-inch pieces
1 (8-ounce) package cream cheese, softened and cut into 1-inch pieces
4 to 6 tablespoons rum
Ginger cookies
Apple and pear slices

Position knife blade in food processor bowl. Add walnuts; top with cover, and pulse 6 times or until coarsely chopped. Remove walnuts, and set aside.

Position knife blade in processor bowl; add chopped dates, and top with cover. Process 1 minute or until dates are chopped. Add Cheddar cheese, cream cheese, and rum; top with cover. Process 1 minute, scraping sides of processor bowl occasionally.

Line a shallow 7-inch container with plastic wrap, extending over edges. Spoon cheese mixture into mold, pressing firmly with the back of a spoon. Bring ends of plastic wrap over cheese mixture. Chill mixture at least 4 hours.

To serve, unmold cheese, and remove plastic wrap. Press walnuts on top and sides of cheese. Serve with commercial ginger cookies and apple and pear slices. Yield: one 2-cup cheese mold.

Breads For Now And Later

How convenient! Homemade breakfast breads to enjoy right after baking—plus an extra loaf, coffee cake, or batch of biscuits to stash in the freezer for later use. These breads are ideal to have on hand during the holidays for overnight guests or as a convenient treat for a special weekend breakfast—maybe even Christmas morning!

VIENNA BRIOCHE LOAVES

1 package dry yeast
½ cup warm water (105° to 115°)
¼ cup sugar
1 teaspoon salt
1 teaspoon grated lemon rind
1 cup butter, softened
6 eggs
4½ cups all-purpose flour, divided
3 tablespoons butter, softened
⅔ cup firmly packed light brown sugar
2 egg yolks, slightly beaten
2 tablespoons milk
¼ teaspoon vanilla extract
2 cups finely chopped pecans
Melted butter
Powdered sugar (optional)

Dissolve yeast in warm water; let stand 5 minutes. Combine yeast mixture, sugar, salt, lemon rind, 1 cup butter, eggs, and 3 cups flour in a large mixing bowl. Beat at low speed of an electric mixer until well blended; continue beating 4 minutes at medium speed. Add remaining 1½ cups flour; beat at low speed until flour is blended, about 2 minutes.

Cover with wax paper, and then with a damp towel; let rise in a warm place (85°), free from drafts, 1½ to 2 hours or until doubled in bulk. Refrigerate at least 8 hours.

Combine 3 tablespoons butter and next 4 ingredients in a medium bowl; stir until blended. Add pecans; mix well. Set aside.

Punch dough down; divide in half. Place half of dough on a floured surface; refrigerate unused portion. Roll dough into a 14- x 9-inch rectangle. Brush with melted butter. Spread with half of filling to within ½ inch from edges. Roll long ends up, jellyroll fashion, to center. Place in a greased 9- x 5- x 3-inch loafpan. Brush loaf with melted butter. Repeat process with remaining dough. Cover and let rise in a warm

place (85°), free from drafts, 1½ hours or until doubled in bulk. Bake at 350° for 35 minutes or until golden brown. Remove from pans, and place on wire racks. Sprinkle with powdered sugar, if desired. Yield: 2 loaves.

To freeze, bake loaves as directed; let cool. Wrap in foil, and freeze. To serve, let thaw. Reheat in foil at 250° for 10 to 15 minutes, if desired.

Kathleen L. Hayes,
Ballwin, Missouri.

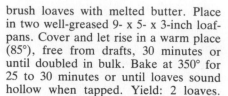

HOMEMADE RAISIN BREAD

2 packages dry yeast
½ cup warm water (105° to 115°)
3 tablespoons sugar
⅔ cup butter-flavored shortening
1⅓ cups milk
½ cup sugar
1½ teaspoons salt
6 to 6½ cups bread flour, divided
2 eggs, beaten
1 cup raisins
2 tablespoons butter or margarine, melted

Dissolve yeast in warm water; stir in 3 tablespoons sugar, and let stand 5 minutes. Combine shortening, milk, ½ cup sugar, and salt in a saucepan, and heat mixture until shortening melts; remove from heat. Let mixture cool to lukewarm (105° to 115°).

Combine yeast mixture, shortening mixture, 2 cups flour, and eggs in a large bowl; beat well at medium speed of an electric mixer. Gradually stir in enough remaining flour to make a soft dough.

Turn dough out onto a floured surface; add raisins, and knead until smooth and elastic (about 8 to 10 minutes). Place in a well-greased bowl, turning to grease top. Cover and let rise in a warm place (85°), free from drafts, 1 hour or until doubled in bulk.

Punch dough down, and divide in half; shape each half into a loaf. Gently

brush loaves with melted butter. Place in two well-greased 9- x 5- x 3-inch loafpans. Cover and let rise in a warm place (85°), free from drafts, 30 minutes or until doubled in bulk. Bake at 350° for 25 to 30 minutes or until loaves sound hollow when tapped. Yield: 2 loaves.

To freeze, bake loaves as directed; let cool. Wrap in foil, and freeze. To serve, let thaw; reheat in foil at 250° for 10 to 15 minutes.

Dee Buchfink,
Oologah, Oklahoma.

APPLESAUCE-HONEY NUT BREAD

2½ cups biscuit mix
1 cup quick-cooking oats, uncooked
2 teaspoons baking powder
½ teaspoon salt
1 egg, beaten
1 cup honey
1 cup applesauce
1 cup golden raisins
1 cup chopped walnuts

Combine first 4 ingredients; make a well in center of mixture. Combine egg, honey, and applesauce; add to dry ingredients, stirring just until moistened. Stir in raisins and walnuts.

Spoon batter into two greased and floured 7½- x 3½- x 2¼-inch loafpans. Bake at 350° for 45 to 50 minutes or until a wooden pick inserted in center comes out clean. Cool in pans 10 minutes; remove from pans, and cool completely on wire racks. Yield: 2 loaves.

To freeze, bake bread as directed; let cool. Wrap in foil, and freeze. To serve, let thaw, and slice. *Alida Garrison,*
Johnson City, Tennessee.

ORANGE-PUMPKIN BREAD

⅔ cup shortening
2⅔ cups sugar
4 eggs
3⅓ cups all-purpose flour
2 teaspoons baking soda
½ teaspoon baking powder
1½ teaspoons salt
1 teaspoon ground cinnamon
1 teaspoon ground cloves
1 (16-ounce) can pumpkin
⅔ cup water
¼ cup orange juice
⅔ cup chopped pecans
⅔ cup raisins
2 teaspoons grated orange rind

Cream shortening; gradually add sugar, beating well at medium speed of an electric mixer. Add eggs, one at a time, beating after each addition.

Combine flour and next 5 ingredients; add to creamed mixture alternately with pumpkin, beginning and ending with flour mixture. Add water and orange juice, mixing well. Stir in pecans, raisins, and orange rind. Spoon batter into two greased and floured 9- x 5- x 3-inch loafpans. Bake at 350° for 1 hour and 10 minutes or until a wooden pick inserted in center comes out clean. Cool in pans 10 minutes; remove from pans, and cool completely on wire racks. Yield: 2 loaves.

To freeze, bake bread as directed; let cool. Wrap in foil, and freeze. To serve, let thaw, and slice.

Romanza Johnson,
Bowling Green, Kentucky.

ALMOND DANISH

2 sticks (1 cup) butter, softened
2 packages dry yeast
½ cup warm water (105° to 115°)
⅓ cup sugar, divided
¾ cup milk
2 eggs
4¼ to 4¾ cups all-purpose flour, divided
1 teaspoon salt
Almond Filling, divided
1 egg, beaten
Sugar
¼ cup sliced almonds

Place 2 sticks butter 1 inch apart between 2 sheets of wax paper; roll into a 12-inch square. Place on a cookie sheet, and chill until ready to use.

Dissolve yeast in warm water in a large bowl; add ½ teaspoon sugar, and let stand 5 minutes. Add remaining sugar, milk, 2 eggs, 3 cups flour, and salt; beat at medium speed of an electric mixer 3 minutes. Stir in enough remaining flour to make a soft dough. Cover dough with plastic wrap, and chill 30 minutes.

Place dough on a lightly floured surface; roll into an 18- x 13-inch rectangle. Peel top sheet of wax paper from butter; place butter on one end of dough to cover two-thirds of dough. Peel off remaining wax paper from butter. Fold uncovered third of dough over middle third; fold remaining third over middle third. Turn dough clockwise so that the open end is away from you. Roll dough into a 24- x 12-inch rectangle. Fold ends to center; then fold dough in half. Turn dough so that the open side is away from you. Repeat

rolling and folding procedure twice; cover and chill dough at least 1 hour.

Divide dough in half. Place half of dough on a lightly floured surface; refrigerate unused portion. Roll dough into a 30- x 9-inch rectangle. Cut lengthwise into 3 strips. Spread about ¼ cup of Almond Filling evenly down center of each strip. Fold edges of strips over filling, and seal. Place 3 ropes, side by side, on a large ungreased baking sheet; braid. Join ends of dough to make a 9-inch ring. Repeat procedure with remaining dough and filling. Let rise in a warm place (85°), free from drafts, 45 minutes or until doubled in bulk. Brush with beaten egg; sprinkle with sugar and almonds. Bake at 350° for 25 to 30 minutes or until golden. Cool coffee cakes on wire racks. Yield: 2 coffee cakes.

Almond Filling:

1 (8-ounce) can almond paste, crumbled
½ cup butter or margarine, softened
½ cup sugar

Combine all ingredients in a bowl; beat at medium speed of an electric mixer until mixture is well blended. Yield: 1⅔ cups.

To freeze, bake coffee cakes as directed; let cool. Wrap in foil, and freeze. To serve, let thaw; reheat in foil at 350° for 15 to 20 minutes.

Sandra G. Souther,
Gainesville, Georgia.

YEAST BISCUITS

5 cups all-purpose flour
1 tablespoon baking powder
1 teaspoon baking soda
1½ teaspoons salt
¼ cup sugar
1 cup butter-flavored shortening
1 package dry yeast
¼ cup warm water (105° to 115°)
2 cups buttermilk

Combine first 5 ingredients in a large bowl, mixing well. Cut in shortening with a pastry blender until mixture resembles coarse meal.

Dissolve yeast in warm water; let stand 5 minutes. Add yeast mixture and buttermilk to flour mixture, stirring just until dry ingredients are moistened. Turn dough out onto a lightly floured surface, and knead lightly 10 times.

Roll dough to ½-inch thickness; cut with a 2-inch biscuit cutter. Place on ungreased baking sheets; cover and let

rise in a warm place (85°), free from drafts, 45 minutes.

Bake at 425° for 10 to 12 minutes. Yield: about 3 dozen.

To freeze, bake biscuits at 425° for 5 minutes; cool. Wrap in foil, and freeze. To serve, place biscuits on lightly greased baking sheets, and thaw. Bake at 425° for 5 to 6 minutes.

Betty Marshall,
Barboursville, Virginia.

Leftover Turkey For Company

Want a new idea for serving leftover turkey? Marcia Felts of Valdosta, Georgia, has a tasty recipe. She uses refrigerated crescent roll dough to enclose a chopped turkey-and-cream cheese filling. With this dish, she often serves a green salad and fresh fruit for a quick luncheon.

TURKEY-CHEESE PUFFS

1 (3-ounce) package cream cheese, softened
2 tablespoons butter or margarine, softened
2 tablespoons milk
2 cups chopped cooked turkey
⅛ teaspoon pepper
1 (8-ounce) can refrigerated crescent dinner rolls

Combine cream cheese and butter; beat on medium speed of an electric mixer until smooth. Add milk; beat until smooth. Stir in turkey and pepper.

Unroll dough, and separate into 4 rectangles; press perforations to seal. Spoon ½ cup turkey mixture in center of each dough rectangle. Moisten edges of each rectangle with water; bring the 4 corners to the center over filling, pinching edges to seal. Place on an ungreased baking sheet. Bake at 350° for 20 to 25 minutes or until puffs are golden. Yield: 4 servings.

Promote Even Cooking With Foil

You may never have considered using aluminum foil in a microwave. Foil is frequently overlooked as a microwave accessory because we're warned against using foil containers in the microwave. However, small pieces of foil used as shields can promote even cooking.

Food in the corners of square and rectangular dishes absorbs microwave energy from more angles and cooks quicker than the food in the center. Smooth triangles of single-layer foil placed around the corners of the dish reflect microwaves to prevent overcooking the food.

A casserole that can't be stirred or food cooked in a round dish, such as pie and quiche, also benefits from the use of foil shields. To prevent the outer edges from getting done before the center, cover the edges with a 3-inch band of foil during the first 5 minutes of cooking time.

Our Tangy Herbed Chicken is a good example of how irregular-shaped foods benefit from shielding. Cover protruding angles and edges to prevent overcooking and uneven defrosting. Use patches of foil to cover any area on a roast, chicken, or turkey that appears to be drying out or overcooking, or feels warm during defrosting. Prevent overcooking the ends of long, narrow pieces of meat, such as pork or beef tenderloins and eye of round, by covering the ends with aluminum foil.

Foil is also used to insulate food, keeping it warm during standing time or while the rest of the meal cooks.

Safe use of foil in the microwave depends on the structural design of each oven. Check the manufacturer's handbook for specific recommendations for your oven. The following simple guidelines also ensure safe use of the microwave oven:

—Always position food so that foil is at least 1 inch from oven walls.

—Remember that wrinkles in the aluminum foil can cause sparks; for that reason, it is important to handle foil carefully.

—Keep in mind that foil shields should fit close to the food and be snug against the dish.

—When shielding meats and poultry, use small pieces of foil, leaving two-thirds of the meat exposed.

CHICKEN LASAGNA

4 chicken breast halves
1½ cups water
6 lasagna noodles
1 (10¾-ounce) can cream of mushroom soup, undiluted
1 cup cream-style cottage cheese
2 (3-ounce) packages cream cheese, cubed
⅔ cup milk
1 teaspoon Worcestershire sauce
½ teaspoon poultry seasoning
½ teaspoon salt
¼ cup thinly sliced green onions
⅓ cup diced green pepper
½ cup diced celery
⅓ cup sliced pimiento-stuffed olives
1 cup soft breadcrumbs
2 tablespoons butter or margarine, melted
¼ cup minced fresh parsley

Arrange chicken breasts in a 12- x 8- x 2-inch baking dish, placing meatier portions to outside of dish. Add water, and cover with heavy-duty plastic wrap. Microwave at HIGH 12 to 18 minutes, giving dish a half-turn after 6 minutes. Cool chicken; cut into bite-size pieces. Set aside.

Cook noodles according to package directions; set aside.

Combine soup and next 10 ingredients in a 2-quart glass bowl; stir well. Microwave at HIGH 3 to 5 minutes or until heated, stirring once.

Place 3 noodles in a greased 12- x 8- x 2-inch baking dish. Layer half each of chicken pieces and soup mixture over noodles; repeat layers. Shield corners of baking dish with triangles of foil, keeping foil smooth and close to dish. Cover with heavy-duty plastic wrap. Microwave at MEDIUM HIGH (70% power) 5 to 6 minutes. Remove plastic wrap.

Combine breadcrumbs, butter, and parsley; sprinkle over top of casserole. Cover with plastic wrap, and microwave at MEDIUM HIGH 5 to 6 minutes. Let stand 10 minutes before serving. Yield: 6 servings.

TANGY HERBED CHICKEN

1 (3½-pound) frozen broiler-fryer
¼ cup butter or margarine
2 tablespoons red wine vinegar
1 tablespoon Worcestershire sauce
1½ teaspoons dried whole thyme
1½ teaspoons dried whole rosemary, crushed
½ teaspoon salt
½ teaspoon pepper
1 small onion, quartered
1 stalk celery, quartered

To thaw, unwrap chicken, and place, breast side down, on a microwave roasting rack in a 12- x 8- x 2-inch baking dish. Microwave at MEDIUM LOW (30% power) 10 minutes. Turn chicken, breast side up; shield wingtips, tail, and ends of legs with foil. Microwave chicken at MEDIUM LOW 10 minutes or until chicken is soft but still very cold. Run cold water inside chicken until giblets can be removed; reserve giblets for other uses. Rinse chicken cavity with cold water until chicken is no longer icy. Pat dry.

Place butter in a 1-cup glass measure. Microwave at HIGH 55 seconds or until melted. Add vinegar and next 5 ingredients. Loosen skin on chicken breast. Spoon half of butter mixture under skin. Place chicken, breast side down, on rack. Stuff onion and celery into body cavity of chicken; pour in remaining butter mixture.

Microwave at MEDIUM HIGH (70% power) 10 to 15 minutes. Turn chicken, breast side up; baste chicken with pan drippings. Shield wingtips, tail, and ends of legs with foil.

Microwave at MEDIUM HIGH 20 minutes or until microwave meat thermometer reaches 185°, or drumsticks are easy to move, giving dish a half-turn and basting once. Cover chicken with aluminum foil, and let stand 10 minutes. Yield: 4 servings.

QUICK BROWNIES

½ cup chopped pecans
2 (1-ounce) squares unsweetened chocolate
½ cup butter or margarine, cut into 4 pieces
1 teaspoon instant coffee granules
1 cup firmly packed light brown sugar
2 eggs, beaten
1 teaspoon vanilla extract
⅔ cup all-purpose flour
½ teaspoon baking powder
Frosting (recipe follows)

Spread chopped pecans in a pieplate. Microwave at HIGH 3 to 3½ minutes. Set aside.

Place chocolate and butter in a microwave-safe glass bowl. Microwave at MEDIUM (50% power) 2½ minutes or until chocolate melts, stirring at 1-minute intervals. Stir in coffee granules. Add sugar, and stir until blended. Add eggs and vanilla, mixing well. Stir in pecans, flour, and baking powder.

Spread mixture into a greased and floured 8-inch square baking dish; shield corners with triangles of aluminum foil, keeping foil smooth and close to dish. Place dish on top of a microwave-safe cereal bowl inverted in oven.

Microwave at MEDIUM 8 minutes, giving dish a quarter-turn at 4-minute intervals. Remove foil.

Microwave at HIGH 1 to 2 minutes or until a wooden pick inserted in center comes out clean. Place directly on counter, and let stand 20 minutes. Spread frosting over brownies. Cut into squares, and immediately remove from dish. Yield: 16 brownies.

Frosting:

1 (1-ounce) square unsweetened chocolate
1 tablespoon butter or margarine
1 cup sifted powdered sugar
Dash of ground cinnamon
Dash of salt
1 to 2 tablespoons milk
½ teaspoon vanilla extract

Place chocolate and butter in a small microwave-safe bowl. Microwave at MEDIUM (50% power) 1½ to 2 minutes or until chocolate melts, stirring at 1-minute intervals. Stir in powdered sugar, cinnamon, and salt. Add milk and vanilla, stirring until mixture is smooth. Yield: ½ cup.

He's A Serious Chili Cook

When Tom Tyler of Mesquite, Texas, cooks a pot of chili, there is nothing haphazard about it. You might say he's a serious chili cook—so serious that he spends up to 40 weekends each year preparing his famous North Texas Red Chili and traveling hundreds of miles just to do so.

During the past seven years he's been cooking chili, Tom and his wife, Linda, have traveled all over the United States and even to Canada to participate in cookoffs. Besides winning numerous contests throughout Texas, he's won first place in the Louisiana State Chili Cookoff twice and even accumulated enough official points from his cookoff winnings to earn invitations to the World Championship Chili Cookoff in Terlingua, Texas.

You would think that after cooking chili every weekend, Tom would opt for something different when he's at home. But he says that chili is on the Tyler menu about two or three times a month. The recipe he prepares at home is a little different from the one he carries to contests. "I use all fresh ingredients at home," he says. "At contests, you can never be sure of the type of produce that will be available where you're going, so I take dried versions of some ingredients, such as garlic and onions, with me."

Having entered more than 200 contests, Tom says when he's in competition, he cooks to meet the judges' specifications and still produce his award-winning flavor. "When they're judging the chili," he explains, "they don't want to see pieces of anything but meat in there, including onions and peppers. It should look like just a mixture of spices in a good gravy sauce with no beans. One of the rules is that there are no beans allowed in it. Beans are considered a side dish to people who eat chili."

But chili isn't Tom's only specialty. "I cook pinto beans and have placed in a few bean cookoffs," he says. "One of the secrets to beans is not to stir them too much and to use a good base of flavoring like bacon or ham hocks."

There's a secret to cooking good chili, Tom claims. "Good meat and good spices are what make a good chili," he says. "I use a cut of beef called chuck tender, which comes from near the chuck roast. A chuck roast will work just fine; just remove the gristle and fat. And then you've got to use fresh chili powder."

The recipe for Tom's North Texas Red Chili, and some of his other favorites are featured here.

NORTH TEXAS RED CHILI

2½ pounds boneless chuck roast, diced
1 tablespoon vegetable shortening, melted
4 cups water
¼ cup diced onion
1 teaspoon garlic powder
1 teaspoon salt
¼ teaspoon red pepper
4 whole jalapeño peppers
2 to 3 tablespoons chili powder
2 teaspoons ground cumin
¼ teaspoon ground oregano
⅛ teaspoon ground bay leaf
2 beef-flavored bouillon cubes
1 (8-ounce) can tomato sauce
2 to 3 tablespoons chili powder
2 teaspoons ground cumin
¼ teaspoon red pepper
1 teaspoon garlic powder

Brown meat in shortening in a Dutch oven. Add water, onion, 1 teaspoon garlic powder, salt, red pepper, and jalapeño peppers. Bring to a boil and simmer, uncovered, 1 hour. Add water as needed to keep liquid ½ inch above meat throughout cooking procedure. Remove jalapeño peppers, and strain liquid from peppers; discard peppers. Add pepper liquid, 2 to 3 tablespoons chili powder and next 5 ingredients; stir well. Simmer, uncovered, 1 hour and 45 minutes. Add 2 to 3 tablespoons chili powder and remaining ingredients and simmer about 15 minutes. Yield: about 6½ cups.

HOME-STYLE BRISKET

½ cup dry barbecue spice
2 tablespoons season-all
2 tablespoons salt-free seasoning
2 tablespoons paprika
1 teaspoon pepper
1 (8- to 10-pound) untrimmed beef brisket
Hickory or pecan chips

Combine first 5 ingredients; rub on brisket on all sides. Wrap in aluminum foil, and chill 24 hours.

Soak hickory or pecan chips in water 1 to 2 hours. Prepare charcoal fire in smoker; let burn 10 to 15 minutes or until flames disappear. Add 6 to 8 pieces of soaked hickory chips to coals.

Place water pan in smoker, and fill with hot water. Remove brisket from foil, and place on rack. Cover with smoker lid, and cook 8 to 10 hours or until tender. Yield: 12 to 14 servings.

PINTO BEANS

2 pounds dried pinto beans
3 tablespoons bacon drippings
4 slices bacon, cut into ½-inch pieces
¼ teaspoon red pepper
½ teaspoon garlic powder
1 teaspoon paprika
¼ teaspoon black pepper
2 teaspoons salt
7 cups water

Sort and wash beans; place in a large Dutch oven. Cover with water 2 inches above beans; let soak 8 hours. Drain.

Combine beans and remaining ingredients in a large Dutch oven. Bring to a boil; cover, reduce heat, and simmer 2½ to 3 hours or until tender, stirring occasionally. Yield: 12 cups.

It's Time For Venison

It's safe to say that venison fills the freezers of many New Braunfels, Texas, residents this time of year, claims Ann Temple Kuehler. "It's very traditional for the men in New Braunfels to go deer hunting and come back and make sausage," she says.

Ann and her husband, Kenneth, usually have fresh sausage, dry sausage, ground venison, steaks, and roasts on hand to use for family meals when the deer season ends. Ann admits that coming up with new ways to serve venison is a challenge. In the recipes here, she shares some of her family's favorites.

VENISON CHILI

6 slices bacon, cut into ½-inch pieces
2 pounds ground venison
1 large onion, chopped
3 cups water
1 (28-ounce) can tomatoes, undrained and chopped
1 tablespoon chili powder
1 teaspoon pepper
1 teaspoon salt
1 teaspoon ground cumin
1 teaspoon garlic powder
1 (16-ounce) can kidney beans, undrained

Cook bacon in Dutch oven until crisp; remove bacon with a slotted spoon, reserving drippings in Dutch oven. Set bacon aside. Add venison and

Serve Venison Chili with toppings of sour cream, green onions, and cheese.

onion to Dutch oven. Cook over medium heat until meat is browned, stirring to crumble. Drain off pan drippings; add bacon, water, and next 6 ingredients. Bring to a boil. Cover, reduce heat, and simmer 1 hour, stirring occasionally. Add beans; cover and cook an additional 30 minutes. Serve with sour cream, green onions, and cheese, if desired. Yield: 2½ quarts.

VENISON BURGERS

1 pound ground beef
1 pound smoked venison sausage
2 to 3 tablespoons lemon-pepper seasoning
Toasted hamburger buns

Combine ground beef, sausage, and seasoning; mix well. Shape into 8 patties about ¾ inch thick. Place patties on a broiler rack. Broil 4 or 5 inches from heat 5 minutes, turning once. Serve on toasted buns. Yield: 8 servings.

Note: Smoked beef sausage may be substituted for smoked venison sausage, if desired.

VENISON STEW WITH POTATO DUMPLINGS

¼ cup shortening
¼ cup all-purpose flour
1½ teaspoons salt
1 (10½-ounce) can beef broth, undiluted
5 cups water
2 tablespoons lemon juice
1 medium onion, sliced
2 cloves
1 bay leaf
3 pounds venison stew meat, cut in 1½-inch pieces
½ cup Burgundy (optional)
2 pounds potatoes, peeled
4 slices white bread
1 teaspoon salt
1 tablespoon grated onion
1 teaspoon parsley flakes
2 eggs, well beaten
All-purpose flour

Melt shortening in a large Dutch oven over low heat; add flour, stirring until roux is the color of caramel. Add 1½ teaspoons salt and next 6 ingredients; boil 5 minutes. Add venison; cover, reduce heat, and simmer 2 hours. Add Burgundy, if desired.

Shred potatoes; drain well. Remove crust from bread, and discard; tear bread into 1-inch pieces. Combine bread, potatoes, 1 teaspoon salt, 1 tablespoon onion, parsley, and eggs. Shape into 2-inch balls. Roll balls lightly in flour.

Drop dumplings into simmering stew. Cover and cook over low heat 20 minutes or until dumplings are done. Remove bay leaf. Yield: 8 servings.

VENISON-VEGETABLE BAKE

2 pounds smoked venison sausage
1 small onion, thinly sliced
1 (14½-ounce) can stewed tomatoes
1 teaspoon dried whole oregano
¼ teaspoon pepper
4 medium potatoes, thinly sliced
4 medium carrots, thinly sliced

Remove casing from sausage, and discard. Brown meat in a large, lightly greased skillet over medium heat, stirring to crumble. Remove sausage, and drain well, reserving drippings in skillet. Sauté onion in drippings; drain well, and discard drippings. Combine onion, tomatoes, oregano, and pepper in skillet. Simmer until thoroughly heated; remove from heat.

Arrange potatoes in a lightly greased 13- x 9- x 2-inch baking dish. Top with carrots. Sprinkle sausage over carrots; spoon tomato mixture over sausage.

Cover with aluminum foil. Bake at 350° for 45 minutes. Yield: 8 servings.

Note: Thinly sliced Polish sausage may be substituted for venison sausages, if desired.

Enjoy A Candlelight Dinner For Two

If you're caught up in a whirlwind of holiday celebrations and activities, you may welcome a quiet dinner for two. And if you're trying to resist the numerous calorie-laden temptations that often accompany festive get-togethers, you'll be glad to know that this menu is less than 500 calories per person. What's more, you can prepare it quickly, and without a lot of fuss.

Our menu begins with Italian Beef Medallions. It features eye of round that's lightly dredged in flour and Parmesan cheese. White wine tenderizes the meat during cooking and adds a delightful flavor and aroma. Although wine itself is high in calories, it's a popular ingredient in many low-calorie recipes. That's because the alcohol and most of the wine's calories evaporate during the cooking.

Rounding out the menu are two tasty side dishes and a salad, followed by a memorable dessert. So set the table, dim the lights, and light the candles—make the evening one to remember.

Italian Beef Medallions
Browned Rice Pilaf
Cauliflower-Snow Pea Medley
Spinach-Kiwifruit Salad
Tangy Cranberry Ice
Coffee

ITALIAN BEEF MEDALLIONS
(pictured on pages 308 and 309)

½ pound lean eye of round, cut into 4 (¼-inch-thick) medallions, well trimmed
1½ tablespoons all-purpose flour
1½ tablespoons grated Parmesan cheese
¼ teaspoon Italian seasoning
¼ teaspoon garlic powder
⅛ teaspoon pepper
Vegetable cooking spray
⅓ cup green pepper strips
2 green onions, cut into ½-inch slices
¼ cup Chablis or other dry white wine
¼ cup water
½ teaspoon beef-flavored bouillon granules
1 teaspoon lemon juice

Place meat between 2 sheets of heavy-duty plastic wrap, and flatten to ⅛-inch thickness using a meat mallet or rolling pin; set aside.
Combine flour, Parmesan cheese, Italian seasoning, garlic powder, and pepper; dredge meat in flour mixture. Coat a large nonstick skillet with vegetable cooking spray; heat over medium-high heat until hot. Add meat; cook 2 minutes, uncovered, on each side or until lightly browned. Remove meat from skillet; set aside. Add green pepper and green onions; sauté 1 minute.

Combine remaining ingredients; add to skillet, and bring to a boil over medium heat. Return meat to skillet. Cover, reduce heat, and simmer 10 to 15 minutes, turning once. Add water, 1 tablespoon at a time, to prevent sticking, if necessary. To serve, spoon vegetables over meat. Yield: 2 servings.

☐ *168 calories, 21.2 grams protein, 5.3 grams fat, 7.9 grams carbohydrate, 49 milligrams cholesterol, 354 milligrams sodium, and 74 milligrams calcium per 3 ounces meat and vegetables.*

BROWNED RICE PILAF
(pictured on pages 308 and 309)

Vegetable cooking spray
¼ cup uncooked long-grain rice
1 small clove garlic, minced
⅛ teaspoon dried whole oregano
⅛ teaspoon dried whole thyme
⅛ teaspoon salt
¾ cup water
2 tablespoons diced carrot
2 tablespoons diced sweet red pepper

Coat a medium saucepan with cooking spray; place over medium-high heat until hot. Add rice and garlic; sauté 3 minutes or until rice is lightly browned, stirring often. Add oregano and next 3 ingredients; stir well. Cover, reduce heat, and simmer 15 minutes. Add carrot and red pepper; toss gently. Cover and cook an additional 5 minutes or until liquid is absorbed and rice is tender. Yield: 2 servings.

☐ *96 calories, 1.8 grams protein, 0.6 gram fat, 20.4 grams carbohydrate, 0 milligrams cholesterol, 157 milligrams sodium, and 15 milligrams calcium per ½-cup serving.*

CAULIFLOWER-SNOW PEA MEDLEY
(pictured on pages 308 and 309)

½ teaspoon chicken-flavored bouillon granules
¼ teaspoon dried whole basil
⅓ cup water
1 cup cauliflower flowerets
¼ pound fresh snow pea pods (about 34), trimmed

Combine first 3 ingredients in a medium saucepan; bring to a boil over medium heat. Add cauliflower; cover and cook 5 minutes. Add snow pea pods; cover and cook an additional 5 minutes. Yield: 2 servings.

☐ *43 calories, 2.9 grams protein, 0.3 gram fat, 7.8 grams carbohydrate, 0 milligrams cholesterol, 212 milligrams sodium, and 46 milligrams calcium per 1-cup serving.*

SPINACH-KIWIFRUIT SALAD
(pictured on pages 308 and 309)

8 spinach leaves
8 Boston lettuce leaves
1 kiwifruit, peeled and sliced
Lemon rind curls (optional)
Sweet-and-Sour Dressing

Arrange salad greens on a platter. Top with kiwifruit. Garnish with lemon rind curls, if desired. Serve with Sweet-and-Sour Dressing. Yield: 2 servings.

Sweet-and-Sour Dressing:

2 teaspoons honey
1 teaspoon prepared mustard
⅛ teaspoon onion powder
½ teaspoon lemon juice
3 tablespoons water
2 tablespoons rice vinegar
1½ teaspoons vegetable oil

Combine all ingredients in a jar. Cover tightly, and shake vigorously. Cover and chill. Yield: ⅓ cup.

☐ *29 calories, 1.3 grams protein, 0.4 gram fat, 5.6 grams carbohydrate, 0 milligrams cholesterol, 13 milligrams sodium, and 24 milligrams calcium per serving plus 21 calories, 0.1 gram protein, 1.3 grams fat, 2.7 grams carbohydrate, 0 milligrams cholesterol, 12.5 milligrams sodium, and 1.5 milligrams calcium per tablespoon dressing.*

TANGY CRANBERRY ICE

1 cup cranberry juice cocktail
½ teaspoon grated orange rind
½ cup unsweetened orange juice
2 thin orange slices (optional)

Combine first 3 ingredients; stir well, and pour into a freezer tray. Freeze until firm. Spoon frozen mixture into small mixing bowl; beat at low speed of an electric mixer until smooth. Spoon into chilled individual freezer-proof compotes; freeze until ready to serve. Garnish with orange slices, if desired. Yield: 2 servings.

☐ *103 calories, 0.5 gram protein, 0.1 gram fat, 26.1 grams carbohydrate, 0 milligrams cholesterol, 6 milligrams sodium, and 10 milligrams calcium per 1-cup serving.*

Entrées With Flair

For some families, decisions about Christmas dinner are as difficult as selecting the tree or the perfect gift for someone special. We're offering a choice of three special entrées ranging from the traditional turkey to beef tenderloin with a flavorful sauce.

A good choice of entrées when serving four is Apricot-Glazed Cornish Hens. The recipe may easily be doubled to serve eight.

APRICOT-GLAZED CORNISH HENS
(pictured on page 307)

¾ cup apricot preserves
2 teaspoons grated orange rind
2 tablespoons orange juice
4 (1- to 1¼-pound) Cornish hens
¼ teaspoon paprika
½ cup cashews
2 tablespoons butter or margarine, melted
½ cup sliced green onions
1 (6-ounce) package long grain and wild rice mix
2⅓ cups chicken broth
Dried-apricot roses (optional)
Spinach leaves (optional)

Combine apricot preserves, orange rind, and orange juice; set aside.

Remove giblets from hens; reserve for other uses. Rinse hens with cold water, and pat dry. Close cavities, and secure with wooden picks; truss. Sprinkle with paprika. Place hens, breast side up, in a lightly greased roasting pan. Bake at 350° for 1¼ to 1½ hours, basting frequently with about ½ cup apricot mixture during the last 30 minutes.

Sauté cashews in butter in a large skillet until cashews are golden. Drain cashews, and set aside, reserving butter in skillet. Sauté green onions in same skillet until tender. Add rice mix, and prepare according to package directions, substituting chicken broth for water and omitting salt.

Arrange cornish hens on serving platter; brush with remaining apricot mixture. Garnish with apricot roses and spinach leaves, if desired, and serve with rice. Yield: 4 servings.

Note: To make apricot roses for garnishing, use a rolling pin to flatten 4 or 5 dried apricots for each rose. Wrap apricots around each other, shaping them to resemble a rose; pinch stem end to make them adhere.

Clairiece Gilbert Humphrey,
Charlottesville, Virginia.

FAST-AND-SAVORY TURKEY

Vegetable cooking spray
1 (10- to 12-pound) turkey
2 teaspoons salt
2 teaspoons lemon-pepper seasoning
1 medium onion
Fresh parsley sprigs
1 teaspoon dried whole rosemary
1 carrot, sliced
1 celery stalk, sliced
1 large onion, sliced
1 teaspoon dried whole rosemary
1 cup dry white wine
½ cup brandy or cognac
1½ cups chicken broth
½ cup tomato juice
¼ cup cornstarch
¼ cup whipping cream
1 teaspoon browning-and-seasoning sauce

Line a large roasting pan with heavy-duty aluminum foil, leaving 3 inches overhang on all sides. Spray foil with vegetable cooking spray. Set aside.

Remove giblets and neck from turkey; set aside. Rinse turkey with cold water; pat dry. Sprinkle cavities with salt and lemon-pepper seasoning. Place medium onion into neck cavity; fold wings under back, and pull neck skin under wings.

Place a handful of parsley and 1 teaspoon rosemary into other cavity. Tie ends of legs to tail with cord. Place turkey in prepared pan, breast side up; arrange carrot, celery, 1 large sliced onion, 1 teaspoon rosemary, and reserved giblets and neck around turkey.

Combine wine and brandy in a saucepan; cook over low heat until thoroughly heated. (Do not boil.) Pour mixture into cavity and over turkey.

Combine chicken broth and tomato juice in a saucepan; cook over medium heat until thoroughly heated. Pour mixture over turkey. Insert meat thermometer into meaty part of thigh, making sure it does not touch bone. Cover turkey with a sheet of heavy-duty aluminum foil. Fold edges of top and bottom pieces of foil together, and crimp edges to seal, making sure it is airtight. (Do not let foil touch turkey.) Bake at 425° for 1 hour on lowest rack of oven.

Remove roasting pan from oven, and cut top of foil lengthwise. Open foil, folding sides back. Reduce heat to 400°, and bake turkey 1 hour and 15 minutes or until meat thermometer registers 185°. (Do not baste turkey.)

Remove turkey; strain drippings, reserving 4 cups. Place 4 cups drippings in a saucepan. Combine cornstarch and whipping cream, stirring until smooth. Gradually stir cornstarch mixture into drippings; bring to a boil, and cook 1 minute or until thickened, stirring constantly. Stir in 1 teaspoon browning-and-seasoning sauce. Serve gravy with turkey. Yield: 10 to 12 servings.

Ursula Knaeusel,
Atlanta, Georgia.

BEEF TENDERLOIN WITH MUSHROOM-SHERRY SAUCE

1 pound fresh mushrooms, sliced
3 tablespoons butter or margarine, melted
1 (5- to 6-pound) beef tenderloin
2 teaspoons lemon-pepper seasoning
1 cup dry sherry

Sauté mushrooms in butter until tender; set aside.

Trim excess fat from tenderloin. Remove 3 to 4 inches of small end; reserve for other uses. Place tenderloin in a roasting pan, and sprinkle with lemon-pepper seasoning. Insert meat thermometer. Bake at 400° for 30 minutes. Reduce oven temperature to 375°, and bake an additional 10 minutes.

Spoon mushrooms around tenderloin, and pour sherry over top. Bake an additional 10 minutes or until meat thermometer registers 140° (rare) or 160° (medium), basting frequently with sherry mixture. Transfer tenderloin to serving platter; arrange mushrooms around tenderloin. Serve with pan drippings. Yield: 10 to 12 servings.

Jane Maloy,
Wilmington, North Carolina.

Right: *For a special dinner, deck the halls, set the table, and serve Apricot-Glazed Cornish Hens (recipe, this page).*

Pages 308 and 309: *This menu trims the calories as well as the preparation time: (on plate) Italian Beef Medallions, Browned Rice Pilaf, and Cauliflower-Snow Pea Medley. Spinach-Kiwifruit Salad is served on the side with its own Sweet-and-Sour Dressing. (Recipes are on page 305.)*

Page 310: *Be adventuresome. Treat your family to extraordinary desserts, such as White Chocolate-Coconut Cake and Chocolate Mousse Cake. (Recipes for these desserts are on pages 263 and 264.)*

Salads That Fit The Season

For a salad that complements holiday entrées, take your pick from these. Some take advantage of fresh fruit, such as cranberries, apples, and avocados, which are abundant this time of year. Others display holiday cheer by virtue of their festive colors.

Leave the peel on the apples for Creamy Waldorf Salad, and the bright-red color will shine through the dressing. Serve it on a bed of lettuce, and the red-and-green salad will look pretty on a holiday buffet.

Choose Lemon-Cranberry Congealed Salad for a new version of cranberry gelatin salad, which is always popular for Christmas. Unmold it onto leafy green lettuce for a festive appearance.

And instead of preparing your traditional green salad for this season, try Cranberry-Topped Green Salad. Just toss fresh greens with avocado, pineapple, and dressing, and then top the mixture with ruby-red, coarsely chopped, fresh cranberries. It's a salad that proclaims, "Merry Christmas."

LEMON-CRANBERRY CONGEALED SALAD

2 cups fresh cranberries
1 cup water
1 (20-ounce) can crushed pineapple, undrained
About 1½ cups cranberry juice cocktail
1 (3-ounce) package raspberry-flavored gelatin
1 (3-ounce) package lemon-flavored gelatin
1 cup chopped pecans
Leaf lettuce

Cook cranberries in water over medium heat until berries pop (about 5 minutes). Do not drain; set aside.

Drain pineapple, reserving juice; set pineapple aside. Add enough cranberry juice cocktail to pineapple juice to make 2 cups; bring to a boil. Add gelatins, stirring until granules dissolve. Chill until mixture is the consistency of unbeaten egg white. Stir in reserved cranberries, reserved pineapple, and pecans. Pour into a lightly oiled 6-cup mold. Chill until firm. Unmold onto lettuce leaves. Yield: 10 to 12 servings.
Dorothy M. Brooks,
Edmond, Oklahoma.

SNOWY EMERALD SALAD

1 envelope unflavored gelatin
¾ cup water
¾ cup mayonnaise or salad dressing
½ cup commercial sour cream
2 (3-ounce) packages lime-flavored gelatin
2 cups boiling water
1½ cups cold water
¾ cup diced, unpeeled cucumber
¾ cup sliced cauliflower flowerets
½ cup sliced radishes
Leaf lettuce (optional)
Radish roses (optional)

Combine unflavored gelatin and ¾ cup water in a heavy saucepan; let stand 1 minute. Cook and stir over medium heat until gelatin dissolves, about 1 minute; remove from heat. Combine mayonnaise and sour cream; stir well. Add gelatin mixture to mayonnaise mixture; stir well. Pour into a lightly oiled 8-cup mold; chill until firm.

Combine lime gelatin and boiling water, stirring until gelatin dissolves. Stir in cold water; chill until mixture is the consistency of unbeaten egg white. Add cucumber, cauliflower, and radishes; stir well. Pour vegetable mixture over chilled layer in mold. Chill until firm. Unmold onto lettuce leaves, and garnish with radish roses, if desired. Yield: 10 to 12 servings.
Mable Stevenson,
Phelps, Kentucky.

GAZPACHO SALAD MOLD

2 envelopes unflavored gelatin
2 cups tomato juice
¼ cup red wine vinegar
¼ teaspoon salt
Dash of hot sauce
1½ cups diced peeled cucumber
1½ cups sliced pitted ripe olives
¾ cup diced green pepper
¼ cup diced celery
2 tomatoes, peeled and diced
Leaf lettuce (optional)

Sprinkle gelatin over tomato juice in a heavy saucepan; cook over low heat, stirring constantly, until gelatin dissolves. Remove from heat; stir in vinegar, salt, and hot sauce. Chill until mixture is the consistency of unbeaten egg white; fold in remaining ingredients except lettuce. Pour mixture into a lightly oiled 6-cup mold; chill until firm. Unmold onto lettuce leaves, if desired. Yield: 10 to 12 servings.
Kathleen Stone,
Houston, Texas.

CRANBERRY-TOPPED GREEN SALAD

1 large avocado, peeled and cubed
1 (20-ounce) can pineapple tidbits, drained
⅓ cup commercial French dressing
1 cup fresh cranberries, coarsely chopped
¼ cup sugar
1 medium head iceberg lettuce, torn

Combine avocado, pineapple, and dressing; let stand 15 minutes, tossing occasionally.

Combine cranberries and sugar; set mixture aside.

Combine avocado mixture and lettuce; toss gently. To serve, place lettuce mixture on individual salad plates; top with cranberry mixture. Yield: 8 servings.
Mrs. Harland J. Stone
Ocala, Florida.

CREAMY WALDORF SALAD

1 (3-ounce) package cream cheese, softened
1½ teaspoons sugar
1½ teaspoons orange juice or pineapple juice
3 large apples, cubed
1 (8-ounce) can pineapple tidbits, drained
2 tablespoons chopped celery
2 tablespoons chopped pecans
2 tablespoons raisins
Leaf lettuce

Combine cream cheese, sugar, and juice in a small bowl; stir well, and set mixture aside.

Combine remaining ingredients except lettuce in a medium bowl. Add cream cheese mixture to apple mixture; toss gently. Cover and chill. Toss again before serving. Serve in lettuce-lined bowl. Yield: 6 to 8 servings.
Mrs. Roy Nieman,
Dunnellon, Florida.

Glossary

à la King—Food prepared in a creamy white sauce containing mushrooms and red and/or green peppers

à la Mode—Food served with ice cream

al Dente—The point in the cooking of pasta at which it is still fairly firm to the tooth; that is, very slightly undercooked

Aspic—A jellied meat juice or a liquid held together with gelatin

au Gratin—Food served crusted with breadcrumbs and/or shredded cheese

au Jus—Meat served in its own juice

Bake—To cook any food in an oven by dry heat

Barbecue—To roast meat slowly over coals on a spit or framework, or in an oven, basting intermittently with a special sauce

Batter—A mixture of flour and liquid that is thin enough to pour

Baste—To spoon pan liquid and/or a sauce over meats while they are roasting to prevent surface from drying

Beat—To mix vigorously with a brisk motion with spoon, fork, egg beater, or electric mixer

Béchamel—A white sauce of butter, flour, cream (not milk), and seasonings

Bisque—A thick, creamy soup usually of shellfish, but sometimes made of pureed vegetables

Blanch—To dip briefly into boiling water

Blend—To stir 2 or more ingredients together until well mixed

Blintz—A cooked crêpe stuffed with cheese or other filling

Boil—To cook food in boiling water or liquid that is mostly water (at 212°F. at sea level) in which bubbles constantly rise to the surface and burst

Boiling-water-bath canning method—Used for processing acid foods, such as fruit, tomatoes, pickled vegetables, and sauerkraut. These acid foods are canned safely at boiling temperatures in a water-bath canner

Borscht—Soup containing beets and other vegetables, usually with a meat stock base

Bouillabaisse—A highly seasoned fish soup or chowder containing two or more kinds of fish

Bouillon—Clear soup made by boiling meat in water

Bouquet Garni—Herbs tied in cheese-cloth which are cooked in a mixture and removed before serving

Bourguignon—Name applied to dishes containing Burgundy and often braised onions and mushrooms

Braise—To cook slowly with a small amount of liquid in a covered utensil. (Less-tender cuts of meat may be browned slowly first on all sides in a small amount of shortening, seasoned, and water added)

Bread, to—To coat with crumbs, usually in combination with egg or other binder

Broil—To cook by direct heat, either under the heat of a broiler, over hot coals, or between two hot surfaces

Broth—A thin soup, or a liquid in which meat, fish, or vegetables have been cooked

Brown—To cook in a skillet or oven or under a broiler until brown

Bruise—To partially crush an ingredient, such as herbs, to release flavor

Capers—Buds from a Mediterranean plant, usually packed in brine and used as a condiment in dressings or sauces

Caramelize—To cook white sugar in a skillet over medium heat, stirring constantly, until sugar forms a golden-brown syrup

Casserole—An ovenproof baking dish, usually with a cover; also the food cooked inside it

Charlotte—A molded dessert containing gelatin, usually formed in a glass dish or a pan that is lined with ladyfingers or pieces of cake

Clarified butter—Butter that has been melted and chilled. The solid is then lifted away from the liquid and discarded. Clarification heightens the smoke point of butter. Clarified butter will stay fresh in the refrigerator for at least 2 months

Coat—To cover completely, as in "coat with flour"

Cocktail—An appetizer; either a beverage or a light, highly seasoned food served before a meal

Coddle—To gently poach in barely simmering water

Compote—Mixed fruit, raw or cooked, usually served in "compote" dishes

Condiments—Seasonings that enhance the flavor of foods with which they are served

Consommé—Clear broth that is made from meat

Cool—To let food stand at room temperature until not warm to the touch

Court Bouillon—A highly seasoned broth made with water and meat, fish or vegetables, and seasonings

Cream, to—To blend together, as sugar and butter, until mixture takes on a smooth, creamy texture

Cream, whipped—Cream that has been whipped until it is stiff

Crème de Cacao—A chocolate-flavored liqueur

Crème de Café—A coffee-flavored liqueur

Crêpes—Very thin pancakes

Crimp—To seal pastry edges together by pinching

Croquette—Minced food, shaped like a ball, patty, cone, or log, bound with a heavy sauce, breaded, and fried

Croutons—Cubes of bread, toasted or fried, served with soups or salads

Cruller—A doughnut of twisted shape, very light in texture

Cube, to—To cut into cube-shaped pieces

Curaçao—An orange-flavored liqueur

Cut in, to—To incorporate by cutting or chopping motions, as in cutting shortening into flour for pastry

Demitasse—A small cup of coffee served after dinner

Devil, to—To prepare with spicy seasoning or sauce

Dice—To cut into small cubes

Dissolve—To mix a dry substance with liquid until the dry substance becomes a part of the solution

Dot—To scatter small bits of butter over top of a food

Dust—To lightly sprinkle with a dry ingredient

Dredge—To coat with something, usually flour or sugar

Filé—Powder made of sassafras leaves used to season and thicken foods

Fillet—Boneless piece of meat or fish

Flambé—To flame, using alcohol as the burning agent; flame causes caramelization, enhancing flavor

Flan—In France, a filled pastry; in Spain, a custard

Florentine—A food containing or placed upon spinach

Flour—To coat with flour

Flute—To make a decorative edge on pastry

Fold—To add a whipped ingredient, such as cream or egg white, to another ingredient by gentle over-and-under movement

Frappé—A drink whipped with ice to make a thick, frosty consistency

Fricassee—A stew, usually of poultry or veal

Fritter—Vegetable or fruit dipped into, or combined with, batter and fried

Fry—To cook in hot shortening

Garnish—A decoration for a food or drink

Glaze (To make a shiny surface)—In meat preparation, a jelled broth applied to meat surface; in breads and pastries, a wash of egg or syrup; for doughnuts and cakes, a sugar preparation for coating

Grate—To obtain small particles of food by rubbing on a grater or shredder

Grill—To broil under or over a source of direct heat

Grits—Coarsely ground dried corn, served boiled, or boiled and then fried

Gumbo—Soup or stew made with okra

Herb—Aromatic plant used for seasoning and garnishing foods

Hollandaise—A sauce made of butter, egg, and lemon juice or vinegar

Hominy—Whole corn grains from which hull and germ are removed

Jardinière—Vegetables in a savory sauce or soup

Julienne—Vegetables cut into strips or a soup containing such vegetables

Kahlúa—A coffee-flavored liqueur

Kirsch—A cherry-flavored liqueur

Knead—To work a food (usually dough) by hand, using a folding-back and pressing-forward motion

Marinade—A seasoned liquid in which food is soaked

Marinate, to—To soak food in a seasoned liquid

Meringue—A whole family of egg white-sugar preparations including pie topping, poached meringue used to top custard, crisp meringue dessert shells, and divinity candy

Mince—To chop into very fine pieces

Mornay—White sauce with egg, cream, and cheese added

Mousse—A molded dish based on meat or sweet whipped cream stiffened with egg white and/or gelatin (if mousse contains ice cream, it is called bombe)

Panbroil—To cook over direct heat in an uncovered skillet containing little or no shortening

Panfry—To cook in an uncovered skillet in small amount of shortening

Parboil—To partially cook in boiling water before final cooking

Pare—To shave away the skins of fruits or vegetables

Pasta—A large family of flour paste products, such as spaghetti, macaroni, and noodles

Pâté (French for paste)—A paste made of liver or meat

Petit Four—A small cake, which has been frosted and decorated

Pilau or pilaf—A dish of the Middle East consisting of rice and meat or vegetables in a seasoned stock

Pipe—To squeeze a smooth, shapeable mixture through a decorating bag to make decorative shapes

Poach—To cook in liquid held below the boiling point

Pot liquor—The liquid in which vegetables have been boiled

Preheat—To turn on oven so that desired temperature will be reached before food is inserted for baking

Puree—A thick sauce or paste made by forcing cooked food through a sieve

Reduce—To boil down, evaporating liquid from a cooked dish

Rémoulade—A rich mayonnaise-based sauce containing anchovy paste, capers, herbs, and mustard

Render—To melt fat away from surrounding meat

Rind—Outer shell or peel of fruit

Roast, to—To cook in oven by dry heat (usually refers to meats)

Roux—A mixture of butter and flour used to thicken gravies and sauces; it may be white or brown, if mixture is browned before liquid is added

Sauté—To fry food lightly over fairly high heat in a small amount of fat in a shallow, open pan

Scald—To heat milk just below the boiling point; to dip certain foods into boiling water before freezing them (procedure is also called blanching)

Scallop—A bivalve mollusk of which only the muscle hinge is eaten; to bake food in a sauce topped with crumbs

Score—To cut shallow gashes on surface of food, as in scoring fat on ham before glazing

Sear—To brown surface of meat over high heat to seal in juices

Set—Term used to describe the consistency of gelatin when it has jelled enough to unmold

Shred—Break into thread-like or stringy pieces, usually by rubbing over the surface of a vegetable shredder

Simmer—To cook gently at a temperature below boiling point

Skewer—To fasten with wooden or metal pins or skewers

Soufflé—A spongy hot dish, made from a sweet or savory mixture (often milk or cheese), lightened by stiffly beaten egg whites or whipped cream

Steam—To cook food with steam either in a pressure cooker, on a platform in a covered pan, or in a special steamer

Steam-pressure canning method—Used for processing low-acid foods, such as meats, fish, poultry, and most vegetables. A temperature higher than boiling is required to can these foods safely. The food is processed in a steam-pressure canner at 10 pounds' pressure (240°) to ensure that all of the spoilage micro-organisms are destroyed

Steep—To let food stand in not quite boiling water until the flavor is extracted

Stew—A mixture of meat or fish and vegetables cooked by simmering in its own juices and liquid, such as water and/or wine

Stir-fry—To cook quickly in oil over high heat, using light tossing and stirring motions to preserve shape of food

Stock—The broth in which meat, poultry, fish, or vegetables has been cooked

Syrupy—Thickened to about the consistency of egg white

Toast, to—To brown by direct heat, as in a toaster or under broiler

Torte—A round cake, sometimes made with breadcrumbs instead of flour

Tortilla—A Mexican flat bread made of corn or wheat flour

Toss—To mix together with light tossing motions, in order not to bruise delicate food, such as salad greens

Triple Sec—An orange-flavored liqueur

Truss, to—To tie or secure with string or skewers the legs and wings of poultry or game in order to make the bird easier to manage during cooking

Veal—Flesh of milk-fed calf up to 14 weeks of age

Velouté—White sauce made of flour, butter, and a chicken or veal stock, instead of milk

Vinaigrette—A cold sauce of oil and vinegar flavored with parsley, finely chopped onions, and other seasonings; served with cold meats or vegetables or as a dressing with salad greens

Whip—To beat rapidly to increase air and increase volume

Wok—A round bowl-shaped metal cooking utensil of Chinese origin used for stir-frying and steaming (with rack inserted) of foods

Zest—Gratings of the colored portion of citrus skin

Glossary 313

Recipe Title Index

An alphabetical listing of every recipe by exact title
All microwave recipe page numbers are preceded by an "M"

Almond Cheese Spread, 292
Almond Cream Confections, 198
Almond Cream with Fresh Strawberries, 93
Almond Danish, 301
Almond Filling, 301
Amaretto Filling, 241
Amaretto-Strawberry Sauce, M165
Ancho Chile Cream, 121
Ancho Chile Sauce, 122
Angel Heart Biscuits with Sausage, 156
Apple-Cranberry Crunch, 178
Apple Dessert Sauce, M165
Apple-Glazed Pork Chops, 35
Apple-Mint Jelly, 134
Apple Muffins, 23
Apple-Nut Cake, 76

Apple Salad, 233
Apple Salad with Blue Cheese
  Dressing, 103
Applesauce-Honey Nut Bread, 300
Apple Veal Chops, 220
Apricot-Cream Cheese Spread, 158
Apricot-Glazed Cornish Hens, 306
Apricot-Kirsch Glaze, 14
Apricot Nectar Salad, 236
Apricot Pinwheels, 276
Apricot-Raisin Bars, 32
Apricot Sauce, 172
Artichoke-Caviar Mold, 239
Artichoke-Parmesan Phyllo Bites, 54
Asparagus-Horseradish Salad, 80
Asparagus in Squash Rings, 68
Asparagus with Cashew Butter, 56
Asparagus with Lemon Butter, M151
Autumn Pumpkin Pie, 213
Avocado, Bacon, and Cheese
  Sandwiches, 279

Avocado-Chicken Salad, 107
Avocado Fruit Salad, 41
Avocado Relish, 120

Baby Clam Pizza, 182
Bacon-and-Tomato Eggs Benedict, 195
Bacon-Beer Cheese Soup, M7
Bacon Spaghetti, 82
Bacon-Wrapped Scallops, 94
Baked Chicken Salad, 176
Baked Clam Shells, 94
Baked Fruit Compote, 228
Baked Fruit Dressing, 253
Baked Lemon Cups, 128
Baked Mustard Chicken, 10
Baked Shrimp, 35
Baked Tomatoes, 197
Baked Zucchini Fans, 243
Bama Brunswick Stew, 4
Banana Bread, 72
Banana Cream Pie, 207
Banana-Oat Muffins, 188
Banana-Oat Tea Loaf, 256
Banana Salad, 80
Banana Smoothie, 160
Banana Split Alaskas, 10
Banana-Strawberry Frost, 199
Barbecued Meat Loaf, 216
Barbecued Stuffed Chops, 229
Basic Processor Crêpes, 289
Basil Butter, 171
Basil Chicken, 171
Béchamel Sauce, 286
Beef-and-Broccoli Salad, 187
Beef-and-Onion Stew, 18
Beef-and-Vegetable Stir-Fry, 22
Beef Madras, 284
Beef Tenderloin with Mushrooms, 115
Beef Tenderloin with Mushroom-Sherry
  Sauce, 306
Beefy Lentil Soup, 282
Beer-Braised Steaks, 96
Beer-Broiled Shrimp, 142
Beer-Marinated Flank Steak, 35
Berry Sauce, 290
Best Baked Veal Roast, 219
Best Ever Refrigerator Waffles, 225
Bite-Size Chiles Rellenos, 246
Black Bean Terrine with Goat Cheese, 120
Black Bean-Tomatillo Relish, 121
Blackberries-and-Cream Parfait, 129
Blackberry-Apple Pie, 130
Blackberry Bars, 130
Black-Eyed Pea Gravy, 12
Blakely Brunswick Stew, 4
BLT Chicken Salad, 144
Blueberries 'n' Cream Cheesecake, 140
Blueberry Chiffon Cheesecake, 76

Blueberry-Oatmeal Muffins, 24
Blueberry-Orange Bread, 140
Blueberry Pinwheel Cobbler, 140
Blueberry Topping, 125
Bourbon Ice Cream, 139
Bourbon-Pecan Pumpkin Pie, 264
Bourbon Sweet Potatoes, 280
Bourbon-Tea Punch, 57
Braised Round Steak, 35
Braised Stuffed Pork Chops, 249
Brandied Carrots, 253
Brandy Slush Punch, 72
Bran Yeast Rolls, 116
Breakfast Eye-Opener, 199
Breakfast Taquitos, 237
Brie Bread, 143
Brie Cheese Bake, 117
Brittle with Crushed Peanuts, 184

Broccoli Casserole, 284
Broccoli-Corn Salad, 24
Broccoli Soup, 288
Broccoli with Sour Cream Sauce, 127
Brown Bread-Cream Cheese
  Sandwiches, M6
Browned Rice Pilaf, 305
Brown Rice Casserole, 118
Brown Sugar Frosting, 296
Brunswick Chicken Stew, 4
Brussels Sprouts in Mustard Sauce, 253
Brussels Sprouts Salad, 233
Bûche de Noël, 241
Burgers au Poivre Blanc, 186
Buttermilk Cake Brownies, 198
Buttermilk Drumsticks, 175
Butternut Squash Pie, 212
Butterscotch Cookies, 58
Butterscotch Cream Pie, 207

Cabbage Kielbasa, 42
Cabbage Salad, 120, 233
Cabbage with Apples and Franks, 42
Cajun Barbecued Shrimp, 95

Cajun Cake, 138
Cajun Chicken over Rice, 268
Cajun-Style Drumsticks, 159
Calico Crumb Cake, 261
Caponata, 166
Caramel Frosting, 265
Caraway Buttered Noodles, 230
Caribbean Snapper, 5
Carrot-and-Raisin Muffins, 24
Carrot Casserole, 285
Carrot Pound Cake, 41
Carrot Puffs, 200
Carrot-Raisin Salad, 10
Cauliflower 'n' Chiles Casserole, 285
Cauliflower-Pea Salad, 231
Cauliflower-Snow Pea Medley, 305
Cauliflower with Pimiento Sauce, 232
Charleston Okra Soup, 156
Cheese and Chutney Ball, 247
Cheese-and-Spinach Puffs, 246
Cheese Biscuits, 78
Cheese Bonbons, 93
Cheese Bread, 11
Cheesecake with Raspberry Sauce, 116
Cheese Loaf, 92
Cheese-Sauced Tuna Salad, M124
Cheese-Wine Bread, 254
Cheesy Beer Spread, 196
Cheesy Fruit-'n'-Nut Salad, 56
Cheesy-Olive Appetizers, 246
Cherry Fruit Salad, 236
Cherry-Pineapple Topping, 126
Cherry Tomato Salad, 156
Chewy Molasses Cookies, 257
Chewy Soft Pretzels, 159
Chicken à la King, 197
Chicken Andalusia, 103
Chicken-and-Broccoli Pasta, 286
Chicken and Tomato with Rotelle, 108
Chicken and Vegetables Vermouth, M37
Chicken Bundles with Bacon Ribbons, 68
Chicken Divan, M218
Chicken Florentine with Mushroom
  Sauce, 250
Chicken, Ham, and Cheese Bake, 217
Chicken in a Bag, 23
Chicken in Phyllo, 286
Chicken Kabobs, 141
Chicken Rolls Jubilee, 118
Chicken Salad Filling, 106
Chicken Spaghetti, 221
Chicken Tortellini Salad, 288
Chile-Cheese Cornbread, 171
Chile-Cheese Dip, 173
Chili, 17
Chili Bean Roast, 268
Chili Chops, 10
Chill-Chaser Soup, 282
Chilled Artichokes with Lemon-Pepper
  Dressing, 55
Chilled Avocado Soup, 37
Chilled Mexican Appetizer, 197
Chilled Zucchini Soup, 90
Chinese Burritos, 181
Chinese Meatballs, 194
Chinese-Style Beef, 50
Chocolate Angel Food Cake, 21
Chocolate-Blueberry Dessert Squares, 299
Chocolate Brownie Delight, 224
Chocolate Charlotte Russe, 74
Chocolate Cheese Spread, 292
Chocolate Cherry Sauce, M165

Chocolate-Coconut Almond Drops, 223
Chocolate-Coconut Crust, 261
Chocolate Cookie Ice Cream
  Sandwiches, 147
Chocolate Cream Pie, 208
Chocolate Crumb Crust, 261
Chocolate Crust, 264
Chocolate Frosting, M97, 198, 199, 293
Chocolate-Ice Cream Pie, 224
Chocolate Lace Cups, 133
Chocolate Macaroons, 57
Chocolate Mousse Cake, 264
Chocolate-Orange Roll, 21
Chocolate Pastry Shell, 262
Chocolate-Peanut Butter Frosting, 222
Chocolate-Peanut Butter Fudge, 257
Chocolate-Peanut Butter Swirl Pie, 262
Chocolate-Peanut Cluster Cake, 184
Chocolate Pound Cake with Fudge
  Frosting, 296
Chocolate-Sour Cream Cake, 222
Chocolate Teasers, 44
Chocolate-Tipped Log Cookies, 294
Chocolate-Topped Amaretto Custard, M37
Chocolate Truffle Filling, 69

Choco-Mallow Brownies, 198
Choco-Maple Frozen Dessert, 178
Chorizo Substitute, 238
Chowchow, 150
Christmas Bread, 296
Christmas Eggnog, 242
Christmas Lizzies, 257
Christmas Strawberries, 293
Christmas-Tree Coffee Cakes, 298
Chunky Piña Colada Topping, 125
Chutney-Chicken Salad, 74
Cider Sauce, 224
Cider-Sauced Pork Chops, 81
Cilantro Cream, 121
Cinnamon Cake Squares, 222
Cinnamon-Pecan Coffee Cake, 69
Citrus Salad, 103
Citrus Salad Bowl, 83
Cloud Biscuits, 15
Cocktail Sauce, 128
Coconut-Caramel Pies, 260
Coconut Cream Pie, 207
Coconut Dressing, 251
Coconut Puffs, 277
Coconut-Spice Cake, 296
Cold Fresh Fruit Soup, 157
Colorful Six-Bean Salad, 82
Colorful Vegetable Lasagna, 19
Commander's Chutney, 245
Company Tuna Salad, 201
Confetti-Stuffed Lettuce, 24
Congealed Avocado Salads, 42

Cornbread, 197
Cornbread Salad, 172
Cornbread-Sausage-Apple Pie, 171
Cornbread Sticks, 15
Corned Beef Dinner, 54
Corned Beef Spread, 196
Corned Beef with Dijon Glaze, 54
Cornmeal Batter Cakes, 16
Corn Moussaka, 190
Corn Relish, 120, 245
Corn Soup, 156
Cottage Cheese-Banana Splits, 56
Cottage Cheese Sauce, 232
Cottage Cheese-Spinach Cups, 190
Cottage Cheese Spread, 107
Country Ham Quiche, 287
Country Ham Spread, 8
Country Pot Roast, 216
County Fair Egg Bread, 68
Crab-and-Corn Bisque, 137
Cranapple-Vodka Punch, 72
Cranberry-Amaretto Chutney with Cream
  Cheese, 244
Cranberry Chicken Kiev, 250
Cranberry-Orange Bread, 244
Cranberry Relish, 245
Cranberry-Topped Green Salad, 311
Cranberry Upside-Down Cake, 8
Cran-Raspberry Pie, 244
Cream Cheese Frosting, 58
Cream Cheese Pinches, 85
Creamed Spring Vegetables, 127
Cream Filling, 198
Cream of Cauliflower Soup, M7
Creamy Baked Mushrooms, 127
Creamy Blue Cheese-Ham Sandwiches, 279
Creamy Chocolate Frosting, 241
Creamy Chocolate Mousse, 133
Creamy Cottage Cheese Dessert, 191
Creamy Ham and Eggs, 286
Creamy Marinated Carrots, 200
Creamy Mustard Sauce, 232
Creamy Orange Dip, 247
Creamy Potatoes with Ham Bits, 191
Creamy Waldorf Salad, 311
Crème Chantilly, 9
Creole Cabbage, 189
Creole Fish, M79
Creole Jambalaya, 210
Creole Potatoes, 138
Crêpes, 126
Crescent Sugar Cookies, 294
Crimson Greens, 153
Crisp Squash-and-Pepper Toss, M152
Crisp Vegetable Aspic with Horseradish
  Dressing, 152
Crispy Pizza Crust, 181
Crunch-Crust Brownies, 198
Crunchy Ice Cream Treats, 178
Crunchy Oven-Fried Chicken, 163
Crunchy Sauerkraut Salad, 9
Crunchy Seasoned Chicken, 217
Crunchy Tuna Salad, 201
Crustless Sausage-Apple Quiche, 70
Cucumber-Mint Dressing, 153
Cucumber-Yogurt Salad, 33
Currant Sauce, 240
Curried Baked Fish, 5
Curried Chicken-and-Orange Salad, 144
Curried Chicken-Stuffed Peppers, 19
Curried Fruit Bake, 241
Curried Shrimp Spread, 158
Curried Tuna Salad with Grapes, 201

Curry Dip, 25
Curry Pea Casserole, 154
Custard Pecan Pie, 184

Date Dressing, 57
Date-Walnut Spread, 292
Decorator Frosting, 86
Deep-Fried Walnut Chicken, 175
Delicate Garden Lettuce, 62
Delightful Crab Salad, 145
Della Robbia Fruit Wreath, 294
Dessert Crackers, 3
Dessert Crêpes, 290
Deviled-Beef Patties, 22
Deviled Dip, 25
Dieter's Cornbread, 164
Dijon Glaze, 54
Dill Marinade, 115
Dill-Spiced Carrots, 200
Double-Crust Chicken Pie, 111
Double-Crust Pastry, 299
Double Good Fudge, M278
Dressed Oysters on the Half Shell, M79
Dressing for Fruit Salad, 81
Dried Apple Filling, 229
Drizzle Glaze, 94
Drunken Bean Soup, 283
Duck Breasts with Raspberry Sauce, 240

Easy Bread, 168
Easy Caesar Salad, 116
Easy Caramel Frosting, 39
Easy Caramel Sauce, 38
Easy-Crust Apple Pie, 11
Easy Eggplant, M151
Easy Green Bean Casserole, 284
Easy Sausage Casserole, M189
Easy Whole Wheat Rolls, 74
Easy Zucchini, 167
Egg Custard Filling, 14
Eggless Quiche, 220
Eggnog Pie, 295
Enchilada Casserole, 287
English Muffins, 49
English Pea-and-Apple Salad, 24

Fast-and-Easy Stir-Fried Steak, 50
Fast-and-Savory Turkey, 306
Favorite Stack Cake, 228
Fennel-Rye Crackers, 2
Festive Braids, 297
Festive Cauliflower Casserole, 232
Festive Chicken Spread, 158
Fiery Tomato-Cheese Spread, 196
Fiesta, 180
Fig Ice Cream, 139

Fire-and-Ice Tomatoes, 92
Fireside Coffee Mix, 241
Fish-and-Vegetable Stew, 220
Fish-Asparagus Divan, 128
Fish Florentine in Parchment, 22
Five-Flavor Pound Cake, 264
Five-Meat Burgoo, 3
Flank Steak and Mushrooms, 61
Flank Steak Pinwheels, 141
Flippo Caesar Salad, 61
Fluffy Chocolate Frosting, 58
Fluffy Nesselrode Pie, 261
Foil-Baked Swordfish, 5
French Bread, 227
French Curled Cookies, 16
French Onion-Beef Soup, 54
French Pear Pie, 213
Fresh Apple-Nut Bread, 256
Fresh Broccoli Salad, 103
Fresh Cranberry-Apricot Sauce, 243
Fresh Cranberry Tartlets, 244
Fresh Fruit Dressing, 134
Fresh Okra and Tomatoes, 89
Fresh Peach Sauce, 167
Fresh Summer Salsa, 89
Fresh Tomato Sauce, 171
Fried Cauliflower with Cheese Sauce, 231
Fried Okra, 89
Fried Parmesan Eggplant, 166
Fried Shrimp with Apricot Sauce, 172
Frosty Fruit Float, 159
Frosty Fruit Shake, 23
Fruit and Spice Cake, M97
Fruit Basket Strudel, 276
Fruited Chicken Salad in Avocados, 41
Fruited Meringue Shells, 32
Fruited Pork Chops, 194
Fruit Kabobs with Coconut Dressing, 251
Fruit Pops, 168
Fruit Salad with Date Dressing, 57
Fruit Salad with Honey Dressing, 129
Fruit Soup, 98
Fruit-Stuffed Pork Tenderloins, 270
Fruit Topping, 225
Fruity Ice Cream Cake, 110
Fudge Frosting, 296
Fudge Pie, 168

Garden Salad, 62
Garden Sauté, 90
Garlic-and-Oregano Marinade, 115
Garlic-Grilled Chicken, 180
Gazpacho Salad Mold, 311
Georgia Quail with Gravy, 240
German Chocolate Cheesecake, 265
German Meat Loaf, 216
Ginger Cake, 222
Gingered Plum Sauce, 175
Ginger-Glazed Carrots, 68
Glazed Carrots and Onions, 128
Glazed Carrots with Bacon and Onion, 200
Glazed Pork Loin, 229
Golden Ham Pie, 78
Good Luck Jambalaya, 11
Good Morning Grits, 156
Graham Cracker Crust, 139, 243
Grandmother's Apple Pie, 212
Greek Salad, 103
Greek-Style Monkfish, M79
Green Bean Bundles, 118
Green Beans, M151
Green Bean Salad, 90

Green Beans and Tomatoes with
    Mustard, 83
Green Beans Italian, 10
Green Beans with New Potatoes, 164
Green Grape Tart, 77
Green Tomato Pickles, 134
Grilled Cantaloupe Wedges, 162
Grilled Corned Beef Sandwiches, 54
Grilled Corn Soup, 121
Grilled Cumin Chicken, 142
Grilled Marinated Shrimp, 173
Grilled Scallops Tostada, 120
Grilled Sour Cream Burgers, 287
Ground Almond Filling, 14
Ground Beef Gumbo, 283
Gruyère-Chicken Pizza, 182
Guacamole Salad, 181
Gumbo Ya Ya, 210

Halibut with Orange-Curry Sauce, 91
Ham-and-Broccoli Rolls, 82
Ham-and-Cheese Casserole, 78
Ham-and-Cheese Pita Sandwiches, 202
Ham and Swiss on Noodles, 108
Ham-Noodle Skillet, 78
Ham-Rice-Tomato Bake, 78
Ham Salad Spread, 92
Harry Young's Burgoo, 3
Hawaiian Cheese Spread, 158
Hawaiian Ham Spread, 106
Hawaiian Pork Chops, 82
Hawaiian Tea, 57
Hearts-of-Palm Salad, 138
Heart Tart Pastry, 14
Heart Tarts, 14
Hearty Beer Bread, 226
Heavenly Chocolate Pie, 260
Heavenly Mushrooms, 281
Herb-and-Cheese Pull Aparts, 143
Herb-Cheese Tart, 98
Herbed Carrots and Onions, 31
Herbed Cheese Spread, 247
Herbed French Loaf, 243

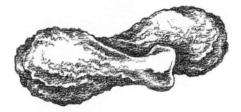

Herbed Fried Chicken, 91
Herbed Mustard, 134
Herbed Potato Salad, 171
Herb-Roasted Chicken, 155
Herb Salad, 90
Holiday Apple Pie, 260
Holiday Broccoli with Rice, 252
Holiday Fruit Salad, 236
Holiday Mincemeat Pie, 213
Holiday Punch, 252
Hollandaise Sauce, 195
Homemade Raisin Bread, 300
Homemade Ravioli, 230
Homemade Ravioli Pasta, 231
Home-Style Brisket, 303
Honey-Curry Chicken, 36
Honeydew Granita, 162
Honey Dressing, 129

Honeyed Chocolate Mousse, 223
Honey French Dressing, 81
Honey-Nut Glaze, 15
Honey-Nut Spread, 157
Honey-Oatmeal Cake, 222
Horseradish Dressing, 152
Horseradish Sauce, 127
Hot-and-Creamy Dutch Slaw, 127
Hot-and-Spicy Kabobs, 193
Hot Apple-Cinnamon Tea, 57
Hot Buffalo Wings, 176
Hot Cabbage Creole, 42
Hot Crab-and-Cheese Sandwiches, 279
Hot Crab Canapés, 239
Hot Dutch Potato Salad, 176
Hot Fruit Dessert Sauce, 299
Hot Green Bean Salad, 176
Hot Mexican Cider, 213
Hot Pimiento Cheese, 173
Hot Pita Sandwiches, M6
Hotshot Bean Dip, 195
Hot Shrimp Dip, 190
Hot Spiced Fruit Tea, 242
Hot Turkey Salad, 176
Hurry-Up Fruit Salad, 236
Hush Puppies, 15

Icy Pineapple-Fruit Salad, 9
Indian Pot Roast, 215
Island Pancakes, 225
Italian Beef Medaillons, 305
Italian Cabbage Casserole, 42
Italian Pot Roast, 95
Italian Salad, 145
Italian-Style Tomato Sauce, 182
Italian Wafers, 36

Jack-O'-Lantern Cookies, 214
Jambalaya de Covington, 211
Jam-It Bars, 159
Jazzy Mashed Potatoes, 192
Jicama Salad, 123

Kahlúa Cream, 134
Kahlúa Smoothie, 242
Kiwi-Berry Pizza, 55
Kiwifruit Muffins, 255
Kiwi Orange Roughy, 193
Kiwi Parfait, 55
Krause's Cafe Bratwurst Dinner, 238
Kyoto Orange-Chicken Stir-Fry, 96

Lamb Pockets with Dilled Cucumber
  Topping, 104
Layered Fruitcake, 265
Layered Sherbet Dessert, 109
Lazy Wife Dills, 149
Lemon Bread, 256
Lemon-Cheese Canapés, 93
Lemon-Chicken Nuggets, 283
Lemon-Cranberry Congealed
  Salad, 311
Lemon Cream Filling, 14
Lemon-Cucumber Mold, 90
Lemon Curd, 139
Lemon Dessert Sauce, M165
Lemon Filling, 293
Lemon Glaze, 41
Lemon-Pepper Dressing, 55
Lemon-Raisin Scones, 69
Lemon-Sour Cream Pound Cake, 38
Lemon Veal with Artichoke
  Hearts, 219
Light Wheat Rolls, 254
Lima Bean Casserole, 284
Lime Cooler, 160
Lime-Honey Fruit Salad Dressing, 81
Linguine Carbonara, 108
Liqueur Cream-Filled Chocolates, 258
Little Phyllo Cheesecakes, 275
Liver in Creole Sauce, 33
Loaded-with-Chips Cookies, 223
Lobster-Stuffed Beef Tenderloin, 248
Low-Calorie Crêpes, 77
Low-Calorie Medium White
  Sauce, 26
Low-Cal Tuna Dip, 25

Macaroni Casserole, 154
Macaroni Salad, 92
Macaroni Shell Salad, 38
Magnolia Blossoms, 72
Mandarin Ham-and-Rice Salad, 145
Maque Chou Stuffed Tomatoes, 89
Marbled Cheesecake, 261
Marinated and Grilled Shrimp, 141
Marinated Artichokes, 250
Marinated Asparagus, 74
Marinated Bean-and-Rice Salad, 152
Marinated Breast of Chicken, 123
Marinated Chicken, 61
Marinated Corn-Bean Salad, 9
Marinated Garden Vegetables, 252
Marinated London Broil, 32
Marinated Roasted Peppers, 90
Marinated Salmon Steaks, 6
Marinated Vegetable Salad, 243
Meat-and-Cheese Appetizers, 7
Meat Loaf Wellington, 284
Medallions of Beef with Ancho Chile
  Sauce, 122
Melba Sauce, 77
Melon Ball Bowl with Cucumber-Mint
  Dressing, 153
Meringue, 207
Meringue Frosting, 84
Mexican Burrito Pie, 287
Mexican Cheese Puffs, 8
Mexican Fried Chicken, 176
Mexican Luncheon, 192
Mexican Meat Loaf, 217
Mexican Rice Dressing, 253
Middle Eastern Salad, 107
Migas, 180

Mincemeat Sweetheart Cookies, 293
Miniature Chocolate Cups, 132
Miniature Cream Cheese Pastry Shells, 190
Mint Dip with Fresh Fruit, 146
Minted Delight, 107
Minted Melon Balls, 162
Minted Peas, 56
Mint Tea, 107
Mixed Baked Beans, 92
Mixed Fruit Cup, 233
Mixed Greens Salad, 62
Mixed-Vegetable Casserole, 154
Mocha Brownies, 93
Mocha Frosting, 224
Mocha Swirl Cheesecake, 262
Mock Country-Fried Steak, 163
Mock Mustard-Hollandaise Sauce, 269
Mock Pâté, 251
Moravian Sugar Cake, 228
Moussaka, 166
Mushroom-Artichoke Casserole, 241
Mushroom-Cheese Crêpes, 289
Mushroom Sauce, 36, 186, 284
Mushroom Scalloped Potatoes, 191
Mushroom Soufflés, 282
Mustard Sauce, 22
My Favorite Applesauce Cake, 263

New-Fashioned Blackberry Cobbler, 164
No-Egg Chocolate Marshmallow Cake, M97
Northshore Jambalaya, 45
North Texas Red Chili, 303
Nutty Burgers, 185
Nutty Cabbage Salad, 42
Nutty Date Dessert Cheese, 299
Nutty Fruit-and-Cheese Spread, 246
Nutty Green Salad, 168
Nutty Phyllo Nests, 277

Oatmeal Brownies, 199
Oatmeal-Raisin Cookies, 221
Oklahoma Sunrise, 67
Okra, Corn, and Peppers, M151
Old-Fashioned Burgoo, 3
Olé Omelet, M124
Omelet Primavera, 71
Onion-Cheese Soup, 81
Onion Cream Sauce, 232
Onion Sauce, 248
Onion-Smothered Steak, M189
Open-Faced Crab Sandwiches, 106
Open-Faced Garden Sandwiches, 105
Open-Faced Salami Sandwiches, 279
Open-Faced Salmon Patties, M218
Open-Faced Vegetarian Melt, 106
Orange Cheese Spread, 292
Orange Chicken Breasts with Parslied
  Rice, 242
Orange Chiffon Pie, 260
Orange-Cranberry Pork Chops, 84
Orange Dessert Sauce, 58
Orange Filling, 84
Orange Fingers, 57
Orange Liqueur Cake, 84
Orange Meringue Cake, 84
Orange Pecans, 292
Orange-Poppy Seed Dressing, 187
Orange Pound Cake, 84, 221
Orange-Pumpkin Bread, 300

Orange-Romaine Salad, 239
Orange Soda Punch, 214
Orange Tapioca Fluff, 31
Orange-Yogurt Pancakes, 225
Oriental Hot Munch, 8
Oriental Salad Bowl, 153
Original Italian-Style Pizza, 182
Oyster-and-Bacon Poor Boys, 40
Oyster-and-Mushroom Soup, 39
Oysters Buccaneer, 40
Oysters in Shrimp Sauce, 40

Palmiers, 277
Pan-Roasted Doves, 240
Parsley Meat Loaf, 22
Parslied Rice, 167, 243
Party Mix, 257
Party Scalloped Potatoes, 191
Pasta and Garden Vegetables, 192
Pasta-Basil Toss, 33
Pasta Salad, 36
Pasta with Broccoli and Sausage, 109
Pastitsio, 12
Pastry, 212, 267
Pastry Shell, 262
Patio Steak, 141
Peach-Berry Sauce, M165
Peach-Caramel Cobbler, 178
Peaches in a Garden Nest, 154
Peach Melba Meringues, 76
Peach-Plum Soup, 157
Peach Sweet Potato Puffs, 280
Peach Upside-Down Cake, 8
Peachy Melt-Away Dessert, 298
Peanut Bread, 184
Peanut Butter Brownies, 199
Peanut Butter Cookies, 58
Peanut Butter Easter Eggs, 86
Peanut Butter-Fudge Frosting, 184
Peanut Butter Muffins, 158
Peanut Clusters, 184
Peanut Divinity, M278
Peanut Soup, 184
Pear-and-Celery Salad, 56
Pear Breakfast Treat, 72
Pecan-Cheese Crispies, 168
Pecan Roulade, 183
Pecan Waffles, 225
Pepper-Cheese Stacks, 80
Peppered Pot Roast, 215
Peppermint Candy-Ice Cream Pie, 260
Pepper Pecans, 137
Pesto-Cheese Pasta Bites, 251
Pesto Pizza, 182
Phyllo-Cheese Triangles, 246
Phyllo-Spinach Triangles, 53
Pickled Beets, 163
Pineapple-Flavored Ham, 160
Pineapple Milkshake, 199
Pineapple-Pecan Loaf Bread, 256
Pineapple Phyllo Bundles, 277
Pineapple Pork Chops, M124
Pinto Beans, 303
Piquant French Dressing, 202
Pizza Burger, 185
Pizza Squares, 168
Pizza with Artichoke and Prosciutto, 182
Plentiful P's Salad, 12
Plum Pudding-Gelatin Mold, 178
Poached Chicken with Black Beans and
    Salsa, 217

Poached Pears with Raspberry Sauce, 69
Polynesian Turkey Salad, 285
Popcorn-Gumdrop Cake, 262
Popcorn Scramble, 185
Pork Arlo, 229
Pork Medallions with Chutney Sauce, 35
Pork-'n'-Bean Salad, 83
Pork Roast with Tomato Sauce, 249
Potato Casserole, 190
Potato Croquettes, 116
Potato-Eggplant Casserole, 166
Potatoes Lorraine, 190
Potatoes with Sweet Red Peppers, 192
Potato Yeast, 53
Potato Yeast Rolls, 53
Pot Roast in Red Sauce, 215
Poulet Rémoulade, 144
Pound Cake with Caramel Frosting, 39
Praline-Flavored Coffee, 69
Processor Devonshire Sauce, 58
Processor Pastry, 67
Prune-Nut Bread, 255
Puffy Apple Turnovers, 276
Pumpkin-Coconut Bread, 255
Pumpkin-Ice Cream Pie, 243
Pumpkin-Pecan Bread, 221
Pumpkin Pie in Spiced Nut Crust, 295
Pumpkin Rolls, 254

Quemada (Burnt-Sugar Candy), 38
Quick Brownies, M302
Quick Chicken Toss, M124
Quick Crab Bake, 192
Quick Orange Salad, 80
Quick Processor Meatballs, 111
Quick Sally Lunn, 16
Quick Shrimp Skillet, 50
Quick Sweet Pickles, 149
Quick Tartar Sauce, 128

Raisin-Pecan Pie, 213
Raisin-Rice Pudding, 46
Raisin Sauce, 127
Range-Top Amaretto Custard, 77
Raspberry Crêpes, 126
Raspberry Dressing, 153
Raspberry-Lemon Vinegar, 134
Raspberry-Peach Topping, 126
Raspberry Ribbon Salad, 236
Raspberry-Rosé Punch, 242
Raspberry Sauce, 69, 117, 183
Raspberry Sweet Potatoes, 280
Red Beans and Rice, 45
Red Cabbage-and-Apple Slaw, 31
Red Roosters, 147
Refrigerator Potato Rolls, 15
Reunion Pea Casserole, 11
Rhubarb Chutney, 245
Ribbon Cookies, 293
Rice-and-Chicken Casserole, 154
Rice Casserole, 45
Rice Mélange, 240
Rice Pilaf, 229
Rice with Green Peas, 45
Roast Leg of Lamb, 96
Romano Sesame Rolls, 144
Rosy Cinnamon Apples, M37
Rotini Romano, 193
Royal Icing, 295
Royal Meatballs, 268

Salad by Committee, 288
Salad Extravaganza, 233
Salad Pizza, 182
Salmon-and-Horseradish Spread, 146
Salmon-Pasta Salad, 9
Salmon-Potato Salad, 285
Salmon Quiche, 38
Salmon-Spinach Salad, 145
Salmon Steaks with Tarragon Butter, 155
Salsa, 217
Salsa Cruda, 180
Salted Peanut Cookies, 92
Satan's Wings, 214
Saucy Carrots, 41
Saucy Chicken Breasts, 167
Saucy Cocktail Sausages, 173
Saucy Potato Salad, 123
Sautéed Chicken Breasts, 36
Savory Meat Loaf, 216
Savory Navy Bean Soup, 282
Savory Pork Chops, 194
Scalloped Apples, 156
Scallop-Vegetable Vermicelli, 143
Seafood Brochette, 96
Seafood Casserole, 109
Seafood Gumbo, 210
Seafood Spread, 146
Seafood Tartlets, 247
Seasoned New Potatoes, M151
Seasoned Potatoes, 253
Sesame Cracker Bread, 2
Sesame Seed Dressing, 81
Seven-Minute Frosting, 296
Sherried Avocado-Crabmeat Cocktail, 95
Sherried Chicken with Artichokes, 143
Sherry-Chicken Sauté, 218
Sherry Sauce, 96
Sherry Snaps, 94
Sherry Sour, 74
Shortbread Cookies, 58

Shrimp-and-Almond Sauce, 282
Shrimp and Feta Cheese on Vermicelli, 108
Shrimp-and-Grouper Sauté, 91
Shrimp Cocktail, 173
Shrimp Creole, 18
Shrimp Dijonnaise, 91
Shrimp Miniquiches, 146
Shrimp Mold, 94
Shrimp Mousse, 196, 251
Shrimp Salad Filling, 106
Shrimp Sauce, 138, 232
Shrimp Spread, 111
Shrimp-Stuffed Artichokes, 55
Shrimp Tart, 70
Shrimp with Herbed Jalapeño Cheese, 112
Skillet Corn Frittata, 90
Smoked Duck Breasts, 121
Smoked Duck Enchiladas with Red
    Pepper-Sour Cream, 121
Smoky Oysters Supreme, 60
Snack Buns, 279
Snowy Emerald Salad, 311
Sole Divan, 21

Sombrero Spread, 111
Sonny Frye's Brunswick Stew, 4
Sour Cream-Bran Muffins, 98
Sour Cream Enchiladas, 37
Sour Cream Sauce, 233
Sour Cream Slaw, 10
Southern Oven-Fried Catfish, 163
Southern Sweet Potato Cream Pie, 260
Southern Turnips, 190
Southern Waffles, 225
Southwestern Scallop Broth with Black
   Beans and Cilantro, 123
Soy-Sesame Dressing, 153
Spaghetti Carbonara, 167
Spanish Avocado Salad, 41
Special Chicken Salad, 183
Special-Occasion Brownie Dessert, 139
Special Pecan Tarts, 224
Special Shrimp Creole, 172
Spice Cookies, M278
Spiced Autumn Fruit Salad, 228
Spiced Carrot Cake, 296
Spiced Christmas Cookies, 294
Spiced Cranberry Lemonade, 292
Spiced Nut Crust, 295
Spiced Peaches with Nutty Dumplings, 164
Spiced Popcorn Snack, 8
Spicy Apple Pancakes with Cider
   Sauce, 224
Spicy Apple Pork Chops, 230
Spicy Apple Topping, 125
Spicy Bloody Marys, 173
Spicy Chicken Dish, 267
Spicy Chili Sauce, 127
Spicy Corn on the Cob, M151
Spicy Taco Salad, 287
Spinach Bread, 144
Spinach Dip, 25, 214
Spinach-Kiwifruit Salad, 305
Spinach Quichelets, 67
Spinach Salad, 62
Spinach Salad with Orange Dressing, 187
Spinach-Stuffed Shells, 20
Spinach-Walnut Pitas, 202
Spirited Beef Kabobs, 142
Spoon Rolls, 15
Spring Salad, 62
Spring Salad Wedges, 62
Squash Casserole, 163
Squash Pickles, 150
Steak-House Burgers, 186
Stir-Fried Asparagus, 52
Stir-Fried Chicken Curry, 51
Stir-Fried Peas and Peppers, 51
Stir-Fried Pork, 51
Stir-Fried Vegetables with Curry, 51
Stir-Fry Sausage and Vegetables, 82
Stir-Fry Shrimp and Vegetables, 91
Strawberry-Banana Float, 160
Strawberry-Banana Topping, 125
Strawberry Ice Cream Crêpes, 290
Strawberry-Lemon Cream Puffs, 75
Strawberry-Orange Breakfast Shake, 186
Strawberry Sauce, 93, 198
Strawberry-Yogurt Shake, 199
Stromboli, 283
Stuffed Carrots, 40
Stuffed Chicken Breasts, 36
Stuffed Chicken Breasts Sardou, 269
Stuffed Leg of Lamb, 248
Stuffed Mushroom Delight, 281
Stuffed Potatoes with Cheese Sauce, 192
Stuffed Snapper, 138

Stuffed Turkey Breast, 270
Summer Garden Salad, 153
Sunshine Sauce, 96
Sweet-and-Sour Beans, 197
Sweet-and-Sour Cabbage, 189
Sweet-and-Sour Dressing, 305
Sweet-and-Sour Marinade, 115
Sweet-and-Sour Shrimp and Chicken, 267
Sweet Potato Delight, 83
Sweet Potato Muffins, 280
Sweet Potato Pancakes, 280
Sweet Potato Puffs, 253
Swirled Melon Soup, 162
Swiss Cheese Sauce, 289
Swiss Chocolate Chip Cake, 85
Swiss Cinnamon Stars, 293

Tahitian Flower, 159
Tangy Beef Salad, M218
Tangy Blue Cheese Dressing, 81
Tangy Broiled Scamp, 5
Tangy Chicken, 35
Tangy Cranberry Ice, 305
Tangy Herbed Chicken, M302
Tangy Vegetable Dip, 196
Tarragon Pasta-Chicken Salad, 155
Tarragon Sauce, 229
Tart Cranberry-Cherry Pie, 299
Tart Milan, 70
Tart Shell, 77
Teaberry Sangría, 147
Tea Party Punch, 147
Teriyaki Lamb Chops, 60
Texas Oyster Nachos, 39
Texas-Style Game Hens, 61
Tex-Mex Wontons, 196
Thick 'n' Crusty Chicken Pot Pie, 267
Three-Egg Cheese Soufflé, 234
Three-Fruit Drink, 199
Tipsy Carrots, 40
Toasted Mushroom Sandwiches, 281
Toffee Ice Cream Dessert, 110
Toffee Meringue Torte, 118
Tomato-Basil Vinaigrette, 89
Tomato-Clam Cocktail, 252

Tomatoes and Okra, 164
Tomato Salsa, 120
Tomato Sauce, 249
Tomato Slices with Lemon Dressing, 167
Topping Glaze, 69
Tossed Bibb Salad, 128
Tournedos Diables, 60
Traders' Punch, 94
Tree-Hunt Chili, 292
Tropical Fruit Crêpes, 77
Tropical Shake, 200
Tulsa Eggs, 95

Tuna-in-a-Pita Pocket, 202
Tuna-Mac in Tomatoes, 188
Tuna-Pecan Ball, 94
Tuna-Rice Salad, 202
Tuna-Taco Salad, 145
Turkey-Cheese Puffs, 301
Turkey-Olive Casserole, 268
Turkey Parmigiana, 193
Turkey Patties in Vegetable-Tomato
   Sauce, 18
Turkey Salad Pita Sandwiches, 202
Turkey Salad with Hot Bacon
   Dressing, 285
Turkey with Squash Dressing, 248

Upside-Down Sunburst Cake, 9
Uptown Welsh Rarebit, 279

Vanilla Frozen Yogurt, 125
Veal Cordon Bleu, 219
Veal Picante, 31
Veal Picatta with Capers, 142
Veal with Green Peppercorns, 220
Vegetable-Egg Spread, 106
Vegetable Kabobs, 116
Vegetable Quiche, M219
Vegetable Soup, 83, 123
Vegetable-Stuffed Flounder Rolls, 6
Venison Burgers, 304
Venison Chili, 304
Venison Sausage Stew, 238
Venison Stew with Potato Dumplings, 304
Venison-Vegetable Bake, 304
Vienna Brioche Loaves, 300
Viennese Sandwich Cookies, 293
Vinaigrette Dressing, 138

Walnut-Cranberry Pie, 259
Warm Lobster Taco with Yellow Tomato
   Salsa and Jicama Salad, 122
Whipped Cream, 225
Whipped Cream Frosting, 263
Whipped Cream Topping, 264
White Cake with Strawberries and
   Chocolate Glaze, 76
White Chocolate Cheesecake, 44
White Chocolate-Coconut Cake, 263
White Chocolate Truffles, 45
White Grape Juice Tea, 57
White Sauce, 166
Whole Wheat-Oatmeal Bread, 85
Wild Goose with Currant Sauce, 240
Wine-Sauced Beef-and-Barley Rolls, 269

Yeast Biscuits, 71, 301
Yellow Tomato Salsa, 122
Yummy Fudge Bars, 158

Zesty Lasagna, M188
Zesty Marinated Shrimp, 173
Zesty Shrimp-and-Orange Rice
   Salad, 155
Zippy Cheese Omelet, 287
Zippy Chili, 110
Zucchini-Apple Bread, 255
Zucchini-Basil Scramble, 34
Zucchini Casserole, 154
Zucchini Relish, 200
Zucchini Salad, 103
Zucchini with Pecans, 31

Month-by-Month Index

An alphabetical listing within the month of every food article and accompanying recipes
All microwave recipe page numbers are preceded by an "M"

JANUARY

Bring On Black-Eyed Peas, 11
Black-Eyed Pea Gravy, 12
Good Luck Jambalaya, 11
Plentiful P's Salad, 12
Reunion Pea Casserole, 11
Burgoo And Brunswick Stew, 3
Bama Brunswick Stew, 4
Blakely Brunswick Stew, 4
Brunswick Chicken Stew, 4
Five-Meat Burgoo, 3
Harry Young's Burgoo, 3
Old-Fashioned Burgoo, 3
Sonny Frye's Brunswick Stew, 4
Fish Is Fine On Your Low-Sodium Diet, 4
Caribbean Snapper, 5
Curried Baked Fish, 5
Foil-Baked Swordfish, 5
Marinated Salmon Steaks, 6
Tangy Broiled Scamp, 5
Vegetable-Stuffed Flounder
  Rolls, 6

From Our Kitchen To Yours, 12
Standard Cooking Procedures and
  Terms, 12
It's A Snap To Make These Crackers, 2
Dessert Crackers, 3
Fennel-Rye Crackers, 2
Sesame Cracker Bread, 2
New Variations On An Old Favorite, 8
Cranberry Upside-Down Cake, 8
Peach Upside-Down Cake, 8
Upside-Down Sunburst Cake, 9
No-Fuss Supper Ideas, 10
Baked Mustard Chicken, 10
Banana Split Alaskas, 10
Carrot-Raisin Salad, 10
Cheese Bread, 11

Chili Chops, 10
Easy-Crust Apple Pie, 11
Green Beans Italian, 10
Sour Cream Slaw, 10
Salads From Your Pantry, 9
Crunchy Sauerkraut Salad, 9
Icy Pineapple-Fruit Salad, 9
Marinated Corn-Bean Salad, 9
Salmon-Pasta Salad, 9
Snacks To Keep You Cheering, 7
Country Ham Spread, 8
Meat-and-Cheese Appetizers, 7
Mexican Cheese Puffs, 8
Oriental Hot Munch, 8
Spiced Popcorn Snack, 8
**Soup And Sandwich—A Natural
Combo, M6**
Bacon-Beer Cheese Soup, M7
Brown Bread-Cream Cheese
  Sandwiches, M6
Cream of Cauliflower Soup, M7
Hot Pita Sandwiches, M6
Try Feta Cheese, 12
Pastitsio, 12

FEBRUARY

Avocado Salad Ideas, 41
Avocado Fruit Salad, 41
Congealed Avocado Salads, 42
Fruited Chicken Salad in Avocados, 41
Spanish Avocado Salad, 41
Bake A Dainty Party Cookie, 16
French Curled Cookies, 16
Cabbage Patch Favorites, 42
Cabbage Kielbasa, 42
Cabbage with Apples and Franks, 42
Hot Cabbage Creole, 42
Italian Cabbage Casserole, 42
Nutty Cabbage Salad, 42
Caramel Makes It Rich, 38
Easy Caramel Sauce, 38
Pound Cake with Caramel Frosting, 39
Quemada (Burnt-Sugar Candy), 38

COOKING LIGHT, 17
*Add A Chilled Vegetable Salad
  To The Menu, 24*
Broccoli-Corn Salad, 24
Confetti-Stuffed Lettuce, 24
English Pea-and-Apple Salad, 24
A Menu For The Two Of You, 31
Fruited Meringue Shells, 32
Herbed Carrots and Onions, 31
Orange Tapioca Fluff, 31
Red Cabbage-and-Apple Slaw, 31
Veal Picante, 31
Zucchini with Pecans, 31
Chocolate—The Ultimate In Desserts, 21
Chocolate Angel Food Cake, 21
Chocolate-Orange Roll, 21

Enjoy Fresh Basil, 33
Cucumber-Yogurt Salad, 33
Pasta-Basil Toss, 33
Zucchini-Basil Scramble, 34
*Iron Is Important In Your Low-Calorie
Diet, 32*
Apricot-Raisin Bars, 32
Liver in Creole Sauce, 33
Marinated London Broil, 32
Lighten Up For A Livelier You, 17
Make Your Own Frozen Entrées, 17
Beef-and-Onion Stew, 18
Chili, 17
Colorful Vegetable Lasagna, 19
Curried Chicken-Stuffed Peppers, 19
Shrimp Creole, 18
Spinach-Stuffed Shells, 20
Tips for Making Frozen Entrées at
  Home, 20
Turkey Patties in Vegetable-Tomato
  Sauce, 18
Sauces Slim On Calories, 26
Low-Calorie Medium White
  Sauce, 26
Variations on White Sauce, 26
Special Equipment, 21
Beef-and-Vegetable Stir-Fry, 22
Chicken in a Bag, 23
Deviled-Beef Patties, 22
Fish Florentine in Parchment, 22
Frosty Fruit Shake, 23
Parsley Meat Loaf, 22
Sole Divan, 21

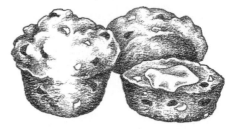

*Start Your Day With A Piping-Hot
Muffin, 23*
Apple Muffins, 23
Blueberry-Oatmeal Muffins, 24
Carrot-and-Raisin Muffins, 24
*Tasty Substitutions Keep Dips Lower
In Calories, 25*
Curry Dip, 25
Deviled Dip, 25
Low-Cal Tuna Dip, 25
Spinach Dip, 25
The Keys To Weight Loss, 34

Dessert For The Sentimental, 14
Apricot-Kirsch Glaze, 14
Egg Custard Filling, 14

Ground Almond Filling, 14
Heart Tarts, 14
Honey-Nut Glaze, 15
Lemon Cream Filling, 14
Enjoy The Taste Of Sour Cream, 37
Chilled Avocado Soup, 37
Lemon-Sour Cream Pound Cake, 38
Macaroni Shell Salad, 38
Salmon Quiche, 38
Sour Cream Enchiladas, 37
Favorite Recipes—Only Faster, M36
Chicken and Vegetables
Vermouth, M37
Chocolate-Topped Amaretto
Custard, M37
Rosy Cinnamon Apples, M37
From Our Kitchen To Yours, 16
Cornmeal Labels and Cornbread
Tips, 16

Oysters Are Versatile, 39
Oyster-and-Bacon Poor Boys, 40
Oyster-and-Mushroom Soup, 39
Oysters Buccaneer, 40
Oysters in Shrimp Sauce, 40
Texas Oyster Nachos, 39
Serve Carrots Anytime, 40
Carrot Pound Cake, 41
Saucy Carrots, 41
Stuffed Carrots, 40
Tipsy Carrots, 40
Simple But Savory Entrées, 35
Apple-Glazed Pork Chops, 35
Baked Shrimp, 35
Beer-Marinated Flank Steak, 35
Braised Round Steak, 35
Honey-Curry Chicken, 36
Pork Medallions with Chutney
Sauce, 35
Sautéed Chicken Breasts, 36
Tangy Chicken, 35
Southerners Love These
Oldtime Breads, 15
Cloud Biscuits, 15
Cornbread Sticks, 15
Cornmeal Batter Cakes, 16
Hush Puppies, 15
Quick Sally Lunn, 16
Refrigerator Potato Rolls, 15
Spoon Rolls, 15
Spice Up Dishes With
Italian Seasonings, 36
Italian Wafers, 36
Pasta Salad, 36
Stuffed Chicken Breasts, 36

MARCH
Accent Meals With Kiwifruit, 55
Kiwi-Berry Pizza, 55
Kiwi Parfait, 55
Bring On The Cookies!, 57
Butterscotch Cookies, 58
Chocolate Macaroons, 57
Orange Fingers, 57
Peanut Butter Cookies, 58
Shortbread Cookies, 58
Cheese Invites A Party, 46
Cheese Chart, 48
Serving Cheese, 49
Varieties of Cheese, 46
English Muffins For Breakfast, 49
English Muffins, 49
From Our Kitchen To Yours, 46
Buying, Storing, and Preparing
Rice, 46
Have Fun With Phyllo Appetizers, 53
Artichoke-Parmesan Phyllo Bites, 54
Phyllo-Spinach Triangles, 53
Have You Cooked Corned Beef Lately?, 54
Corned Beef Dinner, 54
Corned Beef with Dijon Glaze, 54
French Onion-Beef Soup, 54
Grilled Corned Beef Sandwiches, 54
Helpful Hints And A Few Good Tips, M52
Getting the Best Results from Your
Microwave, M52
Offer A Fruit Salad, 56
Cheesy Fruit-'n'-Nut Salad, 56
Cottage Cheese-Banana Splits, 56
Fruit Salad with Date Dressing, 57
Pear-and-Celery Salad, 56
Potato Yeast Rolls, 53
Potato Yeast Rolls, 53
Processor-Quick Frostings And Toppings, 58
Cream Cheese Frosting, 58
Fluffy Chocolate Frosting, 58
Orange Dessert Sauce, 58
Processor Devonshire Sauce, 58
Puzzled About White Chocolate?, 44
Chocolate Teasers, 44
White Chocolate Cheesecake, 44
White Chocolate Truffles, 45
Rice—A Versatile Southern Tradition, 45
Northshore Jambalaya, 45
Raisin-Rice Pudding, 46
Red Beans and Rice, 45
Rice Casserole, 45
Rice with Green Peas, 45
Spring Vegetables Are Here, 55
Asparagus with Cashew Butter, 56
Chilled Artichokes with Lemon-Pepper
Dressing, 55
Minted Peas, 56
Shrimp-Stuffed Artichokes, 55
Stir-Fry To Keep Calories Low, 50
Chinese-Style Beef, 50
Fast-and-Easy Stir-Fried Steak, 50
Quick Shrimp Skillet, 50
Stir-Fried Asparagus, 52
Stir-Fried Chicken Curry, 51
Stir-Fried Peas and Peppers, 51
Stir-Fried Pork, 51
Stir-Fried Vegetables with Curry, 51
Stir-Frying Pointers, 51
Tea Is The Basis Of These Beverages, 57
Bourbon-Tea Punch, 57
Hawaiian Tea, 57
Hot Apple-Cinnamon Tea, 57
White Grape Juice Tea, 57

APRIL
Appetizers And Salads For Two, 80
Asparagus-Horseradish Salad, 80
Banana Salad, 80
Onion-Cheese Soup, 81
Pepper-Cheese Stacks, 80
Quick Orange Salad, 80

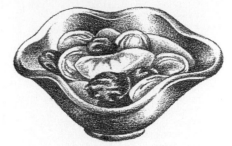

BREAKFASTS & BRUNCHES, 67
Can't Wait For Breakfast!, 67
Asparagus in Squash Rings, 68
Chicken Bundles with Bacon
Ribbons, 68
Cinnamon-Pecan Coffee
Cake, 69
County Fair Egg Bread, 68
Ginger-Glazed Carrots, 68
Lemon-Raisin Scones, 69
Oklahoma Sunrise, 67
Poached Pears with Raspberry
Sauce, 69
Praline-Flavored Coffee, 69
Spinach Quichelets, 67
Cholesterol Is Low In These Dishes, 71
Banana Bread, 72
Omelet Primavera, 71
Pear Breakfast Treat, 72
Yeast Biscuits, 71
Fruit Instead Of Flowers, 73
Using Fresh Fruit in the
Centerpiece, 73
Make The Entrée A Quiche Or Tart, 70
Crustless Sausage-Apple
Quiche, 70
Shrimp Tart, 70
Tart Milan, 70
Plan A Great Brunch, 72
Toast The Morning, 72
Brandy Slush Punch, 72
Cranapple-Vodka Punch, 72
Magnolia Blossoms, 72

Fast-Rising Rolls, 85
Cream Cheese Pinches, 85
Fish In A Flash, M78
Creole Fish, M79
Dressed Oysters on the
Half Shell, M79
Greek-Style Monkfish, M79
From Our Kitchen To Yours, 79
Facts About Fish, 79
Let's Have Lunch!, 74
Chocolate Charlotte Russe, 74
Chutney-Chicken Salad, 74
Easy Whole Wheat Rolls, 74
Marinated Asparagus, 74
Sherry Sour, 74
Look What's Sizzling On The Grill, 60
Flank Steak and Mushrooms, 61
Marinated Chicken, 61

Look What's Sizzling On The Grill
(continued)

    Smoky Oysters Supreme, 60
    Teriyaki Lamb Chops, 60
    Texas-Style Game Hens, 61
    Tips for Successful Outdoor
      Grilling, 60
    Tournedos Diables, 60
Low-Calorie Desserts With High Appeal, 75
    Apple-Nut Cake, 76
    Blueberry Chiffon Cheesecake, 76
    Green Grape Tart, 77
    Peach Melba Meringues, 76
    Range-Top Amaretto Custard, 77
    Strawberry-Lemon Cream Puffs, 75
    Tropical Fruit Crêpes, 77
    White Cake with Strawberries and
      Chocolate Glaze, 76
Luscious Whole-Grain Bread, 85
    Whole Wheat-Oatmeal Bread, 85
No-Frost Cakes, 84
    Orange Liqueur Cake, 84
    Orange Pound Cake, 84
    Swiss Chocolate Chip Cake, 85

Oranges Add Tangy Flavor, 83
    Citrus Salad Bowl, 83
    Orange-Cranberry Pork Chops, 84
    Orange Meringue Cake, 84
    Sweet Potato Delight, 83
**Peanut Butter Eggs For Your Easter
  Basket, 86**
    Peanut Butter Easter Eggs, 86
Pork Pleasers For Two, 81
    Bacon Spaghetti, 82
    Cider-Sauced Pork Chops, 81
    Ham-and-Broccoli Rolls, 82
    Hawaiian Pork Chops, 82
    Stir-Fry Sausage and Vegetables, 82
Salad Dressings To Boast About, 81
    Dressing For Fruit Salad, 81
    Honey French Dressing, 81
    Lime-Honey Fruit Salad Dressing, 81
    Sesame Seed Dressing, 81
    Tangy Blue Cheese Dressing, 81
The Freshest, Prettiest Salads, 61
    Delicate Garden Lettuce, 62
    Flippo Caesar Salad, 61
    Garden Salad, 62
    Mixed Greens Salad, 62
    Spinach Salad, 62
    Spring Salad, 62
    Spring Salad Wedges, 62

Use Up That Leftover Ham, 78
    Golden Ham Pie, 78
    Ham-and-Cheese Casserole, 78
    Ham-Noodle Skillet, 78
    Ham-Rice-Tomato Bake, 78
Use Your Canned Beans, 82
    Colorful Six-Bean Salad, 82
    Green Beans and Tomatoes with
      Mustard, 83
    Pork-'n'-Bean Salad, 83
    Vegetable Soup, 83

MAY

A New Twist For Chicken, 103
    Chicken Andalusia, 103
Appetizers From The Sea, 94
    Bacon-Wrapped Scallops, 94
    Baked Clam Shells, 94
    Sherried Avocado-Crabmeat
      Cocktail, 95
    Shrimp Mold, 94
    Tuna-Pecan Ball, 94
Basil-Cheese Tart, 98
    Herb-Cheese Tart, 98
Celebrate With A Party, 92
    Almond Cream with Fresh
      Strawberries, 93
    Cheese Bonbons, 93
    Lemon-Cheese Canapés, 93
    Mocha Brownies, 93
    Sherry Snaps, 94
    Traders' Punch, 94
Cheese Served With Flair, 88
    Planning and Creating a Cheese
      Buffet, 88
Desserts From The Freezer, 109
    Fruity Ice Cream Cake, 110
    Layered Sherbet Dessert, 109
    Toffee Ice Cream Dessert, 110
Entrées Men Like To Cook, 95
    Beer-Braised Steaks, 96
    Cajun Barbecued Shrimp, 95
    Italian Pot Roast, 95
    Kyoto Orange-Chicken
      Stir-Fry, 96
    Roast Leg of Lamb, 96
    Seafood Brochette, 96
    Tulsa Eggs, 95
From Our Kitchen To Yours, 112
    Cleaning and Storage Tips for the
      Freezer, 112
Get A Crush On Mint, 107
    Avocado-Chicken Salad, 107
    Middle Eastern Salad, 107
    Minted Delight, 107
    Mint Tea, 107
Get Ready For Fresh Vegetables, 89
    Chilled Zucchini Soup, 90
    Fresh Okra and Tomatoes, 89
    Fresh Summer Salsa, 89
    Fried Okra, 89
    Garden Sauté, 90
    Green Bean Salad, 90
    Herb Salad, 90
    Lemon-Cucumber Mold, 90
    Maque Chou Stuffed Tomatoes, 89
    Marinated Roasted Peppers, 90
    Skillet Corn Frittata, 90
    Tomato-Basil Vinaigrette, 89
**Grind, Chop, Or Slice Meat In The
  Processor, 110**
    Double-Crust Chicken Pie, 111
    Quick Processor Meatballs, 111

    Shrimp Spread, 111
    Sombrero Spread, 111
    Tips for Using Your Food
      Processor, 110
    Zippy Chili, 110
Hot Stuffing For Shrimp, 112
    Shrimp with Herbed Jalapeño
      Cheese, 112
Look What's Happening With Pasta, 108
    Chicken and Tomato with
      Rotelle, 108
    Ham and Swiss on Noodles, 108
    Linguine Carbonara, 108
    Pasta with Broccoli and Sausage, 109
    Seafood Casserole, 109
    Shrimp and Feta Cheese on
      Vermicelli, 108
Put A Salad On The Menu, 103
    Apple Salad with Blue Cheese
      Dressing, 103
    Citrus Salad, 103
    Fresh Broccoli Salad, 103
    Greek Salad, 103
    Zucchini Salad, 103
Quick And Easy Cakes, M96
    Fruit and Spice Cake, M97
    No-Egg Chocolate Marshmallow
      Cake, M97
Scrumptious Picnic Fare, 91
    Cheese Loaf, 92
    Fire-and-Ice Tomatoes, 92
    Ham Salad Spread, 92
    Herbed Fried Chicken, 91
    Macaroni Salad, 92
    Mixed Baked Beans, 92
    Salted Peanut Cookies, 92
Surprise Her With Breakfast, 98
    Fruit Soup, 98
    Sour Cream-Bran Muffins, 98

Take A New Look At Sandwiches, 104
    Alternative Bases for Slender
      Sandwiches (chart), 105
    Chicken Salad Filling, 106
    Cottage Cheese Spread, 107
    Hawaiian Ham Spread, 106
    Lamb Pockets with Dilled Cucumber
      Topping, 104
    Open-Faced Crab Sandwiches, 106
    Open-Faced Garden
      Sandwiches, 105
    Open-Faced Vegetarian Melt, 106
    Shrimp Salad Filling, 106
    Vegetable-Egg Spread, 106
Try A Seafood Entrée For Two, 91
    Halibut with Orange-Curry
      Sauce, 91
    Shrimp-and-Grouper Sauté, 91
    Shrimp Dijonnaise, 91
    Stir-Fry Shrimp and Vegetables, 91

JUNE

Add A Chilled Sauce To Meat, 127
Cocktail Sauce, 128
Horseradish Sauce, 127
Quick Tartar Sauce, 128
Raisin Sauce, 127
Spicy Chili Sauce, 127
Come For Dinner!, 115
Beef Tenderloin with Mushrooms, 115
Bran Yeast Rolls, 116
Brie Cheese Bake, 117
Brown Rice Casserole, 118
Cheesecake with Raspberry
Sauce, 116
Chicken Rolls Jubilee, 118
Easy Caesar Salad, 116
Green Bean Bundles, 118
Potato Croquettes, 116
Toffee Meringue Torte, 118
Vegetable Kabobs, 116
End The Meal With Crêpes, 126
Raspberry Crêpes, 126
**Expect The Unexpected In New
Southwestern Cuisine, 119**
Black Bean Terrine with Goat
Cheese, 120
Grilled Corn Soup, 121
Grilled Scallops Tostada, 120
Marinated Breast of Chicken, 123
Medallions of Beef with Ancho Chile
Sauce, 122
Smoked Duck Enchiladas with Red
Pepper-Sour Cream, 121
Southwestern Scallop Broth with Black
Beans and Cilantro, 123
Warm Lobster Taco with Yellow
Tomato Salsa and Jicama
Salad, 122
From Our Kitchen To Yours, 130
Operating and Maintaining Kitchen
Appliances, 130

It's Time To Pick Blackberries, 129
Blackberries-and-Cream
Parfait, 129
Blackberry-Apple Pie, 130
Blackberry Bars, 130
Fruit Salad with Honey
Dressing, 129
It's Yogurt—Not Ice Cream, 125
Blueberry Topping, 125
Cherry-Pineapple Topping, 126
Chunky Piña Colada Topping, 125
Raspberry-Peach Topping, 126
Spicy Apple Topping, 125
Strawberry-Banana Topping, 125
Vanilla Frozen Yogurt, 125
Make Extra Soup, And Freeze It, 123
Vegetable Soup, 123

**Perk Up Vegetables With A Cream
Sauce, 126**
Broccoli with Sour Cream
Sauce, 127
Creamed Spring Vegetables, 127
Creamy Baked Mushrooms, 127
Hot-and-Creamy Dutch Slaw, 127
Pretty To Look At, Good To Eat, 114
Dill Marinade, 115
Garlic-and-Oregano Marinade, 115
Making Garnishes, 114
Sweet-and-Sour Marinade, 115
Quick Cooking For Summer, M124
Cheese-Sauced Tuna Salad, M124
Olé Omelet, M124
Pineapple Pork Chops, M124
Quick Chicken Toss, M124
This Menu Is For Two, 128
Baked Lemon Cups, 128
Fish-Asparagus Divan, 128
Glazed Carrots and Onions, 128
Tossed Bibb Salad, 128

JULY

A Southern Breakfast In Just Minutes, 156
Angel Heart Biscuits with
Sausage, 156
Good Morning Grits, 156
Scalloped Apples, 156
Baked Ham Stretches Summer Menus, 160
Pineapple-Flavored Ham, 160
Casseroles For Potluck Dinners, 154
Curry Pea Casserole, 154
Macaroni Casserole, 154
Mixed-Vegetable Casserole, 154
Rice-and-Chicken Casserole, 154
Zucchini Casserole, 154
Chicken With A Cajun Flair, 159
Cajun-Style Drumsticks, 159
Cool, Crisp Salads To Beat The Heat, 152
Crimson Greens, 153
Crisp Vegetable Aspic with
Horseradish Dressing, 152
Marinated Bean-and-Rice Salad, 152
Melon Ball Bowl with Cucumber-Mint
Dressing, 153
Oriental Salad Bowl, 153
Peaches in a Garden Nest, 154
Summer Garden Salad, 153
Delicious Summer Gifts, 134
Apple-Mint Jelly, 134
Fresh Fruit Dressing, 134
Green Tomato Pickles, 134
Herbed Mustard, 134
Raspberry-Lemon Vinegar, 134
From Our Kitchen To Yours, 150
Recognizing Pickling
Problems, 150
Ice Cream Parlor Beverages, 159
Banana Smoothie, 160
Frosty Fruit Float, 159
Lime Cooler, 160
Strawberry-Banana Float, 160
Tahitian Flower, 159
Kids Will Love These Snacks, 158
Chewy Soft Pretzels, 159
Jam-It Bars, 159
Peanut Butter Muffins, 158
Yummy Fudge Bars, 158
Mighty Flavor From Tarragon, 155
Cherry Tomato Salad, 156
Herb-Roasted Chicken, 155

Salmon Steaks with Tarragon
Butter, 155
Tarragon Pasta-Chicken Salad, 155
Zesty Shrimp-and-Orange Rice
Salad, 155
Party Spreads And Sandwich Fillings, 157
Apricot-Cream Cheese Spread, 158
Curried Shrimp Spread, 158
Festive Chicken Spread, 158
Hawaiian Cheese Spread, 158
Honey-Nut Spread, 157
Pickles: The Quick Way, 149
Chowchow, 150
Lazy Wife Dills, 149
Quick Sweet Pickles, 149
Squash Pickles, 150
**Present Dessert In A Shell Of
Chocolate, 132**
Chocolate Lace Cups, 133
Creamy Chocolate Mousse, 133
Kahlúa Cream, 134
Miniature Chocolate Cups, 132

Quick-Cooking Garden Fare, M150
Asparagus with Lemon Butter, M151
Crisp Squash-and-Pepper Toss, M152
Easy Eggplant, M151
Green Beans, M151
Okra, Corn, and Peppers, M151
Seasoned New Potatoes, M151
Spicy Corn on the Cob, M151

SUMMER SUPPERS, 137
Appetizers For Summer, 146
Mint Dip with Fresh Fruit, 146
Salmon-and-Horseradish Spread, 146
Seafood Spread, 146
Shrimp Miniquiches, 146
Beverages On Ice, 146
Red Roosters, 147
Teaberry Sangría, 147
Tea Party Punch, 147
Blueberries At Their Best, 140
Blueberries 'n' Cream
Cheesecake, 140
Blueberry-Orange Bread, 140
Blueberry Pinwheel
Cobbler, 140
Easy Ways With Dinner Breads, 143
Brie Bread, 143
Herb-and-Cheese Pull Aparts, 143
Romano Sesame Rolls, 144
Spinach Bread, 144
Grilled Meats For Lazy Evenings, 140
Chicken Kabobs, 141
Flank Steak Pinwheels, 141
Grilled Cumin Chicken, 142
Grilling Tips, 141

Grilled Meats For Lazy Evenings
(continued)

    Marinated and Grilled Shrimp, 141
    Patio Steak, 141
Hot Days Call For Cool Desserts, 139
    Bourbon Ice Cream, 139
    Lemon Curd, 139
    Special-Occasion Brownie
      Dessert, 139
Put Together A Summer Bouquet, 147
Set The Mood With Candles, 148
Spirited Main Dishes, 142
    Beer-Broiled Shrimp, 142
    Scallop-Vegetable Vermicelli, 143
    Sherried Chicken with
      Artichokes, 143
    Spirited Beef Kabobs, 142
    Veal Picatta with Capers, 142

Summertime Food And Fun, 137
    Cajun Cake, 138
    Crab-and-Corn Bisque, 137
    Creole Potatoes, 138
    Fig Ice Cream, 139
    Hearts-of-Palm Salad, 138
    Pepper Pecans, 137
    Stuffed Snapper, 138
When The Entrée Is A Salad, 144
    BLT Chicken Salad, 144
    Curried Chicken-and-Orange
      Salad, 144
    Delightful Crab Salad, 145
    Italian Salad, 145
    Mandarin Ham-and-Rice Salad, 145
    Poulet Rémoulade, 144
    Salmon-Spinach Salad, 145
    Tuna-Taco Salad, 145
Yummy Ice Cream Sandwiches, 147
    Chocolate Cookie Ice Cream
      Sandwiches, 147

Try Warm-Weather Soups, 156
    Charleston Okra Soup, 156
    Cold Fresh Fruit Soup, 157
    Corn Soup, 156
    Peach-Plum Soup, 157

AUGUST
Add Eggplant To The Menu, 166
    Caponata, 166
    Fried Parmesan Eggplant, 166
    Moussaka, 166
    Potato-Eggplant Casserole, 166
Chicken—Fried Crisp And Delicious, 175
    Buttermilk Drumsticks, 175

    Deep-Fried Walnut Chicken, 175
    Hot Buffalo Wings, 176
    Mexican Fried Chicken, 176
Cooking Smart Means Cooking Healthy, 174
    Cooking Techniques That Retain
      Nutrients in Vegetables, 174
Cornbread Mix Offers Possibilities, 171
    Chile-Cheese Cornbread, 171
    Cornbread Salad, 172
    Cornbread-Sausage-Apple Pie, 171
Dessert Is Easy With Fruit Sauces, M164
    Amaretto-Strawberry Sauce, M165
    Apple Dessert Sauce, M165
    Chocolate Cherry Sauce, M165
    Lemon Dessert Sauce, M165
    Peach-Berry Sauce, M165
Dinner's Ready In Less Than An Hour, 167
    Easy Bread, 168
    Easy Zucchini, 167
    Fresh Peach Sauce, 167
    Fudge Pie, 168
    Nutty Green Salad, 168
    Parslied Rice, 167
    Saucy Chicken Breasts, 167
    Spaghetti Carbonara, 167
    Tomato Slices with Lemon
      Dressing, 167
Favorite Family Desserts, 178
    Apple-Cranberry Crunch, 178
    Choco-Maple Frozen Dessert, 178
    Crunchy Ice Cream Treats, 178
    Peach-Caramel Cobbler, 178
    Plum Pudding-Gelatin Mold, 178
From Our Kitchen To Yours, 177
    All About Pasta, 177
It's Better With Fresh Basil, 171
    Basil Butter, 171
    Basil Chicken, 171
    Fresh Tomato Sauce, 171
    Herbed Potato Salad, 171
Not Your Everyday Melon, 162
    Grilled Cantaloupe Wedges, 162
    Honeydew Granita, 162
    Minted Melon Balls, 162
    Swirled Melon Soup, 162
Shrimp, Wonderful Shrimp!, 172
    Fried Shrimp with Apricot Sauce, 172
    Grilled Marinated Shrimp, 173
    Special Shrimp Creole, 172
    Zesty Marinated Shrimp, 173
These Appetizers Are Really Hot, 173
    Chile-Cheese Dip, 173
    Hot Pimiento Cheese, 173
    Saucy Cocktail Sausages, 173
    Shrimp Cocktail, 173
    Spicy Bloody Marys, 173
Traditional Southern Foods Go Light, 162
    Crunchy Oven-Fried Chicken, 163
    Dieter's Cornbread, 164
    Green Beans with New Potatoes, 164
    Mock Country-Fried Steak, 163
    New-Fashioned Blackberry
      Cobbler, 164
    Pickled Beets, 163
    Southern Oven-Fried Catfish, 163
    Spiced Peaches with Nutty
      Dumplings, 164
    Squash Casserole, 163
    Tomatoes and Okra, 164
Treats From The Freezer, 168
    Fruit Pops, 168
    Pecan-Cheese Crispies, 168
    Pizza Squares, 168

Try Hot Salads For A Change, 176
    Baked Chicken Salad, 176
    Hot Dutch Potato Salad, 176
    Hot Green Bean Salad, 176
    Hot Turkey Salad, 176

SEPTEMBER
Add Pasta To These Entrées, 192
    Mexican Luncheon, 192
    Pasta and Garden Vegetables, 192
    Quick Crab Bake, 192
    Rotini Romano, 193
A Relish You'll Rave About, 200
    Zucchini Relish, 200
Carrot Dishes That Satisfy, 200
    Carrot Puffs, 200
    Creamy Marinated Carrots, 200
    Dill-Spiced Carrots, 200
    Glazed Carrots with Bacon and
      Onion, 200
Celebrate Victory With A Buffet, 197
    Baked Tomatoes, 197
    Chicken à la King, 197
    Cornbread, 197
    Strawberry Sauce, 198
    Sweet-and-Sour Beans, 197

Color Is The Key To Vitamins, 186
    Banana-Oat Muffins, 188
    Beef-and-Broccoli Salad, 187
    Food Sources of Vitamins
      (chart), 187
    Spinach Salad with Orange
      Dressing, 187
    Strawberry-Orange Breakfast
      Shake, 186
    Tuna-Mac in Tomatoes, 188
Eggs Benedict With A Twist, 195
    Bacon-and-Tomato Eggs Benedict, 195
Energizing Blender Beverages, 199
    Banana-Strawberry Frost, 199
    Breakfast Eye-Opener, 199
    Pineapple Milkshake, 199
    Strawberry-Yogurt Shake, 199
    Three-Fruit Drink, 199
    Tropical Shake, 200
Entrées To Bake Or Broil, 193
    Hot-and-Spicy Kabobs, 193
    Kiwi Orange Roughy, 193
    Turkey Parmigiana, 193
Flavor The Entrée With Fruit, 194
    Chinese Meatballs, 194
    Fruited Pork Chops, 194
    Savory Pork Chops, 194

For The Love Of Potatoes, 191
Creamy Potatoes with Ham Bits, 191
Jazzy Mashed Potatoes, 192
Mushroom Scalloped Potatoes, 191
Party Scalloped Potatoes, 191
Potatoes with Sweet Red Peppers, 192
Stuffed Potatoes with Cheese
Sauce, 192
From Our Kitchen To Yours, 208
Preventing Food Spoilage (chart), 208
Fry This Appetizer, 196
Tex-Mex Wontons, 196
Invite Friends For Dainties, 198
Almond Cream Confections, 198
Kick Off With Snacks, 195
Cheesy Beer Spread, 196
Corned Beef Spread, 196
Fiery Tomato-Cheese Spread, 196
Hotshot Bean Dip, 195
Shrimp Mousse, 196
Tangy Vegetable Dip, 196
Making The Best Cream Pie, 207
Banana Cream Pie, 207
Butterscotch Cream Pie, 207
Chocolate Cream Pie, 208
Coconut Cream Pie, 207
Not The Same Old Pizza, 181
Baby Clam Pizza, 182
Crispy Pizza Crust, 181
Gruyère-Chicken Pizza, 182
Original Italian-Style Pizza, 182
Pesto Pizza, 182
Pizza with Artichoke and
Prosciutto, 182
Salad Pizza, 182

Pecans And Peanuts, Plain And Fancy, 183
Brittle with Crushed Peanuts, 184
Chocolate-Peanut Cluster Cake, 184
Custard Pecan Pie, 184
Peanut Bread, 184
Peanut Soup, 184
Pecan Roulade, 183
Popcorn Scramble, 185
Roasting and Toasting Nuts, 183
Special Chicken Salad, 183
Storing Peanuts and Pecans, 183
Perk Up Your Burgers, 185
Burgers au Poivre Blanc, 186
Nutty Burgers, 185
Pizza Burger, 185
Steak-House Burgers, 186
Picante Sauce Burns With Flavor, 180
Chinese Burritos, 181
Fiesta, 180
Garlic-Grilled Chicken, 180
Guacamole Salad, 181
Migas, 180
Salsa Cruda, 180

Stir In Flavor With Cottage Cheese, 190
Corn Moussaka, 190
Cottage Cheese-Spinach Cups, 190
Creamy Cottage Cheese Dessert, 191
Hot Shrimp Dip, 190
Potato Casserole, 190
Stuff A Pita With Flavor, 202
Ham-and-Cheese Pita Sandwiches, 202
Spinach-Walnut Pitas, 202
Tuna-in-a-Pita Pocket, 202
Turkey Salad Pita Sandwiches, 202
Tex-Mex Dip Starts The Party, 196
Chilled Mexican Appetizer, 197
Try Your Hand At Adapting Recipes, M188
Easy Sausage Casserole, M189
Onion-Smothered Steak, M189
Zesty Lasagna, M188
Tuna Salads To Rave About, 200
Company Tuna Salad, 201
Crunchy Tuna Salad, 201
Curried Tuna Salad with Grapes, 201
Tuna-Rice Salad, 202
Vegetables You Can Rely On, 189
Creole Cabbage, 189
Potatoes Lorraine, 190
Southern Turnips, 190
Sweet-and-Sour Cabbage, 189
You Can't Resist Brownies, 198
Buttermilk Cake Brownies, 198
Choco-Mallow Brownies, 198
Crunch-Crust Brownies, 198
Oatmeal Brownies, 199
Peanut Butter Brownies, 199

OCTOBER
A Bread Made With Beer, 226
Hearty Beer Bread, 226
Cauliflower Is Best Now, 231
Cauliflower-Pea Salad, 231
Cauliflower with Pimiento
Sauce, 232
Festive Cauliflower Casserole, 232
Fried Cauliflower with Cheese
Sauce, 231
Celebrate Fall With A Salad, 233
Apple Salad, 233
Brussels Sprouts Salad, 233
Cabbage Salad, 233
Mixed Fruit Cup, 233
Cooked Up In The Bayous, 210
Creole Jambalaya, 210
Gumbo Ya Ya, 210
Jambalaya de Covington, 211
Seafood Gumbo, 210
Dried Fruit Is Always In Season, 228
Baked Fruit Compote, 228
Favorite Stack Cake, 228
Spiced Autumn Fruit Salad, 228
French Bread Baked Like The Pros, 226
French Bread, 227
Fresh-Baked Sugar Cake, 228
Moravian Sugar Cake, 228
From Our Kitchen To Yours, 211
Cooking Techniques for Making
Gumbo, 211
Fruit And Spices Flavor Pork, 229
Barbecued Stuffed Chops, 229
Glazed Pork Loin, 229
Pork Arlo, 229
Spicy Apple Pork Chops, 230
It's Ravioli, And It's Homemade!, 230
Homemade Ravioli, 230

Keep Chicken On The Menu, 217
Chicken, Ham, and Cheese Bake, 217
Crunchy Seasoned Chicken, 217
Poached Chicken with Black Beans and
Salsa, 217
Sherry-Chicken Sauté, 218
Low In Cholesterol, Not In Flavor, 220
Chicken Spaghetti, 221
Eggless Quiche, 220
Fish-and-Vegetable Stew, 220
Oatmeal-Raisin Cookies, 221
Orange Pound Cake, 221
Pumpkin-Pecan Bread, 221
Make A Soufflé To Brag About, 234
Three-Egg Cheese Soufflé, 234
Meat Loaf, An Old Favorite, 216
Barbecued Meat Loaf, 216
German Meat Loaf, 216
Mexican Meat Loaf, 217
Savory Meat Loaf, 216

**Pancakes And Waffles For Breakfast
And More, 224**
Best Ever Refrigerator
Waffles, 225
Island Pancakes, 225
Orange-Yogurt Pancakes, 225
Pecan Waffles, 225
Southern Waffles, 225
Spicy Apple Pancakes with Cider
Sauce, 224
**Sample A Chip Off The Old Chocolate
Block, 223**
Chocolate Brownie Delight, 224
Chocolate-Coconut Almond
Drops, 223
Chocolate-Ice Cream Pie, 224
Honeyed Chocolate Mousse, 223
Loaded-with-Chips Cookies, 223
Special Pecan Tarts, 224
Savor Veal, 219
Apple Veal Chops, 220
Best Baked Veal Roast, 219
Lemon Veal with Artichoke
Hearts, 219
Veal Cordon Bleu, 219
Veal with Green Peppercorns, 220
Savory Pot Roasts, 215
Country Pot Roast, 216
Indian Pot Roast, 215
Peppered Pot Roast, 215
Pot Roast in Red Sauce, 215
Sheet Cakes To Enjoy, 222
Chocolate-Sour Cream Cake, 222
Cinnamon Cake Squares, 222

Sheet Cakes To Enjoy
(continued)

    Ginger Cake, 222
    Honey-Oatmeal Cake, 222
Spoon On Sauces For Flavor, 232
    Cottage Cheese Sauce, 232
    Creamy Mustard Sauce, 232
    Onion Cream Sauce, 232
    Shrimp Sauce, 232
Timesaving Entrées, M218
    Chicken Divan, M218
    Open-Faced Salmon Patties, M218
    Tangy Beef Salad, M218
    Vegetable Quiche, M219
Traditional Fall Pies, 212
    Autumn Pumpkin Pie, 213
    Butternut Squash Pie, 212
    French Pear Pie, 213
    Grandmother's Apple Pie, 212
    Holiday Mincemeat Pie, 213
    Raisin-Pecan Pie, 213
Treat Your Friends To A Halloween Buffet, 213
    Hot Mexican Cider, 213
    Jack-O'-Lantern Cookies, 214
    Orange Soda Punch, 214
    Satan's Wings, 214
    Spinach Dip, 214
What A Salad!, 233
    Salad Extravaganza, 233

NOVEMBER
A Salad To Rave About, 285
    Salmon-Potato Salad, 285
Beautiful Pastries—Without The Trouble, 275
    Apricot Pinwheels, 276
    Coconut Puffs, 277

    Fruit Basket Strudel, 276
    Little Phyllo Cheesecakes, 275
    Nutty Phyllo Nests, 277
    Palmiers, 277
    Pineapple Phyllo Bundles, 277
    Puffy Apple Turnovers, 276
Casseroles For Busy Days, 284
    Broccoli Casserole, 284
    Carrot Casserole, 285

    Cauliflower 'n' Chiles Casserole, 285
    Easy Green Bean Casserole, 284
    Lima Bean Casserole, 284
Chicken As An Elegant Entrée, 286
    Chicken in Phyllo, 286
Entrées For Everyday, 267
    Cajun Chicken Over Rice, 268
    Chili Bean Roast, 268
    Royal Meatballs, 268
    Spicy Chicken Dish, 267
    Sweet-and-Sour Shrimp and Chicken, 267
    Thick 'n' Crusty Chicken Pot Pie, 267
    Turkey-Olive Casserole, 268
From Our Kitchen To Yours, 238
    Classifications of Sausage, 238
Ground Beef Tastes Better Than Ever, 283
    Beef Madras, 284
    Ground Beef Gumbo, 283
    Meat Loaf Wellington, 284
    Stromboli, 283
Holiday Baking In Minutes, M278
    Double Good Fudge, M278
    Peanut Divinity, M278
    Spice Cookies, M278

HOLIDAY DINNERS, 239
A Different Fruitcake, 264
    Layered Fruitcake, 265
A Fresh Greeting For Guests, 266
Appetizers That Say Cheese, 246
    Bite-Size Chiles Rellenos, 246
    Cheese and Chutney Ball, 247
    Cheese-and-Spinach Puffs, 246
    Cheesy-Olive Appetizers, 246
    Creamy Orange Dip, 247
    Herbed Cheese Spread, 247
    Nutty Fruit-and-Cheese Spread, 246
    Phyllo-Cheese Triangles, 246
    Seafood Tartlets, 247
A Prize-Winning Cheesecake, 265
    German Chocolate Cheesecake, 265
Baked Or Chilled, Pies Make Grand Finales, 259
    Coconut-Caramel Pies, 260
    Fluffy Nesselrode Pie, 261
    Heavenly Chocolate Pie, 260
    Holiday Apple Pie, 260
    Orange Chiffon Pie, 260
    Peppermint Candy-Ice Cream Pie, 260
    Southern Sweet Potato Cream Pie, 260
    Walnut-Cranberry Pie, 259
Bring On The Holidays!, 239
    Artichoke-Caviar Mold, 239
    Bûche de Noël, 241
    Curried Fruit Bake, 241
    Duck Breasts with Raspberry Sauce, 240
    Georgia Quail with Gravy, 240
    Hot Crab Canapés, 239
    Mushroom-Artichoke Casserole, 241
    Orange-Romaine Salad, 239
    Pan-Roasted Doves, 240
    Rice Mélange, 240
    Wild Goose with Currant Sauce, 240
Cakes And Pies For The Season, 263
    Bourbon-Pecan Pumpkin Pie, 264
    Chocolate Mousse Cake, 264
    Five-Flavor Pound Cake, 264
    My Favorite Applesauce Cake, 263
    White Chocolate-Coconut Cake, 263

Delicious Entrées To Carve, 248
    Lobster-Stuffed Beef Tenderloin, 248
    Pork Roast with Tomato Sauce, 249
    Stuffed Leg of Lamb, 248
    Turkey with Squash Dressing, 248
Dinner Entrées For Two, 249
    Braised Stuffed Pork Chops, 249
    Chicken Florentine with Mushroom Sauce, 250
    Cranberry Chicken Kiev, 250
Entertaining: Casual And Easy, 242
    Baked Zucchini Fans, 243
    Herbed French Loaf, 243
    Marinated Vegetable Salad, 243
    Orange Chicken Breasts with Parslied Rice, 242
    Pumpkin-Ice Cream Pie, 243

Food Gifts To Mail, 256
    Chewy Molasses Cookies, 257
    Chocolate-Peanut Butter Fudge, 257
    Christmas Lizzies, 257
    Party Mix, 257
It's Open House, And The Menu Is Light, 250
    Fruit Kabobs with Coconut Dressing, 251
    Holiday Punch, 252
    Marinated Artichokes, 250
    Mock Pâté, 251
    Pesto-Cheese Pasta Bites, 251
    Shrimp Mousse, 251
    Tomato-Clam Cocktail, 252
Make A Cake From Popcorn, 262
    Popcorn-Gumdrop Cake, 262
Make Breads With Fruit And Nuts, 255
    Banana-Oat Tea Loaf, 256
    Fresh Apple-Nut Bread, 256
    Lemon Bread, 256
    Pineapple-Pecan Loaf Bread, 256
    Prune-Nut Bread, 255
Marvelous Marbled Desserts, 261
    Calico Crumb Cake, 261
    Chocolate-Peanut Butter Swirl Pie, 262
    Marbled Cheesecake, 261
    Mocha Swirl Cheesecake, 262
More Flavor In These Breads, 254
    Cheese-Wine Bread, 254
    Kiwifruit Muffins, 254
    Light Wheat Rolls, 254
    Pumpkin-Coconut Bread, 255
    Pumpkin Rolls, 254
    Zucchini-Apple Bread, 255

New Ideas For Side Dishes, 252
  Baked Fruit Dressing, 253
  Brandied Carrots, 253
  Brussels Sprouts in Mustard
    Sauce, 253
  Holiday Broccoli with Rice, 252
  Marinated Garden Vegetables, 252
  Mexican Rice Dressing, 253
  Seasoned Potatoes, 253
  Sweet Potato Puffs, 253

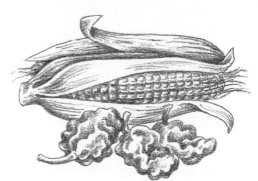

*Relishes And Chutneys Add Color,
  Flavor, 245*
  Commander's Chutney, 245
  Corn Relish, 245
  Cranberry Relish, 245
  Rhubarb Chutney, 245
Sippers For The Holidays, 241
  Christmas Eggnog, 242
  Fireside Coffee Mix, 241
  Hot Spiced Fruit Tea, 242
  Kahlúa Smoothie, 242
  Raspberry-Rosé Punch, 242
Splurge With Cream-Filled Chocolates, 258
  Liqueur Cream-Filled
    Chocolates, 258
The Berries Of The Holidays, 243
  Cranberry-Amaretto Chutney with
    Cream Cheese, 244
  Cranberry-Orange Bread, 244
  Cran-Raspberry Pie, 244
  Fresh Cranberry-Apricot Sauce, 243
  Fresh Cranberry Tartlets, 244
When Dinner Is At Your House, 266

Hot Sandwiches To Satisfy, 278
  Avocado, Bacon, and Cheese
    Sandwiches, 279
  Creamy Blue Cheese-Ham
    Sandwiches, 279
  Hot Crab-and-Cheese
    Sandwiches, 279
  Open-Faced Salami Sandwiches, 279
  Snack Buns, 279
  Uptown Welsh Rarebit, 279
Processor Crêpes And Fillings, 289
  Basic Processor Crêpes, 289
  Dessert Crêpes, 290
  Mushroom-Cheese Crêpes, 289
  Strawberry Ice Cream Crêpes, 290
Sausage—A Texas Tradition, 237
  Breakfast Taquitos, 237
  Chorizo Substitute, 238
  Krause's Cafe Bratwurst Dinner, 238
  Venison Sausage Stew, 238
Sensational Stuffed Entrées, 268
  Fruit-Stuffed Pork Tenderloins, 270
  Stuffed Chicken Breasts Sardou, 269

  Stuffed Turkey Breast, 270
  Wine-Sauced Beef-and-Barley
    Rolls, 269
Serve Chicken Nuggets, 283
  Lemon-Chicken Nuggets, 283
Serve Mushrooms Anytime, 280
  Heavenly Mushrooms, 281
  Mushroom Soufflés, 282
  Stuffed Mushroom Delight, 281
  Toasted Mushroom Sandwiches, 281
**Take A Look At These Sunday
  Suppers, 286**
  Broccoli Soup, 288
  Chicken-and-Broccoli Pasta, 286
  Country Ham Quiche, 287
  Creamy Ham and Eggs, 286
  Enchilada Casserole, 287
  Grilled Sour Cream Burgers, 287
  Mexican Burrito Pie, 287
  Spicy Taco Salad, 287
  Zippy Cheese Omelet, 287
Tangy, Crunchy Holiday Salads, 236
  Apricot Nectar Salad, 236
  Cherry Fruit Salad, 236
  Holiday Fruit Salad, 236
  Hurry-Up Fruit Salad, 236
  Raspberry Ribbon Salad, 236
This Salad Is A Group Project, 288
  Salad by Committee, 288
Toss Turkey Into A Salad, 285
  Polynesian Turkey Salad, 285
  Turkey Salad with Hot Bacon
    Dressing, 285
Try These Sweet Potato Favorites, 280
  Bourbon Sweet Potatoes, 280
  Peach Sweet Potato Puffs, 280
  Raspberry Sweet Potatoes, 280
  Sweet Potato Muffins, 280
  Sweet Potato Pancakes, 280
Warm Up With Dried-Bean Soup, 282
  Beefy Lentil Soup, 282
  Chill-Chaser Soup, 282
  Drunken Bean Soup, 283
  Savory Navy Bean Soup, 282
Wow! Pasta Salad, 288
  Chicken Tortellini Salad, 288

DECEMBER
A Cheese-And-Date Delight, 299
  Nutty Date Dessert Cheese, 299
A Fruit Wreath To Eat, 294
  Della Robbia Fruit Wreath, 294
Breads For Now And Later, 300
  Almond Danish, 301
  Applesauce-Honey Nut Bread, 300
  Homemade Raisin Bread, 300
  Orange-Pumpkin Bread, 300
  Vienna Brioche Loaves, 300
  Yeast Biscuits, 301
Coffee Cake For Christmas, 298
  Christmas-Tree Coffee Cakes, 298
Enjoy A Candlelight Dinner For Two, 304
  Browned Rice Pilaf, 305
  Cauliflower-Snow Pea Medley, 305
  Italian Beef Medaillons, 305
  Spinach-Kiwifruit Salad, 305
  Tangy Cranberry Ice, 305
Entrées With Flair, 306
  Apricot-Glazed Cornish Hens, 306
  Beef Tenderloin with Mushroom-Sherry
    Sauce, 306
  Fast-and-Savory Turkey, 306

From Our Kitchen To Yours, 297
  Using and Storing Spices, 297
He's A Serious Chili Cook, 303
  Home-Style Brisket, 303
  North Texas Red Chili, 303
  Pinto Beans, 303
Holiday Baking Spices The Air, 294
  Chocolate Pound Cake with Fudge
    Frosting, 296
  Chocolate-Tipped Log Cookies, 294
  Christmas Bread, 296
  Coconut-Spice Cake, 296
  Crescent Sugar Cookies, 294
  Eggnog Pie, 295
  Festive Braids, 297
  Pumpkin Pie in Spiced Nut Crust, 295
  Spiced Carrot Cake, 296
  Spiced Christmas Cookies, 294
It's Time For Venison, 304
  Venison Burgers, 304
  Venison Chili, 304
  Venison Stew with Potato
    Dumplings, 304
  Venison-Vegetable Bake, 304
Leftover Turkey For Company, 301
  Turkey-Cheese Puffs, 301
Promote Even Cooking With Foil, M302
  Chicken Lasagna, M302
  Quick Brownies, M302
  Tangy Herbed Chicken, M302

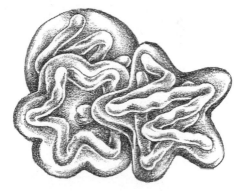

Recipes For A Tree-Hunt Tradition, 292
  Almond Cheese Spread, 292
  Chocolate Cheese Spread, 292
  Christmas Strawberries, 293
  Date-Walnut Spread, 292
  Mincemeat Sweetheart Cookies, 293
  Orange Cheese Spread, 292
  Orange Pecans, 292
  Ribbon Cookies, 293
  Spiced Cranberry Lemonade, 292
  Swiss Cinnamon Stars, 293
  Tree-Hunt Chili, 292
  Viennese Sandwich Cookies, 293
Salads That Fit The Season, 311
  Cranberry-Topped Green Salad, 311
  Creamy Waldorf Salad, 311
  Gazpacho Salad Mold, 311
  Lemon-Cranberry Congealed Salad, 311
  Snowy Emerald Salad, 311
Start With A Can Of Pie Filling, 298
  Chocolate-Blueberry Dessert
    Squares, 299
  Hot Fruit Dessert Sauce, 299
  Peachy Melt-Away Dessert, 298
  Tart Cranberry-Cherry Pie, 299

General Recipe Index

A listing of every recipe by food category and/or major ingredient
All microwave recipe page numbers are preceded by an "M"

Almonds
Cinnamon Stars, Swiss, 293
Confections, Almond Cream, 198
Cream with Fresh Strawberries,
    Almond, 93
Danish, Almond, 301
Drops, Chocolate-Coconut Almond, 223
Filling, Almond, 301
Filling, Ground Almond, 14
Glaze, Honey-Nut, 15
Phyllo Nests, Nutty, 277
Salad, Cheesy Fruit-'n'-Nut, 56
Sauce, Shrimp-and-Almond, 282
Spread, Almond Cheese, 292

Appetizers
Artichoke-Caviar Mold, 239
Artichoke-Parmesan Phyllo Bites, 54
Artichokes, Marinated, 250
Avocado-Crabmeat Cocktail, Sherried, 95
Burritos, Chinese, 181
Canapés, Hot Crab, 239
Caponata, 166
Carrots, Dill-Spiced, 200
Cauliflower with Cheese Sauce,
    Fried, 231
Cheese
    Ball, Cheese and Chutney, 247
    Bonbons, Cheese, 93
    Canapés, Lemon-Cheese, 93
    Crispies, Pecan-Cheese, 168
    Cups, Cottage Cheese-Spinach, 190
    Meat-and-Cheese Appetizers, 7
    Olive Appetizers, Cheesy-, 246
    Pasta Bites, Pesto-Cheese, 251
    Phyllo-Cheese Triangles, 246
    Puffs, Cheese-and-Spinach, 246
    Puffs, Mexican Cheese, 8
Chicken, Deep-Fried Walnut, 175
Chicken Nuggets, 283
Chiles Rellenos, Bite-Size, 246
Chutney with Cream Cheese,
    Cranberry-Amaretto, 244
Cracker Bread, Sesame, 2
Crackers, Fennel-Rye, 2
Dips
    Bean Dip, Hotshot, 195
    Chile-Cheese Dip, 173
    Curry Dip, 25
    Deviled Dip, 25
    Mexican Appetizer, Chilled, 197
    Mint Dip with Fresh Fruit, 146
    Orange Dip, Creamy, 247
    Salsa Cruda, 180
    Salsa, Fresh Summer, 89
    Shrimp Dip, Hot, 190
    Spinach Dip, 25, 214
    Tuna Dip, Low-Cal, 25
    Vegetable Dip, Tangy, 196

Eggplant, Fried Parmesan, 166
Fruit Kabobs with Coconut
    Dressing, 251
Hot Munch, Oriental, 8
Melon Balls, Minted, 162
Mix, Party, 257
Mousse, Shrimp, 196, 251
Mushroom Delight, Stuffed, 281
Oyster Nachos, Texas, 39
Oysters Buccaneer, 40
Pâté, Mock, 251
Pecans, Orange, 292
Pecans, Pepper, 137
Pepper-Cheese Stacks, 80
Pizza Squares, 168
Popcorn Scramble, 185
Popcorn Snack, Spiced, 8
Pretzels, Chewy Soft, 159
Sausages, Saucy Cocktail, 173
Scallops, Bacon-Wrapped, 94
Seafood Tartlets, 247
Shrimp Cocktail, 173
Shrimp Miniquiches, 146
Shrimp Mold, 94
Shrimp with Herbed Jalapeño
    Cheese, 112
Shrimp, Zesty Marinated, 173
Spinach Quichelets, 67
Spinach Triangles, Phyllo-, 53
Spreads and Fillings
    Apricot-Cream Cheese Spread, 158
    Cheese Spread, Hawaiian, 158
    Cheese Spread, Herbed, 247
    Cheesy Beer Spread, 196
    Chicken Spread, Festive, 158
    Corned Beef Spread, 196
    Fruit-and-Cheese Spread, Nutty, 246
    Ham Spread, Country, 8
    Honey-Nut Spread, Lemon-, 257
    Pimiento Cheese, Hot, 173
    Salmon-and-Horseradish Spread, 146
    Seafood Spread, 146
    Shrimp Spread, 111
    Shrimp Spread, Curried, 158
    Sombrero Spread, 111
    Tomato-Cheese Spread, Fiery, 196
Tuna-Pecan Ball, 94
Wings, Hot Buffalo, 176
Wings, Satan's, 214
Wontons, Tex-Mex, 196

Apples
Bread, Fresh Apple-Nut, 256
Bread, Zucchini-Apple, 255
Cabbage with Apples and Franks, 42
Cake, Apple-Nut, 76
Cider, Hot Mexican, 213
Cider Sauce, 224
Cinnamon Apples, Rosy, M37

Crunch, Apple-Cranberry, 178
Filling, Dried Apple, 229
Jelly, Apple-Mint, 134
Muffins, Apple, 23
Pancakes with Cider Sauce, Spicy
    Apple, 224
Pie, Blackberry-Apple, 130
Pie, Cornbread-Sausage-Apple, 171
Pie, Easy-Crust Apple, 11
Pie, Grandmother's Apple, 212
Pie, Holiday Apple, 260
Pork Chops, Apple-Glazed, 35
Pork Chops, Spicy Apple, 230
Quiche, Crustless Sausage-Apple, 70
Salad, Apple, 233
Salad, Creamy Waldorf, 311
Salad, English Pea-and-Apple, 24
Salad with Blue Cheese Dressing,
    Apple, 103
Sauce, Apple Dessert, M165
Scalloped Apples, 156

Slaw, Red Cabbage-and-Apple, 31
Tea, Hot Apple-Cinnamon, 57
Topping, Spicy Apple, 125
Turnovers, Puffy Apple, 276
Veal Chops, Apple, 220

Applesauce
Bread, Applesauce-Honey Nut, 300
Cake, My Favorite Applesauce, 263

Apricots
Bars, Apricot-Raisin, 32
Cornish Hens, Apricot-Glazed, 306
Glaze, Apricot-Kirsch, 14
Pinwheels, Apricot, 276
Salad, Apricot Nectar, 236
Sauce, Apricot, 172
Sauce, Fresh Cranberry-Apricot, 243
Spread, Apricot-Cream Cheese, 158

Artichokes
Casserole, Mushroom-Artichoke, 241
Chicken with Artichokes, Sherried, 143

Chilled Artichokes with Lemon-Pepper
  Dressing, 55
Marinated Artichokes, 250
Mold, Artichoke-Caviar, 239
Phyllo Bites, Artichoke-Parmesan, 54
Pizza with Artichoke and Prosciutto, 182
Salad, Italian, 145
Stuffed Artichokes, Shrimp-, 55
Veal with Artichoke Hearts, Lemon, 219

Asparagus
Cashew Butter, Asparagus with, 56
Fish-Asparagus Divan, 128
Lemon Butter, Asparagus with, M151
Marinated Asparagus, 74
Pork Arlo, 229
Rarebit, Uptown Welsh, 279
Salad, Asparagus-Horseradish, 80
Squash Rings, Asparagus in, 68
Stir-Fried Asparagus, 52

Aspic
Vegetable Aspic with Horseradish
  Dressing, Crisp, 152

Avocados
Cocktail, Sherried Avocado-Crabmeat, 95
Relish, Avocado, 120
Salad, Avocado-Chicken, 107
Salad, Avocado Fruit, 41
Salad, Guacamole, 181
Salad in Avocados, Fruited
  Chicken, 41
Salads, Congealed Avocado, 42
Salad, Spanish Avocado, 41
Sandwiches, Avocado, Bacon, and
  Cheese, 279
Soup, Chilled Avocado, 37

Bacon
Carrots with Bacon and Onion,
  Glazed, 200
Chicken Bundles with Bacon
  Ribbons, 68
Eggs Benedict, Bacon-and-Tomato, 195
Linguine Carbonara, 108
Poor Boys, Oyster-and-Bacon, 40
Salad, BLT Chicken, 144
Sandwiches, Avocado, Bacon, and
  Cheese, 279
Scallops, Bacon-Wrapped, 94
Soup, Bacon-Beer Cheese, M7
Spaghetti, Bacon, 82

Bananas
Alaskas, Banana Split, 10
Bread, Banana, 72
Float, Strawberry-Banana, 160
Frost, Banana-Strawberry, 199
Loaf, Banana-Oat Tea, 256
Muffins, Banana-Oat, 188
Pancakes, Island, 225
Pie, Banana Cream, 207
Salad, Banana, 80
Smoothie, Banana, 160
Splits, Cottage Cheese-Banana, 56
Topping, Strawberry-Banana, 125

Barbecue
Meat Loaf, Barbecued, 216
Shrimp, Cajun Barbecued, 95

Beans
Baked Beans, Mixed, 92
Black Beans and Cilantro, Southwestern
  Scallop Broth with, 123
Black Beans and Salsa, Poached Chicken
  with, 217

Black Bean Terrine with Goat
  Cheese, 120
Black Bean-Tomatillo Relish, 121
Chili Bean Roast, 268
Dip, Hotshot Bean, 195

Green
  Bundles, Green Bean, 118
  Casserole, Easy Green Bean, 284
  Green Beans, M151
  Italian, Green Beans, 10
  Mustard, Green Beans and Tomatoes
    with, 83
  Potatoes, Green Beans with
    New, 164
  Sweet-and-Sour Beans, 197
Lima Bean Casserole, 284
Pinto Beans, 303
Red Beans and Rice, 45

Salads
  Green Bean Salad, 90
  Green Bean Salad, Hot, 176
  Marinated Bean-and-Rice
    Salad, 152
  Marinated Corn-Bean Salad, 9
  Pork-'n'-Bean Salad, 83
  Six-Bean Salad, Colorful, 82
Soup, Beefy Lentil, 282
Soup, Chill-Chaser, 282
Soup, Drunken Bean, 283
Soup, Savory Navy Bean, 282

Beef
Appetizers, Meat-and-Cheese, 7
Brisket, Home-Style, 303
Burgoo, Five-Meat, 3
Burgoo, Old-Fashioned, 3
Chili, North Texas Red, 303
Chili, Zippy, 110
Chinese-Style Beef, 50
Corned Beef

  Dijon Glaze, Corned Beef with, 54
  Dinner, Corned Beef, 54
  Sandwiches, Grilled Corned Beef, 54
  Soup, French Onion-Beef, 54
  Spread, Corned Beef, 196
Kabobs, Spirited Beef, 142
Meatballs, Quick Processor, 111
Medallions, Italian Beef, 305
Medallions of Beef with Ancho Chile
  Sauce, 122

Roasts
  Chili Bean Roast, 268
  Patio Steak, 141
  Pot Roast, Country, 216
  Pot Roast, Indian, 215
  Pot Roast in Red Sauce, 215
  Pot Roast, Italian, 95
  Pot Roast, Peppered, 215
Rolls, Wine-Sauced Beef-and-Barley, 269
Salad, Beef-and-Broccoli, 187
Salad, Tangy Beef, M218
Soup, Beefy Lentil, 282

Steaks
  Braised Steaks, Beer-, 96
  Country-Fried Steak, Mock, 163

Flank Steak and Mushrooms, 61
Flank Steak, Beer-Marinated, 35
Flank Steak Pinwheels, 141
Kabobs, Hot-and-Spicy, 193
London Broil, Marinated, 32
Round Steak, Braised, 35
Smothered Steak, Onion-, M189
Stir-Fried Steak, Fast-and-Easy, 50
Stir-Fry, Beef-and-Vegetable, 22
Stew, Bama Brunswick, 4
Stew, Beef-and-Onion, 18
Tenderloin, Lobster-Stuffed Beef, 248
Tenderloin with Mushrooms, Beef, 115
Tenderloin with Mushroom-Sherry Sauce,
  Beef, 306
Tournedos Diables, 60

Beef, Ground
Burgoo, Harry Young's, 3
Burritos, Chinese, 181

Casseroles
  Enchilada Casserole, 287
  Italian Cabbage Casserole, 42

Chili
  Chili, 17
  Tree-Hunt Chili, 292
Enchiladas, Sour Cream, 37
Fiesta, 180
Gumbo, Ground Beef, 283

Hamburgers
  au Poivre Blanc, Burgers, 186
  Nutty Burgers, 185
  Patties, Deviled-Beef, 22
  Pizza Burger, 185
  Sour Cream Burgers, Grilled, 287
  Steak-House Burgers, 186
  Venison Burgers, 304
Madras, Beef, 284

Meatballs
  Chinese Meatballs, 194
  Royal Meatballs, 268

Meat Loaf
  Barbecued Meat Loaf, 216
  German Meat Loaf, 216
  Mexican Meat Loaf, 217
  Parsley Meat Loaf, 22
  Savory Meat Loaf, 216
  Wellington, Meat Loaf, 284
Moussaka, 166
Moussaka, Corn, 190
Pastitsio, 12
Pie, Mexican Burrito, 287
Ravioli, Homemade, 230
Salad, Spicy Taco, 287
Sandwiches, Hot Pita, M6
Stromboli, 283
Wontons, Tex-Mex, 196

Beets
Pickled Beets, 163

Beverages

Alcoholic
  Bloody Marys, Spicy, 173
  Cider, Hot Mexican, 213
  Coffee, Praline-Flavored, 69
  Eggnog, Christmas, 242
  Kahlúa Smoothie, 242
  Magnolia Blossoms, 72
  Minted Delight, 107
  Oklahoma Sunrise, 67
  Punch, Bourbon-Tea, 57
  Punch, Brandy Slush, 72
  Punch, Cranapple-Vodka, 72
  Punch, Raspberry-Rosé, 242
  Red Roosters, 147

Beverages, Alcoholic (continued)

Sangría, Teaberry, 147
Sherry Sour, 74
Banana Smoothie, 160
Banana-Strawberry Frost, 199
Breakfast Eye-Opener, 199
Coffee Mix, Fireside, 241
Fruit Drink, Three-, 199
Fruit Float, Frosty, 159
Lime Cooler, 160
Milkshake, Pineapple, 199
Punch
Holiday Punch, 252
Orange Soda Punch, 214
Tea Party Punch, 147
Traders' Punch, 94
Shake, Frosty Fruit, 23
Shake, Strawberry-Orange Breakfast, 186
Shake, Strawberry-Yogurt, 199
Shake, Tropical, 200
Strawberry-Banana Float, 160
Tahitian Flower, 159
Tea, Hawaiian, 57
Tea, Hot Apple-Cinnamon, 57
Tea, Hot Spiced Fruit, 242
Tea, Mint, 107
Tea, White Grape Juice, 57
Tomato-Clam Cocktail, 252
Biscuits
Cheese Biscuits, 78
Cloud Biscuits, 15
Heart Biscuits with Sausage, Angel, 156
Yeast Biscuits, 71, 301
Blackberries
Bars, Blackberry, 130
Cobbler, New-Fashioned Blackberry, 164
Parfait, Blackberries-and-Cream, 129
Pie, Blackberry-Apple, 130
Blueberries
Bread, Blueberry-Orange, 140
Cheesecake, Blueberries 'n' Cream, 140
Cheesecake, Blueberry Chiffon, 76
Cobbler, Blueberry Pinwheel, 140
Dessert Squares, Chocolate-
Blueberry, 299
Muffins, Blueberry-Oatmeal, 24
Sauce, Peach-Berry, M165
Topping, Blueberry, 125
Bran
Muffins, Sour Cream-Bran, 98
Rolls, Bran Yeast, 116
Breads. See also specific types.
Apple-Nut Bread, Fresh, 256
Applesauce-Honey Nut Bread, 300
Banana Bread, 72
Banana-Oat Tea Loaf, 256
Blueberry-Orange Bread, 140
Brie Bread, 143
Brie Cheese Bake, 117
Carrot Puffs, 200
Cheese Loaf, 92
Cranberry-Orange Bread, 244
Easy Bread, 168
French Loaf, Herbed, 243
Herb-and-Cheese Pull Aparts, 143
Lemon Bread, 256
Orange-Pumpkin Bread, 300
Peanut Bread, 184
Pineapple-Pecan Loaf Bread, 256
Prune-Nut Bread, 255
Pumpkin-Coconut Bread, 255

Pumpkin-Pecan Bread, 221
Sally Lunn, Quick 16
Scones, Lemon-Raisin, 69
Spinach Bread, 144
Yeast
Almond Danish, 301
Beer Bread, Hearty, 226
Braids, Festive, 297
Brioche Loaves, Vienna, 300
Cheese Bread, 11
Cheese-Wine Bread, 254
Christmas Bread, 296
Cracker Bread, Sesame, 2
Egg Bread, County Fair, 68
French Bread, 227
Pretzels, Chewy Soft, 159
Raisin Bread, Homemade, 300
Whole Wheat-Oatmeal Bread, 85
Zucchini-Apple Bread, 255
Broccoli
Casserole, Broccoli, 284
Divan, Chicken, M218
Pasta, Chicken-and-Broccoli, 286
Pasta with Broccoli and Sausage, 109
Rice, Holiday Broccoli with, 252
Rolls, Ham-and-Broccoli, 82
Salad, Beef-and-Broccoli, 187
Salad, Broccoli-Corn, 24
Salad, Fresh Broccoli, 103
Soup, Broccoli, 288
Sour Cream Sauce, Broccoli with, 127
Brussels Sprouts
Mustard Sauce, Brussels Sprouts in, 253
Salad, Brussels Sprouts, 233
Burritos
Chinese Burritos, 181
Pie, Mexican Burrito, 287
Butter
Basil Butter, 171
Cashew Butter, Asparagus with, 56
Lemon Butter, Asparagus with, M151
Butterscotch
Cookies, Butterscotch, 58
Pie, Butterscotch Cream, 207

Cabbage. See also Sauerkraut.
Apples and Franks, Cabbage with, 42
Casserole, Italian Cabbage, 42
Chowchow, 150
Creole Cabbage, 189
Hot Cabbage Creole, 42
Kielbasa, Cabbage, 42
Salad, Cabbage, 120, 233
Salad, Nutty Cabbage, 42
Slaws
Hot-and-Creamy Dutch Slaw, 127

Red Cabbage-and-Apple Slaw, 31
Sour Cream Slaw, 10
Sweet-and-Sour Cabbage, 189
Cakes. See also Breads, Cookies.
Angel Food Cake, Chocolate, 21
Apple-Nut Cake, 76
Applesauce Cake, My Favorite, 263
Bars and Squares
Cinnamon Cake Squares, 222
Crumb Cake, Calico, 261
Ginger Cake, 222
Honey-Oatmeal Cake, 222
Bûche de Noël, 241
Cajun Cake, 138
Carrot Cake, Spiced, 296
Cheesecakes
Blueberries 'n' Cream
Cheesecake, 140
Blueberry Chiffon Cheesecake, 76
Chocolate Cheesecake,
German, 265
Chocolate Cheesecake, White 44
Marbled Cheesecake, 261
Mocha Swirl Cheesecake, 262
Phyllo Cheesecakes, Little, 275
Raspberry Sauce, Cheesecake
with, 116
Chocolate
Brownie Delight, Chocolate, 224
Marshmallow Cake, No-Egg
Chocolate, M97
Mousse Cake, Chocolate, 264
Peanut Cluster Cake,
Chocolate-, 184
Roll, Chocolate-Orange, 21
Sour Cream Cake, Chocolate-, 222
Swiss Chocolate Chip Cake, 85
Coconut
Chocolate-Coconut Cake, White, 263
Spice Cake, Coconut-, 296
Coffee Cakes
Christmas-Tree Coffee Cakes, 298
Cinnamon-Pecan Coffee Cake, 69
Sugar Cake, Moravian, 228
Cranberry Upside-Down Cake, 8
Fruitcakes
Layered Fruitcake, 265
Spice Cake, Fruit and, M97
Ice Cream Cake, Fruity, 110
Orange Liqueur Cake, 84
Orange Meringue Cake, 84
Peach Upside-Down Cake, 8
Pecan Roulade, 183
Popcorn-Gumdrop Cake, 262
Pound
Caramel Frosting, Pound Cake
with, 39
Carrot Pound Cake, 41
Chocolate Pound Cake with Fudge
Frosting, 296
Five-Flavor Pound Cake, 264
Lemon-Sour Cream Pound Cake, 38
Orange Pound Cake, 84, 221
Stack Cake, Favorite, 228
Torte, Toffee Meringue, 118
Upside-Down Sunburst Cake, 9
White Cake with Strawberries and
Chocolate Glaze, 76
Candies
Brittle with Crushed Peanuts, 184
Chocolate-Coconut Almond Drops, 223
Chocolates, Liqueur Cream-Filled, 258
Divinity, Peanut, M278

Fudge
  Chocolate-Peanut Butter Fudge, 257
  Double Good Fudge, M278
Peanut Butter Easter Eggs, 86
Peanut Clusters, 184
Quemada (Burnt-Sugar Candy), 38
Truffles, White Chocolate, 45
Cantaloupe. *See* Melons.
Caramel
Cobbler, Peach-Caramel, 178
Frosting, Caramel, 265
Frosting, Easy Caramel, 39
Pies, Coconut-Caramel, 260
Sauce, Easy Caramel, 38
Carrots
Brandied Carrots, 253
Cake, Carrot Pound, 41
Cake, Spiced Carrot, 296
Casserole, Carrot, 285
Dill-Spiced Carrots, 200
Glazed Carrots and Onions, 128
Glazed Carrots, Ginger-, 68
Glazed Carrots with Bacon and
  Onion, 200
Herbed Carrots and Onions, 31
Marinated Carrots, Creamy, 200
Muffins, Carrot-and-Raisin, 24
Puffs, Carrot, 200
Salad, Carrot-Raisin, 10
Saucy Carrots, 41
Stuffed Carrots, 40
Tipsy Carrots, 40
Casseroles
Bean
  Green Bean Casserole, Easy, 284
  Green Beans Italian, 10
  Lima Bean Casserole, 284
Enchilada Casserole, 287
Macaroni Casserole, 154
Meat
  Moussaka, 166
  Moussaka, Corn, 190
  Pastitsio, 12
Pork
  Ham-and-Cheese Casserole, 78
  Ham Pie, Golden, 78
  Ham-Rice-Tomato Bake, 78
  Sausage Casserole, Easy, M189
Poultry
  Chicken Casserole, Rice-and-, 154
  Turkey-Olive Casserole, 268
  Turkey Parmigiana, 193
Rice Casserole, 45
Rice Casserole, Brown, 118
Rice Mélange, 240
Rotini Romano, 193
Seafood
  Crab Bake, Quick, 192
  Seafood Casserole, 109
Vegetable
  Broccoli Casserole, 284
  Broccoli with Rice, Holiday, 252
  Cabbage Casserole, Italian, 42
  Cabbage with Apples and Franks, 42
  Carrot Casserole, 285
  Cauliflower Casserole, Festive, 232
  Cauliflower 'n' Chiles Casserole, 285
  Mixed-Vegetable Casserole, 154
  Mushroom-Artichoke Casserole, 241
  Pea Casserole, Curry, 154
  Pea Casserole, Reunion, 11
  Potato Casserole, 190
  Potato-Eggplant Casserole, 166

Potatoes, Bourbon Sweet, 280
Potatoes, Jazzy Mashed, 192
Potatoes Lorraine, 190
Potatoes, Mushroom Scalloped, 191
Potatoes, Party Scalloped, 191
Potatoes with Ham Bits,
  Creamy, 191
Squash Casserole, 163
Venison-Vegetable Bake, 304
Zucchini Casserole, 154
Cauliflower
Casserole, Cauliflower 'n' Chiles, 285
Casserole, Festive Cauliflower, 232
Fried Cauliflower with Cheese Sauce, 231

Medley, Cauliflower-Snow Pea, 305
Pimiento Sauce, Cauliflower with, 232
Salad, Cauliflower-Pea, 231
Soup, Cream of Cauliflower, M7
Caviar
Mold, Artichoke-Caviar, 239
Celery
Salad, Pear-and-Celery, 56
Cheese. *See also* Appetizers/Cheese.
Bake, Brie Cheese, 117
Bake, Chicken, Ham, and Cheese, 217
Banana Splits, Cottage Cheese-, 56
Biscuits, Cheese, 78
Breads
  Brie Bread, 143
  Cheese Bread, 11
  Cornbread, Chile-Cheese, 171
  Herb-and-Cheese Pull Aparts, 143
  Romano Sesame Rolls, 144
  Spinach Bread, 144
  Wine Bread, Cheese-, 254
Buns, Snack, 279
Casseroles
  Ham-and-Cheese Casserole, 78
  Potatoes, Mushroom Scalloped, 191
  Turkey Parmigiana, 193
Crab Bake, Quick, 192
Cream Cheese, Cranberry-Amaretto
  Chutney with, 244
Cream Cheese Pinches, 85
Crêpes, Mushroom-Cheese, 289
Crispies, Pecan-Cheese, 168
Dessert Cheese, Nutty Date, 299
Dessert, Creamy Cottage Cheese, 191
Dressing, Tangy Blue Cheese, 81
Eggplant, Fried Parmesan, 166
Frosting, Cream Cheese, 58
Grits, Good Morning, 156
Loaf, Cheese, 92
Noodles, Ham and Swiss on, 108

Omelet, Zippy Cheese, 287
Pastry Shells, Miniature Cream
  Cheese, 190
Pizza, Gruyère-Chicken, 182
Puffs, Turkey-Cheese, 301
Quiche, Eggless, 220
Rarebit, Uptown Welsh, 279
Salad, Cheesy Fruit-'n'-Nut, 56
Sandwiches, Avocado, Bacon, and
  Cheese, 279
Sandwiches, Brown Bread-Cream
  Cheese, M6
Sandwiches, Creamy Blue
  Cheese-Ham, 279
Sandwiches, Ham-and-Cheese Pita, 202
Sandwiches, Hot Crab-and-Cheese, 279
Sauces
  Cottage Cheese Sauce, 232
  Potatoes with Cheese Sauce,
    Stuffed, 192
  Swiss Cheese Sauce, 289
  Tuna Salad, Cheese-Sauced, M124
Soufflé, Three-Egg Cheese, 234
Soups
  Bacon-Beer Cheese Soup, M7
  Onion-Cheese Soup, 81
Spreads and Fillings
  Almond Cheese Spread, 292
  Apricot-Cream Cheese Spread, 158
  Beer Spread, Cheesy, 196
  Chocolate Cheese Spread, 292
  Cottage Cheese Spread, 107
  Fruit-and-Cheese Spread, Nutty, 246
  Hawaiian Cheese Spread, 158
  Herbed Cheese Spread, 247
  Orange Cheese Spread, 292
  Tomato-Cheese Spread, Fiery, 196
Tart, Herb-Cheese, 98
Tart Milan, 70
Terrine with Goat Cheese, Black
  Bean, 120
Vermicelli, Shrimp and Feta Cheese
  on, 108
Wafers, Italian, 36
Cheesecakes. *See* Cakes/Cheesecakes.
Cherries
Cake, Upside-Down Sunburst, 9
Pie, Tart Cranberry-Cherry, 299
Salad, Cherry Fruit, 236
Sauce, Chocolate Cherry, M165
Topping, Cherry-Pineapple, 126
Chicken
à la King, Chicken, 197
Andalusia, Chicken, 103
Bag, Chicken in a, 23
Bake, Chicken, Ham, and Cheese, 217
Baked Mustard Chicken, 10
Barbecued
  Cumin Chicken, Grilled, 142
  Garlic-Grilled Chicken, 180
Basil Chicken, 171
Breasts, Saucy Chicken, 167
Breasts with Parslied Rice, Orange
  Chicken, 242
Bundles with Bacon Ribbons,
  Chicken, 68
Burgoo, Five-Meat, 3
Burgoo, Harry Young's, 3
Burgoo, Old-Fashioned, 3
Cajun Chicken over Rice, 268
Casserole, Rice-and-Chicken, 154
Divan, Chicken, M218
Drumsticks, Cajun-Style, 159

Chicken (continued)

Florentine with Mushroom Sauce, Chicken, 250
Fried
    Drumsticks, Buttermilk, 175
    Herbed Fried Chicken, 91
    Mexican Fried Chicken, 176
    Nuggets, Lemon-Chicken, 283
    Oven-Fried Chicken, Crunchy, 163
    Walnut Chicken, Deep-Fried, 175
    Wings, Hot Buffalo, 176
Gumbo Ya Ya, 210
Herbed Chicken, Tangy, M302
Honey-Curry Chicken, 36
Kabobs, Chicken, 141
Kiev, Cranberry Chicken, 250
Lasagna, Chicken, M302
Marinated Breast of Chicken, 123
Marinated Chicken, 61
Pasta and Garden Vegetables, 192
Pasta, Chicken-and-Broccoli, 286
Peppers, Curried Chicken-Stuffed, 19
Phyllo, Chicken in, 286
Pie, Double-Crust Chicken, 111
Pie, Thick 'n' Crusty Chicken Pot, 267
Pizza, Gruyère-Chicken, 182
Poached Chicken with Black Beans and Salsa, 217
Roasted Chicken, Herb-, 155
Rolls Jubilee, Chicken, 118
Rotelle, Chicken and Tomato with, 108
Salads
    Avocado-Chicken Salad, 107
    Baked Chicken Salad, 176
    BLT Chicken Salad, 144
    Chutney-Chicken Salad, 74
    Curried Chicken-and-Orange Salad, 144
    Filling, Chicken Salad, 106
    Fruited Chicken Salad in Avocados, 41
    Pasta-Chicken Salad, Tarragon, 155
    Poulet Rémoulade, 144
    Special Chicken Salad, 183
    Tortellini Salad, Chicken, 288
Sautéed Chicken Breasts, 36
Sauté, Sherry-Chicken, 218
Seasoned Chicken, Crunchy, 217
Sherried Chicken with Artichokes, 143
Spaghetti, Chicken, 221
Spicy Chicken Dish, 267
Spread, Festive Chicken, 158
Stew, Bama Brunswick, 4
Stew, Brunswick Chicken, 4
Stew, Sonny Frye's Brunswick, 4
Stir-Fried Chicken Curry, 51
Stir-Fry, Kyoto Orange-Chicken, 96
Stuffed Chicken Breasts, 36
Stuffed Chicken Breasts Sardou, 269
Sweet-and-Sour Shrimp and Chicken, 267
Tangy Chicken, 35
Toss, Quick Chicken, M124
Vermouth, Chicken and Vegetables, M37
Wings, Satan's, 214

Chili
Chili, 17
Red Chili, North Texas, 303
Sauce, Spicy Chili, 127
Tree-Hunt Chili, 292
Venison Chili, 304
Zippy Chili, 110

Chocolate
Bars and Cookies
    Almond Cream Confections, 198
    Brownies, Buttermilk Cake, 198
    Brownies, Choco-Mallow, 198
    Brownies, Crunch-Crust, 198
    Brownies, Mocha, 93
    Brownies, Peanut Butter, 199
    Brownies, Quick, M302
    Chips Cookies, Loaded-with-, 223
    Fudge Bars, Yummy, 158
    Log Cookies, Chocolate-Tipped, 294
    Macaroons, Chocolate, 57
    Sandwiches, Chocolate Cookie Ice Cream, 147
    Teasers, Chocolate, 44
Cakes and Tortes
    Angel Food Cake, Chocolate, 21
    Brownie Delight, Chocolate, 224
    Bûche de Noël, 241
    Cheesecake, German Chocolate, 265
    Cheesecake, Marbled, 261
    Cheesecake, Mocha Swirl, 262
    Cheesecake, White Chocolate, 44
    Coconut Cake, White Chocolate-, 263
    Crumb Cake, Calico, 261
    Marshmallow Cake, No-Egg Chocolate, M97
    Mousse Cake, Chocolate, 264
    Orange Roll, Chocolate-, 21
    Peanut Cluster Cake, Chocolate-, 184
    Pound Cake with Fudge Frosting, Chocolate, 296
    Sour Cream Cake, Chocolate-, 222
    Swiss Chocolate Chip Cake, 85
Candies
    Coconut Almond Drops, Chocolate-, 223
    Cream-Filled Chocolates, Liqueur, 258
    Fudge, Chocolate-Peanut Butter, 257
    Fudge, Double Good, M278
    Truffles, White Chocolate, 45
Charlotte Russe, Chocolate, 74
Crust, Chocolate, 264
Crust, Chocolate-Coconut, 261
Crust, Chocolate Crumb, 261
Cups, Chocolate Lace, 133
Cups, Miniature Chocolate, 132
Custard, Chocolate-Topped Amaretto, M37
Dessert, Choco-Maple Frozen, 178
Dessert Squares, Chocolate-Blueberry, 299
Frostings, Fillings, and Toppings
    Chocolate Frosting, M97, 198, 199, 293
    Creamy Chocolate Frosting, 241
    Fluffy Chocolate Frosting, 58
    Fudge Frosting, 296
    Glaze, White Cake with Strawberries and Chocolate, 76
    Mocha Frosting, 224
    Peanut Butter Frosting, Chocolate-, 222
    Peanut Butter-Fudge Frosting, 184
    Truffle Filling, Chocolate, 69
Mousse, Creamy Chocolate, 133
Mousse, Honeyed Chocolate, 223
Pies and Tarts
    Cream Pie, Chocolate, 208

Fudge Pie, 168
Heavenly Chocolate Pie, 260
Ice Cream Pie, Chocolate-, 224
Peanut Butter Swirl Pie, Chocolate-, 262
Sauce, Chocolate Cherry, M165
Shell, Chocolate Pastry, 262
Spread, Chocolate Cheese, 292
Christmas. See also Cookies/Christmas.
Bread, Christmas, 296
Coffee Cakes, Christmas-Tree, 298
Cookies, Spiced Christmas, 294
Lizzies, Christmas, 257
Strawberries, Christmas, 293
Wreath, Della Robbia Fruit, 294
Clams
Cocktail, Tomato-Clam, 252
Pizza, Baby Clam, 182
Shells, Baked Clam, 94
Coconut
Bread, Pumpkin-Coconut, 255
Cake, Coconut-Spice, 296
Cake, White Chocolate-Coconut, 263
Crust, Chocolate-Coconut, 261
Dressing, Coconut, 251
Drops, Chocolate-Coconut Almond, 223
Pie, Coconut Cream, 207
Pies, Coconut-Caramel, 260
Puffs, Coconut, 277
Coffee
Mix, Fireside Coffee, 241
Mocha Brownies, 93
Mocha Frosting, 224
Mocha Swirl Cheesecake, 262
Praline-Flavored Coffee, 69
Coleslaw. See Cabbage or Salads.

Cookies
Bars and Squares
    Almond Cream Confections, 198
    Apricot-Raisin Bars, 32
    Blackberry Bars, 130
    Brownies, Buttermilk Cake, 198
    Brownies, Choco-Mallow, 198
    Brownies, Crunch-Crust, 198
    Brownies, Mocha, 93
    Brownies, Oatmeal, 199
    Brownies, Peanut Butter, 199
    Brownies, Quick, M302
    Fudge Bars, Yummy, 158
    Jam-It Bars, 159
Chocolate-Tipped Log Cookies, 294

Christmas
  Lizzies, Christmas, 257
  Spiced Christmas Cookies, 294
  Strawberries, Christmas, 293
Curled Cookies, French, 16
Drop
  Butterscotch Cookies, 58
  Chips Cookies, Loaded-with-, 223
  Chocolate Macaroons, 57
  Jack-O'-Lantern Cookies, 214
  Molasses Cookies, Chewy, 257
  Oatmeal-Raisin Cookies, 221
  Peanut Cookies, Salted, 92
Orange Fingers, 57
Refrigerator
  Chocolate Teasers, 44
  Peanut Butter Cookies, 58
  Ribbon Cookies, 293
  Shortbread Cookies, 58
  Wafers, Italian, 36
Rolled
  Cinnamon Stars, Swiss, 293
  Mincemeat Sweetheart Cookies, 293
  Sherry Snaps, 94
  Sugar Cookies, Crescent, 294
Sandwich Cookies, Viennese, 293
Spice Cookies, M278
Cooking Light
Appetizers
  Artichokes, Marinated, 250
  Dip, Curry, 25
  Dip, Deviled, 25
  Dip, Low-Cal Tuna, 25
  Dip, Spinach, 25
  Fruit Kabobs with Coconut
    Dressing, 251
  Mousse, Shrimp, 251
  Pasta Bites, Pesto-Cheese, 251
  Pâté, Mock, 251
Beverages
  Fruit Shake, Frosty, 23
  Punch, Holiday, 252
  Shake, Strawberry-Orange
    Breakfast, 186
  Tomato-Clam Cocktail, 252
Breads
  Banana Bread, 72
  Biscuits, Yeast, 71
  Cornbread, Dieter's, 164
  Muffins, Banana-Oat, 188
  Pumpkin-Pecan Bread, 221
Crêpes, Low-Calorie, 77
Desserts
  Bars, Apricot-Raisin, 32
  Cake, Apple-Nut, 76
  Cake, Chocolate Angel Food, 21
  Cake, Orange Pound, 221
  Cake with Strawberries and
    Chocolate Glaze, White, 76
  Cheesecake, Blueberry Chiffon, 76
  Cobbler, New-Fashioned
    Blackberry, 164
  Colada Topping, Chunky Piña, 125
  Cookies, Oatmeal-Raisin, 221
  Cream Puffs, Strawberry-Lemon, 75
  Crêpes, Tropical Fruit, 77
  Custard, Range-Top Amaretto, 77
  Ice, Tangy Cranberry, 305
  Meringue Shells, Fruited, 32
  Meringues, Peach Melba, 76
  Peaches with Nutty Dumplings,
    Spiced, 164
  Roll, Chocolate-Orange, 21

  Sauce, Melba, 77
  Tapioca Fluff, Orange, 31
  Tart, Green Grape, 77
  Tart Shell, 77
  Topping, Blueberry, 125
  Topping, Cherry-Pineapple, 126
  Topping, Raspberry-Peach, 126
  Topping, Spicy Apple, 125
  Topping, Strawberry-Banana, 125
  Yogurt, Vanilla Frozen, 125
Filling, Chicken Salad, 106
Filling, Shrimp Salad, 106
Low Sodium
  Fish, Curried Baked, 5
  Flounder Rolls, Vegetable-Stuffed, 6
  Salmon Steaks, Marinated, 6
  Scamp, Tangy Broiled, 5
  Snapper, Caribbean, 5
  Swordfish, Foil-Baked, 5
Main Dishes
  Beef-and-Barley Rolls,
    Wine-Sauced, 269
  Beef-and-Vegetable Stir-Fry, 22
  Beef, Chinese-Style, 50
  Beef Kabobs, Spirited, 142
  Beef Medallions, Italian, 305
  Beef Patties, Deviled-, 22
  Catfish, Southern Oven-Fried, 163
  Chicken Breasts Sardou, Stuffed, 269
  Chicken, Crunchy Oven-Fried, 163
  Chicken Curry, Stir-Fried, 51
  Chicken in a Bag, 23
  Chicken Spaghetti, 221
  Chicken with Artichokes,
    Sherried, 143
  Fish Florentine in Parchment, 22
  Liver in Creole Sauce, 33
  London Broil, Marinated, 32
  Meat Loaf, Parsley, 22
  Pear Breakfast Treat, 72
  Pork, Stir-Fried, 51
  Pork Tenderloins, Fruit-Stuffed, 270
  Quiche, Eggless, 220
  Shrimp, Beer-Broiled, 142
  Shrimp Skillet, Quick, 50
  Sole Divan, 21
  Steak, Fast-and-Easy Stir-Fried, 50
  Steak, Mock Country-Fried, 163
  Turkey Breast, Stuffed, 270
  Veal Picante, 31
  Veal Picatta with Capers, 142
  Vermicelli, Scallop-Vegetable, 143
Omelet Primavera, 71
Pasta-Basil Toss, 33
Rice Pilaf, Browned, 305
Salad Dressings
  Coconut Dressing, 251
  Cucumber-Mint Dressing, 153
  Horseradish Dressing, 152
  Orange-Poppy Seed Dressing, 187
  Raspberry Dressing, 153
  Soy-Sesame Dressing, 153
  Sweet-and-Sour Dressing, 305
Salads
  Aspic with Horseradish Dressing,
    Crisp Vegetable, 152
  Bean-and-Rice Salad,
    Marinated, 152
  Beef-and-Broccoli Salad, 187
  Broccoli-Corn Salad, 24
  Cucumber-Yogurt Salad, 33
  Garden Salad, Summer, 153
  Greens, Crimson, 153

  Lettuce, Confetti-Stuffed, 24
  Melon Ball Bowl with
    Cucumber-Mint Dressing, 153
  Oriental Salad Bowl, 153
  Pea-and-Apple Salad, English, 24
  Peaches in a Garden Nest, 154
  Spinach-Kiwifruit Salad, 305
  Spinach Salad with Orange
    Dressing, 187
  Tuna-Mac in Tomatoes, 188
Sandwiches
  Crab Sandwiches, Open-Faced, 106
  Garden Sandwiches,
    Open-Faced, 105
  Lamb Pockets with Dilled Cucumber
    Topping, 104
  Vegetarian Melt, Open-Faced, 106
Sauces and Gravies
  Mustard-Hollandaise Sauce,
    Mock, 269
  Mustard Sauce, 22
  White Sauce, Low-Calorie
    Medium, 26
Soups and Stews
  Fish-and-Vegetable Stew, 220
Spread, Cottage Cheese, 107
Spread, Hawaiian Ham, 106
Spread, Vegetable-Egg, 106

Vegetables
  Asparagus, Stir-Fried, 52
  Beans with New Potatoes,
    Green, 164
  Beets, Pickled, 163
  Cabbage-and-Apple Slaw, Red, 31
  Carrots and Onions, Herbed, 31
  Cauliflower-Snow Pea Medley, 305
  Peas and Peppers, Stir-Fried, 51
  Squash Casserole, 163
  Stir-Fried Vegetables with Curry, 51
  Tomatoes and Okra, 164
  Zucchini-Basil Scramble, 34
  Zucchini with Pecans, 31
Corn
  Bisque, Crab-and-Corn, 137
  Cob, Spicy Corn on the, M151
  Frittata, Skillet Corn, 90
  Moussaka, Corn, 190
  Okra, Corn, and Peppers, M151
  Relish, Corn, 120, 245
  Salad, Broccoli-Corn, 24
  Salad, Marinated Corn-Bean, 9
  Soup, Corn, 156
  Soup, Grilled Corn, 121
Cornbreads
  Chile-Cheese Cornbread, 171
  Cornbread, 197
  Dieter's Cornbread, 164
  Hush Puppies, 15
  Pie, Cornbread-Sausage-Apple, 171
  Salad, Cornbread, 172
  Sticks, Cornbread, 15
Cornish Hens
  Glazed Cornish Hens, Apricot-, 306
  Texas-Style Game Hens, 61

Crab
Bake, Quick Crab, 192
Bisque, Crab-and-Corn, 137
Canapés, Hot Crab, 239
Cocktail, Sherried Avocado-
Crabmeat, 95
Salad, Delightful Crab, 145
Sandwiches, Hot Crab-and-
Cheese, 279
Sandwiches, Open-Faced Crab, 106
Crackers
Bread, Sesame Cracker, 2
Dessert Crackers, 3
Fennel-Rye Crackers, 2
Cranberries
Bread, Cranberry-Orange, 244
Cake, Cranberry Upside-Down, 8
Chicken Kiev, Cranberry, 250
Chutney with Cream Cheese,
Cranberry-Amaretto, 244
Crunch, Apple-Cranberry, 178
Ice, Tangy Cranberry, 305
Lemonade, Spiced Cranberry, 292
Pie, Cran-Raspberry, 244
Pie, Tart Cranberry-Cherry, 299
Pie, Walnut-Cranberry, 259
Pork Chops, Orange-Cranberry, 84
Red Roosters, 147
Relish, Cranberry, 245
Salad, Cranberry-Topped
Green, 311
Salad, Lemon-Cranberry
Congealed, 311
Sauce, Fresh Cranberry-Apricot, 243
Tartlets, Fresh Cranberry, 244
Creams
Chantilly, Crème, 9
Chile Cream, Ancho, 121
Cilantro Cream, 121
Kahlúa Cream, 134

Crêpes
Crêpes, 126
Dessert Crêpes, 290
Fruit Crêpes, Tropical, 77
Low-Calorie Crepes, 77
Mushroom-Cheese Crêpes, 289
Processor Crêpes, Basic, 289
Raspberry Crêpes, 126
Strawberry Ice Cream Crêpes, 290

Cucumbers
Dills, Lazy Wife, 149
Dressing, Cucumber-Mint, 153
Mold, Lemon-Cucumber, 90
Pickles, Quick Sweet, 149
Salad, Cucumber-Yogurt, 33
Topping, Lamb Pockets with Dilled
Cucumber, 104
Curry
Casserole, Curry Pea, 154
Chicken Curry, Stir-Fried, 51
Chicken, Honey-Curry, 36
Chicken-Stuffed Peppers, Curried, 19
Dip, Curry, 25
Fish, Curried Baked, 5
Fruit Bake, Curried, 241
Salad, Curried Chicken-and-Orange, 144
Sauce, Halibut with Orange-Curry, 91
Spread, Curried Shrimp, 158
Tuna Salad with Grapes, Curried, 201
Vegetables with Curry, Stir-Fried, 51
Custards
Amaretto Custard,
Chocolate-Topped, M37
Amaretto Custard, Range-Top, 77
Filling, Egg Custard, 14
Pie, Custard Pecan, 184

Dates
Cheese, Nutty Date Dessert, 299
Dressing, Date, 57
Spread, Date-Walnut, 292
Desserts. *See also* specific types.
Apple-Cranberry Crunch, 178
Cheese Dessert, Creamy Cottage, 191
Cheese, Nutty Date Dessert, 299
Chocolate
Charlotte Russe, Chocolate, 74
Cups, Chocolate Lace, 133
Cups, Miniature Chocolate, 132
Squares, Chocolate-Blueberry
Dessert, 299
Crackers, Dessert, 3
Crêpes, Dessert, 290
Frozen
Banana Split Alaskas, 10
Choco-Maple Frozen Dessert, 178
Fruit Pops, 168
Honeydew Granita, 162
Ice Cream Sandwiches, Chocolate
Cookie, 147
Ice Cream Treats, Crunchy, 178
Sherbet Dessert, Layered, 109
Toffee Ice Cream Dessert, 110
Vanilla Frozen Yogurt, 125
Kahlúa Cream, 134
Lemon Cups, Baked, 128
Meringue Shells, Fruited, 32
Orange Tapioca Fluff, 31
Parfaits
Blackberries-and-Cream Parfait, 129
Kiwi Parfait, 55
Peaches with Nutty Dumplings,
Spiced, 164
Peachy Melt-Away Dessert, 298
Pears with Raspberry Sauce, Poached, 69
Sauces
Amaretto-Strawberry Sauce, M165
Apple Dessert Sauce, M165
Apple Topping, Spicy, 125
Berry Sauce, 290
Blueberry Topping, 125

Caramel Sauce, Easy, 38
Cherry-Pineapple Topping, 126
Chocolate Cherry Sauce, M165
Fruit Dessert Sauce, Hot, 299
Lemon Dessert Sauce, M165
Melba Sauce, 77
Orange Dessert Sauce, 58
Peach-Berry Sauce, M165
Peach Sauce, Fresh, 167
Piña Colada Topping, Chunky, 125
Raspberry-Peach Topping, 126
Raspberry Sauce, 69, 117, 183
Strawberry-Banana Topping, 125
Strawberry Sauce, 93, 198
Strawberries, Almond Cream with
Fresh, 93
Dove
Roasted Doves, Pan-, 240
Dressings. *See* Stuffings and Dressings.
Duck and Duckling
Breasts with Raspberry Sauce, Duck, 240
Enchiladas with Red Pepper-Sour Cream,
Smoked Duck, 121
Gumbo Ya Ya, 210
Smoked Duck Breasts, 121
Dumplings
Potato Dumplings, Venison Stew
with, 304

Eggnog
Christmas Eggnog, 242
Pie, Eggnog, 295
Eggplant
Caponata, 166
Casserole, Potato-Eggplant, 166
Easy Eggplant, M151
Fried Parmesan Eggplant, 166
Moussaka, 166
Eggs
Benedict, Bacon-and-Tomato Eggs, 195
Bread, County Fair Egg, 68
Ham and Eggs, Creamy, 286
Migas, 180
Omelets
Olé Omelet, M124
Cheese Omelet, Zippy, 287
Primavera, Omelet, 71
Peanut Butter Easter Eggs, 86
Soufflé, Three-Egg Cheese, 234
Spread, Vegetable-Egg, 106
Tulsa Eggs, 95
Enchiladas
Casserole, Enchilada, 287
Duck Enchiladas with Red Pepper-Sour
Cream, Smoked, 121
Sour Cream Enchiladas, 37

Figs
Ice Cream, Fig, 139
Fillings. *See* Frostings.
Fish. *See also* specific types and Seafood.
Asparagus Divan, Fish-, 128
Baked Fish, Curried, 5
Catfish, Southern Oven-Fried, 163
Creole Fish, M79
Florentine in Parchment, Fish, 22
Flounder Rolls, Vegetable-Stuffed, 6
Grouper Sauté, Shrimp-and-, 91
Halibut with Orange-Curry Sauce, 91
Monkfish, Greek-Style, M79
Orange Roughy, Kiwi, 193

Scamp, Tangy Broiled, 5
Snapper, Caribbean, 5
Snapper, Stuffed, 138
Sole Divan, 21
Stew, Fish-and-Vegetable, 220
Swordfish, Foil-Baked, 5
Food Processor
Appetizers
Artichoke-Caviar Mold, 239
Mousse, Shrimp, 251
Pasta Bites, Pesto-Cheese, 251
Pastry, Processor, 67
Pâté, Mock, 251
Salsa Cruda, 180
Spread, Country Ham, 8
Spread, Fiery Tomato-
Cheese, 196
Spread, Shrimp, 111
Spread, Sombrero, 111
Coffee, Praline-Flavored, 69
Crêpes, Basic Processor, 289
Crêpes, Mushroom-Cheese, 289
Desserts
Cheese, Nutty Date Dessert, 299
Coconut Puffs, 277
Crêpes, Dessert, 290
Crêpes, Strawberry
Ice Cream, 290
Frosting, Cream Cheese, 58
Frosting, Fluffy Chocolate, 58
Phyllo Nests, Nutty, 277
Main Dishes
Chicken Pie, Double-Crust, 111
Chili, Zippy, 110
Meatballs, Quick Processor, 111
Pizza, Pesto, 182
Salad, Guacamole, 181

Sauces and Gravies
Berry Sauce, 290
Dessert Sauce, Orange, 58
Devonshire Sauce, Processor, 58
Tomato Sauce, Italian-Style, 182
Soups and Stews
Brunswick Stew, Blakely, 4
Melon Soup, Swirled, 162
Spread, Corned Beef, 196
Terrine with Goat Cheese, Black
Bean, 120
Frankfurters
Cabbage with Apples and Franks, 42
Frostings, Fillings, and Toppings
Almond Filling, 301
Almond Filling, Ground, 14
Amaretto Filling, 241
Apple Filling, Dried, 229
Apricot-Kirsch Glaze, 14
Brown Sugar Frosting, 296

Caramel Frosting, 265
Caramel Frosting, Easy, 39
Chicken Salad Filling, 106
Chocolate Frosting, M97, 198, 199, 293
Chocolate Frosting, Creamy, 241
Chocolate Frosting, Fluffy, 58
Chocolate-Peanut Butter Frosting, 222
Chocolate Truffle Filling, 69
Cream Cheese Frosting, 58
Cream Filling, 198
Crème Chantilly, 9
Custard Filling, Egg, 14
Decorator Frosting, 86
Drizzle Glaze, 94
Fruit Topping, 225
Fudge Frosting, 296
Glaze, 85
Glaze, Dijon, 54
Glaze, Topping, 69
Honey-Nut Glaze, 15
Lemon Cream Filling, 14
Lemon Filling, 293
Lemon Glaze, 41
Meringue Frosting, 84
Mocha Frosting, 224
Orange Filling, 84
Peanut Butter-Fudge Frosting, 184
Royal Icing, 295
Seven-Minute Frosting, 296
Shrimp Salad Filling, 106
Whipped Cream Frosting, 263
Whipped Cream Topping, 264
Fruit. *See also* specific types.
Cake, Fruit and Spice, M97
Cake, Fruity Ice Cream, 110
Compote, Baked Fruit, 228
Crêpes, Tropical Fruit, 77
Curried Fruit Bake, 241
Dressing, Baked Fruit, 253
Dressing for Fruit Salad, 81
Dressing, Fresh Fruit, 134
Dressing, Lime-Honey Fruit Salad, 81
Drink, Three-Fruit, 199
Float, Frosty Fruit, 159
Fresh Fruit, Mint Dip with, 146
Fruitcake, Layered, 265
Kabobs with Coconut Dressing,
Fruit, 251
Pops, Fruit, 168
Pork Chops, Fruited, 194
Pork Tenderloins, Fruit-Stuffed, 270
Salads
Avocado Fruit Salad, 41
Cherry Fruit Salad, 236
Chicken Salad in Avocados,
Fruited, 41
Date Dressing, Fruit Salad with, 57
Holiday Fruit Salad, 236
Honey Dressing, Fruit Salad
with, 129
Hurry-Up Fruit Salad, 236
Mixed Fruit Cup, 233
Nut Salad, Cheesy Fruit-'n'-, 56
Pineapple-Fruit Salad, Icy, 9
Spiced Autumn Fruit Salad, 228
Wreath, Della Robbia Fruit, 294
Sauce, Hot Fruit Dessert, 299
Shake, Frosty Fruit, 23
Shells, Fruited Meringue, 32
Soup, Cold Fresh Fruit, 157
Soup, Fruit, 98
Spread, Nutty Fruit-and-Cheese, 246
Strudel, Fruit Basket, 276

Tea, Hot Spiced Fruit, 242
Topping, Fruit, 225
Game. *See also* specific types.
Doves, Pan-Roasted, 240
Goose with Currant Sauce, Wild, 240
Quail with Gravy, Georgia, 240
Venison Burgers, 304
Venison Chili, 304
Venison Sausage Stew, 238
Venison Stew with Potato
Dumplings, 304
Venison-Vegetable Bake, 304
Garnishes
Marinade, Dill, 115
Marinade, Garlic-and-Oregano, 115
Marinade, Sweet-and-Sour, 115
Goose
Wild Goose with Currant Sauce, 240
Grapes
Tart, Green Grape, 77
Tea, White Grape Juice, 57
Tuna Salad with Grapes, Curried, 201

Gravies. *See also* Sauces.
Pea Gravy, Black-Eyed, 12
Grits
Good Morning Grits, 156
Gumbos
Beef Gumbo, Ground, 283
Seafood Gumbo, 210
Ya Ya, Gumbo, 210

Ham. *See also* Pork.
Appetizers, Meat-and-Cheese, 7
Bake, Chicken, Ham, and Cheese, 217
Bake, Ham-Rice-Tomato, 78
Casserole, Ham-and-Cheese, 78
Cordon Bleu, Veal, 219
Country Ham
Quiche, Country Ham, 287
Spread, Country Ham, 8
Eggs, Creamy Ham and, 286
Jambalaya, Creole, 210
Jambalaya de Covington, 211
Noodles, Ham and Swiss on, 108
Pie, Golden Ham, 78
Pineapple-Flavored Ham, 160
Potatoes with Ham Bits, Creamy, 191
Prosciutto, Pizza with Artichoke and, 182
Rolls, Ham-and-Broccoli, 82
Salad, Mandarin Ham-and-Rice, 145
Sandwiches, Creamy Blue
Cheese-Ham, 279
Sandwiches, Ham-and-Cheese Pita, 202
Skillet, Ham-Noodle, 78
Spread, Ham Salad, 92
Spread, Hawaiian Ham, 106
Stew, Blakely Brunswick, 4
Tart Milan, 70
Hearts of Palm
Salad, Hearts-of-Palm, 138

Honey
Bread, Applesauce-Honey Nut, 300
Cake, Honey-Oatmeal, 222
Chicken, Honey-Curry, 36
Dressing, Honey, 129
Dressing, Honey French, 81
Dressing, Lime-Honey Fruit
   Salad, 81
Glaze, Honey-Nut, 15
Mousse, Honeyed Chocolate, 223
Spread, Honey-Nut, 157
Honeydew. *See* Melons.
Hors d'Oeuvres. *See* Appetizers.
Hot Dogs. *See* Frankfurters.

Ice Creams and Sherbets
Banana Split Alaskas, 10
Beverages
   Banana Smoothie, 160
   Fruit Float, Frosty, 159
   Lime Cooler, 160
   Strawberry-Banana Float, 160
   Tahitian Flower, 159
Bourbon Ice Cream, 139
Brownie Dessert, Special-Occasion, 139
Cake, Fruity Ice Cream, 110
Cranberry Ice, Tangy, 305
Crêpes, Strawberry Ice Cream, 290
Dessert, Layered Sherbet, 109
Fig Ice Cream, 139
Pie, Chocolate-Ice Cream, 224
Pie, Peppermint Candy-Ice Cream, 260
Pie, Pumpkin-Ice Cream, 243
Sandwiches, Chocolate Cookie Ice
   Cream, 147
Toffee Ice Cream Dessert, 110
Treats, Crunchy Ice Cream, 178

Jams and Jellies
Apple-Mint Jelly, 134
Jicama
Salad, Jicama, 123

Kabobs
Beef Kabobs, Spirited, 142
Cantaloupe Wedges, Grilled, 162
Chicken, Garlic-Grilled, 180
Chicken Kabobs, 141
Fruit Kabobs with Coconut Dressing, 251
Hot-and-Spicy Kabobs, 193
Seafood Brochette, 96
Shrimp, Grilled Marinated, 173
Shrimp, Marinated and Grilled, 141
Kiwi
Muffins, Kiwifruit, 255
Orange Roughy, Kiwi, 193
Parfait, Kiwi, 55
Pizza, Kiwi-Berry, 55
Salad, Spinach-Kiwifruit, 305

Lamb
Burgoo, Five-Meat, 3
Chops, Teriyaki Lamb, 60
Leg of Lamb, Roast, 96
Leg of Lamb, Stuffed, 248
Moussaka, 166
Pockets with Dilled Cucumber Topping,
   Lamb, 104

Lasagna
Chicken Lasagna, M302
Vegetable Lasagna, Colorful, 19
Zesty Lasagna, M188
Lemon
Beverages
   Cranberry Lemonade, Spiced, 292
Bread, Lemon, 256
Butter, Asparagus with Lemon, M151
Canapés, Lemon-Cheese, 93
Chicken Nuggets, Lemon-, 283
Desserts
   Cake, Lemon-Sour Cream Pound, 38
   Cream Puffs, Strawberry-Lemon, 75
   Cups, Baked Lemon, 128
   Lemon Curd, 139
   Filling, Lemon, 293
   Filling, Lemon Cream, 14
   Glaze, Lemon, 41
Dressing, Lemon-Pepper, 55
Dressing, Tomato Slices with Lemon, 167
Mold, Lemon-Cucumber, 90
Salad, Lemon-Cranberry Congealed, 311
Sauce, Lemon Dessert, M165
Scones, Lemon-Raisin, 69
Veal with Artichoke Hearts, Lemon, 219
Vinegar, Raspberry-Lemon, 134
Lime
Cooler, Lime, 160
Dressing, Lime-Honey Fruit Salad, 81
Salad, Snowy Emerald, 311
Linguine
Carbonara, Linguine, 108
Liver
Creole Sauce, Liver in, 33
Lobster
Beef Tenderloin, Lobster-Stuffed, 248
Taco with Yellow Tomato Salsa and
   Jicama Salad, Warm Lobster, 122

Macaroni
Casserole, Macaroni, 154
Salad, Macaroni, 92
Salad, Macaroni Shell, 38
Tomatoes, Tuna-Mac in, 188
Marinades
Dill Marinade, 115
Garlic-and-Oregano Marinade, 115
Sweet-and-Sour Marinade, 115
Marshmallows
Brownies, Choco-Mallow, 198
Cake, No-Egg Chocolate
   Marshmallow, 97
Meatballs
Chinese Meatballs, 194
Processor Meatballs, Quick, 111
Royal Meatballs, 268
Melons
Balls, Minted Melon, 162
Bowl with Cucumber-Mint Dressing,
   Melon Ball, 153

Cantaloupe Wedges, Grilled, 162
Honeydew Granita, 162
Soup, Swirled Melon, 162
Meringues
Cake, Orange Meringue, 84
Frosting, Meringue, 84
Meringue, 207
Peach Melba Meringues, 76
Shells, Fruited Meringue, 32
Torte, Toffee Meringue, 118
Microwave
Apples, Rosy Cinnamon, M37
Desserts
   Brownies, Quick, M302
   Cake, Fruit and Spice, M97
   Cake, No-Egg Chocolate
      Marshmallow, M97
   Cookies, Spice, M278
   Custard, Chocolate-Topped
      Amaretto, M37
   Divinity, Peanut, M278
   Frosting, Chocolate, M97
   Fudge, Double Good, M278
Main Dishes
   Chicken and Vegetables
      Vermouth, M37
   Chicken Divan, M218
   Chicken Lasagna, M302
   Chicken, Tangy Herbed, M302
   Chicken Toss, Quick, M124
   Fish, Creole, M79
   Lasagna, Zesty, M188
   Monkfish, Greek-Style, M79
   Oysters on the Half Shell,
      Dressed, M79
   Pork Chops, Pineapple, M124
   Quiche, Vegetable, M219
   Salmon Patties, Open-Faced, M218
   Sausage Casserole, Easy, M189
   Steak, Onion-Smothered, M189
Omelet, Olé, M124
Salads
   Beef Salad, Tangy, M218
   Tuna Salad, Cheese-Sauced, M124
Sandwiches
   Brown Bread-Cream Cheese
      Sandwiches, M6
   Pita Sandwiches, Hot, M6
Sauces and Gravies
   Amaretto-Strawberry Sauce, M165
   Apple Dessert Sauce, M165
   Chocolate Cherry Sauce, M165
   Lemon Dessert Sauce, M165
   Peach-Berry Sauce, M165
Soups and Stews
   Bacon-Beer Cheese Soup, M7
   Cauliflower Soup, Cream of, M7
Vegetables
   Asparagus with Lemon
      Butter, M151
   Beans, Green, M151
   Corn on the Cob, Spicy, M151
   Eggplant, Easy, M151
   Okra, Corn, and Peppers, M151
   Potatoes, Seasoned New, M151
   Squash-and-Pepper Toss,
      Crisp, M152
Mincemeat
Cookies, Mincemeat Sweetheart, 293
Pie, Holiday Mincemeat, 213
Mousses
Cake, Chocolate Mousse, 264
Chocolate Mousse, Creamy, 133

Chocolate Mousse, Honeyed, 223
Shrimp Mousse, 196, 251
Muffins
Apple Muffins, 23
Banana-Oat Muffins, 188
Blueberry-Oatmeal Muffins, 24
Bran Muffins, Sour Cream-, 98
Carrot-and-Raisin Muffins, 24
English Muffins, 49
Kiwifruit Muffins, 255
Peanut Butter Muffins, 158
Potato Muffins, Sweet, 280
Mushrooms
Baked Mushrooms, Creamy, 127
Beef Tenderloin with
  Mushrooms, 115
Casserole, Mushroom-Artichoke, 241
Crêpes, Mushroom-Cheese, 289
Heavenly Mushrooms, 281
Potatoes, Mushroom Scalloped, 191
Sandwiches, Toasted
  Mushroom, 281
Sauce, Beef Tenderloin with
  Mushroom-Sherry, 306
Sauce, Chicken Florentine with
  Mushroom, 250
Sauce, Mushroom, 36, 186, 284
Soufflés, Mushroom, 282
Soup, Oyster-and-Mushroom, 39
Steak and Mushrooms, Flank, 61
Stuffed Mushroom Delight, 281
Mustard
Herbed Mustard, 134
Sauce, Creamy Mustard, 232
Sauce, Mock Mustard-
  Hollandaise, 269
Sauce, Mustard, 22

Noodles
Caraway Buttered Noodles, 230
Ham and Swiss on Noodles, 108
Skillet, Ham-Noodle, 78

Oatmeal
Bars, Yummy Fudge, 158
Bread, Whole Wheat-Oatmeal, 85
Brownies, Oatmeal, 199
Cake, Honey-Oatmeal, 222
Cookies, Oatmeal-Raisin, 221
Loaf, Banana-Oat Tea, 256
Muffins, Banana-Oat, 188
Muffins, Blueberry-Oatmeal, 24
Okra
Corn, and Peppers, Okra, M151
Fresh Okra and Tomatoes, 89
Fried Okra, 89
Soup, Charleston Okra, 156
Tomatoes and Okra, 164
Olives
Appetizers, Cheesy-Olive, 246
Casserole, Turkey-Olive, 268
Omelets
Cheese Omelet, Zippy, 287
Omelet, Olé, M124
Primavera, Omelet, 71
Onions
Carrots with Bacon and Onion,
  Glazed, 200
Glazed Carrots and Onions, 128
Herbed Carrots and Onions, 31
Sauce, Onion, 248
Sauce, Onion Cream, 232

Soups
  Cheese Soup, Onion-, 81
  French Onion-Beef Soup, 54
Steak, Onion-Smothered, M189
Stew, Beef-and-Onion, 18
Oranges
Beverages
  Breakfast Eye-Opener, 199
  Magnolia Blossoms, 72
  Punch, Orange Soda, 214
  Shake, Tropical, 200
Breads
  Blueberry-Orange Bread, 140
  Cranberry-Orange Bread, 244
  Pumpkin Bread, Orange-, 300
Chicken Breasts with Parslied Rice,
  Orange, 242
Chicken Stir-Fry, Kyoto Orange-, 96
Desserts
  Cake, Orange Liqueur, 84
  Cake, Orange Meringue, 84
  Cake, Orange Pound, 84, 221
  Chocolate-Orange Roll, 21
  Filling, Orange, 84
  Fingers, Orange, 57
  Pie, Orange Chiffon, 260
  Tapioca Fluff, Orange, 31
Dip, Creamy Orange, 247
Dressing, Orange-Poppy Seed, 187
Halibut with Orange-Curry Sauce, 91
Pancakes, Orange-Yogurt, 225
Pecans, Orange, 292
Pork Chops, Orange-Cranberry, 84
Salads
  Chicken-and-Orange Salad,
    Curried, 144
  Ham-and-Rice Salad, Mandarin, 145
  Quick Orange Salad, 80
  Romaine Salad, Orange-, 239
  Shrimp-and-Orange Rice Salad,
    Zesty, 155
Sauces and Glazes
  Dessert Sauce, Orange, 58
Shake, Strawberry-Orange Breakfast, 186
Spread, Orange Cheese, 292
Oysters
Buccaneer, Oysters, 40
Dressed Oysters on the Half Shell, M79
Gumbo, Seafood, 210
Nachos, Texas Oyster, 39
Poor Boys, Oyster-and-Bacon, 40
Shrimp Sauce, Oysters in, 40
Smoky Oysters Supreme, 60
Soup, Oyster-and-Mushroom, 39

Pancakes
Apple Pancakes with Cider Sauce,
  Spicy, 224
Cornmeal Batter Cakes, 16
Island Pancakes, 225
Orange-Yogurt Pancakes, 225
Potato Pancakes, Sweet, 280
Pastas. *See also* specific types.
Bites, Pesto-Cheese Pasta, 251
Broccoli and Sausage, Pasta with, 109
Chicken-and-Broccoli Pasta, 286
Crab Bake, Quick, 192
Mexican Luncheon, 192
Ravioli, Homemade, 230
Ravioli Pasta, Homemade, 231
Rotelle, Chicken and Tomato with, 108
Rotini Romano, 193
Salad, Italian, 145

Salad, Pasta, 36
Salad, Salmon-Pasta, 9
Salad, Tarragon Pasta-Chicken, 155
Sauerkraut Salad, Crunchy, 9
Shells, Spinach-Stuffed, 20
Tortellini Salad, Chicken, 288
Toss, Pasta-Basil, 33
Vegetables, Pasta and Garden, 192
Vermicelli, Scallop-Vegetable, 143
Peaches
Cake, Peach Upside-Down, 8
Cobbler, Peach-Caramel, 178
Dessert, Peachy Melt Away, 298
Meringues, Peach Melba, 76
Nest, Peaches in a Garden, 154
Puffs, Peach Sweet Potato, 280
Sauce, Fresh Peach, 167
Sauce, Peach-Berry, M165
Soup, Peach-Plum, 157
Spiced Peaches with Nutty
  Dumplings, 164
Topping, Raspberry-Peach, 126
Peanut Butter
Brownies, Peanut Butter, 199
Cookies, Peanut Butter, 58
Eggs, Peanut Butter Easter, 86
Frosting, Chocolate-Peanut Butter, 222
Frosting, Peanut Butter-Fudge, 184
Fudge, Chocolate-Peanut Butter, 257
Muffins, Peanut Butter, 158
Pie, Chocolate-Peanut Butter Swirl, 262
Peanuts
Bread, Peanut, 184
Brittle with Crushed Peanuts, 184
Cake, Chocolate-Peanut Cluster, 184
Clusters, Peanut, 184
Cookies, Salted Peanut, 92
Divinity, Peanut, M278
Salad, Nutty Cabbage, 42
Salad, Nutty Green, 168
Soup, Peanut, 184

Pears
Breakfast Treat, Pear, 72
Cake, Upside-Down Sunburst, 9
Pie, French Pear, 213
Poached Pears with Raspberry Sauce, 69
Salad, Pear-and-Celery, 56
Peas
Black-Eyed
  Casserole, Reunion Pea, 11
  Gravy, Black-Eyed Pea, 12
  Jambalaya, Good Luck, 11
  Salad, Plentiful P's, 12
Casserole, Curry Pea, 154
English
  Minted Peas, 56
  Rice with Green Peas, 45

Peas, English *(continued)*

    Salad, Cauliflower-Pea, 231
    Salad, English Pea-and-Apple, 24
  Snow
    Medley, Cauliflower-Snow Pea, 305
    Stir-Fried Peas and Peppers, 51
Pecans
  Ball, Tuna-Pecan, 94
  Bread, Pineapple-Pecan Loaf, 256
  Bread, Prune-Nut, 255
  Bread, Pumpkin-Pecan, 221
  Cake, Cinnamon-Pecan Coffee, 69
  Crispies, Pecan-Cheese, 168
  Crust, Spiced Nut, 295
  Dumplings, Spiced Peaches with
    Nutty, 164
  Glaze, Honey-Nut, 15
  Orange Pecans, 292

  Pepper Pecans, 137
  Pie, Bourbon-Pecan Pumpkin, 264
  Pie, Custard Pecan, 184
  Pie, Raisin-Pecan, 213
  Roulade, Pecan, 183
  Spread, Honey-Nut, 157
  Tarts, Special Pecan, 224
  Waffles, Pecan, 225
  Zucchini with Pecans, 31
Peppermint
  Pie, Peppermint Candy-Ice Cream, 260
Peppers
  Chile
    Cream, Ancho Chile, 121
    Sauce, Ancho Chile, 122
    Sauce, Medallions of Beef with
      Ancho Chile, 122
  Green
    Stacks, Pepper-Cheese, 80
    Stuffed Peppers, Curried
      Chicken-, 19
  Jalapeño Cheese, Shrimp with
    Herbed, 112
  Okra, Corn, and Peppers, M151
  Red Peppers, Potatoes with
    Sweet, 192
  Roasted Peppers, Marinated, 90
  Stir-Fried Peas and Peppers, 51
  Toss, Crisp Squash-and-Pepper, M152
Pickles and Relishes
  Avocado Relish, 120
  Black Bean-Tomatillo Relish, 121
  Chowchow, 150
  Chutney
    Commander's Chutney, 245
    Cranberry-Amaretto Chutney with
      Cream Cheese, 244
    Rhubarb Chutney, 245
  Corn Relish, 120, 245
  Cranberry Relish, 245
  Dills, Lazy Wife, 149
  Salsa Cruda, 180

  Salsa, Fresh Summer, 89
  Salsa, Tomato, 120
  Salsa, Yellow Tomato, 122
  Squash Pickles, 150
  Sweet Pickles, Quick, 149
  Taco with Yellow Tomato Salsa and
    Jicama Salad, Warm Lobster, 122
  Tomato Pickles, Green, 134
  Zucchini Relish, 200
Pies and Pastries
  Apple
    Easy-Crust Apple Pie, 11
    Grandmother's Apple Pie, 212
    Holiday Apple Pie, 260
    Turnovers, Puffy Apple, 276
  Apricot Pinwheels, 276
  Banana Cream Pie, 207
  Blackberry-Apple Pie, 130
  Butterscotch Cream Pie, 207
  Cheese
    Phyllo-Cheese Triangles, 246
    Puffs, Mexican Cheese, 8
  Chocolate
    Cream Pie, Chocolate, 208
    Fudge Pie, 168
    Heavenly Chocolate Pie, 260
    Ice Cream Pie, Chocolate-, 224
    Peanut Butter Swirl Pie,
      Chocolate-, 262
  Cobblers
    Blackberry Cobbler,
      New-Fashioned, 164
    Blueberry Pinwheel
      Cobbler, 140
    Peach-Caramel Cobbler, 178
  Coconut-Caramel Pies, 260
  Coconut Cream Pie, 207
  Coconut Puffs, 277
  Cranberry-Cherry Pie, Tart, 299
  Cran-Raspberry Pie, 244
  Cream Puffs, Strawberry-Lemon, 75
  Eggnog Pie, 295
  Ice Cream Pie, Peppermint
    Candy-, 260
  Main Dish
    Burrito Pie, Mexican, 287
    Chicken in Phyllo, 286
    Chicken Pie, Double-Crust, 111
    Chicken Pot Pie, Thick 'n'
      Crusty, 267
    Cornbread-Sausage-Apple Pie, 171
    Ham Pie, Golden, 78
  Mincemeat Pie, Holiday, 213
  Nesselrode Pie, Fluffy, 261
  Orange Chiffon Pie, 260
  Palmiers, 277
  Pastries and Crusts
    Chocolate-Coconut Crust, 261
    Chocolate Crumb Crust, 261
    Chocolate Crust, 264
    Chocolate Pastry Shell, 262
    Cream Cheese Pastry Shells,
      Miniature, 190
    Double-Crust Pastry, 299
    Graham Cracker Crust, 139, 243
    Heart Tart Pastry, 14
    Nut Crust, Spiced, 295
    Pastry, 212, 267
    Pizza Crust, Crispy, 181
    Processor Pastry, 67
    Shell, Pastry, 262
    Tart Shell, 77
  Pear Pie, French, 213

  Pecan
    Custard Pecan Pie, 184
    Raisin-Pecan Pie, 213
  Phyllo Cheesecakes, Little, 275
  Phyllo Nests, Nutty, 277
  Pineapple Phyllo Bundles, 277
  Pumpkin-Ice Cream Pie, 243
  Pumpkin Pie, Autumn, 213
  Pumpkin Pie, Bourbon-Pecan, 264
  Pumpkin Pie in Spiced Nut Crust, 295
  Strudel, Fruit Basket, 276
  Tarts
    Cheese Tart, Herb-, 98
    Cranberry Tartlets, Fresh, 244
    Grape Tart, Green, 77
    Heart Tarts, 14
    Milan, Tart, 70
    Pecan Tarts, Special, 224
    Seafood Tartlets, 247
    Shrimp Tart, 70
  Vegetable
    Squash Pie, Butternut, 212
    Sweet Potato Cream Pie,
      Southern, 260

  Walnut-Cranberry Pie, 259
Pimientos
  Sauce, Cauliflower with
    Pimiento, 232
Pineapple
  Bread, Pineapple-Pecan Loaf, 256
  Cake, Cajun, 138
  Ham, Pineapple-Flavored, 160
  Meatballs, Chinese, 194
  Milkshake, Pineapple, 199
  Phyllo Bundles, Pineapple, 277
  Pineapple Topping, Cherry-, 126
  Pork Chops, Pineapple, M124
  Salad, Icy Pineapple-Fruit, 9
  Spread, Hawaiian Cheese, 158
Pizza
  Artichoke and Prosciutto, Pizza
    with, 182
  Burger, Pizza, 185
  Clam Pizza, Baby, 182
  Crust, Crispy Pizza, 181
  Gruyère-Chicken Pizza, 182
  Italian-Style Pizza, Original, 182
  Kiwi-Berry Pizza, 55
  Pesto Pizza, 182
  Salad Pizza, 182
  Squares, Pizza, 168
Plums
  Pudding-Gelatin Mold, Plum, 178
  Sauce, Gingered Plum, 175
  Soup, Peach-Plum, 157
Popcorn
  Cake, Popcorn-Gumdrop, 262
  Scramble, Popcorn, 185
  Spiced Popcorn Snack, 8
Pork. *See also* Bacon, Ham, Sausage.
  Burgoo, Five-Meat, 3
  Burgoo, Harry Young's, 3

Chops
  Apple Pork Chops, Spicy, 230
  Arlo, Pork, 229
  Chili Chops, 10
  Cider-Sauced Pork Chops, 81
  Fruited Pork Chops, 194
  Glazed Pork Chops, Apple-, 35
  Hawaiian Pork Chops, 82
  Orange-Cranberry Pork Chops, 84
  Pineapple Pork Chops, M124
  Savory Pork Chops, 194
  Stuffed Chops, Barbecued, 229
  Stuffed Pork Chops, Braised, 249
Eggs, Tulsa, 95
Meat Loaf, Savory, 216
Roasts
  Glazed Pork Loin, 229
  Tomato Sauce, Pork Roast with, 249
Salad, Pork-'n'-Bean, 83
Stew, Bama Brunswick, 4
Stew, Sonny Frye's Brunswick, 4
Stir-Fried Pork, 51
Tenderloin
  Medallions with Chutney Sauce,
    Pork, 35
  Stuffed Pork Tenderloins, Fruit-, 270

Potatoes
Casserole, Potato, 190
Casserole, Potato-Eggplant, 166
Creamy Potatoes with Ham Bits, 191
Creole Potatoes, 138
Croquettes, Potato, 116
Dumplings, Venison Stew with
  Potato, 304
Lorraine, Potatoes, 190
Mashed Potatoes, Jazzy, 192
New Potatoes, Green Beans with, 164
New Potatoes, Seasoned, M151
Peppers, Potatoes with Sweet Red, 192
Rolls, Potato Yeast, 53
Rolls, Refrigerator Potato, 15
Salads
  Dutch Potato Salad, Hot, 176
  Herbed Potato Salad, 171
  Salmon-Potato Salad, 285
  Saucy Potato Salad, 123
Scalloped Potatoes, Mushroom, 191
Scalloped Potatoes, Party, 191
Seasoned Potatoes, 253
Stuffed
  Cheese Sauce, Stuffed Potatoes
    with, 192
Turnips, Southern, 190
Yeast, Potato, 53

Potatoes, Sweet
Bourbon Sweet Potatoes, 280
Delight, Sweet Potato, 83
Muffins, Sweet Potato, 280
Pancakes, Sweet Potato, 280
Pie, Southern Sweet Potato
  Cream, 260
Puffs, Peach Sweet Potato, 280
Puffs, Sweet Potato, 253
Raspberry Sweet Potatoes, 280

Pralines
Coffee, Praline-Flavored, 69

Pretzels
Soft Pretzels, Chewy, 159

Prunes
Bread, Prune-Nut, 255

Puddings. *See also* Custards.
Plum Pudding-Gelatin Mold, 178
Raisin-Rice Pudding, 46

Pumpkin
Bread, Orange-Pumpkin, 300
Bread, Pumpkin-Coconut, 255
Bread, Pumpkin-Pecan, 221
Cookies, Jack-O'-Lantern, 214
Pie, Autumn Pumpkin, 213
Pie, Bourbon-Pecan Pumpkin, 264
Pie in Spiced Nut Crust, Pumpkin, 295
Pie, Pumpkin-Ice Cream, 243
Rolls, Pumpkin, 254

Quail
Gravy, Georgia Quail with, 240
Quiches
Eggless Quiche, 220
Ham Quiche, Country, 287
Salmon Quiche, 38
Sausage-Apple Quiche, Crustless, 70
Shrimp Miniquiches, 146
Spinach Quichelets, 67
Vegetable Quiche, M219

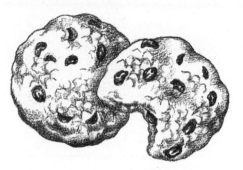

Raisins
Bread, Homemade Raisin, 300
Cookies, Oatmeal-Raisin, 221
Muffins, Carrot-and-Raisin, 24
Pie, Raisin-Pecan, 213
Pudding, Raisin-Rice, 46
Salad, Carrot-Raisin, 10
Sauce, Raisin, 127
Scones, Lemon-Raisin, 69

Raspberries
Chocolate Cups, Miniature, 132
Crêpes, Raspberry, 126
Dressing, Raspberry, 153
Pie, Cran-Raspberry, 244
Potatoes, Raspberry Sweet, 280
Punch, Raspberry-Rosé, 242
Salad, Raspberry Ribbon, 236
Sauce, Duck Breasts with Raspberry, 240
Sauce, Melba, 77
Sauce, Peach-Berry, M165
Sauce, Poached Pears with Raspberry, 69
Sauce, Raspberry, 69, 117, 183
Topping, Raspberry-Peach, 126
Vinegar, Raspberry-Lemon, 134

Relishes. *See* Pickles and Relishes.

Rhubarb
Chutney, Rhubarb, 245

Rice
Bake, Ham-Rice-Tomato, 78
Beans and Rice, Red, 45
Broccoli with Rice, Holiday, 252
Casserole, Brown Rice, 118
Casserole, Rice, 45
Casserole, Rice-and-Chicken, 154

Dressing, Mexican Rice, 253
Mélange, Rice, 240
Parslied Rice, 167, 243
Peas, Rice with Green, 45
Pilaf, Browned Rice, 305
Pilaf, Rice, 229
Pudding, Raisin-Rice, 46
Salads
  Bean-and-Rice Salad, Marinated, 152
  Ham-and-Rice Salad, Mandarin, 145
  Shrimp-and-Orange Rice Salad,
    Zesty, 155
  Tuna-Rice Salad, 202

Rolls and Buns. *See also* Breads.
Bran Yeast Rolls, 116
Cream Cheese Pinches, 85
Potato Rolls, Refrigerator, 15
Potato Yeast Rolls, 53
Pumpkin Rolls, 254
Romano Sesame Rolls, 144
Snack Buns, 279
Spoon Rolls, 15
Wheat Rolls, Easy Whole, 74
Wheat Rolls, Light, 254

Salad Dressings
Blue Cheese Dressing, Apple Salad
  with, 103
Blue Cheese Dressing, Tangy, 81
Coconut Dressing, 251
Cucumber-Mint Dressing, 153
Date Dressing, 57
French Dressing, Honey, 81
French Dressing, Piquant, 202
Fruit Dressing, Fresh, 134
Fruit Salad, Dressing for, 81
Honey Dressing, 129
Horseradish Dressing, 152
Lemon-Pepper Dressing, 55
Lime-Honey Fruit Salad Dressing, 81
Orange-Poppy Seed Dressing, 187
Raspberry Dressing, 153
Sesame Seed Dressing, 81
Sour Cream Sauce, 233
Soy-Sesame Dressing, 153
Sweet-and-Sour Dressing, 305
Vinaigrette Dressing, 138

Salads
Apple Salad, 233
Apple Salad with Blue Cheese
  Dressing, 103
Asparagus-Horseradish Salad, 80
Aspic
  Vegetable Aspic with Horseradish
    Dressing, Crisp, 152
Avocado Salad, Spanish, 41
Banana Salad, 80
Bean
  Green Bean Salad, 90
  Green Bean Salad, Hot, 176
  Marinated Bean-and-Rice Salad, 152
  Marinated Corn-Bean Salad, 9
  Pork-'n'-Bean Salad, 83
  Six-Bean Salad, Colorful, 82
Beef-and-Broccoli Salad, 187
Beef Salad, Tangy, M218
Broccoli-Corn Salad, 24
Broccoli Salad, Fresh, 103
Brussels Sprouts Salad, 233
Cabbage Salad, 120, 233
Cabbage Salad, Nutty, 42
Caesar Salad, Easy, 116

Salads *(continued)*

Carrot-Raisin Salad, 10
Carrots, Creamy Marinated, 200
Cheese-Banana Splits, Cottage, 56
Chicken
    Avocado-Chicken Salad, 107
    Baked Chicken Salad, 176
    BLT Chicken Salad, 144
    Chutney-Chicken Salad, 74
    Curried Chicken-and-Orange
        Salad, 144
    Filling, Chicken Salad, 106
    Fruited Chicken Salad in
        Avocados, 41
    Pasta-Chicken Salad, Tarragon, 155
    Poulet Rémoulade, 144
    Special Chicken Salad, 183
    Tortellini Salad, Chicken, 288
Citrus Salad, 103
Citrus Salad Bowl, 83
Committee, Salad by, 288
Congealed
    Apricot Nectar Salad, 236
    Avocado Salads, Congealed, 42
    Emerald Salad, Snowy, 311
    Fruit Salad, Cherry, 236
    Fruit Salad, Spiced Autumn, 228
    Gazpacho Salad Mold, 311
    Lemon-Cranberry Congealed
        Salad, 311
    Lemon-Cucumber Mold, 90
    Raspberry Ribbon Salad, 236
Cornbread Salad, 172
Crab Salad, Delightful, 145
Cucumber-Yogurt Salad, 33
Extravaganza, Salad, 233
Fruit
    Avocado Fruit Salad, 41
    Date Dressing, Fruit Salad with, 57
    Holiday Fruit Salad, 236
    Honey Dressing, Fruit Salad
        with, 129
    Hurry-Up Fruit Salad, 236
    Mixed Fruit Cup, 233
    Nut Salad, Cheesy Fruit-'n'-, 56
    Pineapple-Fruit Salad, Icy, 9
    Wreath, Della Robbia Fruit, 294
Greek Salad, 103
Green
    Bibb Salad, Tossed, 128
    Caesar Salad, Flippo, 61
    Cranberry-Topped Green Salad, 311
    Crimson Greens, 153
    Garden Salad, Summer, 153
    Lettuce, Confetti-Stuffed, 24
    Lettuce, Delicate Garden, 62
    Mixed Greens Salad, 62
    Nutty Green Salad, 168
    Spinach-Kiwifruit Salad, 305
    Spring Salad, 62
    Wedges, Spring Salad, 62
Guacamole Salad, 181
Ham-and-Rice Salad, Mandarin, 145
Ham Salad Spread, 92
Hearts-of-Palm Salad, 138
Herb Salad, 90
Italian Salad, 145
Jicama Salad, 123
Macaroni Salad, 92
Macaroni Shell Salad, 38
Melon Balls, Minted, 162

Middle Eastern Salad, 107
Orange-Romaine Salad, 239
Orange Salad, Quick, 80
Oriental Salad Bowl, 153
Pasta Salad, 36
Pasta Salad, Salmon-, 9
Pea-and-Apple Salad, English, 24
Peaches in a Garden Nest, 154
Pear-and-Celery Salad, 56
Pepper-Cheese Stacks, 80
Pizza, Salad, 182
Plentiful P's Salad, 12

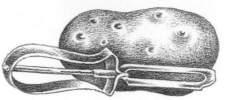

Potato
    Dutch Potato Salad, Hot, 176
    Herbed Potato Salad, 171
    Salmon-Potato Salad, 285
    Saucy Potato Salad, 123
Salmon-Spinach Salad, 145
    Sauerkraut Salad, Crunchy, 9
Shrimp-and-Orange Rice Salad,
    Zesty, 155
Shrimp Salad Filling, 106
Slaws
    Cabbage-and-Apple Slaw, Red, 31
    Hot-and-Creamy Dutch Slaw, 127
    Sour Cream Slaw, 10
Spinach Salad, 62
Spinach Salad with Orange Dressing, 187
Taco Salad, Spicy, 287
Tomato-Basil Vinaigrette, 89
Tomato Salad, Cherry, 156
Tomato Slices with Lemon Dressing, 167
Tuna
    Cheese-Sauced Tuna Salad, M124
    Company Tuna Salad, 201
    Crunchy Tuna Salad, 201
    Curried Tuna Salad with Grapes, 201
    Rice Salad, Tuna-, 202
    Taco Salad, Tuna-, 145
    Tomatoes, Tuna-Mac in, 188
Turkey Salad, Hot, 176
Turkey Salad Pita Sandwiches, 202
Turkey Salad, Polynesian, 285
Turkey Salad with Hot Bacon
    Dressing, 285
Vegetable
    Cauliflower-Pea Salad, 231
    Garden Salad, 62
    Marinated Garden Vegetables, 252
    Marinated Vegetable Salad, 243
Waldorf Salad, Creamy, 311
Zucchini Salad, 103
Salmon
Patties, Open-Faced Salmon, M218
Quiche, Salmon, 38
Salad, Salmon-Pasta, 9
Salad, Salmon-Potato, 285
Salad, Salmon-Spinach, 145
Spread, Salmon-and-Horseradish, 146
Steaks, Marinated Salmon, 6
Steaks with Tarragon Butter,
    Salmon, 155

Sandwiches
Avocado, Bacon, and Cheese
    Sandwiches, 279
Beef Sandwiches, Grilled Corned, 54
Brown Bread-Cream Cheese
    Sandwiches, M6
Cheese-Ham Sandwiches, Creamy
    Blue, 279
Crab-and-Cheese Sandwiches, Hot, 279
Crab Sandwiches, Open-Faced, 106
Garden Sandwiches, Open-Faced, 105
Ham-and-Cheese Pita Sandwiches, 202
Lamb Pockets with Dilled Cucumber
    Topping, 104
Mushroom Sandwiches, Toasted, 281
Oyster-and-Bacon Poor Boys, 40
Pita Sandwiches, Hot, M6
Rarebit, Uptown Welsh, 279
Salami Sandwiches, Open-Faced, 279
Snack Buns, 279
Spinach-Walnut Pitas, 202
Tuna-in-a-Pita Pocket, 202
Turkey-Cheese Puffs, 301
Turkey Salad Pita Sandwiches, 202
Vegetarian Melt, Open-Faced, 106
Sauces. *See also* Desserts/Sauces.
Apricot Sauce, 172
Béchamel Sauce, 286
Cheese
    Cottage Cheese Sauce, 232
    Swiss Cheese Sauce, 289
Chile Sauce, Ancho, 122
Chili Sauce, Spicy, 127
Cider Sauce, 224
Cocktail Sauce, 128
Cranberry-Apricot Sauce, Fresh, 243
Currant Sauce, 240
Devonshire Sauce, Processor, 58
Hollandaise Sauce, 195
Horseradish Sauce, 127
Mushroom Sauce, 36, 186, 284
Mustard-Hollandaise Sauce, Mock, 269
Mustard Sauce, 22
Mustard Sauce, Creamy, 232
Onion Cream Sauce, 232
Onion Sauce, 248
Plum Sauce, Gingered, 175
Raisin Sauce, 127
Salsa, 217
Sherry Sauce, 96
Shrimp-and-Almond Sauce, 282
Shrimp Sauce, 138, 232
Sour Cream Sauce, 233
Sour Cream Sauce, Broccoli with, 127
Sunshine Sauce, 96
Tarragon Sauce, 229
Tartar Sauce, Quick, 128
Tomato Sauce, 249
Tomato Sauce, Fresh, 171
Tomato Sauce, Italian-Style, 182
White Sauce, 166
White Sauce, Low-Calorie, Medium, 26
Sauerkraut
Salad, Crunchy Sauerkraut, 9
Sausage
Biscuits with Sausage, Angel Heart, 156
Bratwurst Dinner, Krause's Cafe, 238
Casserole, Easy Sausage, M189
Chorizo Substitute, 238
Cocktail Sausages, Saucy, 173
Gumbo Ya Ya, 210
Jambalaya de Covington, 211
Jambalaya, Northshore, 45